Publications

of the

State Department of Archives and History

THE PAPERS OF
WILLIE PERSON MANGUM

Printed by
WINSTON PRINTING COMPANY
Winston-Salem, N. C., U. S. A.

Silhouette of Willie P. Mangum by Augustin Edouart, made February 4, 1841. Original in the possession of Mr. Mangum Weeks of Alexandria, Virginia.

Willits P. Mangum Senr of Nth Caro.
Red Mountain Orange 4th Feby 1844.

THE PAPERS OF
WILLIE PERSON MANGUM

Edited by
Henry Thomas Shanks

Volume One
1807 - 1832

Raleigh
State Department of Archives and History
1950

CONTENTS

PREFACE

In 1902 before the death of Willie Person Mangum's last surviving children, Pattie and Mary Mangum, Doctor Stephen B. Weeks obtained and began working with their father's papers. Later he was appointed by the North Carolina Historical Commission to edit the papers but, unfortunately, died before he had completed his undertaking. Upon his death in 1918 the originals were deposited by Mrs. Weeks in the Library of Congress, where they now are. In the course of his editorial labors Dr. Weeks made and deposited in the North Carolina Historical Commission (now the North Carolina Department of Archives and History) typewritten copies. In editing these papers, I have found the significant work which Dr. Weeks did in collecting and deciphering these manuscripts of great assistance.

Dr. Weeks also planned a biography of Mangum but died before he had gone far with it. Because of his wealth of information on North Carolina history and because of his high standards of scholarships, it is unfortunate that he did not complete the editing or the biography. Fortunately, he did write an excellent short study in the *Biographical History of North Carolina,* which is still the most complete sketch of the eminent United States Senator and Whig Party leader.

Several other attempts have been made to write sketches of Mangum. Miss Penelope McDuffie, formerly of Converse College, made an excellent study of Mangum's life to his resignation from the Senate in 1836. This was published after her death by Professor William K. Boyd in the *Trinity College Historical Papers.* She left an incomplete draft of the remainder of Mangum's life. Professor Boyd added some to this study but died before he could complete it. This is in the Mangum Papers at Duke University. One of the students of Professor Fletcher M. Green of the University of North Carolina began a very careful and readable biography, but also died before he had carried the study beyond 1825. Dr. J. G. de Roulhac Hamilton has a highly satisfactory, brief sketch of Mangum in the *Dictionary of American Biography.* A full length life of Mangum should be written. As a step in that direction and with the hope that I may, upon the completion of the present publication, undertake such a biography, I am editing these volumes of the Mangum Papers.

In addition to the large collection of Mangum Papers in the Library of Congress, there are smaller collections at Duke University, the North Carolina Department of Archives and History, the Southern Collection at the University of North Carolina, and in the hands of the descendants of Mangum. The best of those still in the family's possession are owned by Mangum Turner at Winston-Salem. Unfortunately, only a few of the letters in these several collections were written by Mangum himself. Apparently, he did not keep letter books. Some of his papers were lost when he left Washington and despite all of my efforts and those of Mr. Mangum Weeks, of Alexandria, Virginia, no trace of them has been found.

Fortunately, there are many letters written by Mangum in the papers of W. A. Graham, Duncan Cameron, and James Webb at the University of North Carolina. Occasional letters have been discovered in other collections. I have attempted to locate in numerous depositories of the country as many of these as possible. If, as a result of the publication of this first volume or the preparation of the subsequent volumes, other letters are discovered for this first period, they will be included as an addendum in the last volume.

In editing these papers, I have made no alterations in spelling, capitalization, or punctuation. Sometimes it is very difficult to determine for the letters of the early 1800's whether the writer intended a period, a dash, or a capital letter. In every case, however, even at the risk of doing the writer an injustice, I have tried to reproduce the letter as I found it. Although Dr. Weeks deciphered and verified the copies with the original, I have also compared them myself. Needless to say, I found his verifications of great value.

On a subsequent page I am including a key for determining the present location of the original manuscripts included in this volume. Some of the manuscripts in the collections of Mangum Papers do not relate to Mangum or, in the opinion of the editor, have insufficient value for publication. For these reasons and for the reason of limited space, I have omitted some manuscripts. Whenever one is omitted, its nature, date, and present location is given.

The Mangum Papers constitute a large collection, the publication of which is expected to require four volumes. In the letters are many things that are not easily identified. I have made a particular effort to locate as many as possible and to write brief identifications or explanations of them. My purpose in the notes has been to identify and explain rather than to discuss. For this reason, I have made the notes brief and factual.

In preparing these papers for publication, I owe particular gratitude to the two direct lines of descendants of the Willie P. Mangum family. Mrs. John A. Livingstone and Miss Anne Leach Turner of Raleigh, Miss Pattie Mangum Turner of Milledgeville, Ga., Mr. Mangum Turner, an attorney at Winston-Salem, Miss Sally Preston Weeks, of Washington, D. C., and Mr. Mangum Weeks, an attorney with the Department of Justice at Washington, D. C., have contributed Mangum letters, illustrations, and advice which have enriched the publication. Mr. Mangum Turner, who in his childhood heard from his great aunts, Sally and Patty Mangum, the daughters of the Senator, the stories and traditions of his great grandfather, had not only furnished me with valuable manuscripts and illustrations which are included here, but also has helped me by his reminiscences to obtain a better understanding of Mangum. Mr. Mangum Weeks has been of particular service in reading the manuscript of the first volume and in offering valuable criticism. He has prepared the genealogy of the Mangum Family, which will be included in a subsequent volume, and with the generous assistance of other members of the family has selected most of the illustrations herein included. Miss Mary Thornton, Mrs. Lyman Cotton, Dr. J. G. de Roulhac Hamilton, Dr. James W. Patton, and others at the University of North Carolina library have patiently put up with my inquiries and use of their great collections. The staffs of the manuscript divisions of the Library of Congress and Duke University graciously assisted me in my work with them there. The New York Public Library, Yale University Library, Henry E. Huntington Library, Buffalo Historical Society, Tennessee State Library and Archives, University of Rochester Library, and the State Historical Society of Wisconsin very generously provided me with microfilms or photostats of Mangum letters which they had.

A grant from the Research Fund of the Carnegie Foundation has made possible the completion of this study. To Mr. Christopher Crittenden, Mr. D. L. Corbitt, and the other members of the staff of the North Carolina Department of Archives and History, I want especially to express my appreciation for their advice, assistance, and suggestions. I also owe a particular sense of gratitude to this Department for providing the funds for the publication of these papers.

Birmingham, Ala.   H. T. S.
October 31, 1950

CHRONOLOGY OF WILLIE PERSON MANGUM, 1792-1861

1792, May 10. Born near Red Mountain, Orange County, (Now Rougemont, Durham County) North Carolina.

1809-1811. Attended Hillsboro, Fayetteville, and Raleigh Academies.

1811. Student at the University of North Carolina.

1812, Spring Term. Instructor at Raleigh Academy.

1812-1815. Student at the University of North Carolina.

1815-1817. Read law under the direction of Judge Duncan Cameron and tutored Paul Cameron.

1817. Obtained his law license.

1818. Received his M.A. degree at the University of North Carolina.

1818-1819. Member of the House of Commons of North Carolina.

1819, September 30. Married Charity Alston Cain, daughter of William Cain.

December 22. Elected Judge of the Superior Court.

1820, November. Resigned as Judge of the Superior Court.

1823, June 4. Announced his candidacy for Congress.

August. Elected to Congress over D. L. Barringer.

1824, January 6. Birth of his daughter, Sally Alston.

1825, August. Re-elected to Congress over Josiah Crudup.

1826, August 18. Appointed Judge of the Superior Court.

Autumn. Resigned his seat in Congress.

December. Defeated in the legislature for re-election as judge.

1827-1828. Financial difficulties. Bankruptcy of his father.

1828, April 6. Birth of his daughter, Martha ("Pattie") Person.

Presidential Elector for Jackson.

December 10. Elected Judge of the Superior Court.

1829, March 11. Death of Mangum's mother.

1830, April 3. Resigned as Judge of the Superior Court.

Birth of his daughter, Catherine Davis, who died in infancy.

December. Elected United States Senator by the legislature.

1832, July 8. Birth of his daughter, Mary Sutherland.

1833, December. Openly broke with President Jackson.

1834, January 23. Presented to the Senate resolutions from the people of the western part of his state against the removal of deposits.

February 25. Delivered in the Senate what his friends called a "Philippic" against Jackson.

August-September. Trip, along with other members of the special Senate banking committee, to New York, New Haven, and Boston.

December. The North Carolina legislature instructed Mangum and Bedford Brown to vote for expunging the censure resolutions.

1835. Refused to obey the legislature's instructions.

1836, November 24. Resigned as Senator.

Received the electoral vote of South Carolina.

1836-1840. Private practice of law. Helped build the organization of the Whig Party in North Carolina.

1837, July 13. Birth of his son, William Preston.

1839. Delegate to the National Whig Convention at Harrisburg, Pennsylvania.

1840. Presidential Elector for Harrison and Tyler.

December. As a member of the State Senate, he proposed and helped pass through the legislature the important Educational Act of 1840.

December 9. Took his seat in the United States Senate after being elected by the legislature.

1841. September. Led the fight in the Whig caucus against Tyler.

1841-1842. Supported Clay's program of tariff, bank, and distribution.

1842. Built "Walnut Hall."

1842, May 31-March 4, 1845. President *pro tempore* of the United States Senate. (Since there was no Vice President at this time Mangum was the next in line for the presidency).

1843-1844. Led the movement in the South for the nomination of Clay.

1844. Declined the Whig nomination for Vice President.

1844-1845. Opposed the annexation of Texas.

1845, June. Received the LL.D. degree from the University of North Carolina.

1846. Re-elected to the United States Senate.

1848. Declined the nomination for President by the National American Party.

Campaigned for Scott for the Whig nomination.

1849-1850. Opposed Calhoun's efforts to unite the South. Supported Clay's Compromise.

Member of the Committee of Thirteen.

1850. With George E. Badger, he induced Webster to make his "Seventh of March" speech.

Voted for the New Mexico Bill, the Fugitive Slave Law, and opposed the abolition of the slave trade in the District of Columbia.

1851, Autumn. Had a fall which later resulted in a stroke of apoplexy.

1852, April 4. Endorsed Scott for President. The Whigs in North Carolina had already endorsed Fillmore.

April 20. As chairman of the Whig caucus, he refused to allow a vote on the endorsement of the Compromise of 1850.

Declined the vice-presidency on the Whig ticket.

1853, March 4. Returned to private life and the practice of law.

1854. Became justice of peace of Orange County.

1856. Suffered a stroke of apoplexy.

1856-1861. Almost an invalid. He rarely left his plantation.

1861. Opposed secession but after the Civil War started he supported the Confederacy and induced his son to join the Southern army.

July 28. Death of his only son, William Preston Mangum.

September 7. Mangum died.

LIST OF ILLUSTRATIONS

WILLIE PERSON MANGUM—
A BIOGRAPHICAL SKETCH

Willie Person Mangum was born on May 10, 1792, in what was then Orange and is now Durham County, North Carolina. The Mangums had come into North Carolina from Sussex County, Virginia. They probably first settled in Granville County before eventually locating in Orange where Mangum's grandfather, Arthur, obtained public land grants as early as 1763.[1] Mangum's own father, William Person Mangum, ran a country store and a plantation. Although never a wealthy person, he was able to send his three boys to preparatory schools and two of them to college. Before the father's death the home estate included 2500 acres. Mangum's mother, Catherine Davis, was of the Scotch-Irish stock which came to North Carolina from the Schuykill region of Pennsylvania.[2]

At the time of Willie Person Mangum's boyhood, Orange County was inhabited mainly by farmers although there were some large planters. The soil was conducive to the production of tobacco and grain crops. It had not been depleted by the wasteful methods of farming which impoverished the section during Mangum's manhood. The county seat, Hillsboro, was the most important town in the western part of the state. Here the provincial council had met; here Revolutionary leaders such as William Hooper, Thomas Burke, and General Francis Nash resided; and here Regulators were hanged in the edge of the village.[3] Being at the intersection of the main east-west and the Virginia-Raleigh highways, it was the stopping place for many people of political importance. In Mangum's early manhood the town boasted of a good newspaper, several taverns, an academy, several lawyers and mercantile establishments. A little later it had, at the same time, a branch of the state bank, two United States Senators, a governor, and a chief justice of the state supreme

---

[1]S. B. Weeks, "Willie Person Mangum," *Biographical History of North Carolina from Colonial Times to the Present,* edited by Samuel A. Ashe, 8 vols. (Greensboro, N. C.: C. L. Van Noppen, 1905-1917), V, 237-238. Hereafter cited as Weeks, "W. P. M.," *Biog. Hist. of N. C.* Compare also a list of omitted documents, below, p. xlv.
[2]Penelope McDuffie, "Chapters in the Life of Willie Person Mangum," in *The Historical Papers, published by the Trinity College Historical Society* (Durham, N. C.: The Duke University Press, 1925), Series XV, 12. Hereafter cited as McDuffie, "Willie P. Mangum."
[3]For a colorful account of the life of Hillsboro in the Colonial and Revolutionary periods see Francis Nash, *Colonial Hillsboro* (Raleigh, N. C.: Edwards and Broughton, 1903).

court. Duncan Cameron, the wealthy planter from the same
county, was for some years the political boss of North Carolina.
William Norwood, Thomas Ruffin, Edmund Strudwick, William
Montgomery, James Mebane, W. A. Graham, and George Badger
were all neighbors and contemporaries of Mangum. No county in
the state was more promising for a prospective political leader.

In his youth, Mangum worked in his father's country store.
Although the records of his experiences in this venture do not indicate how successful a helper he was, it is reasonable to assume
that the friends he made, the conversations he heard, and the
personality he developed in a country store were of great value
in shaping his political ambitions and abilities. The records do
indicate that he had a share in the responsibilities of the business for some of the accounts were in his and his father's names.

Mangum studied with some of the most famous teachers of his
section. Probably the Reverend Andrew Flinn, who had formerly
headed the Hillsboro Academy, tutored Mangum before the latter
entered the Academy itself.[4] In 1809-1810 he was enrolled at
the Fayetteville Academy which was under the supervision of
the Reverend Colin McIver.[5] After a year under this able teacher,
Mangum transferred to the Raleigh Academy which was headed
by the most notable principal of the state, the Rev. William Mc-
Pheeters.[6] Apparently Mangum was a satisfactory student here,
for in 1812 after he had had one term of study at the state University he was asked to return to teach. On July 4, 1812, he delivered what the Raleigh *Star* labelled a "handsome and appropriate oration." Here Mangum came in contact with such future
political rivals and friends as Weston Gales, Josiah Crudup, Will
and John Haywood, William Polk, and Daniel L. Barringer.

In 1811 he entered the university at Chapel Hill where he
roomed with Archibald Haralson, the nephew of A. D. Murphey.
The two students read and discussed together the writings of
Hume and Rousseau. Mangum did not make as good an academic
record as his younger brother, Priestley, who won high honors
and, therefore, was asked back as an instructor. Willie, however,
was active in the politics of the day: he displayed such Federalist tendencies that they later embarrassed him. At the University even more than at Raleigh, he made friends which were
to affect his later career. James K. Polk, John H. Bryan, Isaac

---

[4]McDuffie, "Willie P. Mangum," 13.
[5]Colin McIver to Mangum, Nov. 21, 1833, Mangum Papers, Library of Congress, Washington, D. C. Hereafter cited as Mangum Papers.
[6]Weeks, "W. P. M.," *Biog. Hist. of N. C.*, V, 239.

Croom, Edward Hall, and Richard Dobbs Spaight, Jr., were all in attendance.

Shortly after graduation in 1815 he began reading law under the direction of Duncan Cameron, one of the wealthiest and most progressive leaders of the state. As partial payment for this privilege Mangum tutored Paul Cameron, Duncan's son, in preparation for admission to the University. This association later bore fruit for Mangum's political life.

After obtaining his license to practice law before the superior court in 1817, Mangum followed the circuits. Two years later he wrote his brother, Priestley, April 20, 1819, that he had made a "good deal of money this spring, say upwards of $1,900 in actual receipts, and nearly that sum in good bonds & accts. My prospects in the practice continue to grow more flattering." At Franklin Court he obtained a single fee of $1,000.00.

As a result of his successful practice he bought a sulky which was "elegant and suited to all the purposes of country life." He had the Raleigh tailor, James J. Selby, make him a coat, a silk velvet cape, pantaloons and a vest of "superfine black cloth @ $15.00 a yard."[7] In the same spring he wrote Priestley that he was considering marriage. At Judge Henry Seawell's, he continued, he "offered a heart not worth two pence upon the shrine of beauty." Whether this proposal was to Charity A. Cain, whom he married September 30 of that year, or to some other girl he did not make clear.

His marriage proved a happy one. Mrs. Mangum was the daughter of William Cain who had come from Baltimore to Hillsboro where he maintained a profitable mercantile establishment. Charity's father also owned a great deal of land and many slaves in Orange County. Later when Mangum was in financial difficulties, his father-in-law came to his rescue with large loans. At the time of their marriage Charity received some slaves and much land from her father.

Mangum's letters to his wife are tender and affectionate. In his busiest periods at Washington he wrote her love letters which had the warmth of an ardent suitor. In fact they are so full of love-making that they contain little about his Washington life. He did not take her into his confidence on political affairs. On January 15, 1826, he wrote: "I don't reckon that you can understand it [his speech] for it is connected with a subject that ladies

---

[7]Bill of J. J. Selby to Mangum, Aug. 16, 1820, for a purchase of March 27, 1819, Mangum Papers.

know but little of." Instead of politics he advised her on the edu-
tion and care of the children and on the way the plantation
should be run. He often expressed the desire to be with her and
the children, although he did not take them to Washington until
1850 when Mrs. Mangum went for her health. Frequently he expressed the desire to resign from Congress in order that he
might be at home with his family and on his plantation.

Mangum had scarcely established his law practice when he
entered politics. If this urge was inherited it probably came
through his Grandmother Person's side of the family, for members of the Mangum side of the family had never been active in
politics. They were farmers and merchants. His grandfather,
Arthur Mangum, had married Lucy Person, a cousin of Thomas
Person, the Colonial and Revolutionary leader.[8]

Starting as a protege of Duncan Cameron, Mangum was elec-
ed to the state House of Commons in 1818 and 1819. As a member of the judicial and educational committees of that house, he
worked with William Gaston and Archibald D. Murphey. These
two great leaders remained his advisers until their deaths. In
the legislature he followed their leads for a strong state supreme
court, a broad educational program, and a constitutional convention.[9] The popular response to his first term in the legislature
was favorable, for he wrote Priestley April 20, 1819, "I could go
to Congress without difficulty," but he felt that it was unwise
at that time. Instead he accepted the position of judge of the
superior court. According to tradition his election to this office
was due to Cameron's endorsement after his failure to obtain
the election of his friend William Norwood.[10]

As Judge Mangum traveled throughout the western part of
North Carolina, he became acquainted with leaders who later
helped his political advancement. Nevertheless he was not happy
in his work. On March 20 and April 25, 1820, he wrote Mrs.
Mangum that he did not like the duties of his office because of
the "intense labor, great responsibility," the distance from home,
and the fact that the people with whom he worked were "little
congenial to my habits and tastes." In consequence he resigned
in November, 1820, giving "poor health" as his reason. For this
resignation he was criticised to the extent that several years
later when he sought reelection as judge he was defeated.

[8]Weeks, "W. P. M.," *Biog. Hist. of N. C.,* V, 239.
[9]Weeks, "W. P. M.," *Biog. Hist. of N. C.,* V, 240; *Journal of the House of Commons, 1819,* 38, 90.
[10]McDuffie, "Willie P. Mangum," 21.

By the end of 1822 Mangum was considering running for Congress. He had made a favorable reputation in the legislature in his fight for the democratic measures so dear to the West, and as attorney and judge visiting the various courthouses he had made friends necessary to promote his campaign. He proved to be a shrewd campaigner. He had a frankness and friendliness of manner which "charmed" people.[11] According to W. A. Graham he was "particularly good on the hustings where he had but few equals in our country. . . . His tall and commanding figure always becomingly dressed, his rich and melodious voice . . . , his sympathetic nature, and perfect acquaintance with all the springs and motives of human action, gave him an almost mesmeric sway over the multitude."[12] E. G. Reade who knew Mangum well wrote Miss Pattie Mangum on December 18, 1865, that on the campaign with his own people he was "almost irresistible."

In preparation for his candidacy for Congress, Mangum spoke to a gathering at Hillsboro in the spring of 1823 supporting the western demands for a more democratic state constitution. In the legislature in 1818 and 1819, he had been a member of the committee recommending constitutional changes. At Hillsboro in 1823 he connected internal improvements with constitutional revision.[13] Although this attempt to revise the fundamental law[14] brought no immediate reforms, it made Mangum a hero in his section. Having laid the foundation for his candidacy, on June 4 Mangum announced his candidacy for Congress to oppose Daniel L. Barringer from Wake County.[15]

The campaign which followed centered around the issue of constitutional revision.[16] Orange, Person, and Wake counties comprised the congressional district. Wake, the most populous of the counties, was in the eastern part of the state, and, therefore, opposed constitutional changes; Orange and, to an extent, Person were for altering the state's fundamental law. Mangum knew that he could count on the support of the voters of Orange and, to a large degree, Person, but to win he needed many supporters in Wake. He, therefore, tried to convince the Wake

[11]Orlando Brown to J. J. Crittenden, Feb. 11, 1836, Crittenden Papers, Library of Congress, Washington, D. C. Hereafter cited as Crittenden Papers.
[12]"Sketch of Willie P. Mangum," Raleigh Weekly Register, Sept. 18, 1861 (Taken from a clipping in Mangum Papers, Duke University Library, Durham, N. C.)
[13]Hillsborough Recorder, June 11, 1823.
[14]Raleigh Register, Nov. 14, 21, 28, 1823.
[15]Hillsborough Recorder, June 11, 1823.
[16]For a good discussion of the constitutional controversy prior to the convention of 1835 see William K. Boyd, "Antecedents of the Constitutional Convention of 1835," South Atlantic Quarterly, IX, 83-93, 161-171.

voters that Barringer was also in favor of democratic changes in the constitution. He obtained from respected Orange County leaders letters which were designed to prove that Barringer had in their presence endorsed constiutional reforms. At the same time Mangum gathered evidence to prove that Barringer had supported the United States Bank which was at that time unpopular in these counties. These letters were published in the form of a circular and distributed in Wake County but not in Orange and Person. Barringer replied in another circular accusing Mangum of breaking his promise not to run for Congress. Barringer's circular also emphasized Mangum's vote in the legislature and at the Hillsboro gathering for constitutional changes. In Wake Barringer denied that he had supported these changes. Mangum won the election by a vote of 2,523 to 1,729, thanks to his large plurality in Orange and Person counties.

The contest resulted in a personal quarrel with Judge Henry Seawell, who prior to this campaign had been one of Mangum's staunchest friends. Seawell had shifted from Mangum to Barringer and, according to some, had written the scurrilous Barringer circular. Friends of both men prevented a duel developing. This was one of many of Mangum's personal controversies which provoked challenges but which because of his good sense or that of his friends failed to result in actual duels.

Mangum entered his new duties with great enthusiasm. At Washington he made friends readily, especially with young men and with such important figures as the state's rights leaders, Nathaniel Macon, John C. Calhoun, and William C. Preston. Like most Southerners he opposed the tariff and Federal aid to internal improvements. Unlike Macon, he warmly endorsed the financial aid given to LaFayette on his visit to this country. In fact he was appointed to serve on the committee which received Lafayette.

Mangum's first term, like that of most new members of Congress, was not distinguished, but he looked after his constituents sufficiently to be reelected. Numerous petitions for new or for changes in old mail routes in his district were passed on to the post office department. He wrote innumerable letters and sent many documents to the people of his district whose names and adresses were furnished by friends and especially by Priestley whose astute political sense and general ability was relied upon by the elder brother. Mangum's papers reveal that he performed many personal services for his friends and constituents. These ranged all the way from subscribing to and paying for Washington and Philadelphia newspapers and magazines to helping the trustees obtain Tennesse lands for his alma mater. Although he was bombarded with requests for favors until the end of his stay in the National Capital, he gave more attention in this first term than he did later to the entreaties.

During his first term much of his time and attention was given to the heated presidential campaign of 1824. A reading of his correspondence for that period will lead one to believe that, outside of political appointments, this election was of chief interest to his constituents. When elected in 1823 Mangum indicated that he favored William H. Crawford. As Jackson became stronger among the people of North Carolina, Mangum was accused of losing interest in his original candidate. In December, 1823, he wrote Duncan Cameron a long letter explaining in an objective manner the chances of success of the different candidates and, since he did not reaffirm his earlier intention to support Crawford, word got out that he was deserting his candidate. In Raleigh when the legislature was in session this talk caused Priestley and J. J. Carrington to write Mangum strong warnings against going back on his word. Mangum immediately squelched the rumors. To Seth Jones he wrote February 11, 1824, that the rumors were "wholly without foundation." He did refuse to attend the caucus which nominated Crawford, but that was due to the unpopularity of the caucus as a method of selecting a candidate rather than to any lukewarmness toward Crawford. In the election which followed North Carolina voted for Jackson. Nevertheless, Mangum stuck with Crawford even after he realized that the Georgian had no chance of success. Apparently his consistency and loyalty strengthened him at home.[17]

Upon his return home in the spring of 1825 at the close of his first term in Congress, Mangum faced Josiah Crudup for reelection. The contest which followed was hard fought. Crudup was a shrewd campaigner. An ardent Jacksonian and pious Baptist preacher, he used the pulpit for electioneering purposes. A large rain at the church in Wake County where Crudup closed his campaign on the last Sunday before the election reduced the crowd and according to Mangum accounted for his victory. The Congressman received in Person and Orange counties a majority

---

[17]D. F. Caldwell to Mangum, Dec. 4, 1825, Mangum Papers.

of 1,017 which more than balanced Crudup's majority of 561 in Wake. The difference of 56 was possibly due to the rain.[18]

At first Mangum seemed sympathetic to the John Quincy Adams administration. He was encouraged in this sympathy by his friend, John Chavis, the Presbyterian Negro preacher who urged Mangum in his numerous letters to put on his "coat of federalism" and line up with Clay and Adams. But like other Crawford men Mangum early changed to a course of aloofness toward the new administration. He sought through correspondence with Bartlett Yancey the sentiment at home.[19] He was flattered by the invitations he received to the splendid levees of the Adamses. Nevertheless, pressure from home and Clay's American system soon convinced him that he could not support the Adams administration. He joined the efforts to wreck the Panama Congress. He opposed Webster's bill to reorganize the judiciary because it proposed greater federal jurisdiction at the expense of state courts. Soon he was writing Yancey: "I verily believe [that this administration] will be conducted upon as corrupt principles, indeed more corrupt, than any that has preceded it."[20] A few weeks later, April 8, he wrote his wife that the administration was "both weak and wicked." As a result of his attacks on the Adams-Clay program and leaders, he became stronger at home.[21]

During the summer of 1826 he sought another appointment as judge of the superior court. He wrote his wife that he was sick of Washington where "everything goes against my judgment." Contrary to his idea of judicial ethics he wrote out a letter to the Council of State soliciting such an appointment. Although a personal application was in poor taste, he justified it on the grounds that others were applying. There is no evidence that the letter was sent. In fact it was not necessary since the governor, a close friend, was pushing his candidacy. The appointment was made August 18, 1826.[22] Unfortunately for his political reputation Mangum did not immediately give up his seat in Congress. He wanted to serve out his term in Washington before resigning. With so many seeking office, this was a

[18]E. G. Reade to Pattie Mangum, Dec. 18, 1865, Mangum Papers. See also Weeks, "W. P. M.," *Biog. Hist. of N. C.*, V, 241.
[19]"Letters to Bartlett Yancey," *The James Sprunt Historical Publications*, X, No. 2, pp. 51-52, 62-65, 106-111. Hereafter cited as "Letters to Bartlett Yancey."
[20]"Letters to Bartlett Yancey," 106-111; also quoted in McDuffie, "Willie P. Mangum," 38.
[21]Letters of W. C. Clement, March 8, Priestley Mangum, March 29, Henry Seawell, April 9, to Willie P. Mangum, Mangum Papers.
[22]Governor H. G. Burton's Letter Book, 1824-1827, MS, State Department of Archives and History, Raleigh, N. C.

poor policy as Priestley frankly wrote him in a letter of September 1, 1826. He resigned but too late to prevent criticism. When the legislature met in the following December, it refused to re-elect him as judge.

During the years 1827-1828 Mangum was out of politics except for the presidential campaign in which he served as an elector on the Jackson ticket. His hostility to Clay and Adams drove him to support the great Tennessean. In this shift he was following the sentiment of his state, which had endorsed Jackson in the election of 1824. In December, 1828, after J. D. Toomer had resigned, Mangum was again elected without opposition to be judge of the superior court.[23] The criticism of 1826 had subsided.

Mangum was not satisfied with his new duties. Justice Strange gave him the Wilmington Circuit in the spring which Mangum felt should not have been assigned to him in that his last circuit in his previous term had been in the unhealthy region of the East. Although, as a result of his protest, he was relieved of this circuit, he drew the Edenton district in the next spring. His health was not good. He had to follow a strict diet. He wrote his wife on March 28, 1830, "I neither use pepper, pickle nor have I taken but one drink of spirits on the circuit." In the following fall he was relieved to get what he considered the healthier Morganton district.

In the years since he began practicing law, Mangum had given much of his life to public office. As a result he had neglected his private business. In the same period his father had become bank-rupt and, therefore, had made the son's financial difficulties greater. His resignation as judge in the early twenties was partly due to his financial difficulties. He was never a wealthy man, although his early law practice had given promise of wealth. In the early period when money came easy he invested heavily in real estate and internal improvement projects. These did not prove successful. Like many of his North Carolina contemporaries, he bought lots in the boom town of Haywood and stock in the proposed Deep River Bridge Company, which proposed to make possible a connection of Haywood with the East. This development was a part of a great wave of enthusiasm for internal improvement in North Carolina. Murphey, Ruffin, the Nashes, and Strudwicks were involved. Mangum went into part-

[23]Weeks, "W. P. M.," *Biog. Hist. of N. C.,* V, 243.

nership with his old college roommate, Archibald Haralson, to buy up lots and stock worth several thousand dollars. Haralson was unable to redeem his pledges and Mangum and Haralson's uncle, Archibald D. Murphey, had to pay Haralson's part. The boom soon burst and Mangum found himself deeply in debt.

In the early twenties Mangum also bought real estate property in Hillsboro and Orange County. He helped the state treasurer, John Haywood, to support the free Negro, John Chavis. Moreover, Mangum had to assume much of the debt of his father. As a result of all these obligations, Mangum was practically bankrupt by 1827. To help his situation his father-in-law, Wiliam Cain, Sr., endorsed his notes for $1,773.73. This did not save Mangum. The next year, therefore, Mangum turned over all of his property to Thomas D. Watts to create a trust fund for settling his debts. According to the indenture of that year he owned 1,600 acres of land in his home section, 4 lots in Hillsboro, an unenumerated number of lots in Haywood, sixteen slaves, 9 horses, an undesignated quantity of cattle, utensils, corn, furniture, and household supplies. The indenture does not give the amount of his debts, but they included notes to Duncan Cameron, Thomas Alston, and William Cain. His father's notes alone amounted to $3,000.

In trying to settle the debts, James Webb, the designated trustee, sold the slaves for $3,390. Most of these slaves had come to Mangum as a gift of his father-in-law to Mrs. Mangum. Except for the home estate, the real estate was sold. Mangum continued to make small payments on his debts until after he returned to Washington in 1830. Despite his straitened circumstances, he endorsed personal notes for Robert Potter and Governor Burton for he was exceedingly generous to these friends who were rarely solvent. Gradually Mangum's debts were reduced until in 1830 he owed only his father-in-law, who continued to allow him to borrow. Consequently, when William Cain died, the Mangums received little property as their share of the Cain estate.

Mangum's long stay in Washington was expensive. His wife was a good manager but profits from farming in North Carolina in the 1830's and 1840's were not large even for good managers. In the 'forties, therefore Mangum had his wife hire out his slaves to planters in Georgia and Alabama. In 1842 he received $1,050 for their hire.[24] By 1850 Mangum was again in

---

[24] William Cain, Jr., to Mangum, Jan. 4, 1842 and Jan. 19, 1844, Mangum Papers.

such financial straits that except for the assistance of Priestley he would have been obliged to sell his slaves to pay off his debts.

With all of his financial difficulties, Mangum held on to the home place. In the 1840's he built on the site of an earlier house a larger and more commodious house in the style of the Greek Revival, which at the suggestion of Duncan Cameron he called "Walnut Hall." Dominated by two gigantic black walnut trees and surrounded by a walnut grove and boxwoods, it was an impressive country seat, similar in plan and architectural style to the Cameron place, "Fairntosh." He took great pride in the plantation and the house. He sent home seeds of great variety and exotic trees, some of which are standing today, although the house was burned in 1933 and the two great walnut trees were destroyed some years before. Mangum longed for his home and family. His letters to Mrs. Mangum are full of advice and instructions for improvements. His friend, C. P. Green, of Warrenton and Boydton included in his letters about politics information on horse races. In one of these letters he offered Mangum a "thoroughbred" mare for improving his race horse stock.[25] Mangum was a country gentleman of the Whig tradition, whose friendship with one of the Orange County magnates and whose marriage into the family of another laid the economic and social foundation for his position.

Despite Mangum's love for his family, his people, his home, and his horses, he was like his race horses in his desire to return to the race track of national politics. By 1828 he was thinking of the Senate. Upon the resignation of Nathaniel Macon in that year his friends urged him to become a candidate, but family tradition has it that he declined in favor of his friend, James Iredell.[26] In December, 1830, he agreed to have his name presented to the legislature. The election which followed was one of the bitterest senatorial contests of the state's history.

In 1830 party lines in North Carolina were not clearly drawn. Instead of organized parties bound together by issues, the state was divided into sections held together by certain leaders. The strongest of these was the Spaight faction led by R. D. Spaight, Jr., Charles Fisher, and Joseph N. Bryan. Before the convening of the legislature in the late fall of 1830, these leaders decided to support Judge Donnell for the Senate and Spaight for governor. The opposition's candidates were John Owen and Jesse

[25]See, for instance, Green to Mangum, March 22, 1841, Mangum Papers.
[26]Weeks, "W. P. M.," Biog. Hist. of N. C., V, 243; McDuffie, "Willie P. Mangum," 40.

Speight or if Owen failed in his race for the Senate he would replace Speight for governor. This was not a strong opposition
ticket. Mangum's friends, William M. Sneed, of Granville, William J. Alexander, of Mecklenburg, and C. L. Hinton, of Wake,
prevailed on Mangum who was above factions to run for the
Senate. Sneed wrote him November 18, "You are decidedly the
most powerful man in the state." Owen and Donnell each agreed
that if he discovered that he could not win, he would throw his
strength to Mangum.

In the early ballotting enough unattached legislators scat-
tored their votes to prevent either of the faction candidates'
winning. Everything was working as the Mangum strategists
planned. Sneed wrote him November 25, "I am afraid you will
be spoiled by the flattery and adulation which you are receiving." Then things went wrong. C. L. Hinton was supposed to
nominate Mangum as soon as Owen and Donnell had proved that
they could not win. Hinton waited too long to make his nomination speech. In his place a Donnell man, Edward Ward, presented Mangum's name himself. This infuriated Owen who felt
that Hinton had made a deal with the Spaight faction. Therefore, he made a personal fight on Mangum. Many were already
disgruntled that Mangum had not been down to Raleigh to court
their favors and that earlier he had resigned his judgeship after
they had given it to him. Mangum himself made a serious mistake
by writing a blunt letter to Owen informing him ahead of time
that he was sending to Hinton and Ward a criticism of Owen's
political principles. Doubtless he felt that his personal friendship
for Owen demanded that he tell him frankly ahead of time what
he was writing others. Owen used this letter to great advantage.
Leaders of the Spaight faction now saw a chance to split the opposition and elect one of their own men. They divided their support between Owen and Mangum with the hope that they would
soon destroy each other. Mangum's friends begged him to come
to Raleigh to save the day. Instead, thinking his chances gone, he
ordered that his name be withdrawn. Sneed ignored Mangum's
instructions and began courting Owen's followers and those who
had formerly been for Donnell. As a result Mangum won on the
seventh ballot by a vote of 103 out of a total of 195.[27]

Owen was bitter over the outcome. On December 4 he wrote
Mangum a letter which was intended to lead to a challenge.

[27]Weeks, "W. P. M.," *Biog. Hist. of N. C.*, V, 243; McDuffie, "Willie P. Mangum," 41; letters of Sneed and Hinton to Mangum, Nov.-Dec., 1830, Mangum Papers.

Louis D. Henry and D. F. Caldwell intervened to prevent the duel. On December 8 Mangum wrote Owen that as a judge he could not fight a duel. He also explained that his attack was on Owen's political principles and not his character. "I hold it as a maxim, never to touch the character of a Gentleman in any respect." He had originally written Owen, he said, because he believed in striking openly rather than behind a person's back. This was the last of Mangum's quarrels to result in a threatened duel. Maturity made him calmer. Later he and Owen were active in the same party and apparently held no grudge against each other.

Immediately upon receiving news of his election, Mangum set out to take his seat at Washington. Except for a brief period in the late thirties he remained in the Senate until 1853. It was in this body that he made his great reputation. By 1830 he had developed into a political leader of considerable reputation in his own state. Before his withdrawal from public life this reputation had become national. In the Senate he became a hard worker, forceful debater, and capable party leader, although he was not always consistent in his stand on the issues of the day.

Mangum went to the Senate as a supporter of Jackson. He had been a presidential elector on the Jackson ticket in 1828. In Washington he was soon associating with the South Carolina congressmen. He disliked Jackson's position in the Peggy O'Neal affair.[28] Soon he began writing home to determine the sentiment on the tariff and nullification.[29] Priestley wrote him a long letter warning him not to go ahead of the sentiment of his state on "unconstitutional resistance." At the same time pressure was being put upon him by Gaston, Murphey, and Cameron to support the recharter of the United States Bank. He replied that he considered that institution an "indispensable necessity." He regretted that Clay brought up the bank question at the time he did. Jackson, he asserted, would have supported a renewal of the Bank's charter if Clay had delayed until after the election.[30]

In keeping with Priestley's advice Mangum made a moderate speech in February, 1832, on the tariff. Like most North Carolina leaders he was opposed to the tariff but he was careful not to emphasize its unconstitutionality. He knew that the state

---

[28]McDuffie, "Willie P. Mangum," 43.
[29]John Scott to Mangum, Dec. 18, 1831, Mangum Papers.
[30]Mangum to Gaston, Jan. 19, 1832, Mangum Papers; Herbert Dale Pegg, "The Whig Party in North Carolina, 1834-1861" (Ph.D. dissertation, University of North Carolina, Chapel Hill, N. C., 1932. Typescript copy in Library of the University of North Carolina, Chapel Hill, N. C.), 13. Hereafter cited as Pegg, "Whig Party in N. C."

legislature had already pressed resolutions denouncing the tariff as "unjust and inexpedient" rather than illegal.[31] Mangum worked hard to frame a speech which would endorse the states' rights view without going too far. For two and a half hours each day on two successive days he spoke to a crowded Senate. He wrote his wife, February 11, that the "almost universal opinion of the Senate is that it was eloquent and powerful." Several thousand copies were printed for distribution.[32] Judging from the numerous congratulatory letters which are in the Mangum papers the speech was well received in North Carolina. Only John Long who was a protectionist wrote a letter of disapproval.[33]

In this speech Mangum was restrained in his position. He argued that the tariff was sectional and selfish. He denied that the power to regulate commerce gave Congress the authority to levy a protective tariff for it destroyed commerce. Although he did not specifically deny the constitutional authority to levy a tariff under the taxing powers, he argued that it was an unfair tax since it fell most heavily on one section. He questioned the authority of Congress to make the tariff more than one for revenue.

Mangum's speech was interpreted by some to mean that he was on Calhoun's side.[34] It was a states' rights document but Mangum was careful not to endorse nullification. He was still loyal to Jackson for he voted for Van Buren's nomination as minister to Great Britain. He also voted against the recharter of the bank, largely because he disliked the bill itself and the political consequences of its passage. His conduct was endorsed by numerous public meetings including one in New York.[35] In the presidential election which followed he remained loyal to Jackson although with no great enthusiasm.

When Mangum returned to the Senate in December the nullification fight was in full swing. Calhoun's Fort Hill letter on August 28 was followed in October by a call for a state convention. On November 24, the South Carolina convention passed its ordinance of nullification and three days later the reassem-

[31]Pegg, "Whig Party in N. C.," 7.
[32]*Speech of the Honorable Willie P. Mangum (of North Carolina) on the Tariff. Delivered in the Senate of the United States on the 7th and 8th of February, 1832, on Mr. Clay's Resolution on the Tariff* (Washington, D. C.: Printed at the office of Jonathan Eliot, 1832), 26 pp.; McDuffie, "Willie P. Mangum," 44.
[33]Letters of A. Lockhart, April 3, C. P. Mallett, April 4, John Hall, April 4, R. B. Gilliam, April 5, Long, April 5, to Mangum, Mangum Papers.
[34]Chavis to Mangum, Nov. 3, 1832, Mangum Papers.
[35]M. L. Felt to Mangum, Oct. 25, 1832, Mangum Papers.

bled state legislature authorized the governor to call out the militia to enforce the laws. Jackson, who until the fall had doubted that South Carolina would go as far as actual nullification, began taking the military steps necessary for the enforcement of the tariff law. On December 10 he issued his belligent proclamation.

In North Carolina there was little sympathy for the extreme position of her southern neighbor. The press vigorously opposed nullification. In the fall of 1832 mass meetings were almost unanimous in their condemnation of South Carolina's position. When the legislature met in November it resolved that while it considered the tariff "impolitic, unjust, and oppressive", it labelled nullification "Revolutionary in character [and] subversive of the Constitution of the United States."[36]

Until the fall of 1832 Mangum did not make his position on nullification clear. His friends became afraid that he had "caught the South Carolina fever."[37] He, therefore, made a speech at Hillsboro explaining in no uncertain terms that he did not approve the South Carolina position.[38] He still held to states' rights and was later indignant with Jackson's proclamation which in his opinion was too "violent and dangerous in its principles."[39] He wrote Priestley in December that he "would sooner resign than sanction the mad project of the administration." In the forthcoming session of Congress he opposed Jackson's "coercive" policy. On February 2, 1833, he wrote his wife: "I fear we shall make war upon her [South Carolina]—I am opposed to harsh measures, and shall make as strong a speech against [it] as I can." When the force bill came up in the Senate, he opposed it.[40]

The nullification fight definitely turned Mangum against Jackson. He began working with Clay and Calhoun in their effort to build up an opposition party. The Bank issue was important in Mangum's shift, partly because the Bank had many supporters in his state.[41] In the congressional election of 1833 the Jackson candidates denounced the Bank as federalism. Despite Jackson's strength two of the pro-Bank candidates won.[42] Prior to 1833 Mangum had been uncertain on the Bank. He wrote William

[36]Pegg, "Whig Party in N. C.," 8.
[37]Charles R. Ramsey to Mangum, Oct. 19, 1832, Mangum Papers.
[38]Chavis to Mangum, Nov. 3, 1832, Mangum Papers.
[39]McDuffie, "Willie P. Mangum," 47.
[40]*The Register of Debates of Congress*, 29 vols. (Washington, D. C.: Gales and Seaton, 1825-1837), 22 Cong., 1 sess., 174-175, 236, 237.
[41]Pegg, "Whig Party in N. C.," 12-13; A. C. Cole, *The Whig Party in the South* (Washington, D. C.: American Historical Association, 1913), 28.
[42]Pegg, "Whig Party in N. C.," 15.

Polk on February 11, 1832, that the Bank was an "indispensible institution" and yet he voted against rechartering it.

In the fall of 1833 Secretary of the Treasury Taney issued his order for the removal of deposits from the United States Bank and in December he reported to Congress the reason for the removal. By the time Congress met Mangum had not officially broken with Jackson, although the rumor was current that he was no longer a supporter of the President's policies. With the opening of Congress he lined up with the pro-Bank party. William Montgomery from Mangum's home county indignantly wrote him December 27: "We are (your old friends) more than mortified at the course you are taking in the Senate." The state was in a political ferment. Jackson's popularity in North Carolina kept most of the people with him, but the pro-Bank leaders tried to counteract this sentiment by holding public meetings and condemning the removal of deposits. Copies of these county resolutions were sent to Washington. On February 3, 1834, in his speech against the removal of deposits, Mangum declared that it was not a question of "bank or no bank" but of "law or no law." A few days later he presented some resolutions of Burke County strongly condemning Jackson's action.[43] Bedford Brown, the other United States Senator from North Carolina, denied that these resolutions represented the sentiment of Burke. Other resolutions from other counties caused similar disagreements between Brown and Mangum.[44] On February 25 Mangum delivered his philippic against the administration, accusing it of usurping power and of corruption.[45] The only motive, he asserted, that he could find for the removal of the deposits was the desire for more political plums. The New York Central Committee was so pleased it published and circulated the speech for political purposes.[46] As chairman of the Senate Committee of Reference, Mangum also attacked Jackson for refusing to turn over to the Senate a copy of his communication to the Cabinet on the removals. These steps made Mangum the leader of the opposition party in North Carolina.[47] His colleague in the Senate, Bedford Brown, continued to support Jackson. These two men became the recognized state leaders of the two parties, Democratic and Whig. The dele-

[43]*Senate Document* 143, 23 Cong., 1 sess., 2 pp.
[44]Letters of Chavis, Feb. 26, J. Busbee, Feb. 27, J. T. Avery, Feb. 28, Priestley Mangum, March 7, and H. T. Clark, March 12, to Willie P. Mangum, Mangum Papers.
[45]Pegg, "Whig Party in N. C.," 18; *Senate Documents* 252 and 310, 23 Cong., 1 sess., 2 pp.
[46]*Register of Debates*, 23 Cong., 1 sess., 272.
[47]Pegg, "Whig Party in N. C.," 17-19.

gation in the House of Representatives divided evenly between the two.[48]

During the session of 1833-1834 Mangum was appointed a member of a Senate Committee to investigate the Bank in order to ascertain if Jackson's criticisms were valid. Ewing, Tyler, and Webster were also members. The committee visited Baltimore, New York, New Haven, and Boston and planned a trip to Philadelphia. From the branches of the Bank in the South and West the committee gathered its information by letters of inquiry addressed to local men connected with the institution. In their investigations they raised questions on whether the Bank had violated its contracts, whether money was safe in its vaults, and whether the institution had changed its policies since 1832. On December 18, 1834, Tyler, the chairman, made the report exonerating the Bank on all of these counts.[49]

Mangum played an important part in this investigation. In his papers are several communications from Bank leaders of North Carolina answering the questions raised by the committee. Even more significant to him was the experience of being in the East and New England for the first time. He attended the Harvard College Commencement and the Phi Beta Kappa Dinner. He paid his respects to John Quincey Adams and dined at the Websters. He wrote at great length on conditions and his reflections on what he found. He was greatly impressed with the beauty and pretentiousness of the houses in and near Boston, with the cleanliness of the town, and with the "gentility" of the well-to-do inhabitants. He was shocked at the working conditions in the textile mills and disappointed at the premium which New Englanders placed on wealth and political position in determining one's entertainment. Frequently in his letters he revealed his provincialism by reminding his wife that his own state was more wholesome and its people more sincere.[50]

In the summer of 1834 after Mangum had become the recognized leader of the party which opposed Jackson, public meetings within North Carolina endorsed or condemned the divergent stands of Mangum and Brown on the Bank. For the first time since Mangum had entered politics there were two definite national parties in the state. Each side proceeded to organize local and central committees. In the work of organization Man-

---

[48]Pegg, "Whig Party in N. C.," 19.
[49]*Daily National Intelligencer*, Dec. 19, 1834; L. G. Tyler, *The Letters and Times of the Tylers*, 3 vols. (Richmond, Va.: Whittet and Shepperson, 1884-1896), I, 503-505.
[50]Mangum to his wife, Aug. 19, Sept. 2, 13, 1834, Mangum Papers.

gum made a significant contribution to the Whigs. He was a
"genius for allaying prejudices and for harmonizing differences."[51] When he returned to Washington he kept in touch with
state Whigs. With others he encouraged the state leaders to support internal improvement, constitutional reforms, public education, and distribution.[52]

Just as Mangum was becoming a recognized national leader of
his party and was being mentioned for the vice-presidency, the
Jackson forces within North Carolina tried to clip his wings by
having the legislature instruct him to vote for Benton's motion
to expunge the resolutions of censure of Jackson for removing
the deposits. In the state election of 1834 the Democrats succeeded in gaining control of both houses of the legislature. Upon
the meeting of the General Assembly, therefore, Bedford Brown
was reelected to the United States Senate. This was followed by
a resolution instructing Mangum and Brown to vote for Benton's
motion. A heated constitutional argument ensued. The resolution
passed the legislature although by a close vote.[53]

What should Mangum do? For the first quarter of a century of
the Federal Constitution such a resolution had usually resulted
in compliance or resignation on the part of the Senator. Mangum
insisted that the conditions in his controversy were different
from the earlier ones because he was being asked to vote for the
unconstitutional action of Jackson. He, therefore, presented the
legislature's resolution of instruction to the Senate and announced that since the assembly, like himself, was a servant of
the people he would wait until after the next election to see
which his constituents approved.[54]

Mangum continued to be uncertain on the course he should follow. On December 16, 1834, he wrote W. A. Graham to discuss
it with his friends and give him advice. He considered resigning
before the election but was afraid such a course would set a
precedent which would weaken the Senate and Constitution. The
next day he wrote Graham again that Senators Black and Moore
of Mississippi and Alabama respectively would be strengthened
in their fight against instructions if he retained his seat. If all
three should resign, the Jackson forces would gain control of the

[51]Pegg, "Whig Party in N. C.," 19.
[52]W. K. Boyd, "A Draft of a Life of Willie P. Mangum," Chapter V, 13, in the Mangum
Papers at Duke University Library, Durham, N. C. After Miss McDuffie died without completing her life of Mangum, Boyd continued her study. Unfortunately he died before he had
gone very far with it.
[53]Earl R. Franklin, "The Instruction of United States Senators by North Carolina," Trinity College Historical Papers, Ser. VII (1907), 1-15; Pegg, "Whig Party in N. C.," 35-36.
[54]Register of Debates, 23 Cong., 2 sess., 722.

Senate. As a result of these arguments his friends urged him not to resign. Despite constant attacks from the Jackson forces he held his seat until after the next election in 1836 when his party was defeated.

These attacks tended to make the Whig party in North Carolina a more homogeneous group. The press and public meetings were the chief agencies for strengthening the organization. Most of the state's newspapers supported the party. The public Whig meetings endorsed Mangum's stand against instructions. In December, 1835, a statewide organization with a central committee was perfected. In the race for governor which followed, the Whigs won but their victory gave them such overconfidence that they failed to carry the legislature. Already Mangum had been discouraged by the way things were going in Washington. On April 23, 1836, he wrote Mrs. Mangum: "I feel extremely little interest in the progress of the public business here, so little goes according to my notion of right." A month later he wrote her again: "I am sick and tired of my daily attendance on Congress —The business is dull and uninteresting, and everything is going wrong, and almost to ruin." As a result of this discontent and the election of a Democratic legislature, Mangum resigned his Senate seat November 24, 1836; Robert Strange, a Democrat, was elected to succeed him.

Mangum returned to his law practice. In 1836 he was mentioned for vice-presidential candidate on a Whig ticket with Hugh Lawson White.[55] In the electoral college of that year South Carolina, probably under the influence of W. C. Preston rather than Calhoun, cast its electoral vote for Mangum for President.[56]

Although Mangum campaigned for White in 1836, his enthusiasm for politics was temporarily on the wane. The next year some of his friends tried to induce him to run for Congress, but he refused. He did agree in 1840 to serve in the legislature when as chairman of the educational committee he drew up an educational act which was one of the important steps in the development of the state's public school system.[57]

Mangum did not remain out of national politics for long. In the year following his resignation from the Senate he kept up his correspondence with Preston, Crittenden, and Clay with a view to keeping in touch with the national scene. In that same year

[55]Weeks, "W. P. M.," Biog. Hist. of N. C., V, 247.
[56]Weeks, "W. P. M.," Biog. Hist. of N. C., V, 247.
[57]Weeks, "W. P. M., Biog. Hist. of N. C., V, 250.

2

he began campaigning for Clay's nomination. As a step in that direction he organized district conventions and primary meetings throughout the state. In 1838 the legislature became Whig. The party's success gave the Whigs confidence for their convention the next year. This was the first state convention of the party in North Carolina. Here Mangum pushed the cause of Clay. Along with John Owen and others, he was appointed as delegate to the national party convention at Harrisburg where Owen was urged to accept the vice-presidential nomination. Upon his refusal some advocated Mangum. According to family tradition he was offered the post but refused because the convention had sidestepped Clay for Harrison.[58] Wise and Tyler asserted that this was not true.[59]

If Mangum was disappointed at the Whig national ticket he did not let his disappointment interfere with his effectiveness as a campaigner. W. A. Graham wrote J. W. Bryan, August 15, 1840, "Mangum kept the field consistently until the day of the election."[60] Invitations to speak at political rallies were received by him from many places within the state, from Virginia, South Carolina, and Alabama. One of the literary societies at the University of Alabama elected him an honorary member. In his home county at Hillsboro he engaged Bedford Brown in a joint debate from 11 a. m. to sundown on two successive days.[61]

The Democrats in the legislature in 1835-1836 had insisted on Mangum's resigning or voting as they directed. In consequence of the Democratic victory of 1836 he resigned but at the same time denied the right of the legislature to instruct a Senator. In 1838 the Whigs won the control of the General Assembly, but because of their previous position refused to instruct the Democratic Senators Strange and Brown. They did, however, demand that the Democrats comply with their position of 1835 and have their Senators give up their offices. Strange and Brown agreed to resign if the Whig legislature would admit the right of instruction. This the Whigs refused to do. Again in 1840 the Whigs gained control. This time Strange and Brown resigned. Along with Mangum, Gaston, Badger, Williams, Caldwell, Graham, Owen, Dudley, and W. B. Shepard were proposed for the two vacancies. There were two wings to the Whig party in the state,

[58]Weeks, "W. P. M.," *Biog. Hist. of N. C.,* V, 250-251.
[59]J. G. deR. Hamilton, *Party Politics in North Carolina, 1835-1860,* in *The James Sprunt Historical Publications,* XV, Nos. 1-2 (1916), 64. Hereafter cited as Hamilton, *Party Politics in N. C.* See also Weeks, "W. P. M.": *Biog. Hist. of N. C.,* V, 251.
[60]Graham Papers, Southern Collection, University of North Carolina, Chapel Hill, N. C. Hereafter cited as Graham Papers.
[61]Pegg, "Whig Party in N. C.," 80.

the states' rights and nationalist Whigs. A caucus resulted in the selection of Mangum from the states' rights group and, after Gaston refused, Graham from the nationalists.[62] Both men were elected without difficulty. Mangum immediately went to Washington to take his seat.

In the Senate in 1841, Mangum lined up with Clay who, it was assumed, would dominate the Whig Administration. On February 13, 1841, Mangum wrote his wife that he was "rushed" in preparing for the new administration. He was determined, he continued, to obtain as many appointments for his state as possible. Earlier he had proposed Owen and later Badger for the Cabinet. The latter won and became Secretary of the Navy. Being close to Clay, Mangum found the pressure for assistance in obtaining public office especially strong. His correspondence for the period is evidence of the extent of the pressure and of his influence.

Upon the death of Harrison and the assumption of power by Tyler, Mangum continued to cooperate with Clay. He was a member of several important committees, which made his duties much more strenuous than in his previous congressional terms. By the summer he was sick with fever and almost ready to quit. He voted for the recharter of the Bank against Tyler's veto, for the Whig tariff, and for Clay's distribution bill.[63] On September 11, 1841, in the congressional caucus he introduced the resolutions calling for an address to the people to blame Tyler for the Whig failures, to accuse him of deserting his party, and, therefore, to read him out of the party.[64]

As a result of the split with Tyler, Mangum and others proceeded to make the Whig organization a Clay party. Efforts were made to establish friendly newspapers. To accomplish this, correspondence with New York business friends was renewed. At home he tried to purge the party of Tyler supporters.[65] Although the pressure of duties in Congress prevented his attending the state convention, his influence there must have been strong for the New York *Herald* called it "your convention."[66] Some wanted to nominate Clay in 1842 for the campaign of 1844, but Mangum successfully urged delay.[67]

On May 31, 1842, Mangum was elected president *protempore*

---

[62]Hamilton, *Party Politics in N. C.*, 70; Pegg, "Whig Party in N. C.," 106-108.
[63]Pegg, "Whig Party in N. C.," 210-211, 219.
[64]Cole, *Whig Party in the South*, 92.
[65]C. P. Green to Mangum, Dec. 10, 1841, Mangum Papers.
[66]Green to Mangum, April 18, 1842, Mangum Papers.
[67]Boyd, "Draft of a Life of Mangum," Chapter VII, 4.

of the Senate—a position that he held until 1845. Since the Vice President, Tyler, had assumed the office of President on the death of Harrison, Mangum was by virtue of his office next in succession to the presidency. Tyler's narrow escape from the tragic accident on the *U. S. S. Princeton* in 1844 measured the margin of chance by which Mangum failed to become President. When his position of presiding officer drew to a close on March 4, 1845, he initiated the practice of turning back the clock to lengthen the legislative day of the out-going administration.[68] Caleb Atwater of Ohio wrote in 1844 that as a presiding officer Mangum was at ease, always dignified, courteous, and in brief, was "the best presiding officer that I ever saw in any legislative assembly."[69] He apparently had new social obligations too, for on December 16, 1842, Phineas Janney wrote that he was sending him a basket of champagne and several dozen bottles of his best wines.

He continued to campaign for Clay. On February 24, 1843, he advised C. P. Green to have the Whig convention of North Carolina meet and endorse the Kentuckian for President and leave the vice-presidential choice until the national convention. If North Carolina should lead, he continued, New York would follow. His correspondence with Reverdy Johnson, Clay, Nicholas Carroll, Thurlow Weed, and other Whig leaders indicates his importance in the approaching campaign. In this period there are, in his papers, fewer letters to his wife and to his constituents. He was invited to join a literary society at Dickinson College, to deliver a commencement oration at his own university, and to attend the usual political rallies. Apparently he ignored most of them. C. L. Hinton wrote him on November 16, 1844, that he did not see his constituents enough. Priestley also wrote him that his failure to give attention to his constituents "has been a prolific source of complaint."[70] He was accused of being too busy with national politics to look after local interests.

North Carolina Whigs who were enthusiastic for Clay in 1844 urged Mangum to run for the second place on the ticket. Mangum reminded them that the Whigs would have a better chance if the running mate were not from a slave-holding state. North Carolina's endorsement of the Kentuckian was followed in Georgia and several other Southern states. Invited to Raleigh, Clay

---

[68]Weeks, "W. P. M.," *Biog. Hist. of N. C.,* V, 252; Boyd, "Draft of Life of Mangum," Chapter VII, 5.
[69]Quoted in Weeks, "W. P. M.," *Biog. Hist. of N. C.,* V, 253.
[70]January 30, 1846, Mangum Papers.

toured many of the Southern states, although he failed to carry
any south of North Carolina. His success in the latter was partly
due to Mangum's untiring efforts. By this time Clay's platform
was acceptable to many Southern Whigs. Mangum, Badger, and
Graham from North Carolina were completely reconciled to the
tariff, distribution, and the Bank. In the state government the
Whig leaders supported internal improvements, a stronger state
banking system, and a state-supported school system.

Before the election, Mangum had been little concerned over
the annexation of Texas question. Although a slave owner he
rarely said anything in his political speeches or letters about
slavery expansion. In this he represented the sentiment of his
party in North Carolina.[71] Until Clay's Raleigh letter, Mangum
had taken no stand on Texas. He was afraid annexation or its
agitation would provoke war with Mexico and reduce the price
of cotton. Later when the joint resolution of annexation came
before the Senate he voted against it. He insisted that the adoption of the resolution would agitate the slavery issue, increase
sectional animosities, and possibly provoke war.[72]

Although most North Carolina Whigs seemed little concerned
about Oregon, Mangum saw in the Democratic program a cause
for war with Great Britain. He, therefore, made a strong speech
and introduced resolutions in the Senate calling for arbitration.
On March 24, 1846, George C. Collins of Philadelphia wrote
Mangum congratulating him on his speech and suggesting that
many leaders in his section felt that Mangum's position on Oregon and Mexico made him a popular candidate for President.
Mangum seemed more concerned, at this time, over the danger of
a foreign war than over the slavery struggle. To him the Wilmot
Priviso was of "exceeding slight importance," although he
thought it unconstitutional. He denied that Congress had the authority to exclude slavery from the territories; and yet he voted
for the extension of the Missouri Compromise to the Pacific. Unlike Badger he later supported the Clayton bill which was designed to leave the legality of slavery in the territory to the
Supreme Court.

The threats of war with Great Britain and Mexico caused
Mangum to lose respect for the administration. On May 11,
1846, he wrote his wife that he was afraid that Polk's policies
would drive the country into a war which would be disastrous.

[71]Pegg, "Whig Party in N. C.," 222.
[72]Mangum to W. A. Graham, Feb. 26, 1845, Graham Papers; Mangum to D. F. Caldwell,
Feb. 20, 1845, Mangum Papers.

Discouraged by the course of events he wrote her that he could do no good in Washington and that he would not return to the Senate after his term was up. Once his country got into war, however, he promised to support it.[73] Mangum's threat to withdraw from the Senate alarmed his political friends who urged him to run again.[74]

Along with other Southern Whigs Mangum opposed Polk's domestic policies. He voted against the Walker Tariff.[75] By 1846 he was for moderate protection. He had lost interest in the Bank as an issue.[76]

In the presidential campaign of 1848 he worked for the nomination of Scott. Some of his friends endorsed Mangum for Vice President.[77] The National American Party of Pennsylvania offered him the first place on its ticket but he declined.[78] Apparently Mangum expected the Whig nomination for Vice President.[79] He soon gave up this hope when he saw that the North Carolina delegation, according to Graham, did "not seem inclined to his support."[80] Mangum was also proposed as a running mate with Judge McLean of Ohio.[81] He did not approve Taylor's nomination for he felt that the General was not strong on Whig principles.[82] With Morehead of Kentucky, Clayton of Delaware, and Crittenden, Mangum was selected to visit Taylor and win him to the Whig principles. Mangum refused to serve on this committee although he had no personal dislike for Taylor. When he saw that Scott could not win the nomination he tried to push Clay into the arena. Despite Mangum's opposition the North Carolina delegation supported Taylor on the first ballot.[83]

Although displeased with the party's nominees, Mangum campaigned for Taylor and Fillmore. He charged the Democratic candidate, Lewis Cass, with using different campaign documents in the South and the North. Northern and Southern Whig newspapers made much of this charge.[84] Partly as a result of his efforts twenty-one of the state's thirty-eight counties voted for Taylor.[85]

[73]Mangum to his wife, Jan. 22, 1846, Mangum Papers.
[74]Clingman to Mangum, Aug. 25, Gales to Mangum, Sept. 22, 1846, Mangum Papers.
[75]Pegg, "Whig Party in N. C.," 213.
[76]Pegg, "Whig Party in N. C.," 222.
[77]James Graham to W. A. Graham, Feb. 20, June 9, 1848, Graham Papers; Nicholas Carroll to Mangum, March 19, 1845, Mangum Papers.
[78]Peter S. Smith to Mangum, April 16, 1847, Mangum Papers; Weeks, "W. P. M.," Biog. Hist. of N. C., V, 252.
[79]W. A. Graham to James Graham, June 9, 1848, Graham Papers.
[80]W. A. Graham to James Graham, June 9, 1848, Graham Papers.
[81]Weeks, "W. P. M.," Biog. Hist. of N. C.," V, 252.
[82]Mangum to W. A. Graham, Feb. 15, 1848, Graham Papers.
[83]Pegg, "Whig Party in N. C.," 252.
[84]Boyd, "Draft of Life of Mangum," Chapter VIII, 1.
[85]Pegg, "Whig Party in N. C.," 254.

Despite his part in carrying his state for Taylor, Mangum soon realized that his influence in the new administration would be slight, especially in the State Department which Clayton headed.[86] When asked by Crittenden which of the North Carolina Whigs should be put in Taylor's cabinet, Bedford Brown suggested Mangum in preference to Badger because the former did not have the latter's "ultraism." Besides, Brown added, Mangum's "generous bearing as a man gives him much more popularity" in North Carolina.[87] Other North Carolinians did not feel so kindly toward Mangum at this time because of his refusal to cooperate with Taylor. R. T. Paine, from Chowan County, wrote W. A. Graham June 14, 1849: "Is there no way by which you can prevail on our Senator [Mangum] to return home? This [is] a thing very greatly desired and if you can accomplish it I beseech you. Do so for his sake and for North Carolina."[88] Others were displeased that he did not return home during his vacation to find out the public's reaction to his course. When Duncan Cameron and C. L. Hinton who had been his close political advisers for thirty years tried to see Mangum in Washington, he refused to see them, because of this political rift.[89]

In the conflict over Clay's compromise measures of 1850 Mangum took an active part. He had been indifferent to the Wilmot Proviso, but later he had accepted the Calhoun doctrine that slavery was legal in the new territories as soon as they were acquired by the United States. He accepted the Clayton Compromise as a way out of the territorial difficulties, although most of the North Carolina Whigs opposed this measure.[90] He disapproved Calhoun's efforts to unite the Southern Congressmen in a common program; and yet a little later he presented to Congress the Wilmington resolutions in favor of the Nashville Convention.[91] To some Mangum was leaning to the extreme Southern view; and to others he did not appear "zealous enough, for the rights of slavery, or at least [he was guilty] of appearing too tolerant of the abolition feeling at the North."[92] Actually Mangum was neither for one side nor the other. He refused to go along with Taylor whose policies he had never liked. Instead he worked with Clay to put through the compromise measures. In the de-

---

[86]Mangum to W. A. Graham, March 1, 1849, Graham Papers.
[87]Boyd, "Draft of Life of Mangum," Chapter VIII, 2.
[88]Boyd, "Draft of a Life of Mangum," Chapter VII, 4.
[89]W. A. Graham to James Graham, March 24, 1850, Graham Papers.
[90]Pegg, "Whig Party in N. C.," 228.
[91]Mangum to W. A. Graham, March, 1849, Graham Papers; Boyd, "Draft of Life of Mangum," Chapter VIII, 3.
[92]W. A. Graham to James Graham, March 24, 1850, Graham Papers.

bate which developed he and Badger held Webster's feet to the
fire until he delivered his famous 7th of March speech which
helped create sentiment for the passage of the Compromise.[93]
He eased up on his former expression of states' rights, and both
in the Committee of Thirteen and in an able speech in the Senate
he supported the compromise proposals.[94] He did not vote on the
Texas boundary, Utah, or California bills, but he voted in the
affirmative for the New Mexico, and Fugitive Slave laws, and in
the negative on the abolition of the slave trade in the District
of Columbia.

In June, 1850, he went home to see his constituents. Immediately Clay and D. R. Atchison frantically urged his return to
help pass the measures.[95] Although Mangum had not been too
consistent on the Compromise he had worked for most of Clay's
proposals.

When Fillmore became President, Mangum was more friendly
although not enthusiastic toward his administration. In the autumn of 1851 he had a fall from which he never completely recovered. Through the assistance of his son who went to Washington to take care of him, Mangum was soon back in the Senate
where he engineered through Congress a bill to reorganize the
State Department. He was, however, quite unhappy in the national capital. He quarreled with Webster over appointments,
when he felt Webster was giving the best places in the State Department to New Englanders. Webster was upheld by the President. As a result Mangum wrote Graham that he was considering going over to the Democrats.[96] He felt that everything was
going wrong. On December 31, 1851, he wrote Graham that the
world was heading for a catastrophe. These, he added, "are the
imagining of old age, and I am old and yet have little faith."[97]
He stayed away from the President's levees. In poor health and
unhappy over the political trends, he was a broken man.

Most North Carolina Whigs endorsed Fillmore for renomina-
tion in 1852. It was, therefore, a great shock to them when Man-
gum in a speech in the Senate on April 4 endorsed Scott. In the
North Mangum's endorsement was enthusiastically received. The
New York papers began championing him for Vice President.[98]
In the South the reaction was reversed. On April 20, he refused

[93]Cole, *Whig Party in the South*, 165n.
[94]Pegg, "Whig Party in N. C.," 310.
[95]Clay to Mangum, June 25 and Atchison to Mangum, June 28, 1850, Mangum Papers.
[96]Boyd, "Draft of Life of Mangum," Chapter VIII, 4.
[97]Graham Papers.
[98]Boyd, "Draft of Life of Mangum," Chapter VIII, 7.

as chairman of the Whig caucus to entertain a resolution endorsing the Compromise of 1850. Whereupon a majority of the Southern Whigs bolted. Most North Carolina Whig papers condemned Mangum's ruling.[99] The state Whigs who soon thereafter endorsed Fillmore and Graham refused to follow Mangum.[100] Nevertheless, the national convention which nominated Scott offered the vice-presidential place on the ticket to Mangum. He declined because his own state was against him.[101] He recommended Graham who was nominated.[102] Mangum actively campaigned for the Whig candidates in North Carolina but refused invitations to speak in New York and neighboring states. In the election which followed his own state supported the Democratic candidates.

Mangum returned to his native county in March, 1853. For some months his health had been bad. The repudiation of his own people also hurt him. Before leaving Washington he had written his wife that he was taking no part in public affairs except to vote and that he regretted that he had stayed away from home these several years for the empty honors of Washington. Upon returning home he began again his law practice and the improvement of his estate. In 1854 the Whigs tried again to get him into the campaign for the party but he refused. As a result of a petition of citizens of his county he was appointed justice of the peace. About 1856 he had a stroke of paralysis from which he never recovered. His son wrote Fannie Mangum May 21, 1858, that as a result of the stroke which came from the fall of 1851 he could walk only with great difficulty and he could scarcely speak at all. More and more his wife and daughter, Pattie, took over the management of his plantation. Although opposed to secession, when the Civil War came he encouraged his only son to volunteer in the Confederate States Army. This son, Lieutenant William Preston Mangum, named for William C. Preston whom Mangum greatly admired, enlisted in the 6th North Carolina Regiment and was mortally wounded in the First Battle of Manassas. He died on February 28, 1861. The news of the son's death was such a blow to the father that he never spoke again. Within a few weeks thereafter on September 7, 1861, Mangum died.

[99]Pegg, "Whig Party in N. C.," 336.
[100]R. B. Gilliam to W. A. Graham, June 2, 1852, Graham Papers.
[101]He wrote his daughter on June 23, 1852, "I might have been second, but declined—the ill temper of North Carolina is such that I thought it might hazard the vote." Mangum Papers.
[102]Pegg, "Whig Party in N. C.," 336.

In politics Mangum was a controversial figure. His enemies accused him of being inconsistent. In June, 1842, the partisan *North Carolina Standard* declared that Mangum "has been Federal and Anti-Federal; Jackson and Anti-Jackson; Calhoun and Anti-Calhoun; Clay and Anti-Clay; Nullifier and Anti-Nullifier. . . . [Every political leader of the state remembers the] period when Mr. Mangum has been upon his side and upon the other also."[103] There seems some basis for this criticism although the *Standard* greatly exaggerated Mangum's inconsistency. But what successful political leaders of that period were not inconsistent! Certainly Clay, Webster, and Calhoun were. Like other leaders Mangum was greatly influenced by public opinion. He made conscious efforts to ascertain what his constituents were thinking. Apparently he was very adept at this for he remained in Congress almost continuously from 1823 to 1853. There were times, however, when Mangum ignored public opinion as in his support of Crawford and the Bank after his state had turned against both. In 1852 near the end of his career he supported Scott although he knew his act was political suicide.

Mangum's effectiveness as a leader was not so much due to his ability as a speaker as to his work in the cloakroom. Nevertheless he was a good speaker. Alexander H. Stephens reported that he spoke with "clearness, conciseness, terseness and power." He rarely spoke in Congress and then from brief notes. In the Mangum Papers at Duke University is a crumpled piece of paper on which are jotted down a few topics he wished to develop in a speech in the 1840's in defense of Whig policies. It included about a dozen topics. They served as the basis for a two-day speech.

He was a commanding figure in appearance and a good conversationalist. Daniel L. Goodloe said he was a better conversationalist than Clay.[104] He had the reputation of being kindly and gracious although he could withstand an attack. After Mangum's defense from an attack by Calhoun, Webster wrote Mangum, "No man could be more unjustly attacked—no man could repel an attack better."[105] Dr. Weeks says he was the "life and soul of a dinner party."[106] He read extensively, especially newspapers.[107] John B. Fry of New York wrote Crittenden that Mangum was a

[103]Hamilton, *Party Politics in N. C.*, 72.
[104]Weeks, "W. P. M.," *Biog. Hist. of N. C.*, V, 254.
[105]Webster to Mangum, no date, Mangum Papers.
[106]Weeks, "W. P. M.," *Biog. Hist. of N. C.*, V, 254.
[107]D. L. Swain to Paul Cameron, Jan. 20, 1862, Cameron Papers, Southern Collection,

man of "great intellectual capacity" and a statesman of "foremost rank."[108] Orlando Brown asserted that there was a "frankness and manliness about him and at the same time an ease and friendliness of manner that charmed me."[109]

University of North Carolina, Chapel Hill, N. C.
[108]Sept. 25, 1861, Crittenden Papers.
[109]Brown to Crittenden, Feb. 11, 1836, Crittenden Papers.

A CALENDAR OF MANUSCRIPTS IN THE MANGUM PAPERS FOR THE PERIOD ENDING DECEMBER 31, 1832, OMITTED IN THIS PUBLICATION

The reasons for the omissions are that the papers omitted do not relate directly to Mangum or they are not, in the opinion of the editor, sufficiently important or pertinent to the subject of this publication to justify their inclusion. After each listing, the present location of the manuscript is indicated.

1. May 2, 1763. A deed of sale of 320 acres of land on Dyals (Dials) Creek, Orange County, by James Horton of Orange County to Arthur Mangum of Granville County. Mangum agreed to pay £30 current Virginia Money. MS at Duke University.

2. July 30, 1779. A plot of survey for Asa Bishop of a tract of 640 acres which joined the land of William Alston and which lay north of the Little River and on both sides of Mountain Creek, a tributary, in Orange County. MS at Duke University.

3. July 30, 1779. A plot of a survey for Asa Bishop of a tract of 200 acres which adjoined the tract listed in No. 2 above. MS at Duke University.

4. August 12, 1779. A plot of a survey for Arthur Mangum of a tract of 550 acres on Dyals (Dials) Creek in Orange County. MS at Duke University.

5. January 1, 1780. An indenture of sale for £3000 North Carolina currency of a tract of 275 acres called the "Red Cobbin Tract" in Orange County by William Alston and wife, Charity, to John Carrington, Jr. MS at Duke University.

6. March 13, 1780. A certificate of a grant by the state of North Carolina, at the rate of 50/ per 100 acres, to Asa Bishop of a tract of 640 acres adjoining the tract in No. 5 above. MS at Duke University.

7. March 13, 1780. A certificate of a grant by the state of North Carolina, at the rate of 50/ per 100 acres, to Arthur Mangum of a tract of 550 acres in Orange County. MS at Duke University.

8. March 31, 1780. An indenture of sale by William Alston to John Carrington for the sum of £200 North Carolina currency of a part of the Alston plantation in Orange County. MS at Duke University.

9. January 6, 1781. An indenture of sale by Asa Bishop to James Powell of Hertford County of a tract of 1000 acres on Mountain Creek adjoining the lands of Red Cobbin, Rich Mountain, Horton, Clark, and Alexander Tarrintine for the sum of £20,000 North Carolina currency. MS at Duke University.

10. October 25, 1782. A certificate of a grant of 200 acres of land in Orange County by the state of North Carolina, at the rate of 50/ per 100 acres. MS at Duke University.

11. November 4, 1784. A certificate of a grant to Arthur Mangum by the state of North Carolina, at the rate of 50/ per 100 acres, of a tract of 186 acres in Orange County. MS at Duke University.

12. October 4, 1785. A deed of Arthur Mangum to Sion Bobbitt and his

wife Sally (the daughter of Arthur Mangum) for 117 acres of land adjoining Mangum's tract for the price of 5/. MS at Duke University.

13. July 6, 1788. An abstract of a deed from Blake Baker to John Carrington for 500 acres in Orange County. MS at Duke University.

14. May 18, 1789. A copy of a certificate of a grant of 253 acres in Orange County, at the rate of 50/ per 100 acres, by the state of North Carolina to Arthur Mangum. Certified by William Hill, March 30, 1835. MS at Duke University.

15. October 27, 1789. An indenture of a sale of a tract of 170 acres in Orange County by James Carrington to John Carrington for the sum of £1000 current money. MS at Duke University.

16. May 10, 1795. An indenture of sale of 382 acres along Mountain Creek in Orange County by John Carrington to George Carrington for the sum of £620 currency. MS at Duke University.

17. September 16, 1796. An abstract of a deed of sale of 200 acres in Orange County by John Cummins to George Carrington. (This abstract is written on the back of No. 13 above). MS at Duke University.

18. May 15, 1798. An indenture of sale by John Carrington to William Cain, Sr., for the sum of £270 North Carolina currency for 170 acres of land on Mountain Creek in Orange County. MS at Duke University.

19. May 15, 1798. An indenture of sale by James Carrington to William Cain, Sr., for the sum of £560 10/ North Carolina currency of a tract of 275 acres of land (The Red Cobbin Tract) in Orange County. MS at Duke University.

20. August 4, 1801. A deed of Samuel Turrentine, sheriff, to William Cain, David Ray, James Yarborough for a lot in Hillsborough formerly seized by the court from Samuel Clenny and Henry Thompson to cover the cost of court, £30. MS at Duke University.

21. March 24, 1804. An indenture of Sharock Forrest to William P. Mangum. (This manuscript is faded to such an extent that it is illegible). MS at University of North Carolina.

22. April 6, 1804. An indenture of sale by James Powell formerly of Orange County and at the time of this indenture of Glenn County, Georgia, to William Cain for the sum of $1000 three tracts of 1000 acres of land in Orange County. (This was more than half of land willed to Powell by his father.) MS at Duke University.

23. October 4, 1806. An assignment by Joseph Brittain of his land (the amount is not given) to William P. Mangum. MS at Duke University.

24. September 10, 1809. A plot of a survey of a tract of 570 acres on Flat River in Orange County for William P. Mangum. MS at Duke University.

25. May 15, 1812. A certificate of a grant of 570 acres of land in Orange County, at the rate of 50/ for 100 acres, by the state of North Carolina to William P. Mangum. MS at Duke University.

26. May 17, 1814. A copy of a certificate of a grant by the state of North Carolina to John Carrington of 26½ acres on Mountain Creek in Orange County. Verified by Wm. Hill, March 30, 1835. MS at Duke University.

27. March 2, 1815. A certificate of membership for Priestley H. Mangum

in the Dialectic Society at the University of North Carolina. Typed
copy at the State Department of Archives and History, Raleigh.

28. June 28, 1815. Priestley H. Mangum's diploma for the A.B. degree at
the University of North Carolina. Typed copy at the State Department
of Archives and History, Raleigh.

29. March 2, 1816. A copy of the will of Jacob Umstead. MS in the possession of Mangum Turner, Winston-Salem, North Carolina.

30. April 20, 1816. A deed of George Carrington to William Cain, Sr., for
a tract of 500 acres on Mountain Creek in Orange County for the sum
of $2000 United States money. MS at Duke University.

31. July 9, 1817. A plot of a survey of 324 acres of land on Flat River in
Orange County owned by William P. Mangum. MS at Duke University.

32. August 4, 1817. License of Priestley H. Mangum to practice law before
the superior court of North Carolina. MS in the Library of Congress.

33. September 20, 1817. A deed of George Carrington to William Cain, Sr.,
for a tract of land of 200 acres on Mountain Creek in Orange County.
MS in possession of Mangum Turner, Winston-Salem, North Carolina.

34. April 8, 1818. Letter of A. R. Ruffin to Robert Henry introducing
Priestley H. Mangum. MS in the Library of Congress.

35. May 13, 1818. A plot of a survey of disputed land lying between the
tracts of W. P. Mangum, Robert Hall, William Cain, Robert Cate, and
John J. Carrington in Orange County. MS at Duke University.

36. October 7, 1818. License of Priestley M. Mangum to practice law in
Randolph County Superior Court, North Carolina. MS in the Library
of Congress.

37. March 30, 1820. A bond for £2000 of W. W. Erwin as clerk of Burke
County Superior Court, North Carolina. MS in the Library of Congress.

38. April 11, 1820. A bond for £2000 of Robert Henry as clerk of Buncombe County Superior Court, North Carolina. MS in the Library of
Congress.

39. May 10, 1820. A bond for £2000 of George Graham as clerk of Mecklenburg County Superior Court, North Carolina. MS in the Library of
Congress.

40. February 22, 1821. The sheriff's execution of the deed for the home
place of William P. Mangum to Walter A. Mangum who was the
highest bidder. Walter paid $75 for the 100 acres in this forced sale.
MS in possession of Mangum Turner, Winston-Salem, North Carolina.

41. February 23, 1821. The sheriff's execution of the deed for a tract of
1200 acres of Arthur Bobbitt and William P. Mangum on Dials Creek
to John Fort for $350. MS in possession of Mangum Turner, Winston-
Salem, North Carolina.

42. August 19, 1821. Letter of William Walker of Wilson County, Tennessee, to Mrs. Martha Taylor of Franklin County, North Carolina, about
her lands in Tennessee. He advises her to get someone else to handle
her land claims. MS in the Library of Congress.

43. February 18, 1822. Letter of William Gaston to Samuel Hillman giving his legal opinion on a case between Abigail Haywood and her creditors, Sneed and Herndon, involving her ownership of a slave of her
second husband, Lamon. MS in the Library of Congress.

44. February 20, 1824. Letter of Richard Smith of Raleigh to Willie P. Mangum asking his aid in obtaining bounty land for Sion Bunn, a Revolutionary soldier. (He refers to enclosures which are not in the Mangum Papers.) MS in the Library of Congress.

45. February 25, 1825. A copy in Willie P. Mangum's handwriting of the correspondence between John Randolph and Daniel Webster in 1825 over their quarrel in 1816. The correspondence almost resulted in a duel. (The original correspondence and that which resulted from subsequent controversies over the correspondence is published in G. H. Van Tyne, *The Letters of Daniel Webster from Documents owned principally by the New Hampshire Historical Society*, New York, 1902, 111, 157, 169-173; and in William Cabell Bruce, *John Randolph of Roanoke, 1773-1833*, New York, 1922, I, 258-9, 442-3.) MS in the Library of Congress.

46. December, 1825. Copy of the resolutions of the legislature of North Carolina about the Cherokee lands. (This is published in the *N. C. Laws*, 1825, p. 37.) MS in the Library of Congress.

47. February 10, 1826. Notice of appointment of W. P. Mangum as attorney to receive the Revolutionary pension of Edward Johnson. MS in the Library of Congress.

48. April 29, 1826. A plot of land claimed by John Carrington and others. MS at Duke University.

49. October 20, 1826. Bond of John Bragg as Clerk of Superior Court, Warren County, North Carolina. MS in the Library of Congress.

50. July 6, 1827. Printed resolutions of South Carolina leaders, including W. C. Preston and Thomas Cooper, protesting against the Woollens Bill. (This was widely circulated among governors and congressmen.) MS in the Library of Congress.

51. March 23, 1828. Letter of Ezekiel Laws to W. P. Mangum asking the latter to defend him in a legal case with John Brown. He states that the water backing up from Brown's mill dam was injuring his land. MS in the Library of Congress.

52. October 20, 1828. A notice of Wiley Wheeler to Thomas Jones that on November 7 he will take the benefit of the insolvent debtors' law at Granville Court, North Carolina. MS in the Library of Congress.

53. February 18, 1829. A printed letter of Lewis Williams *To the Citizens of the Thirteenth Congressional District*, Washington, n.d., 3 pp. (Copies of this are available elsewhere, one being in the North Carolina Room, University of North Carolina.) MS in the Library of Congress.

54. June 20, 1830. A printed list of commencement speakers at the University of North Carolina. (This list is published in Kemp P. Battle, *History of the University of North Carolina*, I, 324.) MS in the Library of Congress.

55. November 5, 1830. Letter of Samuel King, a political leader of Iredell County, North Carolina, to Joseph Caldwell, the President of the University of North Carolina, describing some peculiarly shaped bricks and structures he found in 1826 on a trip to West Tennessee on the Hatchie River in Tipton County. (The letter was mailed by Willie P. Mangum.) MS in the Library of Congress.

56. November 14, 1831. Letter of John Wells of St. Charles City, Missouri, to————————————asking aid in obtaining a pension for Adam Zumalt, a soldier of the Revolution. MS in the Library of Congress.

57. January 2, 1832. Letter of James Grant, Jr., to Willie P. Mangum requesting his aid in obtaining an appointment as superintendent of the Live Oak Plantation in Florida to replace General Whitaker who was resigning. (Grant's father, James Grant, Sr., was Mangum's classmate at Chapel Hill and state comptroller of North Carolina from 1827 to 1834.) MS in the Library of Congress.

58. February 12, 1832. Letter of Thomas Flint of Roxboro to Willie Mangum asking his assistance in obtaining a pension for his services in the Revolution. MS in the Library of Congress.

59. March 27, 1832. Letter of Joseph B. Skinner of Edenton to Willie P. Mangum asking his assistance in obtaining an appointment of the son of Mr. Hoskin as midshipman. MS in the Library of Congress.

60. May 13, 1832. Letter of Clement Wilkins of Granville County to Willie P. Mangum asking him to subscribe to the *Globe* for him. He promises to reimburse Mangum when the latter returns from Washington. MS in the Library of Congress.

61. August 28, 1832. Letter of George and Sarah Waggoner of Allen County, Kentucky, to John Waggoner of Orange County, North Carolina. The letter is concerned with family news. (The letter was sent through Mangum.) MS in the Library of Congress.

62. August, 1832. A sworn statement of William Duke that his younger brother, Hardeman Duke, was entitled to a pension for his Revolutionary services. MS in the Library of Congress.

63. October 3, 1832. Letter of John Tyler to A. L. Botts, the brother of John Minor Botts, introducing a person whose name has been torn from the letter. He asks that this person be presented to the men of the turf in New York. MS in the Library of Congress.

64. November 24, 1832. Letter of Memucan Hunt to Willie P. Mangum asking assistance in obtaining an appointment as commissioner to the Indians west of the Mississippi. MS in the Library of Congress.

65. November 16, 1832. A deed of Walter A. Mangum to Joe Umstead, a man of color, of 52½ acres of land in Orange County for the sum of $127.50. MS at Duke University.

66. 1832. A statement that Walter A. Mangum bought from his father the "home place" on Dials Creek in Orange County. It included 100 acres. (See No. 67 below). MS in possession of Mangum Turner, Winston-Salem, North Carolina.

67. 1832. A deed of sale to Walter A. Mangum for the "home place." He paid $2000. (See No. 66 above.) MS in the possession of Mangum Turner, Winston-Salem, North Carolina.

68. No date (before 1833). A plot and description of the extent of the Rich Mountain tract of John Carrington which was granted to George Carrington. (See above No. 16). MS at Duke University.

69. No date (before 1833). A plot of a survey of a tract of "Mrs. White's" land lying south of the Oxford Road in Orange County. It included 1073 acres. MS in possession of Mangum Turner, Winston-Salem, North Carolina.

70. No date (before 1833). A statement of William Norwood who was appointed by William Cain, Sr., and Samuel Turrentine to arbitrate their differences on land claims. Norwood awarded the disputed 111¾ acres to Turrentine. MS at Duke University.

71. No date (before 1833). A deed of a grant of 172 acres of land by Thomas Carrington to George Carrington. MS in possession of Mangum Turner, Winston-Salem, North Carolina.

72. No date (before 1833). An indenture of Arthur Mangum granting Sion Bobbitt and his wife, Sally (Arthur Mangum's daughter), 117 acres of land in Orange County for 5/. (See above No. 12.) MS at Duke University.

73. No date (before 1833). Letter of John Watson to Willie P. Mangum giving a two-page "Statement of my services rendered in the revolutionary War." MS in the Library of Congress.

74. No date (before 1833). "An attack on Mr. M." This is a short (5 pages) attack on Monroe's request for reimbursement from Congress for his expenses in connection with his mission to France in 1794. This is not in Mangum's handwriting. MS at Duke University.

CHRONOLOGICAL LIST

of the

MANGUM PAPERS (TO 1833) INCLUDED

IN THIS VOLUME

li

SYMBOLS USED TO DESIGNATE DEPOSITORIES
OF MANGUM PAPERS

(The location of papers from other collections is indicated by footnotes.)

WPM-D. Willie P. Mangum Papers at Duke University, Durham, North Carolina.

WPM-LC. Willie P. Mangum Papers in the Library of Congress, Washington, District of Columbia.

WPM-NC. Willie P. Mangum Papers in the State Department of Archives and History, Raleigh, North Carolina.

WPM-UNC. Willie P. Mangum Papers, Southern Collection, University of North Carolina, Chapel Hill, North Carolina.

THE MANGUM PAPERS
1807 - 1819

Account[1] of William P. Mangum and Willie P. Mangum,
May 30, 1807, with Harts & Wright[2]

Mr. William P. Mangum[3]
1805   *in* a/c with Harts & Wright
June 24. To Merchandise /per Bill - - - - 78.5.6
1806
August 11 - " ditto per Order at 60 Days - - 54.0.6

                              £132.6.0

Messrs Wiley & Wm P. Mangum
               in a/c with Harts & Wright
       To Amt of W P Mangums account   - - 132. 6.0
1805 " balance due P & T Hart per acct rendd - - 1 - -
June 24 " Merchandise p bill - - - - - - - - 77.13.8
Decem 7 " ditto - - - " - - - - - - - - 107.11.2
1806
Jany 7 -" ditto dtd A C Mangum[4] - - - - - - 21.16.3
May 13 - " Cash for Picking Tobacco - - - - 10.6
June 7. " 3 bbls Brandy 95 Galls 60 Days - - - - 19. - -
July 11 -" Merch per Order - - - - - - - - 20.11.5

                              £380. 9.0

1806
Feby 20 - By Cash - - - - - - - - 29.14. 8
             " Tobacco - - - - - - - 20. 1. 4
May 10 - " Cash - - - - - - - 15. 4. 6
    "   13 - " Tobacco - - - - - - - 44.14.11
June 7 - " ditto - - - - - - - - - 19. 8. 8
August 14 - " Cash per A. C. Mangum - - 19. 1. -
1807
May 30 - " ditto - - - - - - - - - 30. - - 178.5. 1

                              £202.3.11

[1]The original is in the Cameron Papers, Southern Collection, University of North Carolina, Chapel Hill, N. C.
[2]Harts & Wright were local merchants in Hillsboro.
[3]Father of Willie P. Mangum. William Person Mangum was a merchant and farmer in Orange County. Weeks "W. P. M.," *Biog. Hist. of N. C.*, V, 237-238.
[4]Probably Arthur Mangum, a brother of William P. Mangum.

WPM-LC

Thomas Gales[5] to William P. Mangum

RALEIGH, Augst. 31st. 1809.

I acknowledge myself indebted to W. P. Mangum,[6] one hundred and forty dollars, for value recd. Witness my hand

THOMAS GALES

[torn] - - 70
[Addressed:]
W. P. Mangum

WPM-LC

John Harper Hinton[7] to Willie P. Mangum

CHAPEL HILL. January the 10th 1810

My worthy friend.

Previous to our leaving school at Raleigh,[8] by mutual consent, it was agree'd upon, that we should keep up a correspondence this promise has not been observed by either party until this time. I therefore take the liberty of writing you a few lines to remind you of your promise, and let you know I have not entirely forgotten mine, I have waited for some time to receive a line from you, but have finally determined that you did not intend making the first advance. I of course thought that I must, or a correspondence would not exist. I hope no other apology is requisite for my long silence.

I will now tell you something about the manner in which I spent my vacation after the examination. I spent two or three

---

[5]Thomas Gales, son of Joseph Gales, editor of the *Raleigh Register*, and brother of Joseph Gales, Jr., who edited the *National Intelligencer*, studied law in Raleigh and then moved to Louisiana. He was Jackson's aide-de-camp with the rank of major in the New Orleans campaign. Willis G. Briggs, "Joseph Gales, Editor of Raleigh's First Newspaper," *North Carolina Booklet*, VII, No. 2: John Spencer Bassett (ed.), *Correspondence of Andrew Jackson*, 7 vols. (Washington, D. C.: Carnegie Inst., 1926-1935), II, 98.

[6]Probably William P. Mangum.

[7]John Harper Hinton of Wake County graduated at the University of North Carolina in 1813 and served there as tutor in 1814. In 1818-1828 he was principal of the Caswell Academy at Yanceyville, N. C. In 1819 he married a Miss Puckett of Chapel Hill. Later in 1813 he moved to Clarksville, Tenn., and in 1842 died in Greene County, Illinois. D. L. Grant, *Alumni History of the University of North Carolina* (second edition, published by Alumni Association, 1924), 285. Hereafter cited as Grant, *Alumni Hist. of U. N. C.* See also Charles Lee Coon (ed.), *North Carolina Schools and Academies, 1790-1840; A Documentary History* (Raleigh, N. C.: Edwards and Broughton, 1908), 25-26, 807. Hereafter cited as Coon, *Doc. Hist. of Educ. in N. C.* See also Carrie L. Broughton, "Marriage and Death Notices from the *Raleigh Register* and the North Carolina *State Gazette*, 1799-1825," in *Biennial Report of the State Librarian of North Carolina from July 1, 1842, to June 30, 1944*, (Raleigh, N. C.: n. page, n. d.), 81. Hereafter cited as Broughton, "Marriage and Death Notices."

[8]Mangum later attended the Raleigh Academy under the Reverend W. McPheeters, one of the most noted teachers of the state. McDuffie, "Willie P. Mangum," 1-6. See also Weeks, "W. P. M.," *Biog. Hist. of N. C.*, V, 239.

Willie Person THE 11s Mangum

SELECT DIALOGUES

Book

Bought of OF *J. H. Hinton*

LUCIAN.

1811

TO WHICH IS ADDED,

A NEW LITERAL TRANSLATION

IN

LATIN,

WITH

NOTES IN ENGLISH.

BY EDWARD MURPHY, M. A.

........verbum verbo curabis reddere fidus.   Hor.

Cæca regens *Filo* vestigia.   Virg.

PHILADELPHIA:

AT THE 𝕮𝖑𝖆𝖘𝖘𝖎𝖈 𝕻𝖗𝖊𝖘𝖘, FOR THE

PROPRIETORS

WILLIAM POYNTELL & CO.

....

1806.

weeks in visiting my relatives in Wake after that I went to Warrenton where I staid a week, which time I spent very agreeably
in the company of a fine parcel of girls, after that I went to
Greeneville where I staid a few days, and then returned home,
and spent the christmas among some angels, then after christmas I came to this place, and so ends the chapter, but why talk
of such things as these, which are neither edifying nor amusing.
Since I came to this place I have not been engaged in my studies,
nor did I conclude until to-day what course to pursue, as Mr.
Caldwell[9] did not arrive until last evening, and he advised me
to-day to enter as a private student to Mr. Johnson,[10] as I wish
to qualify myself for the freshman class at Yale Colledge, you
know when we were at school together I frequently expressed a
wish to go on to that place but was never determined whether I
would or not until I received a letter from my father during the
vacation stating that he had some time previous to that received
a letter from my uncle living in Baltimore, who has promised
that if I will go on to the northward he will educate me I expect
to finish at Yale or Princetun. My dear friend it should be our
greatest desire while at school to obtain a g[ood] stock of useful
knowledge, if we neglect [it] we not only disgrace ourselves but
treat with contempt the exertions of our Parents, than which
nothing is more infamous. Hitherto I have not studied with half
that avidity with which I should but for the future

[torn off]

of all folks   [torn]

J. H. HINTON

[Addressed:]

Mr Wilie P. Mangum[11]
Fayetville [sic]
No Carolina

---

[9]Joseph Caldwell, who came to Chapel Hill from Princeton in 1796 as professor of mathematics, served as president of the University of North Carolina in 1804-1812, 1817-1835.
E. W. Knight, "Joseph Caldwell," *Dictionary of American Biography, under the Auspices of
the American Council of Learned Societies,* edited by Allen Johnson and Dumas Malone, 20
vols. (New York, N. Y.: Charles Scribners' Sons, 1928-1936), III, 409. Hereafter cited as
D. A. B.
[10]George Johnston, a graduate of the University of Edinburgh, was the master of the
grammar school at the University of North Carolina from 1795 to 1819. Kemp Plummer
Battle, *History of the University of North Carolina,* 2 vols. (Raleigh, N. C.: Edwards and
Broughton, 1907, 1912), I, 190. Hereafter cited as Battle, *Hist. of U. N. C.*
[11]At the time Mangum was studying at the Fayetteville Academy under the Rev. Colin Mc-
Iver. Weeks, "W. P. M.," *Biog. Hist. of N. C.,* V, 239.

WPM-LC

Lethe E. Read[12] to Charity A. Cain[13]

WAKEFIELDS[14] April 30th 1812

My dear friend-

I have taken my pen for the first time to address you, and tho I never wrote to you I never think of you but with Sensations of the highest esteem, I am now entirely alone, undisturbed by any noise but the Singing of birds and the huming of insects around, me Sister R[15] left me this morning to visit Sister Mary I think its probable she will stay two months perhaps longer - we had the pleasure of receiving a letter from Sister Mary last evening informing us that she was quite well, and fatter than we ever saw her, Sister Rebeccah Calculated on writing to you before she left home but numerous indispensible engagements have prevented, I am now looking for Company to spend several days with me it would be truly gratifying to me if you could be one of the party, I wish to visit you but I fear that privilege will be denied me for some time you must write to me and give me all the news present my my [*sic*] most affectionate respects to Sister Mary,[16] and all your Fathers family) and kiss William[17] for me) May peece and tranquility long be Inmates of my dear Cs, breast may she ever possess that happiness which she so Justly deserves is the wish of

Your
Sincere
Friend
LETHE, E, READ

[Addressed:]

    Miss Charity A Cain
      Orange C,y
      North Carolin[a]
by p- [torn]

---

[12]Probably a sister of Rebecca Sutherland who married Priestley H. Mangum, the brother of Willie P. Mangum.

[13]Charity A. Cain, wife of Willie P. Mangum, was a daughter of William Cain, merchant of Hillsboro.

[14]Home of Col. Ransom Sutherland, near Wake Forest in Wake County. Rebecca Sutherland was Col. Ransom Sutherland's daughter. Col. Ransom Sutherland was a Revolutionary leader who held such important positions as membership in the Council of State. R. D. W. Connor, (ed.), *A Manual of North Carolina* issued by the North Carolina Historical Commission for the use of the members of the General Assembly session 1913 (Raleigh, N. C.: E. M. Uzzell and Co., State Printers, 1913), 425-427. Hereafter cited as *N. C. Manual*.

[15]Rebecca Sutherland.

[16]In 1815 Mary Cain, sister of Charity, married Solomon Sutherland, the son of Col. Ransom Sutherland. Broughton, "Marriage and Death Notices," 79.

[17]William Cain, Jr., of Hillsboro, was a student at the University in 1800-1801, Grant, *Alumni Hist. of U. N. C.*, 93. He continued the mercantile business of his father at Hillsboro.

WPM-LC

Stephen K. Sneed[18] to Willie P. Mangum

CHAPEL HILL September 24th 1814

My D[r] Friend Mangum
Alias Webb.

To make an apology for my long silence, I deem it altogether unnecessary; sufficient to say, that unavoidable avocations precluded the possibility of my writing. When I was in Raleigh last, I merely saw you, but regretted very much that I was disappointed in the enjoyment of your company a few hours, and when I heard that you had left the place, I returned to my Uncles to enjoy the company of the charming Miss L - - - - -e. As for news about College there is none, good, bad or indifferent, only old[e] Jeffreys[19] is over head and ears in love with Miss Louise Yarby & Eliza Henderson.[20] The Democrats here are completely mute, consequently the good old cause of Federalism continues triumphant. Priestly[21] is about to abjure his allegiance to old Cavallo & Simson[22] & incorporate himself in the society of a certain Miss Rebecca Wood; what will be the result, I know not as he has to combat with a very formidable competitor Doc[r]. Yeargin.[23] It is reported in Raleigh that Joseph Lane[24] is to be married to Miss Patsy Moy of Pitt. Joel Lane[25] to Louisa Tool of Franklin, Bedford Brown[26] to Miss - - Baker of Norfolk & Jhonny Puffy Graves[27] to Miss M. Hinton the last of which is to take

[18]Stephen Kutusoff Sneed, son of a large planter in Granville County, graduated from the University of North Carolina in 1815. He was clerk of the court in Granville in 1826. He died in La Grange, Tennessee, in 1841. *Raleigh Register*, April 13, 1841; *Laws of North Carolina for 1826*, appendix.
[19]George W. Jeffreys of Person County was a student at the University in 1813 and a trustee from 1842-1848. He was a progressive farmer who wrote the *Farmers' Own Book (1819)* and *Papers on Agriculture*, (c. 1824-1829). Battle, *Hist. of U. N. C.*, I, 789, 825; Guion Griffis Johnson, *Ante-Bellum North Carolina: A Social History* (Chapel Hill, N. C.: The University of North Carolina Press, 1937), 796. Hereafter cited as Johnson, *Ante-Bellum N. C.*
[20]Daughter of Major Pleasant Henderson of Chapel Hill. Elizabeth Henderson married Hamilton C. Jones. See below, p 155n.
[21]Priestley H. Mangum, the brother of Willie P. Mangum. See below, p. 14n.
[22]Authors of a text on philosophy. President Caldwell's copy of Tiberius Cavallos' *Elements of Natural or Experimental Philosophy*, 2 vols. (Philadelphia, Pa.: Dobson Co. 1813) is in the University of North Carolina Library.
[23]Probably Mark Morgan Yeargin who was a student at the University in 1807. His father was a large planter and school teacher of Orange County. Battle, *Hist. of U. N. C.*, I, 29.
[24]Joseph Lane of Raleigh married Martha Moye of Pitt County on November 23, 1814. He moved west and became a major in the Mexican War. Broughton, "Marriage and Death Notices," 78.
[25]Joel Hinton Lane was the son of the Revolutionary patriot, Joel Lane. Joel Hinton Lane was born in 1790. In January 1815 he married Mary Freeman of Warrenton. He served in the War of 1812 from Wake County. After the war he moved to Giles County, Tennessee, where he died in 1832. Broughton, "Marriage and Death Notices," 81.
[26]Bedford Brown of Caswell County, 1795-1820, was a student at the University in 1813-1814, and in the state legislature in 1815. As supporter of Andrew Jackson against Clay and Adams, he served in the U. S. Senate from 1829 to 1840. In the nullification and bank fights he supported Jackson. In 1840, replaced by Mangum, he moved to Missouri but returned to North Carolina, and then moved to Maryland, from which state he was elected to the House of Representatives. He married Mary L. Glenn. S. A. Ashe, "Bedford Brown," *Biog. Hist. of N. C.*, I, 181-185.
[27]John W. Graves of Caswell County married Martha Hinton, October 26, 1814. Broughton, "Marriage and Death Notices," 77.

place next month. Old Granny Boon[28] lies very ill in Louisburg. And I have also been informed that a certain . . . . [Sneed's dots] has been seen skulking about the Piney Woods of Wake; & it is said he has been courting; however I should like to be better informed upon this subject, before I make any comments. You wished to know where our friend Gaither[29] lives, old Joe[30] has never received a letter from him, but says as soon as he does he will inform you. - - - When you left this place I promised you that I would have your Diploma[31] filled up & sent to you, I accordingly had it signed & thought that Priestly had carried it to you, untill a few days ago; when he told me he had not, On the face of it has been some ink spilt, which disfigures its appearance some but not so much as to injure its virtue. I'll send it to you by the first opportunity.

Priestly requested me to inform you, that he had received your letter & done your business & that he would write to you shortly. I must now conclude (as the bell is ringing for our breakfast) with requesting you to wr[ite m]e a long letter very soon. & believe me to remain

Your Sincere friend

STEPHEN KUTUSOFF SNEED

W. P. Mangum, Esqʳ.

N. B. Old Quiper has been draughted lately consequently there were a few execrations poured forth upon poor Jimmy Madison & this glorious war. Old Cuffy has gone to Norfolk in the capacity of Aid-de-camp

[SKK S]

[Addressed:]
  Willie P. Mangum Esqʳ
      Near
          Staggville
  Mail   Orange
              N C

---

[28]William Augustus Boon of Johnston County graduated from the University in 1814. He became a captain in the U. S. army and died in 1834. Grant, *Alumni Hist. of U. N. C.*, 60.

[29]Alfred M. Gaither of Iredell County, a student at the University in 1813, later practiced law in Iredell County. Grant, *Alumni Hist. of U. N. C.*, 212; Colin McIver, *The North Carolina Register and the United States Calendar for the Year of Our Lord 1823* (Raleigh, N. C.: Jos. Gales and Son, 1822), 47. Hereafter cited as McIver, *N. C. Register.*

[30]Students at the University frequently referred to President Joseph Caldwell as "Old Joe." For an interesting account of the students' attitude toward this professor, see Wm. Hooper, *Address before the Alumni of the University of North Carolina* (n. p., 1859), 10.

[31]Possibly he refers to Mangum's certificate from the Dialectic Society, for he did not graduate until 1815.

Omnibus et Singulis has Literas Lecturis,[32]

SALUTEM

NOTUM SIT, Willie Person Mangum, Socium esse Societatis Dialecticae,[33] institutae apud Academiam Carolinae Septentrionalis, anno millessimo septingentesimo nonagesimo quinto, ad Scientiam, Virtutem, Amicitiamque colendam. Comites quoque, propter Virtutes ejus Eximias Animique Dotes, ei dedisse hanc Membranam, se denique hunc Adolescentem commendare, ut Fide dignum, et valde estimandum.

Quorum in Testimonium, Sigillum Societatis supradictae, Nominaque nostra huic Membranae sunt affixa.

DATUM IN AULA DIALECTICA, vigesimo quarto die Aprilies
Anno Domini millessimo octingentesimo et quarto decimo

SAMUEL PICKENS PRAESES.[34]

J. O. Mitchell Scriba.	Chas. P. Manly	Tryon M. Yancey
Matthew M. Clung.	David F. Caldwell	Alfred Gaither
Isaac Croom [?]	Jnᵒ. W. Graves	W. A. Boon
Stephen Kutusoff Sneede	Charles L. Smith	Bedford Brown
Geo. W. Jeffreys.	Wilie J. Croom	Alfred Slade
Abraham Moore	Jaˢ. B. Yellowley	Peter O. Picot

[Seal attached on 1½ inch light-blue satin ribbon. Inscribed: Love of Virtue and Science. D. L. 1795].

University of North Carolina (Seal)

Omnibus et Singulis has Literas Lecturis,[35]

SALUTEM IN DOMINO

QUONIAM nobis commissum est legibus hujus Reipublicae Carolinae Septentrionalis, ut probis moribus, Religione et Scientia

---

[32] The original is in the possession of Mr. Mangum Turner, Winston-Salem, N. C.

[33] One of the two literary societies at the University: students from the eastern part of the state usually joined the Philanthropic Society, while those from the western section joined the Dialectic.

[34] Nearly all of these students later became active in the politics of the state. Manly became governor of the state; Caldwell became lieutenant governor and congressman; Brown became U. S. Senator; and Gaither, Jeffreys, Sneed, Moore, Graves, and Boon held county offices.

[35] The original is in the possession of Mr. Mangum Turner, Winston-Salem, N. C.

omnes instituamus, qui has eximias animi dotes exoptent, et qui sub tutela nostra diligenter Studeant: Pro manifesto itaque habeatur

WILLIE PERSON MANGUM,

periculis universis in literis ex ordine comprobatum esse, quibus Universitatis alumni Carolinae Septentrionalis exerceri solent; hoc etiam diplomate ARTIUM BACCALAUREI a nobis eundem condecoratum esse, ut omnibus ad quos haec pervenerint de his liqueat.

In Quorum Testimonium nos Senatus Academicus chirographa nostra, et commune sigillum huic Membranae affiximus.

DATUM IN AULA PERSONICA, tertio ante kalendas Julii, Anno Domini millesimo octingentesimo decimo quinto.

Thos. D. Bennehan	Robertus H. Chapman Praeses.[36]
Thomas Brown	Josephus Caldwell M. P.
Jeremiah Slade	Gulielmus Miller Pro.
Thomas Ruffin	Ed. Jones
Gulielmus McPheeters	Dan Cameron
	Jacobus Wallis
	Rob[t] Williams

Willie P. Mangum to Duncan Cameron[37]

HILLSBORO 18th. June 1816

Dear Sir,

Inclosed you will find a receipt for M[r]. Williams—A few days since I saw Mr. Dickens in Person County, and he seems in pretty high spirits—Indeed you would have been most astonished at his success among some of the Flat river democrats., it was so brilliant that I would not be surprised were he to get a responsible majority at Carrington's[38] Doc. Smith,[39] persons to the contrary notwithstanding.—

[36]Robert H. Chapman was president of the University from 1812 to 1816.
[37]The original is in the Cameron Papers, University of North Carolina.
[38]John J. Carrington, Lt. Col. of the militia of Orange County, was a neighbor and relative of Mangum. Later he moved to Tennessee. McIver, *N. C. Register*, 91. See below the letter of W. A. Tharpe to Willie P. Mangum, Aug. 19, 1832.
[39]James Strudwick Smith, 1790-1859, a graduate of Jefferson Medical College, practiced medicine near Hillsboro, served in the House of Representatives of the United States from 1817 to 1821, was a member of the state legislature in 1821, 1822, and was a member of the state constitutional convention of 1835. His opponent for Congress in this election was Samuel Dickens. Smith was elected. *Biographical Director of the American Congress, 1774-1927.* (Washington, D. C.: U. S. Government Printing Office, 1928), p. 1538. Hereafter cited as *Biog. Dir. of Cong.*

Mr. Dickens requests that his friends will point out such public places as he may [at]tend with the greatest probability of success.—

On Friday he will be in Hillsboro. Should you therefore be able to give him any directions with respect to Wake, he will be much obliged to you.

Doct. Smiths prospects are indeed flattering to him and unless Mr. Murphey[40] and his friends make some exertion Smiths election may be expected.—That Mr. Murphey's popularity is in the wane cannot be doubted, and in the Southern & South Eastern parts of the County Smith will get an overwhelming majority. At the sale of Standfords I have understood that Smith was greatly flattered as yesterday. Those flatteries with his own presumption have confirmed him in the opinion that he will be elected.—That the result will be as he (Smith) could wish I cannot believe, but it would be well that Mr. Murphey & his friends should be aware of the Puffing Doctors strength.

I am D. Sir Yrs
With great Esteem
WILLIE P. MANGUM

WPM-LC

License to Practice Law[41]

[2 March, 1817]

State of North Carolina

To all whom it may concern.

We the undersigned Judges of the Superior Courts of Law and the Courts of Equity, in and for the State of North Carolina, do by these presents, license Willie P. Mangum to plead and practice law in the several Superior Courts of Law and the Courts of Equity in the said State during his good behavior with all and singular the rights privileges and emoluments, belonging to the practitioners of the Law, in the said Courts. He the said Willie P. Mangum having just taken the oaths prescribed by Law for his qualification.

---

[40]Archibald D. Murphey, 1777-1832, was one of the most respected and significant North Carolina leaders in politics, and especially in the promotion of education and internal improvements. W. H. Hoyt (ed.), *The Papers of Archibald D. Murphey,* 2 vols., Publication of the North Carolina Historical Commission (Raleigh, N. C.: E. M. Uzzell and Co., State Printers, 1914). Hereafter cited as Hoyt, *Papers of Murphey.* See also Wm. K. Boyd, "Archibald D. Murphey," *D. A. B.,* XIII, 345.

[41]The body of the license is in the autograph of W. P. Mangum.

In Testimony whereof we have hereunto set our hands and affixed our seals, Done at Raleigh the 10th day of January, A. D. 1817.

JNO. HALL[42]   (Seal)

J. J. DANIEL[43]   (Seal)

THOMAS RUFFIN[44] (Seal)

J. L. Taylor[45] Ch. J. (Seal)

Henry Seawell[46]   (Seal)

State of North Carolina }

Granville County }

Superior Court of Law
March Term
A. D. 1817

Willie P. Mangum Esq. having produced the foregoing license to this court, having also paid the sum required by Law as a Tax to the State, and having taken the several Oaths necessary for his qualification, is permitted to practice as an Attorney in the same.

In witness of all which I William M. Sneed Clerk thereof do hereby subscribe my name & affix my seal of office this 2nd March 1817.

W. M. SNEED[47] Clerk.

[Endorsed:]

Mʳ. Mangum's
License.

---

[42]John Hall, 1767-1833, judge of the superior court from 1800 to 1818 and of the Supreme Court of North Carolina from 1818 to 1832, was a Democratic presidential elector in 1829. Marshall deL. Haywood, "John Hall," *Biog. Hist. of N. C.*, V, 117-121.

[43]Joseph John Daniel, 1784-1848, state legislator from 1807 to 1811, and judge of the superior court from 1816 to 1832, was judge of the Supreme Court of North Carolina from 1832 to 1848. Ashe, *Biog. Hist. of N. C.*, VII, 90-94.

[44]Thomas Ruffin, 1787-1870, one of the most eminent of state judges in the U. S. before the Civil War, held numerous state, church, financial, and agricultural positions in North Carolina. He was judge of the superior court from 1816 to 1818 and from 1825 to 1828, and of the state Supreme Court from 1829 to 1852. He served for nearly twenty years as chief justice. He supported Crawford in 1824 and the Whigs after 1832. J. G. de R. Hamilton (ed.), *The Papers of Thomas Ruffin*, Publication of the North Carolina Historical Commission, 4 vols. (Raleigh, N. C.: Edwards and Broughton, State Printers, 1819-20), I, 19-43. Hereafter cited as Hamilton, *Papers of Ruffin*. Walter Clark, "Thomas Ruffin," *Great American Lawyers*, edited by William Lewis, IV (1908), 277.

[45]John Louis Taylor, 1769-1829, was judge of the superior court from 1798 to 1818 and the first chief justice of the North Carolina Supreme Court, 1818 to 1829. He received an LL.D. in 1828 from Georgetown University. He wrote a biography of Associate Justice Alfred Moore of the United States Supreme Court, and various law reports and revisals. He married Julia Rowan and later Jane Gaston, sister of Judge William Gaston. Marshall de L. Haywood "John Louis Taylor," *Biog. Hist. of N. C.*, V, 394-397.

[46]Henry Seawell, 1774-1835, who served in the state legislature in 1802, 1810, 1812, 1821 to 1826, 1831, 1832, was attorney general of the state in 1811, judge of the superior court in 1813 and from 1832 to 1835, and commissioner for settling claims arising from the Treaty of Ghent. He was an able lawyer and sometimes political rival of Mangum. Marshall de L. Haywood, "Henry Seawell," *Biog. Hist. of N. C.*, V, 402-407.

[47]William M. Sneed of Granville County, a graduate of the University, was in the state legislature from 1822 to 1823, 1825 to 1826, and 1829 to 1831. He was for many years clerk of Granville court. Grant, *Alumni Hist. of U. N. C.*, 579; McIver, *N. C. Register*, 42.

WPM-LC
COPY

[28 April, 1818]

A List of Subscribers to the Books of the Neuse River Navigation Company,[48] with the number of Shares at one hundred dollars subscribed by each—taken as on the 28th day of April 1818,
immediately after the General meeting of the Stockholders, when
the shares were reduced & the excess stricken off according to
the provisions of the acts of Assembly in such case provided—
with remarks applicable to the present time.

Subscribers Names	Number of shares	Remarks
Benjamin H. Barham	1	Nothing paid.
William Boylan	19	do
Johnson Busbee	1	$10. paid
A. S. H. Burges	1	$10. paid
Thomas Cobb	1	$10. paid
Wm. F. Clark	1	$10. paid
Mark Cooke	1	$10. paid
James Coman	1	Nothing paid
Thomas P. Devereux	1	$10. paid
John Dunn	1	$10. paid
Beverly Daniel	1	Nothing paid
John D. Delacy	218	Nothing paid & his name stricken off the books.
Thomas Emond	1	Nothing paid
W. J. Franks	1	$10. paid
Joseph Gales	19	$190. paid
Samuel Goodwin	1	Nothing paid
John Holloway	1	do
Thomas Henderson	19	$190. paid
Charles L. Hinton	1	$10. paid
State of North Carolina by John Haywood Treasr.	60	$600. paid

[48]The Neuse River Navigation Company was incorporated in 1812 with a capital stock of $50,000. Under the law the promoters were required to raise $10,000 by 1814 for it to be ef-
fective. Under the charter the company was given the authority to build canals and to have a monopoly of freight on these canals provided the rates conformed to those set forth in the charter. In 1816 under the influence of a report of A. D. Murphey, the state subscribed $6,000. In 1819 he proposed that the state increase its subscription to $25,000. The construction of the canals was to be completed by 1826. Hoyt, *Papers of Murphey*, II, 25, 40-41, 172, 174, 183; *N. C. Laws, 1812, 1816;* Charles C. Weaver, *Internal Improvements in North Carolina Previous to 1860.* (Baltimore, Md.: The Johns Hopkins University Press, 1903), 64.

John Haywood	1	$10. paid
William Hill	19	$190. paid
Sherwood Haywood	1	$10. paid
Lewis Holloman	1	Nothing paid
John Hinton junr	19	$50. paid
John Hinton Senr	1	Nothing paid
Robt. H. Helems	1	$10. paid
Theos. Hunter	19	$190. paid
David Hinton	1	$10. paid
Ransom Hinton	1	$10. paid
James P. Hubbard	1	$10. paid
Calvin Jones-	1	$10. paid
Benjn. S. King	1	$10. paid
John King	1	$10. paid
Alfred Lane	1	$10. paid
James McKee	1	$10. paid
George Nichols	1	$10. paid
Henry Potter	1	$10. paid
Will. Peck	1	$10. paid
William Polk	20	Nothing paid
Thomas Price	1	Nothing paid
Joseph Peace	1	$10. paid
William Peace -	1	$10. paid
John S. Raboteau	1	$10. paid
Wm. Ruffin	1	$10. paid
David Royster	1	Nothing paid
John Rex	1	$10. paid
David Stone	20	$200. paid
Wm. Scott	20	$100. paid
Susan Schaub	1	$10. paid
Richd. Smith	1	$10. paid
John Stuart	1	Nothing paid
James J. Selby	1	$10. paid
Henry Seawell	1	$10. paid
John Scott	1	$10. paid
Jas. F. Taylor	1	Nothing paid
Randolph Webb	1	$10. paid
John F. C. Wiatt	1	$10. paid
Haute C. Wiatt	1	$10. paid

We the President & Directors of the Neuse River Navigation Company do hereby certify that the foregoing List is correct, and do hereby return the same to the office of the Secretary of State, there to be recorded as the Laws directs. Given under our Hands at Raleigh, the 17th day of April 1819.

> H. Potter[49] President
> Theos. Hunter[50]
> Wm. Scott[51]
> Jo. Gales[52]
>
> Directors

A true Copy
> Given 13th Augt. 1819
> Wm. Hill[53] Secretary.

[Endorsed:]
> A List of Subscribers &c. to the
> Neuse River Navigation Company.

COPY.

> [Note enclosed in the foregoing List
> of Subscribers to the Neuse River
> Navigation Company.]

Mr. Delacy

Having advised with other gentlemen of the bar I am induced to decline receiving your paper unless you give Security.

> R. Hinton.[54]

Endorsed:
> Augst. the 30th this note was handed to me at B. S. Kings[55]Store by Mr. Pulley the partner of Mr. King as left with him by Ransom Hinton Esq r. for me.
>
> J. D. Delacy.[56]

---

[49]Henry Potter, 1765-1857, was United States judge of the North Carolina District from 1802 to 1857, a trustee of the University of North Carolina from 1799 to 1857, and director of the State Bank of North Carolina. Kemp P. Battle, *The Early History of Raleigh, the Capital City of North Carolina—a Centennial Address delivered . . . on the Centennial Celebration of the Foundation of the City, October 18, 1892* (Raleigh, N. C.: Edwards and Broughton, 1893), 63. Hereafter cited as Battle, *Hist. of Raleigh*.

[50]Theophilus Hunter, a large landholder and business leader of Raleigh, was on the commission to build the state capitol at Raleigh. He was also a director of the state bank, a member of the Council of State and the House of Commons. Battle, *Hist. of Raleigh*, 19-21; *N. C. Manual*, 827, 428.

[51]Unable to identify.

[52]Joseph Gales, 1761-1841, was founder of the Jeffersonian paper, *Raleigh Register*, and was mayor of Raleigh for nineteen years. He compiled the first two volumes of the *Annals of Congress*. He was father of the editor of the *National Intelligencer*. See W. E. Smith, "Joseph Gales."

[53]William Hill of Rockingham County was secretary of state of North Carolina from 1811 to 1859. *N. C. Manual*, 441.

[54]Ransom Hinton of Wake County was a student at the University of North Carolina in 1804. For several years he was clerk of the superior court in Wake County. Grant, *Alumni Hist. of U. N. C.*, 285.

[55]Benjamin S. King, who for several years was clerk of the court of common pleas in Wake County, operated a store in Wake County. McIver, *N. C. Register*, 285.

[56]In 1817 John Devereux Delacy came to North Carolina from New York to organize a steamship company for Robert Fulton. Failing in this, he helped promote the Neuse River Navigation Company. He subscribed to 218 shares but made no payments. His name, therefore, was stricken from the list of subscribers. He practiced law in Raleigh until his death in 1837. *Raleigh Register*, April 25, 1837.

WPM-LC

Willie P. Mangum to Priestley H. Mangum[57]

GREENSBOR°. 20th. April 1819

Dear Sir,

I rec[d]. yours of last month, and paid to M[r]. Selby[58] the account against y[ou] [torn] this had been omitted through forgetfulness until that late period. Your letter to Walter[59] I rec.[d] but had not an opportunity of forwarding as early as would have been necessary to meet your Wishes. I however thought of an arrangement that will probably meet your views. That is in June You will visit orange & be at the commencement at Chapel Hill, at which time you will be accommodated, if not otherwise with my sulkey which is elegant and suited to all the purposes of country life. - I have been Well- I have made a good deal of money this spring, say upwards of $1900 in actual receipts, and nearly that sum in good bonds & accts. My prospects in the practice continue to grow more flattering.

You know that I have made a considerable purchase in Haywood.[60] I think I have made more by that than all the rest of the labours of my life. I expected to see you at Salisbury Sup[r] Court, but was induced to go to Franklin Sup[r] Court, where I did much better in a pecuniary point of View- In one case of M[rs]. Patty Taylor,[61] I have secured a fee at six months of One Thousand dollars. that's large business, is it not? and an equal share with the first in the other business of that Court which is profitable.

I may be married this Summer, I am not certain because my movements have been too sluggish to ascertain- More of this when I know more The next Visit to Raleigh I mean to settle

[57]This letter has been previously published in McDuffie, "Willie P. Mangum," 19. Priestley Hinton Mangum, younger brother of Willie P. Mangum, was born April 3, 1795, and died September 17, 1850. They were classmates at the University of North Carolina, where Priestley graduated with the A.B. degree in 1815 at the head of his class and with the A.M. degree in 1817. He became a successful lawyer and until his marriage to Rebecca Sutherland, lived in Hillsboro. After his marriage he resided at Wakefields, the home of his father-in-law, Colonel Ransom Sutherland. He frequently considered entering politics but was so outspoken in his views that he antagonized many voters. In 1832 he served his county of Wake in the state legislature, and in 1823 he was county solicitor for Orange County. S. B. Weeks, "Willie Person Mangum, Sr.," and S. A. Ashe, "Priestley Hinton Mangum, Jr.," *Biog. Hist. of N. C.*, V, 253, 258; McIver, *N. C. Register*, 45.
[58]Joseph J. Selby was a tailor of Raleigh.
[59]Walter Alvis Mangum was born January 28, 1798, and died January 20, 1868. He was Willie P. Mangum's youngest brother. He married Eliza P. Bullock of Granville County. He moved to Tennessee and then to Mississippi in 1832 where he became a successful planter. *Raleigh Register*, Dec. 31, 1829; Weeks, "W. P. M.," *Biog. Hist. of N. C.*, V, 236, 239.
[60]A. D. Murphey and others proposed making the Cape Fear navigable up to Haywood, a mushroom town laid out where the Deep and Haw rivers come together to form the Cape Fear River. Lots were sold at inflated prices. Efforts were made to make Haywood the state capital. Plans were developed to connect Haywood and the Yadkin River by a canal. Land speculation was, therefore, rampant. Today the town does not exist and it never was more than a village. Hoyt, *Papers of Murphey*, I, 106n.
[61]Mrs. Martha Taylor owned much land in Tennessee.

the business- You see what a romantic lover I am, speak of *settling the business* when speaking of love, how Cold, how business like, & how ridiculous Dont Speak of this to any of our friends from Hillsbor.° I mean J. S.[62]

22nd. April.

Greensbor.° certainly presents no prospect that would thrill with delight the heart of Midas. I had intended going to Rockingham, but Judge Toomers[63] health will not enable him to do business. Sir, he is a considerable Judge, but what is more than all, he is a good man.- I have exhausted every resource of egotism, but I love to be particular & our friends also are more pleased with it when it interests the hero of his own tale.- Mark me! In this I take no example from your elegantly laboured letters, of which In point of conciseness, Tacitus could find no fault- But not done yet. I am a candidate in the commons. No opposition as yet known, perhaps Wm. McCawley[64]- he is spoken of & will hold I suppose a considerable poll. & may be elected. I have understood but cannot believe his views are hostile to me. The intimate & friendly association that has subsisted between us, and his candour & integrity of conduct & character, repels the idea that his wishes are inimical to me. tho his friends might wish with him to defeat my Views.

I cannot believe that my strength has all diminished, since last year. & that I could go to Congress with out difficulty I entertain no doubt. The dangerous diadem has flitted before my vision & Ambition frequently lingers with delight in tracing the outline of the delusion but interest & in my opinion sound judg.ᵗ forbid the thought. - I have seen Miss Teany Badgers[65] she has returned to Hillsbor°. all are Well,—and the light airy & volatile manners that formerly charmed with an expression of playful sarcasm under the covert of simplicity, have been converted into the most impenetrable & immoveable gravity "femina semper est varium et mutabile"- In an evening's interview, not a smile

[62]This is probably John Scott who was an attorney from Hillsboro then on the circuit with Priestley H. Mangum. See below, p. 18n.

[63]John de Rossett Toomer, 1798-1856, was a member of the legislature from Cumberland County and Fayetteville in 1826 and from 1831 to 1832. He was a member of the Constitutional Convention of 1835, judge of superior court from 1818 to 1819 and from 1836 to 1840, judge of the Supreme Court of North Carolina in 1829, and trustee of the state university from 1818 to 1856. Grant, *Alumni Hist. of U. N. C.*, 625; Battle, *Hist. U. N. C.*, I, 823.

[64]William McCauley, 1788-1835, a student at the state university in 1813, taught law to Jesse Turner in 1826. He was a member of the House of Commons from Orange County from 1822 to 1825. *N. C. Manual*, 737-738; Grant, *Alumni Hist. of U. N. C.*, 384.

[65]This was probably a sister of George E. Badger, 1795-1866, U. S. Senator and Secretary of the Navy, who lived in Hillsboro at this time. His sister, Frances Lucretia Badger, died there in 1822. His other sister was Elizabeth Ann.

brightened those features that frolic and laughter formerly seemed to have marked as their own. & the hard wrung expressions that fell from her lips were more reluctant than the portentious *Guilty* that the prisoner pleads upon his trial for life—

From Franklin Court I returned to Raleigh with Judge Seawell[66] who would have me to stay with him two or three days. and there I offered a heart[67] not worth two-pence upon the shrine of beauty- Whether it will be an acceptable offering I can't say whether or not the sacrifice to me is cheap—if it had been a Hecatomb of oxen, they should have ploughed, or more judiciously have been consigned to the beautiful little hands of the tender & most loving butcher. Judge Seawell makes all the Money say $500 & upward actual receipts at each Court & more than two or three times that amount in bonds & accounts.—

He is a great advocate, and certainly [has] more promptitude of remote association than any man I ever knew. it is [a] faculty, that enables him to look in to the secret corners of heart & eviscerate the motives of the most impenetrable Witness, and the versatility of his talent before a Jury & his faculty of adapting his address to the most powerful motives in their bosom, give him a decided ascendancy over any man in the Circuit, & where is the Sup^r in the State. As a lawyer his is great. & his astuteness & ingenuity, seem to correspond with the exegencies of his cause.—

Our family is well & all going on well

I am Yrs

WILLIE P MANGUM

[Addressed:]

Priestley H. Mangum Esq-
    To meet him at
        Randolph

Mr. Shepperd)[68]
)'

---

[66]Judge Henry Seawell. See note 46, p. 10.

[67]Mangum married Charity Alston Cain, daughter of William Cain of Hillsboro, Sept. 30, 1819.

[68]Probably Augustine Henry Shepperd, 1792-1864, a lawyer of Surry County. He was a member of the state legislature from 1822 to 1826, presidential elector on the Jackson-Calhoun ticket in 1824 and the Clay ticket in 1844, and a member of Congress from 1827 to 1839, 1841 to 1843, and 1847 to 1851. *Biog. Dir. of Cong.*, 1517.

Agreement Between Willie P. Mangum & Arch^d. Haralson[69]

The agreement between Arch^d. Haralson[70] Esqr. & Willie P. Mangum. Mangum buys of Haralson his interest in the point or New Town of Haywood, which Paoli Ashe & Co.[71] purchased from Jno Farrar.[72] Mangum is to have a fee Simple interest in one fifth of s^d purchase, together with a fee simple interest in the Seven lots of the old Town of Haywood which the P. Ashe & Company purchased at the sales of the lots in s^d Town. Mangum is to be entitled to draw a fifth part of the two payments for the lots which s^d Company sold of the New Town or point except fourteen hundred dollars or not exceeding that sum which Haralson has drawn from the Company being part of the proceeds of the Sale of Lots by the said Company. Also the s^d Mangum is to account with the Company for one thousand dollars being the purchase money of a lot which Sd. Haralson bought of the Company, which sum however Mangum is not to account for until the final settlement of the Company concerns; Mangum takes upon himself to pay this proportion of the balance of the purchase money being $15,000 which the s^d Company gave for the s^d New Town or point, also Mangum takes upon himself to pay an equal proportion for a bridge Contracted for & built for the Company.[73] Mangum is to have the benefit of a payment made by Haralson for the lots bought by the Company in the Old Town, which payment exceeds the proportionable share of Haralson the precise sum unknown. Mangum is to have the benefit of a part payment made by Haralson towards the building of the said bridge amounting to $175 or thereabouts. And that Mangum is to step into the place of said Haralson and have & enjoy all the rights previleges & immunities & benefits as a member of s^d Company that Sd. Haralson enjoyed or by right might have enjoyed. For all of which considerations the s^d Mangum is to give the said Haralson One Thousand Dollars.—

---

[69]The original is in the possession of Mr. Mangum Turner, Winston-Salem, N. C.

[70]Archibald Haralson, 1792-1840, nephew of Archibald D. Murphey, was a student at the state university from 1808 to 1811. He then went to Princeton. He practiced law at Hillsboro and Chatham in North Carolina before he migrated to St. Francisville, Louisiana, where he became a successful attorney. In North Carolina he was constantly in debt and unable to pay out. Hoyt, *Papers of Murphey*, I, 53n, 177.

[71]Paoli Pasquale Ashe & Company was a large business firm of Hillsboro. A. D. Murphey did much business with this firm. Hoyt, *Papers of Murphey*, I, 56, 160, 164.

[72]Colonel John Farrar was in the state legislature from Chatham County in 1804-1808, 1813, 1815-1817, and 1819. He invested heavily in the Haywood town development. *N. C. Manual*, 549-550; Hoyt, *Papers of Murphey*, I, 158.

[73]This was probably the Deep River Bridge which was projected by Murphey and others across the river at Haywood.

Witness
W. P. Mangum (s)
John Scott.[74]
Arch^d Haralson (s)

[Endorsement on back:] Agreement between Willie P. Mangum
& Arch^d. Haralson.

---

*Promissory Note of Archibald Haralson and Willie P. Mangum
to Jonathan P. Sneed & Co.*[75]

$25.85
On or before the 25th December next we or either of us promise
to pay or Cause to be paid to Jonathan P. Sneed & co.[76] on order
the Sum of Twenty five Dollars and Eighty five cents for value
received with Interest from the date hereof Witness our hands
& Seal this 27th aug^t 1819.

ARCH. HARALSON   Seal
WILLIE P MANGUM   Seal

[Written across this] Judgment 12 February 1820 J B Jp [Jus-
tice of Peace]

WPM-LC

James Thompson to Willie P. Mangum

[4 Oct. 1819]
Willie P. Mangum Agent for Robert Hamilton[77] & Co.
Petersburgh, Take Notice that on the 18th of October Instant at
the Publick Jail of Orange County in Hillsborough I intend to
take the Benefit of our Act of Assembly passed for the Relief of
Insolvent debtors When and Whare you may attend if You think
proper

JAMES THOMPSON

October 4th 1819.
[Addressed:]
Willie P. Mangum Esq.

---

[74]John Scott was a successful lawyer of Hillsboro. He was a member of the legislature in 1816, from 1818 to 1820, and from 1824 to 1827. He was Solicitor General of North Carolina in 1827. Levi M. Scott, "The Bench and Bar of Guilford County," in *Publications of the Guilford County Literary and Historical Association* (Greensboro, N. C.: Jos. J. Stone and Co., 1908), I, 52-53; *N. C. Manual*, 445.
[75]This is a copy of a photostat from the Charles A. Brown Autograph Collection, Rush Rhees Library, University of Rochester.
[76]Jonathan P. Sneed & Company was a Hillsboro firm. Jonathan P. Sneed, 1794-1841, was a magistrate in Hillsboro in 1823. In 1833 he moved to La Fayette County, Mississippi, where he died in 1843. *Hillsborough Recorder*, Sept. 28, 1841; *Raleigh Register*, June 2, 1843.
[77]A Petersburg merchant who handled the cotton of many Orange County planters. In 1826 this firm changed its name to A. & P. Hamilton & Kwan.

WPM-LC

Willie P. Mangum to Mrs. Charity A. Mangum

RALEIGH 29th. Nov. 1819.

I have but a moment, My Dear to inform you that I have bought nothing for Martha[78] because I found nothing, that I thought would please her taste—but new goods are expected in one or two days when I hope I shall succeed more to her wishes. I have nothing to communicate of the slightest importance, for Raleigh is as dull & uninteresting to me as the squeaking of a scotchman bagpipes. Indeed My Dear I feel oppressed with heaviness & low spirits, when I reflect that I am condemned to this vapid society for a month, excluded from the endearments & loves that afford me the chief, I might almost say my only delight. But I shall look forward with anxiety to see you on Saturday evening at Col. Sutherlands.

The Legislature is doing but little, nothing indeed of public importance.

I sit alone in my rooms & cheat myself of half my dulness by plunging into tales of fiction.

What a contrast between this & last Winter, At that time I plunged into the vortex of fashionable dissipation, & my golden moments sped away on swiftest wing, now those pleasures would disgust, at least they are dull and lifeless—And I fixed my fancy ever reverting from those empty pleasures, & turning to those dear joys, those exquisite moments—that visit none but the bosom of virtuous love.—Indeed My Dear, absence teaches me how rich a jewel my heart has treasured up, in my Dear lovely Wife. Tender my love to your Mamma,[79] & Sister Sutherland[80]— & give the girls a hearty smack in my name.

Inform your Papa that there will be nothing here of importance until thursday, when the Convention resolution will be discussed in the Senate, If he comes down this week, I should wish him to be here on that day—

The next week however he will be perhaps equally entertained & when a visit will best suit, I expect with his convenience.—

---

[78]Charity's sister Martha Ann.
[79]Sarah Alston Dudley Cain.
[80]Mary Cain, Charity's sister, married Solomon Sutherland, the son of Colonel Ransom Sutherland of Wake County.

But a moment.—Can you read this—

I am My Dear Wife Yrs
most affectionately
WILLIE P. MANGUM

Mrs. Charity A. Mangum.

[Addressed:]
Mrs. Charity A. Mangum
Orange

Mr. W. Cain Jr. will oblige me by giving this the speediest passage.

W. P. M.

—————

1820 - 1822

WPM-LC

A. D. Murphey to Willie P. Mangum

[21 Jan., 1820]

Mr Mangum.

Upon reaching this place I learned that Mr. Franks[1] had sued out a Writ against Messrs. Ashe,[2] Strudwick,[3] Haralson[4] & myself, for the Balance due him for the Bridge—I immediately paid Mr. Franks $310 [?], the Sum which he said was due him for Mr. Haralson's Part of the Bridge, and he Settled with me the entire Bridge Account, and agreed to take up the Writ—He tells me you will be here by the 25th. of this month and will be prepared to pay the Balance of the Sum which I have paid on Mr. Haralson's Share in the Bridge—I will thank you to pay this Sum to Mr. Franks, who agrees to place it to my Credit for building my House in Haywood—

Yours with great respect—

A. D. MURPHEY

Haywood—
21t. Jany. 1820:

[Addressed:]
Honbl. Willie P. Mangum esqr.
Orange.

—————

[1]W. J. Franks, a justice of the peace of Chatham County, subscribed to the stock of the Neuse River Navigation Company and the Deep River Bridge Company. See above p. 11 and below p. 150.
[2]Paoli P. Ashe. See above p. 17n.
[3]S. Strudwick, another Hillsboro subscriber to the bridge company.
[4]Herndon Haralson, Murphey's brother-in-law. Hamilton, *Papers of Ruffin*, I, 260n.

WPM-LC

Willie P. Mangum to Mrs. Charity A. M\angum

WILKESBORO, Saturday Evening 20th March 1820.

My Dear Love,

This evening is the first spare time, that I have had from inde-
fatigable employment since my courts commenced,[5] and I know
of noway in which I can use it more pleasantly than in writing
to you.—for it is with but little effort that the pen delineates the
feelings of the heart. You will be no way surprised when I inform you that I am not at all pleased with my new profession—it
requires more intense labour, more awful responsibility, and indeed it is in every respect less suited to my circumstances, and
my disposition.—It is not in the scope of my powers of language
to describe my feelings on the first occasion that a man was tried
before me for his life—For I have just passed through two trials
of that awful character.—The first was so critical that the
weight of a hair would have saved or lost his life, & in that trying moment I was compelled to decide.—I am now just at the
foot of the Mountains, Tomorrow I expect to cross them. & indeed My Dear I am sufficiently oppressed with low spirits when
I look forward to the immense labours before me, and the tedious
period to elapse, before I shall again be restored to the smiles of
love, & the bliss of friendship. In those moments of despondent
feeling, how cold & Joyless does the world with all its splendid
promises & false allurements appear unless sweetened with the
delicious infusion of virtuous love & tender affection. In those
moments I sometimes feel an intenseness of melancholy that borders so much on what this wise world has been pleased to de-
nominate weakness, that I will not tell you a very ridiculous oc-
curance that happened at Salem[6] when I was reviewing the
scenes of your childish sport, & youthful gambols—Those are
moments My Love, that the cold hearted & weak may ridicule,
but the wise will treasure them up as the richest jewels, that are
to be gathered in a life of cares, trouble & vexations.—It is
strange what effect absence produces on the affections of the
human mind. It is when happiness is removed that we look

---

[5] In December 1819 after considerable political maneuvering, the legislature elected Mangum judge of the superior court. Duncan Cameron, in whose office Mangum had read law,
was chiefly responsible for the election. In the winter of 1820 Mangum went to the western
part of the state on the sixth judicial circuit. His health was not good. Becoming quite unhappy, he resigned the same year, 1820. For an account of his election and experience see
McDuffie, "Willie P. Mangum," 20.
[6] Probably Salem, Virginia, where the Cains frequently went to the mineral springs.

back to it with the fullest conviction of its excellence: and never have I so fully appreciated my happiness in possessing the affectations of an excellent & virtuous heart, as I have since my sojourn in this wild and romantic country—& Oh may the angel of Love seal upon that heart the richest rewards of a virtuous, tender & disinterested attachment.

This is My Dear a most delightful country, in the summer it must be enchanting. — Nature seems to have delighted in the grand & magnificent, when she was piling in such whimsical combinations the vast alleghenies.—we have now a warm & soft spring day, & the last two or three hours before I sat down to my letter, I was rambling among the knolls as they call them here, but indeed they are mountains that command a most extensive view of the surrounding Country.—This Country tho at the present is far behind ours in moral improvement, yet it is the most desirable part of North Carolina that I have seen.— And by way of exemplifying the remark You may tell your Pa, that I have seen in one stock at Col. Welbourns[7] 340 Cattle, & 70 or 80 of them that are fattening are in better order than I ever saw any animal of that description.—They are raised without expense by sending them into the inexhaustible range of the mountains in the warm season of the year—

I will select in these mountains some secluded spot for My lovely sister whose fortune when told to her pointed out a seat buried in the very silence of seclusion & retirement.—Tell her the selection shall be made with all imaginable taste—and that she is to be very much obliged to me for my trouble and make a very low curtesy.—But if in that retirement she would like occasionally to see a beau, that there are a plenty with Deer skin leggins & bear skin Coats—and if the fur of their Jackets is as warm as it looks to be, they must have very warm hearts. For all this M.[8] is to give my friend J. S.[9] a kiss the next time they meet.

You must write to me My Dear immediately on the receipt of this, and Direct your letters to *Morganton* Burke County—Don't fail, for I am inexpressibly anxious to hear from you, & know whether your health is better, than it was when I left you.—You must be careful, but take exercise in good [weather], and if you are not relieved, you must take m[ore] medicine.—I feel great

---

[7]Probably Col. James Welborn who was in the state legislature from Wilkes County for many years from 1795 to 1834. *N. C. Manual*, 852-854, 905.
[8]Probably Charity's sister, Martha Ann, who never married.
[9]Probably John Scott. See above p. 18n.

anxiety to know how you are therefore My Dear write imme-
diately, don't let any circumstances put it off. Give my love to
Sister Sutherland,[10] & who indeed has more of it excepting my
Dear lovely Wife—

To your Mamma give my love & seal it with a kiss from me &
tell her that by these presents I give and transfer to her full
power & authority to rule over and govern you according to Law,
& all her acts therein I will duly & legally ratify. To Martha &
Anne[11] I give & bequeath full power to aid & assist in all these
matters & things, & herein to fail not. Given under my hand &
seal—

Farewell My Dear, May Angels of peace guard you from every
harm.

WILLIE P. MANGUM

[Addressed:]
    Mrs. Charity A. Mangum,
        Hillsboro,
            No. Ca.

Mr. Cooke[12] The post-master
will please to hand this to
Mr. Wm. Cain Jr.

WPM-LC

Willie P. Mangum to Mrs. Charity A. Mangum

Tuesday night 25th April 1820

My dear Love,

This evening I had hoped I should have time to avail myself of
the opportunity afforded by M[r]. Turner[13] of writing to you in
detail touching the strange things in this Wild Country. M[r].
James Turner arrived here this evening & sets out at sun rise in
the morning.—M[r]. Arch[d]. Henderson[14] called at my room & engaged my politeness until 10 oclock & never was politeness more
reluctantly bestowed. But now I return to the duty I love to dis-

---

[10]Mary Cain.
[11]Ann Lillington Cain who married Edward Davis.
[12]Richard L. Cooke, postmaster at Hillsboro.
[13]Probably James Turner, 1766-1824, born in Southampton County, Virginia. He was a
member of the North Carolina legislature from Warren County from 1799 to 1802, governor
of North Carolina from 1802 to 1805, and United States Senator from 1805 to 1816. He died
January 15, 1824. Ashe, *Biog. Hist. of N. C.*, III, 412-415.
[14]Archibald Henderson, 1768-1822, was born in Granville County but lived most of his life
in Salisbury where he had a large law practice. He was in the legislature in 1807-1809, 1814,
1819-1820, and in the United States House of Representatives from 1799 to 1803. *Biog. Dir.
of Cong.*, 1085.

charge, and acknowledge the receipt of yours of the 27th of March which never came to hand until last week, in consequence of my passing Morgan & going over the mountains before its arrival.—I was exceedingly concerned to understand my Dear that you still remained the victim of bad health, but this evening felt most pleasantly relieved from gloomy apprehensions by understanding from Mr Turner that you were all well.—I have been in very bad health for three weeks in succession but am now tolerably well again.—My labours have been most arduous. indeed the intellectual labour of this circuit for unremitted application & difficulty has transcended all that I should have performed in 12 months at the Bar.—

And Indeed all your ridicule upon me will not convince me that I love my present employments.—

I have never been able until this circuit to appreciate the agonized feelings of an exile from home, family and friends.—And nothing but hope, dear heaven-born hope affords an alleviation to the afflictive pangs of separation. The far away at one time at 300 miles distance, on the borders of the Wilderness, surrounded with a population as little congenial to my habits & taste as the Wild savage, yet even there a gleam of delight would break in upon my gloom occasioned by excessive bad health, labour & fatigue, when I look to the silent tho joyous moment of meeting you—Indeed you must not think it romantic that my bosom would throb with pleasure's purest ecstacy, while my wayward fancy would hover around your pillow where all my hopes, my happiness & love lay in the sweet embrace of sleep.—

I have once more set my face towards home, and I am now in the pleasant little village of Lincolnton.—Spring is rapidly clothing in her rich & verdant robes the lovely landscape.—The weather is soft, & delightful, and nought but my anxiety to get home disturbs the sweet serenity of the scene. Yet four long weeks must slowly move their round before I have the prospect of seeing you.—I hope to be at home, next saturday night three weeks.—and bid my last adieu to tremendous mountains, frightful precipices & lover's leaps.—My time will be completely taken up, the balance of the circuit with business—I have seen a great deal of pleasant country—some so whimsically romantic that it would even incline trembling old age to strike the harp to the measures of joy—some agreeable society—some polish—a great deal of rudeness—& some primitive simplicity such as would charm you My Dear into pleasing enjoyment.—

Primitive simplicity & a pure & unsophistocated heart constitute the most lovely points of character—And if My Dear I were
to select in you those points of character that are most calculated
to endear you to a husband capable of feeling your worth.—I
certainly should not hesitate to mark out those that discriminate
between the excellence of virtue, & the odiousness of vice—And
so long My Love as you may prize the exclusive devotion of a
warm heart so long cling to those sentiments that reflect upon
you such delicate loveliness in the eyes of your husband—

Tender my love to the family— & bestow upon your Mamma,
Sister Mary & Martha the warmest kiss in my name. I must
sleep—Adieu My Dearest Love, May Heaven smile upon & bless
you—

WILLIE P MANGUM—

[Addressed:]
        Mrs. Charity Mangum
            Orange
                No. Ca.

politeness of   ⎱
Mr. Jas. Turner ⎰

WPM-LC

Thos. N. L. Hargis et. als. to Mrs. Mangum

The pleasure of Mrs. Mangum's company is respectfully solicited at a Tea party to be given at Mr. T. N. L. Hargis' on Tuesday evening 4th July 1820.

THOS. N. L. HARGIS[15] ⎱
W. H. WHITTED   ⎬ Managers
E. STRUDWICK   ⎰

[Addressed:]
        Mrs. Mangum.

WPM-LC

Pherraby Grimes to Willie Mangum

RALEIGH 17th July 1820

Sir,
    You promised me last Session when you called at my house

---

[15]Thos. N. L. Hargis and W. H. Whitted were business partners in Hillsboro. Hargis was
also magistrate of the police. Edmund Strudwick was a physician in Hillsboro.

about 6 miles from this place on the Hillsboro road that you would eneavor to ascertain whether my husband Wm. Grimes[16] (who enlisted in this place and went to Charleston So Ca where it is supposed he died,) was dead or not. Not having heard from you since I have become somewhat uneasy, and beg you will do me the favor to let me know whether you have made the enquiry and if not whether you will do so.

Excuse this trouble, and drop a line directed to me in the Raleigh post office.

Yours Obt. Servt.
PHERRABY GRIMES.

[Addressed:]

> The Hon. Wille Mangum,
> Hillsborough,
> No Ca.

_____

WPM-LC

Jas. J. Selby to

RALEIGH Aug. 16th 1820

Dr. Sir;

This comes to inform you that I am now in extreme want of Money you will be confering a Singular favour on me by Sending me the amt. of ballance of your acct. I do assure you it's pure Necessity compells me to send to you at this time or I Should not trouble you, Your complyance with the above will Greatly Oblige

Yours Respectfully

JAˢ. J. SELBY

1819

March 27th Judge Willie P Mangum   **Dr.**
                To James J Selby

To Makg a Coat ....$ 8.00
To 1¼ yd laventeen at $1.50 to a Sett twist
  buttons $1.25 .... 3.12½
To ¾ yd bombazett at 80 to a Silk Velvet Cape $1.50.. 2.10.
To thread Silk twist pading Staying &c.............. 1.85.
To Makg pr pantaloons $2 to 1 yd hollow 60ct........ 2.60

---

[16]According to the *Roster of Soldiers from North Carolina in the American Revolution* (Printed for the North Carolina Daughters of the American Revolution by the Seeman Press, Durham, N. C., 1932), 129, 261, 527, a William Grimes enlisted in North Carolina Continental Line in Dixon's Company of the 10th Regiment. His pay was received by John Grimes in 1784.

To thread silk twist buttons Stays & ties............ 1.00
To Makg a Vest $2 to 1½ yd bombazett at 80ct....... 3.20
To 1 yd hollow 60 ct thread silk twist moulds & 50ct... 1.10
To 3½ yds Superfine Black Cloth at 15 dollars per yd.. 52.50
To 1¼ yd Florentine at $3........................ 3.75

$79.22½

1819
Apl. 5th C^r by Cash............................$32.97½

Due $46.[25]
N. B. When you send the Money please Send the Bill and I will
return it with a receipt annexed thereto.
Yours Obt.
JA^s. J. SELBY

Jas. J. Selby to
Dr. Sir,
    Enclosed I Send you your Brothers acct. praying the favour
of you to interceed with him for me and inform him of my Situation and hard pressure for Money in so obliging me you^l Confer a great favour on   Your^s. Respectfully
JAS. J. SELBY

Judge W. P. Mangum
N. B. please Send me an answer by the next Mail if possible
JJS

Mr. W. P. M.)
[Addressed:]
        Judge Willie P Mangum
            Hillsboro
                Orange County N. C.—

[April 26, 1819]
1819

Apl. 26th Mr. Priestly H. Mangum
            To James J. Selby

To Makg a Coat ....$ 7.00
To Trimmings in full 6.57½
To 2¼ yd of Superfine Black Cloth at $13.50........ 30.37½
To makg pr. pantaloons 2.00

To trimmings in full	1.60
To 2¾ yds Cassimer at $4	11.00
To Mkg a Vest	2.00
To trimmings in full	2.30
To 1¼ yd. florentine at $3	3.75
To 1 yd Hollon to fold the above in	0.50.
	$67.10

[Addressed:]
> Mr. P. H. Mangum's
> *acct.*

WPM-LC

Willie P. Mangum to Charity A. Mangum

LAKE PHELPS,[17] 10th September 1820

My dearest Love,

Since I have been in this country I have been looking with eagerness and painful disappointment for a letter from you which by a note I requested the post master at Edenton to forward upon its arrival. Almost a month has now elapsed since a syllable respecting you has reached me, but I am sure if you have as adequate conception of my keen desire, & whetted impatience to hear from you *constantly* that you will not permit the delay to be attributable to you.—I am at a loss, My Dear Love, for the powers of language to convey an idea of my solicitude & anxiety respecting you in your present situation, and the Evil of which I am most apprehensive, & which you should most deprecate is that depression of spirits and despondency of feeling, that too frequently diffuse their blighting energy through the heart of the finest and most lovely sensibility.

At this very moment my fancy draws with painful accuracy your very look & countenance at the instant I left you and my heart almost melts at the picture, a look so forlorn, so friendless —a lip quivering with mental agony, an eye swimming in tears— and yet this tempest of feeling that raged in your bosom, yielding to your unshaken resolution, & firmness of resignation—it was a moment short & transient, yet it was the bitterest that my

---

[17]In the fall of 1820 Mangum was assigned the first circuit which included the northeastern counties. Because of his own ill health and the financial difficulties of his father, Mangum resigned his judgeship in November 1820 to return to his law practice.

heart ever knew—My memory loves to retrace the painful scene, and altho its fruits are mingled with bitterness, yet there is *that* in it which warms into a sacred glow the purest feelings of an affectionate husband.

When oppressed & worn down with the cares the troubles and turmoils of business, I retire from them with aversion.—It is then my heart turns to the object of all its love, and treasures up the remembrances of the delights, the endearments & all the loves that have marked our union—And how many are there that can say with me, that in reviewing the scene, nought presents itself that is not endeared by a thousand tender recollections, & nought but what the heart loves to contemplate & dwell on—The all wise disposer of events never intended that frail and forward man should enjoy in this life un-mingled happiness, but whatever may be my destiny the consummation of my misery can never be complete, while blessed with the love of her towards whom my heart feels not an emotion that she would not warmly approve.

May Heaven keep our hearts united in the dearest ties of Love, bestow upon us its blessings here, & prepare us to be united in those regions where temptation can never reach us, where misery is unknown, & where happiness is to be enjoyed throughout the countless ages of Eternity.—This world with all its bright dreams its gay visions & splendid pageantries, is worse than dross, if not combined with a virtuous heart, & the consolation of an approving conscience—& even these are not sufficient.

My Dearest jewel, I love you even beyond the grave; and when this world of vanities shall have shut in its scenes from the eye that is closed in death. O then if I had a heart to feel with what agonizing throes would it yearn for your felicity in the eternal world! But Merciful God spare me the trial! may never the temple of happiness that my heart & affections have erected, fall into ruin while I survive—Perhaps I am too solemn, indeed I have a tinge of melancholy, but it is of that species which is consistent with the warmest enthusiasm & yet not inconsistent with my happiness.—

It is not quite two weeks since I left your Pa's in Orange. I have held only one court, tomorrow I open another if spared at the distance of 30 miles from this place. Our friends in Orange were all well. You however I expect have heard since I have Patsy[18] promised to write to you frequently, she was very anx-

---

[18]Martha Cain.

ious to go [to] the springs to stay with you, but had no means of conveyance—I wrote to you from Orange, in which I stated that you might expect Mr. Davis[19] for you between the 10th & 15th of October. Your Papa however told me the day I set out, that if anything should interfere with Mr. Davis' arrangement, that he would send for you—I am now in a country at the distance of nearly 500 miles from you where you may travel 100 miles without seeing a hill as steep or high as that from Mrs. Benson's dining room to the gate. It is a country filled with swamps, sounds, lakes, flies & musquitoes. It is very unhealthy, the coolest water as warm as branch water in Orange—I have not been well —indeed last evening I weighed in the scales at this place & have lost 9 lb. since I weighed in Union. I have been taking active medicines & to day feel better than for 10 days. I am very apprehensive of an attack, altho I take every precaution—I left Tyrrell Court Thursday evening, on Friday visited the sound—a sheet of water 70 miles in one direction & from 14 to 30 in the other—It is Albemarle sound—the largest body of water that I had ever seen.—Yesterday I came to see Lake Phelps & am now in the residence of a private gentleman within 35 feet of its brink—here is the finest estate in No. Ca. Sixty three thousand Acres of land in one body as rich as the banks of the Nile a canal of 6 miles in length. & 20 feet wide emptying the waters of the lake in Scupperanong river—the lake 9 miles long & 6 in width & the surface of the lake from 6 to 18 feet higher than any of the country around it except the Margin—On the canal there is the greatest variety of useful & ingenious machinery that I ever saw—

My Dear write to me frequently—if I am deprived of y[our] society. It is yet a pleasure dear to my feelings to receive y[our] letters—The paper that your fingers have touched independent of the sentiment is endeared to me.—My heart almost revokes & my blood chills when I reflect that even if I live to get home that in all probability I shall not enjoy your company more than 8 or 10 days between this & next May—My design is to visit the Western Country on my return home—Farewell my dearly beloved—May Heaven spread around you its protection & guardian care, & re[s]tore you in health & happiness,

to your husbands Arms—

WILLIE P. MANGUM

---

[19]Edward Davis, who married Ann Lillington Cain, later moved to the gold region in the western part of the state.

Give my respect & esteem
to all the excellent family
with whom you reside.

W. P. M.

[Addressed:]

Mrs. Charity A. Mangum
Union[20]
Monroe County
Virginia

Via

Richmond, Va. }

WPM-LC

[20 Sept., 1820]

Jhon Harp Parkerson et als. to[21]

State of North Carolina
Chatham County

this day personally appeared before me William Franks one of the States Justices of the peace John Harp Parkerson who being duly Sworn deposeth Testefieth and Sayeth that he Served as a Soldier in the Same Company and Regiment with William Tallen and Titus Jennings Turner and he Sayeth also the military Service proved by the oath of William Tallen as performed by the Said Titus Jennings Turner was begun and entered into by the said Turner in the year one thousand Seven hundred and Seventy Six and that the Said Turner Continued in the Said military Service in the Same Said Company and Regiment till in the year one thousand and Seven hundred and Seventy seven on the Continental establishment of the United States of america in the Revolutionary War.

Sworn and subscribed before me this 26th day of Sept. 1820.

his
Jhon Harp   X   Parkerson
Mark

Test.
Wm. Franks (J. P.)

---

[20] A watering place near the Salt Sulphur Springs in southwestern Virginia.

[21] Although most pension requests are omitted from this publication, these papers on Titus J. Turner are included because they illustrate the type of requests which came to Mangum, and because there are several additional papers about him. See below pp. 156-158, 174-182.

State of North Carolina
Chatham County

I Thomas Ragland Clerk of the Court
of Pleas and quarter Sessions for the
County aforesaid do hereby certify
that William Franks Esq. who witnessed the above certificate is
an [illegible] Justice of the Peace &c for the said County of
Chatham; And that due faith & credit is & ought to be given to
his official acts In Witness whereof I have hereto set my hand
under Seal of said County at office this 28th Sept. 1820.

THOS. RAGLAND, C. C.

I hereby Certify that John harp parkersen is considered as a
Credetable person and that hes oath is to taken and releyed on.

WM. FRANKS J. P.

It appears to my Satisfaction that the years 1776 and 1777 mentioned in the oath of John harp parkerson was the Dates when
the Military Service of the Said Titus Jennings Turner was performed and I am also Satisfied that the said parkerson was
totally uninterested in his oath in behalf of the Said Turner.

WM. FRANKS (J. P.)

Will H. Murfree to Willie P. Mangum[22]

MURFREESBORO ' Decr. 7. 1820 -

Dr Sir.

I am informed by the Clerk & Master that you omitted to send
to him the Bill of Injunction of Picketts[23] from Edenton as we
expected.

As your attention about that time as well as my own was
much occupied with the fever & ague, I presume it escaped
your recollection. I have to request the favor of you to inclose
it to me or Mr. Yancey[24] at this place with your determination
on it -

[22]A typed copy of this letter is in the Willie P. Mangum Papers, State Department of
Archives and History, Raleigh, N. C. The original has not been located. Mr. Stephen B.
Weeks had the original copied from the Willie Mangum Person Collection. See below p 53n.
[23]Probably Col. Joseph Pickett, 1776-1828, of Anson County. He was in the state legislature in 1805, 1813 to 1816, 1817, and 1825 to 1827. *Hillsborough Recorder*, July 23, 1828;
N. C. Manual, 487-488.
[24]Bartlett Yancey, 1785-1828, a graduate of the state university and a member of Congress
from 1813 to 1817 and speaker of the state senate from 1817 to 1827, declined appointment
as U. S. Minister to Peru by President Adams. He became a member of the North Carolina
Supreme Court. He was a lawyer of prominence in Caswell County. *Biog. Dir. of Cong.*, 1734.

I regret to perceive by the papers you have sent your resignation to the legislature - it is hoped by some, tho' I fear ill founded, that they would this session have rendered the situation of the Circuit Judges less laborious-

Early in the summer I expect to finally remove to the western Country and should any thing carry you there should be happy to be informed of it.

> Very respt
> Your O Sert
> WILL H MURFREE[25]

[Addressed:]
> Willie P. Mangum Esqr.
> Hillsboro'
> N. C.

WPM-LC

Jo. Gales to Willie P. Mangum

[24 April, 1821]

1821. W. P. Mangum, Esq.
> of Jo. Gales.

		Dollars
Apl. 24,	Law Repository & Term Reports, 3 vols	18 ....
	Conference Reports	5 ....
	No. 1 to 3 Murphey's Reports	4.50
		27.50

D.ʳ Sir,

I send you the above, agreeably to your wish; and will forward you the succeeding Nos. of the Reports as they appear.

> Yours respectly.

> JO. GALES

Raleigh, Apl. 24, 1821.

---

[25]William Hardy Murfree, 1781-1827, attorney and planter in Chowan County, was a member of the state legislature in 1805, 1812 to 1818; he served in the United States Congress from 1813 to 1817. He moved to Williamston County, Tennessee in 1823. Benjamin B. Winborne, *The Colonial and State Political History of Hertford County, N. C.* (Printed for the author by Edwards and Broughton, Raleigh, N. C., 1906), 328; *Biog. Dir. of Cong.*, 1345.

Augustus Benton[26] to Willie P. Mangum

[May 24, 1821]

Respected Sir,

Having recently been informed that you have again returned to the Bar, I have taken the liberty to appoint you My agent by letter of Attoy which M.ʳ McCawley[27] will hand you, and requesting your professional attention and aid in some business which Judge Ruffin[28] has had in charge a long time to manage for me against John Taylor Junr.,[29] but has for some cause delaid it to this late period. The Judge, A. B. Bruce,[30] and M.ʳ Mc-Cawley can fully explain to you every thing relative to the nature of My several demands and how shamefully I have been treated respecting them and I have now Sir, in the Most particular Manner to beg and request that you will in Conjunction with Judge Ruffin, put the business immediately in Motion and bring it to a close with all possible expedition in your power.

I am at this time short of funds but your fee shall be paid—parden the liberty which I have here taken which is partly from a former acquaintance with yourself & all your family, and believe that I am Sir, in the greatest haste Your Obᵗ. friend & Servt.

A. BENTON.

N. B. I will write you again shortly when I shall have more time than now.

Moore Courthouse
        24th May 1821

It is proper that you should be inform'd of the peculiarity of My present Situation that you May know how to govern yourself in all things which relates to My person &c &c &c. all of the within named personages can inform you. My particular respects to your father.

[Addressed:]
        Judge Mangum,
                Hillsborough
                        No Ca.

---

[26]An attorney of Franklin County. McIver, *N. C. Register*, 46.
[27]William McCaulay.
[28]Judge Thomas Ruffin.
[29]Probably John Taylor of Hillsboro who was clerk of the superior court in Orange County in 1820.
[30]Abner B. Bruce, 1765-1835, was clerk of the superior court in Orange County in 1823. McIver, *N. C. Register*, 43; *Hillsborough Recorder*, Apr. 3, 1835.

Omnibus et Singulis has Literas lecturis,

SALUTEM IN DOMINO.

QUONIAM nobis commissum est legibus hujus Reipublicæ Carolinæ Septentrionalis, *ut probis moribus*, Religione *et* Scientia *omnes instituamus, qui has eximias animi dotes exoptent, et qui sub tutela nostra diligenter* Studeant : **Pro manifesto itaque** *habeatur*

Willie Person Mangum,

periculis universis in literis ex ordine comprobatum esse, *quibus* **Universitatis alumni Carolinæ Septentrionalis** *exerceri solent ; hoc etiam diplomate* ARTIUM BACCALAUREI *a nobis eundem condecoratum esse, ut omnibus ad quos hæc pervenerint de his liqueat.*

In Quorum Testimonium *nos Senatus Academicus chirographa nostra, et commune sigillum huic* Membranæ *affiximus.*

DATUM IN AULA PERSONICA, *tertio ante kalendas Julii, Anno Domini millesimo octingentesimo decimo quinto.*

Mr. McCawley)
[Endorsed:]
Augustus Benton
    Letter & power.

WPM-LC

Martha A. Cain to Charity A. Mangum

RED SULPHUR SPRINGS[31] August 30th 1821.

My Dear Sister

As I expect you are a little anxious to hear from us, I will write you a few lines by Mr. Sanders[32] who intends leaving here in the morning for milton[33] & says he will post my letter in the office.

We reached the Salt Sulphur after 9 days disagreeable travelling, we staid there seven or eight days, & then come on here, my cough mended a little during our stay at the Salt Sulphur. But it has mended much faster, since my arrival here. Sister & Stephen[34] are both quite well. they left me last Friday to visit the Salt Sulphur. & returned on tuesday. Mr. & Mrs. Sanders staid with me untill they returned. Our old acquaintance, Mr. Baker, arrived at the Salt S. a few days after we did, & is here at this time, but speaks of leaving here tomorrow, I am [anxious to] stay here a week longer & if I conclude to do so, Sister will return to the salt sulphur with Mr. Baker.

We expect to start home in about a fortnight, or perhaps sooner. (I expected a letter from you last mail, but I was disappointed, only to think I have not heard a word from you or my beloved parents since I left home).

Mr. Scott[35] arrived at the salt sulphur after we did, he come on here with us & staid a day & returned to the Salt Sulphur with the intention of staying a week there, but was taken sick & went on to the warm springs.

---

[31]Near Monroe, Virginia.
[32]Romulus N. Saunders, 1791-1867, an attorney and political leader of Caswell County, served in the North Carolina House of Commons in 1815, 1817, and 1819, and from 1852 to 1856; he was speaker from 1817 to 1819. He was in the House of Representatives of the United States from 1821 to 1827 and 1841 to 1845. He was state attorney general from 1828 to 1831 and judge of the superior court from 1835 to 1840 and from 1852 to 1856. He was defeated by one vote for governor of North Carolina in 1840. He served as U. S. minister to Spain from 1846 to 1849 and was a member of the commission to revise the North Carolina laws. He was a frequent rival of Mangum. Ashe, *Biog. Hist. of N. C.*, III, 381-390.
[33]County seat of Caswell County.
[34]Mary Cain had a son whose name was William Stephen.
[35]Probably John Scott.

Mr. A. Carter[36] arrived here today from the Salt Sulphur and says he left but one person there. I expect there is about twenty here at this time, or perhaps more.

A gentleman died here about 4 weeks ago - with the consumption & there is a gentleman in the cabin next to us that the Dr's have despaired of, with the bilious fever, he has the most attentive & affectionate wife I ever saw.

Sister Mary joins me in love to you & Mr. Mangum and William and a dozen kisses for Will,[37] if you should see Mama & papa before I do, give my warmest love to them.

Adieu Dear Sister, may kind providence smile upon & bless you is the sincere wish of your affectionate Sister,

MARTHA A. CAIN.

excuse this bad writing
for I am in a hurry.

[Addressed:]
    Mrs. Charity A. Mangum,
        Hillsborough,
            N. Carolina.

WPM-D

Thomas Alston to Willie P. Mangum

13th Octr 1821

Dear Sir

Will you be so good as to apply to the Sheriff of Halifax for the payment of the enclosed receipts, should you be going to Halifax County, and it appears to me, I have a feint recollection of your haveing mentioned you should attend that Court, Mr Robert H. Jones[38] informed me, that he attended to the business, Mr. Plummer[39] being unwell, He observed the suit was brought in the County Court Mr. Tunstall appealed and that this is the Court for the Money to be ready, should you not return by the way of my House, you will please place it in hands of some person who will be passing my way or Raleigh, I dislike to be

---

[36]Archibald Grayson Carter was a planter and lawyer of Caswell County. He was in the state legislature in 1832. Grant, *Alumni Hist. of U. N. C.*, 103.
[37]William Cain, Jr.
[38]A member of the state legislature from 1816 to 1818, 1823 to 1824, and 1826 to 1827 from Warren County, United States district attorney under President Jefferson, and attorney general of North Carolina in 1828. Hamilton, *Papers of Ruffin*, I, 165n; *N. C. Manual*, 836-837.
[39]Probably Kemp Plummer, an attorney of Warren County. McIver, *N. C. Register*, 48.

troublesome, that it is some distance to Halifax and should have
no other business, your complyance will be remembered

Yours respectfully

T[HOS] ALSTON[40]

Mr. Willie P. Mangum

[Endorsement:] Thos: Alston Letter & receipt

[Enclosure][41]

In continuation & esplanation of articles between W P Mangum & Archd. Haralson touching the purchase of the point at Haywood. The meaning of them is that Mangum & Sneed are to pay sixteen hundred & sixty six & two thirds dollars of the second payment to Col Farrar for sd. purchase of the point by Paole Ashe & Co & that Sneed & Mangum are to pay no more - - & Haralson binds himself to make deeds to Mangum & Sneed & their heirs for the sd. point in fee simple

In testimony whereof the sd Haralson hath hereunto set his hand & affirmed his seal this 29th Feby 1820

Test   S. Strudwick   Arch. Haralson seal

[on back]

[illegible]   366

   944

      Cash $300   Scott 200
      Bradalow 180   100
      Hargis   98

                      $100

Deed of lot 148 in Hillsboro to W. P. Mangum[42]

[15 Oct., 1821]

D. HEARTT, Printer, Hillsborough

This Indenture, Made this Fifteenth day of October in the year of our Lord one thousand eight hundred and twenty one between Thomas N. S. Hargis, magistrate of police, and James Child, John Young, John Taylor, William Huntington, Jonathan P. Sneed, William Whitted, Jun. and John Scott, commissioners of the town of Hillsborough, in the county of Orange and state

[40]Thomas Alston, 1781-1850, was a man of much property in Halifax County. Joseph A. Grove, *The Alstons of North and South Carolina; also Notes of some allied Families* (Atlanta, 1901), 310-311. Hereafter cited as Grove, *Alstons of N. & S. C.*
[41]See above, pp. 17-18.
[42]The original is in the possession of Mr. Mangum Turner, Winston-Salem, N. C.

of North Carolina, of the one part, and Willie P. Mangum of the other part, WITNESSETH, that the said magistrate of police and commissioners, for and in consideration of the sum of One hundred and twenty one Dollars - - - to them in hand paid by the said Willie P. Mangum - - - - - at and before the sealing and delivery of these presents, the receipt whereof is hereby acknowledged, have granted, bargained, sold, enfeoffed and conveyed, and by these presents do grant, bargain, sell, enfeeof and convey unto the said Willie P. Mangum - - - - - - - his heirs and assigns, a certain lot in said town, on the South side of Union - - - - - - street, known and distinguished in the plan of said town as number One hundred and forty Eight, bounded on the North by Union Street, One the West by Lot Number One hundred and forty nine, on the South by Lot number Sixty four, and on the East by Lot number One hundred and forty Seven, containing One acre of Land with all and singular the hereditaments and appurtenances thereunto belonging, or in any wise appertaining, to have and to hold the said lot to the said Willie P. Mangum - - - his heirs and assigns, in fee simple and for ever. And the said magistrate of police and commissioners, for themselves and their successors in office, do hereby covenant and agree to and with the said Willie P. Mangum - - - - - his heirs, executors, administrators and assigns, that they the said magistrate of police and commissioners shall and will for ever warrant and defend the above described lot, with the hereditaments and appurtenances thereunto belonging, from and against the lawful claim or claims of all and every person or persons claiming by, from or under them. In witness whereof, the said magistrate of police and commissioners have hereunto set their hands and affixed their seals the day and date first above written.

SIGNED, SEALED AND DELIVERED
  IN THE PRESENCE OF

Jos. A. Woods

Tho. N. S. Hargis	Seal
James Child	Seal
John Young	Seal
J. Taylor	Seal
Wm Huntington	Seal
J. P. Sneed	Seal
Will Whitted	Seal
John Scott	Seal

[Endorsement:] Commissioners Deed to Willie P. Mangum
Lot No. 148.

Deed of lot 149 in Hillsboro to Willie P. Mangum

[15 Oct., 1821]
D. HEARTT, Printer, Hillsborough.
This Indenture, Made this Fifteenth day of October in the
year of our Lord one thousand eight hundred and twenty one
between Thomas N. S. Hargis, magistrate of police, and James
Child, John Young, John Taylor, William Huntington, Jonathan
P. Sneed, William Whitted, Jun. and John Scott, commissioners
of the town of Hillsborough, in the county of Orange and state
of North Carolina, of the one part, and Willie P. Mangum of
the other part, WITNESSETH, that the said magistrate of
police and commissioners, for and in consideration of the sume
of One hundred and Twelve Dollars - - - - to them in hand paid
by the said Willie P. Mangum - - - - - at and before the sealing
and delivery of these present, the receipts whereof is hereby
acknowledged, have granted, bargained, sold, enfeoffed and conveyed, and by these presents do grant, bargain, sell enfeoff and
convey unto the said Willie P. Mangum - - - - - - his heirs and
assigns, a certain lot in said town, on the South side of Union
- - - - street, known and distinguished in the plan of said town
as number One hundred and forty nine, bounded on the North
by Union Street, on the West by Lot number One hundred and
fifty, On the South by Lot number Sixty three, and on the East
by Lot number One hundred and forty Eight, - Containing One
Acre of Land with all and singular the hereditaments and
appurtenances thereunto belonging, or in any wise appertaining, to have and to hold the said lot to the said Willie P. Mangum - - - - - his heirs and assigns, in fee simple and for ever.
And the said magistrate of police and commissioners, for themselves and their successors in office, do hereby covenant and
agree to with the said Willie P. Mangum - - - his heirs, executors,
administrators and assigns, that they the said magistrate of
police and commissioners shall and will for ever warrant and defend the above described lot, with the hereditaments and appurtenances thereunto belonging, from and against the lawful claim
or claims of all and every person or persons claiming by, from
or under them. In witness whereof, the said magistrate of police

and commisioners have hereunto set their hands and affixed
their seals the day and date first above written.

SIGNED, SEALED AND DELIVERED
    IN THE PRESENCE OF

       Jos. A. Woods

Tho. N. S. Hargis	Seal
James Child	Seal
John Young	Seal
J. Taylor	Seal
Wm Huntington	Seal
J. P. Sneed	Seal
Will Whitted	Seal
John Scott	Seal

[Endorsement:] Commissioners Deed to Willie P. Mangum
Lot No. 149.

WPM-LC

Henry Seawell[43] to Willie P. Mangum

LOUISBURG 13th June 1822.

Sir,

Your note of this date is now before me, and I have read it
with some surprise.[44] I Joined you last evening most heartily in
consigning to "oblivion" a transaction which at all times would
be remembered by me with the deepest regret. & can only be
known to others as reproachful to us both- it was done in darkness, & I had hoped it would have slept in everlasting silence -
In your note however you say, there was one expression used
by me which escaped you at the moment of reconciliation and
which you now call upon me to explain.

If you can for a moment believe any part [of] my conduct
which was offensive proceeded from a *deliberate* design, then I
admit, your right to have that part explained. but if on the other
hand, the whole resulted from the excitement of the moment, as
I think both of us must admit, there can be no ground for ex-

---

[43]See above, p. 10n.
[44]Mangum was in frequent quarrels with political leaders of his day. Apparently this difficulty was settled without any duel. The same was true of the quarrel with Henry Seawell
in 1823. See below, pp. 70-76.

amining the merits of any one expression, which does not equally apply to the whole transaction.

All that I said & did, as I presume was the case with you, was of a piece & of precisely the same character; it was intended to be affrontful, and was dictated alone by the same excitement which influenced the whole of my conduct. You have admitted that your conduct & expressions towards me were affrontful, "that both offended in that respect and that you were desirous the whole might be forgotten." This has been as frankly reciprocated on my part, and with equal sincerity. but if any thing like atonement is to [be] made on either side, I must then insist the merits of the whole affair shall be investigated. and whether we are not equally interested in avoiding such a course, I submit to your consideration - that I may not be misunderstood I repeat, my conduct on that occasion was the result of passion - this you must perceive at once is as far as I can go at this stage of the business- for nothing said or done by you has been palleated in any other way -

Yours &c
HENRY SEAWELL

W. Mangum Esqr
[Addressed:]
      Willie P. Mangum Esr
Present -

WPM-LC

John Chavis[45] to John Haywood[46]

July 3rd. 1822

My dear Sir

I have written two letters respecting my note in the bank &c but forgot to mention the amount of the note, & what sum it

[45]John Chavis, a free man of color, fought in the American Revolution, and according to tradition was educated at Princeton. There is no evidence that he was ever at Princeton although there is proof that he attended the Academy (later Washington and Lee) at Lexington, Virginia. In 1800 he was licensed by the Lexington Presbytery to preach. For some twenty years after he went to North Carolina in 1805, he preached in Orange, Granville, and Wake counties. In 1808 he began teaching, which he continued into the 1830's. He taught several prominent North Carolinians and according to tradition taught Mangum and his children. I find no proof of this. He was an ardent Federalist and constantly in his frequent letters to Mangum urged his "son," as he called him, to return to the true doctrine of Washington and Hamilton. Edgar W. Knight, "Notes on John Chavis," *North Carolina Historical Review,* VII (1930), 326-345.

[46]John Haywood, 1755-1827, was born in Edgecombe County but later moved to Raleigh where he was state treasurer from 1787 to his death in 1827. Ashe, *Biog. Hist. of N. C.,* VI. 282-288.

would take to renew it.[47] The amount is 270 dollars so that the sum required to renew is about 31 dollars which I hope it will be in your power to pay, & for fear you have Mislaid the notes or assignments which I enclosed to you, some time ago, I have enclosed another, that there may not be a disappointment on that acc.[t]

> I am your Obt Hmbl
> Srvt.
> JOHN CHAVES

P. S. Next Tuesday is the day of renewal.

> J. C.

[Addressed:]
> John Haywood Esq.,
> Raleigh

Capt Pullen[48]
with great care.

WPM-LC

E. Littell[49] to Willie P. Mangum

[14 Aug., 1822]
To E. Littell Dr.

Willie P. Mangum Esq
Hillsboro N. C.
For New Monthly Magazine Nos 13 to 18 . . . .$3......

Philad: 14th Aug, 1822.

Sir

I transmit yr acct. to this date. Having sold to W. O. Everett, Boston, the publication of the New Monthly Magazine, I cannot afford to send it out of town unless paid for in advanced.— Should you wish to continue yr. subscription please remit either to Mr. E. or to me.

---

[47]Chavis had much difficulty meeting his expenses. His white friends frequently gave him support. The Orange Presbytery in 1832 and thereafter voted him sums of money. Knight, "Notes on John Chavis," *North Carolina Historical Review*, VII, 326-345.

[48]Samuel H. Pullen was the deputy sheriff of Wake County. *N. C. Comptroller's Statement of the Disbursements at the Public Treasury of North Carolina, 1822-1823*, bound with the *North Carolina Laws, 1823*, 7.

[49]Eliakim Littell, 1797-1870, was an editor of a magazine under several names beginning in 1819 and continuing until past 1850. In 1822 his magazine, which was published in Philadelphia, was called the *Museum of Foreign Literature and Science*. It was about 96 pages long and had a wide circulation. *D. A. B.*, XI, 295.

I solicit yr. patronage for the Museum (advertised on the cover of No 18 New Monthly) & remain Sir,

Very Respectfully Yrs
E. LITTELL.

[Addressed:]
Willie P. Mangum
Hillsboro, N. C.

———

WPM-LC

Deed[50] of William Cain to Charity A. Mangum

[21 Oct. , 1822]

Know all men by these presents that I William Cain senr of the County of Orange & the State of North Carolina, for and in consideration of One Dollar to me in hand paid, & for the further Consideration of the love and affectionate regard that I bear towards my daughter Charity A. Mangum, have given, granted & transferred, & by these presents I the said William Cain for the considerations aforesaid, do give, grant & transfer to my daughter Charity A Mangum her heirs and assigns & executors &c. the following slaves, To Wit a Woman named Winny, her sons Isham, Jefferson, Madison & Ben, also a negro girl named Sally—also Ellen; & also Polly. To Have & to hold the said slaves to the said Charity A. Mangum her Executors &c for ever.

I the sd. W. Cain Sr. for the considerations aforesaid do warrant & defend the title to the said Slaves to the said Charity A. Mangum her heirs, & Executors, & assigns forever.

Witness my hand & Seal this 21st Octo. 1822.

WILLIAM CAIN   (Seal)

Signed Sealed &
delivered In presence
of
    Mary Sutherland

---

[50]This is in the autograph of W. P. Mangum.

P. H. Mangum to Willie P. Mangum

HILLSBORO' Dec: 18th 1822.—

Dear Sir,

I am still anxious that you should make up your mind, to reside in Hillsboro'.[51] Every week affords additional evidence of the preference of a residence here, to one in the Country.— You may flatter yourself that it is not true, but you may depend upon it, that you are daily sliding out of public view; and there is as little doubt, that you will, if you continue where you are gradually sink in public estimation.

I have thought proper to commit to writing the reasons, which give me decided impressions in favour of your coming to this place—and that too, in a short time.— In the first place, you would make yourself a better lawyer. You would read more, and to better purpose. The competition you would surely bear—and the opposition you would most likely have to encounter, would incite you to exertions, which you would never make in the country—and without which, neither you nor any other person, can make a good lawyer, or a useful man. Then on this point, the only question is, shall I continue to indulge my case—or shall I labour? Again: It is a desideratum, to possess weight and respectability of character; as regards, as well, political advancement, as professional emoluments. There are appointments & honours, within the gift of the people & Legislature of the State, which no man in his senses, or with due respect for himself & his friends, would spurn from him.

If he were so spell-bound by an austere religion—or so wedded to the inglorious ease & luxurious indulgence of a negative existence, as to have no relish for these things, for *himself*; and be prepared to call them bright toys, fit for madmen & fools—still he might perhaps be induced to consider whether he should not bestow some attention on them, to advance the interests of his friends or family. A residence here, would reasonably ensure a better chance for a participation in the distributions of public favor.—But independently of these considerations an argument of a flimsey nature, may be drawn from self-defence. Mr. Ruffin[52] is already here, whose influence never

---

[51]At the time of this letter, W. P. Mangum was living near Flat River in what is today Durham County. He later built his home, Walnut Hall, in this community.
[52]Judge Thomas Ruffin.

coins golden apples—Mr. Strange,[53] I learn from a respectable source, is determined on removing to this place— and Mr. Murphey[54] has, I understand from Wm. Cain, come to a similar determination. If these three men were stationed in Hillsboro', with their feelings and dispositions towards each other, & with that conduct past experience has so abundantly proven, to exist between two of them, which conduct would acquire increased force from the facilities of local situation— Who that is here, would be able to resist successfully that torrent of favoritism, intrigue & talent, which would spring up & sweep over this country?

Where is to be found a balsam for wounded pride, consequent on being elbowed out, by these or any other Gentlemen?— Altho' I should be conscious of my inability, to contend successfully with them, single-handed—yet my pride as well as my interest, would impel me on to an honorable contest: I know not why the same motives should not influence you. My feelings are alive on this subject. I have no idea of passively submitting to the domination of a set of starveling Virginian Gentry[55]— who leave honors for reasons best known to themselves, and flock into No. Ca. & presume here to build up their prosperity, at the expense of native growth. It is a correct maxim, that there is no office, any where, that a Virginian would not presume to aspire to.— There [is I a]ᵈmit, some illiberality in these re-[marks, but] they are true.—

Doc: Smith[56] offers his House & Lot for sale. He would take $2500.00 & accommodate the purchas[er] by charging paper in Bank. He wishes to write to you— Will you think of it.[57] If the House be suitable, the situation is eligible. The Doc: is about to locate himself at Raleigh.

Yrs
respectfully
P. H. Mangum

---

[53]Robert Strange, 1796-1854, a Hampden-Sidney graduate who settled at Fayetteville to practice law was in the state legislature from 1821 to 1823, was judge of the superior court of North Carolina from 1827 to 1836, and was a Democratic Senator of the United States from 1836 to 1840. He was a literary figure of local note, and for some years served as state solicitor of the fifth judicial district. *Biog. Dir. of Cong.*, 1579.

[54]Archibald D. Murphey.

[55]Priestley Mangum never went very far in politics partly because he was undiplomatic. This attack on the Virginians who held numerous offices in North Carolina is indicative of his frequent thrusts. His views, however, were not unlike those of many others of his section.

[56]James S. Smith.

[57]Although Priestley was urging his brother to locate in the town of Hillsboro, shortly after this Priestley himself upon his marriage to Colonel Ransom Sutherland's daughter, Rebecca, moved to the country in Wake County where he lived the rest of his life.

[Addressed:]
    Willie P. Mangum Esquire
        Flat [River]

————

WPM-LC

P. H. Mangum to Willie P. Mangum

HILLSBORO'. Dec: 31ˢᵗ.. 1822.

Dear Sir,

M.ʳ Moses Guess[58] will hand you this— who visits you to employ you in business with myself. He will state all the facts— upon which I think you will advise him as I have done.—Joseph Pickett[59] has died leaving a will by which he bequeaths all his property to his wife [f]or widowhood, remainder to a natural child forever.— Mr. Trice claims the whole of the old Man's estate in two ways, first by virtue of a Deed of Gift, executed several years ago, & lastly, by virtue of a Bill of sale executed in the old man's illness just before his death. In the first Deed, is a reservation of a power to dispose by will— the last no doubt was obtained by improper practices. If you advise Mr. Guess the Executor, to contend for the property— you can fix upon our fees— The opposite party has applied to me, to retain me with Mr. Ruffin— but after I had been spoken to, by Guess. Trice will employ Ruffin[60] & Murphey,[61] I expect, and will give *good fees. This* you will attend to likewise.

I have written this, without having seen any of the papers— from the representation of the parties.

Yrs
P. H. Mangum

[Addressed:]
    Willie P. Mangum Esq.
        Orange
Mr. Guess.

————

[58]Unable to identify.
[59]See above, p. 32n.
[60]Thomas Ruffin.
[61]Archibald D. Murphey.

1823

WPM-D

Deed of relinquishment from Ellison G. Mangum
to William P. Mangum[1]

Jan 20, 1823

State of North Carolina
  Orange County.

Be it known to all persons to whom
these presents may come Greeting
Whereas William P. Mangum of the County & State aforesaid in the year of our Lord one thousand seven hundred and
Eighty Eight purchased from his father Arthur Mangum sen.ʳ
late of the said County & State a tract of land lying & being in
the County aforesaid, on both sides of Dials Creek, on the West
joining Schon Bobbitts line on the South, John Maizes line, and
bounded on the east by the Ridge Path, containing in quantity
Two hundred Acres, afterwards its Northern boundary to be
ascertained by actual survey — & Whereas the said Arthur
Mangum executed & delivered to the said William P. Mangum
a bond bearing date 21ˢᵗ Octo. 1788. in the penalty of twelve
hundred pounds, conditioned to make to the said William P.
Mangum a good & sufficient title for the said two hundred acres
of land & acknowledged the same, and whereas the said William
P. Mangum hath paid the whole of the purchase money for the
said land, and the said Arthur Mangum departed this life without having executed to the said Wm. P. Mangum a Deed for the
said Land, Whereupon the said land as to its legal title descended upon the said Wm. P. Mangum, Arthur Mangum Junʳ.
and Willie Mangum who were the heirs at Law & the only heirs
at Law of the said Arthur Mangum senʳ. deceased, and whereas
the said William P. Mangum for nearly thirty years after the
execution of the said Bond, held in actual & exclusive occupation
the said land, & Whereas in the year 1819 or thereabouts the
said William P. Mangum by his Deed conveyed to Walter A.
Mangum & his heirs the whole of the said land that lies on the
east side of Dials Creek, and whereas in the year 1821. that part
of said land that lies on the west side of Dials Creek was exposed to public sale by virtue of sundry Executions, at which
sale Willie P. Mangum became the last and highest bidder,

[1]See below, p. 332n.

whereupon the Sheriff of Orange made to the said Willie P. Mangum & his heirs a Deed for that part of said tract that lies on the west of Dials Creek, and Whereas in the year one thousand eight hundred & twenty two the said Willie P. Mangum purchased from the said Walter A. Mangum all that part of the said tract of land that lies on the East of Dials Creek. Whereby the said Willie P Mangum has acquired an Equitable title in the said two hundred acres of land—Whereas Willie Mangum aforesaid one of the heirs at Law of said Arthur Mangum sen^r. deceased, & upon whom the legal title to an undivided third part of the said tract of land descended, departed this life in the year 1809, or thereabouts, & Whereas upon Judgment signed agt the adm^{rs}. of the said Willie Mangum upon fully administered being friend in their favour, a scire facias issued to the heirs at Law of the said Willie Mangum whereby & whereupon the whole of the undivided interest of said Willie Mangum in the undivided lands upon Dials Creek, Dry Creek & Camp Creek, that descended upon him from the s^d. Arthur sen^r. deceased were subjected to be sold & were actually sold by the sheriff — Orange aforesaid by virtue of a good & sufficient process, at which sale Ellison G. Mangum became the purchaser of the whole of the undivided interest of the said Willie Mangum in the lands descended as aforesaid, & lying upon the waters aforesaid and obtained the said Sheriffs Deed for the same. & Whereas the said Ellison G. Mangum is fully impressed with the fair & equitable title of the said Willie P. Mangum to the said two hundred acres of Land, and being desirous to render effectual justice without the coercion of the forms of Law. To that End.

The said Ellison G. Mangum doth by these presents for the considerations aforesaid and for the further consideration of One Dollar lawful money to him in hand paid by the said Willie P. Mangum Give, grant, enfeoff & relinquish to the said Willie P. Mangum his heirs & assigns forever all his right title & interest both legal & Equitable in a certain tract of Land lying on both sides of Dials Creek, adjoining the lands formerly owned by Schon Bobbitt on the west, the lands of John Maize sen^r. deceased on the south, and the Ridge parh on the East, containing two hundred Acres, including the old dwelling of W^m. P. Mangum on the east of Dials Creek & also the old plantation of W^m P Mangum —

And the said Ellison G. Mangum for himself & his heirs &

Executors & adm^{rs}. doth covenant to & with the said Willie P. Mangum his heirs Executors & administrators that he the said Ellison G. will make good the title in fee simple to the s^d. land to the said Willie P. Mangum against all claims, rights or titles to the said land derived by any person or persons by from or through the said Ellison G. Mangum, but it is distinctly understood that the said Ellison doth not warrant the title of the said Land further than against any conveyance or encumbrance that he the said Ellison may have made or put upon it.

In Testimony Whereof I the said Ellison G Mangum have hereunto set my hand & seal this the 20th. day of January A. D. 1823.

ELLISON G. MANGUM (Seal)

signed sealed & delivered
In presence of.
    Hugh Muhollan
    Wm Howard

[Endorsed on back]

Deed of Relinquishment From Ellison G. Mangum
to Willie P. Mangum.   200 acre tract on
Dials Creek.   1823

WPM-LC

T. N. Mann to Willie P. Mangum

GREENSBORO: 24th. apl. 1823.

Dear Judge:

The bond of N.[athaniel] & W. G. Hill was endorsed in blank the day on which I saw you. Mr. Hunt denied that he was under any obligation to endorse it, but he expressed so much confidence in the solvency of the papers, that he thought he incurred no danger by doing so.

I expect to get the money at Huntsville, which will amount to about $450, the half of which will be set apart for you, and if a more direct conveyance sh^d. offer will send it to N. C. if none such sh^d. offer I will bring it myself.

---

*Thomas N. Mann, attorney of Nash County, N. C., was a graduate of the University of North Carolina, a member of the state legislature in 1822-1823, and *charge d'affaires* to Guatemala in 1825. Grant, *Alumni Hist. of U. N. C.*, 411.

I have no time to spare, having called here for refreshment, and in the hope of seeing you. I wish you to farewell personally & hope that opportunity will be given you to take a seat in the senate this winter.

I remain yr. obt. servt.

TH. N. MANN

Mr. P. Mangum

[Addressed]
    Hon Willie P. Mangum
        Hillsboro
            N. C.

———

WPM-LC

Samuel Hillman[2] to Willie P. Mangum

OXFORD 10th May 1823—

Dear Sir,

Having determined to relinquish Person Court altogether I have taken the liberty of sending you my papers and have to request that you will attend to what few Clients I have in Person and see that they have justice done them— There is one case Royster[3] assignee vs McGhee[4] & Irving[5] the suit is brought vs Erving alone and stands for trial at this Term— Please give it your particular attention as Mr. Royster is very anxious to obtain Judgment at this Term— I will thank you also to look into the case of Richard Inge[6] assignee vs John McGehee obtained some Courts ago if the Judgment has been standing so long as to become dormant revive it by Sci Fa. and endeavor to collect as speedily as possible— I have refrained from taking any coercive measures from representations made by Mr. Thomas McGehee who has given me assurances the money should have been

———

[2] Samuel Hillman, an attorney of Oxford, N. C., who was in the legislature in 1819-1821 and who was solicitor for Granville and Franklin counties in 1823, was a close political friend of Mangum. He wrote Mangum frequently to give him advice on political matters. *N. C. Manual,* 622; McIver, *N. C. Register,* 47.

[3] Possibly S. S. Royster of Granville County who was a large property owner, an attorney, and member of the secession convention of 1861. *N. C. Manual,* 881.

[4] Thomas McGehee, a member of the legislature from Person County in 1826, 1829, 1831, and 1833, was a progressive farmer who made significant experiments in tobacco culture. Hamilton, *Papers of Ruffin,* I, 346; *N. C. Manual,* 758. John McGehee was a justice of the peace in Person County in 1823. McIver, *N. C. Register,* 36.

[5] Probably a planter near Roxboro.

[6] A neighbor of W. A. Tharpe.

[7] Benjamin Chambers was a member of the legislature from Person County in 1809, 1811, 1813, and 1819-1820. *N. C. Manual,* 757.

received about the first of January last— Perhaps on application he may pay the money or the greater part if so it may save the necessity of coercion— I will thank you to mention the subject to him— Please also look into the State of the case Lewis Taylor assignee vs Benjamin Chambers[7]— I ordered a Ca. Sa. [*capias ad satisfaciendum*] some Courts ago if it has never been issued see to it if you please. I am in great haste.

Very respectfully yours &c
SAML. HILLMAN

Willie P. Mangum Esqr.
or
    Priesly C. Mangum Esqr.

N. B. Please attend particularly to the bond Royster vs Royster.

[Addressed:] Willie P. Mangum Esqr
       or
          Priesly C. Mangum Esqr.

To meet them at Person
County Court

Mr. Sneed.

WPM-LC

Charles L. Hinton[8] to Willie P. Mangum

WAKE COUNTY June 10th 1823

Dear Sir

I received yours this day inquiring of me whether I was not present and heard a conversation between Gen. Barringer[9] and yourself in relation to your becoming a candidate for the next Congress and whether you did not state to General Barringer in my presence at Wake Superior Court that you believed the upper country would have opposition and that circumstances might occur that would bring you out as a candidate, and whether you did not state that you wished the General to un-

[8]Charles L. Hinton was a student at the University of North Carolina with Mangum. He was a member of the legislature from Wake County from 1820 to 1821, 1827 to 1830, and 1832 to 1833. He was state treasurer from 1839 to 1843 and 1845 to 1852. Grant, *Alumni Hist. of U. N. C.*, 285; *N. C. Manual*, 829-830, 442.

[9]General Daniel L. Barringer, 1788-1852, a native of Cabarrus County, had been in the state legislature from Raleigh in 1813 and from 1819 to 1822. Defeated by Mangum for Congress in 1823, he was elected in 1826 to fill the vacancy caused by Mangum's resignation. He served from 1826 to 1835 when he moved to Bedford County, Tennessee. He was a member of the Tennessee legislature from 1843 to 1845. *Biog. Dir. of Cong.*, 674.

derstand distinctly that he must not be surprised if you became a candidate, for it was not unlikely that such an event might happen, and whether the General indicated any disposition to yield to you or any other person.

To these inquiries I should be very unwilling to answer if I believed the subjects were likely to be matter of dispute between you and the General, and more especially as I feel personally friendly to both of you.

I however can not believe that if you and General Barringer were to meet that any disagreement in relation to these matters would happen. Therefore I the more readily will state what I remember on the subjects of your inquiry.— At Wake Superior Court in a conversation between you and the Gen. relative to your becoming a candidate, the Gen. stated that you could not consistently become a candidate because you had said to him you had no idea of it, to which you replied in substance that it was true you had said so, and that it was equally true at the time you had said so that you then had no idea of it. but that owing to some circumstances that had taken place your mind had undergone some change, and that you took that early opportunity before either party had publicly declared himself a candidate to inform him that it was likely you might become a candidate, and that he must not be surprised at such an event. From all of which conversation the impression was made distinctly on my mind that you would become a candidate and that General Baringer felt no disposition to yield to you or any other person—

I hope you and the General will go on in a smooth and friendly manner and leave the decision between you fairly and without dispute to the choice of the people.

Your Obt Servant

CHAS L HINTON

[Addressed:]

Willie P Mangum Esqr

Now at Raleigh

WPM-LC

Laurence Stacy[10] to Willie P. Mangum

LOUISBURG JAIL 9 July 1823

D Sir,

I am confined in this place for killing a Man & am to be tried for it at the next Superior Court. & wish to employ you—to appear for me, and it [is] my unfortunate situation to be without money & have no chance to get any only from my friends who have promised to aid me all they can—Judge Seawell[11] & Col Robards[12] have promised to appear for me & if you will be so good as to appear with them what money I can raise shall be given, & if I shall be ever able I will make you further satisfaction provided I should be acquited—I am a very poor Man with a wife & six children—by occupation & overseer—I hope I shall see you at Court when the Circumstances which led to this unfortunate affair will be made known to you— please write a few lines informing me whether you will appear for me or not. & oblige Your friend &

humble Servant—
Laurence Stacy—

[Addressed:]
    Wiley P. Mangum, Esquire
        Orange County
            North Carolina
Mail

———

Seth Jones[13] to Willie P. Mangum

WAKE COUNTY Sunday 3rd August 1823.

Dear Sir,

This day I was at Hezebah [Hepzibah] meeting house near the Rev. Josiah Crudups[14] and about 13 miles from Genl. Bar-

———

[10]Unable to identify.
[11]Judge Henry Seawell.
[12]Colonel William Robards, an attorney of Granville County, represented his county in the legislature in 1806 and 1808. He was state treasurer from 1827 to 1830 and was for many years clerk of the Supreme Court of North Carolina. He was a close political friend of Mangum. Hamilton, *Papers of Ruffin*, I, 138n; *N. C. Manual*, 442, 621-622.
[13]A number of letters to and from Seth Jones are not available in the original. When Dr. Weeks had this material copied he obtained the originals from Willie Mangum Person of Louisburg, N. C. Since then Person has died and so far his relatives have been unable to locate the papers. I am, therefore, forced to use the typed copies which are in the State Department of Archives and History, Raleigh, N. C.
[14]Josiah Crudup, 1791-1872, was one of Mangum's strongest political rivals in the 1820's. A powerful Baptist preacher and successful farmer of Wake County, he was elected to the state legislature in 1820, but being a minister, he was not permitted to serve. He served in the national House of Representatives from 1821 to 1823. Mangum defeated him for Congress in 1825. *Biog. Dir. of Cong.*, 866.

ringers[15]— During Divine service I happened at the Spring in company with Genl. Barringer and many others— The subject of the approaching Congressional Election was mentioned and it was stated to Genl. Barringer that you had been through this part of the District last week & that you had said Genl. Barringer was as much in favour of amending the Constitution[16] of the State equalizing the Representation as you were, to which statement Genl. Barringer dissented to and said he was not in favour of and [sic] amendment to the Constitution, or in other words he was opposed to any amendment to the Constitution whatever, and said that you had no grounds for saying so,— I have shown the above which this is a copy to Mr. Newton Wood who is willing to testify to the same as well as myself and perhaps many other bystanders.—

I am fearful the people will believe the Genl. and if they do (which is doubtful) your Election will be much injured in this part of the District. I should be glad if you could extricate yourself from this difficulty and send Hand-Bills in this part of the District or the whol[e] county proving by 3 or more witness that he had been in favour of amending the constitution of the State   There are several Pamphlets of the Convention Committee of Orange[17] circulating in this part of the District for no other purpose but to injure your election, and I herd Genl. Barringer say to day at Preaching that he had left one with Mr. Lawrence one of the Editors of the Star Press which led me to go and see if the Star press was not printing them to circulate to the injury of your Election, when I got to the Star press I was not at all surprised to find that they were then in the act of printing extracts from the said pamphlet to be circulated no doubt to the injury of your election. I have inclosed several of them here for your inspection.[18]

Your friend & Obt Servnt
SETH JONES

---

[15]General Daniel L. Barringer.

[16]At this time a very bitter fight was raging in North Carolina over a revision of the state constitution. In the congressional election of 1823, this became an issue. Mangum's congressional district included Orange, Person, and Wake counties. Orange was western and, therefore, for revision; Wake, being eastern, was against revision. For this sectional fight, see W. K. Boyd, "The Antecedents of the North Carolina Convention of 1835," *The South Atlantic Quarterly*, IX, 83-93, 161, 176.

[17]At a meeting of the captains of the county militia at Hillsboro May 9, 1823, which was called to consider a revision of the state constitution, Mangum spoke strongly for revision in conformity with western ideas. A committee composed of Thomas Ruffin, J. W. Norwood, James S. Smith, Michael Holt, and Mangum was appointed to represent Orange County in an extra legal convention called to meet in Raleigh in November, 1823. *Hillsborough Recorder*, June 11, 1823.

[18]None was found.

Willie P. Mangum
N. B. I [f] this letter will be any advantage to your Election
you may make use of it.
                           S. J.
W. P. M. Esqr.

_____

                                              WPM-LC

            Thomas Clancy[19] to Willie P. Mangum

                              HILLSBOROUGH august 6th. 1823—
Dear Sir
Yours of yesterday is before me— making enquiry— whether
General Barringer did or did not state to me in Raleigh during
the last Session of our legislature & elsewhere. that he was in
favour of an amendment of our State Constitution & whether
the Gen[1]. did not make declarations of posessing as strong
western feelings as any man in the State on that Subject. and
whether he expressed his opinion in favour of amending the
Constitution as resulting from the Clamour of the West or
whether he Said it was correct & right in principle— Situated
as I am feeling personally friendly to both Gen.[1] Barringer &
your self I feel great delicacy in saying any thing on the Subject, but being called on to make the Statement I feel my self
bound to do so. during the last Session of our legislature I
frequently heard Gen[1]. Barringer Speak favorably to an
amendment of our State Constitution, and since that time in
Hillsborough I have heard the Gen[1]. Say that he had drawn up
a string of resolutions for that purpose during the last Session
of our legislature with a view of submitting them to that body.
but from some cause or other (I think because his Colleague[20]
did not agree with him) he did not do so. in Justice however to
Gen[1]. Barringer I must here state that when Speaking on that
subject he always declared himself unfriendly to a general or
unlimited Convention and that in fact he thought the work
might be done by the legislature without Calling a Convention
at all— with regard to the Genl's speaking of his Western feeling, I have heard him say frequently that he had as strong
Western feeling as any man in the State, having to use his own

_____

[19]Thomas Clancy, of Hillsboro, 1781-1845, was a partner in a mercantile establishment in
Hillsboro. He was at one time sheriff of Orange County and was a member of the state legislature from 1822 to 1823. *Hillsborough Rcorder,* Apr. 24, 1845; *N. C. Manual,* 737.
[20]Samuel Whitaker served in the House of Commons from 1822 to 1830. *N. C. Manual,*
830.

words made his first awkward step in the West it is my impression that when ever I have heard Gen¹. Barringer Speak of amendments of our State Constitution that he has uniformly given it as his opinion that it was *correct in principle*

Respectfly yours &. C
THOS. CLANCY

Willie P. Mangum Esqr—

[Addressed:]

> Willie P. Mangum Esqr—
>   Flat River
>   Orange County

WPM-LC

James Mebane²¹ to Willie P. Mangum

PLEASANT RETREAT augst. the, 6th, 1823—

Dear Sir

In compliance with your request I will state as nearly as I recollect the conversation of Genral Baringer, during the first week of the last session of our general assembly, in the house of Daniel Peek [Peck] in Raleigh,²² (in the presence of Judge Cameron²³ and myself if I mistake not.) on the subject of a convention, or amending the constitution of this state, which was to this effect, that he had for a long time been convinced of the propriety and expediency of the measure, that whenever he had been called to act on that subject he had oposed it against the dictates of his conscience, and that he [had] determined he would do so no more, [tha]t if it was necessary that some member of assembly in the eastern part of this state should offer up himself a sacrifice, to public opinion or eastern prejudices, by bringing the subject before the assembly in some shape, he

---

²¹James Mebane, 1774-1857, the son of General Alexander Mebane of Revolutionary fame, frequently represented Orange County in the state legislature. In 1821 he was speaker of the House of Commons. He was a director of the North Carolina Bank, and at one time was a member of the Council of State. *N. C. Manual*, 429, 738-740.

²²Assistant postmaster of Raleigh in 1823. *N. C. Comptroller's Statement, 1824-1825*, 4.

²³Duncan Cameron, 1777-1853, in whose office Mangum read law and who was Mangum's political adviser and guardian, was one of the wealthiest and most influential leaders of the state. He was president of the North Carolina State Bank, chairman of the board for internal improvements, chairman of the committee which built the present state capitol, a superior court judge, a prominent leader in the Episcopal Church, and one of the largest planters of the state. His home, "Fairntosh," is still a "show place." Ashe, *Biog. Hist. of N. C.*, III, 43-48.

was willing to be the person, & he did think that propositions to amend the constitution, which should ultimately be submitted to the people of this state for their adoption or rejecton, would very probably pass the assembly if brought forward by an eastern man, and promised that he would bring forward some resolutions to that effect,

yours respectfully

JAMES MEBANE

P. S. Probably you would do well to obtain a certificate from Judge Cameron, you know his memory is very good   JM—

[Addressed:]
    Willie P. Mangum Esqr   Hillsboro.

[Printed]

Circular Letter[24]

ORANGE COUNTY, August 6, 1823.

Sir,

It is with unfeinged reluctance that I address you in this way, and at this period, on the subject of the approaching congressional election. I dislike it, because all extraordinary efforts on the eve of an election, wear too much the semblance of electioneering trick; I trust, however, that every honest mind will discover in the following details sufficient reasons to acquit me of such an imputation, and a satisfactory apology for this unexpected letter.

I received this day by the mail, a letter from Seth Jones, esq. of Wake county, from which the following is a correct extract:

"August, 3d, 1823.

"Dear Sir—   This day I was at Hezibah meeting house, near to the Rev. Josiah Crudup's and about thirteen miles from Gen. Barringer's. During divine service I happened at the spring in company with Gen. Barringer and many others. The subject of the approaching congressional election was mentioned, and it was stated to Gen. Barringer, that you had been through his part of the district last week, and that you had said that Gen. Barringer was as much in favour of amending the constitution of this State, and equalizing the representation, as you were.—

---

[24]A typed copy of this circular is in the State Department of Archives and History, Raleigh.

To which statement Gen. Barringer dissented, and said *he was not in favour of any amendment to the constitution,* or, in other words, *he was opposed to any amendment of the constitution whatever,* and said you had no *grounds* for saying so.

"I have shown the above to Mr. Newton Wood, who is willing to testify to the same, as well as myself, and perhaps many other bystanders."

It is apparent, from the above extract, that my competitor has not only disavowed his attachment to principles of reform, and his desire to see our state constitution amended; but, in that disavowal, had indirectly assailed my character for integrity and veracity. I have no ambition, by way of retaliation, to emulate the example; nor shall it be my purpose to indulge in a strain of invective or unworthy viturpation [*sic*]. Mine is a plain, simple. unvarnished tale, and I submit it with confidence to the great tribunal of the people.

I have, in all my public addresses to the people of Wake county, stated that Gen. Barringer was as friendly to the amendment of the state constitution, as I or any other person; and that the objection which was urged with such vigor against me, applied with equal force to him, though in truth neither of us as a member of congress could ever be called to act on the subject. If any discrimination, however, was to be made, I thought I might, without presumption, be permitted to lay in some claim upon the score of consistency: and whether my competitor had been *consistent,* I was willing to submit to the determination of all candid and honest minds. For the *proof* that Gen. Barringer was friendly to the amendment of the constitution, I referred the people to Samuel Whitaker, esq. who served with him the last legislature; and I have reason to believe that Mr. Whitaker, on divers occasions, *when called on,* STATED THE FACT TO BE SO. Indeed, it is a fact of public notoriety, that Gen. Barringer, in the county of Orange, has constantly professed his wish to see the constitution of the state so amended as to equalize the representation in the legislature.

I had hoped that no additional evidence would be deemed necessary to establish the fact that Gen. Barringer is completely a western man in feeling, and that he is firmly attached to convention principles.—But with the view that all doubts on the subject may be removed, and that the fact may stand naked and exposed for every eye to look upon, I will subjoin the letters and statements of several of the most respectable gentlemen in Orange.—

The following is a copy of a letter this day received from James Mebane, esq.

"PLEASANT RETREAT, August 6th, 1823.

"Dear Sir—In compliance with your request, I will state as nearly as I can recollect the conversation of Gen. Barringer during the first week of the last session of our general assembly, in the house of Daniel Peck in Raleigh, (in the presence of Judge Cameron and myself, if I mistake not), on the subject of a convention, or amending the constitution of this state, which was to this effect: That he had for a long time been convinced of the propriety and expediency of the measure; that whenever he had been called to act on that subject, *he had opposed it against the dictates of his conscience,* and that he was determined he would do so no more; and if it was necessary that some member of the assembly in the *eastern part* of this state should offer up himself a *sacrifice* to public opinion or *eastern prejudices,* by bringing the subject before the assembly in some shape, *he was willing to be the person;* and he did think, that propositions to amend the constitution, which should ultimately be submitted to the people of this state for their adoption or rejection, would very probably pass the assembly if brought forward by an eastern man, and promised that he would bring forward some resolutions to that effect.

"Yours respectfully

"JAMES MEBANE."

The following is a copy of a letter this day received from Thomas Clancy, esq.

"HILLSBOROUGH, August 6th, 1823.

"Dear Sir—Yours of yesterday is before me, making inquiries whether Gen. Barringer did or did not state to me, in Raleigh during the last session of the legislature, and elsewhere, that he was in favour of an amendment of our state constitution, and whether the general did not make declarations of possessing as strong western feeling on that subject as any man in the state; and whether he expressed his opinion in favour of amending the constitution as resulting from the clamour of the west, or whether he said it was correct and right in principle.

"Situated as I am, feeling personally friendly to both Gen. Barringer and yourself, I feel great delicacy in saying any thing on the subject; but being called on to make the statement, I feel myself bound to do so,

"During the last session of our legislature, I frequently heard Gen. Barringer speak favourably to an amendment of our state constitution, and since that time in Hillsborough. I have heard the General say that he *had drawn up a string of resolutions* for that purpose, during the last session of the legislature, with a view of submitting them to that body; but from some cause or other, (I think because his colleagues did not agree with him,) he did not do so. In justice, however, to General Barringer, I must state here, that when speaking on that subject he always declared himself unfriendly to a general or unlimited convention; and that is fact he thought that the work might be done without calling a convention at all. With regard to the General's speaking of his western feeling, I have heard him say frequently that he has as strong western feeling as any man in the west, "having (to use his own words) made his first awkward step in the west." It is my impression, that whenever I have heard Gen. Barringer speak of amendments to our state institution, he has uniformly given it as his opinion, that it was *correct in principle*.

"Respectfully, yours &c.

"THOS. CLANCY."

"CHAPEL HILL, August 6th, 1823.
"By the request of Willie P. Mangum, esq. we do hereby freely certify, that a few weeks past, we heard Gen. Barringer say that he was in favour of amending the constitution of North Carolina, as far as respects equalizing the representation; that Mr. Mangum, in his address to a collection of people at the same place, mentioned his plan of amendment; and Mr. Barringer in answer, said that he believed he was the first who suggested the plan.
"Given under our hands.

"T H. TAYLOR,[25]
"HUDSON M. CAVE."[26]

Is there any candid and dispassionate man who, with this mass of evidence before his eyes, can doubt that Gen. Barringer is friendly to the amendment of our state constitution? and that heretofore, when he opposed the movements of the west towards that object, he acted in violation of his principles, and with a

---

[25]Thomas H. Taylor was in the House of Commons from Orange County in 1829. *N. C. Manual*, 740.
[26]A physician in Orange County in 1823. McIver, *N. C. Register*, 57.

total disregard to the *"dictates of his conscience."* These last are his own words, and though the General and myself are now arrayed against each other in a political contest, I will be one amongst the last who will [be] so ungenerous and so unkind as to dispute his declaration on *this point*. The foregoing is the ground upon which I have made the statement that Gen. Barringer is friendly to the reformation of our state constitution; and I submit to all candid and intelligent men, whether I am not completely sustained in the assertion.

Should any additional apology be required for the publication of this letter, at this late period, I hope it will be found in the following circumstances:

I understand that publications have very recently been issued from the Star press, at the instance of my competitor; and that they have been circulated with the view of affecting the approaching election.

It is further known, that by virtue of an agreement entered into between Gen. Barringer and myself, on the 30th of July last, at Mr. Wm. Dilliard's,[27] in the presence of twenty or thirty people, I am debarred the liberty of visiting Wake again before the election.—I am therefore compelled to resort to this mode of correcting misrepresentation.

Gen. Barringer and myself agreed at Mr. Dilliard's, in the presence of many people, that neither of us should visit any company except on the next day, and then without the liberty of making address—that we should forthwith return to our respective homes, and remain there until Person county court, and visit NO PLACE WHATEVER, except the residence of our relations, and our respective county towns; reserving to ourselves, however, the liberty of going on errands of charity. You may smile at this last reservation, but it is certainly true that it was a part of our agreement. And for the fulfilment of this agreement, we mutually pledged our honor in the presence of the company. It is true that I was utterly astonished to understand that Gen. Barringer was, on Sunday the 3d instant, thirteen miles from home, at a meeting house, not attending to divine worship, but talking to the people on the subjects of elections and amending the state constitution. Of this, however, I will not complain, inasmuch as it is *barely possible* that Gen. Barringer may have misconceived the true import of our agreement, or that the visit may have been made upon some *kindly errand of charity.*

[27]Postmaster at Dillardsville, Orange County, in 1823. McIver, *N. C. Register*, 70.

Many of my friends think that by reason of this breach of the part of my competitor, I am absolved from all obligation, and may rightfully and justifiably resume electioneering. I think differently. My notions of morality may be stale and unfashionable, but still I prefer *sticking* to them. I will in no event violate my engagement, though an adherence to it should result in the loss of my election. The people will see and appreciate my situation, and to their generosity and sense of justice I am willing to commit all my hopes and prospects in the present contest.

I am, sir, your obedient servant,

WILLIE P. MANGUM.

Seth Jones to————————[28]

RALEIGH 8th August 1823.

Dear Sir,

From the small acquaintance I have with you I have good reason to believe you need only to be informed rightly to decide correctly.—I have understood that while our candidate for Congress Mr. Mangum was passing through your part of the county that he showed to you and several others the yeas & nays, where Genl. Barringer voted against a Bill introduced into the Legislature in the year 1820 to provide more effectually for the payment of specie by the several banks in this State, and since that I have understood that Genl. Barringer has showed to you that he has voted every time in favor of the above named Bill to compel the Banks to pay specie for their notes—I now have the Journals of the House of Commons before me and in page 70 you will find the truth to be this, that on the second reading of the Bill Mr. Graves[29] (of Caswell county) moved that it be definitely postponed, the meaning of which motion is to kill & reject the Bill intirely here Genl. Barringer voted in yeas which is [in] favour of the motion & against the Bill—The Bill passed its second reading notwithstanding Genl. Barringer voted against it— Three days after the Bill was again read for the 3rd & last time & then Genl. Barringer wheels around from what cause I know not & votes for it this you may find in page 75—The reason my writing this letter to you is that you may know the fact how

[28]A typed copy is in the State Department of Archives and History, Raleigh.
[29]Barzilla Graves was in the House of Commons in 1813, 1818 to 1822, and 1832. *N. C. Manual*, 543-544.

Genl. Barringer did vote & to justify Mr. Mangum so far as the truth will do it. It is true that I shall vote for Mr. Mangum but for many other substantial & good substantial reasons.

I am very respectfully
Sir your friend &
Obt. Servant
SETH JONES

Willie P. Mangum to Seth Jones[30]

ORANGE 8th Augt. 1823.

My Dear Sir,

I cannot sufficiently express to you my thanks for the friendly interest you take, and the friendly services you are constantly rendering me—I comply with your wishes & send you some certificates in the form of a hand-bill—I think they will stop the General's mouth on the subject of his friendlyness to amending the constitution of this State—500 men know his *declarations* to that effect in Orange—what his *sentiments* are God only knows —for I expect the Gen: at the first guess could hardly tell himself.—

I need not give you instructions as to their circulation—I will only request you to make out the line the Young man who carries them shall take on his return home—

I wish some left in the neighbourhood of H. Smith's Store— Col. Sutherlands[31] &c for [distribution] through the northern side of the County. I wish Mr. Suit[32] to return—I have sent 100. of these letters to Col Cooke in Raleigh with a request to send them into the south of the County—& towards Upchurches—and with instructions to have more printed if he thinks it necessary —I should be glad [if] you would give your opinion to the Col if it is convenient as to the propriety of printing more—I have written as little in the Bill as I could—my object being to bring the Gen into a bad fix by the testimony of others—

As to the last circumstance in the hand bill of The Gen. has in my opinion disgraced himself—Our honour was most solemnly pledged repeatedly & repeatedly not *even to attend preaching*— I thought proper to omit that fact, except by implication, lest it

---

[30]The original of this letter is not available, but a typed copy is in the State Department of Archives and History at Raleigh.
[31]Probably Col. Ransom Sutherland.
[32]Mangum's overseer.

might hurt the feelings of some religious people — Wm. H. Adams the deputy Sheriff is the only person living in Hillsboro who heard the agreement. He was out of Town when the Bill went to the press—otherwise I should have annexed his certificate—on my return from Town last night I met him—read that part of the letter to him & he distinctly remembers it & will furnish me with a certificate at Person stating every fact. He says the Gen must be without principle—for that the Gen: after the solemn pledge of Honour to it—repeated *"honour bright"* several times.—

I stake my character upon the truth of the statement—

I have been in Hillsboro the most of this week—Give me 500 votes in Wake, & my election is sure.

In great haste, I am yr. sincere friend

WILLIE P. MANGUM

[Addressed:]
Seth Jones Esquire
    Wake County
Mr. Suit

WPM-LC

[Certificate]

[W. H. ADAMS]

HILLSBOROUGH August 9th 1823

I William H. Adams do certify that on the 30th July last I attended as deputy sheriff at William Dilliard's for the purpose of collecting the taxes of this county and that Gen¹. Daniel L Baringer & Willie P Mangum were there and on the evening of that day they both pledged their honours to each other in the most sacred manner, that neither of them should attend any public gathering (except the next day & then not to address the company) reserving to themselves the priviledge of visiting their county towns and the private residence of a relation and going on an errand of charity but going to any preaching was expressly forbidden, and to meet at Person court which should be the first place either of them should electionere with which understanding after being several times repeated while [they] were about gettin[g their] horses & with which understan[ding] they parted—

W. H. ADAMS

Done in the presents of
    J. P. SNEED

[*Printed Circular*]³³   [August 9, 1823]

To the Freemen of the Counties of Orange, Person and Wake.
Fellow-Citizens:

Were I to say that I have been surprised at the publication of
my *worthy* and *honorable* competitor, I should be uncandid. I
had not expected it, but was not surprised by seeing it, I have
known him for years, he was my school-mate; and dare say that
all who know him, have long since discovered *trick* and *strate-
gem,* to be the prominent features in his character. It is a fact
which Mr. Mangum knows; and which I can *prove* if he denies
it, that by agreement, I was to have been at his house on my way
to Person, the very evening, on which his circular arrived at Raleigh. Mr. Mangum no doubt calcuiated that *should I meet his
overseer,* who I understand was the bearer of his handbills, I
should be nothing the wiser on that account. Business however
of a private nature required, I should pass through Raleigh; and
being unexpectedly detained, his messenger arrived, and I have
one of his handbills before me. I shall not pursue him as a victim, or copy him as a model; suffice it to say, that his handbill
was shewn to Mr. Whitaker,³⁴ on whom he relies for much support, and this gentleman has said before a regimental court martial of Wake County, that every reference in Mr. Mangum's
handbill to him, is without foundation and false.

I have not applied to my *friends* for certificates, nor should I
have time if I desired it; but I can prove it, and Mr. Mangum
will hardly deny it publicly, that though on the first outset of
the campaign in Wake County, he was very warm upon the subject of convention, and when in fact, the principal ground of
argument between us, before the people, was on that subject;
yet, in the language of a worthy gentleman, who often heard him
in his public exhibitions, the "further he went the shorter he
got" on that subject. I can also prove (for it is necessary to
bring proof against Mr. Mangum,) that he has *finally* said, upon
reflecting on the subject, and seeing the length Judge Cameron,
and *others* were disposed to go on the Convention question, he
cared so little about it, that he was not willing to have a Convention, to whom should be committed the constitution of our state,
to be "cut and hacked" as it thought proper; that in fact he was
as much opposed to Judge Cameron upon that question (putting

³³A typed copy of this circular is available in the State Department of Archives and History at Raleigh.
³⁴Samuel Whitaker.

the ends of his fingers in opposition) *as that;* how far this corresponds with Mr. Mangum's *professions* to Judge Cameron, or to the people of Orange, I leave them the task of judging. I would barely, by way of caution, suggest to the *honorable* gentleman, that his worthy coajutors in the Convention meeting on the 29th May at Hillsborough, may not have forgotten his energetic and forcible appeal to them, in favor of *unanimity* upon this *all important* question, calling upon them to array in solid phalanx all the force of Orange, for one great and mighty effort in the "good cause," all which was probably the *price* of the distinguished honor done him, in recommending him to the people as a delegate. This may appear very strange, to those who do not know Mr. Mangum, but it is nevertheless true.

Mr. Mangum has attempted to *gull* the people upon the Convention question: he now affects to feel great solicitude for the integrity of the Constitution: but permit me to ask the honorable gentleman, how long it is since those *qualms* have come upon him? They were not felt on the 1st December 1819, when he introduced a string of Resolutions for calling a Convention and amending the Constitution—he was then prepared to immolate this charter of our liberty by twelve vital stabs—for that was the number of his amendments. He seemed to have no compunctions visitings of conscience upon the subject, so late as the 29th of May last, the day before he became a candidate for Congress. When then, do these scruples date their commencement? Why, even after he had made some little trial of the force of argument, and finding the people incorrigible, and remembering the old adage, that it is easier for one man to change than a thousand— so he changed himself.

If, Fellow-Citizens, you should entertain doubts, whether Mr. Mangum ever introduced Resolutions for calling a Convention, I refer you to the Journals of 1819, page 39; and if you do not there find him the introducer of convention resolutions, when then *believe* him and turn your backs upon me.

Mr. Mangum's course upon the Convention question, which he *has brought* before the people, is but a piece of the whole of his conduct. He has carried the Journals of several years past in his saddlebags, and is charging me with various notes, which can having no bearing upon the general government; and has on several occasions, even attempted to cast the odium of the *high sal-*

Charity Alston (Cain) Mangum, wife of Willie P. Mangum, 1795-1873. From original daguerreotype in the possession of Miss Sallie Preston Weeks of Washington, District of Columbia.

aries of the Judges of the Supreme Court[35] upon me, though he very well knows that I was not then a member, and that *he was,* and was among the warmest advocates of the law. This I can prove by his *relation* and witness, Mr. Seth Jones. It would be endless to undertake a recital of the various means employed by Mr. Mangum to obtain his election. In Wake, calling me a *Western*-man, in Orange, an *Eastern*-man, and in Person, I suppose he will call me a *Convention*-man—sometimes calling me a *Bank*-man, when Mr. Mangum knows that I never owned a share of Bank stock in my life; and when he should have remembered, that in 1820, he supported Judge Cameron, a *Bank*-man, against Mr. Holt,[36] when the election turned mainly upon that question —and then charging me with having voted against compelling the Banks to pay Specie in the same year, though upon the third reading of the Bill, when the vote is decisive of every member's sentiments, I voted for it—(See Journals of 1820, page 75.). Yet Mr. Mangum wishes the people of *Wake, at least,* to *believe,* that he is very much opposed to Judge Cameron, and complains, as it is said, that the Judge attempts to swing by his *skirts.*

Believe me, fellow-citizens, this same patriotic Judge Mangum, (for I ask his pardon for omiting his title) is not other than the same gentleman, who, a very short time before I was publicly announced as a candidate, importuned me, to resign my pretensions to Judge Cameron, the same Judge Cameron whom he now seems so unwilling, in some parts of the District, to recognize, I perhaps, to make some apology for bringing a name before the public, not connected with Mr. Mangum or myself; but it will be recollected, that Mr. Mangum has had access to his room, and though he is not cited as his authority, yet he brings forward Mr. Mebane, a visitant: as for Mr. Mebane, Dr. Cave and T. H. Taylor, they appear to be *willing* witnesses; they, I presume, vote for Mr. Mangum, though the testimony of the two latter, would have *looked* a little better, if they had started as the *fact* was, that the principal dispute between Mr. Mangum and myself, at Chapel Hill, was upon the subject of Convention. If we *both* agreed, how could we differ? those sapient gentlemen can answer; and indeed, as for Mr. Mebane, *the people of Orange*

---

[35]In 1818 Judge Gaston was supported in the legislature by Mangum who was on the judiciary committee in an effort to reorganize the Supreme Court of North Carolina. In this effort Gaston proposed an increase of the salaries of judges. For many years after this, attacks were made on the high salaries of judges. McDuffie, "Willie P. Mangum," 18; William K. Boyd, *History of North Carolina: The Federalist Period, 1783-1860* (Chicago, Ill.: The Lewis Publishing Co., 1919), II, 69-70.

[36]Michael Holt, 1778-1842, was state senator from Orange County, 1820 to 1821. Ashe, *Biog. Hist. of N. C.,* VII, 168.

can testify, that the time has been, when *James Mebane* told
them, there was no difference between a Federalist and a Royal-
ist; and on one occasion, his conscience urged him so irresistably,
that he was compelled to oppose his own brother-in-law, (Richard Stanford) [37]—because he fancied he had become tinctured
with Federalism; yet now, when Mr. Mebane finds it necessary
to gain his election, he can *vote* and harange the people in favor
of down-right Federalists. If this is doubted, who has supported
in his country? who has he supported in his county? who does he
now support? But poor good man, he has almost grown old in
hunting for an office, and should be in his *great* and over anxiety
to obtain one, sometimes lose his way, and grope a little in the
dark, it is hoped his friends will excuse him. I am, however, far
from being his enemy, and as proof of it, I will inform him, that
my worthy competitor, under whose banners he has *now* enlisted himself, and for whose interest he has made *sacrifices,*
which must ever prey upon his conscience, has not scrupled to
avow, that in a contest between me and Mr. Mebane, he would
give his support to me.

I have much wondered why my *worthy* competitor has so unceasingly laboured to lug this Convention question into the Congressional contest. Perhaps the solution will be found in the
known conduct of a clamourous bird—which screams and flut-
ters at a distance, for the purpose of drawing the huntsman
from the prey. Enquiry is always on the alert; scrutiny and investigation are characteristic of free and jealous voters. Public
conduct and even *private* character are sometimes rudely en-
quired into and investigated. But from matters of this sort, it is
the interest of certain candidates to divert the public-attention,
by treating men as fishermen do whales—a tub must be thrown
out. And in that sort of management my *worthy* competitor has
given you a fair sample of his skill.

Mr. Mangum, after having placed, as he thought, both himself
and me upon the same ground, as respects the Convention, advances in his claim very pressingly upon you, upon the score, of
consistency. Where I ask you, is the evidence of that *consistency*
upon which he builds such *high hopes.* It is to be found in the
fact, that he attacked with violence the friends of their country,
during the darkest period of our late war, and afterwards attempts to appropriate to himself the rewards of patriotism. Is

---

[37] A native of Maryland, Richard Stanford moved to North Carolina in 1793 as a school
teacher and established an academy at Hawfield. From 1797 to 1816 he served in the United
States Congress. *Biog. Dir. of Cong.,* 1559.

it to be found in his warm support of the Supreme Court in 1818, and his present persecution of that establishment? Is it to be found in the warmth with which he introduced and advocated unlimited Convention Resolutions in 1819,[38] and the lukewarmness and hesitancy with which he now affects to treat that measure? Is it to be found in the zeal with which he advocated the election of Judge Cameron in 1820, upon the Bank question, and the abhorrence with which he affects to view the conduct of the Banks at the present? Is it to be found in the warmth with which the blood rushed through his heart in favor of Henry Clay for the Presidency, at all times and on all occasions before he became a candidate for Congress—and the zeal which he *now seems* to manifest in favor of Mr. Crawford? or is it to be found in the high approbation that he has at *some* muster grounds expressed of Mr. Monroe's administration, or the *"viturpation"* with which he has assailed it at others? Or, lastly, is it to be found in the friendship he has at various times professed to individuals, and the violence of invective and opposition with which he has assailed them at others? I fear, if his *"consistencies"* are too closely looked for, they will, like the purer gems, be found buried in "the vasty deep; impervious to mortal eye, impenetrable by human ken."

My acts whilst a member of the Legislature, were not done in a corner. I have in every instance endeavored to do my duty, and where the subject was of importance, I have ventured to record my course.

It must be *apparent,* notwithstanding the *affected* regrets of my *worthy* competitor, that the appearance of his hand-bill was the effect of pre-concertion, and it was ushered forth to the world, under circumstances, which seemed to forbid *even* the chance of reply; and like all ephemeral productions, when it shall have served its purpose, will disprove itself.

Fellow-Citizens, the subject is before you, "the people will indeed see" and *"appreciate my situation,"* and to their generosity, and abhorrence of trick and stratagem, I freely commit all my hopes in the present contest.[39]

Ever your obedient servant,

DANIEL L. BARRINGER.

Saturday Evening, August 9th, 1823.

---

[38] Mangum in the House of Commons in 1818 and 1819 supported the proposal for a constitutional convention. McDuffie, "Willie P. Mangum," 18.

[39] Mangum won by a majority of 964 popular votes. McDuffie, "Willie P. Mangum," 25.

WPM-D

Willie P. Mangum to Henry Seawell

RALEIGH the 30th September 1823.

Sir

I have received your letter of this date by the hands of Mr. Manly,[40] stating that you have understood from General Barringer, that at Person Court, in a public address to the people on the subject of the Congressional election, I used expressions implying your want of character & respectability; and avowing it to be your object to ascertain from me whether your information is correct.—

I could have hoped that your information had pointed to mere matter of fact & not to matter of mere implication & inference. The difficulty of conceiving what Gentlemen may imply or infer from remarks made under the usual excitement of such occasions is manifest, and the difficulty of recollecting *precisely* expressions used in the agitation and bustle of an electioneering address, is equally embarrassing.—

I have no recollection however, of being betrayed on that occasion, into the indecorum of using expressions, that denied to you the enjoyment of character & respectability.—Having heretofore understood that such an impression had gone abroad in the County of Wake, I took the earliest opportunity of enquiring of respectable Gentlemen who were present, touching my remarks & find my belief corroborated by theirs that no such expressions were used by me.

I conceive it due to myself however to state that your name was mentioned on that occasion by me, in a tone & with a manner that might have been offensive, & under a full conviction that you would be informed of it.—

I spoke under the belief that you had aided & abetted in concocting the venom that diffused itself through Gen: Barringer's scurrilous hand-bill, & countenanced that bold & desperate effort to give a vital stab to my character.—

It is perfectly well known to you, that when we first met in the campaign & constantly afterwards when the subject was mentioned, you professed it to be your fixed resolution not to interfere in the Congressional contest in any respect whatever,

---

[40]Charles Manly, 1795-1871, of Chatham County, was clerk of the House of Commons, and in 1840 a Clay supporter. He was governor of North Carolina from 1849 to 1850, and clerk of the commission for arbitrating the provisions of the Treaty of Ghent. Ashe, *Biog. Hist. of N. C.*, VI, 349-357.

except to vote—that it was a contest you had very much deprecated, & had used your best endeavors to avert it.—& further
that you considered Gen. Barringer & myself both your friends,
& that you were the personal friend of us both, & that you would
upon no account change a vote for or against me.—

I felt gratified at these declarations, but was afterwards induced to believe that you had acted in violation of them & utterly
inconsistent with your uniform professions of respect for me
personally—Under this impression I adverted to your name in
the tone & manner I have mentioned.

I further deem it due to myself and to candour & fair dealing
to state that on divers occasions since the election when speaking under the same impression, I have impugned your sincerity
in the most unequivocal manner,—and I have frequently said
that if you aided & assisted in preparing that hand-bill, in so
direct a violation of your professions, that your conduct was
characterized with neither the principle, the sincerity nor the
candour of a Gentlemen.—

I have the honor to be,
Your obedient
Servt.

(Signed)   WILLIE P. MANGUM
Henry Seawell, Esqr.

The within is a true copy of a letter that I delivered to Judge
Seawell on the morning of the first of October A. D. 1823.
JNO. H. GREENE.[41]

[Addressed:]
   Henry Seawell, Esquire
   Mr. Green.   Present
Copy. 4p.

WPM-D

Willie P. Mangum to Henry Seawell

RALEIGH the 1st October 1823.

Sir
I have received your letter of this date, and have given the
subject of it as mature and deliberate consideration as my time
& circumstances would admit.

----

[41]A political leader from Warren County. He was in the state legislature in 1829. *N. C.
Manual*, 837.

I cannot but regret Sir, that you deem the information contained in my note of yesterday, touching an allusion to you in my address at Person Court, not sufficiently full and explicit.—

In that note, I disavowed the recollection of any expression used by me on that occasion, denying to you the possession of character & respectability. Nor do I remember using any *language* at that time calculated to affect either.

The offensiveness of the allusion to you, and of the mention of your name, (if any there was) consisted entirely as I conceive in *the tone & the manner* of the speaker—and until my pen shall be more highly gifted in catching the hues, in touching off the shadings, and pouring into its page the very tones, looks & other accompaniments of a public speech, I must beg leave to decline any further attempt, at rendering that scene more obvious & palpable to the senses.—

I must be permitted here to enter my most solemn protest against the principle contained in your last note, that I have no right, "*to know of you* whether you were in any way concerned" in the concoction of a poison *designed* to be so powerful & active as to "destroy the whole Well in which truth is said to reside."—

In Law, in Morality, or in Honour, is he who punctures an apple, & infuses into it a poison to be held guiltless, innocent, and without a stain upon his escutchion, while he who lays it for the devoted & unsuspecting victim to eat, is to swing upon the Gallows?—

Is it consistent, that in the very note in which you call upon me to state what *expressions* I have used offending *you,* that you should claim exemption from enquiry touching *acts* affecting *me?* Is this distinction maintained upon the ground, that *Words spoken* which are evanescent & usually limited to one crowd, are more likely to work injury to character, than *Words Written,* capable of unlimited diffusion, and permanent duration?—

I had though that Honor never quailed or blenched at inquiry. —I must further be permitted to enter my protest, against your right, "to know of me" the evidence I had of your agency in bringing into existence that hand-bill, the "first born" of Wit & Intelligence, *before* you condescend to deny the *fact* of your agency.

That point *for the present* I conceive rests with my own conscience, For if I am satisfied that the belief of your agency, which you may deem so injurious, has not been adopted upon light, trivial, & unsatisfactory evidence, it is all that my sense of honour or my conscience requires.

In your last note you say you will "reserve to yourself the privilege of considering as an outrage any thing spoken by me that was or might be considered offensive, though spoken under a full knowledge of the fact" of your agency.—I will beg leave here Sir, to observe that besides a certain tone of peremptoriness in this part of your letter which I dislike; you shall with my unqualified assent be entitled to the full benefit of this reservation.—In another paragraph you say "that you never circulated a single hand-bill, nor read one out of the walls of your own house, or gave any opinion of the merit of the production, or added anything to its weight beyond what it acquired by the signature it bore."—Am I to infer from your claim of exemption, & this long & minute string of negatives that you actually had an agency in preparing that hand-bill? Or am I to consider the studious avoidance of the *main fact,* the satisfactory denial of which would have removed all ground of controversy, as a fresh instance of inquiry, or insult added to injury? It may seem that in my last note, I wantonly travelled beyond the reach of the ground embraced in your inquiry & I know some of my valued friends think it questionable & perhaps improper. Yet I appeal to the searcher of hearts for the sincerity of mine that I was actuated by no wish to excite hostility, or injure your feelings, but was regulated solely & exclusively by considerations (not of pride I hope) but of self respect & what I deemed due to candour & fair dealing. But at the same time that I make this assertion, I feel anxious to impress upon your mind the *grounds* of the language you deem exceptionable.—I must still be permitted to add that I neither regret it, nor repent of it.—If these grounds were fallacious, nothing could have been more easy than for you to have removed them. I gave you the *grounds* & I gave you the *language,* & I shall pertinaciously adhere to the *latter,* until the *former* are removed.—

You say "you were under no *pledge* to Gen. Barringer or me." —Granted—But between Gentlemen I hardly think it worth the pains of drawing a distinction between direct *statements* & *pledges.*—And I still hold that according to your uniform statements & professions, you had not the liberty of going into *secret conclave* or elsewhere, with a man to aid and abet in preparing a hand-bill, *designed* to give a fatal blow to my prospects. Whether

you did so or not or had any agency in it, you have not condescended to inform me. When you shall deny the *fact* of your
agency I shall then give the grounds of my belief—and if in
adopting that belief I have injured you, I am prepared to suffer
the consequences. But I still must be permitted to say, that if you
had such agency "in so direct a violation of your professions,"
I am still of opinion that no language of reprobation & detesta-
tion, that would not be unbecoming my character, could be too
severe towards you.—I feel a firm conviction of the propriety of
this, and I appeal to God for the truth of the assertion that when
I say it, it is dictated *only* by a sense of that firmness & self respect which I think due to my own character.—I have been particular & even tedious in these details.—I have said all that I can
say on these subjects, & shall consider this correspondence closed
on my part, should you think proper to reclaim the ground taken
in your last note.—I could wish not to stay in Raleigh longer
than tomorrow at 10 oclock or thereabouts.—I regret I have put
you to the inconvenience of waiting so long for this note.—
I have the Honor to be Sir
Your obdt. Servt.
WILLIE P. MANGUM.

Henry Seawell Esq
This is a correct & true copy of a note I delivered to Charles
Manly Esq. the friend of Henry Seawell Esq. on the evening of
the 1st October 1823.
WM. H. HILL[42]

WPM-LC

Chas. Manly to Willie P. Mangum

RALEIGH 3rd— Oct. 1823.

Sir,
Your note of Yesterday offering an apology for a certain expression made in my presence by you in your room in relation to
a third person is now before me.—
At the moment the observation was used I confess I felt hurt
& insulted; but upon further reflection I was induced to consider
it an unguarded ebullition of the angry passions, unattended
with a deliberate attempt to injure my feelings.

[42]Probably William Hill, the North Carolina secretary of state from 1811 to 1859. Battle,
Hist. of Raleigh, 52.

I am happy to find that my construction was correct.—
The apology I think Sir, is entirely commensurate with the
supposed injury & is received with the frankness & liberality
with which it is given.—

You desire me to state whether it will be "agreeable to me to
receive your communication for the Gentleman already alluded
to? Permit [me] to decline it. I shall be very busy to-day in arranging some matters previously to my leaving home, which
would render it extremely inconvenient for me to see him, & perhaps it would be disagreeable & improper for the reasons which
you are doubtless aware of.

I am Sir
Very respectfully
CHAS: MANLY

[Addressed:]

 Willie P. Mangum Esqr.
 Present.

WPM-NC

W. P. Mangum to Wm. Robards

ORANGE 12th. October 1823.

Dear Sir,

I received by the hands of Mr. Newell your favor of the 10th.
Instant, covering a Note from Mr. Seawell—I presume that the
previous correspondence between that person & myself has not
been submitted to you, or if it has that you have overlooked the
fact of my declining to receive from him any other communication except upon *one subject.*—which was distinctly understood
to be an *ultimatum*—

I therefore decline giving any notice to the communication. It
is too vague— & if upon its face it were unequivocal, it is totally
inadmissible to be dictated to in relation to the time or place of
meeting the person in question.—Reasonable time was given to
him after my last communication in Raleigh, two days additional
at Louisburg— & now I will not submit to be called to any place
that does not suit my convenience.—

My presence at Warrenton depends upon the contingency of
the Judge holding the Court, & can in no respect be regulated or
influenced by the note alluded to.—

At Raleigh the individual in question was distinctly informed that no communication from him to me would be received unless it were first submitted to & came through the hands of my friend at that place M^r. Hill.—I cannot therefore but advert to the indelicacy of addressing me *directly*, after that *verbal* communication.—Mr Robert Potter[43] is authorized on my behalf—& he can be found at Oxford.—& on next Thursday at Warrenton His acts will be deemed obligatory upon me.

Permit me to say that I deem all the information contained in this note as an act of supererrogation.—& that it is given as a mark of my sincere respect for you personally

I am Dear Sir

Yours with regard

WILLIE P. MANGUM

This is a true copy of the note
sent by M^r. Mangum on the 12th.
Octr. to Co^l. Robards[44]

Rob Potter

Co^l. Roberts.
W^m. Robards

W^{ms}boro.

Mr Newell

WPM-LC

Thomas Henderson[45] to Willie P. Mangum

JACKSON (Ten.) October 14, 1823.

My Dear Sir,

Col. A. R. Alexander,[46] who will hand you this, is our Representative in Congress:—He is my friend and a man of sterling

---

[43]Robert Potter, 1800-1842, was a midshipman in the U. S. Navy from 1815 to 1821. He was an attorney in Halifax and Oxford most of his life, a member of the state legislature in 1826, 1828, and 1834, and a Jackson Democrat in Congress from 1829 to 1831. He moved to Texas in 1835 where he contributed to the independence of that republic. He was a person of violent temper. His extravagance and conflicts later greatly embarrassed Mangum. *Biog. Dir. of Cong.*, 1426.

[44]Col. William Robards.

[45]Thomas Henderson was one of the editors of the Raleigh *Star* from 1808 to 1823 when he sold his interest to Bell and Lawrence and left for settlement in the Chickasaw lands in western Tennessee. Johnson, *Ante-Bellum N. C.*, 767.

[46]Adam Rankin Alexander, a native of Virginia, moved to Tennessee in 1801. He became a member of the state legislature, the register of land, and a member of the House of Representatives from 1823 to 1827. In 1834 he was a member of the state abolitionist convention. *Biog. Dir. of Cong.*, 630.

integrity, I therefore take pleasure in recommending him to your friendly attention.

I continue to be well pleased with the country.

Your friend

THO. HENDERSON

W. P. Mangum Esqr.

[Addressed:]
> Honble
> Willie P. Mangum
> > Washington City

Col. Alexander.

WPM-LC

Saml. Hillman & James F. Taylor[47] to
Messrs. Robards & Potter

WARRENTON—[17 Oct., 1823]

Messrs Robards & Potter,
Gentlemen,

Having understood from you both the nature of the correspondence between Mr. Seawell and Mr. Mangum, and the *facts* connected with the transaction, we are induced to believe that the present unfortunate difference between them has been produced entirely by a misunderstanding of those facts: And we are satisfied that if your principals understood each other, and the part which each has respectively acted, their differences might be easily & honourably adjusted—In the present state of the correspondence however, this understanding cannot be effected, and consequences, much to be depredated, must be the result. We therefore propose as the mutual friends of the parties concerned, and request you both as an act of Justice to your principals and to the publick, that you should restore the correspondence to such a situation that explanations can properly be made between them; and to this end we request your interference as the friends of the parties, to effect a withdrawal of all the letters and of course the sentiments contained in them, with the exception of Mr. Seawell's first letter and Mr. Mangums answer to it; and that an interview take place between you upon the subject—

---

[47]James Fauntleroy Taylor, a member of the state legislature and attorney from Wake County, became the attorney general of the state from 1825 to his death in 1828. *N. C. Manual,* 444; McIver, *N. C. Register,* 48; Grant, *Alumni Hist. of U. N. C.,* 611.

With the strongest hopes and expectations that you will use your influence & present situation as the respective friends of the parties to bring about a proper reconciliation
Sir and with Sentiments of great respect
Y^r. obt. Ser^{ts}—
SAML. HILLMAN
JAMES F. TAYLOR
Octr. 17th. 1823

A copy of the within
was handed by Mr Taylor
& myself to Col Robards
S. Hillman

[Addressed:]
Messrs Robards & Potter
Present—

WPM-LC

William Robards to Robert Potter

WARRENTON October 17th, 1823

[Torn]
It being understood in our interview this morning [torn] at the request of James F Taylor & Samuel Hillman esqrs, contained in their letter of this date that the correspondence between Mr. Seawell and Mr. Mangum be considered as withdrawn simultaneously as proposed [b]y them. I am authorized to say in behalf of Mr. Seawell that if the expressions used by Mr Mangum, and alluded to in Mr Seawell's first letter, derogatory to his character [torn] ed from an impression that Mr. Seawell's agency in the hand [torn] Barringer flowed from a hostile and *unusual* intent [torn] from the character of Mr Mangum: That in this impression [torn] mistaken; that the agency which Mr Seawell had [torn] of that hand bill was in conquence of the [torn]y Genl Barringer to him as his friend; and from their relative situation the General had a right to presume he was authorized to make such an application—that Mr Seawells agency was intended by him as evidence of friendship to Genl Barringer and not done with any hostility towards Mr Mangum or with an intent to detract from his character—

I am persuaded you will readily give such an [torn] [a]S you
are authorized to make—
With sentiments of esteem I am

Yr Obdt.

WM ROBARDS

[Addressed:] Robert Potter esqr.
Present—

———

WPM-LC

R. Potter to W. Robards

WARRENTON
Octr. 17th. 1823

Sir,
I have the honor to acknowledge the receipt of your note of
to day from which it appears that the agency of M^r. Seawell in
Barringer's publication against Mr Mangum did not proceed
from disrespect to that gentleman or from a design to injure his
character M^r. Mangum's expressions disrespectful of M^r. Seawell growing out of that transaction having originated in a mis-
apprehension of the true character of his agency in it are consequently withdrawn

V^{ry}. Rep^{ly}.

Y^r, Ob^t, Sv^t, Sir

ROB, POTTER

Co^l,
    W^m. Robards
        Present
            (a copy)

[Addressed:]
    Co^l,
        W^m. Robards
            Present——

WPM-LC

James Somervell to Willie P. Mangum[48]

STINKING QUARTER, ORANGE COUNTY Nov. 1823.

Dear Sir,

I take the liberty to refer my friend & your's Mr. Alexander Allbright of this neighborhood to you for information and assistance in the case of The Counselmans who now reside here but whose Ancestors lived in Maryland near Baltimore.

Jacob Counselman one of the children of George Counselman of Maryland moved (as it was supposed under the displeasure of his parents) some forty years ago to Orange County, where he married a Miss Loy, by whom he had three daughters who married George Thomas Jacob Iseley & Henry Boggs and one son, George the younger; all of which children of Jacob & grandchildren of George the elder are alive & residents of this vicinity. Jacob Counselman has been dead for some time, and his children have lately understood by a Mr. Adams who resides near Chapel Hill that George Counselman, their Grandfather, died posessed of considerable property near Baltimore, to a part or the whole of which they are entitled either by bequest or descent from George of Maryland in right of Jacob their father.

They have appointed Mr. Alexander Allbright their agent who is a brother in law of my overseer Seymour Purryear their agent to enquire into the truth of Adams' statement and if true to procure for them whatever they may be entitled to—which Adams said would appear of Record in Baltimore, or by enquiry of Jacob's Brethren who have married into the Turnpole family & reside near Royster's Town.

Mr. Allbright applied to me for advice & I could conceive of no mode of obtaining the information more feasible than an application to your kindness which I have not a doubt will do for Mr. Allbright & the Counselmans all that can be done.—As you will have an opportunity through some of the members from Maryland or otherwise of pursuing the enquiry without expence, & I hope with not much trouble & compleat success.

I should be glad to hear from you but your letters upon this subject you will be please to direct to Alexander Allbright, Allbright's Post Office, Orange County, N. C.

---

[48]See below the letter of Alexander Allbright to Mangum, Dec. 13, 1823.

Wishing you good luck, an agreeable session, & to see your name at all times on the side of the people against all their real enemies.

I remain, dear Sir,

most respectfully
Your friend
JAMES SOMERVELL

Hon.
> Willie P. Mangum
>> H. R.
>>> Washington

[Addressed:]
> The Hon.
>> Willie P. Mangum
>>> H. R.
>>>> Washington

Mail.

WPM-LC

M. M. Henderson[49] to Willie P. Mangum

OXFORD December 7th 1823.

Dear Sir

Mr. Benjamin Barham requested me to write to you, stating his situation, and asking if there is any relief He is confined in Hillsborough jail at the instance of the United States as a defaulter while post Master at Chapel Hill.

I suppose you know that he is not worth a cent—that he has a family of small children depending on his individual exertions for bread, and that they must suffer if he is not relieved, I don't know what course is pursued in cases of this kind, but I do know that there is not the least chance of his being relieved by his friends paying the money for him.

If you can do any thing for him I have no doubt that you would be assisting a well meaning man from a situation from which it is impossble from him to relieve himself.

---

[49]Mark M. Henderson, who was a student at the University with Mangum, became an attorney at Oxford until his removal to Carroll County, Tennessee, where he died in 1833. Grant, *Alumni Hist. of U. N. C.*, 273; McIver, *N. C. Register*, 46.

There is nothing new here. Potter[50] is full of Missiouri and Hillman[51] is at a certain house in Wake County and Priestly Mangum is there too—How they will make it the Lord knows, But I should of all things like most to see them. You can well conceive them moving in distinct orbits around the same center with all the regularity but not all the harmony of the sphere. Fisher[52] the self elected champion of the west has brough in a string of resolutions concerning a caucus prefaced with about fifty reasons, the least of which are life limb and member, constitution and law aristocracy corruption and intrigue As they will no doubt have stormy time of next week in Raleigh on the question I shall make it my business to be there.

With sentiments & respect yours &c.

M. M. HENDERSON

The Hon[ble]. Willie P. Mangum

W. P. Mangum to Duncan Cameron[53]

WASHINGTON CITY 10th. Decem. 1823

Dear Sir.

In reviewing the proceedings of the Legislature it would seem that your body is more agitated on the subject of Presidential election than those nearer the grand political focus.—I observe that the election of M[r] Clay to the chair is taken abroad as an unequivocal indication of the State of parties at this place whereas nothing can be more erroneous.

That election having been decided almost exclusively upon the consideration of his superior qualifications and transcendent abilities as a speaker.

Further the friends of M[r]. J. W. Taylor[54] of New York were busily engaged to bring him forward with success, but finding these efforts vain & his chance hopeless, they went over en

[50]Robert Potter.

[51]Samuel Hillman.

[52]Charles Fisher from Salisbury and later congressman, on December 2, 1823, in the House of Commons as the representative of western North Carolina and as a supporter of Calhoun, introduced a resolution instructing North Carolina congressmen not to cooperate in the national caucus for nominating a presidential candidate. This provoked a bitter fight in the legislature between the Crawford and anti-Crawford men. The resolution was tabled by a vote of 82 to 46, not so much because of pro-Crawford sentiment as because of the opposition to the idea of instruction. A. R. Newsome, "Debate on the Fisher Resolution," *N. C. Hist. Rev.*, IV, 428-470; V, 65-96.

[53]The original is in the Duncan Cameron Papers, Southern Collection, University of North Carolina, Chapel Hill, N. C.

[54]John W. Taylor, 1784-1854, a member of Congress from New York from 1813 to 1833, served as Speaker of the House from 1820 to 1821 and from 1825 to 1827. *Biog. Dir. of Cong.*, 1600.

masse to Mr Clay, against their former adversary M^r. Barbour.[55]—M^r. Taylor by the bye, I should think very little more than a very ordinary man.

It is true that the Presidential question is here a topic of frequent, I might almost say, constant conversation—but I observe but little of that *spirit of devotion* which seems to characterize the friends of the two most prominent candidates, before the Legislature of N^oCarolina.—Admitted political sins lie at the door of each of the candidates—

The thorough going '98 men complain of essential departures by the '23 republicans, from the good, old, orthodox, democratic republican faith—Whereas the old Federal party take up a candidate some from one consideration & some from another without regard to any broad & obvious principle by which they are regulated in their selection.

From all that I have heard however from the different states —I should form the following opinion, upon which however I know there can be but little reliance.—M^r. Crawford first, in some parts losing ground & in others gaining upon the whole nearly stationary.—M^r. Adams second evidently I sh^d. think on the wane.—M^r. Calhoun third—unquestionably gaining—as regards his own intrinsic strength and with the best chances for the contingent remain is for M^r. Adam's interest.—On this point there is however some doubt. It being pretty clear that a suspicion of some unfairness on the part Mr Calhoun, and of highly exceptionable conduct of his friends near him towards M^r. Adams, has produced a feeling of displeasure amongst those who cherish with most ardour the hopes & prospects of M^r. Adams.—Gen Jackson has received very great attention since his arrival—more indeed than any person at Washington—but all concur in the belief that he has no chance of success.

Mr Clay is very popular in the House of Representatives, but that popularity is of a species not very enviable.—It is a high admiration of his talents in debate, & his adroitness in the management of individuals & deliberative bodies—all of which is sustained & enforced with manners the most dignified, & yet the most fascinating & popular.—You have seen Mr Clay—All admire him—but that admiration wants an indispensible requisite—The column that presents so beautiful a Corinthian capital does not rest upon the broad basis of Moral confidence.—

---

[55]Philip Barbour of Virginia who was Speaker from 1821 to 1823.

M^r. Crawford evidently has more friends in Congress than others of the candidates—His friends in the general are anxious for a caucus, while the friends of the other candidates deprecate it as the greatest evil—It is amusing to see these old caucus men who once had the hardihood to advocate caucusing as tho it were almost a fundamental principle in the great Bill of rights of the Reb. party at this day when they are split so widely; proclaiming war against it, as tho it were an engine to sap [illegible]the great foundations of constitutional principle—So little of principle enters into the context of ambitious men for power!

M^r. Crawford is in very bad health [faded] to see him & found him confined in his c[hair]. Many doubt his recovery.—

Nothing has been yet done of importance.—You will have seen M^r. Webster's resolution[56] in response to the Kings speech.

A strong disposition manifests itself to us a little against the Holy alliance as the Grand Turk.—Would we not do better to mind our own business? If you have leisure I will thank you for your views on these subjects.—

Accept Dear Sir assurances

of my sincere regard for

You

W. P. MANGUM

M^r. Duncan Cameron

WPM-LC

Jas. C. Mangham[57] *to Willie P. Mangum*

MILLEDGEVILLE December the 11th 1823.—

Dr Sir on Examining the Congressional Election of My Mother State I find you have been elected from the Eighth District. I on this occasion open a correspondence with you—and have to State that on Examining the Register of

---

[56]On December 8, 1823, Webster introduced in Congress a resolution to send an agent to Greece. In a subsequent speech supporting these resolutions he attacked the Holy Alliance and monarchy. *Proceedings of the Debates of Congress* (Washington, D. C.: Gales and Seaton, 1856), 18 Cong., I sess., 805, 1084-1099.

[57]One tradition in the Mangum family is that the family was originally from Wales, and was called Mangolus; another tradition has the family of French Hugenot origin and called Manigault. In the 17th and 18th centuries W. P. Mangum's ancestors lived in Sussex County, Virginia. Arthur Mangum, the grandfather of Willie P. Mangum, settled in Orange County, North Carolina, before the Revolution. One of his sons, Arthur Mangum, 1773-1813, married Dicey Carrington, and left many children who migrated to Georgia, Mississippi, and Missouri. It is probable that James C. Mangham was a descendant of one of these. *Virginia Magazine of History and Biography*, II, 108; Weeks' Genealogy of the Mangum Family.

names from England Ireland and wales—I find that the original
name In Ireland—Is Spelt—Mangham—which Has been the
cause of the alteration in the Spelling the same—the family is
Numerous here—and some of them fills the first Stations in publick Searvice—if my memory serves me—I saw you when a
small boy—and am Proud to hear of your prosperity—and
would that I could personaly commune with your Grand Ma Ma
[*sic*]—and others—I have been in the Legislature of Georgia
alternetly since the year 1813—and have been in the Senate for
the Last 2 years— there is considerable excitement in this State
relative to our next President—which has caused the Legislature to Notice the Same, the, Senate this Day has past a resolution recommending Wm. H. Crawford as our next president and
Inclosed you have the names and votes—Stating from which
county & you will oblige me to Inform me by Letter Directed
to Brunswick Ga—what is his prospects after a caucus on the
subject—and after perusial—of the Inclosed to Shew it To Wm.
H. CRawford—I will thank you to attend in any shape or way
—to the Interest of the Citizens of Georgia who lost negroes
by the British In the late war—as the Majority was Taken from
the Small County of Glynn—in which I live—my connections
there lost considerable & yours also—by the name of Piles—is—
the Daughter and Grand Children of old W^m. Mangum—your
Grand fathers Brother—national Sircumstances requires national attention—you will Please excuse this in hast—as the
Mail is wating I Expect the Legislature will adjourn the 20th
Inst—I am your obt. Svt.

JAS C. MANGHAM

P. S.

The number of negroes taken from our small county is about
five hundred which Mr. Cuthburt[58] of Tatnal Can certify.

[Addressed:]

Wiley P. Mangum Esq.
City of Washington
U. S. A.

Mail.

---

[58]Alfred Cuthbert, a Princeton graduate who practiced law and served in the state legislature in Georgia from 1805 to 1813, 1817 to 1819, and 1832, was a member of the national
House of Representatives from 1813 to 1816 and 1821 to 1825, and was the U. S. Senator
from 1835 to 1843. *Biog. Dir. of Cong.*, 873.

WPM-LC

Alexander Allbright[59] to Willie P. Mangum

December the 13th 1823

Sir not long since I saw Mr. Summerville from the lower part of this state [county] at his plantation not far from where I live & mentioning to him some business I had lately undertaken as an agent to perform for some poor people of this County he kindly offered to write you a letter upon the subject which he did in my presence & also promis'd that If you should still be in Raleigh he would in a few days deliver it to you personally but should he fail seeing you there he design'd sending it on to you.

As the letter written by my friend contain'd nearly or quite as much information relative to the business as I can or need communicate to you I principaly write because it is uncertain with me whether you ever saw his letter. Mr. George Counselman of the state of Mariland liv'd I suppose within 15 or 16 miles of Balitmore, perhaps near or in Roystertown whose Son Jacob Counselman left him when yet single (perhaps for some misdemeanour) and came to this County and in it married a Miss Loy after the death of George Counselman of Maryland Jacob his son understood there was something decended or bequeathed to him by his father but he neglected going for it. Jacob at length died also and left 4 children one Son & three daughters who are all living in this County—the Son's name is George Counselman the three daughters are name[d] & married as follows Catherine is married to George Thomas Elizabeth to Jacob Isley and Sally to Henry Boggs these poor children have repeatedly understood there is something due them from their Grandfather and one Mr. Adams has told me that it is absolutely a matter of record in Baltimore. these Heirs of Jacob Counselman have proceeded to constitute me their agent and as you will be for some time no great distance from Baltimore I suppose if dispos'd you can perhaps transmit to me a true statement of the matter in order to distinguish the Family it will be nothing amiss for you to understand that we have been inform'd that some of Jacob Counselamn's brothers married in the Turnpough Family I will here state that I have likewise understood that one of Jacob's sisters (who was an Idiot) died without marrying leaving property also some of his brothers may have died without

---

[59]See above the letter of James Somervell to W. P. Mangum, November, 1823.

any nearer heir. Sir I hope you will make some inquiry into the matter and send me a letter as soon as possable when you write to me direct your letter to Allbright's office. Should their be anything comeing you will likely be called on to manage the business

Sir if you feel Indispos'd to do anything in it I hope you will let me know by a few lines.

Acting in compliance with the above request you will not fail to oblige your's

ALEXR. ALLBRIGHT.

Mr. Wiley P. Mangum

[Addressed:]
Honr. Judge Mangum, Member of the House of Representatives in Congress Washington City   Now in Session

[Postmarked:]   Allbrights, N. C.

WPM-LC

R. Vanhook⁶⁰ to Willie P. Mangum

RALEIGH Decemr. 14ᵗʰ. 1823

Dear Sir

When you left this place you requested me to send you a list of names in our County which you wished to write too [sic] you will find them inside of this Sheet & the Post offices you will Direct them to.

I want you to examine the claim of John Chatham⁶¹ & wife Mrs. Chatham is the mother of John Barns I think his given name is John who enlisted under Capt. Henry Atkinson⁶² I believe in the year 1808 & died I think Some where on the Mississippy whilst in the army of the U States. I wish you to write what is coming to him in money & whether he gets Land or not & what way the claim can be drawn as they are anxious to know when I return home all about it

As to the news of this place I must refer you to newspapers

⁶⁰Robert Vanhook was a political leader from Person County. He served in the House of of Commons from 1807 to 1812 and in 1814, and in the state senate from 1815 to 1816, 1821 to 1827, and 1830 to 1834. He died in 1834. *N. C. Manual*, 757-758; *Hillsborough Recorder*, Oct. 10, 20, 1834.
⁶¹John Chatham received a pension for his services as was indicated by the report of the Secretary of State to Congress in 1835. Walter Clark, (ed.), *State Records of North Carolina*, XXII, (1907), 55.
⁶²Col. Henry Atkinson became a soldier of some prominence in the Black Hawk War. *D. A. B.*, I, 410.

Published here I can only add that Since the Death of Fishers resolutions the Crawford Ticket is gaining very fast I remain
Yrs respectfully
R. VANHOOK

(wrote 11-March)

[Addressed:]

The Hon.
Willie P. Mangum
Washington City

[Endorsed:]

written to Mr Vanhook
3rd. March.

[Two pages of names with post offices, all from Caswell County follow. These are not included here. At the bottom of the names is the following note:] Sir the above is a list of names Scattered over the County perhaps you will think of others yourself that you wish to write to. Yrs. &c   R. V.

Willie P. Mangum[63] to Thos. D. Bennehan[64]

WASHINGTON 15th. Dec. 1823

Dear Sir.

When I last past your house we had some conversation in relation to a new post route through the upper part of Wake County —At that time I suggested the convenience of getting a route to cross the one at Stagville & so on to Person [County].

It will be necessary that petition should be forwarded, & you will therefore not only do the people in the neighborhood of the Fishdam a favour, but one to me also, if you will urge upon Col. Tharpe[65] & Gen. J. J. Carrington[66] the necessity of preparing one at each neighborhood & obtain as many subscribers as practicable.—The route leaving Raleigh by Jos. Brasfields to the Fishdam, Thence by F. Morges' to Sim's Mills—thence by Stag-

---

[63]The original is in the Duncan Cameron Papers, University of North Carolina.
[64]Thomas D. Bennehan, 1781-1847, brother-in-law of Duncan Cameron, inherited his father's (Richard Bennehan) estate. He was one of the wealthiest planters in North Carolina. He was a close neighbor of Mangum. Hoyt, *Papers of Murphey,* I, 289n.
[65]Col. W. A. Tharpe, a commander of the militia in the northern part of Wake County in 1823. McIver, *N. C. Register,* 91.
[66]J. J. Carrington, who was related to Mangum and who lived near him, was a lieutenant colonel of the militia in 1823. McIver, *N. C. Register,* 91.

ville to J.J.C. Store. Thence by Mount Ferze to Roxbor°.—
Whether such a route can be had I think very doubtful as No-
Carolina is deficient about $8000 on the Gen Post office this
year.—If however I shall not succeed I have but little doubt that
I can succeed according to your suggestion in getting the mail
to return from Oxford to Raleigh by way of the Fishdam.
Nothing has yet occurred at this place in congress worth your
attention—We have had no debates of any consequence.—

You have seen that the President's Message contains some
novel & important matter, and that portion of it which relates
to the probable views of the allied powers[67] has created some
sensation here, and I doubt exceedingly whether Congress will
be found prepared to sustain the views of the Executive if it
shall become necessary to try the question.—

The principal movements of the members here is in relation
to the next presidency—there is considerable effort & canvassing
on that subject, but still I think even at this place in point of
devotion, Gentlemen fall short of the N°. Cª. legislature—I am
somewhat surprized to see so much excitement upon a question
in which No Carolina, cannot have a great deal of interest.—

The result I think very doubtful, tho I think the chances are
considerably in favour of Mr Crawford.

Mr. Adams cannot succeed—this I think perfectly clear.—And
if Crawford does not, his defeat will be effected by some compromise & transfer of interest. Tho Mr Calhoun has not at this
time much certain intrinsic strength yet upon a question of
compromize it is impossible to say what accession of strength
may be his.—Mr Crawford is very ill & tho his Physicians
pronounce him out of danger, yet many entertain doubts of his
final recovery.—

Be pleased to present my respects to your Father, and Mr.
Yarborough[68]

> And accept for yourself
> Dear Sir assurances of my
> sincere regards
>
> WILLIE P. MANGUM

Mr Thos. D. Bennehan

---

[67]He probably refers to the Monroe Doctrine.
[68]Samuel Yarborough was in business with the Bennehans in 1824.

WPM-LC

Th. N. Mann to Willie P. Mangum

RALEIGH Decr. 16th 1823

My Dear Sir,

Being anxious about the proper representation of a fact, which I suspect you more correctly to remember than most other persons, I trust you will excuse this immediate application to yourself.

There is a bill before the senate to entitle a man to be bailed on an appeal to the S. court in all cases not capital; that is to remove the discretion exercised by a judge in such cases. On its discussion a few days since it was stated by a member, Mr. S.[69] of Wake, that at Franklin Superior court last Spring, on a motion to appeal on an indictment for assault &C. it was intimated to the counsel, or declared to him by the court that the party sh^d. not be bailed. This was the case of Jac^b. Cooly, who was defended by you. As it is my impression that no motion was submitted for an appeal in that case, or if submitted, that it was withdrawn in a few minutes, and that the judge made no intimation or declaration at all on the subject, or at least gave no opinion as to the disposition of the prisoner pending the appeal, I am mortified that a representation so unwarranted and so prejudicial to the reputation of the judge, sh^d pass uncontradicted. For this purpose it has been thought proper by Judge Badger,[70] and some of his friends, that the most correct source of information should be appealed to. The counsel concerned seemed to be that source. I am aware of the delicacy of our correcting such statements; I am aware of the peculiarities that may distinguish your situation in the present instance, I assure you that I deeply regret it, but hope as you do not volunteer, that upon this appeal you will be so good as to furnish us with your recollection of the *facts*. I know, and Mr. J. F. Taylor certifies that, that there was a conversation at the bar about an appeal but does not recollect nor does he whether there was a motion to that effect submitted to the court.

I can offer you little information of our proceedings, which you may not derive from the gazettes. There is much talk in both houses, and more out of doors. We are in great perplexity

---

[69]Henry Seawell.

[70]George E. Badger, 1795-1855, after making a brilliant record at Yale, read law and became one of the great lawyers and political leaders of the state. He held such important offices as judge of superior court, Secretary of the Navy under Harrison, and United States Senator. *Biog. Dict. of N. C.*, VII, 35-44; *D. A. B.*, I, 485.

on the state of sentiment at Washington, and through the union on the question about the presidency. We hear the most contradictory statements. The letters are so opposite as light to darkness. Pray give me your opinion as to the prospect of the several men in nomination; and your opinion of the men themselves. In the hope that you will furnish us with the information, which it is the object of this letter more especially to request, I remain as ever

With much respect & sincere regard
Yrs
TH. N. MANN

[Addressed:]

Honble Willie P. Mangum
H. of Representatives

Mail)   Washington City.

WPM-LC

James Mebane to Mangum

RALEIGH December 19th 1823.

Dear Sir,

Our session is drawing near the usual time of adjournment and as yet there has been as little done, likely to be of any benefit to our country as I have ever known in any session of our State legislature, We have however several important bills on their passage, but I think the fate of all of them doubtful, The principle subjects are regulations in the Judiciary, and internal improvement, Prejudice against the lawyers operated against the first, & certain prejudices & illiberality against the latter. And indeed the presidential election is made to bear on many questions even the passage of a bill to erect a bridge over Roanoke at Halifax has been opposed by some of the friends of Crawford, because some of Calhoun's friends were in favor of it—And thus you may see that from, ignorance, illiberality & prejudice of different kinds it is very difficult for any important Measure to prevail—

The proposition to choose electors hereafter by districts[71] has

---

[71]In Charles Fisher's Resolution on the caucus was a recommendation of an amendment to the Federal Constitution to permit the selection of presidential electors by districts. This was a continuation of a similar fight that had raged in North Carolina since 1792. For a good discussion of this controversy see A. R. Newsome, *The Presidential Election of 1824 in North Carolina,* in the *James Sprunt Historical Studies,* XXIII, (1939), 38-40. Hereafter cited as Newsome, *Election of 1824.*

failed, and I believe arrangements are making, to prepare at least two general tickets to be submitted to the people, and I believe that the active & zealous friends of both Crawford and Calhoun, promise themselves ultimate success—So that we may calculate on electioneering on a large scale for near twelve months to come

My principle object in writing you was to call your attention to the papers I put into your hands at this place, after you have ascertained whether any more evidence is necessary you will please to inform me by letter.

Please to remember me respectfully to my old friends Messrs. Macon,[72] Branch,[73] John Long[74] and any others acquaintances I expect we will be able to leave this in eight or ten days—I remain most respectfully Yours &c.

                                JAMES MEBANE

WPM-LC

Will H. Haywood, Jr.[75] *to Willie P. Mangum*

                                RALEIGH 20 Dec 1823.

My dear Sir

I may not be far from a proper conclusion when I suppose that however much a man may be occupied with great matters —*abroad* it by no means abates the interest he feels in affairs *at home* though trivial in the comparison.—

At all events under this impression I have determined to scribble you a short letter of the *"carrying on"* among us and beg that when leisure permits you will favor me with a small portion of the news at the Metropolis.

Our Legislature, as you will discover from the papers, are full of new schemes, none of which seem likely to obtain the asent of a majority of both Houses.—The Senate have been engaged 2 or 3 weeks in perfecting our Superior Court System and—after much labor have produced a Bill providing for an additional Circuit Judge which has passed the Senate the 3rd &

[72]Nathaniel Macon, who was in the Senate in 1823.
[73]John Branch, who was in the Senate in 1823.
[74]John Long, who represented the Randolph County district in Congress from 1821 to 1829.
[75]William Henry Haywood, Jr., 1801-1852, a graduate of the University of North Carolina, was an attorney in Raleigh. He was a member of the state legislature in 1831 and from 1834 to 1836, and speaker of the state House of Commons in 1836. From 1843 to 1846 he was a Democratic Senator from North Carolina. He broke with Mangum after the nullification fight when Mangum went over to the Whig Party. Van Buren offered Haywood the post of charge d'affaires to Belgium but he declined. Ashe, *Biog. Hist. of N. C.*, VI, 296-304.

last reading by a majority of 2 only—yet it is generally believed that its death will be met at crossing the passage of the Capital.—The H[ouse] of C[ommons] on the other hand have divided the State into 6 Chancery districts and require the Judges of the Supreme Court to hold one ch. Co: every 6 m°. in each—This was yesterday objected to upon its *first* passage and should I judge from the spirit evinced by the House at that time it will probably meet its fate without ever leaving the walls of the Commons Hall.—The Presidential election seems to agitate the whole representation and should any man unacquainted with the forms & principles of our government visit Raleigh at this time he would readily conclude that North Caro: or its Legislature had the power as well as the right to confer this distinguishing office upon whom she might please.—The friends of each gentleman now before the public are ready to catch at any thing as a indication that their favorite is at the top of the wheel.—You know I am not friendly to Mr. Crawford's election—yet I am firmly persuaded so far as I can judge that he has a very decided majority in our Legislature—what may be the sentiments of North Caro: at large *no man can tell.*—You are aware that according to our mode of selecting Electors by *general Ticket* that one half the people—aye two thirds either feel too little interest to visit the polls at all or else do not understand what they do in voting for a list which may be handed them.—

My favorite Candidate (*Gen¹ Jackson*) seems to be lost sight of in most parts of the Country—yet I must hope for better things before the time arrives for a settlement of this great question—It is humbling to every honest american Citizen to read the scandalous production of our newspapers thro: the country whose main object seems to be to detract & defame— what must be the impression produced upon the minds of foreign nation?

Indeed all the prominent men of our Country are represented in as dark shades as the true character of most of the crowned heads of Europe would now well bear—But I promised in the outset to confine myself to domestic concerns.—

Yesterday Mr. Alston's[76] proposition before the H. of C. to

---

[76]Willis Alston, 1770-1837, a Jeffersonian from Halifax County, who in the Federalist Period lined up with such Republicans as Willie Jones and Nathaniel Macon. He was for the War of 1812 and the Nationalists' program in the years which followed. He retired from public life until 1819 when he was elected to the state legislature where he served in 1819, 1821, and 1823 to 1824. He was in Congress from 1825 to 1831. Ashe, *Biog. Hist. of N. C.,* VI, 1-5.

compel the Banks upon a refusal to pay spe*cie* to pay *12½ per c't* per annum from the demand was rejected by a majority of 9 or 10 votes—We had some sharp talks which Mr Gales will probably give us in his paper shortly since he was there taking them down.—There is a little County Court Lawyer here from the Town of Halifax—*Bynum,*[77] who is nothing but food for Stanly's[78] wit & sarcasm—very much to the amusement of the House and spectators.—

There are no other measures of general importance at this time recollected now before the House—Mr [torn]M t[79] Rockingham without previous concert or without consent of the friends of Convention introduced some resolution on that subject in the early part of the session but they are not to be called up as I understand.—

If you have learned it I should feel somewhat grateful to learn the views of our new Senator on the Presidential question—I mean Gov'r Branch.[80]—

I spoke to you on the subject of having a law passed for transcribing the Records of the Circuit Court of U S. for this district—Since then in searching over my Books I find it will be unnecessary as I have them complete up to this date.—

Your friends and family I learn are all well and in haste I am truly yours

Will H. H. Jr.

[Addressed:]

> The Hon:
> Willie P. Mangum
> House of Representatives
> Washington City,
> D. C.

Free.

---

[77]Jesse Atherton Bynum, 1797-1868, was a member of the state legislature from 1823 to 1824 and from 1827 to 1834, and the national House of Representatives from 1833 to 1841. He was a planter who later moved to Alexandria, La. *Biog. Dir. of Cong.*, 772.

[78]John Stanley of New Bern, 1774-1834, was an attorney who served in the legislature from 1798 to 1799, 1812 to 1815, 1818 to 1819, and 1823 to 1827. He was speaker of the House of Commons from 1825 to 1827, and was in Congress from 1801 to 1803 and 1809 to 1811. *Biog. Dir. of Cong.*, 1560; *N. C. Manual*, 467, 567-568.

[79]Robert Martin, who was in the legislature from 1822 to 1825 and 1829 to 1834, introduced a resolution proposing a bill to take a poll of people on a constitutional convention. The resolution was printed but no other action was taken. *Journal of the House of Commons, 1823*, 128.

[80]Governor John Branch.

P. S.

Be good enough to deliver this letter for me and take a rec't and send me for the ans^r enclosed in it—I send to you that I may be able to get a rec't

W H H Jr

Mr. Mangum[81]—
H.R.—

Mr. and Mrs. Adams request the favor of
Mr. Mangum's—
Company, on Thursday Evening, the 8th of
January, 1824
22d December, 1923.

WPM-LC

James Mebane to Willie P. Mangum

RALEIGH December 24th. 1823

Dear Sir

On looking over the national inteligencer of the 19th instant I observed a resolution introduced by Mr. Moore[82] of Kentucky directing the committee on private land claims to inquire into the expediency of Granting the bounty land to Thomas Pendergrass, the representative of James Albert deceased, &c. This Sir is the land for which Mary Albert of Orange County the Mother of said James has applied to the war department, & Pendergrass can not by any means be his legal representative, Albert was an illegitimate child of Mary Albert & Pendergrass his reputed father, You know something of the Pendergrass, & will no doubt be willing to believe that the will by the authority of which he drew Alberts pay, might have been [deserving] at least some suspicion as to its fairness—I have no doubt but you have noticed this resolution, but not having very much to do this morning, I thought I would call your attention to it—Nothing important has occurred since my last. It is said the friends

---

[81]The original is in the possession of Mr. Mangum Turner, Winston-Salem, N. C.
[82]Thomas Patrick Moore, 1797-1853, a native of Virginia, served in Congress from Kentucky as a Democrat from 1823 to 1829. He was minister to Colombia from 1829 to 1833, and a lieutenant-colonel in the Mexican War. *Biog. Dir. of Cong.*, 1330.

of Mr. Crawford will assemble to night & make out an electoral ticket.[83]—I think we shall not leave this place before the first of January I remain respectfully

Yours &c.
JAMES MEBANE

[Addressed:]

Wiley P. Mangum Esqr
member of Congress
Washington City

1824

WPM-LC

Samuel Hillman to Willie P. Mangum

OXFORD N. C. 2^d. January 1824

Dear Judge,

I will be obliged to you if you purchase me a Ticket in the Grand Maryland State Lottery at Cohen's Office[1]—Please forward it by return Mail—I am in great haste very respectfully your obt. hum¹. servant—

SAMUEL HILLMAN

Hon¹. Willie P. Mangum—

[Addressed:]

Hon¹. Willie P. Mangum
of the House of Representatives
Washington City

WPM-LC

P. H. Mangum to Willie P. Mangum

HILLSBORO, January 4th 1824.—

Dear Sir,

I have in vain expected a letter from you for the last several mails—your engagements at Washington City & your other

---

[83]On December 24, 1823, in response to notices posted on the doors of both houses of the legislature, Crawford's supporters met and selected their electors. Newsome, *Election of 1824,* 73-74.

[1]J. L. Cohen, Jr., & Bros., Lottery Brokers of Baltimore. In North Carolina this was a popular brokerage firm. Archibald D. Murphey bought lottery through this firm. Hoyt, *Papers of Murphey,* I, 326n.

many correspondents, I suppose, must be your apology.—

The political news of the State you have had as good an opportunity of knowing, as I possess. Our Gen¹. Assembly has done nothing, in the way of legislation, of much importance: the valuable business was rejected as usual.—Mr. Yancy² on his return informed me, that Crawford was much the strongest in the Legislature—that he had a handsome majority over the aggregate interest of all the other candedates,—the miserable misrepresentations of the Star paper to the contrary notwithstanding.

Mr. Scott³ requested me to inform you that you should have your eyes open; that some of Calhoun's friends about Raleigh, & Doc. *Baggs* is one I believe, are busy in proclaiming that you and Gov: Branch are deserting Crawford's interest,⁴ & fleeing to the banners of Mr. Calhoun. I don't believe it—for most certainly you stand pledged in the opinion of the public, to Crawford—& I think that unless an especial inquiry were likely to result from your adherence to Crawford, you would not be so unwise or so unstable as deservedly to incurr the imputations of political inconsistency—& that too, on a subject upon which every inteligent man ought to have formed an opinion.—

I am at length enabled & *authorized* to acquaint you with the issue of my courtship. Miss Rebecca⁵ and I are to be married—the particular time not fixed, but some time this Winter. As the least evil among many, I have contracted to purchase Womack's House & Lot without Town, at $2000.—by substituting paper in the Hillsboro & State banks, $1000. in each. Enclosed you will receive two bonds to each of which I wish you to put your name. Mr. Cain⁶ voluntarily offered to do the same.

I would have rented in preference to buying—but could not get a House that I would carry a decent Woman to. I could not do better. Circumstances require that we should get married shortly—& to go to house keeping directly thereafter. In a few days I shall go down to fix upon the day.—Will you return the bonds immediately—I am not to deposit them before our County Court.

---

²Bartlett Yancey.
³John Scott.
⁴In his campaign for election to Congress in 1823, Mangum made it plain that he was for Crawford. Most North Carolina congressmen were of the same opinion. In the winter of 1823-1824, a false rumor spread that Mangum was becoming lukewarm toward Crawford. The fact is he supported Crawford to the end even after he learned that the sentiment in the state had turned to Jackson. McDuffie, "Willie P. Mangum," 27-29; Newsome, *Election of 1824*, 170.
⁵Rebecca Sutherland, youngest daughter of Col. Ransom Sutherland.
⁶William Cain, Sr., whose daughter Mary married Rebecca Sutherland's brother, Solomon.

Danl. Jones[7] says that poor Mr. Hillman[8] *is killed.* He however, has some consolation that of having companions in his
wretchedness.—

I want you to write me at length.—Charity is in common
health & the rest of your friends are well.

Your absence I feel at this moment, very severely. The many
difficulties in the way of furnishing a house, I shall endeaver to
procure what is necessary; only I fear will be a source of vexa-
tion & perhaps unnecessary delay. Were you at home, when I get
married, I could be with you—However M[r]. Cain Junr has
kindly offered his house as a substitute.—

Yrs *P. H. MANGUM*

P. S. Jno. Taylor Junr.[9] has been expecting a letter from you &
begins to complain—His situation is delicate, & little will induce
him to consider himself neglected. You have inspired him with
hopes of an appointment under the Genl. Government: be they
vain or not, you would do well to let him speedily know by letter.—You know his situation.—

P. H. M.

[Addressed:]

The Hombl.
Willie P. Mangum
Washington City,
D. C.

Hillsboro
Jan 5

Free

WPM-LC

Beverly Daniel[10] to Willie P. Mangum

RALEIGH January 6 1824

Dear Sir

If you can spare a few moments I should like to know how
things are working in relation to the pending election of President—what scale is going up and what scale is going down?—

---

[7]Daniel Jones was a member of the legislature from Granville County in 1810 to 1811, 1814 to 1816, and 1818 to 1819. *N. C. Manual,* 622.
[8]Samuel Hillman was probably defeated for political office.
[9]Probably clerk of Orange County Court. Grant, *Alumni Hist. of U. N. C.,* 610.
[10]General Beverly Daniel, 1777-1840, of Raleigh for many years was a United States mar-
shall and adjutant general of North Carolina. He was also the first president of the North Carolina Jockey Club. Johnson, *Ante-Bellum N. C.,* 183; Hamilton, *Papers of Ruffin,* I, 481; *Hillsboro Recorder,* Sept. 24, 1840.

William Preston Mangum (only son of Willie P. and Charity A. Mangum, 1837-1861), Second Lieutenant, Sixth North Carolina Regiment, Confederate States Army. From a daguerreotype made in 1861 and now in the possession of Miss Sallie Preston Weeks of Washington, District of Columbia.

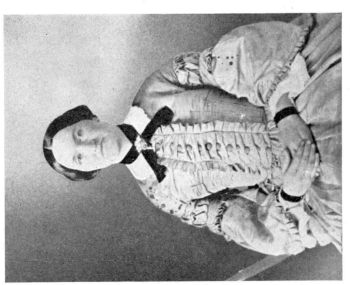

Sallie Alston Mangum (married Col. M. W. Leach), eldest daughter of Willie P. and Charity A. Mangum, 1824-1896. From a daguerreotype made in her twenties and now in the possession of Miss Sallie Preston Weeks of Washington, District of Columbia.

Who ever may be chosen, I hope the following subjects will constitute the most prominent points in his administration—a strict accountability of the Public Funds—Adequate Military works for the defence of the exposed Points of our country— The connection of the Eastern & Western waters, by canal navigation, as being essential to defence of the country, and Union of the States—The continuation of the present system for increasing our Navy—A sufficient Peace establishment. to keep up our Military Works, at least., finally—*May God* enable him to save the *Military Academy* from the hands of the *Radicals*— (I mean those, and such as those who made a bold stroke last session at its existence)

I will take this occasion to call your attention to a subject of minor importance which nevertheless is worthy in my opinion of the notice of Congress—The case is simply this—there is attached to the Military Academy at this time a Band of Music. corresponding with the high character of the Institution, which is partly supported out of the pockets of the cadets—each cadets suffers 25 cts a month to be retained out of his pay for this object, raising in this way $750 annually—Don't you think the Government had better increase the pay of musicians to this amount annually; which would supersede, the necessity of the students making up deficiencies of the Government in relation to the support of the Institution in what is deemed essential to the character & interest

I shall be happy to hear from you when convenient—Our Legislature being over, we have nothing here worth relating— The friends of the different Presidential candidates, continue firm—The matter I I[*sic*] apprehend is not to be easily settled— feelings are too deeply rooted in the subject generally—the strongest prejudices have been provoked and the excitment consequently will not very readily subside

I am very respectfully Sir

Your obed & hb Servant

BEV. DANIEL

The Honble
    W. P. Mangum
[Addressed:]
        The Honorble
           W. P. Mangum
           House of Representatives,
             Washington

6

WPM-LC

H. B. Bunyan to W. P. Mangum

the 6
ORANGE C—N C Jan 4 182
[6 Jan., 1824]

Mr
    W. P. Mangrim Sir   these fu lines With Whot are Inclosed
Will give You to understand how Capt. O W Callis has Cheteed
or trided to Chet Me oute of my land wich I sarved My Cuntry
for five years and almost six months, I *inlisted* in Lewisburg
North Carolina in June the 12, 1812 and Was Discharged in 1817
on the banks off Allebam,, Campe. Mounte pellym And was
drafted in 5 months after—Fight the Siminolans, and in 1818 I
started for N C and pasing by Fort Hawkins, I Met With Capt
O W ,, Callis who told me he would Take my Discharge and
obtain My Land Wornt. wiCh I then left in His hands but have
never yet obtained. Wone sent for. tho I have sent for it By
W. P. Bowans Esqr oxford in Granvill C° N. C. sir by Reeding
the Letter Dayhted Dezem the 28 1818 you will find that he
obtained My land wornte with a very Laffull Charge wiCh I
never heard From him. but I sent him the Full amount of his
Charge by Wm. Bowans Esqs and then he sase he does not
[know] Whot [h]as become of My Land wront. you will Please
to do whot you can for A poor unfortenate soldier And send it
on to CoChtans store And oblige your Friend and I shall Ever
Remane your friend &C

H. B. BUNYAN

    to
W. P. Mangrim Esqe

[Addressed:]

Mr. Willie P. Mangrum
Washington City

Endorsed: Land Warrant N°. *19, 251 iss*^d. for information respecting the *Patent* or *a Copy* of one application to be made to
the Commisⁿ— of the Genl. L. Office 18 Mar 1826

WPM-LC

Seth Jones to W. P. Mangum

RALEIGH 7th. January 1824

Dear Sir,

I have this day had the pleasure to receive the bundle sent to me by you containing Public Documents. We have nothing new in this part of the country except that it is reported in the city of Raleigh that you have changed your opinion for President; I know very well that when you were electioneering you said you would not pledge yourself to vote for Mr. Crawford that you would have yourself at liberty if you saw cause to change your mind to vote for some other person—I should like (as your friend) to know if you have changed your mind & if so your reasons, & who you are for now &C.

I remain as I ever hope
to do   Your friend

SETH JONES

Hon. W. P. Mangum

[Addressed:]

Honbl. Willie P. Mangum Esqr—
Washington City.

WPM-LC

Thomas D. Bennehan to Willie P. Mangum

STAGVILLE 11th January 1824

Dear Sir

Your favour of the 20th of Decemr. only reached me the mail before the last, and I should have replied immediately to it, but wished to have some conversation with Mr. Cameron[11] before doing so—

I am affraid from there being so large a deficit against N. Carolina in the Gen. Post office the last year, you will meet with some difficulty in geting the new Post line established established [sic] from Raleigh to Person, since the receipt of your letter it

---
[11] Duncan Cameron.

has occured to me, & on consulting with Mr. Cameron & others,
that you might effect the object we had in view in this way, Drop
so much of the present line from Raleigh by Oxford to Hillsborough, as from Oxford to Hillsbor°, there is no Post office between Oxford & Hillsbo° but at this place, & so fare as I have
any knowledge is there any person that feels and interest in the
rout but ourselve's in this part of the line (say from Oxford to
Hillsbo°) those place's will still have two mean's of communication by Raleigh & by Person C. Houses, in the place of this
line, let there be one established to leave Raleigh say on Saturday morning after the arrival of the Northern mail, by Joseph
Brasfields,[12] then to Fish Dam, from there crossing Enoe
[River] at my mills on the Bridges, (we all object to its going
up to Sime's [Sym's] mill a's the mail would be frequently
lost by not being able to cross Eno & Little River's) to Stagville, so on to Gen¹. Carrington's Mount Terza & Roxborough at
Stagville we should be as well off as we are at present in having a mail once a week, you will have an office at Carrington's,
& the Fish Dam people will be accommodated, the difference in
distance between Oxford & Hillsborough, & Raleigh & Roxborough you will recollect is only a few miles & I have no hesitation in saying that it will produce to the Government (say the
new line as I propose) at least ten times as much even more,
than the present line, which must be almost a dead expence to
the Government and it will be a great accommodation to a large
& respectable portion of our District, Gen¹. Carrington,[13] Co¹.
Thorpe[14] & Mr Yarbrough,[15] have all Petision's for this new line
& they shall be forwarded to you as soon as practicable. You
will observe that it is important that Saturday morning after
the arrival of the Northern mail should be fixed as the time for
the departure of the new line from Raleigh, as it will give the
Northern paper's of a late date, & I have no hesitation in saying that the new line will scarcely cost the government a Dollar
more than that we propose to abandon, but you have a perfect
knowledge of the country & it is all submited to your better
judgment, I have only stated to you what has occured to u's—

---

[12]Many of the places mentioned in this letter may be located on the map, p. 223, of this volume. Brasfield's was a store northwest of Raleigh in Wake County. Fish Dam was a post office where the Eno River flows into the Neuse River. Sym's Mill was near Mangum's home in what is today Durham County. Mount Tirzah was near Mangum's home. Philip Moore was postmaster. It was near the present hamlet of Timberlake in Person County.
[13]John Carrington.
[14]Col. W. A. Tharpe.
[15]Sam Yarborough.

It affords me much pleasure to say to you that I a few day's since understood that Mrs. Mangum[16] had a fine Daughter & as the *old saying* is, is herself doing as well as could be expected, a report has also reached me that your Brother is soon to be married to Miss Southerland of Wake, I congratulate you also on his forming so respectable a connection, though I have not the pleasure of an acquaintance with this young Lady, I have heard her spoken of in the highest term's, but I have no doubt of all those matters, you have much better information than I can give you—

I have nothing new to communicate to you, our immediate section of country is blesed with good health, my Father whose health is only tolerable, desire's me to present to you his best wishes, & to thank you for the Pamphlet that you forwarded to him, M^r. Yarbrough desire's his best respects to you, it will afford me much pleasure to hear from you, Believe me to be with much regard & esteem

Dear Sir
Your's Sincerely

THO^s. D BENNEHAN

Willie P. Mangum Esq.

[Addressed:]

The Honble.
Willie P. Mangum
Washington City

WPM-LC

Jno. J. Carrington to Willie P. Mangum

ORANGE N^o. Ca. 12th. January 1824.
Dear Sir, I have expected before this to have heard from You, but I freely excuse You, as You have probably to write to so many, & Your knowing that I cou'd see by the papers the most that was doing in Congress—I have nothing of importance to write to You, Our neighborhood is quite healthy, no person dead since You left home & but few married, I must congratulate you, with Your fine daughter, which I expect You have received intel-

[16]Mangum's first child, Sallie Alston Mangum (1824-1896), who later married Col. Martin W. Leach, was born Jan. 6, 1824.

ligence of, before this reach's You,—I will now turn to the subject that induced me to write this letter, that is respecting a mail rout through our section of the country—I expect You recollect our chat upon that subject,—I really think there might be a rout established from Raleigh to Person court house, that wou'd be of advantage to the General Government, Say from Raleigh to the Fish Dam, to Staggville, on by my house to L. V. Hargis's[17] & on to Roxborough—The mail might be carried very low, the distance would only be 48 miles Col. Thorpe thinks that if a rout of that kind was established, there wou'd be immense persons that wou'd take the papers in his neighborhood that doe's not, Staggville being the nearest officc to him—in our neighborhood there wou'd be a great many subscribers and in the neighborhod of L. V. Hargis' we might reasonably expect a vast number of subscribers as it is Generally a neighborhood of good livers—From Roxborough to Staggville there is no post office (a distance of 24 miles)—When the Stage Rout from Oxford to Milton was established the Mount Tirzah post office was dispensed with—There is the Moore[18] family that formerly took papers more or less they now do not, because of no post office within their reach—I really think it is a grievance and I sincerely think that we might petition as such,—In the way spoken of—there wou'd be no impediment whatever respecting water courses as You well know that there is good bridges across all the streams of any size.—Some people think that a Rout from Oxford to Hillsboro. wou'd answer a good purpose by the way of Gooch's Bridge & our neighborhood by Jamieson's You know the Routs as well as myself.—Therefore I cou'd not instruct You on that point,—But I think that the rout last spoken of wou'd be an expense to the Government & the other wou'd be of Profit—However I shou'd like very muct to have a Rout either way, For I am very fond of reading the papers, But when I dont get them for two or three weeks, & then they come sometimes not all, & some times all in a lump they are of but little satisfaction, And to Send 8 or 10 miles & then upon an uncertainty is rather to severe,—I think it is a duty You owe our Section of the country to use Your best endeavours to procure us a rout in some way—Your knowing the situation of the country so well You can point out to the post master General,

[17]A large planter of Person County who lived at Point Pleasant. Johnson, *Ante-Bellum N. C.*, 535-536.
[18]Philip Moore became postmaster at Mount Tirzah. He was a large planter who kept a country store and had an overseer. Johnson, *Ante-Bellum N. C.*, 490-491.

the necessity of the rout, And the great disadvantage we labour
under,—Sir I saw & read a letter From You to Judge Cameron
written in some short time after You reach'd the Federal city,—
in which letter, You said a good deal about the Presidential
Election—and I thought You appeared something wandering &
did not know well which side to take, this is only an conjecture
of my own, & I did not even say to Mr. Cameron what I thought,
—I only slightly read the letter over once, I might have mistaken Your meaning—But you must recollect Your open declaration at Roxbor°. when You told the people that notwithstanding the Electorial Colledge of North Carolina might Give
to some other man besides Crawford their votes, You wou'd not
if You had a vote, vote any other way than for Crawford,—I
dont write this to You, because I am a sticler to Mr. Crawford's
election, for If you will recollect that I have always told You
that I was not in favour of his Election,—I am no friend to the
Tariff bill, say (the protection of the) northern or southern
manufactures farther than is right, but I am & always have
been decidedly in favour of John Q. Adams—I plainly see that
there is no chance for him to be elected,—next to him I wou'd
prefer Crawford or Calhoun & I have but little choice between
them—The representation from our county in the last Legislature were divided, Messrs Clancy[19] & McCauley[20] were in favour
of Crawford & attended the caucus in Raleigh when Crawford's
friends met,—Mr. Mebane[21] is in favour of Adam's Mr. Cameron
dont say who he is in favour of—but did not attend the meeting
of Crawfords friends—I have no more nonsense at present to
write You, therefore will content myself by subscribing myself
Yours respectfully
JNO. J. CARRINGTON

WPM-LC
Michael Holt[22] to W. P. Mangum

January 16 1824 (ORANGE N C)

Respected Sir
The subject of our proposed new constitution is for the
present at rest, but will no doubt come upon the carpet again

---

[19]Thomas Clancy.
[20]William McCauley.
[21]James Mebane.
[22]Michael Holt, 1778-1842, who lived near Allbright in Orange, was in the legislature in
1804, 1820, and 1821. He was a leader for education and internal improvements. Ashe. *Biog.
Hist. of N. C.*, VII, 168.

at the breaking up of the Ice in the Spring—all still nothing stirring untill a few days past, The subject of post roads, post routes, and post offices, how it came to be a subject before the people I no not, for I was absent from Home near Three weeks, on a trip to Virginia, trudgeing through the mud with my crop of tobacco & cotton, performing this trip & the prepareing the same for the trip confined me from the time of my return from Raleigh untill the 27th of December, and from that time to the present I have been much engaged in the selling of my Brother Isaac's,[23] store goods and the whole management of his estate as agent for his representatives

having to transact business with many persons during this time and hereing different talks and remarks upon the subject, I have with the assistamce of Dr. A. Brown, (who is a young Gentleman of a fine mind and much esteemed by all who are acquainted with him, and has the confidence of people here and has a very fine practice as a Physician) digested a rout for a Horse mail to commence at Hillsboro, to David Mebanes,[24] thence to Haw river, thence to my House by Albright's if you choose, thence to John Longs then to Julens in Randolph Cty from Julens to Dr. Worths in Guilford Cty thence to Hunts at Springfield thence to Brumwells Davidson Cty thence to Caldcleughs thence to Lexington (Davidson county court House) once a week The distance is about ninety miles, and I expect the rout could be performed at an expence of from 450 to 500 P. annum—This rout will pass through very welthy settlements and if not at present be sufficient to support itself I think it will in a few years, and will supply places that now are, and embrace others that are entirely neglected, by making some alterations in two other routes, to wit, The mail stage to keep in the Trolinger road through out the country, say from Mason-Hall Mason-Hall [sic] to Trolingers Bridge, to Peter L. Rays thence to the Allemance (Dicks) this change would give news to the rich settlement of Back Creek & Stoney Creek.

I will refer you to the Hon¹. John Long who is well acquainted with the growing wealth & inhabitants of the Allemance and Stinking-quarter, and those in Randolph & Davidson Julens Dr. Worths Springfield & thence to Lexington, I at present know no Post office being neglected but John Newlens, let the mail that

---

[23]Isaac Holt died in 1823. Ashe, Biog. Hist. of N. C., VII, 167.
[24]Most of these places may be located on Wm. L. Spoon's Map of Alamance County, 1893, and the Rural Free Delivery Maps of Davidson and Guilford counties. These maps are available in the North Carolina Room at the University of North Carolina.

runs from Chapel Hill stop at John Newlins and return some
other way, say by Pittsboro or otherwise as you may think
proper—and the same contract that commences at Chappell-Hill
aught to be so changed as to set out from Hillsboro. as above
suggested, I cant discover of any inconvenience by this alteration, only that from Chappell Hill to John Newlins, and should
needs require it let Their be a short rout to extend from Chap-
pel-Hill to said Newlins and I do not know at present of any
other objection, for my new proposed rout will fall in the same
at John Longs and from Longs to Lexington M^r. Long may direct
as he thinks most convenient,—you will take notice my proposed
plan will have a double advantage than the present from Chap-
pel-Hill to Longs, I do not know how many places the mail stops
between the two latter places, but I expect at Clanceys Store &
at John Newlens, from Hillsboro. D^d. Mebanes Hawriver—(you
may say Albrights if you choose, but should their be an office
at Peter Ray's it will be needless,) Haw-river to Holts thence to
Longs. The mail stage will swoop Haw-river for Trolengers &
Albrights for Rays—

Thus sir I have given my views upon the subject by several
repetitions so as you may understand my plan and should you
effect this my wishes, you will do more good and please more citizens than has been done in that way, perhaps in Twenty years,
I need not repeat to you the growing welth & increase of population of all this rout in Orange County, and sir you may add another office, instead of Albrights say William Holts esq. and will
answer every purpose in that neighborhood &c

I will add sir that we have the finest winter I have ever seen,
rather warm for cureing Bacon or rather saving Porke, what
little we have—our little Towns are not yet supplied, and even
many farmers have been looking out for Tennessee Porke, and
no appearance as yet, our acquaintancies at Chapel-Hill & Hillsboro. have, as I have been informed, employed Wm. Adams[25] to
go down into Wayn & Lenoar Countys to purchase their porke,
our country at this time is quite Helthy—with great respect
Ys &c

Honl. Willie P. Mangum   Mich^l. Holt
[Addressed:]

      Honl. Wilie P. Mangum
)   Member of Congress now
Mail)   at Washington City

---

[25]Probably Wm. H. Adams, the police commissioner of Hillsboro.

W. P. Mangum to Thomas Ruffin[26]

WASHINGTON CITY January 20th 1824.

My Dear Sir

I was surprised & indeed mortified to see announced in the Star yesterday that our friend Mr. James Mebane had consented to hold a poll for one of the electors to support the election of Mr. Calhoun.—I was mortified, because the contest will inevitably destroy that harmony which is so desirable in the county, and impair that good understanding which it has been my pleasure to cultivate between him & my friends.—

I have written to Mr. Mebane[27] at great length on the Presidential election two or three times, and laboured to convince him that whatever might be the success of Mr. Calhoun in North Carolina, that he stands no chance of ultimate success, and that division in the South will very probably secure the election of Mr. Clay.

I regret to see Mr. Mebane made the organ through which that party will express their opinions, and to see him with his personal & deserved popularity endeavouring to sustain a cause that cannot but be hopeless.

The result will impair the usefulness of that very excellent man, without a prospect of advancing essentially the interests of his favorite candidate—I still hope that he will decline, and open the way to a gentleman who is ever ready to occupy the breach not where iminent perils are to be encountered but where popular favour can be wooed.—Touching the result, everything is in doubt & uncertainty. — That Mr. Crawford is intrinsically stronger & considerably stronger than either of the candidates cannot be questioned—But that Mr. Calhoun cannot succeed I take to be equally certain—Mr. Adams is evidently on the decline. His best friends abate in their ardour, believing I presume that he cannot be carried through—Gen. Jackson is more caressed here than all them—& is rapidly gaining ground, & could without doubt get Pennsylvania, if she did not think her vote would be thrown away—

You have seen that a convention will be held in Pennsylvania,[28] with the view of designating a ticket. It is believed here that her object is to gain time, watch the progress of events & ultimately

---

[26]The original is in the Thomas Ruffin Papers, Southern Collection, University of North Carolina. This letter has been previously published in Hamilton, *Ruffin Papers*, I, 287-288.
[27]See above, p. 56n.
[28]He refers to the Harrisburg state convention which met March 4, 1824, and nominated Jackson.

throw her strength in favour of the rising candidate—It is believed that both New York & Pennsylvania will make it a point not to be in the minority of the General Government, and therefore I presume that any calculations at this time could not be satisfactorily relied on—If the election shall come to the House of Reps. I assure you that Mr. Clay will be a dangerous Competitor—

Since my arrival at Washington I have become more & more confirmed in the belief that the best interests of this nation require the elevation of Mr. Crawford to the Executive Chair.

You have observed the direction & progress of the present Administration and it seems to me that it cannot be doubted that the present fashionable ultra republicans have gone mad further than the sound Federalists of the old school—& that Mr. Calhoun is at the head of the new school cannot be questioned—I do not believe that there is any intelligent Federalist in No.Ca. that upon his own principles can keep pace with the new school republicans.—The new school has taken the principles of the old Federalists but press their principles much further I mean on the subjects of internal improvement etc., and especially in a latitudinous construction of the constitution generally—

Mr. Macon informs me that even Rufus King told him that he was alarmed at the extent to which the new school were going, and that it had put him upon a reexamination of long established opinions. Mr. Webster yesterday occupied the house 2 or 3 hours on his resolution.[29] The topic would seem to be barren, but he made it most interesting, & it is said that a more able speech has not been made in some years, in the House on the policy & views of the Holy Alliance he was most powerful—& indeed of the great men here he is the only one, that in debate has yet manifested all the strength that I had attributed to him. You know that as a popular speaker Mr. Clay is perhaps unrivalled—Their excellence as you also know is very different in its kind—

Mr. Crawford is still very ill, & has been constantly confined to his chamber since the meeting of Congress—He is now confined in a dark room on account of the inflamation of his eyes. It was thought at one time that he would lose his sight. But at this time no doubts are entertained of his recovery—he amends but slowly, tho surely—

---

[29] See above, p. 84n.

Be pleased to present my respects to Mrs. Ruffin, Mr. & Mrs. Cain and accept for yourself assurances of my high respect.

W. P. MANGUM

Thos. Ruffin Esq.

———

WPM-LC

John Barnett³⁰ to Willie P. Mangum

PERSON 23rd. Jany 1824

Dear Sir,

I have not had it in my power to comply with your Request Sooner But I do herewith transmit you a list I will commence by Captains Companes [Companies] commencing on the north Side of the county first for the post office at Cuningham Store you will corraspond with Thomas McGehee Col. Obdiah Faulker [Falker] Joel Newman James McGehee John Garner (Richard Halliburton Robert Jones Esq pay particular attention to Robert Jones Richard Carnal & David Hemphill To Williamsville) P. office Isham Edwards Capt Edmund Dickson & Sons Capt Charles Sallard Lofton Walton George W Jeffreys Hugh Woods —William L. Allen Esq (William & John Baily to Roxborough) John & James Halwey James Patterson Stephen Jones John Halliburton Thomas Halliburton Esq James King Robert Gill & sons Robert Harris & Sons William Yarbrough Esq Ira Lea & James Dollarhide Kindal Vanhook Vincent & George Lea To Cochrans Store Nathaniel Toryan[?] Robert D Wade John Russel Lemuel Rainey David Hunt George Briggs. Nathaniel Norfleet To Roxborough John Lawson Senr. Robert Brooks Thomas Lawson I leave out a Great many as I know you are well acquainted With them and Know Where they live as Well as I do. I Mean those Who Reside in Capt Sweeneys Company.

I am Respectfully

JOHN BARNETT

Mr Willie P Mangum

[Addressed:]

Willie P. Mangum Esq
Washington City

———

³⁰Sheriff of Person County for many years and state senator in 1836-1837. *Journal of Senate of N. C., 1825-1826,* 90; *N. C. Laws, 1824* and *1831,* appendix; *N. C. Manual,* 758.

WPM-LC
Will. Polk³¹ to Willie P. Mangum

RALEIGH Jany 26th, 1824

Dear Sir.

You are no doubt in possession of much of the acts and doings of the congregated wisdom of the State at their late session; as well from the public prints as from your numerous correspondents—The Presidential question occupied no little of the time and talents of the partizans of Crawford & Calhoun; who were surely the most prominent of all the Candidates for that office in No. Carolina; yet Genl. Jackson had his friends, tho' few in number in comparison with the other two aspirants—I think the number attached to each in the Legislature might be fairly stated; for Crawford from 90 to 100 Calhoun 50 to 65. Jackson 20 to 30.³² There were however some measures taken by the friends of Old Hickory at a late period of the Session to bring him more at large before the public by disemnating sundry pamphlets throughout the State favourable to his pretensions — I think an effect beyond calculation has evidently shown in many sections of the State; particularly to the West in favor of Jackson—I am well aware that you were & may yet be the friend of Mr. Crawford; but I am nevertheless sure that you will not hesitate to give as well to me as to others who may request it of you; what are the standing and expectations of the several candidates.—what *probable* calculations are made with regard to each in the several States and the final result.

For my *own* part I declare to you, that I would be content with either of the Gentlemen—they are all good Democrats I suppose of the Jeffersonian school; from whom I have nothing to hope nor fear, with all; I have a personal acquaintance; not an intimate one; and can come to the poll with as few prejudices or partialities as most voters; yet I have taken Jacksons side and will promote his election; not through *thick* & *thin*, but fairly and honestly.

I wish you would speak freely to me on this subject—I dont wish, nor will I throw away either my vote or my influence; upon a shadow—

³¹Col. William Polk was a trustee of the state university, an ex-colonel of the Revolution, and president of the state bank from 1811 to 1819. A close friend of Major W. B. Lewis of Tennessee, he led the North Carolina forces for Andrew Jackson in 1824. Newsome, *Election of 1824*, 87; Ashe, *Biog. Hist. of N. C.*, II, 361-369.
³²Will H. Haywood estimated Crawford had a decided majority. The Milton *Gazette* estimated from 115 to 120 were for Crawford. Newsome concludes that 77 was a fair estimate. Newsome, *Election of 1824*, 87.

This is the first sheding of ink, I have made to any of the representation from this State in Congress on this, or any other subject; and avail myself in doing so to you from a belief; that what I have said will be received in the same spirit of good will and candour in which it is given.

> I am Dr Sir
>> With much respect
> Yr Mo Obt
>> WILL. POLK

[Addressed:]

> Honbl. Willie P. Mangum
> Washington City

WPM-LC

Dennis Heartt[33] to Willie P. Mangum

HILLSBOROUGH Jan. 31, 1824.

Sir,

I have enclosed an account between Messrs. Gales & Seaton[34] and myself, to whom a balance is due of $9.50. If not inconvenient, you will confer upon me a favour, if you would pay them this balance, and place it to my account.

You must not forget your promise to furnish me with such scraps of information as may fall within your observation, and which will be interesting to the readers of a newspaper in this district. Other printers frequently grace their columns with an "extract of a letter from a member of congress" &c. but mine have been but once so ornamented, though four years have passed since I commenced printing here. Though we do not both support the same candidate for president, though we differ in opinion as to the necessity or propriety of a caucus, and though I cannot surrender to you and those of your side of the question the *exclusive* privilege of retaining the title of republicans; yet I should like to know how these thing[s] go on at Washington. The accounts given in the papers are too contradictory to enable

----

[33]For many years Dennis Heartt was editor of the *Hillsborough Recorder*. Born in Connecticut in 1783 and son of a sea captain, he became an apprentice to a printer in New Haven until he moved to Philadelphia in 1802 where he soon established the *Philadelphia Repertory*. In 1820 he established the *Hillsborough Recorder* which he edited until 1869. He supported Adams in 1824. With the rise of the Whig Party he became a staunch supporter of its cause. He was usually a supporter of Mangum. W. K. Boyd, "Dennis Heartt," *Trinity College Historical Society Papers*, II, 34-43.

[34]Editor of *National Intelligencer*.

us at this distance to come at the truth. Mr. Jefferson, in his inaugural speech, said "we are all federalists, we are all republicans." This expression, in the view of some men at that stormy period, involved a contradiction; but it was, even to the most biggoted a paradox of much easier solution than the various newspaper accounts of parties of the present day. This variance does not exist alone in the complexion of the parties; but the supporters of Mr. Crawford, Mr. Calhoun, Mr. Adams, Mr. Clay and even of Gen. Jackson, do not fail to give to each of their favorites overwhelming majorities. This diversity of opinion, however, need not alarm the friends of the country; it flows from the freedom of our institutions. These candidates are all good, posessed of exalted talents; and we should rejoice that we have so many worthy of so high an office. It is only necessary to give utterance to the voice of the people, by passing the resolutions which you have before you, so to amend the constitution of the United States as to produce an uniform mode of electing electors of president and vice-president, *by districts,* and the country will be safe. Factions may then rage, and ambitions intriegue for power; but the vote of state will not be bartered for office, nor the liberties of the people be trampled upon.

I am, very respectfully,
Sir, yours, &c.
DENNIS HEARTT

[Addressed:]

Hon. W. P. Mangum,
Washington City.

WPM-LC

Jas. C. Manghum to Willie P. Mangum

BRUNSWICK 31st Jan 1824

D^r— Sir   I duly recd your favour of the 23^d Decr. ult, Which afforded me no little Satisfaction to find that you Was friendly to Mr. Crawford and I find that That the Legislature of your State has adopted Measures—friendly which will Militate in his favour —I should have written Sooner after receiving yours But have been trying to Geather matter relitive to the Clames of the Citizens of Georgia—a gainst the British Government—for property

—Carryed off by them at the close of the last war—and find that those who lost property residing in Glynn County—have made an Agent of a Mr Cary Celden Attorney-at-law—to attend to there business with the Commissioners appointed to settle that Business—So Soon as you can ascertain The drift of publick opinion at Washington relitive to the Election for President you Will Confer a favour on Me by Informing Me of your opinion of the result—the Legislature of Georgia adjourned Sine, dy on Satirday 20th December ult—domistick our Stiple [sic]—is Sea Island Cotton on the Seaboard Short Steple Cotton in the upper part of the State and for several years there has been but Short Crops Made and low prices Givn for the Article there is Grater Distress in Georgia then ever was known on account of the high Prices four or five years Since—which caused the Citizens to go in debt with flattering Expectations which has been Cut off—but one blessing we Have Plenty of Land—and a grate opening for Emigrants—I was glad to hear that your Brothers was all dooing well—and would be glad to hear that all your connections was So—Should you see Aunt Nathanial Carrington[35]—present My love to hir—And In form hir that I have not for Got hir kindness to my childhood My best respects, to all friends—at Car[olina]

I shall be glad to hear from you att any time—I am your Most
Obt Svt
JAS C MANGUM

[Addressed:]

Willie P. Mangum Esqr
Member of Congress
City Washington

Mail

Willie P. Mangum to Seth Jones[36]

WASHINGTON CITY 11th February 1824.

My Dear Sir.

I received your favour of the 7th ultimo this morning, and avail myself of the earliest opportunity to acknowledge it. I can-

---

[35]The Carringtons lived within a few miles of Mangum. Dicey Carrington was Willie P. Mangum's aunt and possibly James C. Mangham's mother.
[36]A typed copy of this letter is in the State Department of Archives and History. The original is not available.

not imagine the reason of its delay until this time, and regret that it had not come to hand at an earlier period.—

In relation to the rumor in Raleigh that I have changed my opinion touching the question of Presidency, I have only to say that it is wholly without foundation; so far from it, that I have become more and more convinced since my residence at Washington that the best interests of this Country require the elevation of Mr. Crawford to the Presidential chair—and I cannot refrain from the expression of my surprize, that such rumors should be circulated in the City of Raleigh, and the more especially as I have frankly communicated my sentiments on that subject to several gentlemen residing in Raleigh.—

Permit me to request you to contradict that report whenever you may hear it.

That great question has produced very great excitement at Washington, and absorbs almost every other consideration.— Members of Congress instead of attending to thos[e] avocations exclusively for which they are elected, bestow in many instances both night & day upon the intrigues connected with the subject, —and it is plainly obvious that influence of almost every description is brought to bear upon some of them.—

I conceive that the most discerning politician cannot form an opinion touching the result upon which he can rely with entire certainty.—

Mr. Crawford has sustained much injury from the circumstances of having been confined in his chamber during the whole winter,—and much of the times in a dark room on account of his eyes.—I have seen him only twice, & then he was in his bed, with his eyes closed by bandages—he has therefore had to rely exclusively upon the extrinsic weight of his character (he is recovering) while three of the other candidates have been assiduously engaged in advancing their interests by giving splendid parties, and approaching members of Congress in the most insinuating forms—and it is a remarkable fact, that notwithstanding these striking disadvantages on the part of Mr. Crawford, still he can number as his friends 2 to 1 of any other candidate—You have seen by the papers I presume that the Democratic members of Congress are invited into caucus on Saturday evening next[37] that caucus will consist of about 80 members who will be unani-

---

[37]The caucus met on February 11. Only 66 of the 261 members of Congress attended. Eight from North Carolina were present: Burton, Edwards, Gatlin, Hall, Hooks, Saunders, Speight, and Williams. Branch and Macon, the two Senators, and Connor, Culpepper, Mangum, and Vance of the House were absent. Newsome, *Election of 1824*, 81.

mously in favour of Mr. Crawford—I shall not attend the caucus of course under that invitation—and there are many others sincerely attached to the cause of Mr Crawford that will not attend —among whom I will mention Mr Macon.—

Unless the caucus shall produce considerable effect I am satisfied that an election cannot be made by the people and that the election will ultimately come to the House of Representatives, as much as it is to be deprecated.—Mr. Crawford will be the highest in the electoral college,[38] that is he will get the states of Georgia, No. Carolina, Virginia, New York, & Deleware. I think pret[t]y certainly—and the eastern people have a strong inclination to take him up.—Mr. Adams will be second—and Gen. Jackson or Mr Clay will be third—If Mr. Clay gets into the H of R the American people need not be surprised if he is made President— I think however Gen Jackson will beat him one vote, that is Clay will get the votes of Kentucky, Illinois, Alabama, Indiana, Mississippi, and Pennsylvania making one vote more than Clay—Mr. Calhoun cannot get more than So Carolina & New Jersey unless his prospects shall materially change and even if he should get No. Ca. which I cannot for a moment believe, still the vote will be thrown away, for it will not bring him into the H of Rs.—Since my arrival here, I have felt alarm at the splendid & profuse policy that I think would characterize the administration of either Clay or Calhoun—and Mr. Crawford I think is decidedly preferable on the score of being a sounder constitutionalist, but also inasmuch as there can be no doubt, that his administration would be marked with more oeconomy & a more rigid accountability.—Gen Jackson with all my objections to him, I should prefer to Mr. Calhoun who seems to be a favorite in your county— I am Dr. Sir yours sincerely—

                                                W. P. MANGUM
My respects to Mrs. Jones.

P. S.

The bill for the revision of the Revenue laws will be taken up to day—in which the Tariff is presented in more hideous forms than heretofore—The Yankees will make the Southerners hewers of wood & drawers of water for them. I conceive the line of policy that this Government is to pursue already settled—The Eastern states will be converted into a great workshop & the slave holding states will be compelled to pay them tribute—

---

[38]The electoral votes were: Jackson, 99; Adams, 84; Crawford, 41; and Clay, 37.

The Present Congress since the last increase under the last census, is said by the old members to be more wild & extravagant, than any of it preseccesors [*sic*].

I am your friend

W. P. M.

Mr Seth Jones.

Cary Williams to Willie P. Mangum[39]

WILLIAMSVILLE Feby 12th, 1824

W P Mangum Esq,

Sir

I have sent some papers to the war office for the benefit of George Duncan[40] who was a soldier in the revolutionary war; the old man has been trying for some time to get a pension, and if he is intitled to any thing it wou'd be well for him to have it as he kneeds it much; I have to request you to attend to it as Quick as you can and give me some information on the Subject; you will please not to fail as I have promis'd the old man to write to you for him; If the Deed of trust that Edwards has on his property shoud be forc'd; the Old man must in a verry few years become a publick charge; This leaves me & family well & hope it may find you so; Shou'd be glad to hear from [you] at any time when convenient

CARY WILLIAMS

[Addressed:]   Free

The Honb¹, Wiley P. Mangum
                    Washington City
          Answered

WPM-LC

Priestley H. Mangum to Willie P. Mangum

HILLSBORO' Feb: 20th. 1824.

Dear Sir,

I cant imagine the cause of your silence. Your epistolary

³⁹See below, p. 128.
⁴⁰George Duncan of Granville County enlisted April 20, 1776, and was discharged October 19, 1778. He reenlisted in 1781 and served until 1782. He is listed as receiving a pension under the acts of 1818 and 1835. Walter Clark, (ed.), *State Records of N. C.*, XXII, 62, 1045, 1047.

talent seems to be exhausted—I hope, however, perhaps in vain, to call it forth—unless your parliamentary debating has closed your mouth forever.

You have heard by this time that I was married on the 12ᵗʰ. of this month. I have not yet gone to house-heeping—And it is not certainly known when I shall. I wish to do so as soon as—possible.—On yesterday I came by Mr. Cain's where I found your wife & child well, except a little jaw ache of which Charity complained. She will go home in a few days I expect: & this she can do with perfect safety.—Little Sally looks very fat & well. A Cain forehead & a Mangum nose are a full description of her physiognomy—

You requested me to bond some open accounts for you; I have searched diligently the files of papers you handed me & have failed to find any account for fees that is intelligible.

I wish to know the prospects of Crawford: a caucus seems to have become odious. Genl. Jackson would get the vote of No. Ca., I think, if his friends knew how to manage his interest: An attempt will be made to procure him a ticket[41]—whether they will succeed I know not:—my expectation is that they will fail.—

Yrs
P. H. MANGUM

[Addressed:]

The Honᵇˡ
    Willie P. Mangum
        Washington City
           D. C.

WPM-LC

W. H. Haywood, Jr., to Willie P. Mangum

HILLSBOROUGH 23ʳᵈ. February 1824.

My dear Sir

Your esteemed favour in reply to mine should have been answered before this time, but in consequence of my absence from home for some weeks, and on my return neglected business called

---

[41]Jackson's supporters in North Carolina presented a separate ticket, the People's Ticket. Several electoral candidates on this ticket promised to vote for Adams should he gain a majority of the popular votes. This was designed to gain Adams' supporters. The popular vote of the state in the fall election was 20,415 for the People's Ticket and 15,621 for Crawford's ticket. Newsome, *Election of 1824*, 155-156.

for my undivided attention.—I am now however (as will be discovered from date above) at this place where the small portion
of business I have enables me to devote a few moments to my
friendships.—I think I availed myself of the opportunity afforded in my first letter to return thanks for your confidence in
reposing to my care the interests of your Clients in Franklin
which has at once introduced me into business which I trust
shall be able to preserve by attention to the calls of my profession.—

There is little which has occurred among friends lately that
can interest you unless it be that Priestly has actually got married—of which however you must have been apprized before
now.—You know I am not a man fond of dabbling in the political strifes which occasionally arise among us—though I must
claim the exercise of the priviledge of every one in our country—
that of enjoying my own opinion in regard to the interest of the
publick—and of expressing those sentiments wherever I may
deem it prudent.—And this great political struggle for the presidency which has not only swallowed up the consideration of
every other subject in our State & national counsels but diffused
itself into every private circle seems to strengthen with every
week.—My opinion of the men now before the publick has undergone no change—Genl J. his very enemies will admit can ensure
the vote of this State if they become satisfied that he has any
hopes of success elsewhere but it is useless for North Carolina
obstinately to throw away her influence and weight in the election on a man who is not likely to claim votes elsewhere.—I derive my impressions of his strength in this State—not from the
newspapers which daily contradict their own statements made
but a week before—but by mingling with the people and making
enquiry of those who I know are unfriendly to him and visit portions of our population which I do not [know to be so]—I am
certain I should hazard little in saying that were a ticket formed
in N. C. for the five candidates now before the publick the Genl.
would succeed by a majority of no inconsiderable number over
the whole aggregate of the others.—I feel so perfectly satisfied
of his vast superiority that domestic as I am I would be willing
to give—not to him—but to my country a month of my time to
promote his election.—Let Pennsylvania distinctly declare for
him and you will see the ranks thicken in every quarter—I speak
only of my own native State—though were I the editor of a
Newspaper I might be compelled to extend it beyond those limits

without regard to truth or consequences.—Tell me—Does no one open his mouth among you in Washington for the pride & honor of N. Y. & indeed of our country?—D. Clinton!—Is the faction which party spirit in his own state has raised up against him to exclude the further influence of his talents and greatness upon the interests & welfare of the nation?—obscure their brilliancy it cannot.[42] For you will not have forgotten that though I prefer the General next to him yet he is my first choice.—Neither of them I admit is without fault nor can we find that man among us.—

I begin to feel great apprehensions that Mr Clay will get a chance before the H of R. where the election must fall at last.—I would make any compromise—nay do any thing consistent with the honest duty of a citizen & friend to my country & its liberties sooner than he should be placed at the head of the government.—I fear the influence and power which his eloquence gives him over our H of Rep: will be felt too much—What think you of him? Is he not a great political intriguer? "All things to all men" to promote his ends? I may do him injustice but we have a right to send missiles at publick men and I at least will be generous enough if I can be convinced of my errors to atone for them by withdrawing my prejudices.—

The News papers may squabble & men who are zealous partizans may wish what they please, but I tell you in honest candour that if Gen¹. J. is not run in N. Caro: it is still questionable whether Mr Calhoun or Mr Crawford be favorite among us.—Each one has his party in squads & it is difficult to judge of their relative strength—and more particularly as the friends of the other candidates are unwilling at this period to desert & decide upon another choice.—There is one means I have been surprised to see Mr Calhoun's enemies have never yet used in No. Caro: to break him down.—Don't you know that no man can represent us here who will openly declare for Internal Improvements. — I think I prefer him however to your man The caucus have missed it—What are Mr Crawfords pretensions to the presidency to be supported jointly with those of Gallatin for V. P^res.—I hope we

[42]Van Buren's Albany Regency tried in 1823-1824 to get control of the New York Jeffersonian party. The fight came over the method of electing electors. Van Buren wanted the legislature to elect the electors. The People's Party which supported a popular election of electors defeated Van Buren's plan. This fight went over into the presidential election. Van Buren supported Crawford in place of DeWitt Clinton. To injure Clinton politically he tried to have him removed as canal commissioner of the Erie Canal. The People's Party in reply nominated Clinton for governor. Clinton's forces then gave their support to Adams. John B. McMaster, *A History of the People of the United States, from the Revolution to the Civil War*, 8 vols. (New York, N. Y.: D. Appleton and Co., 1893-1921), V, 71-73.

do not differ in regard to the *latter*.—Have foreign fashions become so dear that while we have so much native talent—5 Men even who are aspiring to the chief magistracy and born in our own land—that we must look out a foreigner for the V Pres't of U: S.[43]—But I will not indulge myself lest not having your views beforehand I may be deemed presumptious.—

While I am opposed to a caucus and believe a large majority of the country are I can not withhold my extreme regret at the indecorous conduct of the opponents in attending their assemblage to *trip* them—as the papers state they did[44]—This is inconsistent with the dignity & decorum becoming a good cause.—But I must not indulge further in my scribbling since my papers warns me tis time to close—

'Tis well this letter will go franked.—

Upon enquiry I learn your wife & *children*[45] are well—I shall look out on your return to see quite a fashionable genteel *beau* & expect a few lessons in etiquette to rub me up for a courting expedition.—

I have to beg an early notice of this that I may get Letter No. 2. so often referred to in your last.—

A word or two on business before I say farewell—First however returning my thanks for the prompt attention bestowed to the little matter with the Clerk of Supreme Co:[46] in my lat.

It will not have escaped your recollection that some time last year you assigned to Mr John Fort a Bond of John Young[47] for $150. or thereabouts and I brought suit on it for Mr Fort ag^t. Tho: D. Watts[48] Executor and obtained judgment for it.—He has now filed a Bill of Injunction—the grounds are too long to state to you. Mr Fort you know to be a man little used to litigation and he has desired I would mention it to you and request as he is in *need* of the money & had made *arrangements* in *reliance* upon the collection of this before this period, that you will relieve him by making him payment of the said monies which I believe with int: amount to him about $175 and taking the said suit to your use & benefit.—Your answer will be necessary to the Bill as he has made you a party to it.—

---

[43]Albert Gallatin was born in Geneva, Switzerland.
[44]Of those who attended the caucus, two were for Adams and one was for Jackson. Newsome, *Election of 1824*, 81.
[45]Mangum had only one child, Sally, at the time this letter was written.
[46]William Robards.
[47]Captain John Young of Orange County died in 1822. Watts carried a notice in the *Hillsborough Recorder* Dec. 25, 1822, advertising a sale of his slaves and household furniture.
[48]He was sheriff of Orange County for several years. *N. C. Laws*, 1826, 1831, appendix.

Tis growing late at night and I have already written enough to weary the patience of any man who has to listen to as many speeches as Members of Congress do—Excuse my haste and believe me as I am truly your friend—And may God bless you & yours

WILL: H: HAYWOOD JR

Don't forget that I do not live in
Hillsboro:—but am only here for a
short season—

[Addressed:]

The Hon:
Willie P. Mangum
House of Representatives
Washington City
D. C.

WPM-LC

James Mebane to Willie P. Mangum

[MASON HALL,] February the 29th. 1824

Dear Sir

I have enclosed you the certificate required in the case of the claim of Lois Albert[49] to the military bounty Land, mentioned in your last, I hope all will be right now, it is made out agreeable to the form you enclosed me, We have had a very busy court, & some talk about the presidents election people, much divided, Crawford, Jackson, Adams, & Calhoun, all have friends, & probably in the order I have named them, but many say Jackson is first in public esteem, The general opinion as to the Congressional caucus is that it is something like a "mouse produced from the labour of a mountain," & that Albert Gallatin will be too heavy for Crawford to carry, & that instead of being assisted by his (Gallatins) strength, he will sink under his weight,[50] so say the Crawford men here, & others are wating to hope this will happen I remain respectfully yours' &c

JAMES MEBANE

---

[49]See above letter of Mebane to Mangum, Dec. 24, 1823.
[50]There was considerable opposition in North Carolina to Gallatin.

[Addressed:]
        Wiley P. Mangum
        Member of Congress
[Endorsed   Washington
by W. P. M.,] 20th, May
    The notification will be sent to me at Hillsboro. The grant will
not be issued unless ordered & thereby save the Taxes—

WPM-LC

John F. Brevard[51] to Willie P. Mangum

LINCOLN COUNTY N. C. March 10th- 1824
Honble—Willie P. Mangum
    Sir
    I think that when I had the pleasure of seeing you last in Ra-
leigh, you promised to write to me from Washington City, the
politicks of the day, prospects before us &C &C. I have not yet
had the honour of receiving a line from you—& write now only
to remind you of your promise—which, as it was given the night
of our hospitable intertainment by the Citizens of Raleigh, it is
possible you may have forgotten.
    Please present my respects to Dr- Vance,[52] & Genl- Sanders[53]—
also Mr- Hayne,[54] Mr- McDuffie[55] & Mr- Carter[56] of South Carolina, the latter of whom *should* spare time to drop me a line now
& then.
    You did well to keep clear of the Caucus—That assemblage,
so far as I have been able to learn the publick sentiment in this
part of the country, is universally reprebate. Happily for us, the
people of this part of North Carolina are not yet influenced by
that spirit of organised faction which exhibits itself so thoroughly in the state of New York, & in Virginia—which is so ab-
surd in principle, & so oppressive & destructive of every republican virtue in practice—which substitutes the dominancy of a

    [51]He was the postmaster at Beatty's Ford in Lincoln County. He was active in the legis-
lature in 1818 for strong state banks. Hoyt, *Papers of Murphey*, II, 91-96; McIver, *N. C.
Register*, 69.
    [52]Dr. Robert B. Vance, 1793-1827, practiced medicine in Buncombe County until his elec-
tion to Congress in 1823. In 1827 he was mortally wounded at Saluda Gap in a duel with
Samuel P. Carson, another congressman from North Carolina. *Biog. Dir. of Cong.*, 1641.
    [53]Romulus M. Saunders.
    [54]Robert Y. Hayne of South Carolina.
    [55]George McDuffie of South Carolina.
    [56]John Carter, 1792-1850, a South Carolina congressman from 1822 to 1829, moved to
Georgetown, D. C., in 1829 to practice law. *Biog. Dir. of Cong.*, 791.

party in the room of the good of the common weal— & directly leads to proscription, feud & the destruction of all genuine patriotism.

I have nothing to communicate which can interest you—But as you are situated you can communicate much which will interest me

Very respectfully
Your Obt-Sert
JOHN F. BREVARD

Direct to Beaties Ford

[Addressed:]

    Honble- Willie P. Mangum
        Washington City
Mail.

WPM-LC

Willie P. Mangum to Charity A. Mangum

WASHINGTON, Sunday 14th March 1824.

My Dear Love,

In your last letter to me, you complained that I do not write to you often enough, & this morning I write more because I hope it will afford you some gratification, than because I have anything to communicate in which you even feel much interest.

My health remains as usual, but one thing of which I feel sure is, that I could not live many winters at Washington without essentially impairing my constitution.—It is more common than I had any reason to know that members of Congress, by a long continuance at this place have got shattered constitutions.—

The fashionable habits of visiting at night, then leaving rooms suffocatingly warm, and going out into a bleak & cutting air for one, two or three miles will gradually undermine the best state of health.—I am as sparing however in these night parties, as I well may be, without incurring the imputation—of singularity —I wish most ardently My Love, that those evenings could be spent in your society, instead of these gay—, flattering assemblages of the beau monde.—The one would reach the heart, & put in lively motion those affections, that constitute the best part of life, while the other is cold, formal insipid, heartless, & wasteful dissipation of the mind.—I look with great anxiety to the approach of the period, when under providence, I may again fold you in my arms, and hug you to my bosom the heart of all others that throbs with warmest affection for me; and feel that the world has nothing as dear to offer me as that of which I am possessed.—If there is any thing on earth, that partakes strongly of angelic beatitude, it is the virtuous loves and affections of two hearts drawn together by inclination by duty, & sealed together by the solemn ordinance.—And whatever My Dear may be my fate, there is one thing I know, & for which I ought to feel deeper gratitude to heaven than perhaps I do—that I have had perhaps more than my share of blessings in that respect. that I have been infinitely blessed beyond my deservings by the kindliest affections that the human heart has to bestow upon its fellow being—and that which more than any other consideration, gives pain to me, is the want of the means of rendering you more happy, as happy as you deserve to be—

But providence tempers the wind to the shorn lamb, and I know full well, that you are willing to try to believe *that* comfort and happiness, under which thousands would repine as a doom of absolute misery—

The mail leaves here directly—I expect by this time you are at home—The spring seems disposed to set in.—I write to Stagville, but not knowing whether letters go there expeditiously if they are delayed I would write to Hillsbor°. if you prefer it.—Write to me My Dear, & tell me whether Priestly has yet flogged his wife—Rebecca would not believe me, & when the fact shall be disclosed—she may regret that she did not. Tell me whether Priestly seems to be in the "melting mood" whether he seems to be conscious that he is married.—I had hoped to hear from him, but he is the very poorest of correspondents—

How does our little daughter, can she talk yet? does she seem conscious & observing?—does she seem to know that she has got into a very naughty world—Does she know where her Pa is? Does she never say a word about him?—I am afraid she is like too many other young ladies—giddy & *unthinking?* Poor dear little thing how I wish to see her—Both you & she not only call home to you many of my waking thoughts, but often have I visited you in the visions of the night. And may God grant that I may visit you both in person in a short time, and find you both in health. I am going this morning to the Catholic Church, where the noble organ shall swell its grand & solemn sounds and they

mingled with a choir of human voices, shall fall upon the ear, &
creep into the heart, & seem to still & hush every human passion
—While this soul composing music softens the heart. The eye is
turned upon our Saviour large as life, with his Crown of thorns
& the blood streaming from his side—and *a countenance, such as
never was human,* all this sustained & enforced by a diversity of
external circumstances—that the eye easily comprehends, but
that I cannot now describe, together with a chaste & impressive
sermon—all indeed impress my imagination with more grandeur
& solemnity, & overpower the heart with more of profound ado-
ration, than any worship that I ever witnessed—It surely is the
most comfortable religion known to man—We know its vices,
better than its virtues—It is as pure as any religion—

Remember to my Mother,—Eliza—& our other friends—My
Love, Time has demolished temples, razed cities to their foundation. It weakens every grief & every affection—But Let us my
Dearest Love, try to encrease the flow of heart, & affection—Remember me often—In kindliest affection—My Love farewell—

WILLIE P. MANGUM

WPM-LC

Petition of W. A. Thorpe et als

[March, 1824]
To the senate and House of Representatives of the United
States in Congress assembled, the memorial of the Undersigned
respectfully sheweth—

That they are Citizens of and residents in the County of Wake
and State of North Carolina—that they live in the North western section of the County aforesaid, district from twelve to twenty five miles from the City of Raleigh—there they have for a
long time past laboured and still labour under the great inconvenience resulting from their local situation in reference to the
Post-office establishment—there is no post office nearer to them
than that in the City of Raleigh, and the post office at Stagville
in Orange County, from which they generally reside at about the
same distance as from Raleigh. —

Your memorialists further state that the section of Country
destitute of the accommodation offered by the Mail establishment of the United States, is extensive in territory; and very

populous—and while they would forbear to ask of the congress the establishment of a new mail rout, which would be necessary for publick convenience, or productive of the expenditure of Publick money improperly—they hesitate not to state that the Interest and convenience of a very large and respectable portion of the Citizens inhabiting the section of Country before mentioned, would be greatly promoted by the establishment of the route hereinafter mentioned—and furthermore that in their opinions the revenue arising therefrom, would be fully equal to the expenditure necessarily incidental to its establishment.— they therefore respectfully pray that a weekly mail may be authorised by law, to go from Raleigh by Joseph Brasfield's, and the Fishdam Ford in Wake County; by Stagville & Carringtons Store in Orange County to Rocksborough (Person Court House) where it will meet the main Western mail from *Warrenton* to *Milton* and Danville, that return by the same route—and that post office[s] be established at such of the places above mentioned, where there are none at Present.

March 1824 - - - -

W. A. Thorpe[57]	Bennett Cooper
Griffin Crook	John Allin
William Thomason	John Estes
Bennett Gooch	Rimber Johnson
John Crook	Calvin Johnson
Thomas Roycroft Junr	Henry Johnson
Joseph Williams	John Reves
William Cash	Thomas Fowler
Major Pollard	Fielding, Leathers
John Singleton	H. S. Vernon
Thos Culverhouse	Alexander Colclough
Jams Lyon	Archabald Rigsbey
Matthew Jones	John Cheek
Kimbrough Jones	T. W. Allen
John Amoree	James Courtes
Gray Singleton	John Nichols Jnr.
Isaac Adams	Aron Sugg—
Jesse Sikes	Masten Critcher
William Clements	Allen Rogers
Gregory Singleton	Jno. W. Pullen
C. W. H. Boyd	Bazil Yates

[57]All names are autographs.

Redding Allen
Hosea Holder
T. Roycroft
Wiley Simmons
Richmond Bledsoe
Zachariah Shaw
Amasa Parham
William Bailey
Joh Bayly
Allen Bailey
Joel Simms
Jesse Gril
Mark Grady
Henry Allen
Jas. A. Allen
C. N. L. Thompson
Alsey Jones
John Nichols S^r
Robet Boyd
Dempsey B. Massey
John Nichols Son of Jas
W. M. Tate
    *All signed in autograph.

Major Bledsoe
Lewelin Wilkins
Joseph Belvin
Solomon Thompson
John Shaw
Thos. Williams
Dennis Grady
Isaac Dawson
Chesley George
John Roycroft
Harbert Hutson
Thos Rochell
William Rigsbee
W. Ship
Zachariah Oneal
John Broadwell
West Pope
E. Parker
Uriah Branton
Robt. Handwek
Westwood A. Jones

WPM-LC

Cary Williams to Willie P. Mangum[58]

WILLIAMSVILLE March 14th, 1824

Wiley P. Mangum Esq.
    Sir
    Yours of the 3rd. & 4th. Instant came to hand last night, with the Coppy of a letter dated 12th, of May 1823 which letter I did rec^d. in a short time after that date; also the schedule of George Duncans property: It being sent to the War Department without the Clerks signature; Agreeable to the terms or instructions laid down in that letter, I applyd to Isham Edwards for a list of the Articles purchased by George Duncan from him; it was several months before he render'd me the account, but so it was he gave me an account of considerable length containing a number

of Articles all of which appeared to be purchas'd by Duncan prior to the 18th day of March 1818, & at Feby term of Person Court he & Duncan both made oath to the same As I thought in proper form, that the articles was sold to Duncan and no other person; that Duncan said they were purch^d by himself and for his own benefit and no other I then had the County seal attach^t to it with the Clerks certificate; which account with the schedule I inclosed to the war Department with a request that if there was any thing else necessary to let me know: Now I am at a loss to know what or how to act untill I know whether or not the papers reached the war office; I inclosed them the same day I wrote to you on the subject; be so good as to Examin whether or not they have got them, and write to me my only doubt on the subject was that the account was fill'd up too much with dram drinking which I thought might make against Duncan but you will recollect that it is like the most of the old soldiers; I have been informed that General Sanders has laid before the committee of Post roads a petition to change the rout from Person C. H. to Milton by Leasburg. I hope that will end it, as I think they might be satisfied with the mail they already have by that place; As to your wish that N. Carolina may study their Interest in the election of President you may rest satisfied in my opinion Crafford [Crawford] will get the whole Interest beleaving no other candidates will be started than what has been and of course the ones in nomination will vote for Crafford & as to the Vice president but little is said   please to Accept of my sincere regard &C

CARY WILLIAMS

[Addressed:]

> The Honorable Wiley P. Mangum
> Washington City

WPM-LC

Michael Holt to Willie P. Mangum

ORANGE N: CAROLINA [23 March, 1824]

Dear Sir

Yours came to hand duly, we are all in a buble for Jackson, but the most considerate and firm men, continue for Crawford and I

think will succeed in this State many new converts for Jackson
are stagerd when they become acquainted with his moral car-
rector—I think much depends upon you, your Judgment freely
made known to your friends by letter, at this time would be of
service, you have it in your power to make yourself acquainted
with each individual who are candidates for the presidency—

I have consented to be a candidate again in the Senate Judge
[Duncan] Cameron declines it is not known who will run against
me if any — many thinks it will be a whipping race between
Crawford & Jackson in this State The most of Calhoun's friends
Turning over to Jackson—will you do me a little favor by paying J. S. Skinner[59] editor of the American Farmer of Baltimore
—he charges me discount on the small sum which I owe for the
4th. & 5th. Vol. of the American farmer—you can procure money
at Washington that will pass at parr in Baltimore and I will pay
you on your return, the sum is eight Dollars which is due Mr.
Skinner—our agricultural Society[60] offers $50 a premium to the
owner of the best cultivated farm in Orange cty owned by a
Member—

With great respect ys.

March 23d 1824—

[Addressed:]

Honl. Wiley P. Mangum
City Washington

W. P. Mangum to Thomas Ruffin[61]
HOUSE OF REPR. 24th March 1824.

Dear Sir.

I have but a few moments before the mail leaves the house, to
inform you that Col. H. G. Burton, cannot in justice to himself
file his answer at his Spring Term of Wake to the Bill filed
against him by the Representative of John Farris decd.—Col.
Burton has been anxious & is still anxious to do anything in his
power to hasten that suit to a conclusion—and with the view of
filing his answer this spring, procured a copy of the Bill to be
sent to him, the service of which he was ready to acknowledge

[59]For the main facts of John Stuart Skinner's life, see *D. A. B.*, XVIII, 199-201.
[60]Orange County Agricultural Society, Duncan Cameron, President, John Taylor, Secretary. McIver, *N. C. Register*, 100.
[61]The original is in the Thomas Ruffin Papers, Southern Collection, University of North
Carolina. The latter part of this letter has been previously published in Hamilton, *Ruffin
Papers*, I, 300.

and also put himself to the expense & trouble of procuring the answer filed by McQuay—after obtaining which he requested me to examine the case & prepare his answer—I advised him to decline answering at this place, unless he could get all his papers which are necessary to refresh his memory in relation to the details of this case—It is true that he could answer but it would be in very general terms and perhaps too much so to meet the views & just expectations of the complainant.

By reference to a letter heretofore written to the complt. you will perceive the grounds of defence that Col. Burton will take, and is as much as his answer will in several important facts be materially variant from McQuay it is the more desirable that he should be entirely accurate even in unimportant matters—

It is to be hoped that no delay will take place on his account for upon Col. B. return he will file his answer as of the Spring Term & so he wishes it to be considered.

There is nothing new or important here, that it is not to be seen in the papers.

I think it perfectly certain that Gen. Jackson, tho strong, cannot in any event be elected President. I should be gratified to feel as sure that Mr. Adams is not to be the man, no material however that I know of—Crawford will get at least 90 votes in the electoral college—It is believed however that no election will be made, unless by the H. of Reps—and there is the difficulty that Crawford has to encounter. If the intrigues that are on foot, I mean of the combination of the other candidates, shall succeed, he will be ultimately defeated—all indeed depends upon that and it is probable before we leave Washington, that the result may be anticipated with some certainty—Congress will not adjourn I think before 15th May, probably not before 1st June as some think.

I am Dr Sir
Yours truly
W. P. MANGUM

WPM-LC

John Louis Taylor to Willie P. Mangum

[WAKE COUNTY, 26 March, 1824]

dear Sir

I am requested by Mr. William Rope [or Rosse], an illiterate,

7

but very honest constituent of yours, to ask you to forward the inclosed letter for him, through the medium of the Secretary of State's office, or in any other mode which you may approve. A son of his impelled by a desire to improve his fortune, left the paternal home three or four years ago, and without capital or friends, made his way to the city of Mexico, where, after as many vicissitudes as could be crowded into such a small space of time, he soon found himself in a prosperous condition as a merchant, and wrote to his father that he purposed to return overland with a drove of mules. This is more than a year ago, since which time no further intelligence has been received from him; and I have taken the liberty to state these circumstances, that you may perceive how very gratifying it would be to the father that a letter should reach his son by you[r] means, and, that, with an act of civility you would be uniting one of real charity and kindness I remain with great respect

Your Obede^t. Servt.
JOHN LOUIS TAYLOR.

Wake Cy
26th. March
   1824)
[Addressed:]

        The Hnble
           Willie P. Mangum Esqr.
             House of Representatives
               City of Washington

WPM-LC

James A. Craig[62] to Willie P. Mangum

HAW RIVER 4th April 1824.

Dear Sir:

I would be glad to know if a Cylinder could be got at Washington City, I would like to obtain one [torn] 6 or 8 inches in diameter—be so good as to make enquiry for me, and at what price one of the above description could be got and if one could be easily forwarded here—

I have all the apparatus belonging to an electrifying machine

---

[62]James A. Craig, 1796-1849, the principal of the Chapel Hill Academy in 1820-1821, became a physician and orator of note in Orange County. *Hillsborough Recorder*, Nov. 28, 1849; Coon, *Doc. Hist. of Educ. in N. C.*, 299-300.

except the Cylinder; I Judge one might be got in Washington
for $3 or 4—As soon as you can ascertain please drop me a
line—

I am much pleased to find, that as far as I know your conduct
in Congress, gives very general satisfaction—It was a fortunate
circumstance for you that you did not Join the *Caucus party* on
the 14th. Feby—

Be so good as to drop me a line on the Prospect in Congress of
the Presidential Candidates—is not the Radical chieftain[63] on
the *wane* throughout the United States? The Current of Popular
Opinion, seems to be setting strongly in favour of Genl. Jackson
in this section of the state.

Ever yours

Hon. Willie P. Mangum   JAMES A CRAIG
        Washington, D. C.

[Addressed:]

    Honourable W. P. Mangum
        Washington D. C.
[Endorsed:]
    To Answer
        James Craig

WPM-LC

Priestley H. Mangum to Willie P. Mangum

ORANGE April 15th. 1824—

Dear Sir,

I have just arrived from Salisbury court & have found our
families very well.—We are anxious to learn when you will be at
home.—You must ere now have become tired of a parliamentary
life. The tedious recurrence of the same things, unchequered, by
diversity or novelty, would I think be almost insupportable—unless you make a good use of the opportunities of acquiring information, which are afforded by your situation. But I suspect
the unvarying phases of the presidential contest excite interest
& relieve the mind from an oppressive littleness, if nothing else
should produce that effect. That seems to be a subject of almost
universal concernment; & were I to say it is one productive of

---

[63]Probably John C. Calhoun.

less reason in argument, & more hardihood in bold operation & uncompromising viturperation than any other, I should stand acquitted of any incorrect statement.

I think I may safely assure you of a fact, which you will dislike to hear & be inclined to disbelieve, that exhibits the character of our people in a very unfavorable point of view. That fact is, that Genl. Jackson will in my opinion get the vote of this State. At this time, from Orange inclusive to the Mountains, he is I think unquestionably the people's President—I except Caswell county & some neighbourhoods, & perhaps might except Lincoln County. When at Salisbury I made it a business to ascertain as nearly as possible what the State of the public mind was on the subject, in the west. I learn't that since Calhoun was withdrawn the people of Lincoln were taking a stand for Crawford—but in every other County there were meetings upon meetings of people at Law-days & Company musters, for the purpose of giving an expression of opinion on the subject of the next President; & Genl. Jackson is always the man.—Genl. Stokes[64] with whom I spent several days— & with him I might mention several men of some distinction—is acting a part I detest with all my heart. He says that *he has not said he would support Jackson*—notwithstanding they have got him as I understand, *on the people's Ticket,* in his country. He says next to Calhoun, Crawford was & is the choice of his understanding—but *h'll G-d D-d if he would go to Heaven with some of Crawford's friends;* therefore he cannot & will not support him. With such men as Cocke,[65] L Williams[66] & Dick Speight,[67] he says that he can't travel.—Judging from what I have heard & seen I must believe that Jackson will get the vote of the State. I have said this exhibits our character in the unfavorable point of view,—I think

---

[64]General Montford Stokes, 1762-1842, a Virginian who after the Revolution in which he was a naval officer became a planter in Rowan County, North Carolina, held numerous local and state offices before being elected in 1804 to the U. S. Senate. He declined this office but accepted when reelected in 1816 and served until 1823. He was governor of the state from 1830 to 1832. In 1830 he was president of the Board of Visitors of the U. S. Military Academy. Stokes was the brother-in-law of W. B. Lewis of Tennessee, and upon the advice of the latter, he shifted his support from Calhoun to Jackson. As a result he was placed on the People's Ticket as an elector in March 1824. He, thereupon, announced that he liked Crawford himself but not his friends. It is this of which Priestley is complaining. Newsome, *Election of 1824,* 81, 99n, 115; William O. Foster, "The Career of Montfort Stokes in North Carolina," *North Carolina Historical Review,* XVI (1939), 237-272; *Biog. Dir. of Cong.,* 1574.

[65]John Cocke, 1772-1854, served in the Tennessee legislature in 1796-1797, 1799-1801, 1807, 1809, 1812, and in Congress from 1819 to 1827. *Biog. Dir. of Cong.,* 829.

[66]Lewis Williams, 1786-1842, after serving in the state legislature from Surry County in 1808, and 1813-1814, went to Congress where he served from 1815 to 1842. Before his death he was called the "Father of the House." *Biog. Dir. of Cong.,* 1707.

[67]Richard Dobbs Spaight, Jr., 1796-1850, a student of the state university about the time of Mangum, was in the state legislature from New Bern from 1819 to 1822, and in 1825 and 1826. He was a member of Congress from 1823 to 1825, governor from 1835 to 1837, a member of the Democratic state convention in 1835, presidential elector on the Jackson ticket in 1828, and an agriculturalist of note. *Biog. Dir. of Cong.,* 1550; *D. A. B.,* XVII, 419.

so, because the people are fascinated & influenced by the splen-
dor of his military fame *alone*. It is not that they think or care
about his being an able statesman that they will vote for him—
consideration of this sort never enter into their minds. The
sto[ry is] he has done much for his country, he has slain the Indians & flogged the British & spilled his blood in defence of his
country's rights—therefore he is the bravest, wisest & greatest
man in the nation—even the memory of Washington is lost in
the blaze of the Genl's Glory & in the glare of his bloody laurels.
These remarks are not intended to apply to the Genl's enlightened friends; they pretend to give to him other & more plausible
claims, if they were true—but even they can't after all their efforts at the expense of truth & good sense & correct feeling,
make him the man of the full choice of their heart—and then to
fill out the sketch of their president & touch off the shades of
their portrait, they fall upon Crawford, cover him with filth—
& with a sudden mental throe, relieve themselves by a bold self-
important assertion that the Genl. is better than *Crawford*.
Write me & give some sketches of the great men of the nation &
the prospects of the presidential candidates.—Rebecca has been
at your House since we were married, but we shall leave it in a
few days. I am ready to house keep

Yrs

P. H. MANGUM

[Addressed:]

The Honb^l. Willie P. Mangum   Free
House of Representatives
Washington City
(D. C.)

WPM-LC

William H. Haywood, Jr., to Willie P. Mangum

RALEIGH 17 April 1824.

My dear Sir

Your last favour was received in due course of mail and should
have been noticed before this, but I have been so constantly occupied with professional *travelling* and business that I really
could not do so with any satisfaction to myself or to you,

I thank you sincerely for your long and interesting account of the men & measures at Washington and I suppose I ought for the *latter* part of your letter in *particular* where I am so highly complimented by the proposal even of being your successor. But my Dear Sir, were I qualified for such a station I thank God I do not desire political preferment, there is but one office in the gift of my country I could at this time be induced under any circumstances to seek or to accept and that principally from a desire to serve my country—and you will think me singular indeed when I tell you that is that of a prosecuting officer—and this were it now vacant the want of sufficient standing and experience in my profession would forbid me at this time to aspire after.—The criminal Law of our country is administered with so much laxity as holds out an inducement rather than a terror to evil doers—and if there be any situation in our profession in which a man may move on with an unstrained conscience it is where we have no inducement to arm ourselves with anything more than the truth & justice of a cause.—This leads me to the case of one Hainds who you will recollect was to be tried at our Superior Court for the murder of J. Boylan—On behalf [of] the State I prosecuted him and it seemed that not only able counsel —the influence of bribery & corruption were enlisted on his behalf, but even the Judge—Paxton[68]—was determined to save his neck from a halter long since merited—I went into the case on the eve of the trial—the State made out a clear case—but in vain—he escaped with a brand—The daring villain in an hour afterwards paraded our streets—visited the scene of his bloodshed & owned his guilt & crime but exultingly said "it is too late now I am free.—" I do not know when so much publick excitement has prevailed among us—and but for the *untimely* interference of the Judge & the dexterous management of Counseller Ruffin[69] in turning it to the best advantage & the Atto: Genl's[70] 2 or 3 hours speech I think I should have been able to swing the rascal.—I cannot however write upon the subject with any degree of patience—I was stopped 4 times!! abruptly by his counsel in my short talk of 10 min. and that old granny of a Judge

---

[68]John J. Paxton moved from Virginia to North Carolina to settle as a merchant at Morganton. Unsuccessful in his business, he began the study of law. Soon after he was admitted to the bar he enlisted and served in the War of 1812. Then he moved to Rutherfordton where he was very successful in legal practice. He served as superior court judge from his selection in 1818 until his death in 1826. Clarence W. Griffin, *History of Tryon and Rutherford Counties, North Carolina, 1730-1926* (Asheville, N. C.: Clarence W. Griffin, 1937), 166-167.

[69]Probably Thomas Ruffin.

[70]William Drew, an attorney of Halifax County who served as attorney general of the state from 1816 to 1825. *N. C. Manual*, 444.

would not protect me from such decorum.—Enough of such for the present.—

I should like much to see you and talk much more than I can write—When will you Congressmen finish your long talks and "gang hame" to your wives & children?-!.-

I am still fully satisfied that without a great revolution in the publick sentiment of this State that Genl Jackson will be the favorite for the next preidency:—You do not get fair news at Washington City.—If the vote of No. Car: will secure the election of the Gen¹. he may calculate on it and we may begin to prepare ourselves for it—This is no *party feeling* or prejudice—Mr Crawford's friends *here* admit there is *danger,* but when they write to the Metropolis they think it might work a prejudice to do so.—The people with us are astonished at Nat: Macon for saying that "Congress always have elected the President & always *will* elect him.—" If it be so and there is balm in Gilead all good republicans must admit that 'tis time to apply it to this breach in our constitution.—If so old & respectable a man had not said it *first,* it would have almost been treason in another.— It may be & no doubt is matter of perfect indifference to a man so much courted as I learn he is what *I* an humble individual may think—but I say it now and will stick to it that Nat Macon is no man for my ruler—I would not have such a man after such a speech.—It surely must have been a slip in the old cock.—Fie! Fie! Natty! you place too much confidence in the weight of your dicta.—

Manly & the Arbitrata⁷¹ have just returned & both seem run mad on the pres: election—But it will not do.—Until the prospects of Genl J. success brightened the great body of the people seemed to take no interest in the election—but now there is not a farmer in our country but has formed his opinion & determination on the subject as far as my opportunities have enabled me to Judge and I have taken some little pains to do so correctly and inpartially.—We talk of nothing else and think of little besides in our part of the country.—I have the fullest confidence in the integrity of the people of the country and shall submit *aequo animo* to their will.—

If you can tell me I should like to know why it is that Mr.

---

⁷¹Charles Manly was the clerk of the committee appointed to arbitrate the value of slaves to be paid for in the Treaty of Ghent. Henry Seawell and Langdon Cheves were on this commission for the United States. George Jackson and John McTavish represented Great Britain. J. B. Moore, *History and Digest of the International Arbitration to which the United States has been a Party,* 6 vols. (Washington, D. C.: Government Printing Office, 1898), I, 366-382.

Caucas and Messrs. Crawf: & Galletin have had no correspondence published according to custom? This however may be an improper enquiry from one of his friends (I mean Mr. Crawford's)
and if it be I must rely upon y'r friendship & kindness to forgive it.—

We are likely to have a warm campaign among those who are
candidates for our Legislature in this County and I fear much
that our friend Taylor[72] will be kept by his Clients to attend to
their suits for them—Though he is a *Craffordite* I must vote for
him yet he has lost many of his most zealous supporters on account of opinion & warmth on that subject.—I try all I can to
dissuade those who think with me on the pres: question to forget
it in the selection of our Legislature but they refuse to hear me
—I think it has nothing to do with it at all.—Taylor poor fellow a day or two since lost his oldest child—a son 5 or 6 years
old. It is a severe visitation upon him & he bears it with but
little fortitude.—

I am gratified to tell you that in attendance to your business
entrusted to my management I have been very successful— &
hope I have given them satisfaction—tho: some of your clients
are the greatest geese I ever saw—they know no more about
their suits than so many goats—I don't speak of them *en masse*
I say some of them.—

Another long letter from you at an early date would be very
acceptable—Tis late at night and I must bid you farewell and in
the perusal of the foregoing I beg you to remember that I have
written in haste and in the confidence that I was addressing a
friend that will be ready to overlook all carelessness & imperfections

Sincerely I [am] your Obt
friend & Servt.
WILL. H. H. JR.

P.S. I forgot to add that Dun Cameron has declined being a Candidate for the next Legislature although he was promised no opposition.

[Addressed:]   Willie P. Mangum esquire
H: of Representatives
Washington City
D. C.

---

[72]James F. Taylor opposed Fisher's resolution and opposed printing the governor's message against the caucus. Taylor was defeated by Johnson Busbee. Newsome, *Election of 1824*,
67n, 76; *N. C. Manual*, 830.

WPM-LC

W. A. Tharpe to Willie P. Mangum

FISHDAM April 17th 1824.

Dear Sir.

Enclosed you will receive two petitions,[73] for the post route you desire, I hope they will reach you in time to enable you to make the arrangements to your satisfaction, though not so early as I wished to forward them—

The Presidential Election appears to excite considerable Interest in this section, General Jackson in all probability will receive the vote of North Carolina, he is gaining strength very fast in Wake.—Since John C. Calhoun boulted, I have become an advocate for old Hickory. previous to that I was in favour of W. H. Crawford, believing that Jackson had but a poore chance for success—I wish to have your opinion as to the probable result of the pending Election—

Respectfully yours &C
W. A. THARPE

[Addressed:]

Willie P. Mangum Esqr.   Free
A Representative in Congress.

WPM-LC

Wm. K. Ruffin[74] to Willie P. Mangum

BALTIMORE April 18th 1824

Dear Friend

I have just finished my Fathers letter, which I now send to you that you may read it, and if you approve of my motive you will please write to Papa, and direct one in which our letters are enclosed to "Mr. Kirkland[75] Fayetteville N. C." and request him to send them on immediately, as I have but few days to determine if you do not write or do not approve of my going, you

---

[73]The petitions have not been located.
[74]William Kirkland Ruffin was the eldest son of Judge Thomas Ruffin. In 1824 he attended St. Mary's School in Baltimore. In 1827 he entered the University of North Carolina, from which institution he graduated in 1830. He became an attorney and settled at Haw River where he managed his father's estate. Hamilton, *Papers of Ruffin.*
[75]William Kirkland, the father-in-law of Judge Thomas Ruffin, was a large merchant and planter. Hamilton, *Papers of Ruffin,* I, 127n.

will not send my letter. I hope you will however, and will ascertain from Mr. Randolph[76] all the circumstances that regards the college in Switzerland, and you will please relate them to my Father. It depends entirely on you, I am pretty well assured, for I know that Papa trusts a great deal on you. at least he is willing to do any thing that you think is profitable for me. I shall consider it a great favour if you write whether I get permission or not.—Mr. G. Moore called to see me the other day, and was much surprised to hear that you had not been in Baltimore. he requested me to tell you that you must not battle with any of the Adamites. when I began to write a letter to Papa I did not intend to mention my desire to go to Switzerland, and I said I scarcely expected to see you here, because I thought you would stay in Washington listening to Mr. McDuffie[77] and the Hon. Mr. Trimble[78] until it would be too late and then you would wish to see Mrs Mangum so much that you would go away without thinking of me which I hope will not be the case I go with Mr Randolph I will not be able to visit N. Carolina before I go.

Write to me if you please by tomorrows mail. I wish to hear from you as quick as possible.

I am yours, with respect

WM K. RUFFIN

Hon. W. P. Mangum

WPM-LC

Willie P. Mangum to Charity A. Mangum

WASHINGTON CITY 25th April 1824

My Dear Love.

You must pardon me for not having written to you before this time, and also for the shortness of this letter—

For the last 10 or 12 days, It was expected constantly that a day would be fixed for the adjournment of Congress—

It is customary to appoint the day of adjournment 2 or 3 or more weeks before the time—and I had hoped that in my letter I should have the pleasure of letting you know at what time the Congress would adjourn & when I should probably be at home—

The Senate some time ago fixed the 15th of May—But the House

---

[76]John Randolph of Roanoke.
[77]George McDuffie of South Carolina.
[78]David Trimble, 1782-1842, a Democratic congressman from Kentucky from 1817 to 1827. *Biog. Dir. of Cong.*, 1627.

of rep. would not agree to adjourn as soon as that day—and as
that day—[*sic*] and as yet no day is fixed—And in consequence
of an event that has recently happened—some high charges
brought against Mr. Crawford by that notorious scoundrel Nin-
iam Edwards[79] late Senator of the U. S. and in consequence of
that matter being now under examination by a committee—And
that committee having despatched an officer to bring Edwards
from Illinois. & Crawfords friends determining to have the matter fully investigated—It is impossible to say when Congress will
adjourn—In the first place it is uncertain whether Congress will
await the arrival of Edwards—If it does which is not at all improbable—it will not rise before some time in the month of June
—My own opinion, all things considered is that we shall leave
here the 20th & 25th of May—though a majority I believe at this
time has no expectation of leaving here before June—I have
been tolerably well—The weather is becoming warm—Yesterday
I threw off my flannel—and feel much better of it, the prospect
from Capitol Hill has become beautifully green within the last 4
or 5 days—and every thing around me & about me seems to be
rejoiced with the approaches of the spring & the loveliness of its
robes—But to me it calls up recollections more melancholy than
delightful—

I am exceedingly anxious to see you my Love & our little
daughter, & once more feel & experience the sensation of free-
ness from Crowds—

I write in great haste—Remember me to *my friends*—and accept for yourself & our dear little daughter my Loves & affection

W. P. MANGUM

[Addressed:]

Mrs. Charity A. Mangum
Orange Co.
No. Ca.

---

[79] In April when Congress was about ready to adjourn, Ninian Edwards, former U. S.
Senator from Illinois, charged Crawford with mismanaging funds while he was Secretary of
the Treasury. Edwards was a supporter of Calhoun. A heated debate followed. Many congressmen were so anxious to get home that they favored delaying an investigation until next
term, but Mangum insisted on an investigation to exonerate Crawford. On May 25 a committee appointed to make the investigation completely exonerated Crawford. *Annals of the
Congress of the United States*, 42 vols. (Washington, D. C.: Gales and Seaton, 1834-1856),
18 Cong., 1 sess., 2654-2660; 2713-2725.

WPM-LC

Charity A. Mangum to Willie P. Mangum

[26 April] 1824

My Dear Husband

I have been looking for 3 weeks for a letter from you expecting to hear when you would return home but have received no
information yet. I cannot tell you my Willie how much I wish to
see you & how painful the separation is to me. I am as well as
usual & our dear little Sally appears to be well & grows very fast
but is a very cross child . . . [*sic*] every thing appears green and
fluorishing & I think Ought to make us all feel cheerful & happy
but I have felt more depressed for two weeks than I have been
for some time to think how long you have been absent & that this
time last year I had my Dear & inestimable mother[80] with me &
now that she is in her silent grave & that we are to meet no more
in this world—almost overpowers me never do I expect to see
the day when I shall cease to regreat her loss had I half this
world in my possession I would give the most of it to recall her
If I could—but that is selfish & more so than I ought to be I
have no doubt but that she is happy & that ought to add greatly
to my happiness None can know the loss of such a Mother but
those that have had the misfortune to loose them I now can think
of a great many things that would have added to her happiness
that I omited to do but the time is gone & there is no such thing
as recalling ones Mother but I have one consolation that I know
it was my sincere desire to please her & that she was satisfied
with me & my Willie. Do my husband write me how you are &
when you will return home. I probably may get a letter from
Stagsville today, as I have not sent yet but have been so often
disappointed that i shall not be certain of one untill I see it if I
should be so fortunate as to get one from you. Priestly & Rebecca left here for Hillsborough last week. Fathers Family are
as well as usual Mother[81] is tollerable well were you happy my
Willie I should not care or mind my distresses I have a hope beyond the grave & my happiness in this world is nothing compared with the reward I hope to receive in the World to come
time is short—Farewell My dear husband May Our dear re-

---

[80]Sarah Alston Dudley Cain. Cain Genealogy in possession of Mrs. Lyman Cotton, Chapel
Hill, N. C.; Grove, *Alstons of N. & S. C.*, 423.
[81]Mangum's mother was Catherine Davis Mangum.

deemer never forsake you is the sincere wish of your devoted
wife

C. A. MANGUM

[Postmarked:]

Stagville N. C.
26th April 1824

[Addressed:]   Free

Willie P. Mangum, Esqr.
Washington City   Virginia

———

WPM-LC

Robert Potter to W. P. Mangum

HALIFAX N⁰. CAROLINA
Tuesday April 27th. 1824

My Dear Sir,

Within the last two months I have moved to this place, where
I am determined to abide the issue of fortune; I think my prospects must mend soon, if they vary at all they cannot do otherwise—I shall go up to Granville Court on Saturday, where I have
to encounter the solicitous demands of my petty creditors; were
they a legion of armed devils hot from the bowels of hell I could
comfront them with more complacency—I shall *indesputably* require a $100 which I have no prospect of raising. can you lend it
to me, and forward it by mail so as to reach Oxford on the Saturday of court week? under the expectation that you can, I must
refer my Shylocs to that day for payment; and if I am disappointed, what then, why—satisfy them as I would a flock of hungry buzzards—with my horse

Your friend
ROB. POTTER

[Addressed:]

Honble--

W. P. Mangum
of the H. R.
Washington

WPM-LC

Samuel Yarbrough to Willie P. Mangum

STAGVILLE 17th--May 1824

Dr- Sir,

Having some expectation that our Friend Thos. D. Bennehan Esqr. will give you a call. on His way from Norwich Vermont where we Have understood. he and His nephew Thomas Cameron.[82] reachd. safely and in good Health. about the first. day of this month,—

I wish you to inform Him that. we are all alive Here. & that His Father. Has declined meeting Him at Halifax as expected. when he left Home mostly on accompt. of the expectation. of keeping a certain Lueco Mitchell, Here untill His return Home—When are you coming Home every man that Has a wife ought to be coming Home. with your Tariffs. & Edwards[83] & Crawfords. I am really afraid. You will ruin the nation you dont suppress any Documents. from Mrs. Mangum for the mail. was full. yesterday. they were soon after sent on. they were markd- public. but. I am fearfull If you stay much Longer. at Washington. you will Loose some of your private Documents. or at Least mislaid or Lost so they'll- not easily be found. I believed your friends are Generally well. Mr. R. Bennehan offers his best respects to you. & believe me to be Sincerely

Yrs

SAMl- YARBROUGH

P.S. If you should see Bennehan You can tell Him He will find a letter at Northampton Ct. House N C

S. Y

[Addressed:]

Willie P. Mangum Esqr.
Washington City
D. C.

---

[82]Son of Duncan Cameron.
[83]Ninian Edwards.

William McMurray to Willie P. Mangum.

McMurry's Store   Person Coty N C[84]
17ʰ. May 1824

Dear Sir

a petition having been—forwarded on to you through the Honorable Mr. Mangum—for the Establishment or rather the removal of a post office called cochrans Store in said county to my place and having recᵈ. an answer from Mr. Mangum that the prayer of the petitioners was granted which communication from Mr. Mangum was dated the 3ʳᵈ. March last post and recᵈ. not long thereafter—and I have been in expectation ever since of receiving the request papers—or credentials to open the post office but as such have not been recᵈ. and the petitioners appears anxious for such has Induced—me to address these lines to you wishing to know how soon such can be done consistent with the press of business of the kind now before you. I being at any time ready to comply with the prerequisits as post-master—at any time—required.

Very Respectfully
WILLIAM MCMURRY

[Endorsements:]
Cochran & McMurrays Store N C   10 June 1824
There has no order been given for the establishment or removal of the off[ice] referred to, Neither any papers [in] my file. [The] paper may have been mislaid—perh[aps] it was a small one. What does the o. proposed to be removed pay?

$9—— p. qʳ.
    00
   100

Has a post master been lately appt at this place. None since 1822.
      rec the other side 9 June.
Write to the P. M. to state any objection he may have to the removal—that it has been recommended. Also write, to the writer of this letter, and inform him of the fact.

Leasbury N C.
May 26ᵗʰ 1824

[Addressed:]

Post Master General
Washington City

---
[84]The original is in the possession of Mr. Mangum Turner, Winston-Salem, N. C.

Willie P. Mangum to Seth Jones[85]

WASHINGTON CITY 24th May 1824

My dear Sir.

Our very long & protracted Session is rapidly drawing [to] a close, the 27th we rise—The tariff has passed, but with a great many & important modifications—

The Bill as passed is not so exceedingly objectionable, instead of being a law for the *protection* of Domestic Manufactures, it is a revenue bill—It was gutted in the Senate—The only question of objection or the greatest, is, whether it is not politic to levy indirectly an additional revenue of three millions of dollars, when the present revenue is entirely sufficient to meet the current expenses of government, and to sink gradually the public debt.

The Committee to investigate the charges prefered against Mr Crawford by N. Edwards will be made tomorrow. The principles of the report (as I understand from the Committee) are agreed upon & settled, & that document will furnish the American people with additional evidence of the integrity, purity & ability of the Secretary—And the vindication will be most triumphant when we advert to the fact that the investigation has been made by the ablest of Mr. Cs. political enemies, and the report (however reluctantly) is dragged out of them.—For Gen. Floyd[86] the Chairman of the Committee who is the friend of Mr, C. has been sick & in bed nearly all the time & Mr Randolph[87] staid until he became satisfied, and upon Crawfords ansr. being given in he said that if Edwards has sworn to the charges, that that oath being put in opposition to his evidence last winter, would convict him of perjury & cut off his ears,—& concluded by calling that ansr. the most triumphant refutation. Gen. Jackson cannot in any event be the President & his friends are throwing away their strength. Of this I feel perfectly sure

Crawford has to contend against the most powerful combination & I fear as unprincipled as powerful But he will be president in my opinion—If he fails it will be Adams.

---

[85]A typed copy is in the State Department of Archives and History, Raleigh. The original is not available.
[86]John Floyd, a physician of southwest Virginia, who became a general in the army during the War of 1812, held numerous state and national offices including the Virginia legislature, the national House of Representatives, and governorship of Virginia. In 1832 he received the electoral vote of South Carolina for President. In 1824 when this letter was written he was in Congress. *Biog. Dir. of Cong.*, 975.
[87]John Randolph.

In great haste
Accept assurances of my sincere regard
W. P. MANGUM

Present my respects to Mrs. Jones.
W. P. M.

[Addressed:]

Seth Jones Esquire   *Free*
Raleigh   W. P. Mangum.
North Carolina.

WPM-LC

Presidential Election[88]

WASHINGTON, May 25th, 1824.

THE friends of Mr. Clay adopted in consideration of political principle, public service, and distinguished talent. Upon a full consultation, with a perfect knowledge of the facts, and a just estimate of all the probabilities connected with the question, they now determine to adhere to him steadily to the end.

It is due to him, to his numerous supporters, and to the respectable States by which he has been nominated, to make this declaration.

They were prepared to make any sacrifice, the country, the cause, or the occasion, might demand. But his withdrawal now could produce no result, as his friends, in the electoral vote, would divide; their weight would be lost, and perhaps increase the doubt and uncertainty. The election must, in any and every event that can be anticipated, come into the House of Representatives.

He is now sustained by a weight of influence equal to that of any other candidate; he has more personal and political popularity, and they believe can compete successfully with any man in the nation.

They now offer to the consideration of the People the following candid statement of the relative strength of the parties— from which they will be able to judge correctly of the views herein taken. It is useless to disguise or misrepresent the facts. It is due to the subject and the People to state the truth; and all other means are disdained.

---

[88]A printed circular letter, 1 p.

It is believed that Mr. Adams will have six States:—

Maine, Massachusetts, New Hampshire, Rhode Island, Connecticut, and Vermont, ... 51
Mr. Crawford will have three States: — Virginia, North Carolina, and Georgia, ... 48
General Jackson will have four States: — Pennsylvania, Tennessee, Alabama, and Mississippi, ... 47
Mr. Clay will have six States:—Ohio, Kentucky, Indiana, Illinois, Missouri, and Louisiana, ... 46

It is believed that New York, New Jersey, Delaware, Maryland, and South Carolina, have given no decided indication, and that in these the question is entirely open. Mr. Clay is known to have numerous influential friends in each of these States. His chances are equal to any, and superior to some of the candidates.

They will not speculate upon the probable votes of those States —the changes that may happen, the combinations that may be formed, and the events that may intervene. But, after the most dispassionate consideration of the subject, they are candidly of opinion that Mr. Clay will be returned to the House of Representatives. To the wisdom of that enlightened body, if it be unavoidable, they with confidence submit their claims.

Entertaining the highest respect for the other candidates, they will not indulge in any insidious comparisons of their strength. But it may perhaps be assumed, that if from any cause Mr. Crawford should not receive the vote of New York—if General Jackson should not receive the support of some of the doubtful States—or if Mr. Adams should not receive the vote of New York—Mr. Clay must be returned to the House without calculating any of the contingent or probable cuts that may render that event certain.

If, contrary to all probability, Mr. Clay should not be returned to the House, his friends, having done their duty, will be able by concentration to control the event—they will hold in their hands the balance—they will determine between the opposing and conflicting interests, and secure to the country a republican administration.

Under all the views taken, it is determined to recommend to his friends to adhere to him steadily—and to await with confidence and patience the issue now pending before the people.

[Addressed:]

    The Hon^{bl}
      W. P. Mangum
        (member of Congress)
        Hillsborough
          Orange County
            N. Carolina

WPM-LC

Lewis Williams to Willie P. Mangum

RALEIGH June 3rd. 1824

Dear Sir.

I arrived here on Tuesday in company with Messrs Spaight,[89] Vance[90] and Kelly [91] of Alabama—

On the road and since my arrival here I have had much talk about the Presidential election—From all I can learn there can be no doubt that Crawford will get the vote of this State—But in politics as in war the enemy should not be dispised—on the contrary the action should be planed as if the most formidable opposition was to be expected, and I trust all of us will do our duty—

Permit me again to solicit your company at Chapel Hill[92]—I shall go up tomorrow, and calculate on leaving the place about next Wednesday in the Stage for Salem—Therefore come before Wednesday—we shall see Dr. Craig[93] at C. Hill I presume—

    Your friend truly and sincerely

        LEWIS WILLIAMS

---

[89]Richard D. Spaight.
[90]Robert Brank Vance who was in Congress from Buncombe County from 1823 to 1825.
[91]William Kelly, 1770-1832, a lawyer of Huntsville, Alabama, who was U. S. Senator from Alabama from 1822 to 1825. *Biog. Dir. of Cong.*, 1172.
[92]It was a custom in those days for political leaders to gather at the state university's commencement.
[93]Dr. James A. Craig. See above, p. 132n.

[On inner edge of p. 1]

A Murphey,[94] Calvin Jones,[95] Wm. Gaston &c I expect we shall
see at Chapel Hill—
Hon. Willie P. Mangum—

[Addressed:]

> Hon. Willie P. Mangum
>   Stagville
>   Orange County
>   North Carolina

———

WPM-LC

Copy of Papers on Deep River Bridge Co.

[31 Aug., 1824]

State of North Carolina[96]
. Chatham County.
    Whereas it is deemed expedient and **necessary to the best
interest** of Haywood, that a bridge shall be **erected over Deep
River** in the said Town at the point where union **Street touches**
said River, And whereas the same is resolved to be erected and
after it is built to be established a Toll bridge, by the company
who subscribe for, & have the same built.

    Now to the end that the same may be effected, We the sub-
scribers by these presents form ourselves into a company for
the purposes herein set forth, and we and each of us bind ourselves respectfully to pay fifty dollars for each share & every of
us respectively taken.

    That the profits of said bridge after it is finished shall be di-
vided between us the subscribers in proportion to the stock that
each of us may hold in the sd Company. That the payments for
the shares taken in said Company shall be made as follows, to
Wit Ten dollars to be paid upon each share at the time that the
contract shall be made with the undertaker for building the

---

[94] Archibald D. Murphey.
[95] Calvin Jones, 1775-1846, who was born in Massachusetts, came to North Carolina and
settled at Smithfield in 1795. He entered every phase of the life of the state—social, political,
economic, religious, military, and professional. He organized the North Carolina Medical Society. He served in the legislature from Johnson and later from Wake County. He became
chief of police in Raleigh. With Thomas Henderson he established the Raleigh *Star*. In the
War of 1812 he was adjutant general and major general in defense of the coast. In 1832 he
moved to Tennessee and enjoyed his plantation at Bolivar for the remainder of his life.
D. A. B., X, 163.
[96] See above, p. 11n.

same, fifteen dollars upon each share to be paid at the time that the commissioners shall adjudge the bridge to be half completed and the balance to be paid at the time the said bridge is completed by the undertaker

That Col. John Farrar,[97] John A. Ramsay[98] Esqr and Wil[l]ie P. Mangum Capt Herndon Haralson[99] & Paoli P. Ashe[100] are appointed commissioners to contract for the building of the same, and that the same shall be commenced as soon as twenty five hundred dollars are subscribed, and that no subscriber is to be bound by his subscription until twenty five hundred dollars are subscribed.

		Shares
Willie P. Mangum		Two
Jno. A. Ramsey		Two
W J Franks	2	Two
Theo. Sanders	1	One
H Haralson		Two
S. Strudwick		Two
R. D. Ashe		Two
A. D. Murphey		Two
Carter Atkinson		Two
P. P. Ashe		Two
J. Farrar		Two
D. Tate		One
H. Branson		Two
Andra. Scott		One
Jacob Levy		One

[Endorsed:]

These are all the papers, relative to the town of Haywood in any way which I have been able to find in my office, after the strictest search.

Aug. 31, 1824.   P. H. MANGUM.

[97]See above, p. 17n.
[98]John Ambrose Ramsay graduated from the state university in 1811; he was a member of the state legislature from Moore County in 1814 to 1820 and in 1823. Grant, *Alumni Hist. of U. N. C.*, 510.
[99]See above, p. 20n.
[100]See above, p. 17n.

Indenture of Sheriff Thos. D. Watts to Willie P. Mangum

Sept. 27, 1824

D. Heartt, Printer, Hillsborough

This Indenture,[101] Made this Twenty Seventh day of September in the year of our Lord one thousand eight hundred and twenty four between Thomas D. Watts—Sheriff of the county of Orange and state of North Carolina, on the one part, and Willie P. Mangum of the county of Orange—and state aforesaid, on the other part, WITNESSETH, That whereas by virtue of Sundry writ of venditioni exponas, issued from the court of Pleas and Quarter Sessions for the county aforesaid against Sihon Bobbitt.[102]—for the sum of Ninety dollars with Interest from 18th. January 1823.—which said sum was recovered by Willie P. Mangum assignee & William P. Mangum Surviving partner & with costs, as on record may appear: And whereas the said writ of venditioni exponas directed and delivered to the said Thomas D. Watts sheriff as aforesaid, commanding him to expose to public sale all the right Titles & Interest of Sihon Bobbitt both legal & equitable in & to a Tract of Land lying on the North Side of Dyals Creek adjoining the Lands of Hardaman Duke, William Cozort, & Arthur Mangum Senr. heirs upon which the said Sihon Bobbitt formerly lived Supposed to contain about one hundred Acres also all the right Title & Interest that the said Bobbitt hath in and to a Tract of Land called the Carey Tract adjoining the Lands of Warren Ball Hardamon Duke & William Lunsford all of which Lands are in the County of Orange.

And the said Thomas D. Watts sheriff as aforesaid, after due advertisement according to law, did put up the said land at public sale to the highest bidder, at the court-house door of the county of Orange on the twenty-eighth day of April A. D. 1823, at which time and place the aforesaid Willie P. Mangum—became the last and highest bidder at the sum of One hundred & Sixteen dollars & Seventeen Cents & an half cent for the said lands, with the appurtenances thereunto belonging: Now this indenture witnesseth, that the said Thomas D. Watts—sheriff of Orange county, for and in consideration of the sum of One hundred & Sixteen dollars & Seventeen & an half Cents to him in hand paid by the said Willie P. Mangum—before the sealing and signing of these presents, the receipt whereof is hereby acknowledged, hath here-

---

[101]The original is in the possession of Mr. Mangum Turner, Winston-Salem, N. C.
[102]Sion Bobbitt married Sallie Mangum, the sister of William P. Mangum.

by bargained and sold unto the said Willie P. Mangum—heirs
and assigns, for ever, and by these presents doth bargain and
sell unto the said Willie P. Mangum—his heirs and assigns, the
aforesaid tract of land, to have and to hold, with all its appurtenances, to the said Willie P. Mangum — and that the said
Thoma D. Watts—sheriff, will warrant and defend the same to
the said, Willie P. Mangum his—heirs and assigns, for ever, so
far as his office of sheriff will admit, and no farther. In witness
whereof, the said Thomas D. Watts sheriff of Orange county,
hath hereunto set his hand and seal, the day and year above
written.

SIGNED, SEALED AND DELIVERED
    IN THE PRESENCE OF

    J. Taylor CC

                              Tho⁹. D. Watts Shff   (Seal)

                                                     WPM-LC

        Willie P. Mangum to Thos. McGehee[103]

                         CITY OF RALEIGH Octo. 1824.
My dear Sir.
    The enclosed letter from Jesse Person Esqʳ.[104] an attorney of
the Town of Louisburg, & who has done much collection business, who is intimately acquainted with the people of that County & more especially with the circumstances of Mʳ. Rainey,[105]
seems to indicate the entire certainty of the loss of your claim
against him—at least for the present.
    I learn from enquiry that the time has never been since his
residence in Louisburg that he could either pay or secure the
payment of any but a very small sum of money—I will however
place your paper in the hands of Mʳ. Person, who is a good collector, & if any contingency shᵈ. happen by which he might be
able to secure anything he will do it—or upon your order return
it to you—
    I regret to perceive in Wake a very strong disposition to sup-
port the Peoples ticket[106]—Every vote is worth something &

[103]See above, p. 50n.
[104]See below for letters of Mangum to Person and *vice versa*, Jan. 25, Feb. 20, 1832; Apr. 24, 1843.
[105]Lemuel Rainey of Person County was a member of the legislature in 1819. *N. C. Manual,* 757.
[106]The ticket of presidential electors which favored Andrew Jackson.

therefore I hope Person County will turn out to a man—It is of vast importance to get the people to turn out—& even in that I fear that we shall not be as active as the opposition—

The upper part of Person is much relied upon—The old & young it is hoped will go to the polls—This district I think will be lost.—but efforts will effect much—

I am Dear Sir

Yours with much regard

WILLIE P. MANGUM

Mr Thos McGehee

[Addressed:]

Thomas McGehee, Esquire
Williamsville P. O.
No. Ca.

WPM-LC

H. G. Burton[107] to Willie P. Mangum

HALIFAX October 4 A. D. 1824

My Dear Sir

It was my Intention to have met you this week at Raleigh—a few days Past I lost my son Willie,[108] and Mrs. Jones is now lying at my house dangerously ill—to a husband and Parent it is unnecessary to describe my feelings—I must beg the favor of you to obtain from Judge Ruffin[109]—further time to answer the Bill filed by Cook—I will meet you at any place you will appoint as soon as I can leave home

I am with much

Esteem Yours

H. G. BURTON

[Addressed:]

The Honble
Willie P. Mangum
Raleigh

Jimmy.

---

[107]Hutchins Gordon Burton, 1782-1836, a native of Virginia, was reared in North Carolina by his uncle, Col. Robert Burton. After being admitted to the bar, H. G. Burton became a member of the state legislature in 1809 and 1817, attorney general of North Carolina in 1810, and a member of the national House of Representatives from 1819 to 1824. He served as governor from 1824 to 1827. Iredell County was his home. Ashe, *Biog. Hist. of N. C.*, IV, 68-71.

[108]Burton married Sarah Wales Jones, the daughter of Willie Jones, the noted North Carolina Jeffersonian. Willie Burton was named for Willie Jones.

[109]Judge Thomas Ruffin.

WPM-LC

John Haywood[110] to Willie P. Mangum

RALEIGH 15th October 1824.—

Dear Sir,

The Note with which you kindly favoured me on the 8th. Curr^t. was handed me by Capt. Ruffin on the day following,— and was Shortly after forwarded to the Cashier of the State Bank here, from whom I received the Mem^o. or statement enclosed; which goes to Show the amount in which we are considered bound at the Bank as the Securities or Endorsers of the Rev^d. Mr. John Chaves,[111] and is forwarded to you in compliance with the Wish expressed in your favour above mentioned.—The accumulation of the interest of this Debt, owing to the neglect of Mr. Chaves to pay the Instalments on any of them as they became due, has augmented the amount beyond what I expected: I was aware, however, that the whole Sum, including Prin.^l and Int[.], was considerable; and submitted to you the advisability of our paying off the Debt at once, rather than Suffer it to hang up and be continually growing, through Chaves's Neglect, as it seemed he would not (or could) not pay nor lessen it:—The Bank too, I was aware, has become impatient of Mr. Chaves's delay:—I wish the Parson could and would assist us in paying off this his Debt; and can but hope he will contribute towards the discharge of it, should it so happen that you can conveniently see him, before you come to Raleigh; but if, unfortunately, his means are so limitted as to p[ut] it out of his power to pay any thing, there can be no doubt but the Sooner we pay it for him, the greater will be the Saving in the end.

I am sorry it so happened I chanced to be absent when you did the favour to call at the Office, on the eve of your Setting out from Raleigh, on friday last.—We remain Sickly here still:— Col^o. Henderson[112] has been confined since Saturday last, but is thought, at present, to be somewhat relieved:—A Brother of Mr. Manly's[113] has been ill for a greater number of days, and is

[110]See above, p. 41n.
[111]See above, p. 41n.
[112]Col. Pleasant Henderson, 1755-1846, of Granville who served in the Revolutionary War was clerk of the North Carolina House of Commons from 1807 to 1830 when he moved to Carroll County, Tennessee. *Hillsborough Recorder*, Jan. 12, 1842; Walter Clark (ed.), *N. C. State Record*, XXII, 129-131.
[113]Matthias E. Manly, 1801-1881, of New Bern, received his A.B. degree at the state university in 1824 and his A.M. in 1829. He was judge of the superior court from 1840 to 1859, and of the state Supreme Court from 1860 to 1865. A member of the constitutional convention of 1865, he became speaker of the state senate and lieutenant governor in 1866. Although elected U. S. Senator in 1867 he was not permitted to take his seat. Ashe, *Biog. Hist. of N. C.*, VI, 357-366.

considered as being very dangerously indisposed—Very many others in this place and around it, are likewise sick.

I trust you continue in health! and greeting you kindly and respectfully, remain much & truly,

Your friend & Ser.

Mr. Mangum,   JOHN HAYWOOD

[Addressed:]
The Honourable
Willie P. Mangum, Esquire,
at his Seat in Orange County,
near
Stagville
No. Carolina.

———

WPM-LC

Titus Jennings Turner's petition for Revolutionary Pension[114]

[8 DECEMBER, 1824]

honourable Nathaniel Macon Senator in Congress and to the honourable Willie P. Mangum Representative in Congress of the united States of America gentlemen the following address is for and in half of a man who Served in the North Carolina Contenental line twelve months and about Twelve months in the north Carolina militia and about Sixteen months in a Regiment —of Regular Soldiers Raised by an act of the North Carolina legislature passed in the summer of the year 1781 which Regiment was to be organised and disciplined in the same manner as Continental Troops but to serve within the State the said man has well authenticated evidence of his said services performed in and during the Revolutionary war but having lost his discharge from the Continental line and persons who had seen it being Dead he used all means heretofore likely in an ingenious manner to avail himself of a part of the money the honourable Congress of 1818[115] granted to the men who suffered

---

[114]See above, pp. 31-32.
[115]The act of 1818 provided that every person, who had served in the Revolutionary War until its close or had served for nine months in any period in a continental unit or in the navy, and who was a resident citizen of the United States, and who was in need of support should receive a pension. The rates ran from $8.00 to $20.00 a month for life. This act resulted in a tremendous increase of pensions and applications. An amendment of 1820 required the applicant to present sworn statements of need. In 1826 a person must have less than $300.00 worth of property to receive a pension. The whole program was greatly liberalized in 1832 to consider two years of service in the state forces sufficient for a pension. W. H. Glasson, *Federal Military Pensions in the United States* (New York, N. Y.: Oxford University Press, 1918), 67-71, 81-83.

in defence of the united States from the [Bri]tish oppression though he has faild to obtain the money he has a Certificate of one of his Captains Company that the Cloathing was not Delivered till about twelve months after enlisting and that he was not present at the time nor the place when and where the last payment was made which was once in Two months he has other written evidence of his performance in life when out of the army and now nearly Seventy-two years of age his constitution being much Debilitated by the hardships he suffered the said debility yet continues his bodily strength much lessened by sickness and hard labour and not possessed of any estate nor property Real nor personal nor income therefore if you please to condescend to consider of this address if it is thought such evidence will support and cause a petition to the national Supreme legislature to prevail or not you can answer if in the affirmative the evidence will be immediately sent with the controlers certificate that the name is not on the list of army accounts the gratuity would be saveing from distress him that suffered to defend Honestly [what] others enjoy him whose name is signed is the man alluded to

TITUS JENNINGS TURNER.

December 8, 1824.

whatever may be the Result of this my application for a public gratuity I shall with Complacency acquiese in the event knowing that if sufferance be my lot others is and future ages will be exemp from the expression of monarchy and that our government and people will ever persevere with the wisdom and patriotism of Congress, in preserving and maintaining to all there posterity our free and liberal political institutions you will please to direct your answer to the post office in Raleigh I assert to you that I have not omitted endeavoring to avail myself of everything Required by the Law Relative to Revolutionary pensioners. I am with all due Respect and difference gentlemen yours a poor distressed Revolutionary Soldier.

TITUS JENNINGS TURNER.

[8 DECEMBER, 1824]

postscript.

I have omitted to send my papers of the said evidence (though authenticated in all Respects Required by law) for fear of loosing (for I set much by them) till I have a likelyhood of availing [prevailing upon] you will Remember that a large number of the North Carolina line had not their names inserted in the muster Roll and as the desertion of them that did desert is inserted in the muster Roll I see no cause why them that prove their Service should not have their names inserted in the muster Roll and be placed in all Respects on the same footing with others whose names are already on the muster Roll pay for twelve months Cloathing and Two months wages is yet owing and due to me for Service in the north Carolina Continental line in the year of 1776 and 1777, and ought to be paid with interest.

[Enclosure:]

State of North Carolina
Orange County

    We the subscribers having movd from Wake County and was there personally acquainted with Titus Jennings Turner and the said Turner as it was understood ameong his acquaintance in Wake County Served a year in the North Carolina Continental line in the forepart of the Revolutionary war and after that served in the militia in equal Relation with others until near the close of said war and served a year in Regiment of Regular soldiers then Raised to serve in the State and the said [Turner] was not accused of leaving the service nor his duty during the said time without authority for the same.

Nicholas Atkins
Paris Pearson

I the undersigned Subscriber a Justice of the peace in and for the County of Wake in the State of North Carolina do hereby Certify that Nicholas Atkins and paris pearson whose names are signed to a certificate on this paper for and in behalf of Titus Jennings Turner are each of them a Respectable and Creditable Character whose information and Testimony are to be Relied on, trusted to, and confided in.

N. Norris, J. P.

W. P. Mangum to Thomas Ruffin[116]

WASHINGTON 15th Dec. 1824.

Dear Sir

I have just returned from Baltimore, where I left William[117] —He seemed never fully to realize his situation until I was about to leave him when he seemed deeply affected—Indeed every thing about St. Mary's[118] wears a melancholy appearance to one from No. Caro.

The dresses of the Catholic teachers, the Gothic tower, the strange appearance of the halls hung with pictures calling up every sort of religious association altogether affected William in almost any other way than pleasantly—He will however I have no doubt become perfectly satisfied in a short time—There are many fine boys in the school—and some of them from the south & from protestant families—

Mr. Damplon indicated every dispostion to put William in a course that will not at first tend to strengthen his dislike of his situation—The intercourse I should think from what I observed, is upon a more easy footing between the Teachers and the Students at St. Mary's than at Chapel Hill, and from all that I have been able to learn on the subject, I should think that it is one of the best institutions in the United States for the acquiring of the ancient & modern languages, and more especially the latter.

I presume you know that Mr. Damplon is a Parisian, that he lived & taught in Paris until he had attained a ripened manhood—and that under the troubles of Napoleon he left Paris for America with no other view than that of paying a visit to some of his friends, but contrary to his expectations was induced to become an officer in St. Mary's.

I had an interview of say 2 hours with him, I left him well pleased, with his affability, easy politeness, and even courteousness—

The check you handed to me was duly paid at the Bank in Baltimore.—I enclose you a prospectus which will give you more fully the information you may desire in relation to the course of study in the College—

---

[116]The original is in the Thomas Ruffin Papers, Southern Collection, University of North Carolina. This letter has been previously published in Hamilton, *Ruffin Papers*, I, 321-322.
[117]Thomas Ruffin's son.
[118]A well-known Roman Catholic institution in Baltimore.

I also enclose to you Mr. Damplon' receipt for the money paid him.—

I have but a moment more to say to you, that Gen. Jackson will in all probability be the president—Everything however depends upon Mr. Clay—Crawford's friends have determined to stand upon their arms, and receive the Cross forces of the enemy—that is to say Virga. No. Ca. Georgia & Delaware—for it is pretty certain that New York true to her character, will abandon Crawford in the House—

The North Ca. vote will remain firm unless under some exigency they shall move en masse, & with unanimity—

I will say more to you on these subjects before long.

I am Dear Sir
Yours with much respect
WILLIE P. MANGUM

Mr. Thos. Ruffin.

[Address:]

Thomas Ruffin Esquire
Hillsborough
North Carolina.

[Endorsed:]

Honble. W. P. Mangum
Decm. 1824.

W. P. Mangum to Bartlett Yancey[119]

WASHINGTON 25th. Dec: 1824.

Dear Sir

I have this morning received yours of the 20th Inst[120] and have only a moment to write to you—I certainly am astonished to hear that anybody can form the slightest pretence, or indulge the remotest expectation that I shall give any other vote, than for Mr. Crawford in the H of Reps.—I have written but very few letters—and have been upon my guard.—I have expressed my opinion in some of them that Jackson is likely to succeed. .In doing so I have expressed what has seemed to me most probable, knowing that the event was in no manner to be controuled by any opinion that I might express—or that other than members might entertain—I write to you at Raleigh, that you may if it should become proper in any conversation, declare my determination not to give up the ship.—I do not know what No. Ca. will do in the event Crawford is de hors. nor does any other person know. Indeed it is here understood that the members from No. Ca. have not looked to any other result than a vote for Crawford. that when it shall become necessary to surrender his claims it will then be time enough to determine as to the Course by them to be taken—But it is generally understood. & I believe the fact to be so. that his claims are not to be surrendered. that our delegation are *unwilling to take the responsibility of making a President, without a choice*—that to vote for *another* is in some degree, *underwriting* for him. This they are unwilling to do.—Late events leave Jackson's prospects more doubtful than they have heretofore been supposed to be. Cooke[121] of Illinois it is pretty certain will vote for Adams—he pledged himself to vote with his State. But the State is divided into 3 electoral districts, & tho Jackson got 2 vote. yet there were powerful minorities in each, & in the dis—where Adams prevailed the majority was large, leaving the parties so balanced that he feels at liberty to pursue the dictates of his own Judgt. He will of course go for Adams & without him, Jackson cannot succeed—

Your calculations as to Mississippi & Louisiana I believe are wrong.

All depends on Kentucky—which is yet doubtful—Ohio & Missouri will go with her, if she takes a decided stand.

I have no time to write now I will write to you before long more at leisure & more in detail.

Yours respectfully,

W. P. MANGUM

None of Crawford's friends from No. Ca. will move unless all move. They will act with perfect harmony, & en masse.

W. P. M.

Hon Bartlett Yancey   Free
    Raleigh   North Carolina   W. P. Mangum
                                              25. Dec 24

---

[121]David P. Cook, the only member of the House of Representatives from Illinois, voted for Adams for personal reasons, although the electoral vote of his state had been cast for Jackson. Upon his arrival in Washington, Cook had announced that he was bound by this vote of his state. J. S. Bassett, *The Life of Andrew Jackson* (New York, 1928), 363.

WPM-LC

Jno. J. Carrington[122] to Willie P. Mangum

ORANGE 27th. Decemr. 1824.

D[r]. Sir,

Elizabeth Lingo requests me to inform you, that her husband William Lingo enlisted in the United States service at Granville court house under one Ridley (who she believes was a captain, he went on to charlestown in South Carolina & died on an Island near that place.— She wish's [you] to attend to the matter for her & try to get the money for her if possible, She says the necessary papers has been before sent on

Yours Sincerely

Jno. J. Carrington

P. S. I will take your crop of cotton if delivered at my machine, at the price you asked me, say three dollars)

JNO. J. CARRINGTON

[Addressed:]

Hon: Willie P. Mangum
Member of the house of
Representative, Congress
of the United States

Mail   Washington City

WPM-LC

John Newlin[123] to Willie P. Mangum

[31 DEC., 1824]

Friend W. P. Mangum

I am Desirous that the Post office Department should be extended Juditiously as far as it will Carry itself on it own productions and no further I discover that on thy motion the house has resolved that the Committee on Post offices & Post roads be Instructed to Inquire into the expediency of a Post rout[124] from Raleigh N C by the fishdam on Neuse by Stagville and Mt Tirza to Roxborough not being acquainted with the direction of Post

------

[122]See above, p. 88n.
[123]Postmaster at Lindley's Store in Orange County near what is today Saxapahaw in Alamance County. McIver, *N. C. Directory*, 70.
[124]See above, pp. 105-107.

Washington 25th Dec: 1824.

Dear Sir

I have this morning received yours of the 20th Inst and have only a moment to write to you — I certainly am astonished to hear that any body can form the slightest pretence, or indulge the remotest expectation that I shall give any other vote, than for Mr. Crawford in the H of Rep. — I have written but very few letters — and I have been upon my guard. — I have expressed my opinion in some of them that Jackson is likely to succeed. In doing so I have expressed what then seemed to me most probable. knowing that the event was in no manner to be controuled by any opinion that I might express. or that other than members might entertain — I wrote to you at Raleigh, that you may, if it should become proper in any conversation, declare my determination not to give up the ship. — I do not know what No 1a will do in the event Crawford is de hors. nor

does any other person know. Indeed
it is here understood that the members from
N Cra have not looked to any other
result than a vote for Crawford. that
when it shall become necessary to surrender his claims it will then be time
enough to determine as to the Course
by them to be taken — But it is generally
understood. & I believe the fact to be so.
That his claims are not to be surrendered.
That our delegation are unwilling
to take the responsibility of making a
President, without a choice — & & to
vote for another is in some degree, un-
-der writing for him— this they are unwilling
to do.— Late events leave Jackson's
prospects more doubtful than they
have heretofore been supposed to be—
Cook of Illinois it is pretty certain will
vote for Adams— he pledged himself to vote
with his State. But the State is divided into
3 electoral districts. & tho Jackson got 2
vote. yet there were powerful minorities in
each, & in the dis— where Adams prevailed
the majority was large. leaving the parties
so balanced that he feels at liberty to

pursue the dictates, of his own judgt
he will of course go for adams & without
him Jackson cannot succeed.
Your calculations as to Mississippi & Louis-
-iana I believe are wrong...

All depends on Kentucky — which
is yet doubtful — Ohio & Missouri
-ri. will go with her, if she takes
a decided stand.

I have no time to write now
I will write to you before long
more at leisure & more in
detail. — Yours respectfully,
Wm G Mangum

None of Crawfords friends from
No Ca. will move unless
all move. They will
act with perfect har-
mony. & on Masse
W.P.

Free
W. P. Mangum

Hon Bartlett Yancey

Raleigh

North Carolina

routs now existing in that Section of the Country am not prepared to say whether it will be a Juditious rout or not I also observe that on John Longs motion there is a resolve that the same Committee be Instructed to Inquire into the expediency of a Post rout from Pittsboro to Joseph Brookes Wm Lindleys Store Albrights Store John Carters (I presume Jehu Carters) Longs Store Hadleys Mill Mcleanes Store to Greensborough N C being somewhat acquainted with the direction of existing routs and the Geography of this Section of Country as thee is a Representative then I feel it my duty both as a citizen and an officer in the Post office department through thee to shew that this will not be a Juditious rout the Stage from Raleigh to Salisbury through Pittsbororugh runs I think within two miles of Joseph Brooks the horse mail from Chapel Hill to Lexington Passes within about three mile of Wm Lindleys and within about One mile of Albrights the beforesaid Stage also Passes through the Neighborhood of Carter at Longs there is now a Post office and the Neighborhood accommodated by the beforesaid horse mail Hadleys is within about two miles of Longs I don know exactly the Situation of Mebanes Store but think the rout by there from Hadleys to Greensborough is no part distant from the Stage line from Raligh to Salem more than Six or eight miles I am of the Opinion that this proposed rout will not Increase the revenue of the department [by] ten dollars and the expence perhaps [by] three hundred my own Opinion is that we have Post routs enough in this Country unless we could make them more productive [than these] that are now existing which I think might be made more accommodating and more productive by aranging their little Cross routs to go one way and return another with very little expence Increased I have No other View in this Statement but public good I regret that our thinly Inhabitted Country will not Justify a mail in every Neighborhood as by that Convenience the mind of the people are much enlightened—but I submit it to thy better judgment All well

I am respectfully
JOHN NEWLIN

Lindleys Store Orange Cty N C
   12th mo 31st 1824
N. B. Please to shew this to
       John Long[125]

---

[125]John Long, 1785-1857, a farmer in Randolph County, was a member of the North Carolina legislature in 1811, 1812, 1814, and 1815. From 1821 to 1829 he was in the national House of Representatives. *Biog. Dir. of Cong.*, 1236.

[Addressed:]

Wiley P. Mangum Esq
        Representative in Congress
                Washington City

WPM-LC

Priestley H. Mangum to Willie P. Mangum

WAKEFIELD,[126] Dec. 31st. 1824.

Dear Sir,

Having removed to this place soon after your departure for Washington City, I am entirely ignorant of the passing events in the Councils of the nation, except what little information I have gleaned from one or two *papers*, which have casually fallen under my observation. This is attributable to the retirement of a country residence & the want of my *papers* which have not yet been directed to this neighborhood. Perhaps the latter cause is not to be regretted, unless the *press* has cast off the weight of moral corruption, which a few months or rather weeks ago filled its pages & disgraced its character. I am anxious to learn who is likely to be the president—yet I almost dread the information. Genl. Jackson is said here to be most prominent in the estimation of the members of Congress—I hope not. But still I know that "like master like man" *almost* universally applies to the *People's men*. If the Genl. is to be President, we ought perhaps to know it, that we may be prepared within ourselves to brook the idea, that a *military leader* can give a direction, at his pleasure, to the popular impulse of the nation.

If your little Irishman[127] continues his paper, I wish you would tell him to send it here, instead of Hillsboro. The little man's spirits are down,[128] I suspect; he has the consolation of having companions in misery.

I am absolutely at a loss to write any thing at this time—unless it be a dissertation on the effects of Broom-sedge upon the eyesight—which would not amuse you much.

---

[126]Home of Col. Ransom Sutherland, Priestley's father-in-law, who lived near Wake Forest.
[127]Dennis Heartt, the editor of the *Hillsborough Recorder*.
[128]Heartt supported Adams for the presidency and at this time it looked as though Jackson would win.

I was at your house a few days ago—and all were well. We are tolerably well.

Write me immediately

Yrs
respectfully
P. H. MANGUM

[Addressed:]

The Honbl.
Willie P. Mangum
House of Representatives
Washington City
D. C.

———————

1825

WPM-LC

John F. Brevard[1] to Willie P. Mangum

LINCOLN COUNTY N. C. Jany. 1. 1825

Honb[le] Willie P. Mangum
Sir

I have just ventured to put you to a little trouble, by laying you under requisition to do a little business—which notwithstanding is of considerable importance to us. A suit has been for some years in pendency in the Federal Court in Nashville, Ten. James Hibbits vs. James Conner & Henry W. M. Conner,[2] for 5000 Acres Land. A trial was had in 1823, which was not decided altogether to the liking of the Defend[ts]— An Appeal was taken, & stands now for trial in the Supreme Court at Washington—The Honb[le] Hugh L. White of Knoxville, Tennessee, has been imployed as the Counsel to attend to the case at the latter place (Washington).

By last Mail he writes me—"It has been, & still is, my intention to apear in this cause at Washington, if I can possibly get

———————

[1]See above, p. 123n.
[2]James Connor of Lincolnton County was the brother of Henry William Connor, 1793-1866, who was a member of the Federal House of Representatives from 1821 to 1841. Henry Workman M. Connor, the son of James and nephew of H. William Connor, became a banker and political leader in Charleston. William L. Sherrill, *Annals of Lincoln County, North Carolina . . . through the years 1749 to 1937.* (Charlotte, N. C.: The Observer Printing House, 1937), 64.

on there this Winter—If I cannot, I will take care to write to
Mr. Henry Will. Conner at Washington in time to engage some
other person, & will advise you &C",

To this I have just replied—"We truly hope that nothing will
intervene to prevent you from attending personally at Washington—But if such should be the Case, we wish you to write
to the Honb^le Willie P. Mangum, a Member of Congress from
this State, as our Agent there, & not to Mr. Henry Will. Connor. The latter Gentleman has been so kind as to carry on the
papers directed to you—but it is probable would not wish to
have any further trouble or agency in the business—as there is
a coolness between our families. By next mail I shall write to
Judge Mangum & request his attention to this business—
(should any accident render it necesary)—which I am assured
will be cheerfully & efficiently bestowed."

Thus Sir you see that I have made free with your name. What
has been stated to Judge White will serve to explain to you why
we wish to put Mr Conner to no further trouble—An additional
reason is, that, in a mater of such importance to us, & a law
case, we should much rather rely upon your judgment than his
in selecting & imploying Counsel. If Sir, you will agree to take
this trouble, you will lay me under very great obligations—I am
interested indirectly one half in whatever profit may be gained
or loss sustained by the decision of the suit. The land is a first
rate tract—& the cost is already *Something*.

How you are to inform Mr Conner[3] of our application to you,
or to obtain the papers from him(should Judge White not go
on) I leave to your own judgment to accomplish in the most
delicate manner—as no contempt or insult is intended to him
(for we duly acknowledge our obligation for what he has done,
& appears willing to do) but still we should very decidedly prefer your acting in this business, to his acting—if you will be so
kind as to undertake it.

It may perhaps become necessary for some one who fully
understands this business to be at Washington at or previous to
the trial of the suit, to put the Counsel imployed, into possession of all necessary information. Should this be the case (tho'
I hope it may not) Mr Henry W. M. Conner of Charleston will
repair to Washington at the shortest notice.

---

[3] He refers here to Henry William Connor.

Be so good as to write to me immediately on the receipt of this letter

With great respect
& esteem
Yours &C
JOHN F. BREVARD

Honb^{le} Willie P. Mangum

    P. S. The attendance of Mr. Conner at Washington will be greatly against his interests in Charleston If he can be done without to equal advantage it would be much preferable. I think the case a plain one—as the Bill—answer & depositions may shew. Perhaps it may not come to a decision this Winter. And as matters have turned out this might be to our advantage. Inform me whether it will or *must* be tried at the ensuing session of Court?

Should it become necessary for you to imploy Counsel in our behalf at Washington I presume it is unnecessary to State that you are authorised to contract for the payment of whatever fee you may think just and proper to allow—And that the Money to the amount will be forwarded according to your Order either by Henry W. M. Conner, Charleston,—or by

John F. Brevard

[Addressed:]

Hon^{le} Willie P. Mangum
Washington City

Mail

[Postmarked] Beaties Ford, N. C.

5th Jany 1825
Free

WPM-LC

John Rogers[4] to Willie P. Mangum

HILLSBOROUGH Jan. 2nd. 1825—

Dear Sir—

I have presumed so far as to solicit your agency in order to the effecting of a settlement with certain persons in Baltimore

---

[4]John Rogers, a graduate of Georgetown College, maintained a classical academy in Hillsboro. In 1826 when he considered moving to Tennessee he had the reputation, according to A. D. Murphey, of being one of the best classical scholars in North Carolina. Hamilton, *Papers of Ruffin,* I, 207n; Hoyt, *Papers of Murphey,* I, 343.

& Washington, who have claims against me—The friendly disposition you have ever manifested towards me, is the only ground upon which my expectation rests, that you you [sic] will, at any rate, excuse the trouble I propose to give you, if there be the smallest impropriety in the present application—Your attention to this business however, if your public duties will permit you to bestow it, shall not be forgotten—

I am indebted to Gales & Seaton as a subscriber to the Intelligencer, for a consideratble time—also to Col. Pechin[5] in Baltimore, for the Commercial Chronicle—to the former Editor of the Baltimore Morning Chronicle, & to Edward J. Coale of Baltimore Bookseller—

By this day's mail, I shall write to each of those persons, requesting that they will forward their respective acc^{ts} to you, with an assurance that so soon as I shall receive from *you* a *memorandum* of their several claims, the whole am^{t}. shall be forwarded to you the moment it comes to my knowledge, in the hope that you will have the goodness to pay their respective demands—

Is there no scourge of impudence, & presumptuous folly in the House, now Mr Randolph[6] is no longer there, to keep the advocate for exploring a N. West Passage, (say for the honor of poor N. Carolina,) in subjection? if there be not, the chaplains, as the last resort, ought to be instructed to pray every morning in a special manner, for the amelioration of the Edenton District[7]—I was scandalized at seeing in the Intelligencer the names of several members of Congress who had rendered themselves conspicuous by their exertions to extingush the fire in the Capitol—how will such a thing read in the saloons of Europe! our Supreme Legislators puffed as Firemen!

Our State Legislature has rendered important service to the venders of turkies & table fare generally—this, at most, is all I can collect from reading the papers, and it is seldom I go abroad to inquire how the world goes.

Will you do me the favor to send me a copy of the "Souvenir

---

[5]*The Baltimore Chronicle* went under various names. In 1807 W. Peckin took it over and remained a member of the firm until 1817 when Robert A. Dobbin got control. Mary Wescott and Allene Ramage, comp., *A Check-list of United States Newspapers in the General Library of Duke University*, 6 vols. (Durham, N. C.: Duke University Press, 1836), II, 178.

[6]Probably John Randolph of Roanoke.

[7]Alfred M. Gatlin was congressman from this district. In 1823 he had been elected over Lemuel Sawyer. He was originally for Jackson but his friends prevailed upon him to shift his vote to Crawford. This made him unpopular. As a result he was defeated in 1825. Newsome, *Election of 1824*, 58n, 82n, 170, 171n.

Atlantique,"⁸ I believe it is called—a sort of Almanac published
either in Philadelphia, or Washington—I should prefer a copy
in the cheapest binding—the price of it shall be remitted along
with the money for the persons mentioned above—
        I am, dear Sir, with the utmost respect,
                Your friend & obedᵗ Servᵗ
                        JOHN ROGERS.—

Hon. Willie P. Mangum—Washington—

[Addressed:]
        The Hon. Willie P. Mangum
                Washington City

                Willie P. Mangum to John Robertson⁹

                WASHINGTON CITY 3rd January 1825.

To Capt. Jno. Robertson.¹⁰
Dear Sir,
    I take the liberty of transmitting to you some documents, that
you may find somewhat interesting, and I also drop you this line
in haste, hoping it will not be unacceptable.
    It is to be presumed that you feel some desire to know, how
the contest, which has so strongly, & so extensively agitated the
union now stands, according to the opinions of those who are
present at the theatre where the final struggle is to be made.—
    It is entirely uncertain as yet, what will be the result, and it is
only upon such indications as present themselves, that I found
not _an opinion,_ but merely _conjecture_ as to the issue.—soon
after my arrival at Washington I took the impression, that Gen.
Jackson would succeed—but later events leave it _now_ very uncertain, and indeed I think his prospects are not as bright as
they were.—Crawford is a long way behind, but I should not be
greatly surprised, if Jackson and Adams friends ultimately
compromize to a certain extent by meeting on Crawford—Much
very much depends on Mr. Clay, and he as yet has given no clear

⁸In 1825 the publishing house of Carey and Legan produced _The Atlantic Souvenir_ which included short stories, essays, and poems, as a gift book. It was so well received that other editions followed until thirty different ones were produced in one year. Ralph Thompson, _American Literary Annuals and Gift Books 1825-1865_ (New York, N. Y.: The H. W. Wilson Co., 1936), 1-4, 156.
⁹A typed copy is available in the Department of Archives and History, Raleigh, N. C. The original was formerly in the possession of Willie Mangum Person.
¹⁰Probably Captain John Robertson of the state militia from Wake County.

indication of the course of policy he will adopt.—Not having seen you during the canvass, I do not know what are your wishes on the subject.—But for myself I am clearly of opinion *now,* as I have always been that the best interests of our country require the election of Crawford—& believing so I have as an honest man but one course to pursue—I know full well that these sentiments do not suit the County of Wake—But I cannot bring myself for mere purposes of popularity, to abandon what in my heart I believe to be those principles that make for the welfare of our common country,—And I am sure that every honourable man would spurn that sort of policy, which *seeks only* for the strongest garrison for shelter & defence—there is at least some loyalty to principle to defend its shattered ruins to the uttermost.—There is much on this subject that I should like to say to every man in the district I represent, but it cannot be said in a letter.—It will be objected to me that I set up my opinion against the will of the State—Every one who knows me is satisfied that I do nothing of that sort in a spirit of defiance, on the contrary it is my anxious wish to give entire satisfaction to my constituents—it is my first wish to discharge conscientiously my duty to myself & my country in all public trusts—& the second wish of my heart would be to have my course approved by those whose interests are placed in my keeping.—

But in this question I have to act, and let me act in what way I will, I shall have to encounter strong opposition. My great object has been to *find out the true course,* & to pursue it steadily & firmly, & leave the consequences to God, & my countrymen.—

I feel it my duty to vote for Mr Crawford as long as he has the remotest prospect of success & for the honour of poor North Carolina, I hope she will be amongst the last to give way from what she believes is right.—

The best rule on a subject of this kind is to do what we think will redound to the best interests of the country, & throw ourselves upon the people—In their decisions I have generally a strong confidence. There may be misled for a while, but only for a while.—

Congress has not done much yet, nor do I think that much important legislation will be done this winter—

You have I presume seen through the Executive communications the state of our finances, they are flourishing and the national debt is gradually extinguishing—Notwithstanding the extensive & profuse expenditures of the present administration, the national debt under the superintendence of Mr. Crawford has been more extinguished within the last 8 years, than it ever has in the same length of time under the management of any other Secretary of the treasury since the foundation of the Government.

Much has been said of the Economy of Mr. Jefferson's Administration, but it is a fact that does not seem to be generally known that since Crawford has managed the treasury that more of our debt has been paid than was under Mr. Jefferson in the same length of time—Upwards of one hundred & one millions of dollars have been paid in 8 years towards the principal & interest of the national debt. And during that time immense sums have been paid away & some of them very uselessly, towards extinguishing indian titles—fortifications &c.—The Gallant little Navy of the U States has been gradually increased & the Army tho reduced (& in my opinion very properly, & ([sic] still the staff might be beneficially more reduced) is in a state of sound health. Upon the whole the presents financial

[The remainder of the letter is missing.]

WPM-LC

Seth Jones to Willie P. Mangum

PLEASANT LEVEL 7th January 1825.

My dear Friend,

I hoped to have answered your favour of the 11th December sooner, but even at this time I have nothing of importance to write you.

I should be glad if you would write me how the Presidential election is going on and likely to terminate, should we not get Crawford I suppose we must have Adams or Jackson, I do not like either of them for President of these United States, but of the two I should prefer Adams as the lesser evil.—

There is not much talk as yet about the next Congressional election in this District some think that Crudup[11] will be a candidate Others think he never will be a candidate again, my opinion is that he only needs incouragement sufficient to think that

---

[11] Josiah Crudup. See above, p. 53n.

he could beat you for him to come out, My opinion is further
that neither Crudup nor any other person in the District can
beat you.

Many of the neighbors as well as myself wish a Post office
established at William Role's[12] in Wake, the expence cannot be
much to the Government, as William Role's is on the Stage Road
from Raleigh to Louisburg and about half way,—Mr. Roles is
willing to be Post-Master to transact the business pertaining to
that office, Mr. Roles has considerable influence in his neighbourhood & it would perhaps be not amiss to write him a letter
or two. The sooner you have the Post office established the better as we have no regular way of getting our News-Papers.

I should like for you to write me the news often I have stopped
the Richmond Enquirer

In your letter of 11th. Decemr. you mentioned you expected to
publish a hand Bill, If you do so any thing I can do for you will
be done with pleasure.

> Your very affectionate and
> Obliged
> SETH JONES

Willie P. Mangum Esqre.

N. B. The Stage stops and shifts Horses at Roles so that it will
be no hindrance to the mail

> S. J.

[Addressed:]

> Honorable, Willie P. Mangum Esqre.
> Washington City

Willie P. Mangum to Duncan Cameron[13]

WASHINGTON CITY 10th Jany. 1825

My dear Sir

Your favour of the 2nd. Instant, came to hand this morning,
and I hasten, by this days mail, to acknowledge its receipt.—I
have laid your letter before Mr. Cobb[14] of Georgia, and made

---

[12]This is the present Rolesville in Wake County.
[13]The original is in the Cameron Papers.
[14]Thomas Willis Cobb, 1784-1830, was in the national House of Representatives from 1817
to 1821, and 1823 to December 1824 when he transferred to the Senate. He served in the
Senate until 1828 when he resigned to become a judge of the Georgia superior court. *Biog.
Dir. of Cong.*, 827.

all the enquiries touching the subject matter of your application that I presumed would be useful to you.—

Mr. Cobb informs me that Mr. Gilmour[15] late a member of Congress, practices in the Court at Oglethorpe, and that his standing as a lawyer is in all respects good, and that your business might be safely entrusted to his care.

Mr. Cobb is however under the impresison that Mr. Gilmour has been retained in behalf of the representative—and mentions to me that he *himself* and his partner a Mr. Foster[16] also practice in that Court, and that should your determination be to place the business in his hands that he will have it speedily & effectually attended to. In that event he desires that any necessary communication may be made to him immediately at this place, and he will speedily take the proper steps.—Should you however think proper to apply in the first instance to Mr. Gilmour, he will upon request give any letters that may be useful.

Under all the circumstances I should presume that you would do well to employ Mr Cobb who evidently has a great ascendancy in the profession in that part of Georgia from what I learn. He will necessarily be occasionally absent, but his place is well supplied by his partner.—

On the subject of the Presidential election, I am *at fault.*— The most knowing ones seem to be but little better off in as that subject.—Soon after my arrival here, I thought the indications of public sentiment decisively favorable to Gen: Jackson. The members of Congress seemed not to have recovered from the astonishment created by his unexpected successes.—Time & reflection have however, I think materially diminished his chances of success.—*The election I think will depend upon the course that Mr Clay may take.* Of this I entertain scarcely any doubt. Mr Clay & his friends have until very recently, maintained the utmost reserve, and the slight departure from that course, is still quite equivocal.—One thing I think sure, that he will not stand still, and that when he moves the *first object* will *be success*—Our notions of patriotism become quite low, when we see a gentleman occupying so much space in the public mind as Mr Clay regulated by no higher considerations.—I learn from a

---

[15]George R. Gilmer, 1790-1859, was a member of Congress from Georgia in 1821-1823, 1827-1829, and 1833-1835. He was governor of his state from 1829 to 1831 and from 1837 to 1839. He became an ardent Whig. *Biog. Dir. of Cong.*, 1014.

[16]Thomas F. Foster, 1790-1848, attended the Litchfield Law School and practiced law at Greensboro, Georgia. He was a member of Congress in 1829-1835 and 1841-1843. He was a Whig. *Biog. Dir. of Cong.*, 984.

source that I deem entitled to full faith, that sad measures have already been taken by Clay & his friends as to prevent Gen Jackson from getting *in any event* the votes of Clay, that is, Clay's interest.

That interest is now believed to be balancing between Mr Crawford & Mr Adams.—They prefer Crawford, but they still more prefer success, And I presume when the final struggle shall have approached, they will be ready to go any way to attain that object.—

Upon the whole, I am of opinion that Gen. Jackson, will not be the next president, and that M^r. Adams has more chances of success than Crawford.—Indeed for myself, I have thought that M^r C's chance is but small.—

If other than the reasons that present themselves to every reflecting mind were working to shew the mischief of submitting the determination of that question to the H. or Rep^s. they would be found in the daily observation of every attentive spectator.—

Clay certainly holds in his hands the vote of 5 States. It is believed that his interest in New York, will incline the scale to Adams or Crawford as he may desire.—He can give the vote of Maryland to Adams & can prevent a vote of that State at all should he go to Crawford—These with divers other calculations that are daily made, exhibit rather an afflicting spectacle to those that have been in the habit of considering ours the purest government that ever existed on the face of the earth[17]

There will be but little regulation this winter, perhaps the less the better.—

Be pleased to present my best respects to Mr Bennehans, the older & younger.

And accept for yourself assurances of my very high respect and esteem.

Mr. Duncan Cameron—   W. P. MANGUM

WPM-LC

Titus Jennings Turner[18] to Nathaniel Macon and W. P. Mangum

[14 Jan. 1825]

To the honourable Nathaniel Macon Seanor; and to the honour-

---

[17] In the House as a result of Clay's support, Adams carried six New England states and Illinois, Missouri, Maryland, Louisiana, Kentucky, Ohio, and New York.
[18] See above, pp. 31-32, 156-158.

able Willie P Mangum Representative in Congress gentlemen I
have Received the letter which your Condescension favoreded me
with and with Defference Due to your Capacity of knowing how
the arrangements between individuals being Claimants on the
public and the united States are digested or defined but to me
Sirs it is of importance and indespensible necessity that a Considerable Sum of money now due and owing to me for my Military Services be paid though I have not omitted endeavouring to
obtain it I have never Receeved it moreover to Comply with the
form of the oath prescribed for Revolutionary pensioners I must
in Conscience and truth mention the money due to me from the
public and Comprise all incidents that have intervened to hinder
me from getting that money would for ought I know be Con-
strued as a defailance   Default neglegence or omission in me
and that I am owner of good property for maintenance and prevent me from getting a pension and it is but of late years that I
Could obtain the evidence I now have on that occasion and previous to my obtaining Such evidence a law was passed here to
prohibit Such payments which law I expect you are not unin-
formed of gentlemen I am Sorry to know that there are others
public defenders in the Revolution who have not obtained the
Compensation Justly due to them and though I am applying in
my own behalf I am not all to whom Revolutionary arrears are
due and as the Constitution of the united States provides that
Congress shall have power to pay the Debts of the united States
and the Revolutionary war was Carried at the Joint expense
of the united States (as by primative Compact of the articles of
Confederation) with all due defference to the wisdom and patriotism of Congress I know not why the national Council invested
with Supreme legislative Jurisdiction might not pass a law to
adjust liquidate Settle and pay arrears due to Revolutionary
Soldiers which arrears was by the Solemnity of law promised
to them who Defended a Comparatively an unarmed and un-
disciplined Small nation of people against a much more numerous nation and one, of the most martial nations on earth with
a formidable and predominant navy while the victorious success of the Revolution has by the interposition of Divine providence been Blessed without military Conquest with an extensive and accelerated of valuable fertil and locally important Territory and with the most Just and equitable government on
earth or that ever existed Sinse the theocracy of the Isaraelites
and as the united States are now much more able to pay arrears

due to Revolutionary Soldiers with the accruing interest than they were to pay the principal at the Close of the Revolution. observe Sirs that it is a Custom and established maxim Sanctioned by law for Creditors to indulge Debtors upon paying interest untill they are able to Discharge the whole moreover by an act of the general assembly of north Carolina 1789 Chapter the Sixth it is Represented that many officers and whole Regiments of privates who Served in the Contenental line of this State are not be found on the musters or war or pay office of the united States and as other law Required the evidence of officers who perhaps was at Such Remot Distance or unknown of or Dead as to Render it impracticable to obtain Such evidence and as John Rogers who was paymaster to the fifth Regiment of the north Carolina Continental line in which Regiment I Served tooke each man's Receipt and as mr Samuel goodwin late Comptroler Said to me that Such papers was Sent away to Seattle with the united States and the British Destroyed Documents from north Carolina in their Depredations at washington in the last war So I am not likely to obtain any Registered evidence when people would agree that the oath of an individual Claimant Should be admitted and when no nation ancient nor modern Sinse the theocracy of the Israelites has obtained as much profit by their military acquisitions as the united has by the military interposition of the Revolutionary Soldiers as those who voluntarily inlisted into the Regular army against the British formadable army and navy with but a Small american force especially in the Commencement and on the likeness of intention without action against a Despotic King his law would take their lives they were actuated by the most pure and pious motives and as it is usual in law to admit the oath of individuals between themselves and between an individual and individual and the public to the taking the life of an accused individual therefore worthy gentlemen the oath of a Revoluntionary Regular Soldier in his own behalf for a stipend he has meritoriously and Richly earned can be no detriment to the public welfare but on the Contrary the more punctual the payments are made the more Certainly to engage men in future occasion and in the Journal of the Congress of north carolina in 1776 the oath of individuals was admitted for pay for horses lost on the expedition against the Cherokee indians and as in law the best evidence the Circumstance and Case will admit is Received I expect you are informed that a law was made in North Carolina

to Raise troops and of the militia for the better Defence of the
State in 1781 by virtue whereof a Regiment was Raised Commanded by Majors Joel Lewes and Bennet Crafton[19] in which
Regiment I served from early in the fall of 1781 to March 1783
pay for Cloathing in Said Regiment is mostly now due to me and
pay for Twelve months Clothing in the North Carolina and Two
months wages is now due to me and by the law of the general
assembly of North Carolina from the 14th of april at newbern in
1778 to January 1779 the time when I was in the militia actual
military Service in aid to the States of South Carolina, and georgia called the five months expetion   I was in that Service from
early in the fall 1778 to late in the Spring 1779 there was twenty Dollars a month bounty allowed to each militia man which
Bounty I did not Receive therefore If you Consider me included
in the national legislative Representation please to Consider the
evidence accompanying this address and on Confering other
gentlemen friendly to the Revolutionary Soldiers it is Considered adequate please to present a petition in my behalf the papers herein inclosed you will Take Special Care of and on the
Close or Result of this my business please to Transmit the Said
papers to the post office in Raleigh to me if I be answered in the
negative (as my Real welfair is Refered to you agency Condescension and interposition) my only Consolation is in the prosperity of the united States (though I am in adversity) and in
the gospel Isaiah or 7 matthew 5-4 Isaiah 57-15 I have not gentlemen bestowed my Service on them that are unable to pay or
I would not have asked it and others having a gratuitious favour
bestowed on them I wish for my pay I am Sirs yours to Serve
                    TITUS JENNINGS TURNER
January 14- 1825
you will observe that it is not usual for the Retentive faculty of
man to Retain all the particulars of long past events So that I
would not prove to a day the precise length of Time of my military Services I have not nor had I money and out of my power
get it to pay the fees for the Seals and Certificates of Clerks to
Some of these evidences

[Addressed:]
    For the honourable Nathaniel Macon: Senator and for
the honourable Willie P Mangum Representative from the State

---

[19]Major Joel Lewis who fought in several battles in North Carolina in the Revolution was
promoted to colonel in November 1781. Bennet Crafton was made a major at the same time.
Walter Clark (ed.), *N. C. State Records*, XIX, 309.

of North Carolina in Congress of the united States of North america
>> City of Washington

[Enclosure 1]

Wee the Subscribers who lived during the Revolutionary war in the militia District in the Southeast Corner of Wake County in the State of North Carolina in the which district Titus Jennings Turner also lived during the said war except when he was in the Military Service of the united States and mustered in Said District and the Said District was his Residence where we had Continual acquaintance with him do hereby Certify that there was no other man whose usual Residence was in Said District during or in time of Said war that Served more than about half as long time nor more than about half as much in the Said military Service as the Said Titus Jennings Turner did perform in the said Military Service of the united States

>> his
>> ephraim X ferril
>> mark

>> his
>> William X Beasly[20]
>> mark

>> William Goodwin

[Enclosure 2]

State of North Carolina)   I Benjamin S. King Clerk of the
>>)
>> Wake County   )   Court of Pleas and quarter Sessions for the County of Wake afors^d. do hereby Certify that Nathaniel G. Rand[21] Esquire before whom the annexed affidavits were made was an acting Justice of the peace in and of the County of Wake afors^d, at the time of the taking the same, and that due faith and credit is and ought to be given to his official acts as such. In Testimony whereof I have hereto set my hand and the seal of office at Raleigh this 14th. January 1825
>> B. S. KING C. C.

---

[20]William Beasley who received a pension for his services is the only one of these three mentioned in the Walter Clark (ed.), *N. C. State Records*, XVII, 195; XXII, 319.
[21]Nathaniel G. Rand was also a member of the House of Commons in 1830 to 1833, and from 1836 to 1843. *N. C. Manual*, 830.

[Enclosure 3]

I Nath¹. G. Rand do hereby Certify that ephraim and William Beasly and William Goodwin whose names are Signed to a Certificate on the other Side of this paper in behalf of Titus Jennings Turner are Considered Creditable men of Reputable Carachtors whose information and Testimony is to be Relied Trusted to and Confided in

N. G. RAND J P

for the County of Wake in the State of North Carolina

[Enclosure 4]

State of North Carolina) this day Came before me Afred Moore
)
Wake County   ) one of the States Justices of the peace

Titus Jennings Turner who being Duely Swern Sayeth on his oath that he did not Receive the Cloathing for hes twelve months Service in the North Carolina Continental line in the Revolutionary war in the Year 1776 and 1777 and that there is yet Due and owing to him Two months wages for the Said Service moreover he Sayeth that he Received only one Coat one pair of Shews and one pair of Breeches and no othe; of the Cloathing for his Service of about Sixteen months in a Regiment of Regular. Soldiers Raised by Law entitled an act to Raise troops out of the militia for the Better defence of this State passed at Wake County Court house in the year 1781 and that the County for his Service in the north Carolina Militia in aid to the States of South Carolina and georgia in 1778 and 1779 he never Received. Sworn to and Subscribed before me this 26th day of november 1824

Titus Jennings Turner

Alfred Moore J P

I Certify that Ttitus Jennings Turner is Considered a Creditable man whose oath is to be trusted to Relied on and Confided in
Alfred Moore J P

[Enclosure 5]

State of North Carolina)
    Wake County   )

I Benjamin S King Clerk of the Court of Pleas and quarter Sessions for the County of Wake aforsᵈ. do hereby Certify that

Alfred Moore Esquire before whom the annexed Affidavit was made was at the time of the taking the same an acting Justice of the Peace in and of the County of Wake, and that faith and Credit is and ought ot be given to his official acts as such.

In Testimony whereof I have hereto set my hand and the Seal of office at Raleigh this 14th. January A. D. 1825

B. S. KING C C

[Enclosure 6]

State of No. Carolina
Secretary's Office 23rd. June 1819.

I William Hill Secretary of State in and for the State aforesaid do hereby certify, that the name of Titus Jennings Turner is not to be found on the musterroll of the No. Carolina Continental line in the Revolutionary War, that it is generally reported and believed that the officers and Soldiers who entered into the service of the United States from this State, early in said war and marched to the Southward, and who were discharged at the end of nine or twelve months after the commencement of their services, were not placed on any musterroll; and it is also further reported that a part of the musterrolls of the line of this State in the revolutionary war, were burnt at an Assembly in Fayetteville after the close of said war.

Given under my hand
the date above—

WM HILL

[Enclosure 7]

All persons who Saw and Read my Discharges are now and for many years Dead so that it is utterly out of my power to prove any of my Discharges for I have had many Discharges and as the laws of north Carolina was that any man who did not perform his Tour of Service in the militia was to be Deemed a Continental Soldier for twelve months or during the war and men who Deserted from the Continental line Could not have appeared in public and Served in the militia and again in the Regular army as I have Served otherwise than by its being well known that I had performed such Service as is Specified in the evidences accompanying this my petition for all vilagence was on

the alert to apprehend such delinquents
I am now in the Seventifourth year of my age and I never Received any pecuniary gratuity nor I never have Received any pension from any individual State nor from the united States for my military Services and am now a Superannuated Revolutionary Soldier and now occasioned by pressing necessity Claim and ask for pay as promised by the Solemnity of the law of north Carolina enacted even in time of the Revolution the part of pay I ask for I never have Received I Sold a Claim for twelve months of the wages for the my last Service thout it has not been paid to the man who bought it I Claim it not but Claim pay for the time I served more than Twelve months in that Regiment Raised by the law of north Carolina dated July 14— 1781 Chap 1 an act to Raise troops of the militia of this State for the better Defence thereof and for other purposes as that Regiments time expired the 20 of September 1782 I was Discharged the 1 of March 1783

TITUS JENNINGS TURNER

February 1—1826

[Enclosure 8]

Supplemental to the petition to Congress Signed with the name of Titius Jennings Turner and bearing date february 1—[torn] one of the laws of north Carolina which is an act under date of May 10—1780 Chap XX Section III Requiring three years Service or to the end of the war of them soldiers as should be entitled to a Slave the war having Terminated ended and Closed within about two year as the last battle was on the 20 of may 1782 and in all instances of Raising men by Drafting enlisting or by any mode of Recruiting it is long after the Business is begun before any Considerable number of men as soldiers Can be assembled So that many of them were entitled to the Slave without having Served three year I have Served between three and four year and I Served more than two year in the Regular military Service and by virtue the law by which the Regiment was Raised that I last Served in I was in the military Service about or at the end of the Revolutionary war under the Same organization and Disipline as Continental troops and having been drafed for twelve months Service in the Regular military Service and for three months Service in the militia in one and the same day which twelve months was to have expired on the

20 of September 1782 I Continued a Regular Soldier till the first
day of March in the year 1783 for the Space of five months
longer than the time that Regular Regiment was to Serve and
there no other Soldiers Raised in the State of north Carolina
neither Regulars nor Militia after I was discharged and others
were Discharged about the Same time before the time they were
engaged was expired because the war was ended and might have
had their bounty which bounty I never Received   february 1—
1826

TITUS JENNINGS TURNER

WPM-LC

J. S. Smith[22] to Willie P. Mangum

HILLSBOROUGH January 23rd 1825

Dr Sir

I wrote you some time since on the Subject of my Ohio Land
I had written to Mr Sloane[23] of Ohio during the last summer
[on] the subject & had not received [an] answer
[torn]
you I fear that my letter did not [rea]ch you I have written
this day to Mr Sloane again on the subject—I am very desirous
to know something of the quality of the land & probable value
of it — It is in the county of Tuscorawas & near new Philadelphia the seat of Justice for that county—Will you be so good
as to say something to Mr. Slone on the Subject & gain what
information you can for me Mr. Sloane has the Nos. of the lots
& the description of the location of the three tracts—

Permit me to as the favor of you not to forget Gales & Seaton
I owe them according to my opinions for 5 years subscription
making Thirty dollars & no more that amount I I[*sic*] want to
be paid to them & a receipt taken in full The only difference between their account & mine, is one year, & that has grown out
of Mr Gales neglect to give me credit for a payment, I made
him, in the loose whilst there— There is no news, here at this
time worthy of your attention— All is very still on the subject

---

[22]James Strudwick Smith. See above, p. 8n.
[23]John Sloane, 1779-1856, was a member of the Ohio legislature from 1803 to 1805 and in
1807. He served in the national House of Representatives from 1819 to 1829. In 1831, and for
several years thereafter, he was clerk of the court of common pleas of Wayne County, Ohio.
From 1841 to 1844 he was the secretary of state in Ohio and from 1850 to 1853 the treasurer of the United States. *Biog. Dir. of Cong.*, 1532.

of the Presidential Election It seems to be the General opinion
here that Gen¹. Jackson will be the President & I think that the
people whom I have heard speak on the subject would rather
prefer him to Mr Adams I mean those who were not [friend]
to either
[torn]
would almost be persuaded to vote for Jackson His want of good
Moral character notwithstanding—I fear That the subject of
Slavery is long to be a bone of contention between the north &
the south & it has been a matter of doubt with me whether Mr
Adams has not been one of the prime movers of the Missouri
question At least we have more to expect from the west than
from the north on that subject—

I beleve that the bounty you have bestowed on Genl. Lafayette
meets the approbation of the people generally.²⁴ Some have
ventured to anathamatize *Uncle Natt*²⁵ for his vote But be
assured that although the good feelings of the house & of the nation gave the money & the land & I rejoiced that they did so—yet
I think that Mr Macons ground is a Just & tenable one & with
me his vote is but an other proof of the Stability of that miserable old Mans principles

I beleve that I can say to you from very respectable authority
that you will not have Mr Crudup on the turf next August. He
avows that   [torn]
fraud I hope that you will [torn] no opposition. I think it
highly probable that you will not—
With much esteem
I am Dr Sir
Your Hmb, Sv, t—
J S SMITH

Willie P Mangum Esqr
N B. please to forward the enclosed letter to Col Watson²⁶

[Addressed:]
Willie P. Mangum Esqr
Member House Representatives U. (S.)
Washington City.

²⁴In December 1824 when Lafayette visited Congress, John Randolph proposed in the House of Representatives a gift of $200,000. Some in the House tried to reduce the amount to $100,000. Mangum spoke with much fervor for the larger sum. *The Register of the Debates of Congress*, 29 vols., (Washington, D. C.: Gales and Seaton, 1825-1837), 18 Cong., 2 sess., 49-50. Hereafter cited as *Register of Debates*.
²⁵Nathaniel Macon voted against the gift of $200,000 for Lafayette. *Register of Debates*, 18 Cong., 2 sess., 32.
²⁶Probably Col. John Watson who was a commissioner in the Land Office in Washington.

WPM-LC

John Chavis[27] to Willie P. Mangum

RALEIGH N. C. Jany 28th. 1825

My dear Sir/

I am truly glad that I came to Raleigh today. Mr. Pullen[28] the sheriff showed me a letter from you respecting my bank business, stating that he had written to you and had informed you that it was at my request, which was not so. Shortly after you had set out to Congress, I was in Raleigh, and he asked me, what I intended to do about the business. I answered that you had told me that you & the Treasurer[29] had promised to pay the debt, he replied that he had understood that you had said, that the Treasurer should not lose by it & this was all that was passed upon the subject. I hope therefore that you will not think hard of me on ac[t]. of his writing to you in the manner he did for it was not my act at all—

Shortly after I conversed with Mr. Pullen I saw, & conversed with the Treasurer upon the subject, & his conversation was that of a father to a beloved son which melted my heart with thankfulness & penitential sorrow—

I am placed in the most unhappy situation I am in want of every thing & without a school & what to do I know not. I hope however that God has in reserve some way of relief. It is commonly said that the darkest time is just before day—

I am anxious respecting the presidency. I am very fearful that Mr Crawford will not be elected. Tho' Mr Western Gales tells me that he saw a letter of yours to some person in this place saying that he was gaining ground. I do suppose that the exertions in the case will be indiscribable and I hope that you will, for Mr. Crawford, fight old [illegible] battle, & if you are killed, I think you will die in a good cause—

There is much rumour abroad that you will not be elected again because you support the election of Mr Crawford. It is supposed that Mr Crudup will oppose you & if he does your election will be doubtful. If you offer & I am alive I will vote for you.[30] I

[27] See above, p. 41n.
[28] Turner Pullen was sheriff of Wake County in 1824-1825. *Statement of the Revenue of North Carolina for the year 1824-1825,* bound with *The N. C. Laws,* 1825.
[29] John Haywood.
[30] Until 1835 free Negroes could vote in North Carolina. Johnson, *Ante-Bellum, N. C.,* 601.

should be glad to know whether the Managers of the colonization society[31] have made any propositions to congress—
I am your ob^t H^b- ser^t.
JOHN CHAVIS
P. S.
Please to give my best respects to Mrs. Seaton[32] & tell her that I am truly glad to find that there is so much friendship between her & Gen Lafayette, and I intend when [he] comes to Raleigh to endeavour to take a peep at him if possible—

[Addressed:]

Hon. Willie P. Mangum Esqr
Washington City
District of
Columbia
Mail

WPM-LC

W. Ruffin[33] to Willie P. Mangum

RALEIGH 1 Feby 1825
Dear Sir.
I am indebted to you for your three several favors, for which you will please receive my acknowledgment and thanks—They should each have ben replyed to in regular succession, if I could have communicated any thing, either interesting or amusing, but alas! There is such a dull monotony in our little circle that I could say nothing in which you could feel an interest—Besides, we are looking to you for *light & knowledge*— you appear to have a strange dense atmosphere about Washington; with almost a continual veering of the wind— at one time, there is a strong breeze from the West, at an other a violent hurricane from the East, the sky is obscured, the sun darkened, and the heavy clouds approach with threatening danger—what is the mariner to do in this perilous situation? Moor fast his vessel— let go the sheet anchor of reason—pay out the cable of consist-

[31]Chavis was opposed to the American Colonization Society or other agencies which worked for the emancipation of slaves.
[32]Probably Sarah Weston Seaton, the wife of William W. Seaton and the daughter of Joseph Gales, Sr. Seaton and Joseph Gales, Jr., edited the *National Intelligencer. D. A. B.*, XVI, 541.
[33]William Ruffin, a Virginian who moved to Warrenton, N. C., and then to Raleigh, was the uncle of Judge Thomas Ruffin. Hamilton, *Papers of Ruffin*, I, 330n.

ency, keep all hands on the deck, and look to him "who rides upon the storm and directs the whirl wind," for safe deliverance—Perhaps a gentle breeze may spring up from the South, drive back the threatening clouds to their native home, and receive the fertilizing influence of a cheering sun—

The course which Clay[34] & his friends are said to be taking is passing strange to us—surely whatever may be the motives which operate on Clay, they can not be equally strong with the others— Should Clay persevere in his present career, altho' he may succeed for the present, he may consider the death warrant to his future prospect signed from the present moment—

To you (all the friends of Crawford) I presume it is unnecessary to say, It is expected you will adhere to the truth, tho' you should suffer like the martyrs of old, in defence of the truth —you however will have nothing to apprehend from that course, your friends will reward your firmness, while your opponents (if you should have any) will observe your consistancy—

The theatre at Washington must exhibit many and strange scenes—the expectation sometimes "riding on the mountain top," and then cowering in the valley of disponding hope! The experience of a long life proves to me that political integrity like moral virtue, carries with it, its own reward

I am, with much respect,
Dr Sir,
Ys. mo. obtst.
W RUFFIN

[Addressed:]
The Honble
Willie P Mangum Esqr.
Washington City
D. C.

————

WPM-LC

Willie P. Mangum to Charity A. Mangum

SUNDAY MORNING 6th February 1825.

My dear Love,

I have waited with great anxiety to receive a letter from you, to learn how our dear little Sally is. I fear that she has relapsed,

---

[34]He refers to Clay's support of Adams in the disputed presidential election of 1824.

or that worse has happened to her, other wise I should have heard from you.—

I have been a good deal unwell for the last 8 or ten days, but I am now tolerably—the weather here has for a few days been very cold, & constant attendance to business, when I was well enough, has kept me with a bad cold.—

I feel gratified that the time [is] approaching, wh[en] I m[ay] leave here, and with pr [torn] ssions I hardly ever expect to see the place again, at least for many years, should I live—I am tired of it—The being seperated from my family, not only my interests are sacrificed, but the life is one of the most uncomfortable kind, that any man can imagine.

I hope my dear that I shall receive a letter from you in a day or two— all my enjoyment at this place & in these miserable pursuit are trash to me when compared with the pleasure I feel in reading those lines that are dictated by the heart & traced by the hand of affection— Wednesday next being only three days off the presidential election comes on—Mr. Crawford will be beaten & Mr. Adams I have no doubt will be elected—

[torn]   to my Mothern   [torn]   & give my de[ar l]ittle daughter her [fath]ers blessing.

I am your affectionate husband
WILLIE P. MANGUM

[Addressed:]
Mrs. Charity A. Mangum
Stagville
Orange County
North Carolina

WPM-LC

Edward Johnston's[35] appointment of W. P. Mangum as his attorney for Revolutionary pension

[8 Feb., 1825]
Know all men by [these pre]sents that I Edward Johnson do hereby nominate and appoint Willie P. Mangum my true and lawful attorney in my behalf to sign for me and in my name to any and every proper Receipt-roll and Vouchers and to receive

---

[35]Edward Johnson was a private in the North Carolina Revolutionary military forces from Person County. Walter Clark (ed.), *N. C. State Records*, XVI, 1091.

for me and in my name Whatever sum of money that may be due to me by the United States as compensation for my services as a soldier in the Detached Militia from Person County—North Carolina under the command of Captain John Bradsher Ordered to rendexvous at Gates Court house, and I do hereby for myself my Heirs, Executors and administrators ratify by these presents all acts and deeds of my said attorney in fact Touching and regarding the pay aforesaid in Witness whereof I have hereunto set my hand and Seal 8th day of February 1825—

his
EDWARD X JOHNSTON   (Seal)
mark

Test—
John Bradsher
State of North Carolina)   [torn] of February 1825 came
)
    Person County   )   Edward John[ston] before me and
acknowledged the Within to be [his o]wn Voluntary act and Deed having signed Duplicate

JOHN BR[ADSHER, justice of the peace]
[torn]

WPM-LC

James Strudwick Smith to Willie P. Mangum

HILLSBORO, February 9th 1825

Dr Sir
   I will request the favor of you, provided you can do it without inconvenience to yourself, to pay to Mr. Secretary [John C.] Calhoun Sum of Money which he advanced to   [torn]
                    [torn]
        one thing   [torn]
dollars—If you can [do so] conveniently, I will reimburse you on your return home without fail It will save me the risque of transmiting it by mail, & also the discount, for Altho., Mr Calhoun would, in all probability, not ask a discount on our money, yet I feel bound to reimbuse him fully with interest for his kindness
   I would also ask the kindness of you, in the name of myself,

& the other trustees of the Hillsboro female Academy,[36] to inquire of your acquaintances from New England, whether a Suitable Lady could not be procured from there, to take charge of the school in this place?

We have a good building compleated for the purpose, & altho., we have no funds to endow the school with, & are therefore unable to guarrantee any specific sum; yet, It is my opinion, that if a suitable Lady & Gentleman, possessing the requisite character, & qualifications were to take the School, that they could make in a year, or two, a handsome business of it—

I think the success of Dr Rogers[37] with the male Academy, without any Guarrantee on the part of the trustees, is sufficient to Justify the opinion I have advanced—

It would be most desirable to have a Gentleman & Lady; Because it   [torn]

of such   [torn]

trustees [could comm]unicate with, the utmost freedom, & without feeling that delicacy, which would be imposed on them, in the event of having none but a female at the head of the school; and in the second place, some of the Branches which should be taught, such as English Grammar & Geography, are never so well taught by a female, as by a male teacher.

If such an arrangement cannot be made—We must do the best we can, & will have to take a lady alone—One that has had some experience in teaching, would be prefered, as she would of course be better skilled in dicipline, than a person who had never been engaged in teaching; & nothing you know, is more important than dicipline in such a school—

I hope, that, from what I have written, you will be able to perceive what we want, & that you will be able to explain the prospects of the place, and the inducements that it holds out, from the state of society, & its relative situation with other Seminaries, as to health &C.—

Altho this will reach you at a time when you will have but a short stay to make at Washington, Yet I hope you will have time to make the necessary inquiry, before you leave there—

I do not expect that you can learn any [thing] more than the [torn]   hardly permit you [to] hear from the person

---

[36]The Hillsboro Female Academy was in operation during the 1820's and 1830's. Mangum sent his daughter, Sally, there in 1835 and 1839. At that time the Reverend Wm. M. Green who later became a famous bishop of the Episcopal Church was in charge of the academy. In 1825 Miss Lavina Brainard was in direct control. Coon, Doc. Hist. of Educ. in N. C., 300-308.
[37]John Rogers. See above, p. 167.

who might be recommended—

But they could write on for further particulars, to you, or to me at this place, and can enclose such recommendations, as they may think proper—

Your little daughter has been very ill some time past, But the last account I had from her, which was a day or two, since, she was convalessent, indeed, almost restored to health again—The balance of your family were well—

Nothing new—It is thought here, that Adams will be president, from the last accounts; & the Jackson people are in an ill humor, as might be supposed—for myself, I shall be content. Tho not pleased—

Very respectfully, Dr Sir
Your fond, & Hub Svt
J. S. SMITH

Willie P. Mangum Esqr

[Addresed:]

Willie P. Mangum Esqr
Washington City

WPM-LC

H. G. Burton[38] to

HALIFAX Feby 11th A D 1825

My Dear Sir

I have just received your letter—Your draft has not as yet been presented—you may be assured of one fact—that whether you had funds in my hands or not—that any draft of yours that could be met by my limited means—It would afford me the greatest pleasure to accept—as to the papers if you have not sent them, I should prefer your not doing so, untill your return, at the time I wrote I expected it would be insisted on that the Bill should be answered in January—but as appears to be waived—I should prefer your answering it the first time you come to Raleigh.—

I presume before this time that the shew is over—and I take it for granted that we are beaten—however, it behoves us as good subjects to submit with cheerfulness to the powers that

---

[38]See above, p. 154n.

be.—Tell my old friend Capt Cobb[39] (of Chesapeake memory) that I expect he has swallowed a poker—since his transfer to the other house, that he promised to write to me, and has never done so—Remember me in a particular manner to all our old mesmates—my hand is cripled and it is painful to write

Yours friend

H G. BURTON

N. B.

my best wishes to Capt Hall[40] Capt Spaight[41] and all the rest of the Captains—

WPM-LC

Willie P. Mangum to Charity A. Mangum

WASHINGTON CITY 12th, February 1825.

My dear Wife.

I have felt very great anxiety on your account; I fear from what I have learned that you have worn yourself down with fatigue.

I hope & trust, My Love, that you will be prudent & not expose yourself too much to fatigue nor loose too much sleep— The life of our dear little daughter is in the hands of our creator, & if it were his will to deprive us of her, I feel that I could sustain the loss, & would expect to acquire after a time a proper resignation—

But my feelings towards you & on your account would be very different—For I feel that no earthly possession could supply in my heart & affections the place that you hold—I therefore beseech you My Love, to keep the guard of prudence over yourself & your health.—

I often fear that I shall never again see Poor little Sally—I cannot account for her cough—unless it proceeds from the want of stamina of constitution—If so, perhaps it would be better for her not to live, to drag after her a wretched existence borne down with affliction—

The Presidential election is over—& we are all beaten—Mr.

---

[39]Thomas W. Cobb. See above, p. 172n.
[40]Thomas H. Hall, 1773-1853, was a physician, agriculturist, and political leader from Tarboro, N. C. He served in Congress from 1817 to 1825 and from 1827 to 1836. *Biog. Dir. of Cong.*, 1048.
[41]Richard Dobbs Spaight, Jr. See above, p. 134n.

John Quincy Adams is elected the President, by looking into the National Intelligencer you will see all on the subject.

Our time here I am glad to say, will not be long—And I shall rejoice not less than any other man at Washington, when the near prospect is afforded me of getting home.— I have been a good deal unwell for the last 2 weeks. I am now well—My indispositon proceeded from cold—

Give My Love to Mother & Eliza Kiss the baby if she lives, and accept My

Love & affection,
W. P. MANGUM

Mrs Charity A Mangum

[Addressed:]

Mrs. Charity A. Mangum
Stagville
North Carolina

WPM-LC

John Louis Taylor[42] to W. P. Mangum

RALEIGH 20th Feby 1825.

Dear Sir,

As one of a commission appointed by last Assembly to digest and report a plan for the education[43] of the children of the poor, I shall esteem it a great favour if you would ask any gentlemen from Massachusetts, N. York, or Connecticut, to indicate the laws, under which the existing systems in their respective States, are now in operation. There may be other States in which the plan has extensively succeeded, whose laws might be useful to us. The statute books are for the most part in the Secretary's office at this place, but it might shorten our labours to have the proper references.

If you can without much trouble open to me any other sources of information on this subject, which may in its effects be so

---

[42]John Louis Taylor. See above, p. 10n.
[43]For many years there had been great agitation for schools for the poor. Archibald D. Murphey had been the leader in this with his significant report in 1817. By 1825 a Literary Fund was created and Taylor as chief justice of the state Supreme Court was on the board which administered it. Johnson, *Ante-Bellum N. C.*, 268-270.

interesting to our common country, I shall always esteem it a great favor conferred on. Sir

Your friend & servt.

JOHN LOUIS TAYLOR

Accept my thanks for the valuable and elaborate tariff book.

[Addressed:]

The Honble W. P. Mangum Esq.
House of Representatives.
City of Washington

To The Freemen of the Counties of Wake, Orange and Person[44]

[8 August, 1825]

A publication in the Raleigh Register of the 5th instant, over the signature "Timoleon",[45] is calculated to mislead the public, and requires to be met and exposed. The object of this publication is to satisfy you that Mr. Crudup has declined publishing a circular prepared by him, because the statement it contains is not supported by the certificate of Maj. Hinton.[46] To expose the falsehood of this imputation, let the public attend to the following statement:

On the 30th of July, Mr. Mangum and Mr. Crudup came to a written agreement regulating their conduct respecting the election. A copy of this agreement before the appearance of Timoleon's piece was placed by Mr. Crudup in my hands, and contains the following stipulation:

"We agree to publish nothing to affect each other's election, *directly or indirectly.* Mr. Crudup having left a *manuscript in the Star Office,* and subsequently having given orders not to publish it, should it not be published before he reaches Raleigh, *it is*

----

[44] A typed copy of this printed circular is available in the Department of Archives and History, Raleigh, N. C. Mr. Weeks had this typed copy made from a printed copy in the possession of Willie Mangum Person.

[45] This article signed by "Timeleon" states that Josiah Crudup, who was running against Mangum for Congress, had written a circular but had delayed its publication until he received a letter from Charles L. Hinton. Hinton wrote his letter, but still the circular did not appear because, according to "Timeleon," Hinton's letter gave out the information that Crudup, in his presence, had stated that if he were elected he would not give up his position as a Baptist minister. *Raleigh Register,* Aug. 5, 1825. The circular included here was issued August 8 in reply to the "Timeleon" article.

[46] Charles L. Hinton. See above, p. 51n.

to be suppressed. Each of us may leave home to attend any election we choose, and allow ourselves a reasonable time to travel the distance, but abstain from electioneering.

"Saturday, 30th July, 1825.

"Willie P. Mangum.
"Josiah Crudup."

"Signed in presence of
    "A. D. Murphey.
    "W. Montgomery."

Three observations are naturally suggested:

1. Mr. Mangum's friend "Timoleon" attempts to persuade you that the Circular of Mr. Crudup was suppressed from an unworthy motive, when it appears it was expressly agreed by Mr. C. with Mr. Mangum, that it should not be printed, and that Mr. Crudup refrained from the publication as an honest man, because he had promised to do so.

2. It was agreed that neither of the Candidates should *directly or indirectly* publish any thing respecting the election; and yet Mr. Mangum's friend "Timoleon" makes a publication to influence the election, and to deceive the public, while Mr. Crudup's friends observe the agreement with fidelity.

3. This publication of "Timoleon", is made at so late a period, as to preclude refutation by a reply in the papers, and, as it was probably hoped, too late for refutation in any other way.

If "Timoleon" was aware of the facts respecting the suppression of Mr. Crudup's Circular, and knew that he had declined to publish it by agreement with Mr. Mangum, then he has attempted to impose upon your understanding by a known falsehood. If he was ignorant of the facts, what shall we say of him who imputes base motives of conduct to another without troubling himself to ascertain the facts from which those motives are to be known?

Could Mr. Crudup's Circular appear before the public, all the objections of his enemies, and doubts of his friends, if they have any, relative to the Certificate of Maj. Hinton, would be entirely removed.

It is proper to remark, that no reflection is intended upon Mr. Crudup's opponent. I am willing to think him too honorable a man to have had any agency in the publication in the Register after his agreement not to publish. But, however that may be, the friends of Mr. Crudup have surely reason to complain that an attempt has been made to pervert so simple a transaction as the supression of his Circular, and to convert that into an imputation upon him, which, in truth, is but a new proof of the sterling integrity of his character: who, "though he promise to his hurt, yet makes his promise good."

As Timoleon says "the facts are now fairly before the people,"[47] and they can and will decide whether a cause which requires to be holstered up by a resort to means like these can be entitled to the support of men like yourselves, honest in your objects and fair and direct in the means of obtaining them. Monday, August 8th, 1825.

A Friend to Mr. Crudup.

WPM-LC

Louis Mc Lane[48] *to Willie P. Mangum*

WILMINGTON [Del.] Aug. 29. 1825

My Dear Sir,

After the "dreadful havoc" made in your congressional ranks at your last election,[49] I beg to offer you my congratulations that you escaped the sword. Your triumph is the more gratifying to your friends, because of your manly and distinguished services during the painful crisis of the last session, and which I presume had its influence in the late elections.—Your trial is fairly over Sir—You have now stood the fire of the enemy, he will not rally again, and your future march will be obstructed only by his slain. I trust it may ever be so with all your publick interprises! But what has occasioned all this slaughter among you? Is it the triumph of the Admn? or a new effort of the old coalition—of the Holy Alliance to exterminate a common enemy? What is the complexion of your new delegation, and what flag do they now nail at the mast—Be pleased my dear Sir, if entirely at leisure to enlighten me upon these topicks—

---

[47]In the election which followed, Mangum won by the small majority of 56 popular votes. Mangum carried Orange and Person counties by a majority of 1017, and Crudup carried Wake County by a majority of 961. *Raleigh Register*, Aug. 19, 1825.

[48]Louis McLane, 1786-1857, who practiced law in Delaware, was a member of the House of Representatives from 1817 to 1827 and Senator from 1827 to 1829. He was minister to England from 1829 to 1831 and from 1845 to 1846. From 1831 to 1833 he was Secretary of the Treasury and from 1833 to 1834 Secretary of State. *Biog. Dir. of Cong.*, 1271.

[49]Of the ten North Carolina congressmen who voted for Crawford in 1825, only five were reelected. These five were W. N. Edwards, John Long, W. P. Mangum, R. M. Saunders, and Lewis Williams. Those defeated were Alfred Gatlin, Thomas H. Hall, Charles Hooks, and Richard Dobbs Spaight. Newsome, *Election of 1824*, 170-172.

9

& pardoning me for a short letter, which I write amid the hurry
of my Court, on hearing of your individual success; believe me
to be

Mo truly & sincerely
Yr. fd. & Humb. Servt
L. Mc LANE.

Hon.
>   Willie P. Mangum

[Addressed:]

The Honble.
Willie P. Mangum
Hillsborough
Orange Co.
North Carolina

WPM-LC

Henry W. Connor[50] to Willie P. Mangum

LINCOLN CTY. 4th Sept[r]. 1825.

My dear Sir—
   I would have offer[d]. you the last mail my congratulations on
your success had I have rec[d]. the intelligence, in time. I was
much surprized to find you had not beaten Crudup farther,
from the intelligence I occasionally had from your district. however the triumph is a great one if the majority was small. I find
lately even in this section of country much was calculated on
from him and Giles:[51] both prostrate. I see not one of the last
congress to the East of you are returned for which I am really
sorry. I presume the talent is not increased by the change. You
have seen that Carson[52] is elected from Buncombe, probably you
know him as well as I do, never having seen him but once, it is
said the district is *much* worsted: My time was rather an easy

---

[50]Henry William Connor, 1793-1866, a graduate of the South Carolina College, was aide-
de-camp to Brigadier General Joseph Graham before settling in Iredell County as a planter
and lawyer. He served in Congress from 1821 to 1841 and in the state senate from 1848 to
1850. *Biog. Dir. of Cong.*, 841. See also above, pp. 165-167.
   [51]John B. Giles, 1788-1846, of Salisbury was defeated for Congress in 1825 by John Long.
Giles, who graduated from the state university in 1808, was clerk of the county court for
many years before he ran for Congress. Later he was elected to Congress but because of poor
health refused to serve. Grant, *Alumni Hist. of U. N. C.*, 219; *Hillsborough Recorder*, Aug.
17, 1825.
   [52]Samuel Price Carson, 1798-1838, served in the state legislature in 1822-1824 and 1834.
He was in Congress from 1825 to 1833. In 1836 he moved to Texas where he was a member
of the constitutional convention, secretary of state of Texas, and Texas commissioner to
Washington. *Biog. Dir. of Cong.*, 791.

one than otherwise: having had no oponent, for some time, there was a goodeale of pow-wow-ing, but as a dutchman would say, *nix-cum-a rouse*, they made out nothing. I should have been exceedingly happy to have passed thro your neighborhood but find I will not be able to leave home untill very late allowing myself only time to get on: and likely will take the upper route.

Accept dear Sir the best wishes of
Your friend & Hble Servt

HENRY W. CONNOR.

[Addressed:]

Hon. Willie P. Mangum
Hillsboro
No. Ca.

[Postmarked]

Sherrilsford, Sept. 5th.

WPM-D

Returns for congressional election between Mangum and Crudup, 1825

	Mangum	Crudup	Mont-gomery	Holt	McCauley	Boon	Mebane	Hoskins	Barber
Hillsboro	297	206	131	103	207	176	249	55	13
Coles	140	91	89	12	125	115	82	102	7
McCauley	70	45	24	31	26	15	92	42	0
Davis	263	8	72	34	213	215	53	4	27
Mason Hall	77	53	39	24	15	47	123	44	10
Holts	168	47	119	24	23	136	62	115	36
Maulders	117	40	68	8	37	106	75	100	8
Newells	169	44	115	5	36	72	81	142	64
Adam's	119	46	52	24	153	32	44	5	11
Nichols	54	17	26	19	16	30	59	7	5
Herndon	74	110	86	4	158	70	44	33	35
	1548	707	822[sic]	288	1059	1015[sic]	904	649	237

Person Co. 373 192

1921 899

[Endorsed on back:]

A statement of the election between Mangum-Crudup 1825—

WPM-LC

John Martin[53] et als. to Willie P. Mangum

Oct., 1825

Willie P. Mangum Esqr.

The undersigned beg leave to state to you, that by the alteration of the post rout from Raleigh to Oxford crossing at Powell's bridge, & by way of "Wake Forest" post office, & then to the Holly Springs[54] instead of the straight forward road by the falls, Highs & Sutherlands as was formerly the case, great in convenience has been produced to a large number of citizens living on or near the former rout, that in consequence of this change which we believe was to accomodate a single individual, at least one dozen citizens have been deprived of taking the public prints, while it is believed that not more than one has been accommodated—We respectfully solicit, that you will have the ancient order of things restored, & that we may be reinstated in the enjoyment of those conveniences which we are entitled to expect, from the mail being carried by the nighest & best rout, & that which all travellers pass in going from Raleigh to Oxford,

John Martin
William Crenshaw   Henry Hunter
Alex^d. M, High   P. H. Mangum
David Justice
Turner Pullen
Daniel Pierce
Robt Fleming
Samuel Crenshaw
Nathl. C Thompson.
T. D. Wynne
Smith Abernathe

[Addressed:]
                    To
          Willie P. Mangum Esqr
By   Orange County
Some friend—

---

[53]John Martin ran the Forest Hill Academy, fifteen miles north of Raleigh toward Oxford. Coon, *Doc. Hist. of Educ. in N. C.*, 526.
[54]This route was almost the present U. S. Highway No. 1. The route by the falls (Neuse Falls) was the old Oxford Road that went about one mile west of Wake Forest. Most of the people who signed this letter have descendents living along that old Oxford Road.

WPM-LC

John Martin to Willie P. Mangum

Dear Sir, Should you alter this rout, the post office may be at
John W. Harrises store formerly Sutherlands old store, Harriss
will Except of the appointment he told me, nothing more but
Remaines Yours with due respect

JOHN MARTIN
oct°. 1825

W. P. Mangum Esqr

WPM-LC

Acct. of Willie P. Mangum to Milo Latimer[55]

[6 Oct., 1825]

Willie P. Mangum
   To Milo Latimer .... Dr—

1823
March 10 To 4 yds Sup^r. Blue cloth @ $11.50............ $46.
  " " 1 vest pattern 150 6½ yds.
      Sheeting. ⁵⁰.325 .... 4.75
  " " 15 hks Silk ¹⁰.150 1 Slip thread 25........ 1.75
  " " 1 yd. Padding 150 1½ doz
      Moulds.⁹ᶜ 18¾ 1.68¾
  " " 2 doz Small Mo.⁶¼ 12½ 1 stck long
      twist 20 .... ".32½
  " " 1½ Yds Bumbazet.⁷⁵ 112½ 1 tape 12½ 1.25
  13 " 1 doz Buttons P Taylor .... ".37½

                 56.13¾
    Int. from June 6 1823 .... 8.12

                 64.25

16th. May 1825 this above acc^t was acknowledged, with a promise to pay the same by Mr Mangum on this day—

THOS. SCOTT[56] M. LATTIMER

---

[55]Milo Latimer was a local merchant.
[56]Thomas Scott was a justice of peace of Orange County and a business partner of A. D.
Murphey in the latter's milling business on the Haw River. Hoyt, *Papers of Murphey*, I,
44, 338; II, 430; McIver, *N. C. Register*, 35.

Acc^t .
W. P. Mangum
56.13¾
11.22   Interest
_____

67.35¾ due the Octr 6. 1826

_____

WPM-LC

Rob. Potter[57] *to Willie P. Mangum*

HALIFAX—No. CAROLINA
Octr. 23rd. 1825—

My Dear Sir,
    Your letter addressed to me at M^r. Bullocks,[58] having disclosed the fact that you had not protested my order, I should cheerfully and promptly, have returned a friendly and apologetical reply, had the parylising influence of a malignant fever, left it in my power to do so; but on the morning after I pen'd the harsh and much regretted note, transmitted to you by the hand of Thos. Bullock, I was seized with a violent billious fever, which detained me in Granville seventeen days: during the first ten of which, I was unable to write a legible note of five lines: and it was only in the afternoon of yesterday that I reached home, after a pilgrimage of four days from Oxford—If you will permit your recollection to travel back over the circumstances which led to my last note—if you will candidly and dispassionately weigh those circumstances, and consider what I conceive to have been, the more than ordinary relationship which existed between us: I think your sense of justice will constrain you to admit, that there was much to palliate the course I have pursued—On leaving Oxford last year, I found it impossible as I have stated to you before, to avoid a transfer of the claim which chance had given me on you; yet such was the delicate regard I cherished for your feelings—such the enthusiastic character of those feelings of friendship I entertained for you; feelings which had been fostered by a frequent and confidential interchange of sentiment, and confirmed by what I conceived to be, demonstrations on your part, of a warm and devoted regard for

---

[57]Potter was in constant financial difficulty.
[58]Probably Thomas Bullock who was a large planter in Granville County. "Genealogical Table of the Bullock Family." A microfilmed copy is in the library of the University of North Carolina.

me; that I addressed you a note, explaining my necessities, and *apologising* for the transfer which I had an undoubted right to make, and which, in the ordinary transactions of business should have excited no surprise—To that friendly note I received no answer, but taking it for granted that the order was discharged, dismissed the subject from my mind, until five or six months afterwards, when I happened in Oxford, it was presented to me for payment by Kyle, with your name endorsed thereon, and the word protested written above it, Kyle informing me, that you had protested the order—I could not but be surprised and offended at the circumstances, as it amounted to nothing less than an impeachment of my integrity and honesty, implying as it did, that I had attempted to evade the payment of a debt, by drawing an order on a man who owed me nothing—injured and insulted as I then thought I was however, my respect for you would not permit me to disclose the affair to any one, and determined me to await some future explanation from you which I was still certain of receiving—The explanation being witheld, it seemed to me that you had acted towards me, on the supposition that the feebleness of my character and the humility of my condition, would enable you to practice an act of injustice on me, without danger to your own reputation or standing—but your letter has perfectly undeceived me, and shewn me the *injustice* I had done you—an injustice however *confined to my own thoughts* as I have communicated the subject to no one—I placed such reliance on the assurance contained in your letter, as not to question Kyle at all about the protest; satisfied as I now am, that affair was a mere trick of his, to force the money out of me—My feelings towards you now, are as warm and unadulterated, and I should be as ready to make a sacrifice for you were it necessary to do so, as in the earlier days of our friendship; and I sincerely trust, that the explanation contained in letter, will banish from your mind, as I think it should do, every resentful or unpleasant feeling connected with this affair—

Y^r, friend
ROB. POTTER

[Addressed:]

    To

      The Honble,

        Willie P. Mangum

          Hillsborough   No. Carolina

WPM-LC

John Chavis to Willie P. Mangum

Oct. 24th 1825

My dear Sir,

I suppose that towards the end of next Month, you will set out to Congress, & will, no doubt, be pretty much engaged in making arrangements which will lead you often from home, & which will make it uncertain when to find you there. As I wish to see you before you go away I have fixed upon the third Saturday in next Month to come to see you as being the most favorable to time for my conveniency. However I fear it will not be so to you, as I know you are in the habit of going to Raleigh about the time of meeting of the Assembly & should you go there at that time, you will probably take my son Priestley[59] on your way which will cause you to Start on Saturday. Should this be the case, Iwd thank you to write & leave your letter at Mr Cain's store in Hillsborough where I expect to be on the first Saturday in next Month. Or should you be going to Raleigh sooner & can make it in your way to call at my school house I sh'd be glad, as I want your advice in to cases as well as to converse with you on your own concerns or affairs.

I am yours &c
JOHN CHAVIS

[Addressed:]
Hon. Willie P. Mangum
        Orange
Care of
Mr. W. Cain.

—————

WPM-LC

H. G. Burton to Willie P. Mangum

RALEIGH Nov. 9 A D 1825

Dear Sir

I hope very much to have seen you before you set out for Washington—but suppose I shall not enjoy that pleasure—Do my good friend enclose me—My Memorandum And any papers

---

[59]Chavis usually referred to a favorite white leader as "my son." Here he refers to Priestley H. Mangum.

you may have realtive to my suit in Equity—My object is to answer—that the matter may be brought to a close. I hope you will be a better correspondent this session than you were the last—tho If I must tell the truth, I have no right to complain of others upon that *score.* for I am convinced it proceeds neither from a want of respect or friendship on my part, but from abomniable laziness.—and why may not Honerable gentlemen, have the same Lawful excuse, more especially—when their heads are filled with Politics "hunting Ghosts" and other such important matters—Robert Potter is anxious to go to Guatamala—I believe him to be well qualified for the appointment, as I have ever considered him a man of extradanary [*sic*] powers of Mind, and unbending Integrity—you know he stands in need of it—and I believe you always helped the "widow" when the call was honor bright—I have your Atlass and will send it whenever directed.

I am sincerely
Your friend
H G BURTON

N. B.
Judge Ruffin I presume for the present has blown all our projects sky high[60]—

[Addressed:]

The Honble
Willie P. Mangum
Orange

WPM-LC

John Chavis to Willie P. Mangum

Nov.r 20th. 1825

My dear sir

I have sent your Pamphlet by Mr C. Bass. The transactions in Hayti have convinced me more fully of the impropriety there wd. be in our Government recognizing the Haytian Government & I

---

[60]Thomas Ruffin was appointed superior court judge in July 1825. Burton, who was governor at the time, apparently wanted to appoint Mangum. In August, 1826, he did appoint Mangum. McDuffie, "Willie P. Mangum," 38; Stephen B. Weeks, "W. P. M.," *Biog. Hist. of N. C.,* V, 242.

hope you will use your best endeavours to prevent it.[61] It appears to me that sh^d. the President of the United States mention it in his Message it w^d. well for Congress to pass it in silence & not agitate it as a question at all & this I sh^d. suppose could be managed out of doors—

Should I fail of a school in Hillsborough Doctor Hunt[62] tells me that he thinks that he can make me a school in his neighbourhood of 25 [sc]holars at $10. each, but he hopes I may succeed in Hillsborough as being a better situation so that I do not expect to continue on Ellibies Creek.[63] But I intend to join the Doct & I hope we shall be able to make converts of your opposers on that stream. I told the Dr. that the most effectual way was to make a dead set at J. N. if we get time to turn [illegible] the matter cud be settled at once, and shall not only shoot at N., but the [illegible] & I think I can at least make them understand. You have my best wishes and may God bless you is the prayer of your Obt Hbl. Servt.

JOHN CHAVIS

State of N. Carolina)
    orange County   )

[Addressed:]
        Hon. Willie P. Mangum
            Orange.

WPM-LC

[21 Nov., 1825]

State of North-Carolina[64]

To the Honorable
        W. P. Mangum Esquire, Greeting:
        It having been officially certified, by the certificates of the returning Officers, bearing date the ....
        day of .... 1825, that you were

---

[61]By 1825 the United States' trade with Haiti was large. The press of New England began agitating for recognition. In that year France recognized the republic. This influenced Clay to champion recognition, but Adams did not push it. The Haitian government, which had gone through frequent revolutions seemed more stable from 1822 to 1825. Rayford W. Logan, *The Diplomatic Relations of the United States with Haiti 1776-1891* (Chapel Hill, N. C.: The University of North Carolina Press, 1941), 188-222; Ludwell Lee Montague, *Haiti and the United States, 1714-1838* (Durham, N. C.: The Duke University Press, 1940), 15-16.
[62]John Hunt was a planter in Granville County.
[63]Ellebee Creek is just north of the present town of Durham. It flows east into the Neuse River just south of the confluence of the Eno and Neuse.
[64]Printed form.

(SEAL)   duly elected by our Eighth Congressional District, to represent us in the Nineteenth Congress of the United States, which commences on the Fifth day of December 1825, and expires on the 4th day of March, 1827—, you are hereby authorized and commissioned to claim and hold a seat as a Member of the House of Representatives of the United States, for the term aforesaid, and vested with all the rights, privileges, and immunities conferred by the Consti tution on members of the said House.

     In Testimony Where His Excellency Hutchins G. Burton— Our Governor, Captain General, and Commander in Chief, hath caused the Great Seal of State to be here- unto affixed, and signed the same at our city of Ra- leigh, on the 21st. day of November A. D. 1825.—

By the Governor,   H. G. BURTON
Jno. K. Campbell.[65]
     Pri. Secretary.
Comⁿ. to W. P. Mangum
    Fee of office $2.00

WPM-LC

J. Taylor[66] to Willie P. Mangum

HILLSBOROUGH N. C. Nov. 28th 1825.

Dear Sir.

    The office of "charge de affairs" to Guatamala having become vacant by the death of the late Gov. Miller[67] and it seeming to be desirous that it should be filled by some native North Carolinian, I have determined to have my name presented to the President of the United States as a Candidate for that appointment. I therefore address you on the subject and request the favor of you, to inquire at as early a day as practicable, whether the office has already been applied for and by whom and to inform me

---

[65]John K. Campbell, a native of South Carolina and a graduate of the South Carolina College, settled in Raleigh as Burton's secretary until he moved to Florida to become the United States attorney. He was killed in 1833 in a duel in Florida. Stephen B. Weeks, "The Duello in North Carolina and Among North Carolinians." *The Charlotte Democrat*, June 15, 1888. This is a clipping in the Weeks' Collection in the North Carolina Room, University of North Carolina.

[66]John Taylor, a large planter, was the clerk of the Orange County court. Grant, *Alumni Hist. of U. N. C.*, 610.

[67]William Miller of Warren County was state attorney general in 1810 and a member of the legislature from 1811 to 1814 and 1821 to 1822. He was speaker of the state House of Commons from 1812 to 1814, and from 1814 to 1817 he was the state's chief executive. Presi- dent Adams made him charge d'affaires to Guatemala where he died in 1825. Ashe, *Biog. Hist. of N. C.*, IV, 328-330.

whether there is any probability of my application meeting with success. I would be glad that you would point out to me the necessary steps to be taken by me, in order to be placed in a proper point of view before the President of the United States.

I was very desirous of seeing you on that subject as well as on the subject of getting my son John Umstead admitted at West Point, before you left home, but my professional business prevented my seeing you—

Your attention and friendly aid on those Subjects will confer a p[art]icular obligation upon me—

I am yours truly

J. TAYLOR

[Addressed:]

The Honble
  Willie P. Mangum
    Washington City
      D. C.

WPM-LC

Gales & Seaton to Willie P. Mangum

Office of the National Intelligencer
December, 1825.

Sir:

As the Reports of the Debates in the two Houses of Congress, published in this paper, become the materials for the Register of Debates, we shall take [it] as a favor if you will on perceiving any material error in such reports, as respects yourself, inform us thereof in writing, to the end that it may be corrected for the Register; and if you should desire what you may say on any occasion to be reported more at large for the Register, your communication to that effect will be thankfully received.

We take the liberty of suggesting, further, that, should you at any time feel a particular solicitude for the accuracy of the Intelligencer report of any remarks which you may make, we should take it as a favor if you would furnish to either of us, on the day of the Debate, your own notes of such remarks; or a sketch of them by your own hand; the latter would be more acceptable, as it would, insomuch, lighten our daily, or rather nightly labor.

We have the honor to be,

Very respectfully, your obt. Servts.

GALES & SEATON

Hon. W. Mangum.

[Addressed:]

Hon. Mr. Mangum.

WPM-LC

D. F. Caldwell[68] to W. P. Mangum

Raleigh Dec[b]. 4th 1825

My dear Sir

I would have written you during the recess of Congress, but from a hope of seeing you at this place before your departure. I have no particular business, save to express my personal thanks, for the able & in my opinion correct stand you took in support of McLane[69] from Deleware. Altho°. I supported Gen[l]. Jackson, I cannot yield assent to the position, that Congress in a great National election or question, is bound by every wild & indiscreet expression of public opinion. Whether the votes for the Gen[l]. in the electoral colleges, be such is not now necessary to determine. In the abstract you were correct & the contrary in my opinion would put an end to our Government.

Much to your credit, you hazarded your popularity & ran the risk of being swept out of view by public indignation. I know of no event in your public career, which has elevated you so much with the reflecting men of No Carolina.

As a republican, for such I hope we all are, I have a due respect for a fair expression of public opinion, but I cannot assent, that Congress or the Legislature shall be degraded into a set of demagogues.

I fear that our session will be a disastrous one We have already the Bank & Sheriffs Bills before us & a Bill to repeal the

---

[68]David F. Caldwell, 1791-1867, was a student at the state university with Mangum. He served as a member of the state legislature in 1816 to 1819, 1825, and 1829 to 1831. In 1830 he was speaker of the state senate. From 1844 to 1859 he was a judge of the superior court. His home was Salisbury. Grant, *Alumni Hist. of U. N. C.*, 93.

[69]Louis McLane of Delaware was an ardent supporter of Crawford. He stuck to Crawford after his election seemed hopeless.

whole subject of internal improvements. From the present temper of the Legislature their success is greatly to be apprehended.
What will be the fate of our chancery Bill I cannot predict. The
great bone of contention seems to be the places of its location.
Mr Gales[70] lost his election to day for public printer, by near
thirty votes. I am glad of it; not from any former political re-
sentment, but because he is rich & his opponent is poor & their
qualifications are equal—Mr Stanly[71] whom I fear you are not
partial to presides over us with impartiality, dignity & ability.
He certainly gives a dignity to the deliberations of the Commons,
& preserves a degree of decorum which I have never witnessed.

The Comptroller[72] has opposition (W^m H Hill[73] & Jno G A Williamson[74]) but I do not believe it will be successful. I hope you
will write me during the Winter frequently, & furnish me with
such public documents as you can conveniently. I am without a
representative. Mr. Long[75] I believe looks on every man as his
enemy who did not vote for him.—

Yours Sincerely

D. F. CALDWELL

[Addressed:]

The Hon^bl. W P Mangum
Washington City

Mail.

WPM-LC

Willie P. Mangum to Charity A. Mangum

Monday Morning the 5th. Decr. 1825

My dear Love,

I have postponed writing to you until this morning, knowing
that my letter could not reach you before next Sunday, and
therefore I wished to write at the latest period.—

---

[70]Weston Raleigh Gales, the son of Joseph Gales, was editor of the *Raleigh Register* after his father went to Washington.
[71]John Stanly. See above, p. 94n.
[72]Joseph Hawkins, 1785-1842, a member of the legislature in 1812 to 1813, was comptroller of the state from 1821 to 1827. He was active as a trustee of his alma mater, the state university, and as a railroad director. Grant, *Alumni Hist. of U. N. C.*, 266.
[73]William H. Hill was probably the son of William H. Hill, the United States attorney for the North Carolina district and member of Congress as a supporter of John Adams. Ashe, *Biog. Hist. of N. C.*, IV, 176-181.
[74]John G. A. Williamson of Person County was in the state legislature from 1823 to 1825 and was charge d'affaires at Caracas in 1830. Grant, *Alumni Hist. of U. N. C.*, 678.
[75]John Long.

I left home a day or two earlier than usual to enable me to stop a day at Petersburg, or Richmond to rest myself from the excessive fatigues of Stage-Coach travelling—but the weather proved so fine, and the roads were in such perfectly good condition, that I travelled with less fatigue & exhaustion than usual, & therefore I kept in the line, without any stop until, I reached Washington, on Thursday morning last at the break of day.—I found a great many members of Congress in this city, and the arrivals on thursday, were more numerous than have heretofore been known at so early a period.—I have taken my lodgings at Dawsons and shall have a better mess than heretofore—

I have been perfectly well, except a slight costiveness, which I hope to remove entirely, by early rising and exercise in the morning—

I was so much beset by business just before I left home, that I came off in a sort of dreamy state—and scarcely had time to think of the long space of separation, that was to take place between us—These reflections always press upon me with most severity after the event has happened, I then feel deeply enough and bitterly enough, the loss of that quiet & comfort which I hope in God at some period I shall enjoy with my family.—I hope my Love, that you will take good care of your health, and often see our dear little daughter—For after all in you two all my hopes of rational enjoyment & happiness in this world are centered—and my severest miseries arise from my inability to place you both in the condition that you deserve, and to enjoy it with you, & to cherish that happiness that has been from necessity chiefly, too much neglected by me.—

Yesterday Mr. Bryan[76] a member of our mess and a very pious man, attended church, where I heard one of the most powerful sermons that I ever listened to.—And while I sat under those powerful & heart searching appeals the world with all its pomps, its grandear & its attractions that lead off the mind & intoxicate the fancy, seemed to fade into insignificance—

For my sake, try to spend your time as well as you can, and do not, My Love permit melancholy to prey upon you too much often think of me,—For it does my heart good even its loneliness, to believe that there is one heart in the world, that has freighted all its earthly happiness on me.—May God save that

---

[76]John Heritage Bryan, 1798-1870, after graduation from the state university practiced law in New Bern. He served in the state senate in 1823 and 1824 and in Congress from 1825 to 1829. *Biog. Dir. of Cong.*, 752.

heart from the pangs of unrequited returns of affections in all its relations in life—and may its happiness be as complete, as its purity and deservings are surpassing.—

Give my Love to my Mother & Eliza, and cherish my dear, the deep assurance, that I am in life & shall be in death, if that event were to happen to me when separated from you, your devoted & affectionate husband, and that my heart constantly turns to you as the being on earth for whom it has the most love, and in whom it has the fullest & most confiding faith—Your value to me is surpassing, and may kind providence enable me to treasure the jewel in my inmost heart at all times and all periods—and at some day be enabled to cherish that heart without absence or without remission as it deserves.

Farewell my dearest Love

WILLIE P. MANGUM

Mrs. Charity A. Mangum

[Addresed:]

Mrs. Charity A. Mangum
Stagville
No Carolina

———

WPM-LC

W. P. Mangum to Charity A. Mangum

SUNDAY MORNING the 11th december 1825.

My dear Love,

I hope I shall receive by this mornings mail a letter from you, I am anxious, very anxious to hear from home and I trust my dear, that you will make it a point, let what may be to do, to write me every week,—If you say nothing but that you are well; it will contribute much to alleviate the burdensome hours— many of which are exceedingly burdensome, that I spend at this place.—I want to hear from our dear little daughter—and would this moment give my high bell-crowned hat, and it is likely the highest that you ever saw, to see & to kiss the little urchin—

After the first of January, that is some little time thereafter, all my letters & papers will go to the *Red Mountain,* that is to Carringtons[77] where it will be less inconvenient to send to the

---

[77] J. J. Carrington and his family were related to Mangum. He lived near Mangum.

post office.—I have not been entirely well since I have been here, I have taken quite a bad cold, I am very hoarse, but have had but little fever.—I have taken to my old habit of bathing in cold water every morning, and I find that it is of much service in this fickle climate.—My hours are regular and I intend that they shall be so this winter.—My mess is composed of Gentlemen of much more regular habits, than it formerly was.—and therefore I shall have to contend with no difficulty in living as best comports with my health and improvement—For with the vastly extensive library belonging to the Capitol, I am engaged when unemployed in public business, in reading—But little public business has been done, nor will much be done until after christmas—we do not spend an hour a day in the capitol—and indeed have met but four days.—The president has set up a splendid court in a style superior to Mr. Monroe's—On Tuesday evening next I shall have the honor to dine with him—The administration opens upon principles that I cannot approve—What may be the future direction I cannot tell—

To day I shall go to the Episcopal church, and in the evening take a family dinner with Jo. Gales the head of the National Intelligencer.—His mother my old acquainance Mrs. Gales[78] of Raleigh is here, and they seek occasions to treat me with great kindness & attention.—

I hope, my Love, that you will not fail to write to me often.—It will afford me much satisfaction—To know my dear, that you are well, and that you bear with a calm fortitude our separaion would give me much comfort.—I hope & trust that the time will come, when we shall yet be happy—

In you my Love, My dearest hopes & richest treasures are embarked.—For where in this wide world have I found, or where should I find, a heart so affectionate, so devoted & so true to me & to my happiness—

Remember me to my mother, & Eliza & the rest.— and you yourself I hope will often think of me with kindness & with love—and always believe me

to be your affectionate husband
WILLIE P. MANGUM

[78]Mrs. Joseph Gales, Sr.

WPM-LC

James W. Armstrong[79] to Willie P. Mangum

ORANGE COUNTY N. C. Decembr. 14th 1825.

Dear Sir,

I am anxious to procure a warrant for to go on to the United States Military Academy, at West Point, next June one year; at which time I will be graduated in the Universiy of N.C.

I wish you to ascertain from the Secretary at War, whether I can procure a warrant one year before hand, and if I can you will confer a great favor by getting me one.—My motive for applying so soon is; that I may be certain of getting a Warrant—Direct your letter to Chapel Hill—

Your friend etc

JAMES W. ARMSTRONG.

Honble. Willie P. Mangum

P. S. Excuse the style of this letter as the mail is just about to start.

Free

[From] Red Mountain, N. C.
December 14th. 1825

[Addressed:]

Honl. Willie P. Mangum
    Washington City
        District of Columbia.

WPM-LC

Paris Pearson[80] to Willie P. Mangum

[14 Dec. 1825]

To the honourable Willie P. Mangum—Representative in Congress from the State of North Carolina—

Sir, as soldiers in the Militia from the state of North Carolina in aid to the State South Carolina and Georgia, I marched from Wake County in 1778 said State and continued to serve tell the spring in the year 1779 and by an act of the Legislature

---

[79]See below, p. 305.
[80]See below, p. 286.

of North Carolina passed at the Spring Session of 1778 each drafted man was allowed twentyfive dollars and each volunteer fifty dollars bounty, and I served as a volunteer, and by another session of the same assembly before a subsequent Election which last session was begun in the fall 1778 continued January 1779, twenty dollars a month bounty was allowed each Militia Soldier that marched to the aid of other States both the salaries in force at the same time I served, and one of them bounties is now due and owing to me, and as the United States are in a condition of unparrelled prosperity and more able to pay the arrears now due to individuals for Military survices performed in the Revolution with Interest, than to have paid the principal only at the termination of the Revoluntionary ware, and so relying on the gratitude of a free people and on the patrotism and wisdom of Congress, I apply to you Sir to present this my claim for fifty dollars with Interest from the Spring of 1779 for the constitution of the United States which in all party of peculer[?] Spirit, should efficient oppression in behalf of those who at the most eminent risk of their lives defended and protected his nation with real and perseverence from the intolarable oppression of the British Government &c.

PARIS PEARSON.

North Carolina Orange County)
Dec. 14th 1825.   )

N. B. Please Sir direct me a letter to Chapel hill office as I live in Orange County.

P. P.

[Addressed:]   To the Honl.   [Endorsed:]
                       Willie P. Mangum   Paris Pearson.
                 in Congress, at Washington City.

WPM-LC

G. A. Mebane[81] to Willie P. Mangum

MASON HALL December 18 day 1825

Dear Sir

After my respects to you, I take this method to inform you that I have a claim in the war department for transportation

---

[81]George A. Mebane was a close relative of James Mebane of Mason Hall.

from Norfolk in Virginia to Orange County North Carolina the
distance of two hundred and twenty miles for which I am entitled to back transporation of the grade of Lieutenant, I was
discharged at Norfolk when peace was made and bore my own
expence and there being a compensation allowed by Congress for
all of the officers transportation, I am at a loss how to draw up
my account I will take it as a particular favour if you will procure the necessary forms and send them by the first mail.

Yours Respectfully
G. A. MEBANE

[Addressed:]

> Willie P. Mangum
> Member of Congress
> Washington City

[Endorsed:]

> Geo. Mebanes claim

WPM-LC

B. Yancey to Willie P. Mangum

RALEIGH 20. Decembr. 1825.

Dear Sir:

Before this I expected to have recd. at least *one* letter from
you since your arrival at Washington—I fear however, that
your engagements of an evening, are too alluring, for me to expect in you a constant correspondent. I should like notwithstanding to hear from you sometimes, if you could not take as
much time to write to me, as you must have employed in the
letter you wrote Gales—

As it is thought you can approach the poltitical bureau of the
Secretary of State with more facility than most men, may I not
expect in a short time to heard from you a full disclosure of
the views & policy of the administration—

I should like to have a few Hours social Converse with Mr.
Clay: I think I could discover from him what they intended &
whether he & his friend Mr. Q,[82] are really searious when they
say, they wish to do something for our State—

---

[82]John Quincy Adams.

We have no news here—We have passed in the Senate a Bill to prevent free negroes from migrating into the State & to regulate the conduct of those resident among us & compel them to follow some industrious employment—I believe & hope it will pass the Commons—It is however to be assialed by Stanly[83] & Sheppard[84]—It is the only thing I believe we shall do worth a cent.

Write me fully & freely—& if you do not continue to write me after I go home, I will abuse by letter Constantly—

Yrs. respectfully
B. YANCEY

[Addressed:]

Hon.
Willie P. Mangum
Washington City.

A. D. Murphey to Willie P. Mangum[85]

HAW-RIVER. N. Car. 20th Dec. 1825

Dear Sir.

I enclose to you an Outline of the Plan of my intended Work on North Carolina, And beg you to look out for Papers, Documents or Books, that will throw any light upon any Part of the proposed plan, particularly the Historical Part. Perhaps you may find some at Washington in your Searches for other Papers.

As to the Memorial,[86] it is presented; but I have no Idea that any such Aid will be given as my Work will require. I thought, however, public Notice might be thereby drawn to the Subject, and some Men be induced rather to send me their old Papers, and Pamphlets, than to cast them into the Fire.

With much Regard, I am, Dear Sir,

Yours.
A. D. MURPHEY

Willie P. Mangum, Esqr.

[Address: Washington, D. C.]

---

[83]John Stanly.
[84]Augustus H. Shepperd. See above, p. 16n.
[85]This letter was previously published in Hoyt, *Murphey Papers*, I, 323.
[86]Murphey requested financial aid of the state legislature to help pay for the publication of his history of North Carolina. See Hoyt, *Murphey Papers*, II, 333-340.

WPM-LC

Dennis Heartt to Willie P. Mangum

HILLSBOROUGH. Dec. 25, 1825.

Dr. Sir,

I have taken the liberty of enclosing to you an account for advertising for Yates & McIntyre and if not too much trouble would request you to procure parts of tickets for the same in the lottery to be drawn on the 4th Jan.

Yours, rspectfully,
DENNIS HEARTT.

Messrs. J. B. Yates & A Mc'Intyre
To Dennis Hearttt   Dr.

To advertising New York State Literature Lottery from 12th Oct. to this date, 11-weeks-57 lines................$10.00
Hillsborough, Dec. 25, 1825.   ——

[Addressed:]

Free

Hon Willie P. Mangum
Washingon City.

———

WPM-LC

John Scott to Willie P. Mangum

RALEIGH, Dec. 25th. 1825.

My Dear Sir.

Yours of the 9th. Inst. is before me. In answer to the interrogations enclosed I have to state that I do know John Scott of the Town of Hillsborough and that he is considered as still alive: nor have I yet heard of the death or removal of John Taylor who is generally considered and believed to reside also in Hillsborough—Mr. David Andrew can receive his distributive share of the estate of James Andrew dec^d. whenever a sufficient receipt or voucher is tendered to me. The precise amount I cannot now give, but will on my return to Hillsborough, ascertain it, and for[ward] it to you for Mr. Lawrence who can take cha[rge] of it for Mr. Andrews. I have been ready and [will]-ing for 12 months for a settlement, the amount is sm[all].

Yesterday we changed the time of our sitting. Next session will commence on the last Monday of Decr. and afterwards on the 2ᵈ. Monday of January in every year.

The Bill to confine the Atto. Genl. to the Supreme Court and to appoint a solicitor for the 3ᵈ. Circuit, passed our House on Friday. On the 3ᵈ. reading, it was amended by adding the 4ᵗʰ. Circuit and a section to repeal the Act creating the Office of Solicitor General. The fate of the Bill in the Senate is quite uncertain.[87] Three candidates are *spoken of*, for each circuit. J. F. Taylor[88] Spruil[89] & Barringer[90] for the 2ᵈ. & Sheppard,[91] Caldwell[92] & myself for the 4th.[93] We have passed the Bill in our House for aiding Murphey in his proposed History of No. Ca. The aid is, to raise by Lottery $25.000.[94]

Yours sincerely,

JOHN SCOTT

For Wake

John Burt	Matthew Strickland
David Holland	John E. Boddie
Wm. McCullows	Lemuel Cooke
Andrew Hartsfield	Thomas Mils
John Robinson	Harrison Terrell
Frederick Israel	Levi Jones
Saml. Harris	James Spaight
John Smith	Thomas L. West
Burwell Temple	James Utley
Newton Wood	Bennett Baucom
Wm. High	Wm. Battle
James Chamlee	Wm. Foot
Reuben Carpenter	John Moore
Joseph Hopkins	

The above list was furnished me a few days past by Pullen,[95]

---

[87]It was defeated.
[87]James Fauntleroy Taylor. See above, p. 77n.
[89]George E. Spruill's name was withdrawn on January 2, 1826. *Journal of the Senate,* 1826, 83, 84.
[90]Daniel L. Barringer.
[91]Augustus H. Shepperd.
[92]D. F. Caldwell.
[93]Taylor was elected.
[94]Archibald D. Murphey, *Laws of N. C., 1825,* 23.
[95]Turner Pullen of Wake County.

former Shff of Wake & consists of such as he supposes you may not be personally acquainted with.

[Addressed:]

> The Honble.
>   Willie P. Mangum
>   Member of Congress
>   Washington City.

—————

WPM-LC

Post Office Dept. to Willie P. Mangum

[28 Dec., 1825]

The Hon. W. P. Mangum is informed by the Postmaster General that he has this day established three Post Offices—at Hollowoy's, Fishdam, and Mount Tirza, N. C. and appointed Wm. Holloway Esq. Col. Wm. Tharpe, and Phillips Moore Esq. Postmasters: and sent the keys with the proper papers for them, the two first to Raleigh, the last to Roxborough, N. C.

Post O. Department)
)
28. Decem. 1825   )

[Addressed:]

> Hon. W. P. Mangum
>   of N. C.
>   House of Repres.

—————

WPM-LC

C. D. Donoho to Willie P. Mangum

RALEIGH, Dec 30th, 1825.

Dear Mangum—

I see you have opened the budget of the ex-President's accounts. I have never been able to learn, whether the report of the select Committee to whom that subject was refered, last winter, was ever printed: if it was, I should be obliged to you, if you'll send me copy of it. It is a subject in which I feel some interest.

THE MANGUM PAPERS 219

The Newspapers will tell you what we are doing here. I think we shall adjourn about the middle of next week

I am with esteem and respect,

yours etc.

C. D. DONOHO[96]

P. S. Address me in Milton.

[Addressed:]

Willie P. Mangum, Esqr
Washington City.

1826

WPM-LC

C. L. Hinton[1] to Willie P. Mangum

January 1st 1826.

Dr Sir

I have to complain of your not complying with with [sic] your promise in not writing me before you left Carolina respecting the settlement between Mrs Sutherland[2] and Mrs Goodloe[3]—I wish to settle the Estate next Franklin Court provided that settlement can be made as has been contemplated, I would be glad you'd write me whether Mrs Sutherland would take Mrs Goodloes note, or what course she expects to be persued.

Our Legislature expects to adjourn the present week—Mr Drew[4] the Atto Genl sent in his resignation yesterday. J F Taylor Barringer & G E Spruill are announced candidates for the appointment—tomorrow it is expected Hillman[5] & Badger[6] will be added to the list—poor Drew it is thought is partially deranged—he has been in Raleigh the past week incompetent to the discharge of any part of his duties

---

[96]Charles D. Donoho, who graduated from the state university in 1820, was a member of the House of Commons from Caswell County from 1824 until his death in 1828. He was an attorney in Milton. Grant, *Alumni Hist. of U. N. C.*, 167; *N. C. Manual*, 543-544.

[1]See above, p. 51n.

[2]Possibly Mangum's sister-in-law, the wife of Solomon Sutherland who lived in Wake County.

[3]Possibly the mother of the anti-slavery leader Daniel R. Goodloe of Louisburg. The Goodloes later felt special gratitude to Mangum because in 1844 he helped Daniel R. Goodloe to find a job with a newspaper in Washington. Ashe, *Biog. Hist. of N. C.*, V, 255.

[4]William Drew. See above, p. 136n.

[5]Samuel Hillman.

[6]George E. Badger.

I have this morning rec^d the Richmond Enquirer which contains your remarks on Mr Monroes claims[7] or rather its reference, in which I felt much interested particularly as coming from you—

respectfully
Your sincere friend
C. L. HINTON

[Addressed:]

> Honbl
>> Willie P Mangum
>> Washingon City

WPM-LC

H. G. Burton to Willie P. Mangum

RALEIGH January 3rd A D 1826.

Dear Sir

The Resolution[8] of Genl Love[9] regularly authenticated I have sent to you—Also the Law ratifying the contract with the Indians—in the course of a few days I will forward the Decision of the Supreme Court—And as soon as the resoluion can be printed I will forward to each of our Senators and Representatives a Copy—I expect to be at Washington in the course of a few weeks—the Legislature is about to adjourn and there is

---

[7]James Monroe was in financial difficulties when he completed his term as President. The expenses of his diplomatic missions of 1794 to France and 1804 to Spain were never completely paid. In 1825, therefore, he asked Congress for $30,000. Congress adjourned before action was taken but not until after Mangum had made a strong fight against the payment. In 1831 Congress finally granted the $30,000, but this came too late to save Monroe from financial failure. W. P. Cresson, *James Monroe* (Chapel Hill, N. C.: The University of North Carolina Press, 1846), 470-477; *Register of Debates*, 19 Cong., 1 sess., 847-849.

[8]By the treaty of 1819 with the Cherokees, the United States agreed to reserve 640 acres of land to each family of the Cherokees when the Cherokees became citizens of the United States. To take care of this agreement the Federal government set aside this land in North Carolina without the state's approval. Already the state had granted this land to the whites. Since the Indians and whites claimed the same land, law suits followed. The state Supreme Court decided in favor of the Indians. Hence the state paid the whites $19,940 for the land. On December 13, 1825, General Thomas Love of Haywood County proposed in the legislature a resolution to request repayment from the Federal Government. This resolution was approved. In Congress in 1828 Samuel P. Carson on the Committee on Indian Affairs proposed the repayment. This was done. Archibald Henderson, *North Carolina: The Old North State and the New*, 5 vols. (Chicago, Ill.: The Lewis Publishing Co., 1941), II, 11-12; *N. C. Laws, 1826*, 87; *Journal of the N. C. Senate, 1825*, 889.

[9]General Thomas Love, 1730-c. 1830, fought in the Revolution. At its close he resided in Tennessee for a few years before he returned to western North Carolina, finally settling in Haywood County. He was in the state legislature from 1797 to 1811, 1814 to 1815, 1817 to 1819, and 1823 to 1828. W. C. Allen, *Centennial of Haywood County and its County Seat, Waynesville, N. C.* (Waynesville, N. C.: Courier Publishing Co., n. d.), 55.

nothing but bustle and confusion I have no time to write more
Yours sincerely
H. G. BURTON

[Addressed:]

The Honble
Willie P. Mangum
Washington
D.-C.-

WPM-LC

Thos. H. Hall[10] to W. P. Mangum
TARBOROUGH N. C. 4th January 1826
Will my friend Mr. Mangum be so good as to pay in advance for
six months for the Intelligencer, 4 dolls I see is the sum required
I wish to see what is said on some of the subjects marked out
for talk If any which may be considered masterly speeches
should assume a Pamphlet form—as they some times do please
send me a copy or two on either side & have the Intelligencer
directed to me at this place. What is likely to be come with the
Constitution in regard to the presidential election. I see many
propositions for altering but whether to amend I cant say Will
Mr Monroe acct.[11] be paid or will Congress at the suggestion of
some one in the papers give him a Pension. If true as stated in
the debate the other day, that he is in penury he is entitled
under the act already in existence. With a certain order of Politicians now nearly extinct Madisons Report on certain Resolu-
tions, settling principles of relation between the State and Genl.
Govt[12] was considered a sort of text book, if you can with the
assistance of Mr. Macon procure and transmit me a copy I shall
consider it an act of kindness. Mr. Macon will know at once
what Document I mean if you will tell him what I say about it
I am with great regard yours
THOS. H. HALL.
Torborough N C
Jany 7th 1826   Free
[Addressed:]
Hon W. P. Mangum
Washington D. C.

10See above, p. 191n.
11See above, p. 220n.
12He refers to the Virginia Resolutions of 1798.

WPM-LC

Thomas H. Blount[13] to Richard Hines[14]

WASHINGTON N. C. 6ᵗ. Jany. 1826

My Dear Sir,

There is a portion of your constituents labouring under much inconvenience and if you could thro' the Secretary of the Treasury or any other means relieve them from it, you would thereby render them an essential service—The Inhabitants on Cape Hatteras banks obtain their subsistence entirely by the wrecks cast on shore there—that is by the salvage in saving the cargoes of the unfortunate & transporting that produce to the inland Towns, a precarious one indeed—but it compels nearly all he men to own small boats of from five to fifteen Tons burthen—beyond this they are of no use, except to carry their *small* stock of provisions to the Banks—These men have always paid hospital money for the employment of the boats and there never has been an instance where they have asked for or obtained assistance from the Hospital fund of the United States—In their old age and poverty they ask for support from their County—They are not *properly* seamen—and yet enough so to pay hospital money—If any relief can be afforded them, 'twill assist them much, for I assure you to the greater portion of the bankers, a small sum is desirable—

The period for which I was appointed Collector of the Customs for this District expires in February, and I should be much gratifyed if thro' you I could be continued—I would therefore request you to solicit it from the President—You have known me many years and can therefore state any fact which may be necessary—I flatter myself that your recommendaion alone would be sufficient, but beg leave to mention that from the intimacy formerly existing between the Secretary of the Treasury[15] and Tho-Blount, and his official acquaintance with me, that he would render me the necessary assistance—If you have become acquainted with Major Eaton[16] of the Senate & Genˡ. Houston[17] of the H. R. from Tenessee please present my

[13]Thomas H. Blount, a lawyer and former member of the legislature, was the collector of customs for the port of Washington, N. C. McIver, *N. C. Register*, 82.
[14]Richard Hines, a lawyer and former member of the state legislature, was Democratic-Republican Congressman from 1825 to 1827. *Biog. Dir. of Cong.*, 1101.
[15]Richard Rush of Pennsylvania was Secretary of the Treasury from 1825 to 1829.
[16]Major John Henry Eaton, Jackson's friend from Tennessee.
[17]General Sam Houston.

respects to them individually—and if you have not, do so by all means, as they are among the most deserving of men—

Yours truly

THOS. H. BLOUNT

Honble.

Richd Hines
House of Repr.

[Addressed:]

Honble
Richard Hines
H. of R^s-
of the Un. States

_____

WPM-LC

W. P. Little¹⁸ to Willie P. Mangum

LITTLETON Jany the 6th 1826

Dear Sir/

I take the liberty for several reasons not now necessary to recite to request that you will use your influence to procure a Warrant for my son George to be admited as a pupil at West Point, George is a youth of Great assiduity Steadiness perseverence and not deficient in Genius and I will Venture to predict that Should he be Successful in his application that he will never leave the place until he graduates unless his health shoud require it he is between fifteen and sixteen years of age has made considerable progress in the Classical part of education and is verry anxious to finish his education at West Point he is about six feet in height has a pretty G[ood] Constitution and I am persuaded shoud you be instrumental in procuring him a Warrant you will never have Occasion to regret it he saw you on your way to Washington and he relyes on your aid much

I am Verry respectfully Yours &c

W P LITTLE

P S

George was recommended last year by Messrs Macon Branch

_____

¹⁸William P. Little, a former state senator from Warren County, was postmaster in Littleton near Warrenton. *N. C. Manual*, 621; McIver, *N. C. Register*, 73.

and Edwards and it was said there was not any Vacancy at that time but that he was placed on the list of applicants for the ensuing year

Yours &C

Littleton   W P L—
   Jany 6th
Mail

[Addressed:]

Mr. Willie P. Mangum
Free
Washington City

WPM-LC

John Garner to Willie P. Mangum

Januy 7th 1825 [1826]

Wyley P. Mangum Esqr
  Dear Sir
    You will be so good as send me the National inteligencer, you will please pay the Subscription and I will pay you on your return, or if the Editers will risk the money by mail will remit it them, at any time—Nothing new in this quater of the World—

I remain very respectfy
Yr ob^t. Sevt

JOHN GARNER

P. S. have the Paper directed to Cunningham Store[19] N. C. via Petersburg Va
J G—

[Addressed:]   [Postmarked:]

Wiley P. Mangum Esqr   Milton, N. C.
Washington City   Jan. 8, 1826
D. C.

----

[19]In the northern part of Person County near the Virginia line.

WPM-LC

Charity A. Mangum to Willie P. Mangum

tt 7, 1826,
SATURDAY NIGHT January - - - -

My Dear Willie,

I have received no letter since the 18 of december & have become quite impatient to hear from you I sent to stagsville last sunday and the boy returned without a letter but I hope my husband that if you have not written to me that it is not owing to sickness, my sincere wish & Prayr is for you to enjoy good health, our Family are as well as usual accept Walter[20] he has a bad cold, I heard from our dear little Sally[21] last Wednesday it was not convenient for me to go & I prevailed on hariet Moore to go that she might see her and tell me all about her Hariet says she is one of the sweetest little creatures that she has ever seen, she says she has never seen any child that was as interesting in her life. she still continues her fondness for Stephen's likeness. hariet says it was shewn to her in her presence and she was so delighted with it that she danced and called it papa she is in very good health she was two years old yesterday, that My Willie was her second birth day and her Father was at neither, I hope if we should live until the next if it is the will of kind providence for her to have another that one will be with her if not both of us. She is a gift My Willie that we ought to render sincere thanks for. I hope my husband that she will live to make you amends for all the imperfections of your Wife, May every blessing attend you both is my dailly wish and Prayr. Mother, Eliza, & the Family Join me in love to you. Farewell My Husband & believe me to be your devoted wife C A M, W, P, Mangum—

[Addressed:]

Mr Willie P Mangum,
Washington City,
D. C,

[Postmarked:]

Stagville, N. C.
8th Jany 1826

---

[20]Walter A. Mangum, the Senator's brother.
[21]Sally was with the Cains in Hillsboro at the time.

WPM-LC

Clemon Stinson's oath on the pension claim of Titus Jennings Turner

[12 Jan., 1826]

State of North Carolina   Wake County
this day Came personally before me H Brown one of the States
Justices of the Peace for the County aforesaid Clement Stinson
who Sayeth on his oath that Titus Jennings Turner was one of
the men that Served in a Regiment of Regular Soldiers Raised
by a law of North Carolina passed in 1781 entitled an act to
Raise troops out of the militia for the Better Defence of the
State the Regiment to be organised and Dessiplened in the Same
manner and do the Same duty as Continental troops and that he
believes the Regiment Continued to Serve till about the Close
end of the Revolutionary war and that the wages was not paid
to any of the private men as he knows of   Sworn to and Subscribed before me January 12—1826

his
Clemon Stinson   x
mark

Test
    H BROWN   J. P.
I hereby Certify that Clement Stinson named on the other side
of this paper as a witness in behalf of Titus Jennings Turner is
Considered a Creditable man whose oath is to be trusted to Relied on and Confided in
                    Henry Brown

WPM-LC

Testimony of Titus J. Turner

State of North Carolina   Wake County
this day Come personally before me H. Brown—one of the
States Justices of the peace for the County aforesaid Titus Jennings Turner who Sayeth on his oath that Clement Stinson was
one of the men that Served in a Regiment of Regular Soldiers
Raised by a law of North Carolina passed in 1781 entitled an
act to Raise troops out of the militia for the Better Defence of

the State the said Regiment to be organised and Disiplined in
the same manner and do the same duty as Continental troops
and was Commanded by majors Jo Lewes [Joel Lewis?] and
Bennet Crafton[22] and that the wages was to any private as he
knows of was not paid

Sworn to and Subscribed before me

TITUS J. TURNER

January 12—1826.

Test H. Brown   J. P.
I hereby certify that Titus Jennings Turner name on ther Side
of this paper as a witness in behalf of Clement Stinson is Considered a Creditable man whose oath is to be trusted to Relied
on and Confided in

Henry Brown

————

WPM-LC

Charity A. Mangum to Willie P. Mangum

January 15, 1826

My Dear
    Willie,
            I omitted writing you yesterday that I wuld have it
in my power to tell how our daughters health was, I am now
writing from My Fathers the Family are all well as usual, sally
is as flirty as you ever have seen her, & has not been sick since
you left her she is one of the most mischievous children I have
ever seen & is an affectionate dear sweet child. I received your
letter dated the 2 of January, and was truly glad to hear from
you, & to hear you were in good health I was afraid by my not
getting a letter mail before last that you were sick, I can not
tell my Willie why you have not received my letters I have
written to you almost every week since you left me. I feel so
disappointed whenever I miss getting a letter from you that I
do not think I shall let one week pass without writing you.
Patsy[23] sends her love to you & says she has received 2 letters
from you in her sleep they generally disappear before she

————
[22]See above, p. 177n.
[23]Martha Cain, Charity's sister.

10

wakes. I dreamed the other night of seeing you, & singing the meeting of the water's for you, I see you frequently in my sleep Mr. James ruffin[24] is to be married next week to Miss Susan Williamson.[25] Walter has found the will I mentioned to you in one of my letters, & I expect will send it to you, Sally has Just given me some kisses for you You see nothing half so sweet in washington as the rosy cheek of our dear little daughter She will be I hope too bright a star ever to honour washington citty with her presence in it. a sincere and candid heart would soon become tired of the vain and gaudy show of that place. I should My Willie as soon expect to forget to live as to forget to think of you in my publick as well as my private hour's. Sister Polly[26] Joins me in love to you, Farewell my Willie may every blessing be yours is the sincere Prayer of your

devoted Wife C A Mangum

Willie P Mangum

[Addressed:]

M[r]. Willie P Mangum   [From:] Hillsboro
16th Jany

House of Representatives
Washington City
D. C,

WPM-LC

Willie P. Mangum to Charity A. Mangum

WASHINGTON the 15th. January 1826.

My dear Love,

I have been so much engaged in public business for the last ten days, that I really have scarce had time to write you a word—This is Sunday morning, yesterday morning I wished to write, but had not a moment to spare; This however I hope will reach Stagville by next Sunday, when you will probably get it—The roads have become so bad, and the ice having stopt the running of the Steam Boats that it takes longer for a letter to pass from this place home, than in better weather.—I have

------

[24]James H. Ruffin was the youngest son of Judge Thomas Ruffin.
[25]Susan Williamson was from Person County. The marriage occurred January 24, 1826. Broughton, "Marriages and Death Notices," 16.
[26]Mary Cain Sutherland.

had some cold but upon the whole have been tolerably well; indeed the only want is the proper degree of exercise, which I have omitted to take for the last fortnight.

I hope my Love that you and our dear little daughter have both been well; I want to see you both I believe as much as I ever did in my life—I have received I imagine all the letters you have written, and this week rec^d. the letter in which you mentioned Mr Moores[27] business—I had not written to him because the business was done before I left home—Mr Shaw[28] obtained the contract, & I learn here that if Mr Moore had not increased the sum after he left our house, that he said to me that he would carry the mail for, he would have got it, but asked $60 or 70 more than Mr Shaw & the post master General gave it to Mr Shaw.—I wish he could have got, and indeed he would have done it if the appointment had not been made before I left home—

As regards Sister Polly's business I shall get Mr. Hinton to have it closed in time for her.

In the national intelligencer of the 16th. January, you may find a speech that I made in Congress[29]—I don't reckon that you can understand it—that is much of it—for it is connected with a subject that ladies know but little of.—I gave the administration a rap over the knuckles, and as I was the first member of Congress that had done it, it seemed for a moment to open a beehive over my head—but none of them have yet stung me—

My old friend Mr Macon is in very bad health and I often much fear that he will never leave Washington,—he has never been confined more than a day or two at a time—but his general health is exceedingly bad.—I hope my Love, you will spend as much of your time as you can with our dear little daughter. It would be painful to see her forget both father & mother.— and My dear drop me a line as often as you can, if be only to let me know how you all are.—

I spend many—many hours at the dark late hour of night in thinking of you both—whenever the affections are called up they turn homewards. In this cold place, the mind may be interested, but the affections lie as cold & frozen as the adder in dead winter—all is affectation & show.

[27]Phillip Moore was postmaster at Mount Tarzah in Person County. See above, p. 218.
[28]Willie Shaw was a member of the House of Commons from 1820 to 1821. Later he went west with his slaves to Mississippi. *N. C. Manual*, 440. See below J. P. Sneed's letter to W. P. Mangum, Jan. 1, 1833.
[29]Mangum spoke against Webster's judiciary bill.

My Love remember me often—remember me to Mother Eliza
& the rest. & believe me as I am your affectionate husband

WILLIE P. MANGUM

[Addressed:]

Mrs. Charity A. Mangum
Stagville
Orange Co.
No. Ca.

Willie P. Mangum to Bartlett Yancey[30]

WASHINGTON 15th January 1826

My dear Sir.

Your favor written while you were at Raleigh has been long
since received, and I should have acknowledged it before this,
but that I had hoped that something would have presented that
might have been of some interest—The session thus far has gone
on smoothly with very slight exception; and nothing has occurred upon which the strength of parties has been arrayed so
that the strength of any might be distinctly known.

The Creek treaty[31] seemed to excite most interest upon the
meeting of Congress, but the final developments have been unac-
countably delayed; and the public interest on that subject seems
at this moment to have subsided.—It is believed that the administration are unwilling to drive that subject to extremity, if it
can be consistently avoided.—The Hostiles as they are called &
the McIntosh party are each represented at Washington by a delegation of 15 or more of either side.—Before Christmas the administration proposed to the Geo. delegation an extinguishment
of the indian title by a new treaty to a river in the nation the
name of which I don't remember, leaving to the indians perhaps
one fourth of the whole of the lands they now possess—The Geo.
delegation declined the offer upon the ground that they were invested with no authority to make any compromise, and upon the
additional ground that the former treaty as they insisted was

[30]The original is in the Bartlett Yancey Papers, Southern Collection, University of North Carolina. This letter has been previously published in McDuffie, "Willie P. Mangum," 30-35, and in Edwin M. Wilson, "The Congressional Career of Nathaniel Macon. Followed by Letters of Mr. Macon and Willie P. Mangum with notes by Kemp P. Battle," *The James Sprunt Historical Monograph,* no. 2 (1900), 106-111.
[31]See above, p. 220n.

good & obligatory. The delegation were then notified that the President would send a message to Congress on the subject in the first week in January—This however has not been done—nor are the members at Dawson's Cobb & Merriweather[32] able to account for the delay except upon the supposition that they are endeavouring to negotiate a new treaty so as to avoid the excitement anticipated upon the discussion—

Some of the Georgians—Tattnall[33] for instance—is prepared & I believe determined to drive to extremities any affair of honor that could be got upon the occasion.—During the last week we have been discussing a bill proposing to add three new Judges to the present Supreme Court and the whole weight of administration is thrown into the scale in favor of the Bill[34]—Though for 6 or 8 years the bill of a similar character, though not going to the extent of this, has had no prospect of success—But now by the aid of the eastern people I doubt not but it will pass by a large majority.

That subject is the only one that has called up any disagreeable retrospections—and I have been the unfortunate wight first to broach those subjects—I felt so indignant at the miserably corrupted policy as I believed it of the yankee nation, that I could not refrain from giving them a touch—I expect to be scaled —But I will come out of it as well as I can.—Sir, this administration I verily believe will be conducted upon as corrupt principles indeed more corrupt, than any that has preceded it. Bargaining & compromise will be the order of the day—I came here hoping that I might be able to lend to it a frank support—The Crawford party will have to stand aloof, they will not be able I fear to support this administration; and the alternative as yet presented is perhaps still more objectionable I mean to stand aloof from all political connection having relation to the next presidency—and support or oppose, accordingly as my best Judgment may dictate in each particular case—The proposed constitutional amendment[35] will probably occupy much time—and upon one point I have not made up my mind & should be obliged to you for your views on that point—I am in favor of uniformity in electing electors, and would as at present advised prefer the

[32]Dawson's was the boarding house where Mangum lived in Washington. Thomas W. Cobb was Senator from Georgia. See above, p. 172n. James Meriwether, 1789-1854, was in the war against the Creeks, a member of the United States Commission to the Cherokee Nation, and a member of Congress from Georgia from 1825 to 1827. Biog. Dir. of Cong., 1306.
[33]Edward Fanwick Tattnall, 1788-1832, was a member of Congress from Georgia from 1821 to 1827. Biog. Dir. of Cong., 1597.
[34]See below, p. 237n.
[35]See above, p. 262n.

district system—But as regards taking the election in the event the people fail to give a majority to one candidate, from the House of Reps.—is the point upon which I have great & serious doubts—

In the first place, it will not do in my opinion to let a plurality elect for the govt would not be able to get along with a monopoly against it.—If still the point has to be settled by some tribunal—cannot the Judgt. and discretion of the H. of Rs. be more relied upon than the electoral colleges.—For in either case a compromise would have to be made & which body is most to be relied upon?—Again, I think it desirable to retain the *Federal* features of the constitution undefaced—and resist the tendencies to consolidation—The equality of reps. in the senate is the strong & strongest Federal feature—another is the *equality of the sovereignties* in the election of Prest. in the event of failure by the people—abolish that, and is it not an approach towards consolidation?

I know that the public sentiment is at this time in favour of destroying that feature—But temporary resentments resulting from disappointment in a favourite object ought not to prevail in making great fundamental changes, & the Representative is not worth a fig who in such a case does otherwise than as he thinks right. I take it that the destines of No. Carolina, will cast her lot with the small states—though in population & territory she is such as to give expectation of better things—Yet her exclusion from commercial importance, will contribute powerfully to give her an interest in common with, tho not the smallest, yet with the smaller states—she has no political views to gratify—her nature is that things should go on calmly & smoothly—should she not therefore endeavour to preserve & keep up the weight & importance of the smaller states? I should like to have your views on this subject.—our members here as far as I know, are in favor of the change, I am the only one perhaps opposed to it or doubting about it in the H. of Reps.—

The present Congress will be administration—"the powers that be" have been gaining strength I should imagine—Our friend Lewis Williams goes in deep enough—the thought, you know, of Gen. Jackson is to him gall & bitterness.—and I fear that sentiment may drive him too far—as regards Gen Jackson, I am sure he has made his best race—& that the "powers that be" have but little to apprehend from that quarter—Williams however is no halfway man—he is agt. Jackson & therefore per-

mits himself when there is not necessity for it, to be for Adams
—For it is clear that this adms. has but few sentiments or
leading political subjects in common with him—The other day
when I had made a feeble act at the new Judiciary bill Lewis
made a long speech, and at every step spoke at me.—It was all
done however with good feeling—and as he said in self defence—

Judging from what I can learn here, I presume that Mr.
Adams will be reelected easily, unless some northern man shall
come, who can carry the south—& whether Clinton could or
ought to do so, must depend upon further developments.—

Our old friend Mr. Macon has been in worse health this winter, than I ever knew him to be—He has had very violently &
still has with diminished violence the influenza, which has prevailed here with unusual severity—I believe the old gentleman
sometimes thinks seriously of quitting—He has not recovered I
think from the shock produced by the death of his daughter[36]—
Mr. Clay has been in very bad health, he is better however—and
has resumed his old tricks of *managing occasionally*—

My confidence in him has been a good deal impaired by a circumstance which I will mention to you *in confidence*—He expects
that his course in relation to the presidential election will be
severely handled in the discussion of the proposed amendments
of the constitution—Gen [Joseph] Vance of Ohio with whom I
have been on terms of great intimacy since our first acquaintance—told me sometime ago, that in the event any reflexions
should be cast upon their party in the debate—they had determined to propose another amendment—to wit that the weight 3/5
of our Slaves shd be no longer operative in that election—indeed
to abolish that feature of Compromise—He further informed me
that he was *fixed upon* to propose it—he held the conversation
with me to prepare my mind for it that I might not be taken
with surprise—Now from the known confidence existing between
Clay & Vance—I cannot doubt, (tho not so informed) that Clay
was at the bottom of it—Indeed he is the only man amongst
them of *boldness* enough to go that length & touch that delegate
subject—Now Sir, any southern man, who is capable of touching
that subject in that manner & at a moment when there is so
much known feeling upon the subject to the North ought to be—
and is reckless of every thing to gratify a bad ambition—Indeed
Clay perceives that he has but little to expect from the South—

[36]Seigniora Macon Eaton died August 16, 1825.

and by a movement of this kind he may effectively secure the
north—*Pennsylvania perhaps inclusive* For it is clear that the
Jackson fever has abated very much with many of that delegation—That communication produced great effect upon my mind
& accounts in some degree for the raps I gave them the other
day[37]—

Mr. Adams gives splendid *levees*—and John II is quite republican in his manners—Mr. Calhoun gives his dinner parties—I
had the honor of being noticed by him quite early—& what do
you think he sd to me when leaving him—holding my hand
"Mangum—Mangum do—do Sir call & see me frequently &
spend some of your evenings with us—without ceremony—Come
Sir, we shall always be glad to see you & bring any friend with
you.—" Ah Sir! he knows a thing or two—It is in that way he
sweeps the young fellows. He is a great friend to the North State
as Mr. Macon calls it. Haven't you seen how some one of his
friends, Hayne it is believed, has taken his friends defend Mr.
Calhoun & laud Mr. Macon—He is in the Senate every day, talks
a great deal about paying off the national debt immediately—I
shd like to know whether a reduction of the expenses of the army
establishment & the consequent reduction of the patronage of
that department, would be as bitter a pill to him now as formerly—He may be considered as entered for the success stake if not
at the next races, certainly at the second.

It would make you laugh heartily to hear Gov. Barbour[38] speak
of the labour of his department. You know him I believe—You
know he is a man of words—but not a business man—He says
he sits down to make estimates on the subject of some fortifica-
tion—he scarcely gets under way before he is applied to & urged
about a pension & every pension case is a suit in equity—he
hardly begins before some would be cadet is introduced & breaks
off the train of his reflections—he returns to the subject again &
before he can collect his thoughts—some damned dispute about
brevet rank is submitted to him about which he knows nothing—
and he hardly gets underway in examining [*sic*] the usages of
the gov't. before some of the Tustanaggee's (little indian chiefs)
are thrust upon him and before he can get his maps & *"count the
broken sticks"* some damned fellow turns him a somerset into a
canal—and after the day spent in these perplexities next morning he begins again, without having advanced a step upon any

[37]See above, p. 229.
[38]James Barbour was Secretary of War under J. Q. Adams.

one subject—His account of his perplexities are truly ludicrous
—But he says a purchaser *with notice* ought not to complain—

Mr. Gailliard[39] has been very & dangerously ill—he is recovering I hope—

Mr. Randolph seems much gratified with his election to the senate, and will I expect become for a while an industrious member of that body—

I have I believe sufficiently tested your patience. It being Sunday night, and having little else to do—I have indulged the cacoethes sufficiently.

I shall let you hear from me occasionally & hope you will reciprocate—

Accept assurances of my regard

WILLIE P. MANGUM

Bartlett Yancey, Esq.

WPM-LC

Willie P. Mangum to Charity A. Mangum

WASHINGTON January 21st. 1826

My dear Love,

I received this morning two letters from you, One of them dated the 7th. January & the other the 15th, I am really at a loss to know to what cause to attribute the irregularity of the Mails —I was however greatly gratified to learn that you, our daughter & our friends were all well.—Indeed My dear, in the midst of my engagements, nothing occurs to give me one tithe of the pleasure, that I feel in receiving your letters, and hearing that all are well.—I recd. two letters also from Walter, which I shall answer in a day or two,—I should do it now but that I have not the time,—

There has been a great deal of sickness here resulting from the Influenza which rages to an extent & with a virulence never heretofore experienced.—

In New York, Philadelphia, Baltimore and Washington as much sickness from that cause has not been heretofore known.—

In our Mess Mr. Macon, has been exceedingly ill—Mr. Ed-

---

[39]John Gaillord, 1765-1826, was United States Senator from South Carolina from 1804 to 1826. *Biog. Dir. of Cong.*, 995.

wards[40] has been very ill, so much so that his Physician has been compelled to resort not only to a very free use of the lancet but also to the strongest & most active medicines Mr. Randolph,[41] has been for a week dangerously ill & still continues so.—Others have been more or less so.—I have at this time a cold, & I think it is encreasing. I hope however it is not the Influenza.—I attribute it to going out the night before last the evening being exceedingly cold, in a thin dress—I dined with the British Minister Plenipotentiary. The Right Hon: Mr. Vaughan.[42]—after I left his dining party I drove to a route that was given by Mr & Mrs. Johnson[43] of Louisiana—Where I found the house exceedingly thronged, dancing & very warm.—I had on thin pumps, & silk stockings, & caught cold.—

I have avoided night parties as much as I could,—and to that cause I owe much of the health I have enjoyed here.—& for the future I shall endeavor to avoid them.—I hope My Love, you will be as good as your promise & write me often—I long for the time to see you, & hope God will preserve you well until that time. Accept My Love, assurances of my

Affectionate fondness

W. P. MANGUM

[Addressed:]

Mrs. Charity. A. Mangum
Stagville
North Carolina

Willie P. Mangum to Col. William Polk[44]

WASHINGTON CITY 23rd January 1826[45]

My dear Sir.

Your kinsman the Hon: M^r. Polk of Tenn: exhibited to me this morning a memorial from the legislature of Tenn: for-

---

[40]Weldon Nathaniel Edwards.

[41]John Randolph.

[42]Sir Charles Vaughan.

[43]Josiah Stoddard Johnston, 1784-1833, was born in Connecticut and lived in Kentucky a few years before he settled in Louisiana. He was a member of the first territorial legislature in Louisiana from 1805 to 1812 before he became a state district judge. From 1821 to 1823 he was in the national House of Representatives. In 1824 he went to the Senate where he remained until his death in 1833. *Biog. Dir. of Cong.*, 1158.

[44]Col. William Polk, 1758-1834, a Revolutionary soldier, was a trustee of the state university, president of the state bank in Raleigh, and brother-in-law of Governor William Hawkins. Although a Federalist in the eighteenth century, he became an ardent supporter of Andrew Jackson even in 1824. Few men in the state were more respected. When Lafayette visited the state, Polk was in charge of his entertainment. He was James K. Polk's greatuncle. Ashe, *Biog. Hist. of N. C.*, II, 361-369; Johnson, *Ante-Bellum N. C.*, 140.

[45]The original of this letter is in the William Polk Papers, Library of Congress.

warded to him by the Gov: of that State: praying the Congress
to relinquish to Tenn: all the public lands lying s°. & west of
the Congressional reservation line; after the satisfaction of the
Claims of the University of No. Carolina.—I learn that the Legislature of Tenn: has passed an act at the last Session in relation
to those claims, but with provision to be void in the event the
Trustees do not accede to its provisions.

I have not seen a copy of the act. Will you do me a favor to inform me whether the trustees have signified their assent or dis-
sent, or if they have not acted as yet, what they are likely to do—

For upon the fact, whether those disputes are finally adjusted,
would depend the propriety of Congress interfering at this time
on the subject.—Tennessee sets up her claim to the relinquishment upon the following case as I understand it. In 1806 or 1807
—Congress passed a law providing for a reservation of the public lands in Tennessee of 640 acres each in every 6 miles square,
for the benefit of public education:—The Legislature of Tenn:
allege that so much of that land has been appropriated under
warrants issuing from N°. Cᵃ. that the beneficient object of Congress indicated in that act has been defeated and that no lands
remain now but fragments of but small value.—

You will readily perceive, that until our claims are satisfied to
the full extent, Congress would not relinquish any lands—should
the Govᵗ. be disposed to do it, *even after* the satisfaction of those
claims.—Hence results the necessity on the part of our delegation of having information touching the acquiescence or refusal
of the Trustees in regards to the offers made by the Tenn: Legislature.

We have but little business of importance, except the Judiciary
Bill[46]—The administration has not submitted its strength to a
fair trial.—Tho it is in vain to expect to resist successfully any
measures recommended by the Executive.—Parties have not had
their lines of distinction yet clearly defined—Mʳ. Polk requests
me to offer you his respects.—You know him personally I believe—He is the cleverest man in the delegation.—

I regret to give you any trouble in this matter, but knowing
your perfect familiarity with the subject of this letter, I thought
it best to apply to you.—

---

[46]Webster as chairman of the Judiciary Committee in the House proposed in December,
1825 the increase of the number of circuit courts in the West and the increase of the number of justices of the Supreme Court. His bill passed the House but the Senate made such
alterations that the House refused to accept the changes. Claude Fuess, *Daniel Webster*, 2
vols. (Boston, Mass.: Little Brown, and Co., 1830), I, 328-329.

Be pleased Sir, to accept assurances of my high respect & consideration.

WILLIE P. MANGUM

Co¹ William Polk

WPM-LC

B. Yancey to Willie P. Mangum[47]

CASWELL. 25th. Jany 1826.

Dear Mangum—

Yours of the 15th. has been rec^d- It gave me great satisfaction affording a much more detailed account of matters and things, than any thing I have rec^d-

Knowing as you do my opinions often expressed in favor of the principle of our Supreme Court, over the former system, it will readily occur to you, that I should be opposed to the Judiciary Bill,[48] now before you—The principle is the same, and I am opposed in principle to any set of Judges acting in the Circuit Courts & on the Supreme Court Bench on the same cause. The Supreme Court of the United States ought to consist of 5 Judges and the Circuit Courts ought to be increased in proportion to the wants of the Country—I am very much inclined to believe, with you, that the present apparent want, is of a temporary kind—perhaps 2 more Circuit Judges would be sufficient.

On the subject of Amendment to the Constitution as respects President and Vice-President, my opinion is, that if you retain 1. The Electoral College and 2^ndly the District plan, it is not very important as to the third principle, whether the election be finally made by the House of Representatives or the Electoral College. If our colored population, be not taken from us, by the force of usurpation; I believe that our State, though She will not be the largest, will Continue to Class, as one of the *large* States. Improvement in our State for the next 50 years, will increase our relative population, and we will then be comparatively to *all* the other States of the union, as great a state as we now are; I think therefore upon the shear score of interest an election by the Electoral College, instead of the House of Representatives, in the last resort, might suit our State. But my opin-

----

[47]This letter has been previously published in McDuffie, "Willie P. Mangum," 35-37.
[48]See above, pp. 231, 237n.

ion on this question, is founded upon purer principles and higher ground, than the mere numerical chances of interest in the election of President. The Constitution of the United States was formed upon liberal principles of Compromise, and with a view to the benefit of *all* the States, by which it was formed, and for the common good. In its formation there were two principals ingrafted into it upon principles of compromise, and without which it cannot be said with truth at this day, it would have been adopted at all: The first is, that, to the small States, was given an equal Representation in the Senate, & in case the election of President & Vice President was not made by Electors, that the small States by vote, in Congress, should have as much power in the election, as a large State. The second principle of Compromise was, that States which held slaves should have 3/5 of them Represented & that the taxes apportioned to the States should be in proportion to Representation, and that Congress should exercise no power over slaves, or the rights of their owners to them: the latter clause is not inserted in the Constitution, but results from the clause, that all power not given to Congress is reserved to the States, or the people. Now if the large States, shall, when they have acquired sufficient political power, so amend the Constitution as to abridge the rights to the small States in the election of President, what can we of the South say to those *pretended* friends of humanity, who prate so much about slavery, and the necessity of altering the Constitution so as to prevent, the representation of 3/5 of our colored population, in the House of Representatives. The fact too, that the election of President by the House of Representatives, is one of the strongest features of *Confederation,* in the Constitution ought not to be forgotten. The tendency of the general government is towards Consolidation: a tendency greatly to be feared, for as Mr. Clinton in his message lately published, declares, upon the rights of the States being maintained, & the principle of Confederation preserved, depends the freedom & permanency of our government:

Against the mode which has been suggested of direct vote by the people, I am entirely opposed—all the South are and will be opposed to it, when properly understood. It will force the government as respects the President, directly into a Consolidation: from which good lord deliver us of the south.

I should not be at all surprized if the proposition you men-

tion as coming from Gen¹. Vance,⁴⁹ should be made—As a southern man I wish they may make it: they can stand no possible
chance of carrying it in the Senate, and I should like to see a
vote on it, in the House of Representatives. It would serve to
produce a state of feeling in the Southern States, which I should
like to see; for depend upon it, in the South, especially in this
State and Virginia we are not sufficently roused upon the subject of securing and maintaining our rights to our Coloured
population. The infernal spirit of emancipation, generated by
Colonizing & emancipating societies, is greatly felt in this State,
and so is the free negro suffrage in many Counties & almost all
the towns—If the people of this State are not more awake to
their rights and interest on this subject, a few years more will
produce an influence here, greatly to be lamented & feared—
Such a proposition to amend the Constitution will have I think
a salutary effect: In the discussion in the legislature, upon the
Bill to prohibit the migration into the State of free negroes,
Stanly supported the principle of the proposition of Mr. King,
openly in debate, declaring "that negroes had the same God, &
the same Redeemer of white has"., which though literally true,
serves to show you the *slang* employed on the question.

If the spirit of our State, this summer, be not roused upon
the subject, so as to enable us to adopt a measure by which our
State can protect itself against the common & constant influx
into it of free negroes from Virginia, Georgia & South Carolina, we shall indeed become the common recepticle of all the
vice & villany from that sort of population. as therefore, I
should like to see good, grow out of such an evil. I should like
to see the proposition of Gen¹. Vance made.

With you I fear, that this administration is to be one of *Contract*; To me it is certain, that the great & national interests of
the South are not to be fostered either by this administration
as one formed by the partizans of Jackson—The policy then of
our State is, to throw itself into the scale of neither—approve
what is manifestly right by permitting it to receive our votes
and condemn what is wrong in the same way—Attach ourselves
to neither party—stand aloof—look on & see the prospect before
us—If I am not very much mistaken, before the termination of
three years, we may find a man in one of the middle States, as
far north as New York, who will meet the present incumbent

with success—He should not be brought on the turf too early—
He may not suit us, as well as some others, but much better
than Adams or Jackson—Let these friends however, *now* wage
the war, but let the South stand by as neutrals—The North
Carolina delegation, that you can trust, ought to understand
each other on this subject—

Upon the whole therefore, my opinion is, as regards the
amendment to the Constitution, the plan first proposed by *this
State,* to lay the Union off in to districts of territory contiguous
& convenient, is the only alteration necessary & proper. It is
one this State, at first proposed with great unanimity in the
legislature & one which is popular with the people all over the
State. It is one our Representatives know not only agreeable
to the legislature but also to the people—It preserves the
Original feature of Compromise; which the South ought always
to adhere to, & by giving it our support, we shall increase our
claims on the influence of the small States to oppose the other
principle of Compromise which will shortly be opposed from
the North.

It will give me great pleasure to hear from you often & in
detail. I will gladly reciprocate with you—Rest assured it will
never tire me to read your communications. tell Bryan & Williams[50] I want to hear from them—

Very respectfully yr. friend
B. YANCEY.

[Addressed:]

> Honble.
> Willie P. Mangum
> Washington City

WPM-LC

Titus Jennings Turner's pension oath

[31 January, 1826]
State of North Carolina, Wake County this day came personally
[torn] Alfred Moore one of the Justices of the peace of said
County Titus Jennings Turner who being sworn sayeth on his
oath that there is two months wages and pay for twelve months

---

[50]John Heritage Bryan and Lewis Williams.

Cloathing now due and owing to him for he served in the fifth Regiment of the North Carolina line and four months wages and pay for twelve months cloathing (excepting a Coat pair of breeches a pair of sheets) now due and owing to him for his service in another Regiment of Regular Soldiers of North Carolina now due and owing to him and for his Service the last Regiment he Received no bounty and that he never did Receive a slave nor the value for it for his military Services and that he never did Receive the years pay as allowed Revolutionary Regular soldiers above the wages.

Sworn to and subscribed before me this 31 day of January 1826

Alfred Moore J. P.   Titus Jennings Turner

I hereby certify that Titus Jennings Turner is considered a Creditable man whose oath is to be truste to Relied on and Confided in.

ALFRED MOORE, J. P.

WPM-LC

Titus Jennings Turner to Willie P. Mangum

[1 Feb., 1826]

To the honorable Willie P. Mangum

I sent to you a Claim for pay for Cloathing and for wages and for bounty last winter with evidence of my Service and my accn of Service and money owing to me a Certificate of my not being present to Receive the (for I was Sick) The Certificate Said the Cloathing was Delivered till about Twelve months after enlisting the was from Mr William Tilton who Served with me if that Claim be allowed to me I do not ask it twice when the business of my Claim is finished I want all the evidences my Service Sent to the post office in Raleigh to me

TITUS JENNINGS TURNER

february 1—1826

[Enclosure   1]

In the Second Secton of the act of assembly of North Carolina passed the 14th of July 1781 entitled an act to Raise troops out of the militia for the Better Defence of this State and for other purposes it is Said that such as had voluntarily enlisted and Served Twelve months in the Continental army Should be exempt from Serving in the Regiment Raised by that law I then had my Discharge from lieutenant Colonel* of the fifth Regiment Certifying I enlisted and Served twelve months but in my absence I was preparing to march in the militia I was Drafted in the Regular Regiment Raised by that law for twelve months when the militia law was only three months I might have availed myself of the exemption from both or either of Services but willing to perform as others in Common Defence I hope to serve in the Regular Regiment and was Discharged from that Regiment on the first day of March in the year 1783 by an officer named Galispy—

TITUS JENNINGS TURNER

february 1—1826
*henry Irvin lieutenat Colonel of the fifth Regiment of the North Carolina Continental line [This is Turner's footnote]

WPM-LC

James Mebane to Willie P. Mangum

MASON HALL February the 1st. 1826

Dear Sir
    John Hobs [Hobbs][51] an old soldier of the revolutionary war called at my house to day & for him I ask the favour of you to examine whether there is any means by which he can be placed on the pension list of the United States. I will here give you all the account he can give of his enlistment &c
    He says, he enlisted in the first Regiment of the continental troops of South Carolina, a man called Captain Cattles enlisted him, that he served three years in said first Regimant at & about Charleston, Sulivans Island &c. under Captain Thomas Pinkney, that William Pinkney was his Lieutenant Colonel, & Colonel Gatson his colonen [?] comandent. The old man knows of no person now living by whom he can prove any of the facts above stated, but if there is in Washington City a copy of the Muster Rolls of South Carolina, possibly his name may be found there, the old man is poor & must soon become entirely incapable of doing any thing to support himself—He is now in the service of

----

[51]See below, p. 286.

my brother Robert as an Overseer, & is of some service for the
attention he pays to the negroes—

If you can do any thing for him you will confer a favour on
one of those old men whose labours & sufferings achieved our
independence I remain respectfully yours &C.

                                        JAMES MEBANE

[Addressed:]

          Wiley P. Mangum Esqr
             Washington City

[Endorsed:]

          John Hobbs

                                             WPM-LC

        *Wm. Clements*⁵² *to Willie P. Mangum*

                    WAKE COUNTY 4th February 1826.
Dear Sir
   I acknowledge the receipt of the documents you sent me for
which I am thankful. I have nothing of importance to communicate only to let you know that I am not unmindful of your
favours, Our Legislature has recently adjourned sine die, and
they have accomplished literally nothing. There was but two
Bills of Public interest before them; that of Establishing a State
Bank and the free Negro Bill, neither of which was passed into
a law, I see from the Journal of Congress as published in our
papers, that Congress is engaged in the discussion of a number
of important questions, and among the Gentlemen engaged therein I find you hold a conspicious part. I am gratified to find that
we have a member from good old North Carolina that is able
to raise a voice in her defence among the counsels of the nation—Your talents and devotion to the interest of North Carolina I never doubted, And having glutted my Vengeance on you
at our last election for the consideration of you know; I am disposed to forgive and be your friend I hope we shall never have
another Occasion to Split in Opinions. I shall however reserve
to my self the right of watching your movements at the end of

---

⁵²William Clement was the deputy surveyor and sheriff of Wake County. McIver, *N. C.
Register,* 48, 52.

the next four years—And as I cannot Sacrifice my old principles it is possible that we may again divide. I know of nothing here about principallities or powers that will be entertaining to you all friends is in good health as far as I know. myself and family is in health. I hope this will find you enjoying that earthly blessing. I should be glad that you would drop me a few lines if you have leisure time but so many friends and subjects to occupy your attention I cannot reasonably expect it.

I am with the greatest respect.
Your humble Servant.
WM. CLEMENTS.

The hon. Willie P. Mangum.

[Addressed:]

    The Honorable
      Willie P. Mangum
        Washington City

WPM-LC

Nat. G. Smith[53] to W. P. Mangum

SPRING HILL CHATHAM COUNTY
N. C. Feb[y] 6th 1826

Hon: W. P. Mangum
Dear Sir

Though our acquaintance is but slight never having had the pleasure to have seen you but once & then but a little while amidst the fervor of an electioneering campaign—yet I hope you will not deem it as impudent in me to address a few lines to you on a subject I feel interested in, to wit, The Columbian College.[54] I observed a Bill introduced in the Senate by Mr. Johnson[55] of Ky. "For the benefit of the Columbian College in the District of Columbia"[56]—Now Sir when I take into consideration

---

[53]Nathaniel G. Smith was a member of the House of Commons from Chatham County.

[54]Columbian College was founded in Washington in 1821 by the Baptists. In 1873, because of the gift of W. W. Corcoran, its name was changed to Columbia University. In 1904 it was combined with other institutions to make George Washington University.

[55]Richard Mentor Johnson, 1781-1850, after serving in the Kentucky legislature from 1804 to 1807 was elected to Congress, where he served from 1807 to 1819 and from 1829 to 1837. He was in the national Senate from 1819 to 1829 and from 1837 to 1841. He was with Harrison in the War of 1812. *Biog. Dir. of Cong.*, 1155.

[56]In December of 1824 a bill was proposed to excuse Columbian College from a debt of $25,000 it owed for the use of government buildings. The bill was defeated but Johnson brought it up several times thereafter. *Register of Debates*, 18 Cong., 2 sess., 94-99; 19 Cong., 1 sess., 590, 2586; 2 sess., 7; 20 Cong., 1 sess., 72, 344.

the very great influence that Education has on the well-being
of a Republic—I deem it to be an indispensable duty of Government to support it—& when we further consider the vast influence of the Clergy in forming the manners and peculiar characteristics of a nation—Those of orthodox faith and practice
should undoubtedly be encouraged—Though I am opposed to
establishing Religion by Law in any respect yet I think a fostering hand should be extended towards the promotion of piety—
The College having Religion connected with it certainly en-
hances its importance & utility—but taken in a different point
of view altogether it should be supported—how much more imperiously does it then demand our support as it is. The District
of Columbia unlike our individual States has no where else to
appeal but to Congress—Will Congress then refuse the College
that efficient aid it so much needs, the boon of Twenty Thousand
Dollars might be perhaps more advantageously bestowed on the
College than any other way—Is not Education of first or primary
importance in a Republic? Should that silver or gold be withheld
then which alone is requisite to its furtherance? In vain is any
thing appertaining immediately to humanity attempted without
money—for agreeable to the declaration of the wise man Solomon—"Money answereth all things." Would it not be a pity for
government to suffer a College so desirable in every point of view
to go to wreck for want of pecuniary assistance? I hope it will
not be the case—I think Sir a large majority of your constituents would be favourable to it—& I hope Sir you will exert that
eloquence which you have so often displayed on other occasions
in the procurement of the sum asked in the memorial—I am Sir

Yours respectfully

NAT. G. SMITH

[Addressed:]

Hon: Willie P. Mangum
Member of Congress
Washington City

Mail)   D. C.

WPM-LC

Charity A. Mangum to Willie P. Mangum

Saturday Night February th10, 1826.

My Dear Husband,

I cannot let one week pass with ease without writing you, Could I have all the world laid at my feet it would not compensate me for your absence no nor a thousand such worlds. If I could have old Mother eve, here now I think, I should be one of the first persons to have her *ducked,* i blame her for putting rambling and restless notions in mankind. I saw Brother Moore this morning just from my Fathers, he saw our dear little Lamb, & says if he had seen her any where else that he would not have known her, he says she has grown so much since he saw her & her cheeks are so blooming that he was surprised to see her look so. I do not wish to bring her home as long as you are absent your Mother wishes to see her very much but the Idea of taking her home is painful to me, & I would not have her home if mother would be satisfied without seeing her. It is a very great cross to let her stay from me, but would be a much greater one to take her home. Sister Matha's cold is better. Mother & her Family are well. I understood from Mr. T. Ruffin that you intended visiting Baltimore again. I have not had it in my power to see your speech yet but have seen Mr. Websters & Wickliffe,[57] against you that I cannot thank them for I wish no person to contradict my husband; but I would wish you always to be in the right if possible. I have been no where since you left me but at my Fathers to see my Dear little lambe. I have not been to see sister yet, & I know she thinks strange of my not going. Eliza sends her love to you. Farewell my Willie. Remember me and believe me to be your devoted Wife

C. A. MANGUM

W. P. Mangum

[Addressed:]

Mr. Willie P. Mangum   Stagville N.C.
House of Representatives   12th Feby. 1826.
Washington City
Mail   D.C.

---

[57]Charles Andrew Wickliffe, 1788-1869, held various state offices in Kentucky, including the legislature, the speakership of the state's lower house, and governor. He was in Congress from 1823 to 1833, Federal judge for the Missouri district, Postmaster General under Harrison and Tyler, and a member of the Peace Conference of 1861. *Biog. Dir. of Cong.*, 1697.

WPM-LC

Willie P. Mangum to Charity A. Mangum

Sunday Morning 12th. Feby 1826.

My Dear Love.

I received your letter yesterday, and it gave me great satisfaction—

I have but a moment, My Love to tell you that I am well again, and hope by great prudence to remain so—

I have been quite sick, & while in that situation, alon in my silent & solitary room, I felt perhaps more strongly than ever, how much I missed your society— & how much you could have contibuted to my confort by all the offices of kindness & affection.— I have a strong wish to see you, & have once or twice & do even now sometimes think strongly of going home upon a visit.— We shall probably be kept here until late in May— tho I cannot now say to what time.—

How is my dear Little Sally— can she talk? My Love to my Mother & Eliza.

& for yourself accept My Love & affection.

W. P. MANGUM

[Addressed:]

Mrs. Charity A. Mangum
Stagville
North Carolina.

Willie P. Mangum to John Haywood[58]

Ho of Reps. 16th-Feby 1826

Dear Sir:

Your attention has doubtless been drawn to the Annual report of the Secretary of the Treasury,[59] recommending a loan of 15 millions for the extinguishment of the War debt of 6 pr Cents.

I herewith transmit to you, the report of Mr. McLane[60] of Del. the Chairman of the Committee of Ways & Means which is considered by Congress, a very able & correct view of our financial condition.—

---

[58]The original is in the Ernest Haywood Papers, Southern Collection, University of North Carolina.
[59]Richard Rush.
[60]Louis McLane.

You will perceive the startling discrepancies between him &
the Secretary of the Treasury. — What may be the permanent
effect of the report I know not. — At the present however there
are indications of a very general distrust of the financial ability
of the Secty.

The friends of the Secty. seem to be extremely apprenhensive
of its effect upon his reputation.

I trouble you with this, trusting, as it lies somewhat within
the range of your own reflections, it may not be wholly unacceptable. —

Your old friend M^r. Macon has enjoyed but little health this
Winter, — he suffered exceedingly from an attack of the Influenza, which has raged in this & the neighbouring cities with unexampled virulence. —

Accept, dear Sir, assurances of
My profound respect
WILLIE P. MANGUM

Mr. John Haywood

To
John Haywood Esqr.
    City of Raleigh
        North Carolina.

————

WPM-LC

Jacob Appler[61] to Willie P. Mangum

Union Town, Maryland
Feb: 17. 1826

Hon: W. P. Mangum
    D. Sir,
        I take the liberty to request the favor of you to inform me
by letter whether my sister Rosanna Wagner was living and
what state of health she was in at the time you left home which
I suppose was sometime in Novr. last —I wish to write to her
soon, and as I discover from her letter to me of last August that
you are acquainted I thought proper to make the enquiry and

————
[61]See below the letter of D. L. Barringer to W. P. Mangum, Feb. 5, 1828.

shall be very thankful for you to answer as soon as convenient. I have been confined to my room for some time past in consequence of the injury I received by a fall from a Horse, but am now recovering and hope to be able in a week or two more to turn out again— I wish you also to state, as near as you can at what time Congress will rise — I have the honor to be Sir Your's very Respectfully

For   Jacob Appler sen^r.
by J. H.

[Addressed:]

Hon: Willie P. Mangum
member of Congress
Washington City

WPM-LC

Samuel Dickens[62] to Willie P. Mangum

Nas'ıville 17th. Feby 1826

Dear Sir,

Since my arrival here I have heard that a proposition is before Congress to ceede to this State the vacant lands South and West of the Congressional reservation line[63]— for the safety of the interest of the University of North Carolina and many of the citizen of your State it is important that the cession should be made for the following reasons viz first to say the least it is questionable whether North Carolina had the right to issue Military Warrants in any case to the University and if she had it is very clear that Tennessee did not possess the right to have *Military* Warrants entered *south and west* of the reservation line consequently if Congress refuses to make the cession and at some future time opens an office for the disposal of the land all the lands entered by virtue of Military Warrants may be lost the University thereby ruined with many of the citizens of No Carolina but if the lands are ceeded to this State she having herself issued Grants will be *Estopt*, nevertheless to make the matter shure it may be well for you to wedge in some word in the bill (if one passes) which will confirm all the Grants issued by Ten-

---

⁶²Samuel Dickens of Person County was a Federalist congressman from 1816 to 1818. In 1820 he moved to Tennessee. There he acted as land agent for Murphey and the University. *Biog. Dir. of Cong.*, 904; Hoyt, *Papers of Murphey*, I, 88n, 165, 222.
⁶³See above, pp. 236-237.

nessee if you can do so it possibly may be obtaining a great point for the University and while I am on this subject it may be prudent to apprise you that Col Alexander and many others of the representative from this state are hostile to the In^t. of the University and the object you have in view they must not be apprised of

Your friend

SAMUEL DICKINS

P. S

In such haste I wrote the foregoing that I omitted to turn this leaf of paper which haste please to excuse

[Addressed:]

The Honble.   S D
Willie P. Mangum
House of Representatives U S
Washington City

WPM-LC

A. G. Glynn[64] to Willie P. Mangum

CITY OF WASHINGTON
Febr'y 20th 1826

Sir

I take the liberty of introducing to you, Mr. Harry Peake, a gentleman with whom I have been acquainted some time and in whose welfare I feel some interest. He is desirous of obtaining the situation of French & Spanish Instructor in the University of N^o. Ca. From the evidence in my possession, I am fully satisfied that he is competent to discharge the duties, if appointed, and from my knowledge of Southern manners and habits, believe he would become popular.

In addition to his accomplishments as instructor he possesses a correctness of morals, amenity of manners and evenness of temper and disposition, calculated to attach those to him, with whom he may be connected.

In recommending Mr P. to your patronage, I feel confident that while I am but barely doing him justice, I am laying the

---

[64]A. G. Glynn was district attorney for Baltimore.

foundation, of a lasting benefit to the youth of No Carolina; should that University have the good fortune to select the present applicant.

I have the honor to be
Your very humble St

A. G. GLYNN

Hon. W. P. Mangum
[Addressed:] H. of Representatives

WPM-LC

Samuel Dickens to Willie P. Mangum

NASHVILLE 20th. Feby 1826

Dear Sir

Since writing you the hasty note by the last mail I have seen and had a conversation with Pleasant M Miller[65] on the subject of the University Land titles in this State and he thinks with me that it is important that the cesson act (if one passes)[66] should confirm all grants used by the State of Tennessee heretofore and has no doubt but that the Representatves from this state will agree to it provided you make it a sine qua non—it will be bad policy for you ever to mention in their hearing the University claims but state to them that many citizens of North Carolina as well as the citizens of this state have had their *Military* warrants entered South and West of the reservation line and that it is the opinion of the first legal characters in this state that Tennessee had no right to pass the law under which it was done—I have had for years to stand almost alone in defence of the University claims and now have to contend against hungry speculators who are Bankrupts in principle and in property but if you can my dear sir get an act of Congress passed which will confirm the Grants* now issued and which may issue on entries already made I shall be enabled to prostrate them and gain a triumph that will give me inexpressable satisfaction the remainder of my days

----

[65]Pleasant Moorman Miller was a member of Congress from the Knoxville district of Tennessee from 1809 to 1811. He moved to the western part of Tennessee in 1824.
[66]See above, p. 250.

I cherish the pleasing hope of spending the ensuing summer in North Carolina

Yours &c
SAMUEL DICKENS

*or rather title to the *Grantees*
Hon. Willie P. Mangum
House of Representatives of the U. S.

[Addressed:] Washington City.

WPM-LC

S. Decatur[67] *to Willie P. Mangum*

GEO. TOWN Feb 21, 1826

My Dear Sir

As I was disappointed in the pleasure of seeing you, I hope you will excuse me for troubling you with a few lines upon the Subject of my Claim—

The Naval Committee in their report upon my Memorial,[68] have entirely overlook'd, what I have always been taught to consider the *Strong hold* of the Claim, and which was the chief object of the Memorial—The prize having been captured by an inferior force, belong'd wholly to the Captors; and if she had been taken to the Squadron, the existing Law wou'd have secur'd her to them—that she was not so dispos'd of, was owing entirely to the peremptory orders of the Commander in Chief, who thought it more prudent not to risk even the possibility of her falling again into the hands of the Enemy; and believing the government cou'd not, under such circumstances, object to pay for her—Now, we ask Congress to pay us for the property we were deprived of by the act of their own Agent whom we had not the right to resist; and which property if we had been permitted to preserve it, the Law wou'd unquestionably have secur'd to us, and this is the only case in which the government has disposed of the property of individuals without paying for it—It is not consider'd honest in an individual to shelter himself under the letter of the Law, to evade a debt whether of honor or of equity; and I shou'd think it wou'd be equally unworthy of a

[67]See below, Benton to Mrs. Decatur, Mar. 8, 1826.
[68]On December 19, 1825, Susan Decatur, Stephen Decatur's widow, petitioned Congress for prize money for the *Philadelphia* which was destroyed at Tripoli in 1804. The House committee recommended compensation but Congress did not carry out the recommendation.

great Nation to avail herself of such subterfuge in settling an
account with the Heroes and benefactors of their Country—for
the whole Naval force belonging to the United States, at that
period cou'd not, if applied in the *ordinary* Mode of warfare,
have brought those Barbarians to terms and releas'd your Citizens from the Dungeon and the lash to which they had then
been subjected nearly two years without any prospect of relief,!
and it appears to me, that if ever there was an account that
ought to be honestly and liberally settled, this is one—It has sav'd
Millions of dollars to your Treasury—It has saved your Merchant vessels from being plunder'd, and your Seaman from
Slavery; and it moreover, sav'd your Navy which was then at
its last gasp; and obtain'd for you all the National glory in
which you have since so proudly exulted; and which had gain'd
for you a name amongst the greatest Nations of the Earth!!!
I hope that you, My Dear Sir, will have the goodness to *read* the
Documents in support of the Claim, and judge for yourself; and
give it all the support you can, consistently with your ideas of
justice and sound policy—

If you shou'd at any time have half an hour to spare, I shou'd
be much oblig'd to you if you wou'd call and see me—either
Morning or Evening—I am always at home—

      I beg you to believe me
             Very Sincerely and Respectfully
                Yours
                S. DECATUR

The Honble
   George [Willie P.] Mangum

                         WPM-LC

Charity A. Mangum to Willie P. Mangum

                      SUNDAY MORNING
                      February 25, 1826,

My Dear Willie,
   I Received your letter Dated th12 of february which gave me
great satisfaction, to hear that you had recovered of your cold,
I was truly thankfull My Willie that you recovered as soon as
you did. do my husband take care of yourself—, & remember the
irreparable loss that would be sustained by your wife, & Daugh-

ter, should they have the misfortune to loose you, a loss that time could never replace, I was at a wedding last week cinthia Mangum[69] was maried to Meeking carrington it is the first couple I have seen maried since, I was maried, & it made me as serious as if it had been myself—it made me think of old times my feelings at such times are past expressing, but I believe there are but few that view such things with as much solemnnity as myself. it certainly is a great change to all thinking persons. every thing was very nice, Walter[70] has returned from Petersburgh sold his cotton & expects to start to raleigh Monday or tuesday to attend to your business, nothing could give me more pleasure than to see you my Willie & for you to see our dear little Sally, I fear very much if she should live that she will be spoiled Patsy says she is one of the most mischievous little buisy creatures in the world, she had sally in her room with her the other day, had a nice little work basket, & while she was buisy with her back to her, sally took her basket put apples in it and set it on the fire & then seated herself very contentedly waiting for the apples to roast in the basket, & when patsy saw it her basket was almost ruined She can talk but will not only when it suits her Sally looks as well as any child . . . I would be rejoiced for you to visit me but cannot conquer my Fear of the steam boats—I am tollerable well Mother is in good health. I sent last night to James stagg[71] for your horse as she is very much wanting, the boy returned without her & said he had swaped her for a trifling horse with John J. carrington, I have sent to mr carrington to day for the mare as mr stagg says she is not yours & have told him if he think's propper to keep her that I shall proceed as you shall direct me to do—you told me to send for the hose & that you certainly would not have done if you had given her to James stagg I shall send Mr stagg's very polite note in your letter. Nead davis[72] has not returned yet. Farewell My Willie, may guardian angels guide & direct you through this life is the sincere Prayr of your devoted wife C. A. M.

W. P. Mangum. william sutherland[73] is waiting with great im-

[69] A cousin of Willie P. Mangum.
[70] Mangum's brother.
[71] Mangum's overseer.
[72] Edward Davis was Charity Cain Mangum's brother-in-law. Later he was interested in the gold mines near Charlotte in North Carolina.
[73] Probably the nephew of Charity Mangum. He was a student at the University of North Carolina from 1832 to 1836. He died in 1838. Grant, *Alumni Hist. of U. N. C.*, 602.

patience to receive a letter from you. your writing him would stimulate him to learn—

[Addressed:]

Stagville   Mr Willie, P, Mangum,
                    House of Representatives
                    Washington City
                        D. C.

WPM-LC

A. Alston[74] *to Willie P. Mangum*

GREENSBOROUGH ALABAMA the 28th Feby. 1826

My Esteemed Friend

I have the pleasure to Introduce to you my friend & neighbour Israel Pickens[75] Esqr who is a Gentlema of Real worth and worthy the attention of any Gentleman He has acted as Chief Majistrate of this State for the last four years And has Discharged his Duty with General satisfaction

Sir I have the Mortifying Intelligence to Inform you I have lost my Dear child Christian Morton & her husband about twelve Months sincence leaving a sone and Daughter for me to scratch of in my old age But thank God they are pretty well provi'd for

Any Communication from you will be gladly Rec^d. at all times

Your favourite leattle Mary is now at school in the Natches Country with her Connection & is a fine sprightly girl and makeing Great progress in learning She is makeing a fine Musitioner & speaks good french

My son Calvin is pretty well advanced in the Lattin & is a fine promising boy he is also boarded out from home And will after about twelve or Eighteen Months be prepaird to Send to Chapel hill

after our Compliments to Genl. Calvin Jones[76] you may say to him about the above named time I shall fetch or send my son & put him under his Charge

---

[74]Absalom Alston came from near Mangum's home in Orange County.
[75]Israel Pickens, 1780-1827, was a member of Congress from 1811 to 1817. He was register of the land office in the Mississippi territory from 1817 to 1821 and governor of Alabama from 1821 to 1825. He became U. S. Senator in 1826. *Biog. Dir. of Cong.*, 1410.
[76]See above, p. 150n.

We have the pleasure to say to you we are all well as for
farther particulars concerning our local Concerns I Refur you
to my friend Govr. Pickins

Sir wife Jones me in Respects to you & lady

Accept of my best wishes
for your welfare & prosperity

A.. ALSTON

W. P. Mangum Esq.

[Addressed]

Willie P. Mangum Esqr Politeness of
Washington City Govr. I. Pickins

―――――――

WPM-LC

Thomas H. Benton to Mrs. Decatur[77]

(Copy)

[8 March, 1826]

My Dear Madam

The vessel to which your Note refers was the sloop of War
Hermes, Commanded by Capt. Sir Wm Henry Percy. This
sloop led the attack upon Fort Boyer, Mobile Point,[78] in Sept
1814, and had the boldness to enter within Musket Shot, where
the fire of the Garrison destroyed her and blew her up. She was
paid for by the Act of Congress, upon the petition of the Garrison in March 1816―

Yours Most Sincerely,

(Signed)   THOMAS H. BENTON
Mrs. Decatur

March 8, 1826.

―――――――

[77]See above, p. 253.
[78]The *Hermes* was the British ship which led the attack against the American forces in
September, 1814 in the battle of Mobile. It was burned by the Americans. For a brief account of the battle see Peter J. Hamilton, *Colonial Mobile, an Historical Study . . . from
the Discovery of Mobile Bay in 1519 until . . . 1821* (New York, N. Y.: Houghton-Mifflin
Co., 1897), 374-380.

WPM-LC

W. C. Clements[79] to Willie P. Mangum

WAKE COUNTY 8th. March 1826

Dear Sir

I received your favour bearing date the 7th. Ultimo. and at Your request. I now write you. But having no Subject worthy of your consideration I fear you will be unpleasant at reading such an epistle: We have no political news here; except what I expect you have almost every day; from a much abler pen than mine. As to your conduct in the present Congress it is generally approved by all classes of men in my Section of the Country with a fewer exceptions: I have heard some of your old friends remark that they thought you was two harsh and rather prejudiced against the administration. But for my part I am unable to see it so. I think you Steadily pursue the Course you laid down in Your letter to me: viz. to Support him when right and firmly Oppose him when rong; indeed this seems to be the course that all enlightened Statesmen should pursue. not only towards the present administration but every other. It is well known that he is not the man of my choise and I moreover despise the way in which he obtained the chair. But as he is constitutionally there I feel desposed to Support his measures for a while, when they are consistantly with the public good but no further: Our Country has been a long time represented in part by men who would go all lengths with the administration for the sake of Popularity. or in the hope to get some appointment to mexico or some where else. But in you I hope to find more Virtue and firmness. I hope you will still pursue your good old rule to Oppose when your better Judgment shall tell you that the measure is wild and extravagant: and in doing so. if you should err I will freely forgive you; And I think a majority of your destrict will also. You are gaining many friends here in the piney Woods. and I think you merret them so far as you have yet proceeded—I have nothing more to write. in fact I have a sore finger and cannot write to be understood— I am in health and sincerely hope these will find you well—If you have time from the abundance of business and the great

---

[79]See above, p. 244.

number of friends you have to attend to I should be glad you
would write me again: If not this will be a Sufficient excuse

I am with respect
Your humble Servt

W. C. CLEMENTS

The Hon
Willie P. Mangum

[Addressed:]

The Hono .
Willie P Mangum
        Washington City

———

WPM-LC

Willie P. Mangum to Charity A. Mangum

WASHINGTON the 13th. March 1826.

My dear Love,

I have but a few minutes to drop you a line, informing you
that I am in very good health.—

I hoped this morning to receive a letter from you but I am
disappointed.

I hope My Love to be at home by the middle of May, but that
is wholly uncertain. The time for the adjournment of Congress
has not been fixed, though several attempts have been made—

Some think we shall leave here earlier, some think later—

I send to you the Book I promised, I am much concerned to
hear that Judge Cameron[80] has had a severe attack. I trust he
will recover.—

I am exceeding anxious, My Love to see you & my little daughter.—My time here is spent unpleasantly enough—Mr William
M Sneed[81] of Oxford has been here for two weeks—He leaves
here tomorrow for home, & I most sincerely wish I could go
with him.—

How little of happiness have I enjoyed.—Driven from post
to pillar, & in each & every situation, much to destroy that
serenity, which under happier auspices I might & I believe,
should enjoy.

---

[80]Judge Duncan Cameron.
[81]See above, p. 10n.

11

I will not, however, add to your unhappiness by unavailingly adverting to my own.—

Accept this short note, with my prayers for your happiness

W. P. MANGUM

[Addressed:]

Mrs. Charity A. Mangum
Stagville
Orange County
North Carolina.

———

WPM-LC

John Haywood to Willie P. Mangum

RALEIGH 24 " March 1826.—

My dear Sir,

Our friend Major Cameron,[82] of Fayetteville, is about to set out on a Visit to Washington City, in the hope of obtaining the appointment of Commissioner for North Carolina under the Bankrupt Law of the United States, in case such Law shall be made or passed; a thing which he is advised will probably happen, in course of the present Session of Congress;—I have not even read the Bill which has been reported for that purpose, and therefore know nothing of its details; but Major Cameron, I apprehend, is better informed on the Subject.—In common with his other friends, I doubt not you have learned of and regretted that Loss of fortune which he has Suffered, in consequence of the unfortunate Result of his late Mercantile Business; a Loss which makes it indispensably necessary to him that he shall now seek some Employment, through which he may be enabled to support a young, growing and helpless family:— Your acquaintance with this Gentleman, added to your knowledge of the distinguished Talents of his family generally, will leave you no difficulty in coming to the conclusion that, but for his sufferings in the Army during the late War and the unhappy consequences of them so far as they affected his Speech or arti-

———

[82]John Adams Cameron, 1788-1838, of Fayetteville, was a major in the War of 1812. A graduate of the University of North Carolina, he served as a member of the Virginia lower house before he became consul in Vera Cruz. In 1829 he was appointed judge of the Florida district. He was Duncan's brother. Grant, *Alumni Hist. of N. C.*; Ashe, *Biog. Hist. of N. C.*, III, 46.

culation, he would have been placed, by his professional Standing, above the necessity of asking the Patronage of his friends, or seeking any other Employment than that to which he was bred.—Remembering you have been acquainted with Mr. Cameron long & well, and assured that you think highly of him, and feel for him all that affectionate Regard and kind consideration which I or any other of his many friends possibly can experience towards him, I am sensible it would be wrong and superfluous in me to say more; well knowing that you are already disposed to favour his Pretensions and to forward his views, as far as shall be in your power; nor would I even have ventured to say thus much, but by way of making known Mr. Cameron's Business to you on his first arrival in Washington, which he might feel some hesitation and backwardness in doing.—Should the Bankrupt Bill fail to be matured or passed into a Law, I have indulged the hope that it may, nevertheless, possibly be in your power to direct the attention of this our friend to some other object or official Employment which may be had, and which would prove profitable to him; as we know his Talents and Qualifications are such as would enable him, promptly and ably to acquit himself of the duties of any Appointment which he would accept.

I greet you kindly and respectfully, and remain,
Much and truly,
Your friend,
JOHN HAYWOOD

The Honble.
Mr. Mangum—Congress.

[Addressed:]
To the Honorable,
Willie P. Mangum,
Congress.

Major Cameron.—

WPM-LC
Priestley H. Mangum to Willie P. Mangum
WAKE FOREST No. CA.
March 29th, 1826.

Dear Sir.
I should be gratified to receive letters from you more fre-

quently. Altho' I am at a distance from the school of political
science, & the scenes of politics—still I feel an interest, in common with others, in such things.

The discussion in the House, of the Judiciary Bill, I have read
with great pleasure—and I was particularly pleased, to find
that you sustained yourself so well. Your speech on that subject, has brought to you, in North Carolina, considerable accession of reputation. Even your most dangerous and bitter
enemies are compelled either, to say nothing about it, or to
speak in respectful terms of it.—

Judge Henderson[83] is well pleased with it *of course*—and was,
at Granville Court after speaking of it, *in a way to spread*, not
only respectfully, but more; and giving to his own opinion the
sanction of Albert Gallitin's [*sic*] who is here represented by
some, to have said, that it was the best made on the subject—
by others, that it was the best, on your side of the question The
only fault found, is that you made a tilt of the Administration
prematurely. I think, However, that one Mr. Wright,[84] of Ohio,
was *very pungent;* I felt as if a *cane* could have measured the
capacity of his scull—such things, I suppose, would not do.—

Mr. McDuffy's[85] speech on the resolutions to amend &c. is
very good—tho' I don't concur with him. With Mr. Everett's,[86]
I am likewise pleased particularly on account of his remarks
about slavery. His views however don't altogether please me.
Some of them are very good.—Mr. Storrs[87] is right good—and
Cambrelings[88] right worthless. I can't help thinking that the
cudgel is an excellent argument sometimes—however unfashionable—or *something else,* by way of equivalent.

I am opposed to amending the constitution in relation to the
mode of electing the Pres.[89] &c. altogether! the motion towards

[83]Judge Leonard Henderson, 1772-1833, was judge of the superior court from 1808 to 1818, and from 1818 to 1829 he was associate justice of the Supreme Court of North Carolina. From 1829 to his death he was chief justice of the latter court. D. A. B., VIII, 529.

[84]John Crofts Wright, 1783-1861, was in Congress as a supporter of Adams from 1823 to 1829. He was a member of the Ohio Supreme Court from 1831 to 1835 before he moved to Cincinnati to edit the *Cincinnati Gazette.* He became a director of the Cincinnati, Hamilton, and Dayton Railroad Company. He was honorary president of the Peace Conference in Washington in 1861. *Biog. Dir. of Cong.,* 1731.

[85]George McDuffie of South Carolina.

[86]Edward Everett of Massachusetts.

[87]Henry Randolph Storrs, 1787-1837, was a member of Congress from New York from 1817 to 1821 and from 1823 to 1831. A lawyer of New York City, he served as judge of the Court of Common Pleas from 1825 to 1829. *Biog. Dir. of Cong.,* 1577.

[88]Churchill Caldon Cambreling, 1786-1862, a native of North Carolina, became a merchant in New York City. He served as congressman from New York from 1821 to 1839 and as U. S. minister to Russia from 1840 to 1841. *Biog. Dir. of Cong.,* 779.

[89]Several attempts between 1810 and 1830 were made to change the method of electing the President. On December 15, 1825, Benton proposed a committee to study the proposals. This committee reported January 19, 1826, recommending that by popular vote each electoral district (the districts would be apportioned by the state legislatures according to population) cast its vote for President and Vice-President. March 8 this was laid on the table. *Register of Debates,* 19 Cong., 1 sess., 16-19, 77-78, 692-697, 940, 1365-1376, 1395, 1397-1417.

it now, proceeds from the writings of disappointed ambition. This would be enough. Another objection is, that such an amendment as proposed, would be another encroachment upon state rights. This with me is all-sufficient in this constructive [lat]itudinarian age.—

My neighbour, Jno Martin Esqr[90] is anxious for you to attend to his Petition about the post route—you ought to write to him.

Send something to Judge [Archibald D.] Murphy—poor man is almost gone—in worse health than any man I know.

We are well—your family were well last week. I expect to bring charity & baby to my house next month.

You know, I suppose, that the appointment of *Carge De Affairs to Peru,* has been tendered to B. Yancey—and declined, upon the ground that it being intended for the State, is unworthy of her dignity and rank.

Yrs respectfully

P. H. MANGUM

[Addressed:]

> The Hon:
>   Willie P. Mangum
>   House of Represent:
>   Washington City
>   D. C.

WPM-LC

J. G. A. Williamson[91] to W. P. Mangum

ROXBORO N°. C. 2nd April 1826.

W. P. Mangum Esq.
  Sir
    Yours under date of the 22nd ult. I recvd. by last evenings mail, the contents have been duly noticed; I should have been glad to have been consulted before the nomination which you speak of, had been made, because in the interview I had with **Mr.** Clay previous to my leaving the City, this Vacancy was mentioned, and that it was much sought after, but at the same time the impressions left upon my mind, was that it was of little *value,*

---

[90]See above, p. 198.
[91]See above, p. 208n, and below, p. 281.

and not of much importance—besides this information I accidently met with a gentleman at Williamsons who I have no doubt was in pursuit of the appointment, but I believe would not have disguised the truth, who informed me that it was lean in perquisites, but as he had been concerned in business with the previous Consul, it would in the way of recommendation increase his business. I am not sufficiently aware of the importance of the Laguayra[92] trade, wheather I could without a previous connection in business with some person render it of any advantages to me, and to depend upon such a contingency as that would not suit me at all—Mr Clay likewise informed me a Gentleman after a little urging into the situation had withdrawn his name as an applicant—These circumstances together with its *extreme unhealthiness*, particularly the information Mr Clay gave me prevented my suggesting the situation when in your place—A situation there at any event, would not altogether realize my expectations, not I conceive being more than barely respectable in a political point of view, and in emoluments I have no doubt inconsiderable—I am very well aware of the old adage 'that beggars should not be *choosers*, nor am I disposed in the least to be very choice But I hardly calculate that Mr Clay would have sugested the Laguayra situation after the conversation I had with him, but at the same time fully sensible that any appointment under our government is honorable, and that all consular situations are of the same importance in the interest they have to overlook—If I had no other objection, the unhealthiness of Laguayra would I think be sufficient not to accept, however if the prequisites were considerable there might be some inducement to hazzard health—I should have much preferred the situation at Canton, but do not know even if I could have obtained it which I certainly had some reasons to suppose I could, before I reached the city, that I would have accepted it, entirely on the grounds that it would not have supported me—I should be sorry that the nomination should reach the Senate before this gets to the City—Perhaps by a little *delay* (an unfortunate word) a vacancy might occur more suitable to my views, and my claims, if I have any, rest upon the executive table—I hope you will not look upon this as fastidiousness, for I believe weighing every consideration If Laguayra was healthly or tolerably so, I

---

[92]La Guaira in Venezuela is nine miles north of Caracas on the Caribbean. It was the most important port in the country and had in 1825 an extensive trade with the United States.

would accept, but indeed Sir I see no inducement and there is certainly every hazzard—My acceptance or not I have no doubt is a matter of perfect indiference to the executive—I am much indebted and feel highly sensable of the interest felt and taken by Mr. Williams[93] and yourself in this business, and permit me to subscribe.

Myself your
obt Servt

J. G. A. WILLIAMSON.

Roxborough
April 2nd 1826

[Addressed:]

Missent to Warrenton N. C.

Honble
    W. P. Mangum
        Washington City
           D. of C.

WPM-LC

Jno. Campbell to Willie P. Mangum

HARMONY HALL April 3rd. 1826.

Mr. Mangum
    Dr Sir

My son John[94] has bought out Mr. Benjⁿ Corey's establishment at Milton and is to take possession the 20th Inst. and expects from that time to conduct the Milton Gazette, Mr Corey is postmaster at that place and promised my son that he would use his influence with the Postmaster General to have him appointed at the time he resigns, which probably will be some time in May. You are no doubt well acquainted with the character of my son as he has lived about 5 years in Hillsboro', we therefore beg the favour of you to be so kind as to mention the subject to the post Master Genl. and speak of my son as you think he may deserve, My son is now about entering into business, and I am not able to render him the aid I wish, and he has to depend on his own exer-

---

[93] Lewis Williams.
[94] He was editor of the *Milton Gazette and Roanoke Advertiser* in 1827 but not in 1830. In 1830 he edited the *Halifax Minerva*. He followed this with the *Roanoke Advocate* and the *Windsor Herald*. N. C. *Free Press*, Oct. 25, 1831.

tions & good conduct to recommend him in life, the post office will be a considerable addition to his business in Milton and any aid in this way will be greatfully acknowledged. He will be able to give such security as may be required. I believe he can if required get as strong recommendations from all the principal characters of Hillsboro', as any young man raised in the place— we shall be glad to hear from you—

yours very respectfully

JNO CAMPBELL[95]

P. S. We will be thankful also for your patronage as a subscriber to his paper.

J. C.

[Postmarked:] Hillsboro

[Addressed:]

Willie P. Mangum Esqr.
Washington City

Willie P. Mangum[96] to John Haywood

WASHINGTON CITY 6th April 1826.

My dear Sir.

I received in due course of mail your several letters, for which you will be pleased to accept my thanks.—I have also received the letter directed to my care for Majr. Cameron.

Yesterday morning I received a letter from Majr. Cameron, dated at Norfolk; informing me that by reason of some irregularity in the departure of the boat from that place to Washington, he was deprived of the opportunity of taking this City in his way for New Jersey. He enclosed to me divers communications to be used, should the Bankrupt Bill become a Law, & I should deem it proper to use them, before his return.—He will return by Washington to the South.—

The discussion upon the proposed amend. to the Constitution has occupied so much of the time of this Session; and the proposed Mission to Panama is likely to employ so much—that I doubt whether the Bankrupt Bill will have a fair trial—

---

[95]John Campbell, Sr., had been a minister in Hillsboro.
[96]The original is in the Ernest Haywood Papers, Southern Collection, University of North Carolina.

The House is worn down with the long and tedious debates, and evinces already a strong disinclination to enter upon the consideration of any other important business—M^r. Webster however will insist upon taking it up—and it is unnecessary to say that he can rally a majority of the House upon almost any question.—

If the Bill shall pass I think the prospects of Maj^r. Cameron are very promising.

I shall feel great pleasure in using my best endeavours for his success.—I am conscious that I have no personal influence with the power that be, but I flatter myself that I can do something in moving *others*, whose influence may prove efficient.—The delegation, generally, I presume, will favour the wishes of Maj^r. Cameron—but they are in "bad odour"—

If he shall succeed it will be highly gratifying to me, not only upon his own account, but upon that also of his excellent brother Judge Cameron to whose wishes upon any subject, I can never feel indifferent.

I learn by the last mails that the Influenza continues to prevail with great exacerbation in Orange & particularly in Hillsborough.

I hope Sir, that your family have recovered.

Our friend M^r. Macon, is in extremely bad health, his spirits are occasionally deeply depressed, and he thinks frequently not only of closing his political but his mortal career.—He never complains however, & in that respect is one of the most remarkable men that I ever saw, at his time of life.

I hope as the warm weather advances, his health will become better, and I cannot doubt that his return to his friends will be essentially benefical to his Sp [irits] & his health.

[Be] pleased Dear Sir, to accept [the] assurances of my profound respect

& regard

WILLIE P. MANGUM

To
John Haywood Esqr.
   City of Raleigh
     North Carolina

Free
W. P. Mangum

WPM-LC

Willie P. Mangum to Charity A. Mangum

WASHINGTON 8th. April 1826.

My dear Love.

I received a day or two ago from Mr [William M.] Sneed a letter informing me that you were all as well as usual, and yours also came to hand yesterday; I was very glad to hear that you & our little daughter continued well.—I have been as well as usual, but am becoming very anxious to leave this City.—The prospect of an early departure however, is exceedingly gloomy & unflattering.—

The committee who have that subject under consideration & to fix a day for the close of the session, are backward, & seem to be of opinion that the session cannot be ended by the 15th of May. I shall however continue to vote for the earliest period.—

I received a letter from Priestley a few days ago, and he stated that he should carry you & our daughter to Wake this month—I perceive no reason why you should not go—Rebecca will be glad to see you.—

I am becoming as usual very tired of this place, & feel but little pleasure in any of my employments, every thing here goes on against my judgment.

The Administration are both weak & wicked I fear,—and the present prospect is that the Members of Congress from the south of Washington will unite to put down Adams, & if they can get no better, they will take up Gen: Jackson for that purpose.

I am in haste & have nothing to say further than that I had rather see you, than to indulge any of these political hopes, or even to witness the reality.

Believe me my Love your affectionate husband

WILLIE P. MANGUM

[Addressed:]

Mrs. Charity A. Mangum
Stagville
Orange County
North Carolina

WPM-LC

W. N. Pratt to Willie P. Mangum

HILLSBOROUGH [ORANGE] COUNTY N. C. April 8th. 1826
Sir

I want you if you please to pay the tax on my Missouri Land
Lying in Howard County near Franklind as I have not had an
oppertunity of Paying the tax since Dct Smith[97] was a member
of Congress my Deed for the said tract of Land was placed in
the hands of Vansant and Rockwell for the purpose of Beeing.
Recorded I allso want you if you please to precure the dead and
bring it on with you I allso want you to precore some person for
me to pay the tax and Keep the title good—and place money in
his hands for that purpose and I will pay you on your Returne
My Clame is for one quarter section the North West of section
Thirty two of Township fifty three north in Range nineteen
West the above Described Tract or parcel of Land I purchased of
one Richard Jones Head a soldier

I Hope Sir you will do Me the favour to attend to this Clame
for Me and you will mutch obliedg Your Humble Servyant

W. N. PRATT

[Addressed:]

To the Honb. Willie P. Mangum
Washington City

————

WPM-LC

Henry Seawell to Willie P. Mangum

RALEIGH 9th April 1826.

(Confidential)
Dear Sir

I had the pleasure of receiving your very kind & obliging letter in answer to mine of a previous date, & feel thankful to you
for the trouble you gave yourself on my account. The causes
which have operated a suspension of the functions of our board
I understand are still a subject of negociation; and I am led to
believe that if the difficulties should be removed, the business

---

[97] James S. Smith.

will terminate in a gross sum being paid by great Britain,[98] which will be to be distributed totally amongst all the sufferers within the treaty, & consequently the board to make this distribution will be altogether American—having been obliged by duty to examine all the claims, & having at this time a note of all the testimony, without pretending more than ordinary capacity to decide upon the sufficiency of the proof and the extent and scope of the treaty, I should hope my friends would excuse me for presuming to be willing to become a member of such board—and especially, as I have been obliged to decline a great deal new business, from the apprehension of an interference with my engagements as a member of the present board. I have been induced to make this communication to you at this time, from the belief that in the event before stated, there will probably, be numerous applications—and though I have not written, nor shall I write to Mr. Macon, on this business from a knowledge of his rule on such occasions; yet I should have no objection to your communicating freely with him on it; & if occasion should require it, I am very well assured that in the Senate I have several friends, who would take pleasure in serving me, when it was not inconsistent with duty—among whom I will mention [Robert Y.] Hayne & [Thomas H.] Benton & would venture to hope Messrs. [John] Randolph, [Littleton Waller] Taswell [Tazewell] and [Hugh Lawson] White would not feel otherwise disposed. Our Superior Court is just over, a full weeks sitting & nothing done; tho hard at it till Saturday night: tomorrow morning (Monday) I set off for Franklin, & expect not to return till after Northampton—*report* says I am to encounter Col. Rogers[99] at the next election,—this if it does happen, will be product of a consultation last week at which the Reverend..............presided. I think however the Col. will not suffer himself to be brought out, whether he comes out or not I am already out, & shall *take the field.* I think you were much misinformed in regard to your strength in this county. I unhesitatingly pronounce it *much* stronger than ever before & I know this to be the opinion of at least one of your most intelligent sturdy friends. I should be very

---

[98]Seawell was on the commission appointed under the Treaty of Ghent to determine the value of the slaves lost in the War of 1812. The English allowed $1,204,960. J. B. Moore, *History and Digest of the International Arbitration to Which the United States has been a Party,* I, 366-382.

[99]Probably Allen Rogers, the postmaster at Rogers' Store in Wake County. He was in the state legislature in 1803, in 1806 to 1808, and in 1812. From 1834 to 1836 he was a member of the Council of State. *N. C. Manual,* 435-436, 829-830.

glad to hear from you & if you have leisure upon your hands, write me to Warren Supr. Court—in the mean time accept my best wishes

                                HENRY SEAWELL.

Honble Mr. Mangum.

[Addressed:]

                Honble
                    Willie P. Mangum
                        of Congress
Mail.   Washington City.

_____

                                        WPM-LC

        A. D. Murphey to Willie P. Mangum

                        HAW-RIVER, 9, April 1826.
Dear Sir,
    Your two last letters were received by me on this Morning, and whilst my fever is off, I will write for a short time. I thank you Sincerely for your friendly Feelings; I never doubted them: & I assure you that no one of your Friends rejoices more at your growing reputation than I do:—As to any little difference in political Opinions, it weighs nothing with me in my Social Intercourse, nor in estimating the Value of a Man's Qualificatons for Usefullness. I wish you a long continuance in Public Life, believing that you will be both useful & respectable, and all the Honours which your Country can bestow on you—
    I am Sorry for Mr. Duffie.[100] He has little Prudence. just as he was recovering from the disagreeable posture in which his Duel with Col. Cummings had placed him, he he [*sic*] falls into an error that will keep him down—He will never recover again. He ought never to *think* of a Duel, much less take part in one. What could be more ridiculous than for him to call on Trimble[101] for an explanation, and then deny to Trimble, an equality with him? This Denial, will under the Circumstances of the Case, be imputed to sheer Cowardice.—He has handsome Talents; but a Want of Prudence will render them of no Value in public life—.

_____

[100]George McDuffie and Col. Cummings of Georgia fought a duel at "Sister's Ferry," S. C., June 8, 1822. McDuffie was wounded. Stephen B. Week's Scrap Book, III, 105, in the North Carolina Room at the University of North Carolina.
    [101]David Trimble of Kentucky was in Congress from 1817 to 1827. *Biog. Dir. of Cong.*, 1627.

I regret to see such bitter Hostility to the Administration. I never liked Mr Adams, as Chief Magistrate; but whilst he seems to labour honestly for the Good of Country, I would give him my Support: Not that I would vote for his re-election; but Justice ought to be done to him—.I had no idea untill the Panama question came on, of the State of Feeling in Congress. I beg you to keep me informed of it, and to Send me a Copy of the Documents? on this Subject—.

I received the Printed Sheets which Mr. Morse[102] had forwarded to Mr. Macon. I was then, long before, & ever since, tortured with Rheumatism, which put it out of my Power to write what I would have gladly done. I am even now Scarcely able to write at all, and am so feverish that a slight mental exertion prostrates me—.I Send to your Care for Mr Morse, my *Memoir on North Carolina,* and Mr. Olmsteads[103] reports on the Geology & Minerology of the State—In these Pamphlets Mr Morse will find much information respecting our State—.If He is not in a hurry to have printed these Sheets, & will return them to me, I will communicate all the information in my Power, as Soon as I get able to write, which I hope will be the Case in two or three Weeks—

—All my Family is Sick. The Influenza prevails here in almost every Family.—

I beg you to remember me Affectionately to Mr Macon. I would have written to him long Since, if I had been able—.

Your Affectionate Friend.

A. D. MURPHY

W. P. Mangum Esq.,

"Can you procure for me a Copy of the Journals of the Continental Congress? I think Congress had a Small edition printed a few years ago. I can't get a copy any where in this State, that I can learn—A. D. M.

Haw River)

April 9th)

---

[102]Jedidiah Morse, 1761-1826, the famous geographer whose geography practically monopolized the field, applied to Macon and Mangum for information on North Carolina to use in a new edition of his *American Geography.* They turned the request over to Murphey who agreed to comply. Hoyt, *Papers of Murphey,* I, 330, 330n; *D. A. B.,* XIII, 245-246.

[103]Denison Olmsted, 1791-1859, a graduate of Yale, taught chemistry at the University of North Carolina. In 1821 he began agitating for a state geological survey. His survey was published in 1824, 1825, and 1827. *D. A. B.,* XIV, 23-24; Johnson, *Ante-Bellum N. C.,* 858.

[Addressed:]

Honble
Willie P. Mangum
Of the House of Representatives,
Washington,
D. C.

WPM-LC

Will. Polk to Willie P. Mangum

RALEIGH April 9, 1826.

My dear Sir.

I have to acknowledge the receipt of your letter of the 28. ult. covering the testimonials in behalf of Mr. Hentz;[104] who comes as well recommended both as regards his moral character and fitness to teach youth, as his competency in the knowledge of the French Language &c. and although he possesses not a proficiency in the Spanish language; yet I am persuaded he could obtain such a knowledge, as to enable him to teach it in a few months; being as he is stated to be; a correct linguist in the Ancient Languages—the Committee so far, are well disposed towards him; but are not at liberty to act finally on the applications before the 15th of May next. Since the receipt of your letter, other Candidates have offered themselves, as well for the Professorship of Modern Languages, as for the Chair of Mathematics, and of whom I have this day *written* to Mr. Macon; to *which*, I beg leave to refer you, with the view of your aiding the Committee in the work which has been assigned to them. Several of our Trustees, are members of Congress; and all, I have no doubt, feel a deep interest, in having the two vacant chairs in our University filled with the very best qualified persons, the Salary will command; to each of whom I would write on the subject; were I not assured, that it is only necessary for them to know the charge committed to the Committee of appt. to claim their aid.

· The Sanhedrins[105] appears to be getting into a state of great fermentation,—the subjects which have produced the most ex-

---

[104]Nicholas Marcellus Hentz was professor of Modern Languages at the University of North Carolina from 1826 to 1831. *Sketches of the History of the University of North Carolina, together with a Catalogue of Officers and Students, 1789-1889.* (Published by the University, 1889), 79.
[105]He refers to the leaders of the Adams Administration.

citement, it would seem, will be supported and maintained by
the Party in Power; if we who are only readers, judge correctly—as far as my information extends the People of N. C.
(I speak of the great majority) are dissatisfied with the doings
of the Administration. I foresee that the Mission to Panama
will [torn] & that no plan will be adopted in [torn] to any alteration in the Constitution.

Accept Dr. Sir
the assurances of my [torn]
and esteem
Yo. Mo. Obt [torn]

WILL. POLK.

[Addressed:]

The Honbl. W. P. Mangum
Washington City.

———

WPM-LC

Willie P. Mangum to Charity A. Mangum

Sunday morning 16th. April 1826.

My dear Love,

Congress has at length fixed the day for adjournment and we
shall break up the 22nd of May—If I live and no accident happens, I hope be at home the 23rd. 24th. or 25th. of May.

If I leave here the Saturday before the adjournment on Monday, I ought to get home by tuesday the 23rd—It will however
depend on the business to be done on Monday the last day,
whether I shall leave here before the close—

I am most anxious my Love, to get home to see you, our dear
little daughter & friends—

I have enjoyed good health—though there has been a good
deal of sickness here—

You have seen in the papers, that Mr. Randolph & Mr Clay
have fought a duel, they shot at each other twice, that is Clay
shot at him twice, R. shot but once, the first time he shot at C's
legs, the second fire reserved & fired his pistol into the air—He
determined before he went out not to try to kill Clay—saying
"I will never make a widow & orphans—It is agt. my prin-

ciples"—I write in great haste. Parties run high & there is a great deal of violence—

John Cameron[106] is here, I invited him to my lodgings, he has been here several days & will stay several more—His situation is most wretched I sh^d think.—

Excuse this short & hasty letter, & believe me My Love, to be your most affectionate husband

W. P. MANGUM

P. S.

I hope to find our daughter at home, & hope she has been so managed that her papa will not be obliged to treat her severely—

W. P. M.—

[Addressed:]

> Mrs. Charity A. Mangum
> Stagville
> Orange County
> North Carolina

WPM-LC

Saml. Yarborough[107] to Willie P. Mangum

STAGVILLE, Orange County
April 17th—1826

My Dear Sir

I ask the favour of you to forward a Ticket to me in the consolidated Lottery for Internal Improvement Literature &C^a. for the Benefit of Sundry States, authorized by acts of Congress. to be drawn in the City of Washington. on the 26th. Inst. If the Tickets, are to be procured, for 20$ the present price, & should I live to see you. I will do the needful at first Sight. I am sorry to see that your Randolph & Mr. Clay Have been pretending to shoot at each other, I fear it will cause some of our Headlong boys in these States' to think they ought to do the same & be foolish enough to take good Aim—I am fearful, you will return too much the partizan. I mean embittered against Johnny Adam^s. administration. whose conduct I have as yet thought

---

[106]John A. Cameron. See above, p. 260n.
[107]See above, p. 89n.

well of. I am surprised at your writing to our Davis & Carrington in the manner you Have I mean about endorsing &C^a. a small sketch. of which I have only Heard, and to conclude I Have the management of a Sir Archy Horse,[108] which Stands at only 6$ the season, & your man George tells me you Have some Mares. I should like for You to think enough of small matters to write for them to be sent down which would help me a little. I shall expect to Hear from you shortly

& Believe me to be sincerely
Yours most obt. Hble St.

SAML. YARBOROUGH

Stagville, N. C.
April 17, 1826   The Honble Willie P. Mangum

[Addressed:]

Member of the House of Representatives
Washington City D. C.

WPM-LC

Joseph Gales to Willie P. Mangum

Dr Sir,

Understanding that you had requested your Acct. to be sent to you here, my Son put it into my hand, with some others, when I left home.

If convenient, you can inclose or hand me the amount. I propose leaving the City in the morning for Philadelphia, but shall return in a few days.

Very respectfully,

JO. GALES.

April 18, 1826.

[Addressed:]

[W.] P. Mangum,
House of Representatives.

----

[108]Sir Archy was one of the most famous race horses in America. John Taylor, III, of Mt. Airy, Virginia, the original owner sold him to William R. Johnson of Warrenton, N. C. William R. Davie and William Amis were subsequent owners. Sir Archy sired a great number of colts, many of which won races from 1811 to 1828. Sir Archy won many races himself. He lived from 1805 to 1833. John Hervey, *Racing in America 1665-1865*, 2 vols. (New York, N. Y.: American Jockey Club, 1944), II, 191-212.

WPM-LC

Willie P. Mangum to Charity A. Mangum

[About 1826]

[The beginning of letter is missing].

in the winter at 7 o'clock. These parties play whist, chat, dance, make bows, look languishingly—squeeze each other—drink tea, eat jellies—& the ten thousand sweet things—& go home.— These parties are generally standing when well attended—and a little saucy minx in the crowd & squeeze, will think no more of running dash against & bruizing your hip with her steel corsets & boards, than I would putting my foot upon the floor—Really you would think all modesty was gone & lost, if you could see the best bred ladies here, squeezing their way through the crowd.

But of these thousand nothings, if you feel the least curiosity about them, I hope I shall tell you, not with pen, but with tongue —I should like to know what sort of figure our Little lady would make in one of these parties. I reckon the poor little thing would be squeezed to death—

Present my Love to Sister Rebecca, in the best manner you can when you see her—to your Sisters & Eliza—Remember me to my mother &c.—And above all remember me often my Love, with affection & prayer.—

And accept for yourself & your little Lady, her fathers dearest Love—

WILLIE P. MANGUM

[Addressed:]

> Mrs. Charity A. Mangum
> Stagville,
> Orange County
> North Carolina.

WPM-LC

William K. Ruffin[109] to Willie P. Mangum

BALTIMORE April 18th 1826

Dear Friend

I have just finished my Fathers letter, which I now send to

---

[109]William Kirkland Ruffin. See above, p. 139n.

you that you may read it, and if you approve of my motive you will please write to Papa, and direct one in which our letters are enclosed to "Mr. Kirkland,[110] Fayetteville N. C." and request him to send them on immediately, as I have but few days to determine, if you do not write or do not approve of my going, you will not send my letter. I hope you will however, and will ascertain from Mr. Randolph all the circumstances that regard the college in Switzerland, and you will please relate them to my Father; It depends entirely on you, I am pretty well assured, for I know that Papa trusts a great deal on you, at least he is willing to do any thing that you think is profitable for me. I shall consider it a great favour if you write whether I get permission or not. Mr. T. Moore called to see me the other day, and was much surprised to hear that you had not been in Baltimore he requested me to tell you that you must not battle with any of the Adamites, when I began to write a letter to Papa I did not intend to mention my desire to go to Switzerland, and I said I scarcely expected to see you here, because I thought you would stay in Washington listening to Mr. McDuffie and the Hon. Mr. Trimble until it would be too late and then you would wish to see Mrs. Mangum so much that you would go away without thinking of me, which I hope will not be the case, for if I go with Mr. Randolph I will not be able to visit N. Carolina before I go.

Write to me if you please by tomorrows mail, I wish to hear from you as quick as possible.

I am yours, with respect

WM. K. RUFFIN.

Hon. W. P. Mangum.

[Addressed:]

Hon. Willie P. Mangum
Washington City
D. C.

WPM-LC

J. A. Cameron to Willie P. Mangum

FAYETTEVILLE May 1st. 1826.

Dear Sir!

I reached home on Thursday evening and found my family all

110William Kirkland. See above, p. 139n.

well. From Petersburg, I came by the way of Halifax and Tarborough: the Superior Court was sitting at Halifax, and such was the crowd of criminal business, that Judge Paxton[111] had entered at once upon it, without touching the Civil Docket. Young Potter[112] was to have tried the day I passed through: the general Opinion there was, that he would be acquitted altogether.—

I have not seen many persons since my return, but incline to think that public opinion is much the same about public Men and public Measures, as when I left home.

The "Journal" will not appear this week, as was intended: the paper on which it is to be printed was shipped from N. York three weeks since, but has not come to hand yet: it will probably be published on the 10th.—

I should be much gratified, and esteem it a great favour, if you and the other Members from this State, would write me occasionally, giving me your views of passing events and Measures, and enclosing me any documents which you might esteem valuable and interesting. Will you send me, as early as may suit your convenience, the report which was made in your house, by the Committee of Claims on the New Orleans negro.—I have not been able to come across it since I came home.—

Captain Cobb[113] passed through this place last night: I did not see him, though I understand he was well.

Be pleased to make my respects to all: the Gentlemen of your Mess and accept assurances of high regard from

Your mo: ob^t. Ser^t.

J. A. CAMERON

Hon: W. P. Mangum
    Washington City

[Addressed:]

The Honb^{le}. Willie P. Mangum
    City of Washington.

---

[111]John Paxton. See above, p. 136n.
[112]Probably Henry H. Potter of Granville who was a student at the state university in 1825. He was the son of Judge Henry Potter. Grant, *Alumni Hist. of U. N. C.*, 501.
[113]Thomas Willis Cobb. See above, p. 172n.

WPM-LC

A. D. Murphey to Willie P. Mangum[114]

HAW RIVER, 6th May, 1826

My Dear Sir

I am still confined by the Rheumatism, but I am getting better as the weather becomes settled and Warm—.

I wish you to write to Mr Morse[115] and say to him if he will forward to me to the Haw River Post Office his sheets on North Carolina, I will endeavor as soon as I can sit up and write to give him satisfactory information on all the subjects on which he requested it from you & Mr Macon—

As to the History of the State,[116] tell him to Strike out every th[ing] that is contained in the former Editions of his Geography a[nd] adopt the Historical account to be found in an Ameri-[can] Edition of Guthries Geography published some years [ago] by Matthew Carey in a small quarto. This Article I [will] endeavour to improve when my health will permit—

I enclose to your care a letter to M^r [Edward] Everett of the House of Representatives. It is open for your perusal. I beg you to present it to Mr Everett, and Solicit his friendly aid on the Several subjects therein mentioned—If I were able to write myself, I would write a long letter to him embracing much detail, but weak & feeble as I am I can only dictate a letter in general Terms—

I am glad to perceive that a better temper seems to prevail in Congress, & hope that you will all break up in peace & friendship—. I wish to get a copy of the Engineers Report on the road from Washington to New-Orleans If you have one to Spare, please forward it to me—

Yours truly & affectionately

A. D. MURPHEY

Willie P. Mangum Esq.
Washington D. C—

---

[114]This letter has been previously published in Hoyt, *Murphey Papers,* I, 330.
[115]Jebediah Morse. See above, p. 272n.
[116]See above, p. 215.

WPM-LC

J. G. A. Williamson to W. P. Mangum

ROXBORO No. C. 9th May 1826.

Honl. W. P. Mangum
  Sir
  Your esteemed favour I rec^d. a few days since under date of
the 24th ult., and at the same time my commission from the Secretary of State as Consul for the Port of La Guayra and Republic of Colombia, which I have accepted, but Sir the great objection I have to the appointment is its situation, but a few degrees
removed from the Equator, an eternal summer reigns there,
and if the situation of La Guayra is upon low and *swampy*
grounds, I must expect to be liable to the diseases incident to
such situation and climate, and those too of the most formidable
kind—to heat I should not have material objection but a combination of heat and moisture is a certain production of inflama-
tory feaver of the most dreadful kind—But the die is cast, and
I may have been in my great anxiety to obtain a situation under
the government, only endeavouring to change the place of my
burial; yet I hope to be able to weather out a year or two there,
when perhaps some more favourable situation for health & equal
in proffits may become vacant in Europe, which with the assistance of my friends at Washington I may be enabled to obtain;
this tho' is but a dim prospect ahead a bare twilight hope—For I
fear even now I see the utmost limits of my horrison bounded
by the mountains that overlook the bay of La Guira—however
Sir we live in hope of better days, and was it not, that universal
medicine for the diseases of accident or bad conduct, we might
at once lay our head down under the stroke of affliction, and
welcome death as a relief from the cares and troubles of this
transitory life—I have requested Mr Williams[117] & I hope you
will use your influence with Mr Clay to delay my arrival in So.
America until Oct., as I wish at least to have the advantages of
the hour of arrival—I feel satisfied that the situation is a good
one & may be improved, and I would oppose no objection
but its climate—Our court is next Monday and the only important busines I presume will be the trial of Cochrum and his two
negroes for the murder of Marshall—
  The news of my appointment appears to *interest* more people

---

[117]Lewis Williams.

in and *out* of my county *than I could suppose,* but I have not much doubt it is that kind of interest which does not wish any good to myself; it is here in the mouth of every man—

It does not interest me half as much, because it is of not so much importance as to excite very exalted prospects—

Yours very Respectfully

J. G. A. WILLIAMSON

[Addressed:]

Hon. W. P. Mangum

Washington City

D. of C.

WPM-LC

M. I. Coman[118] to Willie P. Mangum & Samuel P. Carson

RALEIGH N. C. May 10th 1826

The hon Mesrs Mangum & Carson

Gentlemen

Yesterday I directed a letter to each of you on business of altogether a private character as relates to myself and I have only to request of you respectively that attention to it which you may think it entitled to. I fear that I may be the occasion of giving you some inconvenience but expect to find a ready excuse in your known politeness and liberality—It is not much I solicit at the hands of the Powers that be, but in the language of a worthy Member of the last legislature, if there was one vacancy to be filled, let it be given to the modest yet worthy and deserving citizens of North Carolina—the People of North Carolina have scarcely derived 6ᵈ a head from the bolted doors of the Treasury of the General Government, while the little State of Delaware sometimes called the little Republic of Merino has shared most extravagantly *I will not say undeservedly* the favours of the General Government. her citizens like their Representative Mr Louis McLane have something of merit and qualifications on their side, you will please not omit sending me a

----

[118]Matthew James Coman, 1800-1870, the son of a Raleigh merchant, attended the state university with James K. Polk. He lived in Haywood County before he moved to Texas. W. C. Allen, *Annals of Haywood County,* 480-486.

letter of introduction to Mr White[119] the delegate in Congress from the Territory of Florida.

Respectfully Yours

M I COMAN

Hon Messrs Mangum & Carson

[Addressed:]

The hon Willie P. Mangum & Samuel P Carson
Representatives in the Congress United States
from North Carolina
City of Washington

WPM-LC

John Haywood to Willie P. Mangum

RALEIGH 12th May 1826.—

Dear Sir,

Pressed and fatigued by the public Business in which you have been now for so many months unceasingly engaged at Washington, and worn down by the Cares and Anxieties inseperable from it; I feel it is wrong in myself and should consider it so in any other of your friends likewise, to attempt to add to your present Labours by asking your attention to matters of a private or personal nature, and more especially at the present time when the Session of Congress is fast approaching to a close: and you will do me but justice in being assured I could not do so, if I believed it to be in my power to effect or accomplish the object I have in view, through any other way or mean.

Mr. Hill, our Secretary of State, has an only son, who is known by the Name of William G. Hill:—and the same Gentleman has a Nephew named William R. Hill;[120] both Youths or young Men of high desert as well as of much promise; and each of them willing to obtain a Warrant of admission into the Academy at West Point: Such however was the anxious desire of each of these young Gentlemen last year; both of them could not be

[119]Joseph Masters White, 1781-1839, a native of Kentucky, became a lawyer in Pensacola. He represented the territory of Florida in Congress from 1825 to 1837. *Biog. Dir. of Cong.*, 1691.
[120]A William R. Hill was the state librarian in 1829, and from 1829 to 1830 the superintendent of public buildings. Neither of these boys was admitted to West Point. George W. Cullum, *Biographical Register of the Officers and Graduates of the United States Military Academy* 6 vols. (New York, N. Y.: Houghton-Mifflin Co., 3rd. ed., 1891-1920), I, 566.

gratified, and the Son yielded his Pretentions to the Nephew in the Summer of 1825; since which time nothing further has been known on the subject, although it has been hoped by all and believed by some that the Nephew, Mr. William R: Hill, would be favoured with a Warrant of admission into the Military Academy, at or before the Commencement of the next Session, which will happen in June or July, as it is understood here:—Mr. Hill is an amiable young man—of impeachable conduct and character, and has indeed a respectable and high standing among all who know him:—He has written in the Secretary's Office for some time past, and in course of his Employment⁵ there has rendered to myself as well as to many others of his friends, Services which ought warmly to attach us to him: and indeed his pleasant and obliging manners, added to the politeness and kindness of his general deportment, make for him an Interest with all who know him.—I took the liberty of trespassing on your time and patience lately, on behalf of my *Namesake*, Mr. Hardin: and the Object of the present illy timed intrusion is, to ask your good Offices in favour of my young friend Mr. Hill; so far at least as to ascertain at the War Department, whether a Warrant has been granted & forwarded to him? as none has been received:—or if not, whether he may yet hope to obtain one?— If you know Mr Hill as I do, I know it would give you pleasure to render him this service, and thereby to do away his present suspense:—and I feel I risque nothing in adding, that you would be gratified likewise in forwarding or promoting his Pretentions in this regard, as far as may be in your power; as he is, as I before said, a young man of much promise and of sterling Worth.

Forgive the trouble I would occasion you, and be assured I would do as much and more for yourself or for yours, were it in my power.

Yours respectfully & truly,

JOHN HAYWOOD

[Addressed:]

The Honourable,
    Willie P. Mangum,
        Congress.

WPM-LC

E. W. Reinhart[121] to Mr. Mangum

BOSTON, May 12, 1826.

Hon. Mr. Mangum,

Sir,

Some time since I received a letter from Mr. Saunders,[122] of N. C. stating that you would write me on the subject of establishing a newspaper; upon which subject I had written to Mr. S. Having never heard from you, I am somewhat apprehensive that your letter may have miscarried. Be good enough to write me a line giving your views relative to the expediency of establishing a press in any place known to you. In connexion with this purpose, I must say—that I will be concerned in no press opposing the pretensions of Andrew Jackson, as long as he may be a candidate for the Presidency; nor in any one, that shall support the "puritan and blackleg coalition! !"[123]

Very respectfully

E. W. REINHART

N. B. For any information relative to me, please call on Hon. John Varnum,[124] I, Barlett[125] or R. M. Saunders, M. of H of R. I believe I can easily furnish capital sufficient to establish myself. Provided I can obtain support after that shall have been done, & reasonable assurance of it I know not what should prevent my embarking in the business immediately.

E. W. R.

[Addressed:]

Hon. Mr. Mangum,
M. C.
Washington,
D. C.

---

[121]Unable to identify.
[122]R. M. Saunders.
[123]John Randolph's epithet on the coalition of Adams and Clay.
[124]John Varnum was congressman from Massachusetts from 1825 to 1831. *Biog. Dir. of Cong.*, 1647.
[125]Ichabod Bartlett was congressman from New Hampshire from 1823 to 1829. *Biog. Dir. of Cong.*, 677.

WPM-LC

J. L. Edwards[126] to Willie P. Mangum

War Department
Pension Office
May 18, 1826.

Sir,

Mr. Paris Pearson's letter[127] to you, with it's enclosure, is herewith returned, and I have to inform you, that his claim to back pay for revolutionary service, is barred by an act of limitation. I also return Mr. Mebane's letter[128] to you, and have to state, that although it is contrary to the regulations of this Department, to give any information concerning military service, until a claim to a pension has been presented, yet, in order to save John Hobbs, the unecessary trouble and expense of preparing a declaration, I deem it proper in this case to depart from the rule by stating that it appears from the rolls of the South Carolina line of continental troops, that Hobbs was last reported as a deserter, and is not therefore entitled to a pension.

Mr. Clayton Jones's letter[129] to you is also herewith returned. It appears from our records that the papers in his case, were returned to Mr. William McKissack, at Roxborough, N. C. on the 8th of July last, accompanied by a letter of which a copy is herewith enclosed, & which will shew what is deficient in his case. It does not appear that any document in support of the claim, has been received at this office since Similar regulations to those mentioned in the letter to Mr. McKissack are herewith enclosed for the claimants guidance.

I have the honor to be
very respectfully
your obedient servant

J. L. EDWARDS.

Hon. W. P. Mangum
House of Representatives.

---

[126]James L. Edwards was the clerk in charge of the Pension Bureau of the War Department until 1833. From 1833 to 1850 he was Commissioner of Pensions. Glasson, *Federal Military Pensions*, 87.

[127]See above, p. 212.

[128]See above, p. 243.

[129]This letter was not found in the Mangum Papers.

WPM-LC

John Chavis to Willie P. Mangum

May 24th. 1826

My dear Sir/

I am teaching school, where I did last year, and should you be traveling this road I would thank you to call on me, and I would rather it be on any Saturday, but the last in the Month Or I would much rather you w^d. let it be on some Friday evening, (not the last in the month) and go to our friend J. Nutts. For I wish you to know, that I have fought, as uniformly since you been in Congress, as I did before the election, and I have found nothing else to work upon, but whitleather, & that of the most tough, and durable kind

I wish to see you exceedingly, I have much to talk about & many questions to ask, among other things I wish to know why you have been so silent this session. was it because there were so many spouters, who loved to hear themselves talk? or was it because you discovered too much whitleather in them, for your weapons? I wish to know also why you were opposed to the Panama question, I thought it had the appearance of a good thing, tho, I confess I am no Judge & therefore I want information—

Your opposition to the Judiciary System I was well pleased with, but why you called it an electioneering thing I did not so well understand—

I was pleased that you voted for the amendment of the constitution respecting the choice of the President, but for no other reason then I did not wish you to discover a disposition to trample upon the will of the people; but as to its actual amendment in that case, I am opposed, because once a beginning is made to amend the constitution, a way goes the best of human compacts & therefore I think it be attended with ruinous consequences. The truth is, the constitution as it now stands places the people upon firm ground, that they cannot sink or stop for, not so much so as strain their joints much, & therefore I say let us move on as we have done—

Please to give my respects to Mrs. Mangum & tell her that I join her in acclamations of joy at your return. I am, every attom of my heart, the same old two & sixpence.

JOHN CHAVIS

P. S. I believe that Silas Leak [?] has repented of his conduct in every vein of his heart & therefore I wish you to treat him friendly

       J C

[Addressed:]

      Hon. Willie P. Mangum Esqr.
           Orange
care of Mr.
W[alter] Mangum

                    WPM-LC

Deed of William Cain, Sr., to his daughter

                 [24 May, 1826]
Know all men by these presents that I William Cain Senr of the County of Orange, for and in consideration of the natural love and affection which I have for my Daughter Martha A. Cain[130] do give, grant and deliver to my said Daughter Martha A. Cain a negro man slave, known by the name of Plato, black and about forty five years old—In evidence whereof I hereunto set my hand and affix my seal this 7th day of December 1825.
Signed sealed & delivered

           WILLIAM CAIN, SR. (Seal)

in presence of
Wm. Cain Junr.

        Orange County—February Term 1826.
  The Execution of the within Deed was duly proved in open Court by the oath of William Cain junr. a subscribing witness thereto and ordered to be registered.
             Test
             John Taylor, C. C.

Registers Office)
) 24th May 1826. The above Deed of Gift is
Orange County)
         duly Registered in Book S. page 624.
          Test   J. McKerall P. R.

---

[130]Charity A. Mangum's youngest sister.

Endorsed:

>Deed of Gift
>Wm. Cain Senr.
>to
>Martha A. Cain
>1825   for Plato.
>Decr. 7.
>Registered.

WPM-LC

Joseph Gales, Jr., to Willie P. Mangum

WASHINGTON June 29, 1826

Dear Sir:

Looking over the names of the Speakers on the Panama Mission, I discover yours, as Speaking on an amendment moved by Mr Forsyth[131] to Mr McLane's resolution[132] immediately after Mr Mitchell[133] of Tennessee. Can you recal your remarks so as to furnish them. If so, I should be obliged to you to let us have them, as well for the newspaper as for the Register of Debates.

Mr Cory[134] is here, & I am glad to hear from him that you & your family are well & happy in a seclusion, which must form a fine contrast to your winter life.

>Very truly & respectfully
>your friend & Servant

>JO: GALES JR

Hon. W. P. Mangum.

[Addressed:]

>Hon. W. P. Mangum
>Red Mountain
>Orange Co
>No. Ca.

----

[131]John Forsyth of Georgia.

[132]While the debate over the appropriation of funds for sending delegates to the Panama Congress was at its height, Louis McLane proposed, February 2, 1826, in the House that President Adams be asked to send to that body copies of all documents on the Panama Congress especially on its purpose. Forsyth objected. He said the resolutions did not go far enough. He proposed, therefore, that the President indicate the powers the delegates would have. Apparently, Mangum did not furnish Gales a copy of his remarks for they are not in the *Register of Debates.*

[133]James Coffield Mitchell, 1786-1843, was Congressman from Tennessee from 1825 to 1829. From 1830 to 1836 he was state judge. He moved to Mississippi in 1837 where he was unsuccessful in his race for governor on the Whig ticket. *Biog. Dir. of Cong.*, 1319.

[134]Benjamin Corey. See above, p. 265.

Seth Jones to Willie P. Mangum[135]

POMONA 16th July 1826.

My Dear Sir,

Since your return from Congress I have been anxiously looking for you to visit your little though faithful band of friends— We have not heard a word from you since your return from Congress. We did expect a Circular from you, but since you have not visited us, nor written a Circular I have thought it would not be amiss to inform you there will be three musters in my neighborhood next week and I am satisfied that many of us would rejoice to see you at them. The musters were appointed for, and it is expected that the county Candidates will attend them. The musters are arranged thus.

Wednes. the 26th July muster at Berry Kings.[136]
Thursday the 27th do   do   at Hartwell Hortons
Friday the 28th   do   do   at Alfords (near Crudups)

I could not by any means have you to think me presumptious by dictating to you, but would be very glad if you would come down and attend the above musters, as I have no doubt it would be an advantage to you if you should ever be a Candidate again, (which I have reason to believe & hope you will)

Some of your *real friends* begin to think you slight us by not coming and attending some of our large meetings at Raleigh. Mrs. Jones & myself Present our compliments to Mrs. Mangum and wold be happy to see her at our house, she says you promised to bring Mrs. Mangum to see us, and that you are fair to promise but fears you will not perform.

With great respect I
remain your friend &
Obt. Servant

SETH JONES.

Honble Willie P. Mangum.

[Addressed:]

Honourable Willie P. Mangum
Orange.

---

[135]The original of this was in Willie Mangum Person's possession when Mr. Weeks had it copied. The copy is in Raleigh at the State Department of Archives and History.
[136]All of these musters were in the eastern part of Wake County.

WPM-LC

B. Bullock¹³⁷ to Willie P. Mangum

18th July 182[6 ?]

Dr Sir

The Granville Candidates have Commenced their Campaign and will Come into my neighborhood Wednesday and to my house that night—

I Received a message from Squire Wm M¹³⁸ by Captain Sneed¹³⁹ to this amount. if I would Send you a message that he wish,d to see you at my house on Wednesday Eavening, and that you if possable must see him on Some particular business at my house.

I hope you will Come down with Mrs. Mangum, and give the Squire some Lessons in Congress Campaigns

Respctfully yours

B. BULLOCK

[Addressed:]

Willie P. Mangum Esqr.
Orange
N. C.

By Peter)

WPM-LC

Printed Circular of Philadelphia Committee in behalf of Andrew Jackson for President

(CIRCULAR.)

[20 July, 1826]

FELLOW-CITIZENS:—

The cause of our country seems, at this jucture, so closely blended with the political elevation of General *Andrew Jackson,* that watchful and vigorous efforts to promote the latter, must receive the aid and approbation of all sincerely attached to the former.

---

¹³⁷Benjamin Bullock of Granville was a justice of the peace, physician, and in 1814 member of the House of Commons. *N. C. Manual,* 622; McIver, *N. C. Register,* 29, 56.
¹³⁸William M. Sneed.
¹³⁹Stephen K. Sneed, the brother of William M. Sneed.

12

Our government is based upon the People's will. If this foundation be removed, or if, as in Europe, it be disregarded, the structure of our civil liberties must fall, or be ultimately overthrown. Unless we are willing to change our system: to sink into the condition whence we are but just emancipated: and to entail upon our descendants all the degradation and wretchedness from which our ancestors, at the hazard of life and fortune, rescued themselves and us: we should vigilantly and fearlessly enforce our rights against the encroachments of power and the sublte arts of ambition.

Until the period made memorable by the election of the present President of the United States, the principles of the Revolution of '76, especially in reference to the duty of public agents and the sovereignty of the People's will, had been sacredly pursued and most happily exemplified. On that occasion, however, they were openly violated: and their violation accompanied by indications of corruption truly appropriate to the event, and well calculated to alarm our patriotism. Although the election was, by the provisions of the constitution, rightfully within the power of the House of Representatives, who could expect that the people would be spurned by their delegates? who could expect that the public *servant* would unblushingly deny his *master?* who anticipated that the *representative*—known, existing in no other character—should defy, repel, and insult his *constituents?* and who, in the land of Washington and Jefferson —while the first was yet fresh in immortality, and the second still mortal—could expect to find political promotion to follow upon political infidelity, and the people's offices showered upon his who betrayed and mocked the People?

It will be remembered that in the House of Representatives, the Presidential election is conducted by states—that General Jackson, though far ahead of his competitors on the returns of the electoral ballots, there received but eight votes: that the representatives of Kentucky gave their state vote to Mr. Adams, in favour of whom not a single man of their constituents had, by suffrage, declared himself: that the representative of Illinois, unmindful of a public pledge, acted in the same manner: that the representative from Missouri followed in this wake, even after the repeated and protracted struggles of a conscious sense of duty: and that Louisiana, whose soil had been redeemed, and whose matrons had been shielded by the transcendant heroism of Jackson from the barbarous pursuit of *"beauty and booty,"* abused by two of her representatives, turned upon her preserver, and against the will of her citizens, pierced him with the fang of unparalleled ingratitude. Nor can we forget, that the master spirit, by the power of whose influence, mysteriously exerted, these effects, so opposite to republicanism, were produced, was himself instantly rewarded with the office of Secretary of State, long an object of his ambition.

Such examples warn us to be wary in time; unless speedily and emphatically condemned, they will ripen into precedents, and afford conspicuous apologies for future misconduct. It merits remark, that Mr. Adams, elated perhaps to indiscretion by his triumph over the people, in his very first message to Congress, insinuates that our representatives should not be *"palsied by the will of their constituents:"* in other words, that they should disregard that will, however clearly ascertained, when inconsistent with their own personal views or opinions. Such is the inevitable tendency, as it constituted the ground-work of [t]he prinsiples upon which his election was accomplished.

In the fall of this year, we shall be called upon to select *members of Congress*: and they whom we select, will continue to act as such, until after the choice of another Chief Magistrate. It is within the range of possible contingencies, that they may elect the President for the ensuing four years. Is it not, then, our duty, to exert more than common circumspection? Does not the recent experience to which we have adverted strongly urge us to confide this trust to those only by whom our will cannot be disobeyed or misrepresented? Although it be true, that the existing aspect of public opinion promises an easy and decisive triumph to the People's candidate, can we oppose too much precaution to the management and patronage of intriguing politicians? Ought we not, at once, to make sure, of the distant future, by resolutely restricting our suffrages, for congressional stations, to those who are avowedly and firmly attached to the principles for which we contend?

The town-meeting of republicans in the city and county of Philadelphia, whence this committee of superintendence and vigilance emanated, deemed the subject to which your attention is now drawn, worthy of distinct and strong remark. It was a leading object in their early movement: and they hoped by energetic measures to give a successful circulation in their early movement: and they hoped by energetic measures to give a successful circulation to their sense of its importance. Our fellow-citizens, considering the Presidential election to be remote, do not reflect that its fate may depend upon what they are at this moment doing. Their dexterous adversaries, with honey on their lips, but poison at their hearts, would lull them into apathy— preaching the beauty of tranquillity, and the folly of premature contest: while, in secret, they labor every nerve to make the next Congress of materials hostile to Jackson, and subservient to Adams.

We do not think it necessary to impel you to efficiency and zeal, by dwelling upon the peculiar claims which the Hero of New Orleans has to the untiring devotion of his fellow-citizens. His eminent virtues, his intelligence, his valor, and his pure republicanism, have been known, witnessed and felt by all of us. In war and in peace—in the scenes of retirement, or when surrounded by faction and temptation—at the plough, or in the Senate—he has, every where, uniformly proved that he deserves to be the chosen champion for the cause of his country. In this respect, he is alone in America. Providence furnishes, for the safety and pride of any nation, but one such man at a time. Let us avail ourselves of the gift, and reinstate the principles of Washington under the auspices of Jackson.

It has been made our duty, so undoubtedly will it be our pleasure, industriously to advance the cause for which the people of the United States, and their favorite citizen, have embarked together. We will receive thankfully, and employ appropriately, with all the means in our power, and to the best of our ability, whatever information relating to your district you may be good enough to convey to us, as worthy of general dissemination. Let us, however, not forget, that while steadily bent upon securing the election of our candidate at the close of the present presidential term, we must, in the mean time, avoid the acts, as we disclaim the title, of faction—not suffering our just indignation against those who have by artifice usurped the rights of the people, to mislead us into an undiscriminating opposition to public measures, or a vindictive bitterness against persons. Let us uphold what is beneficial, with the same resolute spirit that we condemn what is injurious, to our beloved country: adopting the frank declaration of an energetic statesman, "We will judge of the measures of the administration by their own intrinsic merits: but we will not judge of the administration by their measures *only, when they come to settle the account of their stewardship, and ask for a renewal of their trust:*" we will, then, advert to the vice of their origin, to the treachery and corroption which characterized their political birth.

We are, fellow-citizen,

respectfully,

your friends,

(Signed on behalf of the Committee,)

CHANDLER PRICE,[140] Chairman.

Jacob Holgate,)
)

Henry Horn,   )

Secretaries.

[Addressed:]

Hon W. P. Mangum

Red Mountain

N. C.

[Postmarked:] New Hope, Penna, July 20.

————

WPM-LC

W. M. Sneed to W. P. Mangum

WILLIAMSBORO

July 31st. 1826

Hon^l. W. P. Mangum,—

Dear Sir,

I was called down yesterday to see my mother who is on the very *brink* of the Grave—

I have this moment by the Stage received a letter from home, giving me information of the arrival last Evening at Oxford of Govr. Burton. He is Expected to spend a day or two with his aunt[141] in this vicinity on his way to his Seat in Halifax C.y—

I shall see him as soon as I can and would have gone up this morning, but at day break I did not think my mother would live two hours—She has revived a little, but I *believe* she cannot survive Ten hours[142]—

---

[140]Chandler Price kept up a considerable correspondence with Jackson in 1824. Bassett (ed.), *Cor. of Jackson*, III.
[141]Mrs. Robert Burton lived near Henderson, N. C.
[142]Mrs. Stephen Sneed of Williamsboro was the mother of William M. Sneed. She died August 3, 1826. Broughton, "Marriage and Death Notices," 300.

I hear Ro. H. Jones,[143] Toomer[144] and Hawks[145] are Candidates for Judge—These were the names spoken of in Raleigh a week ago—There may be others added to the list before this time— I think you had better come down to Oxford—and if the Gov. shall have left there, you would do well to come on to W^{ms}.-Boro[146]

Your friend & Servant

W. M. SNEED

[Addressed:]

Honl. Willie P. Mangum
Orange
N. C.

———

WPM-LC

Jo. Gales to Willie P. Mangum

[RALEIGH, 1 Aug., 1826]

Dr Sir,

Your esteemed favor of the 28th inst. was recd. this morning.

The name of Mr. Seaton's oldest Son is *Augustine,*[147] and I most heartily concur in the opinion which you have heard of his being a promising Youth, and I believe that he would be gratified by obtaining a situation at West Point. So would his Father; though I own I should be better satisfied to see him at a Seminary where he would be less in the way of imbibing a love for a Military Life.

His Parents, I am sure, will feel as his Grandparents feel, deeply impressed with obligation to you for the recommendation you propose to give to their Son, and for the handsome manner in which you are pleased to speak of his family connections.

---

[143]See above, p. 36n.
[144]J. J. Toomer. See above, p. 15n.
[145]Francis Lister Hawks, a lawyer who was the reporter for the state Supreme Court from 1820 to 1826, later became an Episcopal minister and settled in New York. He wrote a history of North Carolina. Sanders Dent, "Francis Lister Hawk," *Trinity College Historical Papers*, I (1897), 56-65.
[146]Mangum was being considered for an appointment as superior court judge by Governor H. G. Burton. The appointment was made August 18, 1826. Weeks, "W. P. M.," *Biog. Hist. of N. C.*, V, 242.
[147]Augustine F. Seaton, the son of William W. Seaton, was a cadet at West Point from 1828 to 1833. He served at many military posts until his death in 1835. Cullum, *Biog. Reg. of U. S. Mil. Acad.*, I, 566.

Excuse this short letter. I am pressed for time, and desirous of writing by the present mail,

Your obliged srvt.

JO. GALES.

Raleigh, Aug. 1, 1826.

[Addressed:]

Willie P. Mangum   Paid
    Red Mountain P. Office
        Orange.

WPM-LC

Willie P. Mangum to a Member of the Council of State[148]

ORANGE 14th. August 1826.

Dear Sir.

Although I have never had the pleasure of a personal acquaintance with you, I have notwithstanding long had an intimate knowledge of both your public & private character: If I have formed a true conception of it; no apology is necessary for introducing to your consideration with freedom & frankness any subject of eith[er] public or private interest.—nor and any apprehension be entertained, that it will not be received [&] considered in a corresponding spirit of frankness & candour.

I therefore take the liberty of informing you that my name will be placed before the Executive Council to fill the vacancy in the Superior Courts of Law & Equity occasioned by the resignation of Judge Nash.[149]—In consequence of the principle insisted on by the Council & acceded to by the Gov. last summer, touching their respective powers & duties. It would seem more fit that the members of the Council should be addressed.

I had however declined, previous to the time fir[st] fixed for the meeting of the council to write to them either collectively or individually—nor had any communication been had between any

---

[148]This letter apparently was never sent.
[149]Frederick Nash, 1781-1858, was a member of the House of Commons from New Bern before he moved to Hillsboro. He represented Orange and Hillsboro in the state legislature frequently from 1814 to 1829. He was judge of the superior court from 1818 to 1826, and from 1836 to 1844. From 1844 until his death he was a justice of the state Supreme Court. Ashe, *Biog. Hist. of N. C.*, I, 405-410.

of them & myself with the exception of my intimate friend Mr Jeffrey[150]

I have now however determined to depart from that original intention, so far as to wr[ite] to you, & to you *only*.—You will readily perceive in the sequel my reasons for this course.—

Upon the happening of the vacancy, I knew that the southern part of the State would strongly urge an appointment in that region.—I felt that they had some claim.—

WPM-LC

H. G. Burton to Willie P. Mangum

[18 Aug., 1826]

State of North Carolina.

To the honble. Willie P. Mangum.

We, reposing special trust and confidence, in your prudence, integrity, abilities and learning in the law, do hereby commission you one of our Judges of the Superior Courts of Law and Equity, you having been thereunto appointed, by his Excellency the Governor, by and with the advice of the Council of State; and authorize you, after taking such oaths as are necessary for your qualification to enter upon and discharge the duties of said appointment and to receive and enjoy the salary thereunto annexed untill the session of our next General Assembly.

In testimony whereof I, Hutchins G. Burton, Governor, &c. have caused the great seal of State to be

(SEAL)

hereunto annexed and signed the same at our city of Raleigh this 18th. day of August A. D. 1826.

H. G. BURTON

By the Governor,
    Jno. K. Campbell
        P. Secty.

[Endorsed:]

Fee of Office $4.00

---

[150]George Washington Jeffreys of Caswell County was a classmate of Mangum's at the state university. He became a successful planter who wrote articles and a significant book on agricultural methods. Johnson, *Ante-Bellum N. C.,* 796. See above, p. 5n.

WPM-LC

P. H. Mangum to Willie P. Mangum

HILLSBORO' Sept. 1st. 1826.

Dear Sir,

On yesterday a letter was received in this place from Stephen Moore which stated that he was at Austenville in Wythe county, Va.—that the health of Martha Cain was getting better—that Charity was well, and that it was uncertain when he should return, but probably next week.

I have this [week] endeavoured to ascertain as well as I could, the state of public opinion as to the propriety of your serving your time out in Congress: I have no doubt but that your warm country friends would be pleased that you would return, & will generally be displeased with you for abandoning their service. But at the same time I am equally certain such a step in you would greatly impair your strength in the State and Legislature upon being run for the jud[g]eship. I understand that you will in all probability *be hard set at* in the Assembly—Mr. Strange[151] seems to be mostly spoken of. In looking at the *representation*, I find that there will be in the Assembly several men of no mean pretensions, who will likely be arrayed against you such [as] Chs. Fisher, Jno. Morehead,[152] Shepherd,[153] Genl. Stokes[154] from the West; and doubtless several from the East. For these reasons, I think that prudence requires that you should *resign* your seat in Congress, if you intend to seek a confirmation of your appointment. This is the opinion of several of your friends.

There is nothing here of any interest. Judge Nash is enchaining these folks by his silvery eloquence. He is elegant, correct & generally successful—But he has not the force of Ruffin—nor has he his roughness. He has lost none of the suppleness of youth.

I brought Rebecca to your house & there left her.

Yrs. respectfully
P. H. MANGUM

[Addressed:]

The Hon:
Willie P. Mangum
Tarborough
No. Ca.

---

[151]Robert Strange.
[152]John M. Morehead, the future Whig governor who championed internal improvements. Ashe, *Biog. Hist. of N. C.*, II, 250-259.
[153]Augustine Henry Shepperd.
[154]Montfort Stokes.

WPM-LC

P. H. Mangum to Willie P. Mangum

OXFORD. No. CA.
September 7th, 1826.

Dear Sir.

Last week I wrote you from Hillsboro; and altho I then touched the subject which induces this address further conversations with our friends have produced an anxiety to be more explicit.—

I am strengthened in the opinion that you should resign your seat in Congress, as you have intimated to me an intention of doing—and I think that you should do so *forthwith*. Some of your friends *here* have expressed their surprise that you had not done so *ere now*—particularly Billy Sneed, who says that it has been a subject of remark about Warrenton. I learn that others at this place this week, who you can conjecture as well as I, have made it a subject of remark—intimating that you did not intend to resign *at all*, & that the love of power or of gain, or both, would be the cause. This is conjectural but not without some ground. I am pursuaded and so are all of your *intelligent* friends, with whom I have conversed on the subject, that it is indispensable to your success before the Legislature[155] that you should resign—& that an *early* resignation is *important*. You know that you have bitter enemies whose friendship by the by I should priz[e] as [li]ghtly as their enmity, and it is politic at this juncture to disarm them of every weapon if practicable—

The few days which have elapsed since I wrote, have not furnished any news worthy of detail.

[Geo. E.] Badger, [Henry] Seawell, [Josiah] Crudup, [James] Mebane & Doc. [James S.] Smith have been spoken of as candidates.[156] I doubt not but that Badger would be very glad to be elected, if he could be without opposition—which I think is the only way in which he could be elected. If Badger or any other man from Wake, except *Crudup*, is a candidate—Mebane will be run from Orange. Against Crudup, Mr. [Mebane] would not run. If Crudup runs I think Doc. Smith will come out—& *I* think Crudup would beat him *easily* tho' the Doctor thinks that he

---

[155]Mangum was defeated by the legislature.
[156]Candidates for Congress.

could beat Crudup easily, which I set down to the Doctor's vanity. These things however have not yet made much stir.

Yrs respectfully

Oxford, N. C.   P. H. MANGUM.
  Sept. 8, 1826

[Addressed:]
    The Hon.
      Willie P. Mangum
        Tarborough
        No. Ca.

WPM-LC

G. E. Badger to W. P. Mangum

[14 Oct., 1826]

Sir,
    I send you a draft of a Decree in the case of Ruffins Creditors vs: Ruffin's Trustees—mentioned by Mr. Haywood[157] & myself— Will you have the goodness to read it & signify your approbation—Mr—H: & myself will then give form to the decree & have it entered.
    We hope you are at length restored to health—As our movements here depend greatly upon yours please drop me a line for the common benefit of the bar saying what you intend to do—
    Pray let me add—do not attempt anything to which your strength is not entirely adequate—I think of starting for Warren on Tuesday morning unless otherwise directed by you—
    With best wishes for your restoration to health I am

Sir
your most obed:
G. E. BADGER
Raleigh 14. Oct: 1826

The Honorable
    Judge Mangum

[Addressed:]
    The Honorable
      W. P. Mangum
      Wake County
by
  Washington).

-----

[157]Probably Will H. Haywood.

1827

Willie P. Mangum to B. Yancey[1]

HILLSBORO the 1st of January 1827.

My dear Sir:

I [torn] learn that a young gentleman [faded] of Raleigh a day or two ago, reports that he heard a public conversation at a dinner table amongst a number of members of the assembly, and that it was confidently said and seemed to be so understood that in consequence of the public excitement indicated at my temporary appointment to the Circuit Co. Bench, I had declined being considered a candidate before the Legislature.[2]—

It is true that I have neither requested any member nor distinctly authorized any one to nominate me; hence it is possible that the inference may be drawn and by reason of my silence on the subjects my friends may not know my inclinations.—I have seen no member since the month of November, nor have I except on this occasion, put pen to paper on the subject.—

My object now is merely to inform you of my wishes on the subject.—I have hitherto abstained from any interchange of sentiment *directly* with you on this matter, and you can readily appreciate my reasons.—I know the delicacy of your situation, & the jealous and illiberal spirit with which you are observed by a certain party in this State, & I should be very reluctant, by any means whatever or for any object to strengthen that spirit.— But to the subject.—My mind was made up in the summer to accept the appointment if conferred; to devote my best exertions to my public duties; to turn my studies exclusively to the law, to endeavor to attain as respectable a standing as my abilities would admit; and to enter upon those duties as a permanent business.—

Early after my appointment,[3] I was astonished to perceive the virulence of public feeling growing out of that occasion.—If I had been elevated over men pre-eminent for legal learning, or distinguished for great or long continued public service, I could not nor ought I to have felt surprised.—Whatever estimate the pub-

---

[1]The original is in the Bartlett Yancey Papers, Southern Collection, University of North Carolina. This letter has been previously published in the "Letters to Bartlett Yancey," *The James Sprunt Publication,* X, no. 2, 62-65. In that publication the date is erroneously given as January 27, 1827.

[2]Mangum was defeated by a combination of the East and West. Robert Strange and James Martin were elected to fill the two vacancies. "Letters of Bartlett Yancey," *The James Sprunt Publications,* X, no. 2, p. 62, n. 4.

[3]Governor Burton had appointed Mangum August 18, 1826.

lic may think that I have formed of my own qualifications, on that occasion at least I don't think I am censurable for over-weening presumption—When Judge Toomer was spoken of, & when it was expected that his name would be before the council; recognizing as I did the reasonable wishes of the Cape Fear district; & the high personal claims of Mr. Toomer; I determined to yield to his pretensions; & that determination was distinctly announced to Gov. Burton—But when the other gentlemen were the only competitors, I was unable to view their pretension in the same imposing light—Nor could I perceive that either their learning, or public services imposed upon me any obligation to yield to them.—After the appointment was received, I expected as matter of course to hold a poll before the Legislature.—Nor have I been deterred from persisting in that determination, by denunciations as virulent as they were unexpected.

I know full well that the confirmation of my appointment will be resisted with great violence & great numerical strength. Nor am I unprepared to meet complete defeat—

But I feel that I have been treated with a rudenes and inde-corum, as unexampled in former cases, as it was uncalled for by my public deportment—and that too upon an occasion, when to grant the most to my opponents the public interest could not have sustained any deep injury by my appointment over the gentlemen *then* before the Council.—Hence my determination is to enter the contest, for I prefer to meet my enemies, & encounter an entire overthrow, rather than make a pusillanimous re-treat.—

A part of the opposition to me savours so strongly of deep political malignity or personal hatred; that my resistance as far as it depends upon me, shall at least be manly, tho unavailing.—

My early resignation when I rec^d. the same appointment in 1819 will be urged against me & not without effect. I have to say to you, (tho I should scorn to enter publicly into domestic reasons for my conduct) that the disastrous turn of my Father's pecuneary affairs[4] took the year after, left me to choose between keeping the appt. and looking coolly on his situation, or to abandon my station & endeavour to save as much of the wreck as w^d. make his situation comfortable.—I did not hesitate in making the choice, nor shall I ever regret it, whatever may be its effects upon my personal advancement.—

[4]See above, pp. xxiii-xxiv.

I learn that Gen Stokes is violently opposed to me, & says amongst other things "that but for that damned fellow the Moravean suits would have slept forever"—This in substance he urged & was urging strongly agt me this fall in Wilkes.—I have to say that my decision on that question after several days argument has been affirmed by the Supreme Court. It was the granting the petition for a review of a decree in Equity.—

My own opinion is, that the lamented death of that firm & honest man Judge Paxton will make against me.—Will it not produce a coalition between the southern & western interests? Whereas if but one vacancy was to supply, the motives to coalition would not exist.—

I wish you to understand me—That however proud, as I really am of your good wishes, yet I know the delicacy of your situation so well, that I neither expect, nor do I wish you to mingle in this contest in any way to your prejudice—For however anxious you may naturally expect me to be in reference to the issue, yet knowing that contests of more consequence to the public are yet in reserve; I hope I should be unwilling to weaken in any way, those upon whom my hopes of success rest.

I wish Mr. Scott[5] of Hillsbor°. to be apprized of whatever is contained herein.—

Believe me yours truly & sincerely

W. P. MANGUM.

WPM-LC

James Barbour[6] to Willie P. Mangum

WASHINGTON
Jany 8th '27.

Dear Sir

Yours of the 29th Ul°. has been received this morning. It would have given me sincere pleasure to have done an acceptable act to you, especially in so doing to have brought in to the public service the youth whose merits you so forcibly present—But in coming into office I prescribed from a conviction of its Justice a rule for my government in the distribution of these appointments—Altho by so doing I reluctantly surrendered my largest

---

[5]John Scott.
[6]James Barbour of Virginia was Secretary of War from 1825 to 1827. *D. A. B.*, I, 590.

branch of patronage. This rule was to send to each state its share
of the federal principle of Representation namely one Cadet for
each Representative and Senator—And to assign one Cadet to
each Congressional District and two at large in the State—I was
sorry to find that two had already been appointed by my Prede-
cessor from your former District—

Hence you find how utterly impracticable it is to meet your
wishes in the appointment, for the present, of Mr. Armstrong.[7]

I feel very sensibly the expressions of kindness you have been
good enough to use towards me. It has been my lot to hold situations in times of difficulty—involving great responsibility—I
thank God that I took as my polarity what I believed was the
welfare of my Country—and often as I may have wandered
from the line what a Superior intelligence would have pointed
out my departure was the result of the infirmity of my understanding—

I beg you to be assured of my
> High respect and friendly regard

> > JAMES BARBOUR

[Addressed:]

> > Judge Mangum
> > Red Mountain
> > No. Carolina.

                                        WPM-LC

Nath¹. Macon to Judge Mangum

                              WASHINGTON 14 Jany 1827

Sir

I heard last night, that you were not elected by the Legislature
to fill the office,[8] to which you had been appointed by the executive: the instant the news was communicated, every member of
the mess immediately expressed their regret, in the most friendly terms; Mr. Randolph stated his in a manner, that would have
made a strong & lasting impression on you could you have heard
them: & asked me, whether I corresponded, with you, I answered, that I had not written to you, but sent you documents,

----

[7]James W. Armstrong. See above, p. 212, and below, p. 309.
[8]Judge of the superior court.

& that I thought, I would do so tomorrow (which is this day) he then requested me, to give you his best respects; every member of the mess desired to be remembered to you

The friends of the candidates for the presidency, are very industrious, both parties I hear, say, that they are sure of success at the next election; & pretend to calculate on the votes of states enough to make good the calculation; those in power, unless more economy be used in the public expenditure, may find an empty treasury, before the election; want of money by the British government, was the primary cause of the Independence of the U. S., & want of money has destroyed the governments, which have existed heretofore, & so want of money may injure an administration in this country; The public burthens & private debts are now a great injury to the mass of the English people, with all their industry, & with all their improved labor saving machines; they want bread, they have enough of nothing except debts & taxes

The constitution of the U. S. provides for an equality of taxation, but taxes may be perfectly equal, and ruinous to our plans & beneficial to another, for example, if all the expenditure be at one place, & none at the other, the first ought to get richer every year, & the last poorer, because the amount is carried from the last to the first, be the sum what it may, it takes that much from the capital of one & transfers it to the other; I speak of places & not individuals because with the last, there must be the difference of paying & receiving; the pension law of Mr. Monroe is a strong illustration in point

It has so happened, that all the free government of old times has passed by; and all of them probably from the same causes, to wit—Debt & extravagance; can a remedy be found for this great evil, which affects the moral as much as it does the political world, can honor & honesty be substituted for courts of law & equity in the dealings of men, gambling & duelling are on honor, & against law, & it would hardly be contended; that every one engaged in either was an honorable man, on this subject I have reflected much, but have not come to any perfectly satisfactory conclusion; News this minute come, that you are not a Judge, two being elected[9]

God bless you & yours

NATH[l] MACON

---

[9]Robert Strange and James Martin were elected. *N. C. Manual*, 448.

during the session, I have sent documents to Hillsborough for
you—
                        N M.

[Addressed:]
        Judge Mangum

                                        WPM-LC

            Geo. Luther¹⁰ to W. P. Mangum

                            RALEIGH 30th Jan^ry 1827.
Dear Sir
    I am Glad to be informd that you intend to commence a prac-
tice in Chatham Court I have Several Suits to commence there
If Its True that you intend Coming please do not engage against
me untill you see me my cases are important and the fees shall
be Liberal
                    Yours Respectfully

                        GEO: LUTHER
the
    Honorable
        W. P. Mangum

[Addressed:]
            The Honourable
            Willie P Mangum
                    Orange County
                        N Carolina
Way

                                        WPM-LC

            Rob. Potter to Willie P. Mangum¹¹

                            HALIFAX 26th April '27
(Confidential)
My Dear Sir,
    I have it in contemplation, as I intimated to you last winter at
Raleigh to migrate to the South or West. My thoughts at this

----

¹⁰George Luther was a justice of the peace in Chatham County.
¹¹See below, letter of Potter to Mangum, May 24, 1827.

time are fixed upon New Orleans, and I am desirous to obtain if
possible before I go there some appointment which will sustain
me for a time and guarrantee an honorable standing there—do
me the favour then to forward to me as early as possible a letter
of introduction to Mr. Clay, with whom I believe you are intimate, and from whom in a personal interview, I propose to solicit
the appointment in question—if I were at leisure I would
promptly unbosom myself, and disclose to you the full extent of
my views—but the court bell is at this moment ringing its sum-
mons, and your knowledge of me moreover would seem to render
that unnecessary—if you think proper to do so, I th[ink it wou]ld
aid me if you were to address a private letter to Mr. Clay—I
address this letter to you in especial confidence, *no one* knows of
it, or of my intended visit to Washington I shall address a similar communication to Govr. Burton & to him *only*

Your friend
& obt. Svt.
ROB. POTTER

Honble.
      Willie P. Mangum
        Hillsborough

[Addressed:]
      The Honble.
        Willie P. Mangum
         Hillsborough.

the P.M. will be so good as to cause this letter to be delivered
as early as possible.

WPM-LC

H. G. Burton to Willie P. Mangum

RALEIGH May 24 A D 1827.

My Dear Sir
   I am nearly out of funds and I am now on my way to Halifax
for the needful, on my return I will send you twenty three Dollars, which I justly owe and unjustly detain, if I meet an opportunity, if not—we shall meet at Chapel Hill

Your friend
H. G. BURTON.

[Addressed:]
Willie P. Mangum Esq.
   Present.

WPM-LC

Robert Potter to Willie P. Mangum[12]

WASHINGTON CITY, 24th May..27 [1827]

My Dear Sir.

I was severely disappointed on my arrival here, at not finding a letter from you, and have now waited nearly a fortnight in anxious, but vain expectation of hearing from you—I left Halifax as soon as I received your letter, in reply to that I had addressed you at Hillsborough on the subject, and acting upon a suggestion contained in your letter, I wrote to you from Richmond, requesting the transmission of the promised draft—relying upon it in my expenditures, I am actually unable to get home without it—do then my good friend remit me fifty or sixty dollars by return of post—you know the expense of living here is great, and if I remain much longer that sum will be insufficient—let me know too if you please if any thing has been done in relation to the object of my visit to this place.

Your friend

ROB POTTER

[Addressed:]

The Honble
    Willie P. Mangum
    Red Mountain P.O.
    Orange County
    No. Carolina

If Mr. Mangum is not at home, Mrs. M. will please cause this letter to be immediately conveyed to him—

———

WPM-LC

James W. Armstrong[13] to Walter A. Mangum

WEST POINT June 23rd. 1827—

Respected friend:

I have determined to devote part of this evening to redeem the pledge which I made you, when I had the pleasure of seeing you last.—

---

[12]See above, letter of Potter to Mangum, April 26, 1827.
[13]See above, pp. 212, 305.

I reached this place on the 11th inst. after a very pleasant journey of 9 days. To a person, who has not been accustomed to survey the wildness of nature, West Point must present a thousand objects to please: At its base the Magestic Hudson rolls its waters in silent grandeur to the wide Atlantic, and bearing on its bosom hundreds of vessels laden with the products of different countries and winding, through the Highlands, whose summits pierce the clouds, at the distance of 4 or 500 feet above the surface of the water. The West bank of the Hudson as far down as New York is the most romantic and picturesque scenery in the United States, the bank is perpendicular [in some] places, at others hanging over some 8 or 10 feet.

The Academic buildings which are made of rock and very large, are situated on a beautiful plane, which seems to have been designed by nature for such an institution, it is completely surrounded by lofty mountains. It was on this very plane on which the traitor Arnold and Major Andre held their conclaves to betray our infant army into the hands of the merciless British.

Yes, I behold, in imagination, the sloop Vulture riding at anchor, and as if conscious of the conspiracy which was going on, on board her: But providence smiled upon us & rescued our army from imminent destruction It was on this Point that Kosciusko cultivated his garden, and the very rose bushes and shrubs, which were planted by his hands more than 50 years ago are now seen—Well may I say:

"Hope for a while bade the world farewell
And liberty shrieked when Kosciusko fell"

What American is there [who can] reflect upon these things, without emotion, yes without the tear of gratitude rising in his eye; and who would not be ready and willing to die in defence of our liberty.

I must confess that I was dissatisfied for a day or two after I got here, but I attribute it to my having no acquaintance on the point. But I begin to like it better every day; and I am now very well pleased. My examination took place yesterday and I was admitted a member of the Academy—the number of new cadets are 113 all of whom were admitted, with the exception of 10 or 12. We are at this time on encampment, where we will remain until the 1st. of Sept.; the duties, during which time will be exclusively military—last night was the first day I slept in camp, it is by no means agreeable to a person who has not been accustomed to sleeping on the ground. The tents look like a small town, being 63 in number [exclu]sive of 6 or 8 marquees.

This is unquestionably the best institution in the United States for getting an education: But we pay dear for it we have a large musket on our shoulders 5 hours every 24 and 13 hours every 4th day, during the encampment besides attending to the duties of the tent—carrying water, rolling dirt from the camp ground &C—

At City Point Va. I took water, and saw a steam boat for the first time, they are a wonderful invention both for expedition and comfort the cabins of all the steam boats in which I was are as handsomely finished & furnished as any hall room in Orange—they have most excellent fare—it is almost worth a visit to the North, if one had no other object in view except the good eating which one gets on board a steam boat. We got to Norfolk about 11 at night, in a storm, and took another boat immediately for Philadelphia, but had to cast anchor, on account of the wind, which blew very hard; the next day we entered the Chesapeake bay—We landed at Seaford in the State of Delaware, and took coaches for Dover and then took another boat for Phila-delphia, and landed in the city about sun down, the appearance was very fine indeed and the thousands of vessels riding at anchor was truly a sublime & beautiful sight—the moon shone bright the night I got there, and I walked over [a] small part of the city the streets were crowded even as late as 11.—I rose early next morning and walked myself down and after all saw but a small part of that handsome city—I remained only 1 day & night—the Ladies of Philadelphia are quite handsome—and look far superior to the Southern ladies at a small distance; but upon a more close inspection they are [torn] delicate. I went up the Delaware river as far as Trenton N. Jer[sey] [torn] farms and country seats on eit[her si]de of the river are extremely [hand]-some. I saw the residence of Jos. Buonaparte his dwelling is almost [torn] by trees, but his observatory is very prominent which appears to be an octagonal, it looks very handsome—At Trenton we took the accommodation coaches for New Bruns-wick where we took another boat for New York at which place we arrived about 10. in the morning—It would be impossible for [me] to give you any sort of description of New York in an epistle [torn] you will please excuse all mistakes, errors &c in this letter, as I am now writing on my knapsack and sitting on the bottom of my tent,—no tables being admitted in the tents.

Henry Clay's son is one of the new cadets, he has just gone out
of my tent, I find him a very clever young man, no pride at all.
Give my respects to Judge Mangum and Lady, Let me hear from
you soon tell me all the news in Orange and particularly all in
our neighborhood—You will not wait for me to answer all the
letters which I expect to receive [from] you, as my situation pre-
cludes the possibility

Your friend &c

JAMES W. ARMSTRONG

[Addressed:]

Mr Walter A. Mangum
      Red Mountain
            Orange Co.
                  (N.) Carolina

WPM-LC

John Boon[14] to Willie P. Mangum

August the 8th— 1827

Dear)
   Sir   I have bean in your neighbourhood but it was out of my
power to call and See you I had undersood that there had bean
Some complaint a gainst me for my not attending the tax gath-
erings Sir I am very sorry that there should be any Complaint
for I am sorry there should be any where I have bean so liberaly
Seportedt but Sir as I understand that you have not forgot your
old friend I hope you will attend the Election[15] and regulate
your & my friends Sir I am sorry to here that is a Split Likely
to take place I understand Sence I left home that there would be
a grate many Single votes given against me by Mr Stockards[16]
friends and Mr Nashes[17] in hilsborough that has pretended to
be my friends, in this way they may run me hard many friends
in the upper ende of the county knows nothing a bout it Sir

---

[14]John Boon, a justice of peace of Orange County in 1823, was a member of the House
of Commons from 1824 to 1825 and from 1836 to 1837. *N. C. Manual*, 740-741; McIver, *N. C.
Register*, 35.
   [15]Boon was running for the House of Commons. He was elected.
   [16]John Stockard, a lieutenant colonel of the militia in 1823, was in the House of Commons
as a representative from Orange County from 1826 to 1830, 1833 to 1839, 1842 to 1843, and
1848 to 1849. Hamilton, *Papers of Ruffin*, I, 513; *N. C. Manual*, 740-741, McIver, *N. C. Register*, 91.
   [17]Frederick Nash represented Hillsboro in the House of Commons from 1828 to 1829.

any thing that you can do to prevent anything of that kinde will nver be forgotten Sir Excuse my blundring scribling

Very respetfuly

JN. BOON

W. P. Mangum

[Addressed:]

Willey P. Mangum
Orange County
N C

Joseph Ross to Duncan Cameron[18]

RALEIGH, 22nd August 1827

Sir,

The note of Willie P. Mangum[19] as principal with William Cain, Senr as security held by the State Bank of North-Carolina, dated the 12th of May 1827 payable Eighty eight days after the 22nd May 1827 and endorsed by Dun Cameron and drawn for One thousand seven hundred & Seventy Three 73/100 dollars, has become fully due, and remains unpaid. The same having been placed in my hands for collection, payment is now demanded of you.

Yours, respectfully,
JOS ROSS Not. Public

Dun Cameron Esqr

WPM-LC

Willie P. Mangum to

RED MOUNTAIN N. C. Octo. 1st. 1827

My dear Sir.

Your favor of the 29th July last. by reason of its direction to the city of Raleigh, was not forwarded in due course, and did not reach me [until] this day.—You appeal to me "as a ma[n] [of ho]nor and as an old friend". to answer [what] ever may be my

---

[18]The original is in the Cameron Papers.
[19]Mangum had incurred debts in the early twenties to help his father who was in financial difficulties. See above, p. xxiii.

political feelings ce[rtain] interrogatories contained in your letter [torn]

I recognize the appeal not only from a sense of justice generally; but the more especially from the warm & unabated personal regard which I most cordially cherish towards you.—In answer to your enquiries it is proper that I should state, that during the whole period of our service together, an unusually open & undisguised personal & political entercourse subsisted between us—and although we were frequently found conbatting against each other upon certain questions of policy with equal zeal; yet th[torn] no event transpired to my knowledge to [torn] our personal regard or to interrup[t] [torn] harmonious & friendly intercourse.

During the session of Congress 1824-5 [torn] held divers political conversations on the s[ub]ject of the Presidential election.—

I received you then as the warm personal and political friend of Mr Clay—He was your first choice upon the list of Presidential candidates—Your attachment to Mr. Crawford as I conceived, was sincere & strong; & but for his precarious health his claims in your opinion yielded to none but those of Mr. Clay.— You professed a high respect for the experience & qualifications of Mr Adams, but he did not seem to possess as strong a hold upon your affections & confidence as either Mr. Clay or [Mr] Crawford.—You uniformly avowed to me from [the] beginning to the end of the session that Gen: Jackson was decidedly your last choice on the list of candidates—

Soon after we assembled at Washington, it was understood that Mr. Clay was excluded from the House by the Electoral colleges—It immediately became matter of universal anxiety & speculation, as to the Course that he & his friends would pursue.

It was believed that they would naturally act together, & that their influence would be decisive of the question.—At this time as well as all others during the session I held a more free intercourse with you; than with any other member of Congress always excepting the friends of Mr. Crawford.—

We both I believe expressed our sentiments, conjectures & speculations without reserve to each other; & with no other restriction than that those [view?]s & opinions were not to be used publicly [torn] otherwise during the pendency of the election.

Your views & opinions were uniform & consistent as expressed to me; that you could not get your consent to vote for Gen: Jackson: nor would those with whom you acted, in your opinion, be prevailed upon to do so.—I considered you as one of the most active & efficient of the Ohio delegation, & knowing that you felt & took a deep interest in the election; I did not doubt your means of information; nor the faithfulness with which you d[torn] it to me.—I believed that (Mr Clay out of the qu[estion] you had strong predilections for Mr Craw[ford]

You seemed to deplore the then bad conditio[n of his] health, and often stated to me that it presented [a] great, if not insuperable obstacle to his electio[n.]

That the embarrassments of you & your friends w[as] increased when you looked to the probability of Mr Calhoun being brought into the Executive, upon the demise of Mr Crawford—a result that you seemed strongly to deprecate—constantly expressing the grea[t]est repugnance towards him as a statesman, as well as on account of his supposed connexion with the unexampled persecutions of that able & virtuous man W. H. Crawford. [On the back in Mangum's handwriting:] To John McLean,[20] Ohio Delegation

WPM-LC

John Chavis to Willie P. Mangum

Nov[r]. 16[th] 1827—

My dear Sir/

After I parted with you that Morning, upon reflection, I found I had forgotten to tell you some more things to say to Mr. Roberts[21]—and that there was an intimacy and a friendship subsisting between myself & Judge [George E.] Badger, that I supposed that you might get something from him Accordingly I wrote to you on these subjects & sent my letter to Granville Court, expecting you w[d]. certainly be there, but I am told you were not—at which I was not a little supprized, however I expect the latter was given to my son Priestley—

I now write to let you know that our supposition respecting my neighbours puting up a house for me cannot be realized.

---

[20]John McLean of Ohio was Postmaster General from 1823 to 1829. A John McLean from Illinois was in the Senate from 1824 to 1825. But in this letter Mangum refers to his vote in the House of Representatives for President. Probably Mangum meant William McLean, John's brother, who was in Congress from Ohio from 1823 to 1829. *Biog. Dir. of Cong.*, 1273, 1274.
[21]Probably William Roberts, justice of peace of Wake County. McIver, *N. C. Register, 40.*

They are engaged in gathering corn sowing wheat &C. . So that
I was oblige to hire hands to do the work & had to go to a different neighbourhood to get them. Being compeled to get out of
the miserable hutt I am in, & that before Christmas. If you can
possibly raise among our friends 20. or 30 dollars for me by
Christmas I can make out for the present I shall be at your house
on my way from school, at Christmas to get you to draw the
writings between me & Mr Rogers[22] respecting the Land—.
I should suppose that you might get something from Gen. B.
Daniel of Raleigh—Governor Burton, the latter being a fellow
student & a particular friend—I think you may get something
from Jack Wilson of Hillsborough either at present or the future. It would be well, I think, to act in all cases for the present
or the future as the case may be—I shall endeavor to send you a
description of the Land before I come, as you may have the writing ready & if you should be from home about Christmas, please
to leave the writings or any thing you may have for me enclosed
in a letter at your fathers and oblige yours &c

JOHN CHAVIS

[Addressed:]
Hon. Willie P. Mangum Esqr
Orange—

Capt. A. Rogers,

WPM-LC

John Chavis to Willie P. Mangum

Dec[r]. 15th. 1827

My dear Sir/
I wrote you that I should call to see you on my way home from
school at Christmas, but finding that w[d]. be quite inconvenient,
I called to day to get you to draw the deed of Trust of the Land
given me by Benjamin Rogers of Wake The Land lies in Wake
& the Trustees is Allen Rogers, & the Land is to be given to me
during life & my wife Frances during her life or widowhood. I
forgot to get a general description of the Land from Mr. Rogers,
but know the Land as well as he does & by whose lands it is
bounded but not the Lines of the Land, as you said a general

------

[22]Allen Rogers. See above, p. 270n.

description was sufficient & Mr. Rogers agreed it was. I suppose
the memorandum I have left will be sufficient. As it will be very
inconvenient for me to call again, I would thank you to draw the
deed & enclose it in a letter & send it by some safe hand to put
in the hands of Judge Cameron who can send it safely to me by
his man James who passes by Mr. Greens to see his wife. Any
other communications, either from Roberts, or any business with
my friends will be thankfully rec^d.—

My buildings are going on & I expect to move in the course of
a few weeks & am yours &C

JOHN CHAVIS

[Addressed:]
Hon. Willie P. Mangum Esqr
Orange

WPM-LC

John Chavis to Willie P. Mangum

Decr. 18th. 1827—

My dear Sir/
Your present & future prospects, to provide for your growing
family, is a part of my daily meditations. I am much concerned
therefore at the thought you have of moving to Hillsborough. I
do conceive it will be the most fatal step to your prosperity that
you have ever taken—

You know, that I have ever opposed every stage of your political life, preferring your continuance at the bar untill you had
acquired a competent fortune. And you are now certainly convinced beyond the shaddow of a doubt, that had you followed my
advice, you would been worth dollars, dollars, where you are not
worth a *Mill*. And in the face of all your destructive steps—you
are about to give the fatal blow, by moving to Hillsborough after
being at the great expense of preparing to live, How can you possibly conceive, that you can better provide for your family, from
a baron lot of ground, than you can from a well prepared &
ample farm? Pray stop and draw the contrast between the prospects Examine and see which of the two is the most likely to
afford you sustenance, your farm with all necessaries provided,
stock of all kinds, farming utensils & wood in abundance or to

go to Hillsborough & leave a Farm & good houses and all other necessaries, to go to dedestruction, & to add to it the purchase of every thing to support your family fire wood & all the necessities of life and many other inconveniences that might be mentioned. Good heavens, you are called a wise man, and so you are, but w^d. that be wisdom, answer me?—

I understand that your friends in Hillsborough are advising you to this step, but will they when you get into difficulties help you out? say no, well behave yourself & stay where you are. I dont blame your friends for wishing your company & your society, but will that fill the belly in plain English? say no, well think for yourself then?

I understand that my son Priestly says that either you or himself must go to Hillsborough, that his house & lot must be taken care of. A pretty story indeed! Pray if he wants his house & lot taken care of why dont he do it himself? The plain reason is this, that altho he was once opposed to living in Wake yet he has found in his wisdom that a Farm in Wake is far preferable to a Lot in Hillsborough with the addition of the business of States Attorney. I hope you will while you a naping, become as wise as him, & stay on your Farm too, as being the most advantageous way of supporting your family & let him dispose his Lot, as I have before advised him, & put the money either to the purchase of Syms's Mill or to the use of his farm—To conclude my opinion is, that Town property is as trifling property as a man can have. For it keeps whoever has it & lives on it, stretched like a bow string, so behave yourself & stay where you are, is the advice of one of the sincerest friends you have on the Nation & you have your choice either to believe it or let it alone but his name is John Chavis.

P. S. I would thank you to attend my next examination in Wake it will be at Revises cross roads where you were once on the last Thursday in July. I shall tell the people that you will be there. I know it will be pleasing & give dignity to my prospects.

[Addressed:]

Hon. Willie P. Mangum Esqr
Orange

1828

WPM-LC

Willis Alston¹ to Willie P. Mangum

WASHINGTON Jay 19" 1828

My Dear Sir

Your expressions that the administration are overthrown are often quoted here I am pleased to see your name brought forward in the present contest,² I have no fears for my native state, altho we are counted upon for the administration, our majority in both houses are firm and decided and act in great concert and harmony mildness and moderation mark every step we take any difference of opinion with our friends of the North and East is marked with great good feeling and temper

On the subject of the revision of the Tarriff I can say nothing I rather am inclined to an opinion that it will be approached with some degree of caution

We have every reason to count on New York, going for Jackson they vote by districts and our friends say 24 certain and perhaps 30 the whole artilery of the coalition will be directed towards Pennsylvania but our friends from that state say it will be all in vain that Pennsylvania is firm and for Jackson Kentucky is safe for 9 if not for 14 each side claims Ohio, & strange to tell you our friends in New Hampshire say Jackson will get the vote of that state of this however I do not count

There has been a warlike speech in the House, which you may have seen in the papers between Desha³ of Tennessee, & Brent⁴ of Louisiana, about Brents denunciation of Genˡ. Jackson & his friends, which was taken notice of in a pointed manner by Desha in a Toast, B. came out in the news paper, as did D, and there the matter now rests, there will be no more of it I believe

I am your friend

WILLIS ALSTON

¹Willis Alston. See above, p. 93n.
²Mangum was a presidential elector on the Jackson-Calhoun ticket.
³Robert Desha, 1791-1849, a merchant from Gallatin, Tennessee, and a former major of the War of 1812, served in Congress from 1827 to 1831 and then moved to Mobile where he reentered the mercantile business. *Biog. Dir. of Cong.*, 900.
⁴William Leigh Brent, 1784-1848, a native of Maryland, practiced law in Louisiana after 1809. He became the deputy attorney general for the western district of the territory of New Orleans. From 1823 to 1829 he was in Congress. *Biog. Dir. of Cong.*, 734.

[Addressed:]
> Honble.
> > Willie P. Mangum
> > Red Mountain
> > > Orange County
> > > > North Carolina

WPM-LC

D. L. Barringer to W. P. Mangum

WASHINGTON 5th Feb. 1828

W. P. Mangum Esqr.

My dear Sir, I rec^d. from you two letters in relation to the Claim of Mr————— a Soldier in the late war, and the other, inquiring in Behalf of Mrs Rosanna Waganer[5] after her brother. I reply to the first I will on a future occasion transmit you the reply of Peter Hagner;[6] and in reply to the other, I have to say, That I call^d. on Mr Washington representing the district in which Mr Appler is said to live, who kindly untertook To ascertain the facts, connected with your enquiries—The result is, that Mr Jacob Appler still lives on the plantation, where Mrs Waggoner and himself were Born—and has in this city a son, David, who has liv^d. here 17 years—keeping a Tavern, at the corner of the square on which P. Thompsons Bookstore stands— and you may remember to have seen the House—I call^d. on him—and he will write in a very short time to his Aunt—and direct to Red Mountain—he appears in the true sense of the term to be quite a *clever* man—You have not in either of your letters —given me a word, on the politics in N. C. I suppose things are pretty much in *statu* quo—The administration party are making great efforts in almost every part of the Union—and it would seem from news paper reports with some success in N. C. as else where—is the fact so? I had not believe^d. that Adams could get one third of our State—We have got the Tariff under discussion—it is a perplexing subject—its friends have many preliminary questions, first to settle—and in the scuffle we may give it a death wound—but if they can a gree upon terms—it will pass by an encreased majority—we have mov^d. slowly—there

---

⁵See above, p. 249.
⁶Peter Hagner, 1772-1850, was third auditor of the Treasury from 1817 to 1849. He handled claims. *D. A. B.*, VIII, 84-85.

was perhaps never such a *talking mania,* as no rages here—
and unless means can be found to limit its exercise within *some*
bounds—the lord knows when we shall get a way—Hailes
resolution[7]—prescribing *one hour* for each speech—would have
a salutary effect—if it were practicable, and ought not to be considered quite so ridiculous as— most things from the same
source, is— If you delight in storms and tornadoes—you might
Be gratified here—there is scarcely a day—which does not elicit
angry feelings in debate—and what would be considered on
other occasions—as of extraordinary—is not told of ordinary
occurrence—you have seen that poor old Genl. Brown is dead—
I hope we shall—settle the question of precedence between
Gaines & Scott[8]—by abollishing the office or command of Maj^r
Genl. I should be much pleased—to hear from you often— this
is not common place—and hope you will gratify me—with Un-
diminish^d. friendship—

D. L. BARRINGER—

[Addressed:]

Hon
W. P. Mangum
Hillsboro, N. C.

WPM-LC

John Chavis to Willie P. Mangum

March 11th. 1828

My dear Sir/
I wrote to you, before I left Mrs Greens, and requested, that
you wd write the deed for the land, and send it to Squire
Walkers Mill, if you did so, it has not come to hand. Col Tignal
Jones,[9] is going to Hillsborough to the superior Court, and tells
me he expects to stay in Town one night. I hope it will be in

---

[7]William Hailes, 1797-1837, was a member of Congress from Mississippi from 1826 to 1828. *Biog. Dir. of Cong.,* 1044.

[8]When General Moses Brown died in 1828 and Jackson resigned to become governor of Florida, Winfield Scott, Edward Pendleton Gaines, and Alexander Macomb were in line to succeed Brown. All three were major generals. Scott was the senior officer, but Gaines and Macomb intrigued for promotion. After the Cabinet decided for Scott, Richard Rush, who was for Macomb, then told Adams that if either Gaines or Scott was appointed the two would fight a duel but that both of them were friendly to Macomb. Adams' horror of duelling led him to change the Cabinet's recommendation to Macomb. Scott, who had been away, re-turned, and a great controversy developed. Arthur D. Smith, *Old Fuss and Feathers: The Life and Exploits of Lt. General Winfield Scott.* (New York, N. Y.: The Greystone Press, ,1937), 166-169.

[9]Col. Tignal Jones was a member of the legislature from Wake County in 1777, 1784, and 1797. *N. C. Manual,* 827-828.

your power to write it and send it by him as he lives a near neighbour to me I shall be certain to get it. I have moved, & am much pleased with my new settlement, & should Mr. Rogers die before I get the deed, you know it w^d. be bad—And that you may be the better able to oblige me, I will give another description of the the Land—

One hundred Acres more or less, bounded on the South by Soloman Thompson, and Jacob Hunter, on the West by the Lands of James Boyd, on the North by Richard Smith, & on the East by Tignal Jones, the Land is well Timbered with pine Oak & other common growth known by the name of the Job Rogers Tract, to be given to me during life & during the life of my wife Frances or her widdowhood—

If your engagements should be such that you cannot write the deed, & send it by Mr Jones; please to write it & bring it to Wake superior Court & send it by him or some of our neighbours. The Thompsons or the Rogers or others—

The presure of the times are such, that I fear that however willing any of friends may be to assist me, that they will not be able. If not I hope God will provide for me, he is all sufficient—

Give my respects to my sons Abram[10] & Priestly, & tell them I never expect to see them again, unless they should condescend to come to see me. I am much more helpless than when you saw me You cannot conceive what it cost me to attend to my school my number at present is 16. and it may probably arrive at to 20. however the people are very mulish.

Pray dont forget to attend my examination on the last Thursday in July I have told my employers that you are to be there—

I am very anxious respecting your affairs I fear John J.[11] will injure you from report. But I hope strict attention to the practice of Law will releive you, & that you will be enabled to lay up for your family. I hope also that you have given out all thoughts of moving to Hillsborough My respects to Mrs Mangum & believe me to be yours with all my heart

JOHN CHAVIS

The Land is bounded on the South by the Lands of Soloman Thompson & Jacob Hunter, on the west by James Boyd on the

---

[10]Abraham Rencher, 1798-1883, was a Democratic Congressman from 1829 to 1839 and 1841 to 1843. From 1843 to 1847 he was the United States minister to Portugal. He declined the appointment of Secretary of the Navy under Buchanan. From 1857 to 1861 he was territorial governor of New Mexico. *Biog. Dir. of Cong.*, 1453.
[11]Unable to identify.

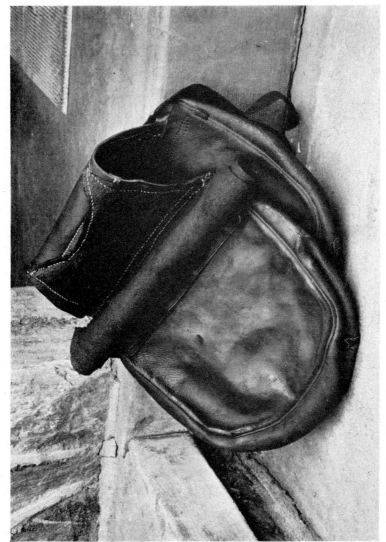

Saddlebags used by Willie P. Mangum on the judicial circuits while he was superior court judge in North Carolina. Original in the possession of Mr. Mangum Turner of Winston-Salem, North Carolina.

North by Edward Rigsby, and on the East by Tignal Jones, and it lies on some of the waters of Bartons Creek, and on the Road leading from Rigsbys cross roads to Raleigh. It is tolerably fine corn Land & well timbered with pine—Oak and other common growth & is known by the name of the Job Rogers tract of Land   100 Acres

[Addressed:]
                    Hon. Willie P. Mangum Esqr
                              Orange
Col. T. Jones

WPM-LC

Willis Alston to Willie P. Mangum

WASHINGTON March 16 1828

My dear Sir
    Your favor of the 6" was this moment handed to me, altho' I had firmly believed the sentiment of N. C. being such as by you stated, nevertheless I assure you it gave me great pleasure to learn it from such a source. The friends of administration realy believe or pretend to believe that N. C. will go for them, unless I am much mistaken many of their calculations are as falacious, (for instance) Virginia Pensylvania and a large majority in New York, These three large states are as certain for Jackson as, N. C. or Tennessee, except that N. Y. votes by districts a majority, will be for Jackson, Kentucky both sides claim. The Friends to J: by far the most sanguine, that state by unanimous consent of the Legislature, altered their law to a general ticket, agreeing to go for the whole, the contest will be warm and animated but Tom Moore[12] says all is safe by not less than 10,000, New Jersey is warmly contesting every inch of the ground, the issue, I put down very doubtful, so is ohio, but Indiana, Illinois is with us, so is Missouri and Lousianea.
    Our friends in Newhampshire say Jackson will get the vote, so says Maine, but I have nothing like confidence of a vote in N. C. Now I will tell what says the other side, They count all the doubtful states I have named as certain, and expect to get either N. Y. Pa. Va. or N. C. to give them the majority. The

---

[12]Thomas Patrick Moore. See above, p. 95n.

13

foregoing is a true account of the calculations here, and the prevailing sentiment is that Nor[th] C. is the most doubtful of the fo[ur] states above

Let me not overlook little Deleware your friend Lewis [*sic*] McLane told me a few days since that Deleware was safe for Jackson, and gave me a hearty shake by the hand, it may be therefore placed among the doubtful, you can see now that our prospects are flattering, I am sure I have not made our side better than the universal impression is here.

On the subject of the Tariff little can be said, to be relied on. The pretended American system is certainly loosing ground with the intelligent, almost every where, if the Tariff is defeated it will certainly be by the administration, in order to keep up the excitement, we at the south will go with any side to defeat it, in truth we all seem very well to understand each other here, that is due to the south vote as we please about Tariff and internal improvement and so will our friends to the west & in Pennsylvania & New York without offence or harm to the great cause of administration or anti.

I am now labouring under severe cold and will promise to write soon more in detail

Give my best respects to Madam and all the family, I wish you would come & see us next summer I want if I can to visit [my] friend in chatham again and if I do will [take] your country in the way

I am
your sincere friend

WILLIS ALSTON

[Addressed:]

Honoble
Willie P. Mangum
Red Mounting
Orange county
North Carolina

WPM-LC

Chauncey Goodrich[13] to Willie P. Mangum

WASHINGTON CITY March 23rd 1828

Willie P Mangum Esq.,

Sir,   Permit me to enclose to you a note against Robert Potter[14] for $170 cash lent last Summer, which I wish you to present to him for payment, as I understand that Mr. Potter is not wealthy, I wish you to take the same course to obtain the same, as you would if the note was yours, with only this exception not subject me to any costs You can retain any part that you please for your trouble.

I am Respectfully &C,

CHAUNCEY GOODRICH,
of Buffalo,
New York

[Addressed:]

Willie P. Mangum
Red Mountain
Orange County
No Carolina.

---

*Indenture[15] of W. P. Mangum to James Webb[16]
and Thomas D. Watts[17]*

[25 April, 1828]

This Indenture made this the twenty fifth day of April in the Year of our Lord one thousand eight hundred & twenty eight Between Willie P. Mangum of the County of Orange and the State of North Carolina of the one part, and Doctor James Webb and Thomas D. Watts of the same County & State of the other part Witnesseth. That the said Willie P. Mangum for & in consideration of one dollar lawful money to him in hand paid

[13]See below the letter of Willis Alston to W. P. Mangum, May 7, 1828, and a letter of Goodrich to E. F. Norton, November 28, 1829.
[14]See above letter of Potter to Mangum, May 24, 1827.
[15]The original is in the James Webb Papers, Southern Collection, University of North Carolina.
[16]James Webb, 1774-1853, a graduate and later a trustee of the University of North Carolina, was a well-to-do physician in Hillsboro. Grant, *Alumni Hist. of U. N. C.*, 653; Hamilton, *Papers of Ruffin*, I, 182.
[17]Thomas D. Watts was the sheriff of Orange County and Hillsboro town treasurer. *N. C. Laws*, 1826, 1830, 1831, appendix; McIver, *N. C. Register*, 87.

by the said Doct Webb & Thomas D. Watts, the receipt whereof
is hereby acknowledged, hath Given, granted, bargained & sold;
& by these presents doth give, grant, bargain & sell to the said
James Webb & the said Thomas D. Watts their heirs, executors,
& administrators & assigns for ever, the following named real
estate & other property & effects, to wit, all the lands of the
said Willie P. Mangum lying & being in Orange aforesaid North
Carolina, on both sides of Dials Creek & Dry Creek consisting of
the W^m. P. Mangum old tract, the Sehon [Sion] Bobbitt tract,
the new entry, & one third of the lands on said Creek situate,
of which Arthur Mangum Senr died seized & possessed in all
consisting of about Sixteen hundred acres. (1600 acres) Also
four lots situate within the corporation limits of the Town of
Hillsborough known & designated in the plan of said Town as
the Numbers (147, & 148. & 149. & 175). Also one half of the
one fifth part of the tract of land lying in Chatham County in
the fork of Haw & Deep Rivers, upon which the new Town of
Haywood is situate, and the half of one fifth of Seven lots in
the old Town of Haywood. The same being one half of the interest conveyed by Arch^d. Haralson to said Mangum & W^m. M.
Sneed of Granville County, a more accurate description of which
can be had by reference to the Deed of s^d Haralson to said Mangum & Sneed.—Also the following Negro Slaves, to wit Jim a
negro man—27 years old—Orange a man 24 years old George
28 years old—Isham 18 years old—Frank 14 years old Madison
13 years old, Ben 7 years old, Harrison, Alfred, Winney, Sarah
Polly - Maria - Letty - Ellen - & Minerva - also a [torn]
The said Mangum's stock of horses consisting of Nine head except one—also all his stock of Cattle, & hogs, also all his farming utensils pt of Blacksmith's tools—a Waggon. A yoke of oxen
& cart. 1 Gig—1 Sulkey & harness. Also all his Corn supposed
to be 150 Barrels. All his oats & fodder. All his Bacon, & all
his household & kitchen furniture except one bed & furniture—
To Have & to hold the said Lands & other property to the said
Webb & Watts their heirs Ex^{rs}. &c forever. The said Mangum
however expressly reserving the use of the Dwelling house in
which he now lives for 8 Months. But notwithstanding the said
Webb & Watts to Have & to Hold the aforementioned land &
other property, upon the conditions & to the uses & trusts herein after expressed, indicated & set forth.—
    The said Mangum having become largely indebted, & being
desirous, as he hopes & believes that he is able, to pay off & dis-

charge all his just debts—This conveyance is made to the said
Webb & Watts with the view & for the purpose that they or
either of them shall & may dispose of the said estate in whatever
manner to them in their discretion they may think fit, for the
purpose of paying the debts of the said Mangum in the manner
& in the order herein after set forth. That is to say—The said
Trustees are first to discharge all executions that now exist
against the said Willie P. Mangum; & especially an execution at
the Instance of the State Bank of No. Ca. against him upon a
debt for which Duncan Cameron is endorser, & this conveyance
to be subject to a conveyance heretofore made to said Duncan
Cameron's benefit to indemnify him against the consequences of
said endorsement. After the discharge of the execution & judg^t.
debts. The next debt that the trustees are to discharge is a debt
due from s^d Mangum to Thomas Alston[18] of Wake for loaned
money, & after the s^d debt to Alston, then to pay all the creditors of said Mangum. The s^d Mangum expecting to change a
part of his debt at Bank. The balance of the debt due from him
to others, are to be paid out of this fund first, and the residue
of the fund if any, is to be applied to discharge the am^t of debt
that s^d Mangum may incur by reason of the changing of any
amount of his debt at Bank.

The said parties have hereby agreed that the Trustees are to
be fully & fairly paid for their trouble &c in executing the
Trusts of this Deed, & if any surplus remains after discharging
all the Trusts & costs of this Deed, the same is to be paid to
W. P. Mangum his Ex^{rs}. &c.

In Testimony Whereof we have hereunto set our hands &
seals this 25th- April 1828.

Test
Wm Moore Jurist

> WILLIE P. MANGUM
> JAMES WEBB
> THO^s D. WATTS
> Orange County May Term 1828.

The execution of the foregoing Deed was duly proved in open
Court by the oath of William Moore and subscribing Witness
thereto & ordered to be registered

[18]Thomas Alston, 1781-1850, was a man of much wealth. In 1808 he represented Franklin
County in the legislature. Grove, *Alstons of N. & S. C.*, 310, 311. See above, pp. 36-37.

Test
J. TAYLOR   C Cl

Registers Office)
)
Orange County)

10th. June 1828. The within Deed
was duly registered in Book U at
Hillsborough
J. Mc. Kirall P. R.
By G. W. Bruce

Willie P. Mangum
)
To (Deed *in Trust.*
)
James Webb
Tho. D. Watts

Registered

North Carolina—
I Thomas Ruffin, one of the Judges of the Superior Courts of
Law & Equity do testify, that before me this 19th. day of July
1828 at Orange County the execution of the within Deed by all
the parties therto was duly proved by the oath of William Moore,
the subscribing witness thereto—Let it be registered—

THOMAS RUFFIN

Registers office   )
(August the 14th. A.D. 1828
Chatham county)

The Within Deed was duly Registered Book A. B. pages 44 & 45.

A. GUNTER Regr.

Robert Cozart vs. Willie P. Mangum and Walter A. Mangum[19]

[26 April, 1828]

STATE OF NORTH CAROLINA,) To any lawful officer to
Orange County   ) execute and return with-
) in Three Months.
YOU are commanded that of the goods and chattels of Willie P.

---

[19]The original is in the James Webb Papers, University of North Carolina.

Mangum & Walter A. Mangum—if to be found in your county, you cause to be made the sum of Sixty Seven dollars which Robt. Cozart lately recovered against them before me one of the Justices of the Peace for said county, at the house of .... on the 19th. day of Jany. last, for his debt, with interest from the 25th day of Decemb. 1827 and eight shillings for costs, whereof the said Willie & Walter A. is convicted, and if you cannot find any of the goods and chattles of the said Willie & Walter A. in this county, you are to levy this execution on their lands and tenements, and make due return thereof. Given under my hand and seal this 26th. day of April 1828.

JNO. J. CARRINGTON J. P. (Seal)
Debt $67
Intest 1.67
Cost 1.20
_____
$69.87

[Endorsed:]

Recd of James Webb Trustee
Sixty Nine Doll 87/100
May 26 1828

H. Parrish Court [?]
Robt. Cozart
vs.
Willie P. Mangum
& Walter A. Mangum

WPM-LC

Willis Alston to Willie P. Mangum

WASHINGTON May 7th 1828

My Dear Sr
Yours with one for Mr Goodrich[20] was yesterday handed to me I accidentally saw him soon after & gave it him he seemed perfectly well satisfied for you to do as to you seems best

If the friends (in N. C.) of the administration take steps other than are set as an example here for them, they indeed outrage

_____
[20]See above, p. 325.

any thing before heard of False statements misrepresentation and mutulated documents are the order of the day But all will not do New York is safe to the back bone Her sons here say every thing is going on well at home In fact you may see from countenances that the enemy are beaten—

The Tariff question not yet finally acted upon in the senate I fear we shall be beaten finally and that some further additions will be made on the imports

Our course however is clear, self defence, raise our Horses, mules & Pork, spin & weave at home buy nothing from these Tariff Gentlemen, that can be dispensed with, we can live as cheaply as they can, Let us take pride in what we can make & raise within ourselves and not in what we buy,

We have nothing here other than the papers convey [?] give my best respects to my old friend Cain if yet alive, My health is bad, I shall try to visit the up country this summer, Chatham and the university particularly, and perhaps quite to Tenessee, I have land there that wants looking to

I am your friend

WILLIS ALSTON

[Addressed:]

Honble
Willie P Mangum
Red Mountain
Orange County
N. C.

---

*Attachment[21] of Thomas Clancy against goods of
Willie P. Mangum for John Wilson*

[17 May, 1828]

STATE OF NORTH CAROLINA) To any lawful Officer to
(execute and return Within
Orange   County   ) Three Months.

YOU are commanded that of the goods and chattels of Wille P. Mangum if to be found in your county, you cause to be made the sum of Twenty six Dollars and forty cents which John Wilson lately recovered against Him before Thos. Clancy one of the Jus-

---

[21]The original is in the James Webb Papers.

tices of the Peace for said county, at the house of....on the 2 day
of February last, for his debt, with interest from the 2 day of
Decemb 1827 and 4/. shillings for costs, whereof the said chattels
of the said Defendant in this county, you are to levy this execution on His lands and tenements, and make due return thereof.
Given under my hand and seal this 17 day of May 1828

THOS. CLANCY J. P. (Seal.)

[Endorsed:]
$27.95 Re^d of James Webb & Thos. D. Watts trustees of W^m P.
Mangum twenty seven dollars 95/100 May 28. 1828

M. Adams & C

```
                    )
John  Wilson  Fi  (  Fa    Wille P. Mangum      $27.95
                    )
```

WPM-LC

Th. J. Green[22] to W. P. Mangum

WARREN May 24th 1828.

Dear Sir:
If you could have a desire to return to the federal city in a
higher character than when you left it, *go* to our next legislature
a Member. A word to the wise is sufficient.
No one knows *these* thoughts. Delicacy forbids me now to say
more; but at a time more propitious to a proper construction of
my *motive* I will explain—
I am your devoted friend
& hm^l. Sev^t..

TH: JEF: GREEN

To Willie P. Mangum, esqr.

[Postmarked:] Ellisville, N. C.

[Addressed:]
Willie. P. Mangum; esqr.
Hillsborough.
N. C.

-----

[22]General Thomas Jefferson Green, 1801-1863, represented Warren County in the state legislature in 1826. He moved to Florida and then to Texas where he became a brigadier general in the Texan Revolution. He held Santa Anna as a prisoner and, in turn, was captured
by the Mexicans. He went to California in the 1849 gold rush. Ashe, *Biog. Hist. of N. C.*,
II, 114-120.

Award²³ between W. P. Mangum and W. A. Mangum

[27 May 1828]

Whereas Willie P. Mangum & Walter A. Mangum have re-ferred their several accounts to the subscribers for final Settle-ment and having examined the several charges vouchers & alle-gation do award that Willie P. Mangum shall Execute a Bond to Walter A. Mangum for one Hundred & Sixty-five Dollars which shall be a full & final settlement of all debts dues demands, Judg-ments & Executions

Given under our hands and seals this 27. day of May 1828

JAMES WEBB   Seal
P. H. MANGUM   Seal

[Endorsed:]   Award between
W. P. Mangum
&
W. A. Mangum

Notes and Receipts of Willie P. Mangum²⁴

$165 One day after date I promise to pay W. A. Mangum or order one Hundred & Sixty five Dollars the amount of an award this day made in Persuence of a Submission of a all matter of account & demand between them
May 27. 1828

$165   *Willie P. Mangum*

Reᵈ of James Webb & Thˢ D. Watts trustees Sixty Nine Doll 02/100 the amount of an Execution R. D. Bumhass or W. P. Mangum   May 27. 1828

69.02   *E. G. Mangum Ct.²⁵*

Recᵈ. of Willie P. Mangum at the hands of James Webb & Thoˢ. D. Watts jointly as Trustees Two Hundred Seventy Dollars Thir-ty three Cents in full Three Fi. Fa

GANARD & SHAW

270.33 $270.33/100   May 27. 1828

---

²³The original is in the Webb Papers.
²⁴The originals are in the Webb Papers.
²⁵Ellison G. Mangum was Willie P. Mangum's first cousin. His son, Addison W. Mangum, became a professor at the state university. Ashe, *Biog. Hist. of N. C.*, V. 238.

R^d of James Webb & Ths. D. Watts trustees twelve Doll 79/100 the amount of an ex. J J Carrington or Willie P. Mangum

May 27. 1828   E. G. MANGUM   Ct.

12.79

$40.80   Rec^d of James Webb Trustee of Wm P. Mangum forty Doll 80/100 Jim's Prison fees
                   May 28. 1828

                                        JAMES CLANCY   Jalor

May 28th 1828
Receve of Doct Jams Webb Two Dollare in full of my Serves for Crying W. P. Mangums Negro^s

                          Wm NELSON

Rec^d James Webb & Ths. D. Watts trustees & of Wm P. Mangum fifteen Doll 23/100
an Execution N. H. Horton or J. R. Sneed
May 28. 1828
$15.23   Wm NELSON   C

Attachment[26] against the property of Willie P. Mangum
for L. & Thos. V. Hargis

                                        [28 May, 1828]
STATE OF NORTH CAROLINA)   To any Lawful Officer to
)
Orange county   )   execute and return with-
                             in Three Months.
YOU are commanded that of the goods and chattles of Willie P. Mangum if to be found in your county, you cause to be made the sum of Forty Dollars & Seventy nine cents which L & Thos V. Hargis lately recovered against him before Andrew Watson one of the Justices of the Peace for said County, on the 16 day of July last, for his debt, with interest from the 22nd. day of March 1827 and 4/. shillings for costs, whereof the said is convicted, and if you cannot find any of the goods and chattles of the said W. P. Mangum in this county, you are to levy this execution on

---

[26]The original is in the James Webb Papers.

his lands and tenements, and make due return thereof. Given under my hand and seal this 28th. day of Apl. 1828.

J. P. WOMACK   J. P.   (Seal.)

$44.34 Red of James Webb & Ths. D. Watts trustee of Wm P. Mangum forty four Doll 34/100 May 28. 1828

M. Adams & C

)
Larune & L V Hargis   Fi   (　Wm P. Mangum   Lend the
) Fa
20th March on the old Execution

M. A. & c.

$43.54
　80

──────

$44.34
27.95

──────

73.29

Due this day 3

May 1828

M. Adams

$44.34
27.95

──────

$72.29 Due

$43.54
29.95

──────

$72,49

Lend 20th—March 1828

──────

Judgments[27] against Willie P. Mangum and Walter A. Mangum

State Bank) Ex[n]. to Febr. 1828
)
vs) Judgment $8.50
) with Int
Walter A, Mangum) Office cost 10.02½
& others)

Bank of Cape Fear) Ex[n]. May 1828
)
vs) Judgment .... $210.
) with Int from 15—June
Willie P. & P. H.) 1826 24.68
) Office cost 8.90
Mangum)
) Shffs coms. 7.35

250.93

The Same) Judgment .... $250.
vs) Int. from 26th Febr. 33.75
) 1826
) Office Cost 10.90
Willie P. Mangum) Shffs Coms. 8.59
& others)
) 303.24

J. P. Sneed & Co) Judgment $131.96
) Interest from 3d March 9.90
vs) 1826
) Office Cost 8.02½
Willie P. Mangum) Shffs coms. ....

Extract from Records—

J. Taylor C C

Robert Dickins	)	Judgmt Sept 1828 Ex N° 28
	)	Judgment ....$ 85.70
vs	)	Costs 19.93½
	)	————
Walter A. Mangum	)	115.63

(Endorsement)

W. P. Mangum
Trustees

————

WPM-LC

W. H. Haywood, Jr., to Willie P. Mangum

[RALEIGH, June 7, 1828]

Dear Sir

I enclose you Mr. Thornton's[28] letters to me and on one of them a note of introduction to him.

I have neither time to write or news to tell you, but I hope your trip to the West may prove both pleasant and profitable to you— and upon your return I shall expect the pleasure of a long account of it from you—

The Central Jackson Committee have in *press* a publication of "Militia Documents"[29] accompanied with a pretty *spicey* introduction of 15 or 16 pages—Badger is engaged under *orders* in writing an *address to the people of North Caro: upon* the presidential election[30]—He regards his reputation as being in some degree staked in the character of the production & we have great

---

[28]Probably Francis A. Thornton who was in the legislature from Wake County in 1821 and 1822 and from 1848 to 1850. *N. C. Manual*, 837-838.

[29]In the spring of 1814 Governor Blount of Tennessee called out 1000 drafted militiamen for garrison duty in the Creek War. They were to serve for six months. Hard work was used to fortify the forts. Dog days and the Coosa fever added to the troubles. At Fort Jackson about 200 of the Tennessee militia mutinied and Andrew Jackson ordered a court martial. Six were shot in Jackson's absence, although he later approved the action. See *The Case of the Six Militia Men Fairly Stated, with an appendix of Public Documents and other Papers, in which the imputations cast upon General Jackson respecting that transaction are shown to be illiberal and unfounded columnies, published by order of the Central Jackson Committee, an address to the Freemen of North Carolina.* (Raleigh, 1828), 47 pp.

[30]George E. Badger wrote the pamphlet, *Address to the Freemen of North Carolina: Electoral Ticket of North Carolina, for President, Andrew Jackson, for Vice-President, John C. Calhoun.* (Raleigh, 1828), 16 pp. See also Lawrence F. London, The Public Career of George Edmund Badger (Ph.D. Thesis at the University of North Carolina, Chapel Hill, N. C., 1937, Typescript), 13-16, 17.

reason therefore to expect *his best*—which of course must be *very good*

I am with great respect & esteem
Your friend

WILL H. HAYWOOD JR

Raleigh 7 June 1828.

[Addressed:]

Willie P. Mangum Esq
Hillsborough
N. C.

Wm. Cain, Jr., to Duncan Cameron[31]

HILLSBORO. 12th June 1828—

Dear Sir

Upon enquiries from my Father I find he is bound for Mr. Mangum for the following sums with me To the State for 2500 dollars & the Newbern Bank for 500 dolllars, these notes Mr. Watts who carried them to Raleigh informs me are made payable 88 days after the 30th May last & I believe are dated about or on the 25 April last past—

As you were making some enquiries about the Sales of the Negroes I inform you the whole were sold for some few dollars over the sum of Thirty three Hundred & ninety Dollars; Those which my father gave him & the increase sold for $2075—
Your friend

Wm CAIN JR.

P. S—Suppose you were merely suggest to my Father to place Mr. Priestly H. Mangum in my place in the business. We were talking of. I leave the propriety of the measure of it to yourself.

Wm CAIN JR.

---

[31]The original is in the Cameron Papers, University of North Carolina.

Wm. Cain, Jr., to Duncan Cameron[32]

PLEASANT GROVE July 3rd 1828

Dear Sir

My father desires me to write to you & begs that you will come up & do the business he is very desirious of having done; he thinks his health is on the decline & I believe the strong interest he feels in that business makes him low spirited & much worse than he otherwise would be—

Permit me to explain to you one observation to you, which I made use of when I saw you last, that is, That I would have no hand in securing the money whcrein my father & myself gave our notes for $3000 to the state & Newbern Bank—When I offered that act of Kindness to M[r]. Mangum in my fathers & my own name it was intended as a pure act of Kindness & with the hopes & expectation (relying wholly on his honor) That I believed he would by his attention to business soon be enabled to pay the money from his profession. Now allow me to say that, if I was concerned either directly or indirectly in securing myself in that way he might & perhaps would say that all my pretended Kindness towards him and his family proceeded from interested motives[33] & that I might be & was instrumental in prevailing on my father to make his will in the way you were speaking of & further, that it was concluded by us before this offer of Kindness was made—I thought relying on his honor might make him use exertions, where all other things would fail—I hope you understand me—Hoping you will come to see my my [sic] father as soon as convenient.

I subscribe myself in haste
Your friend—

W[m]. CAIN JR.

WPM-LC

Henry Pranham[34] *et als. to Wiley Mangham*

EATONTON GEO 14th July 1828.

Sir,

At a meeting of the citizens of Putnam County held in this place, on friday the 11th Inst. for the purpose of taking into

---

[32]The original is in the Cameron Papers, University of North Carolina.
[33]Later Mangum and his wife, Charity Cain, felt that William Cain, Sr., in his will left too much of the property to Mary Cain.
[34]Dr. Henry Branham. See Stephen F. Miller, *The Bench and Bar of Georgia Memoirs and Sketches* . . . 2 vols. (Philadelphia, Pa.: Lippincott, 1858), I, 188.

consideration the Tariff act[35] passed by the last Session of Congress, and of adopting measures to counteract as far as possible its pernicious & oppressive operation upon the Southern States, the undersigned were appointed a committee to corrispond with our distinguished and enlightened fellow citizens both in & out of the State with a view to the acquisition of all the information practicable in relation to the means best calculated to accomplish the object of the meeting.

Another meeting is to be held by the citizens of this County on the second tuesday in August at which time we are to make known the result of our corrispondence. We do not purpose now to discuss the various principles involved in the Tariff act. Suffice it to say that in our opinion all constitutional barriers have been overleaped & all considerations of common justice disregarded and outraged by its advocates.—We find ourselves placed in this awful dilemma, either to submit patiently to the operations of this act, or to resist or counteract its influence. *Submission* will add greatly to the distress and embarrassment under which the people of the South already labour, and will go very far toward completing our ruin.—If we resort to *resistance* and attempt to redress our wrongs, we are Surrounded with difficulties of the most embarrassing and perplexing character. As far as we know the feelings and intentions of the people *Submission* is out of the question. and the main question now to be settled is, as to the mode or manner of resistance. This is a Subject vitally interesting to the people of each one of the Southern States, and to make our resistance effectual, it will at once be seen how important it is, that we should determine upon & prosecute to the last extremity the same policy & measures, and by no means to suffer discord or confusion to mingle in our deliberations. Our resistance should be temperate, deep, solemn, firm, uniform, & universal. The citizens of this county as well as ourselves, repose, great confidence in your prudence, wisdom & experience in the various questions involved; we therefore take the liberty respectfully to invite your attention to this matter & to request that you will favor us with your opinion as to the course which ought to be pursued in counteracting or resisting the act in question, and particularly your opinion is respectfully requested upon the questions—whether the Legislatures of the different States have the right or power by law to impose a tax

---

[35]This was the so-called "Tariff of Abomination."

upon all horses, mules, hogs, cotton bagging of American manufacture &c. introduced into any State for sale or barter? Wheter
if this power exists, it is at all probable that such a law would in
its operation tend to a repeal of the Tariff? if it would—are
there any other articles of American manufacture which ought
to be included in such law? & what are they? We also respectfully request your advice & opinion as to the power, propriety
of good policy of the several Southern States taking any, and if
any, what steps to prevent or embarrass the collection of duties
in our ports under the late Tariff act? And any other suggestions in reference to this matter of so high concernment, which
you may consider material, we should be glad to receive.—

We are apprised that you will have but little time to bestow
upon the subject of this communication, if you answer it in time
to enable us to lay it before the meeting of our citizens in
August; but we earnestly hope you will neverthelss bestow upon
it, all the attention in your power.—It is also desirable that we
should know as far as you have the means of informing us,
what course will probably be pursued by the people or Legislature of your State in relation to the matter under consideration,—

Respectfully, yours
obnt. Servts.
Henry Pranham
Eli S. Shorter
Irby Hudson   Corrisponding
Alford Clopton   Committee
Mark A. Cooper

[Addressed:]
    Genl. Wiley Mangham
        Hillsboro,
            North Carolina.

—————

WPM-LC

John H. Green[36] *to Willie P. Mangum*

WARREN COUNTY, 21st July, 1828.

Dear Sir:

It is my opinion, from what I have heard, that if you are a

—————

[36]John H. Green was a member of the House of Commons from Warren County in 1829.
N. C. Manual, 837.

Candidate for the Office of Attorney-General, which is at present
vacant and also pretty profitable, that you will succeed in obtaining the appointment both from the Executive Council and
the Legislature, and it is also my opinion that your appointment
would be a popular one in this Circuit.—The Executive Council
is to be convened on the 30th Inst.

I am, very respectfully

JNO. H. GREEN

Willie P. Mangum, Esq.
    Hillsborough

[Addressed:]

Willie P. Mangum, Esq.
    Hillsborough
    North - Carolina.

The Post Master is
requested to send this
to Judge Mangum immediately.

Priestley H. Mangum to Archibald D. Murphey[37]

RALEIGH, July 22nd, 1828.

My Dear Sir:

I have not heard from you about your health since Orange
Court when it was bad—and I much fear, that you are now in
bed. I hope in God, it is not so.—At this time, being roused to
look around me for friends, I have gladly and confidently turned
my thoughts to you.—

On the 30th Inst. the Council of State will convene at Raleigh
to make a *temporary* appointment of an Atto: Genl: I have requested the Gov. to submit my name. Being very [only] partially acquainted with any of the council, except Washington
Jeffreys, I am anxious that the members might receive more
knowledge of me than they probably have.

If your health will permit and the return mail would be in
time—I would be glad that you would write to such of the Council as you might deem expedient.

Were you to write to Raleigh "to the care of Jno. L. Hender-

[37]The original is in the Archibald D. Murphey Papers, State Department of Archives and History, Raleigh, N. C.

son."[38] Mr. Henderson would take them out of the office & deliver them.

All that I could ask of my friends, would be, to say what they know & believe of my character, & qualifications for the office to be filled. You know that I have been at the Bar more than ten years, & the greater part of that time, engaged in prosecuting for the state.

Your friend

P. H. MANGUM

[Addressed:]   Archibald D. Murphy
Murphy's Mills
Orange County   [Endorsed:]
N.C.   Priestley H. Mangum
22 July 1828

WPM-LC

[OXFORD, N. C. 10 August, 1828]

UNION TAVERN.

Mr. Willie P. Mangum

To Parker F. Stone Dr.

To 6 Days' Board, per self			4.50
— Breakfast	-	-	
— Dinner	-	-	
— Supper	-	-	
— Lodging			
— Children			
— 6 Night for Horse	-		4.50
— Feed for Ditto			
— Servants' Bill			
To Sundries at the Bar			25
			$9.25

Receiv'd Payment

PARK F. STONE.

Oxford, N. C. Augt. 10, 1828.

---

[38]John L. Henderson, 1778-1843, a frequent member of the legislature from Salisbury, became the State's comptroller in 1827. He was the brother of Archibald and Judge Leonard Henderson. Grant, *Alumni Hist. of U. N. C.*, 273.

WPM-LC

M. A. Patrick to Willie P. Mangum

HILLSBORO' N. Carolina.
September 13th 1828.

Dear Sir,

With my thanks, I beg you to accept the enclosed, as a partial compensation for the trouble you have given yourself in procuring the acquittal of my men—*King, Morris and Griffin,* from the punishment which appeared to hang over them. I need hardly say that the affair gave me no little anxiety. If my means corresponded with my feelings, the note should have been much larger.

I have the honor to be, Sir,
With sincere respect & esteem
Your Most Obdt. Servt.

M. A. PATRICK
Lt. 1st Regt. U. S. Artly.

To the Hon: Mangum
Hillsboro
N. C

[Addressed:]
For/
The Hon: W. P. Mangum
Hillsboro'
N. C.

———

WPM-LC

*Sheriff's Certification of results of Presidential election
in Orange County*

State of North Carolina)
)
Orange County)

[14 Nov., 1828]

I Thomas. D. Watts Sheriff of the County aforesaid do hereby certify that an Election was held on thursday the thirteenth day of November in the year of our Lord one Thousand Eight

Hundred & Twenty eight (1828) and at the places Fixed by
Law Within the said County for that purpose, and that the
Number of Votes herein specified opposit the Names of the sev-
eral persons following was given by Voters Qualified to Vote
for this purpose for such persons as Electors for the State of
North Carolina—of President and Vice President of the United
States—

Namely For Robert Love[39]   one Thousand & fifty Sevin Votes . . . 1057
"   "   Montford Stokes   one Thousand & fifty|Sevin Votes . . . 1057
"   "   Peter Forney   one Thousand & fifty Sevin Votes . . . 1057
"   "   John Giles   one Thousand & fifty Sevin Votes . . . 1057
"   "   John M. Morhead   one Thousand & fifty Sevin Votes . . . 1057
"   "   Walter F Leak   one Thousand & fifty Seven Votes . . . 1057
"   "   Willie P Mangum   one Thousand & fifty Seven Votes . . . 1057
"   "   Josiah Crudup   one Thousand & fifty Sevin Votes . . . 1057
"   "   John Hall   one Thousand & fifty Sevin Votes . . . 1057
"   "   Joseph J Williams one Thousand & fifty Seven Votes . . . 1057
"   "   Kedar Ballard   one Thousand & fifty Sevin Votes . . . 1057
"   "   Louis. D. Wilson one Thousand & fifty Seven Votes . . . 1057
"   "   Richard.D.Spaight one Thousand & fifty Seven Votes . . . 1057
"   "   Edward.B.Dudley   one Thousand & fifty Seven Votes . . . 1057

For Isaac. T. Avery   Four Hundred & forty Votes . . . 440
"   Abner Franklin   Four Hundred & forty Votes . . . 440
"   Robert. H. Burton   Four Hundred & forty Votes . . . 440
"   Edmund Deberry   Four Hundred & forty Votes . . . 440
"   James T Morhead   Four Hundred & forty Votes . . . 440
"   Alexander Gray   Four Hundred & forty Votes . . . 440
"   Benjamin Robinson   Four Hundred & forty Votes . . . 440
"   James. S. Smith Four Hundred & Thirty nine Votes . . . 439
"   William Hinton   Four Hundred & forty Votes . . . 440
"   Edward Hall   Four Hundred & forty Votes . . . 440
"   Samuel Hyman   Four Hundred & forty Votes . . . 440
"   Isaac N Lamb   Four Hundred & forty Votes . . . 440
"   William Clark   Four Hundred & forty Votes . . . 440
"   William. S. Blackledge Four Hundred & forty Votes . . . 440
"   Daniel L Kenan   Four Hundred & forty Votes . . . 440
"   William A Graham   one Votes 1

Given under my hand & seal this 14th day of November 1828

THOˢ. D. WATTS Shff (Seal)

[Addressed:]
         Willie. P. Mangum esqr
                Raleigh
                   No Carolina

---

[39]This was the Andrew Jackson ticket.

WPM-LC

Sheriff's Certification of results of Presidential election in Granville County

[18 Nov., 1828]

I Nathaniel Robards Sheriff of Granville County do hereby certifiy that an Election was held on Thursday the Thirteenth day of November A. D. 1828 at the places fixed by Law within said County for this purpose and that the number of votes herein specified opposite the names of the several persons following was given by voters qualified to vote for this purpose—for such persons as Electors for the State of North Carolina of President and Vice President of the United States namely

for Robert Love Eight Hundred & forty two votes
for Peter Forney Eight Hundred & forty two votes
for John Giles Eight Hundred & forty two votes
for Abraham Phillips Eight Hundrd & forty two votes
for John M. Morehead eight Hundred and forty two votes
for Walter F Leak Eight Hundred & forty two votes
for Willie P. Mangum Eight Hundred & forty two votes
for Josiah Crudup Eight Hundred & forty two votes
for John Hall Eight Hundred & forty two votes
for Joseph J. Williams Eight Hundred & forty two votes
for Kedar Bullard [*sic*] Eight Hundred & forty two votes
for Lewis D Wilson Eight Hundred and forty two votes
for Richard D Spaight Eight Hundred & forty two votes
for Montford Stokes Eight Hundred & forty two votes
for Edmund B Dudley Eight Hundred & forty two votes
for Isaac T. Avery one Hundred & sixty two votes
for Abner Franklin one Hundred & Sixty two votes
for Robert H Burton one Hundred & Sixty two votes
for Edmund Deberry one Hundred & Sixty two votes
for James T. Morehead one Hundred & Sixty two votes
for Alexander Gray one Hundred & Sixty two votes
for Benjamin Roberts one Hundred & Sixty two votes
for James S Smith one Hundred & Sixty two votes
for William Hinton Senr. one Hundred & Sixty two votes
for Edward Hall one Hundred & Sixty two votes.
for Samuel Hyman one Hundred & Sixty two votes
for Isaac N Lamb one Hundred & Sixty two votes
for William Clark one Hundred & Sixty two votes

for William S. Blackledge one Hundred & Sixty two votes
for Daniel L. Kenan one Hundred & Sixty two votes

Given under my hand this Eighteenth day of November in the
year of Our Lord Eighteen Hundred & Twenty eight.—

NATHI. ROBARDS Shff
of Granville County

WPM-LC

J. M. Henderson⁴⁰ et als. to Rev. Josiah Crudup

RALEIGH Novr 16th 1828

Dr Sir

We have learnt from Thomas D Watts Esqr of Hillsboro' that
he desires the appointment of carrying the Electoral vote of
North Carolina to Washington City. You know Mr Watts personally, we presume, and therefore we deem it unnecessary to
enlarge upon his promptness, caution and great fidelity in the
discharge of any public trust committed to his charge

He has been amongst the most efficient friends of Gen¹ Jackson. This added to his well known fitness for the appointment
induce us to recommend him to your particular regard & shall
consider it no small personal favor to ourselves can you favor
his pretensions

JA^s. M. HENDERSON
HUDSON M CAVE
Wm D. MURPHEY
JOSIAH TURER [TURNER]

[Addressed:]

Rev Josiah Crudup

WPM-LC

Thos. D. Watts to Rev. Josiah Crudup

RALEIGH 17th Novr 1828

Sir

I have thought proper to drop you this line to say to you that
owing to business that will require my attention at Washington

---

⁴⁰James M. Henderson was a physician of Wake County. McIver, *N. C. Register*, 58.

City—I have thought fit to ask at the hands of the Elec [tors] to git the appointment to Carry [the] votes My Friend W. P. Mangum will hand this to you & if you can feel a Willingness to aid me this Favour will be remembered

Yours respectfully

THOS. D. WATTS

[Addressed:]   Rev. Josiah Crudup

WPM-LC

Rufus A. Yancey⁴¹ to Willie P. Mangum

CHAPEL HILL Nov^br 20th 1828

Sir

As the presiding officer of the Dialectic Society I am empowered to inform you that on the 6th of the present month the Society resolved that, if consistent with your pleasure, you should appear as our *Orator* on the day preceding our next annual Commencement. Permit me to add, as I have long admired your talents, and considered you as an ornament to your native Carolina—, that I am extremely happy to be the organ of the present communication—If convenient please inform us *shortly* whether you accept the appointment.

respectfully

RUFUS A. YANCEY—

[Addressed:]

Hon
Willie P. Mangum
Raleigh
No C

Mail
the P. M. will please deliver this immediately
or if Mr M. is absent forward it to him—

---

⁴¹Rufus A. Yancey, son of Bartlett Yancey, graduated from the University in 1828. Hamilton, *Papers of Ruffin*, I, 528n.

WPM-LC

D. Turner[42] to Willie P. Mangum

WARREN COUNTY Nov[r] 25th 1828

Sir

Permit me to introduce to your acquaintance Mr Wm Collins[43] of Warren County. Mr. C—has some idea of offering his services to the Electoral College as Messenger—should it not interfere with a previous determination, you will find him worthy your support.

Yr obdt. Servt.

D. TURNER.

[Addressed:]

Wiilie P. Mangum Esq
   Raleigh
     N Carolina

Mr Collins)

WPM-LC

W. K. Ruffin to Willie P. Mangum

CHAPEL HILL Decm. 1st 1828—

My Dear Sir—

It has been some time since I wrote to you. I have nevertheless always remembered the debt of gratitude I owed you for your kind offices to me when you were my only friend in a land of strangers[44]—This debt I shall in after time endeavor to the best of my power to repay—I am sensible of the great obligations I am under, and am sorry that can only manifest my gratitude by words. I know you have been a good friend, and perhaps you will have occasion one day to observe that I am not insensible to benefits you have conferred on me—Since you have done so much for me, and have always manifested so much friendship for me—I take the liberty of writing this letter to you by way of an introduction to my fellow-student F. L.

[42]Daniel Turner, 1796-1860, after attending the U. S. Military Academy fought in the War of 1812. He served in Congress as a Democrat from 1827 to 1829. He moved to California in the 1850's. *Biog. Dir. of Cong.*, 1631.
[43]He was the comptroller of the state from 1836 to 1851. *N. C. Manual*, 443.
[44]See above, pp. 277-278.

Smith[45]—He is desirous of visiting Washington this Winter, and not being in the best circumstances, would be glad to be the bearer of the electoral votes—Being an elector, you can render a service to this young man for which he will be very much obligated to you—I have great esteem for Mr Smith; an esteem founded not only upon the many good offices he has conferred on me, but on the exalted integrity of his *heart* and the singular modesty with which all his virtues are accompanied—Let me therefore earnestly entreat you to confer this favour on him— You will find him, be assured a man of a most generous and well natured disposition—And the honor with which you shall distinguish this my friend, will not only indissolubly unite to you an excellent and grateful young man, but at the same time confer a very singular obligation upon myself—

We are all here astonished why you do not answer a letter written to you by Mr R. Yancey, Pres. of the D. S. in which you received the appointment of our next orator—it is the greatest honor we can bestow and we all hope that you will accept of it— Mr. Smith nominated you, and there were but three dissenting votes—

Smith leaves here shortly—a letter from you would be received with the greatest pleasure and at the same time be thought a great honor.

by Your obd. Servant

W. K. RUFFIN.

Hon. Willie P. Mangum

[Addressed:]

Hon[ble].
    Willie P Mangum
      Raleigh
        N. Ca.

Mr. F. L. Smith)

---

[45]Franklin Lafayette Smith of Mecklenburg County who received his A. B. degree from the state university in 1829 was an exceptionally good student. He settled in Charlotte where he practiced law until his death in 1835. Battle, *Hist. of U. N. C.*, I, 323.

WPM-LC

B. B. Blume⁴⁶ to W. P. Mangum

JACKSON, December 1ˢᵗ. 1828

Willie P. Mangum Esq.—

I take great pleasure in presenting to your particular, my friend Mr. Shirley Tisdale of Northampton—Mr. T. is desirous of being intrusted with the Electoral vote of this State—So far as I am competent to judge of the matter, I should say that no man is better qualified to discharge the duty—His attachment to the cause of the people has not been surpassed by any person of my acquaintance, in continuance or zeal. It would afford Mr. T. a great pleasure to receive the confidence of those Electors, for whose promotion he has labored much and successfully.

With sentiments of much respect
Your obt. Sᵗ.

BEN B. BLUME

[Addressed:]

To the Honl. Willie P. Mangum
Raleigh
N. C.

By S. Tisdale Esq)

———

WPM-LC

N. J. Drake⁴⁷ to Willie P. Mangum

NASHVILLE N. Ca. Decr. 1ˢᵗ: 1828.

Dear Sir,

Permit me to introduce to your acquaintance my friend Majr. Wm. F. Collins.

Major Collins visits Raleigh with the hope of obtaining the appointment to bear the electoral vote of N°. Ca to Washington City.—.In behalf of Major Collins I take the liberty to assure you, that to an elegant person uniting all the accomplishments of a gentleman, being a distinguished pupil of Capt. Patridge &

---

⁴⁶Benjamin Byrum Blume, a student at the University in 1824, became a lawyer and settled for a while in Stokes County. Later he moved to Memphis. Grant, *Alumni Hist. of U. N. C.*, 56.

⁴⁷Nicholas J. Drake, a physician from Nash County, was in the legislature in 1824-1825 and in 1827. *N. C. Manual*, 717.

the early & devoted Friend of Genl. Jackson, he is eminently fitted to be the bearer of such despatches—.

In haste—very respectfully yrs etc—

N. J. DRAKE

Willie P. Mangum Esq.

[Addressed:]

The Hon: Willie P. Mangum
            Raleigh
                  N. C.

Fav' by
Maj. Collins.

WPM-LC

F. Nash[48] to W. P. Mangum

RALEIGH the 17th Dec[r]. [1828]

D[r]. Sir

Your favor of the 13th inst. has been duly received—I have not been concerned in the case of Garrards will, that I recollect of, & will appear in behalf of the widow, your client—The issue I presume was made up last court — & will stand for tryal at February Term—The books you mentioned, Stockie & Maddox, shall be purchased for you as you request—the sale takes place on Saturday next—Accept my congratulations upon the attainment of your wishes—May all your hopes be realised

We are literally doing nothing—you have heard of my defeat —yesterday the house killed Swains consolidation Bill[49] after an animated & too warm discussion—considerable personality took place, be Messrs Swain[50] & Wyche[51] on the one side & Messrs Potter,[52] Fisher[53] & Bynum[54] on the other—I know of no good we shall do by remaining here—& am ready to adjourn at a mo-

---

[48]See above, p. 297n.
[49]A bill to consolidate several banks of the state and to establish a new Bank of the State of North Carolina. *Journal of the House of Commons, 1828*, 204.
[50]David L. Swain, the future governor of the state and future president of the state university.
[51]James Wyche was a member of the House of Commons from Granville from 1828 to 1831 and in 1833. He was in the state senate in 1834-1835. *N. C. Manual, 623.*
[52]Robert Potter had sponsored in November an investigation of the state banks. See *Hillsborough Recorder*, Apr. 8, 1827; *Journal of House of Commons*, 1828, 144, 149-150.
[53]Charles F. Fisher.
[54]Jesse A. Bynum.

ments notice—I shall to day introduce a resolution to fix the day
—There will be two reports on the subject of the Banks one from
Mr Potter the other from the committee—I should not be the
least surprised if the former were adopted by the house—

Your friend

F. NASH

[Addressed:]

> Honorable
> > W. P. Mangum
> > Red Mountain
> > Orange County
> > No. Carilina

Mail

———

WPM-LC

James Martin,[55] Jnr., to W. P. Mangum

Saturday Dec 26th 1828.

Dear Sir

Permit me to greet you in the most hearty manner on your
late elevation to the Bench It is the more honorable to you as
you were elected without rival or opposition. I apprehend that
you will find the appointment is rather desirable as a relief from
the severe labor of the bar than as a scource of increased emolu-
ment.

Upon the subject of the arrangement of the circuits for the
next year I had written to each of the other Judges before I
heard of your appointment, from Judge Strange I have received
an answer acquiescing in the proposal that I make one which is
subjoined, although he says that he would prefer the Wilmington riding in the Spring The only answer except the one mentioned is from Judge Daniel who wishes to assign me to the
Hillsborough circuit in the Spring, and in reply to my objection
to that on the score of what is due to public justice arising from
my old suits still pending in three of the counties in that circuit,
he says that "there will be other business to occupy your attention" all the week As if Public Justice did not entitle my old

---

[55]See above, p. 306n.

clients to at least an equal chance for a trial as those, whose
suits have been commenced since their suits were brought, and
as if in those counties where it is known the Docket is never
gone through, it is sufficient that the presiding Judge should be
engaged the whole week. My dear Sir, the suitors have rights
that cannot be neglected without we endertake to exercise "power without the right." But in addition to the argument that by
assigning me to the Hillsborough circuit my old clients must be
posponed to more recent ones, there are peculiar trials pending
in Rowan on the State Docket where my relatives are parties
and where I could not judicially act. But Judge Daniel says further that he has business at Fayettevill which will demand his
personal attention or he would swap that for Hillsborough. As
if my dear Sir we should permit our private business to interfere with that which concerns the justice of the public. I believe
that in the distribution of the circuits we should still feel that
we were in the exercise of a Judicial discretion. For two years I
have been confined to the low country without a murmur and in
the plan I propose I shall be assigned to the Wilmington circuit
where I have not rode for two years. The circuits assigned you
in the plan proposed are the Morganton and the Raleigh Neither
of which, I trust, will you find inconvenient I would thank you
to write to me upon the subject as soon as convenient.

Yous respectfully

JAMES MARTIN JU^r

	Spring	Autumn
Edenton[56]	Daniel	Donnell
Newbern	Norwood	Daniel
Raleigh	Daniel	Mangum
Wilmington	Martin	Strange
Hillsborough	Strange	Norwood
Morganton	Mangum	Martin
	Spring	Autumn
Edenton	Donnell	Daniel
Newbern	Norwood	Donnell
Raleigh	Daniel	Mangum
Wilmington	Martin	Strange

[56]This first list is crossed out in the original.

Hillsborough .....Strange .... Norwood
Morganton ....Mangum .... Martin

Hon^{le}. W. Mangum

[Addressed:]

> The Hon^{le}
> Wilie Mangum
> Orange Country
> N. C.

1829

WPM-D

W. P. Mangum's commission to judgeship of Superior Court

State of North Carolina

To the Honorable
Willie P. Mangum.   Greeting

We reposing special trust & confidence in your prudence, integrity, abilities and learning in the law: do commission you Judge of the Superior Courts of Law & Equity of this State; you haveing been thereunto appointed by joint ballot of both houses of the General Assembly; [SEAL]   and authorize you after taking such oath or oaths as are necessary for your qualification, to enter upon the said office, exercise and perform its authorities and duties, & to receive and enjoy the salary thereunto annexed, during your good behaviour therein.—

Given under my hand as Governor and under the great seal of the State, at the City of Raleigh this 12th day of January A. D. 1829.

By the Governor   JNO. OWEN
Jno B Muse Secy

[Endorsed on back:]

Price $400 [*sic*]

Mary Sutherland Mangum, youngest daughter of Willie P. and Charity A. Mangum. From a photograph made in Philadelphia in 1876 and now in the possession of Miss Sallie Preston Weeks of Washington, District of Columbia.

Martha Person Mangum, second daughter of Willie P. and Charity A. Mangum. From a photograph made in Philadelphia in 1876 and now in the possession of Miss Sallie Preston Weeks of Washington, District of Columbia.

WPM-LC

J. B. Muse[1] to Willie P. Mangum

RALEIGH Jany. 16th 1828 [1829][2]

Sir

I have made out your Commission as Judge. and as I intend to leave town tomorrow, I have deposited it in the Post office, where you may have it on application—You will please pay the Secretarys fee to the P M—

Yours & C

JNO B. MUSE

Hon.
    W. P. Mangum

[Addressed:]

Hon.
        Willie P. Mangum
            Stagville
                Orange Co.

WPM-LC

Henry Seawell to Willie P. Mangum

Confidential

RALEIGH 9th Feby 1829

My Dear Sir

Having always spoken to you in the most perfect frankness, in whatever concerned my interest or flattered my pride; I shall make no apology for the freedom used in the present letter: and as I have at the same time considered you one of my firmest friends, I shall offer no excuse for the appeal I am about to make —nor are you for a moment to suspect, that I have felt it neces-

---

[1]John B. Muse was the clerk of the court in 1823 and the private secretary to Governor James Iredell in 1827 and 1828, and for Governor John Owen and Governor Montfort Stokes who followed. He was in the House of Commons from Pasquotank County from 1835 to 1836 when he resigned. He was also a large planter. McIver, *N. C. Register*, 43; Grant, *Alumni Hist. of U. N. C.*, 450; Comptroller's Statements bound with the *N. C. Laws* from 1827 to 1832.

[2]Mangum was elected judge of the superior court in December, 1828. See above the letter of James Martin to W. P. Mangum, Dec. 26, 1828.

sary to put a Seal upon your lips, by the heading of this letter by the mark *"confidential"* it being only intended as a barrier to its publicity in the event of its falling into other hands. After this long preface I proceed to the subject—I wish to be appointed on the supreme court bench. and I want your assistance with the legislature[3]—I say legislature, because I think I have a very fair prospect of success with the executive & Council I have had no intimation from any quarter, but writing what my vanity prompts, with my acquaintance with the Council, I have strong hope that the result may be favorable. Now my dear Sir I know your talents in serving a friend, & you will have two circuits before the meeting of the legislature, I should be very much obliged by your assistance & venture to hope, you will bring no mischief upon the Country by extending me a helping hand. It is rumored that Wilson[4] & Donnell[5] will be candidates for it—; and I have thought it not beyond the range of probability, if Mr. ————— of the State Bank, shoud have some slight hankering that way— The situation wood be agreable to me on many accounts, independently of the salary—and that to be Sure would be acceptable enough—I have lived to become an old man in the practice, & am the oldest now at the Bar—I should be glad to hear from you as it will enable me to learn that you have received this letter—If you come to Raleigh, or can come before the circuit I should be glad you woud come to my house—I have much to say to you & should be much gratified in an opportunity to impart it.

I offer you my best wishes

HENRY SEAWELL

Judge Mangum

[Addressed:]

Honorable Willie P. Mangum
Red Mountain
Orange County

---

[3]Chief Justice John Louis Taylor died January 29, 1829. As a result, Judge Leonard Henderson was appointed chief justice and the legislature elected Thomas Ruffin as associate justice. John Hall was the other associate justice. Johnson, *Ante-Bellum N. C.*, 626.
[4]Probably Joseph Wilson of Stokes County, an attorney and state solicitor. McIver, *N. C. Register*, 21.
[5]John R. Donnell was state solicitor from 1815 to 1819. From 1819 to 1835 he was a superior court judge. Grant, *Alumni Hist. of U. N. C.*, 167.

WPM-LC

Lewis Williams to Willie P. Mangum

WASHINGTON February 23rd, 1829

Dear Sir.

I take the liberty to inclose you a copy of my circular letter[6]—you will find that I continue yet a good radical—On your circuit I hope you will feel a freedom in speaking a word for me if it comes in the way—

We have had as many different reports in relation to Cabinet appointments as there have been days intervening since the arrival of Gen. Jackson—At last it has settled down to this: Van-buren to be Secretary of State: Ingham of the Treasury: Eaton of Tennessee for the war: Branch (our friend) for the Navy and Berrien for Atto. Gen[l] I understand the friends of Gen[l]. Jackson give out this arrangement as the one finally agreed on—They appear (some of them) a good deal despleased with it—The friends of Mr Adams say nothing, being resolved to Judge the next administration, not by the men who compose it, but by its measures—

Accept my best wishes for your health and prosperity—

LEWIS WILLIAMS

Hon Wilie P Mangum—

[Addressed:]

Hon. Wilie P Mangum
To meet him at
Rockford
Surry County
North Carolina

WPM-LC

W. M. Green[7] to Willie P. Mangum

HILLSBORO' March 12th— 29

Dear Sir

Your Wife has requested me to convey to you the painful in-

[6]Lewis Williams, *To the Citizens of the Thirteenth Congressional District of North Carolina.* (Washington, D. C.: n. pub., February 18, 1829). 3 pp.
[7]William M. Green was at this time superintendent of the Hillsboro Female Seminary. He later became a member of the faculty at the University, bishop of the Mississippi Diocese, and chancellor of Sewanee. *The National Cyclopedia of American Biography* . . . (New York, N. Y.: James T. White and Co.), IX, 326.

telligence of your Mother's death,[8] which occurred on Tuesday morning last. Her complaint was the bilious cholic, with which, I believe that she has been frequently afflicted.—Your family was, at the time, with Mr Cain where I saw them on Monday last in good health. May this dispensation, which must be a sore one to you, be blessed by the Disposer of all things, to yr eternal good!—

With sincere regard
Yrs & —

W. M. Green

Hillsboro N. C.   To the
    March 14   Hon. Willie P. Mangum

[Addressed:]

Ashe Court-house
N. Ca

If Judge Mangum shall have
left Ashe Court-house before the arrival of this
letter—the P. Master will please forward it to Morganton

WPM-LC

Priestley H. Mangum to Willie P. Mangum

Hillsboro'. March 14th. 1829—

Dear Sir,

It falls to my lot to communicate to you the mournful intelligence of the death of our Mother. She died on the morning of the 11th Inst. viz: tuesday morning 3 or 4 o'clock. I heard of it on tuesday about 11 oclock, & went down from Hillsboro' immediately, & there remained untill thursday morning when the corpse was decently interred, at a place set apart *years ago* by my Father & Mother for their graves—as I understand from my Father. It is South of the *old place*, on the ridge beyond the first branch. The grave yard is not at the place I should have selected —but I could not think for a moment of even intimating an opposition to my Father's wishes on a subject of such delicate, deep & holy feeling to him.—The old man is powerfully affected,[9]

---

[8]Mangum's mother was Catharine Davis Mangum. Her father moved to Orange County from Pennsylvania.
[9]Mangum's father died in 1837.

as is the whole family of us—who feel as the best & dearest of our family is taken from us.—

On my way from the County Court here, to Granville Superior Court, last Monday was a week, I called to see my Mother— & spent a few hours with her, when she informed me that she was in the enjoyment of better health than she had had in 5 or 7 years—which I don't remember.—The last conversation I had with her was, that if she should have another attack, which I thought probable, & the medicine on hand should fail to give her speedy relief, I wished that Doctor Smith[10] should be sent for without delay. For I was sensible of the extremely dangerous character of the attacks she had had & was liable to—and was altogether unwilling that her life should be left in the hands of Doc: Bullock,[11] who, tho' a friend for whom I have respect, is not & can not be a safe practitioner.—She was according to my expectations again attacked in the old way—on friday evening after dinner; she instantly took of the medicine on hand, & unfortunately without any beneficial results; and poor old woman, who loved her children better than herself, was unwilling to send for Smith because of the *consequent expense*, & of being flattered with the hope that she would shortly be relieved as she had been on former occasions. Walter however, called in Bullock, who did not arrive before Sunday night—he did not & could not afford any effectual relief. Possibly the same result would have ensued under any physician—but I think that if Smith had been called in on Saturday, her life would have been saved. She suffered immensely—died in the full possession of her senses, & talked to the moment death struck her, & died without a struggle or a groan. I saw her corpse, it was herself—Poor woman, the goodness of her heart, & her love for her children will live with me as long as life—Charity had gone on the day before she was attacked, to her Father's, to return on Sunday—My Mother was unwilling to put her to the trouble of coming home sooner than she had designed—or on Monday when the weather was bad— & therefore Charity did not know of her illness untill she arrived on tuesday morning, when the old lady was no more.—

The family are all well.

Yrs. respectfully

P. H. MANGUM

---

[10]Doctor James S. Smith.
[11]Probably Dr. Benjamin Bullock of Granville County near the Orange County line. He was the father of Elizabeth Bullock who married Walter A. Mangum.

[Addressed:]

His Honor
Willie P. Mangum
Morganton
No. Ca.

If the Judge should have left Morganton before this letter arrives, the postmaster will confer a favor upon me by forwarding it to him safely by mail or otherwise, speedily.

P. H. Mangum.

WPM-LC

J. Wilson¹² to W. P. Mangum

CHARLOTTE May 9th 1829

Dear Sir

On monday a vacancy of the Clerk of the Superior Court of this County is to be Supplyed by you the present incumbent (James Hutchison)¹³ has been Clerk for the last four years and during *all* that time he has so far as I know or have ever understood discharged the duties of the office with integrity and ability—he together with Doctor Lemuel Henderson will be applicants for this appointment as I understand—It may be asked why shoud Hutchison be displaced—My answer is that although his qualifications are undoubtedly such as all ready stated; yet his deportment in the office has been supercilious and arbitrary to the ignorant and poor, who are compelled to have recourse to him—this alone might be viewed a Sufficient objection to his reappointment—the claims of his opponant are to my mind conclusive—his qualifications in every respect are equal—his affabillity and courteous deportment to *all* will be sattisfactory—He is *Honest* he is Poor and even needy He has a family solely dependant on him—the other has none, and is in easy circumstances—It may be further stated and *I state it as of my own knowledge* that Doctor Henderson woud have been the Clerk four years ago but from the *fact* of his having withdrawn his name

---

¹²John Wilson was a member of the House of Commons from Mecklenburg from 1816 to 1818. *N. C. Manual,* 699.
¹³Samuel M. Hutchinson. See the next letter.

as a candidate—It is Submitted to you under the various aspects
in which I have here truly placed the claims of the parties—
which of them shall be appointed.

Yours very respectfully

J. WILSON

The Honbl. Willie P. Mangum—

[Addressed:]

Honbl. Willie P. Mangum
Present

WPM-LC

Wm. Davidson[14] et als. to Willie P. Mangum

CHARLOTTE N. CAROLINA.—
[11 May, 1829]

To the Honble Judge Mangum
Sir,

We the undersigned do hereby certify, that Samuel M. Hutchinson Esqr. as Clerk of our Superior Court has discharged the
duties of the office. we believe to the entire satisfaction of the
community. He is uniformaly attentive; and punctualy accounts
for, and pays over all moneys that come into his office: Is a man
of *integrity* and *correct moral habits*, and is considered a *useful,
efficient public officer;*

Given under our hands this 11th day of May 1829.—

Wm. Davidson
Saml. McComb
John Irwin
David Banks
Jas. H. Blake
Wm Smith
William Carson
Thomas Harris
J. D. Boyd

<hr>

[14]William Davidson was in the legislature in 1813, 1815, 1818, 1821 to 1823, 1825, and
from 1827 to 1829. He was also a member of the Council of State from 1821 to 1823. *N. C.
Manual,* 432.

[Addressed:]

The Hon^able. Willie P. Mangum

(Charlotte
(
(No. Ca.

_____

Thomas Alston to James Webb[15]

[12 Oct. 1829]

Doctor James Webb,
 Sir,
 You will please to pay over to my Nephew, James J Alston,
three hundred dollars, or whatever sum, you have in your hands,
of the funds of Willie P. Mangum—which when paid will be
applied to the reduction of my claim against him—My nephews
receipt by virtue of this order, will be available for whatever
sum you may pay him. October 10th. 1829.

Wake County   T Alston[16]
 N^o. C^a.—

_____

The above order was signed in my presence by M^r. Thomas
Alston—M^r. Alston would be glad to receive $50. in United
States paper, having recently agreed to give a premium for
that amount.   P. H. Mangum
or return it in kind.—

[Endorsement:]

Oct 12th. 1829 then rec^d. Three hundred dollars ($300) from
Dr James Webb—James J Alston

Tom Alston
 Rect
  $300.

Doc. James Webb
 Hillsborough
  N^o. C^a.

_____

[15]The original is in the James Webb Papers, University of North Carolina.
[16]Thomas Alston. See above, p. 327n.

WPM-LC

Chauncey Goodrich[17] to E. F. Norton[18]

BUFFALO Nov. 28th 1829.

Hon Ebenezer F. Norton
  Sir,
  You will soon receive a note against Robert Potter Esq of
170$ from the Honbl. Willie P Mangum of No Carolina which
please deliver to Maj. John G. Camp[19] as he will have more
time to attend to its collection than yourself.

I am Respectfully &C,

CHAUNCEY GOODRICH

[Addressed:]
  Hon E. F. Norton
  Washington City.

WPM-D

Romulus M. Saunders to Willie P. Mangum

RALEIGH Dec. 30. 1829

Dear Sir—
  Permit me to introduce to your acquaintance Judge Farman[20]
from New York a particular friend of *our* friend Van Buren—
He calls upon you on official business—if you can afford the relief asked for it will save him much trouble and confer a great
favour—

Very respectfully
Yr. friend
R. M. SAUNDERS—

—The Bill for altering my circuit still before the Legislature.

[Address:] Hon. Willie P. Mangum
    Politeness   Orange
        Mr. Farman

[17]See above, p. 325.
[18]Ebenezer Foote Norton, 1774-1851, was an attorney for the Niagara Bank at Buffalo,
N. Y. He served in Congress as a Democrat from 1829 to 1831. *Biog. Dir. of Cong.*, 1362.
[19]Major John G. Camp was appointed a midshipman, November 15, 1809. He resigned in
1811. After that he read and practiced law. Edward W. Callahan, *List of Officers of the
Navy of the United States and of the Marine Corps from 1775 to 1900.* (New York, N. Y.:
L. R. Hamersly and Co., 1901), 98. Hereafter cited as Callahan, *List of Officers of U. S.
Navy.*
[20]Probably Joshua Farman of Onondaga County, New York. While Van Buren was governor, Farman was nominated by the legislature in 1829 for the Safety Fund System to pro-
tect depositors against bank failures. John C. Fitzpatrick, *The Autobiography of Martin
Van Buren*, in the *Annual Report* of the American Historical Association for the year 1918
(Washington, D. C.: The Government Printing Office, 1920), II, 221.

1830

WPM-LC

Ro. Strange[1] to Willie P. Mangum

FAYETTEVILLE Feby 4th. 1830

Dear Sir

You have no doubt understood from Judge Norwood[2] my dissatisfaction with the arrangement proposed by him and yourself and some of the reasons of my dissatisfaction.[3] At the same time that I wrote to him I wrote also to Judges Daniel[4] Donnel[5] and Martin[6] all of whom disclaim having given any assent to that arrangement and have voted for the plan originally proposed by Judge Martin; which then together with myself constitute a majority of the Judges. I have with their approbation published the correction which you will see in the papers—

I am sorry that any of us should be compelled to ride the Edenton circuit in the Fall, but justice and the opinion of the majority Judges are both in favor of its being ridden in rotation in the Fall; so that the bitter dose will have to be taken by each but once in six years—You have not as yet ridden it since your last elevation, if ever; and if a man is not called upon to ride it oftener than his turn it matters but little when that turn comes and the sense of justice in each one of us must be too strong to make us willing to throw upon another an unpleasant task which it is our own duty to perform. When I rode the Edenton circuit the Fall before last I did it as a child takes physic, I knew it was a bitter dose but then I consoled myself with the reflection that when once taken it would not have to be done soon again, and therefore courageously swallowed it. And be assured I was not a little surprised and disappointed when I found the cup so soon again presented to my lips— Accept my assurances of high respect

Yr. ob. ser[t].

RO. STRANGE

---

[1]Robert Strange was judge of the superior court from 1827 to 1836.
[2]William Norwood of Hillsboro was a judge of the superior court from 1823 to 1836.
[3]By the act of 1806 the legislature created six judges and six districts of the superior court. No judge was to ride the same circuit twice in succession. Until 1856 the judges met and allotted ridings. All of the judges disliked the Edenton district for the autumn. When Mangum was judge in 1826 he had ridden the Morganton circuit in the west and the Edenton circuit in the east. Johnson, *Ante-Bellum N. C.*, 623. See below William Norwood's letter to Mangum, Feb. 9, 1830.
[4]Joseph John Daniel was judge of the superior court from 1816 to 1832.
[5]John R. Donnell of New Bern was judge of the superior court from 1819 to 1836.
[6]James Martin, Jr., was judge of the superior court from 1827 to 1835.

The following is the arrangement now published

[Circuit]	Spring	Autumn
Edenton	Norwood	Mangum
Newbern	Strange	Donnell
Raleigh	Martin	Daniel
Hillsboro'.	Donnell	Strange
Wilmington	Mangum	Martin
Morganton	Daniel	Norwood

[Addressed:]
> To
> The Honl. Willie P. Mangum
> care of Mr Wᵐ Cain Junr.
> Hillsborough
> N. C.

WPM-LC

William Norwood to Willie P. Mangum

POPLAR HILL 9ᵗʰ Feby 1830.

Dear Sir—

As our allotment was not expressly agreed to by any of the Judges by you and I it is not legal.[7] Judge Strange complained greatly, and has induced Martin, Donnell and Daniel to assent to the following allotment—and published it. To avoid any further misunderstanding on the subject, and to do you that Justice you are entitled to, I am willing to exchange with you, and to ride your two circuits as if they had been originally alloted to me. Neither of the allotments is legal. Let me hear from you as soon as possible—

Yours &c. WM. NORWOOD

[Circuit]	Spring	Autumn
Edenton	Norwood	Mangum
Newbern	Strange	Donnell
Raleigh	Martin	Daniel
Hillsborough	Donnell	Strange
Wilmington	Mangum	Martin
Morganton	Daniel	Norwood

[7]See above, p. 352.

[Addressed:[The Honble Willie P. Mangum
Stagville
Orange

The Postmaster is requested to send [this] immediately.

WPM-LC

Priestley H. Mangum to Willie P. Mangum

At Mr. Cain's, Sunday 1 O.Clock P.M.
Feb: 22nd. 1830.

Dear Sir,

I am here on my way to Hillsboro' with my family, & all
well. The recent fall of snow deranged my plan of operations, &
made it impracticable to come up by your house.—

I drop these lines, to call your attention to a fact, which I
fear from the recent date of the last *announced* allotment of the
Sup: Court circuits, may not have occurred to you. I have seen
by the last week's papers of Raleigh, that it was announced in
the Fayetteville Obse[rver] as the result of a *majority* of the
Judges, an allotment or assignment of the Circuits, different
from the one previously published.—By this arrangement, you
are placed on the Wilmington riding in the Spring—and by
reference to the Almanack, you will perceive that that circuit
commences on the 4th Monday of Feb:. This fact was suggested
to me by Mr. Cameron in Raleigh, 'tother night—& I call your
attention to it, lest you may loose a Court.

Mr. Cain, I am pleased to find, is up.—
I go to Hillsboro' this evening.

Yrs

P. H. MANGUM

[Addressed:]

His Honor
Willie P. Mangum
Mr. Fitts)   Orange

WPM-LC

Willie P. Mangum to Charity A. Mangum

WINTON: HERTFORD COUNTY 28th March 1830.

My dear Love,

I have been looking with great anxiety for a letter from you, but have not received one.

This is Sunday Morning, at the close of my fourth Court, and as soon as I finish writing & pack up, I shall set out for Gates County My fifth Court—It is only 12½ Miles. I have had a very bad cold, and my bowels have been in bad condition—but by great abstinence, I am now very Well—You know, I thought that every sort of stimulus injured me—and spoke of neither chewing tobacco, nor drinking any sort of spirit on my circuit.— As to chewing we will say no more on that subject — But I neither use pepper, pickle, nor have I taken but one drink of spirits on the circuit & that flushed my face & gave me headache—

It is the stomach which is sensitive, and if I enjoy health, it must be procured by perfect abstemiousness—and this I shall try—But as to Tobacco, "No more of that Hal, an thou lovest me"—

I hope my Love, to-morrow morning to get a letter from you— I am very anxious to hear from you and our dear little children.

As the season advances, I feel more & more anxiety to see you & the children—In all our lives, we have never been with each other during the spring that most delightful of all the seasons, except one; & that one was clouded & overcast by so deep & black distresses that I was unfitted for the enjoyment of it— I mean the Spring, when our dear little Patty was born[8]—Home, dear, delightful home, is at last the only place where anything approaching to happiness is to be enjoyed—And there with a proper & wise regulation of the mind & passions, if not happiness, at least more of tranquility & content may be enjoyed, than any where else in this wide cold and selfish world. This wise regulation I have never retained—Much of the fault was in myself & a good deal of it in my unhappy circumstances & connexions. I hope for more of it—, & I pray God that more of it may fall to My Lot.—I know not, why I ought not to enjoy it.—

---

[8]At the time of this letter, Mangum had two children, Sallie Alston who was born in 1824, and Martha (Patty) who was born in 1828.

To a heart like mine, nothing can contribute more to it than the deep & devoted affections of those we love—

And this happiness at least I enjoy, and let what may come, & much has come, almost enough to desolate my heart & affections, yet in the deepest & darkest moments, when the brain was almost ready to turn, when in the wild & gloomy paroxysm, existence itself seemed almost a burden & a curse, the mild beam of that bright star of affection, has often broke through the gloom, and reassured me that it was as fixed as it was mild.— With a heart that is affectionate and a disposition once cheerful. Yet I am aware that at the lowest depths of my heart there is an awfully dangerous mine, inherited I think from my poor Mother, that ought to be guarded as a magazine, for its explosion, might spread desolation over all my hopes of happiness.— I therefore seek as much as I can to cut off myself as much as I may, from this heartless, cold & vexatious world—& hope in time to be able to be as cheerful & happy, as I desire to see you My Love.

I have received a letter from Doct Bullock[9] & find as I expected, a blow up about the Gold & Money is the root of all evil, saith the wise man—

Give My dear Sally & Patty their father's kiss—& tell Sally father says she must be a good Girl—& mind Mother.

Farewell My Love, & remember often & kindly

Your affectionat husband,

W. P. MANGUM

[Addressed:]

Mrs. Charity A. Mangum,
    Red Mountin,
        Orange County,
           No. Carolina.

Via   )
)
    Fayetteville &   )
)
      Raleigh   )

---

[9]Benjamin Bullock who was the family physician. At this time Mangum was in financial difficulties.

WPM-LC

Chas. Manly[10] to W. P. Mangum

RALEIGH 28th May 1830.

Dear Sir,

I am instructed by His Excellency Govr. Owen, Prest. of the Board of Trustees of the University to invite specially and earnestly your attendance at a meeting of said Board at Chapel Hill on Monday preceeding the next Commencement: viz on the 21—June next—

The depressed condition of the financial concerns of the Institution is deplorable:[11]—The active & zealous cooperation of the Board is required to avert its threatened dissolution.—

This special invitation is given to such of the Trustees as, it is hoped & believed will on this Occasion not fail to give their attendance.

I am Sir, very respectfully,

Your obt. Servt.

CHAS. MANLY,
Secty.

[Addressed:]

Hon. W. P. Mangum
　　Red Mountain P. O.
　　　　Orange Co.,
　　　　　　N. C.

Thomas Alston to James Webb[12]

WAKE COUNTY Sept 4. 1830[13]

Dear Sir

The rect. which I hold against Judge Mangum and a certificate from him for compound interest will be handed you by James Alston

---

[10]See above, p. 70n.
[11]North Carolina, like the other seaboard slave states, was in an economic slump in the 1820's. The University lost the income from the western lands. Enrollment declined. An effort to build three new buildings was made. The result was that the trustees had to borrow money to pay the salaries of the professors. By 1830 the University was on the verge of financial collapse. Some of the trustees met in January, 1830, and upon Mangum's motion a special committee was appointed to present a plan at a full meeting of the trustees. The legislature was asked to take over the University debt and appropriate $25,000 from the Literary Fund. This was done. Battle, *Hist. of U. N. C.*, I, 325-334.
[12]See above, p. 325n.
[13]The original of this letter is in the James Webb Papers, University of North Carolina.

I am in want of the money if *it can be had*—otherwise I will take M^r. Canes[14] note which you offered me—If you have not the mony you will oblige me by instructing James Alston how to proceed with M^r. Canes note, so as to get the money the shortest possible way—You will perceive that the Judges certificate bears date August 1825—but it is my pervailing custom to renew annually—and it was my understanding with him, that he should pay me compound interest from the time the money was due, and I thought the certificate was to that effect, until after I arrived home, when upon an examination I found it only bears date from August 1825—I think the Judge has *certainly* made a mistake respecting the dates—

Yours vy respectfully

T ALSTON

Doctor———Webb

(Endorsements)

On Mrs Southerlands Note
I R^d Interest 32.56
on Do 22.87
on W. A. Mangums Note   7.50

D^r.———Webb
      Hillsborough

)
Ja^s Alston)
)

Receipt of James Webb for two notes[15]

[6 Sept. 1830]

Rec^d of James Webb trustee[16]of
Willie P. Mangum two Notes
one on Mary Southerland balance

[14]William Cain, Sr.
[15]The original of this receipt is in the James Webb Papers, University of North Carolina.
[16]See above, p. 325.

```
due and Intest ........................$330.45
one on W. A. Mangum for            75
Interest  ..........................   7.50
                                      _____
                                       412.95
```
Sept. 6. 1830

JAMES J ALSTON
for THOMAS ALSTON

[Endorsement]
Ths. Alston
Ret $412.

Statement of Willie P. Mangum's Trust Fund[17]

[6 Sept. 1830]

```
Bal of the trust fund after satisfying
Executors in the hands of J. Webb
        Int May 27. 1828              $935.97
        2 year     7 My. 27 ..............  37.16
                                          _____
                                           973.13
        Rent Plantation ........$ 75.
                                 9.30     84.30
                                _____  _____
                                          1057.43
        Lde Haywood ..........$106
        Int 2 year             12.72     118.72
                                _____
        Lotts in Hillsboro ........ 150.
        Int one year ...........   9.00    159.00
                                _____  _____
                                          1335.15
1829   By last Pd. T. Alston    300.
       " Int May 19 one          30.75    330.75
         year 8 Mo 15           _____  _____
                                          1004.40
1830   By last ................ 412.95
Sept. 6. Int 4. 18 ................   9.33    422.28
                                _____  _____
                                           682.12
```

[17]The original of this statement is in the James Webb Papers, University of North Carolina.

WPM-LC

Lewis Williams to Willie P. Mangum

SURRY COUNTY September 14th 1830.

Dear Sir.

While at our Superior Court last week some of my friends in Surry had so much partiality for me as to suggest the propriety of offering my name to the Legislature at the next Session for the appointment of Senator in Congress— The same suggestion has been made by other persons from other quarters

I regret that my business compelled me to leave Court so soon as to deny all opportunity for consulting you on the subject—as it will be out of my power to see you at Wilkes or Ashe Court I take the liberty to write to you in confidence and to request your opinion

I am opposed totally to the doctrine of nullification and deny to any State either in convention or the ordinary legislature the right to secede from the Union unless she proceeds upon the revolutionary principle—

The decision of the supreme Court in all questions of constitutionality should be binding on the States and submitted to by them—

I hold the Tariff not to be unconstitutional but merely inexpedient and on this ground have opposed it—

As to internal improvement I believe the power contended for by the advocates of that system, to be doubtful, and for this reason as well as the inexpediency of the system itself at this time, I have from first to last, voted in the negative—

These are the leading topics of the day and if you think an anti-Jacobson man (whose claim to consistency of principle will I trust bear comparison with that of the President himself), would have any prospect of success I will thank you to say so— I am not insensible of the prejudice which may be excited against me, but if the Legislature regard measures and not men; if they look to realities & rather than names I should think that prejudice might be over come— General Iredell[18] told me at our Court that he should not again be a candidate —The East will now

---

[18]James Iredell, 1788-1853, a Princeton graduate, lawyer and soldier of considerable prominence in the eastern part of the state, was governor of the state in 1828 and United States Senator from 1828 to 1831. From 1840 to 1852 he was the reporter of the North Carolina Supreme Court. Iredell had been selected in 1828 to finish Nathaniel Macon's term in the Senate. Tradition has it that Mangum would have been selected in 1828 but he generously gave way to Iredell. *Biog. Dir. of Cong.*, 1138; W. K. Boyd, "Draft of a Biography of Willie P. Mangum," Chapter V, p. 1. This is a manuscript in the Mangum Papers at Duke University. Hereafter cited as Boyd, "Draft of Life of Mangum."

probably claim the Senator, and this in the absence of political considerations, would likely be the greatest obstacle to the success of a candidate from the West—The friendship which has subsisted between us induces me to request that whatever may be your opinion you will state it without reserve—
I am Dr Sir with great respect
Your most obt & very Hble. Servt—

LEWIS WILLIAMS

Hon Wilie P. Mangum—

[Addressed:]
Hon Wilie P. Mangum
Wilkesborough
North Carolina.

WPM-LC

Order of Slave Patrol of Hillsboro

[21 Sept., 1830]
[?]

TOWN OF HILLSBOROUGH, ss[19]

To John A. Faucett Captain of a Company of Patrol, No. 11.[20]
You are hereby commanded and required to summon all the members of the company of Patrol of your class to attend, and you are to patrol said town for one week from the date hereof, at least three times in said week, in the night time, and three hours in each night, after nine o'clock; and you are to apprehend, or cause to be apprehended, all such white persons, free negroes, mulattos and slaves, as shall be found acting contrary to the ordinances of said town, and bring them before me, to be dealt with according to the ordinances established by the commissioners of said town! and if the person so apprehended can-

---

[19]This is a printed form filled in.
[20]In 1829 David Walker, a free Negro who formerly lived in Wilmington, published in Boston his *Appeal . . . to the Colored Citizens of the World.* Subsequent editions were more inflammatory than the first. A copy appeared at Savannah in the fall of 1829 and caused much excitement. In 1830 another copy was discovered at Wilmington. Excitement ran high, and as a result in November of 1830 the governor was ready for drastic action. In the succeeding session of the legislature it was forbidden to teach slaves to read or write. Probably this excitement accounted for the action in Hillsboro. The year of this document is not clear. There is a possibility that it was issued in September of 1831 after the Nat Turner insurrection of August 21. Clement Eaton, "A Dangerous Pamphlet in the Old South," *Journal of Southern History*, II (1836), 325-334.

not immediately be brought before me with convenience, you
are commanded to carry such person to the keeper of the jail of
Orange county, who is hereby authorized and required to receive
the body of such person, and to keep him or her safely until duly
discharged. You are farther required to make return to me at
the end of your week as captain how you shall have executed
the same. Given under my hand, as Magistrate of Police for said
town, the 21 day of September 183

James Boling   B. Cheek M. P.
Pater Thompson
Stephen Dollar.

[Endorsed:]   Section 18 of the Ordinances. "It shall be the duty
of the Town Constable, and *the Captain of each Patrol,* to disperse all collections or assemblies of negroes or mulattos in the
streets, and to quell rioting, quarrelling, loud and profane curs-
ing and swearing, and disorderly behaviour of every kind: to
effect which purpose they shall have it in their power to call to
their assistance any citizen of the town, who on refusing to give
his assistance shall be fined not exceeding four dollars; and the
Magistrate of Police shall fine not exceeding ten dollars, or im-
prison at his discretion, all persons behaving in such riotous
and disorderly manner, and commit him, her or them to jail
until such fine and the costs be paid."

Endorsed:

John A. Faucett Captn.
James Boling
Pater Thompson
Stephen Dollar

Executed agreeable to Law
John A. Faucett.

WPM-LC

H. G. Burton to Wm J. Alexander[21]

Morganton Nov. 7th A D [torn] [1830]

My Dear Sir
I was unable to close the busness with our friend The Genl[22]—

---

[21]William J. Alexander was speaker in 1829-1830.
[22]Probably Romulus M. Saunders.

he was very unwell and kept his bed a considerable part of the
time I was Salisbury—he promised however it should be done
at Charlotte—knowing the delacy you felt on the subject—I
thought it best to execute a Deed which I left with Alfred Burton[23] to be delivered when he paid the money or gave his Note—
I made a considerable payment towards the Note in Bank when
last at Milton which I hope will make all matters easy in that
quarter—but if I do not sell the horse or get that money—I may
want you and my friend Sneed[24] to Endorse once more for the
residue—that will however be towards Christmas—when I hope
to have the pleasure of seeing you—It will not be in my power
to leave this part of the Country for some weeks as I now think
I have gotten in way of rubing out old scores—I must make my
arrangements for the ensuing year before I leave this part of
the Country. I have my corn and Pork to purchase, and this is
the proper time of doing it—If Capehart does not continue with
me, he is willing to Endorse for me believing that I will be able
to Square of, or nearly so the ensuing year—As to the appointment of Senator I feel no great anxiety on the subject—but as
I should not have to go on untill the expiration of twelve months
—if you and my friend Ship[25] thought I could be elcted[26] without my being present I must confess it would be gratifying to
me—I have been so overwhelmed and bedeviled the last few
years that I should like an opertunity of once more standing
erect—Should you and Ship think the chances in my favor be so
good as to consult my particular friends Cols Matthews[27] and
Nicholson[28] and Genl Ward[29] who upon all occasions has proved
as true as steel to me, also my friend Gary[30] must not be neglected—Mhoon[31] McGehee[32] and Sneeed[33] I have no doubt would
lend a hand—and last tho not least my friend Caldwell[34]—it is

[23]Alfred Burton, the son of Robert Burton, was a first cousin of H. G. Burton.
[24]William M. Sneed.
[25]Bartlett Shipp was in the House of Commons in 1824, 1826, 1828-1830 and in the state
senate in 1834. Sherrill, Annals of Lincoln County, 201-202.
[26]See the letters which follow for the political maneuvering in the legislature. Mangum
was elected.
[27]Isham Matthews was in the senate from Halifax County from 1824 to 1833. N. C.
Manual, 640-641.
[28]Thomas Nicholson was in the House of Commons from Halifax County from 1829 to
1831. N. C. Manual, 640.
[29]Edward Ward was the state senator from Onslow County in 1811, 1815, and 1822 to 1830.
N. C. Manual, 733-734.
[30]Roderick B. Gary was a member of the House of Commons from 1821 to 1830 and in
1832, 1835-1837. N. C. Manual, 728-729.
[31]William S. Mhoon of Bertie County was in the House of Commons from 1828 to 1830
and was state treasurer from 1830 to 1835. N. C. Manual, 442, 503.
[32]Thomas McGehee represented Person County in the House of Commons in 1826, 1829,
1831, and 1833. He was a member of the Council of State from 1838 to 1840. N. C. Manual,
436, 758.
[33]Wm. M. Sneed.
[34]David F. Caldwell. See above, p. 207n.

a matter I shall submit entirely to the discretion of you my
friend Ship and those above mentioned—and whatever may be
your decision—you may rest assured will be entirely satisfactory to me—I do not wish to be nominated unless I can get a
respectable vote—You are one of the few friends who have stood
by me in good and bad report. and I hope never while I breathe
to forget your kindness, and my constant desire is, to have in
my power to make a proper return—

Sincerely your
friend,
H. G. BURTON.

[Addressed:]
Wm. J. Alexander Esq
   Charlotte
     No Carolina.

WPM-LC

Saml. Hillman to Willie P. Mangum

MORGANTON 12th Nov. 1830.

Dear Judge,
   I presume ere this you have been informed of the death of
Mr. E. A. Erwin the la[te] Clerk of Burke Superior Court of
Law and that you have been presented with a recommendation
in favour of Mr Roane[35] to supply the vacancy occasioned by
his death—At or about the time or receiving this, you will have
been presented with a letter with several signatures to it recommending Mr. Gaither as a suitable person to succeed Mr. Erwin
—Both these gentlemen have applied to me for letters to you
upon the subject of the appointment—I declined signing Mr
Roane's recommendation because I did not wish to commit myself before I knew who would be applicants for the office, because having resided so short a time in the County I felt unwilling to be considered as taking sides in any appointment for
which there should be fair competition and because I thought
the application premature on the part of Mr Roane—I do not
wish by the statement of this latter reason to prejudice the
application of Mr Roane, but merely to say that Mr Erwin hav-

---

[35]William Roane, a close relative of Thomas Ruffin, became an attorney in 1818 and later
a state solicitor in Burke County. In 1823 he represented his county in the House of Commons. McIver, *N. C. Register*, 44, 46; Hamilton *Papers of Ruffin*, I, 162, 205.

ing been of the profession and a fellow boarder in the same house with me, it would have been in *me* a mark of disrespect for *his* memory and disregard for the feelings of his friends, for me to have lent my name even, in favour of the appointment of his successor before he was buried—Having declined recommending Mr Roane I had made up my mind at one time to decline saying any thing in favour of Mr Gaither,[36] leaving them [to] depend upon the recommendation of others and your knowledge of both the men—I have been induced to change that determination from a suggestion that being of the profession who are much interested in the appointment and living on the spot it might be thought that I had some reason for being silent which if made known would militate against their appointment—I have deemed it therefore advisabe to state to you what I know of both the gentlemen—Of Mr Roane's skill in penmanship either as regards neatness or dispatch, I know but little—In other respects I think he would make a good Clerk—He has the reputation of a man of strict integrity and his legal attainments would soon enable him to accommadate himself to the rotine of the business of his office—Those gentlemen who have recommended him have had much better opportunities of judging of his skill in penmanship and talents for business than I have— The above is the substance of what I should have said if I had written you by Mr Roane—With Mr Gaither my acquaintance has been of a more intimate kind, arising probably out of the accidental circumstance of our having boarded the greater part of the year in the same house—We have been thrown frequently together and when in each others company the topic of conversation has generally been the subject of law and the business of the Courts—I can say [of] Mr Gaither that he too has the reputation of a man [of gre]at integrity that he writes a good business hand, is of [in]dustrious habits, posesses an investigating and d[iscr]iminating mind and would I think make a good Clerk. For both these gentlemen I entertain a sincere regard— I would not willingingly prejudice the claims of either and I trust I have done them both ample justice—

---

[36]Burgess S. Gaither, 1807-1892, was appointed clerk by Mangum. He was a Whig who served in the constitutional convention of 1835. Under Tyler he was superintendent of the Federal mint at Charlotte in 1840. He served as solicitor for the seventh judicial district in 1844. He was in the legislature from 1840 to 1841 and from 1852 to 1853. Ashe, *Biog. Hist. of N. C.*, II, 93-99.

STATE DEPARTMENT OF ARCHIVES AND HISTORY

I am my dear sir as ever your
sincere friend and obt. svt.
SAML. HILLMAN.

Hon. Willie P. Mangum.

[Addressed:]
Honble.
Willie P. Mangum,
Cabarrus Court
By Mr Erwin

WPM-LC

Robt. H. Burton[37] *to W. P. Mangum*

BEATY'S FORD November 14th 1830

My dear Sir

The subject of the appointment of a Clerk for Burke Superior
Court to fill the vacancy occasioned by the death of Mr A. Erwin,
was somewhat discussed before I left Charlotte. At that time I
was at a loss who would apply, and indeed who could be selected
in that County, who would perform the duties of the office, in
justice to it. Mr. B. Gaither never entered into my thoughts. He
has called on me today & signified his intention of applying to
you for the appointment. I take great pleasure in saying to you,
that I most heartily & cordially recommend him as a proper person for the place. Since my acquaintance with him, he has ever
conducted himself with the utmost propriety. His habits are temperate & moral and amiable and gentlemany in his deportment
to others. His capacity is equal to the duties of the office, and I
do expect that he would give as much satisfaction in the office as
any other person, could give. In addition to all this, he has a
small family & but little to support on, except his own exertions,
& this office would assist him. I would feel highly gratified if you
could in justice to your duties confer it on him

With sincere regard & esteem
Your Obt Servant
ROBT H. BURTON

[Addressed:]
The Honble. W. P. Mangum
Concord
Mr. B. Gaither.

---

[37]See below, p. 525.

WPM-LC

W. M. Sneed to Willie P. Mangum

RALEIGH Nov. 18th. 1830—

My Dear Sir,

Your valued letter dated the 9th instant was handed to me on Monday Morning by Mr. Caldwell;[38] and you must pardon me for saying, that from it I could not but come to a conclusion diametrically opposite to that expressed by you vizt "I consider myself out of the question"[39]—and the letter received from your brother Priestly the next morning has fully justified that opinion—

I shewed your letter to your fast friend Charles L. Hinton soon after it was received—Although he and myself are both very friendly to Gov. Owen[40] yet we know that his talent is not of that order which the Station of Senator imperiously at this time, calls for; and however much we are willing to evidence our regard for him, and however anxious we are to defeat the machinations of the party who are likely to ride "rough shod" over us; yet we feel well assured that with him, that cannot be effected. And of this opinion are all, or almost all, of the party opposed to the Spaight faction,[41]—for I cannot give it a better name—You see that Fisher[42] has displaced Alexander,[43] and Caldwell[44] succeeded in the Senate against Spaight by mere luck —for it was nothing more nor less—The Party consists of R^d. D. Spaight, Charles Fisher, Romulus M. Saunders & Joseph H Bryan as leaders and followed by Stokes[45] Montgomery[46] OBrien,[47] Steadman,[48] Bynum,[49] "'*et citeris paribus*"—Saunders[50]

---

[38]David F. Caldwell.

[39]He refers to the proposed election of Mangum to the United States Senate.

[40]Governor John Owen, 1787-1841, of Bladen County, was in the legislature in 1812-1813 and 1827. He served as governor from 1828 to 1830. An ardent Whig, he was acting president of the National Whig Convention at Harrisburg in 1839 when tradition has it he refused the nomination of vice president. Ashe, *Biog. Hist. of N. C.*, VIII, 399-402.

[41]In 1830 political parties in North Carolina were not yet divided along national lines. Instead, there were factions. One of these, the Spaight faction, was led by R. D. Spaight, Charles Fisher, and Joseph H. Bryan. In the legislature which met in November 1830, the Spaight faction was in control. Consequently, Mangum's friends decided to support one of the Spaight faction against the choice of that faction's leaders and thereby split the faction. Mangum, it was argued, would come in as a compromise candidate. McDuffie, "Willie P. Mangum," 40.

[42]Charles Fisher, the speaker of the House of Commons.

[43]William J. Alexander was speaker in 1829-1830.

[44]David F. Caldwell was eleted speaker of the senate over R. D. Spaight.

[45]Montfort Stokes was in the legislature from Rowan County in 1829 and 1830.

[46]William Montgomery of Orange County was state senator from 1824 to 1827 and from 1829 to 1834. He was a Democrat in Congress from 1835 to 1841. *Biog. Dir. of Cong.*, 1325.

[47]Spencer O'Brien represented Granville County in the House of Commons from 1829 to 1832. Later he moved to Tennessee. Grant, *Alumni Hist. of U. N. C.*, 463.

[48]William W. Steadman represented Gates County in the House of Commons from 1823 to 1830. *N. C. Manual*, 616.

[49]Jesse A. Bynum represented Halifax County in the legislature in 1823, 1824, and 1827 to 1830. He was in Congress from 1833 to 1841 when he moved to Alexandria, Louisiana. *Biog. Dir. of Cong.*, 772.

[50]R. M. Saunders.

Bryan[51] & Obrien were most active Caldwell & Alexander & their friends are exceedingly *exasperated* with Saunders They had taken him by the hand & cherished him—, brought him forward & made him what he is—now he turns upon them viper like— Caldwell says he will never speak to him again—

So firm, and closely allied is this party and so well disciplined is it, that opposition is deemed useless—There is but one way and that is to devide them—In the Election for Senator Owen & Donnell[52] are the prominent candidates and we are well assured that Donnell will prevail over Owen and that by a smart number of votes—It is true that Stokes, Swain[53] and Caldwell have been thought of but little talk has been made of them—I consider them out of the question The issue then will be that Donnell will beat Owen for Senator and Spaight will beat him for Governor— This catastrophe cannot be endured—We cannot & will not submit to it—Owen has ever been and we now think he will be willing (but reluctantly perhaps as it has gone thus far) to yield to you—Neither owen nor Donnell are considered fit in point of Talent for the Station and a sentiment is felt by almost all (the swiss of the faction) and the personal friends of each of the candidates excepted that a man of more talent would come out—The almost universal sentiment is that you are the man and the only man that can effect the object that we all have so much at heart—

Gary,[54] Bynum, Williams[55] (of Martin) Bateman[56] also OBrien and very many others who unite in this party have expressed their great desire that you would come out—That they will vote for you, but that if you are not a candidate, they vote for Donnell—

Alexander and his friends are all in your favor and Despair of Success with Owen—Alexander told me last night and came over this morning to insist upon my writing to you—He says he & his friends agreed that as I had received a Letter from you they would request me to convey their wishes to you. [He] says he hopes and requests that you will come down by, not sooner than, Monday next—We very much fear that with the offices of Senator that of Governor will follow—and that in the Train will follow many of our most valued institutions—Nothing can be ex-

[51]Joseph H. Bryan.
[52]Judge John R. Donnell was judge of the superior court from 1819 to 1836. See above, p. 356n.
[53]David L. Swain.
[54]Roderick B. Gary.
[55]Joseph J. Williams represented Martin County in the senate from 1826 to 1831. *N. C. Manual*, 693.
[56]Daniel N. Bateman was in the legislature from Tyrrell County in 1815, 1817 to 1822, 1827 to 1832, and in 1834. *N. C. Manual*, 822-823.

pected of them, but gratifications to their dependants in their
favored projects without reference to the General Welfare—
I hope and Trust you will not disappoint our ardent wishes
and that you will come down and aid us with your presence even
if you do not choose to have your name put in nomination—The
message has given food for the vipers—They are roasting the
Gov. for the fees paid Badger,[57] Swain & Seawell and me for my
little *"Agency"*[58] but it cannot succeed—All are Federalists that
do not go with them—Saunders is I fear not what he should be—
I ought not to say fear for facts speak his course—I must close
my letter by renewing the assurance of my regard—
Yours
W. M. SNEED

[Addressed:]
Honl. Willie P. Mangum
Red Mountain P. O.
Orange County
North Carolina

WPM-LC

C. L. Hinton to Willie P. Mangum

RALEIGH Nov. 18th 1830.

My Dear Sir
I received a letter from Priestley a few days ago in which he
authorised me to say, if your friends thought the emergency of
the times required you should be put in nomination for Senator
they were at liberty to do so which letter I have shewn to such of
the members as I supposed wer your friends particularly the Roanoke members[59] who are anxious you should run—You are expected down on monday or Tuesday your friends think it advisable you should come, I however have some doubts on that subject, I have never known party feeling run half so high, both
sides claim you, I leave it to your own consideration whether it
would not excite a jealousy that might operate on the election

---

[57]George E. Badger, D. L. Swain, and Henry Seawell received $500.00 each as fees for handling the state's cases before the Federal courts against the purchasers of the Cherokee lands. *Comptroller's Report, 129-1830,* p. 10.
[58]As state commissioner, William M. Sneed received $1000.00 for adjusting the claims of the state against the Federal government for money spent in the War of 1812. *Comptroller's Report, 1829-1830,* pp. 10-11.
[59]Members from the counties along the Roanoke River, especially Warren, Halifax, and Northampton.

My own opinion is you would probably go without opposition. Gov Owen would not oppose you I feel almost certain, for he has expressed himself all along as desirous that you should offer and and I cant believe that Donnels friends would risque his election. Bynum Williams Mathews[60] and Gary are decided for you and the general impression is you are decidedly the most powerful man in the state—You must determine and let us know your feelings immediately for we are waiting to hear from you before we act—You must come or send an express as you think best.

I had intended writing you at length but being interrupted by company was prevented and must hurry this on to the office before the mail closes.

respectfully

C L HINTON.

[Addressed:]

Honble Willie P. Mangum
Red Mountain
Orange County
N. C.

WPM-LC

Isaac T. Avery[61] to Willie P. Mangum

MORGANTON Nov. 20th 1830.

The Honble. Willie P. Mangum,

My Dear Sir,

This will be presented to you by Mr. Gaither;[62] an applicant for the clerkship of this county, rendered vacant by the death of my much lamented Friend, and Brother in law, Elam A. Erwin—

of Mr Gaithers qualifications for the discharge of the duties of the appointment; the Members of the Bar who are acquainted with him, are the persons whose opinions ought to have most weight, and I presume they would be in his favour—

---

[60]Isham Matthews.

[61]Isaac Thomas Avery , 1785-1864, represented Burke County in the House of Commons in 1810-1811. He was a presidential elector in 1824 on the Jackson ticket. After that he held no political office. Instead he gave his time to his law practice and to his duties as cashier of the Morganton branch of the State Bank. He created a large estate, had a large family, and was something of a social leader in his section of the state. Ashe, *Biog. Hist. of N. C.*, VII, 6-8.

[62]Burgess M. Gaither.

I should be gratified if he could receive the appointment. your uniform friendship and kindness to Colo. Erwin, and his Family leaves no doubt on my mind; that his wishes, with regard to the appointment, will be permitted to have their full weight with you. & as little doubt that if on reflection you should decide against the application that it will be from a sense of duty, which we will cheerfully acquiesce in.

The late incumbent received the appointment at a time, when age and infirmity, had impaired The energy, and capacity of his Father, to transact the business, he purchased the best set of Dockets I ever saw, erected an office at his own expense, systematized his business, and arranged his papers, so that, I doubt whether any office in the State except the office at Plymouth, was in better order. I should be gratified that some friend should reap the benefit of his Labour, & expenditures. Whether the long period for which the Office has been held by Colo. Erwin, should operate for or against, a Member of his Family, is for you to decide—the unfeeling haste of an applicant at least, for the office; has excited an interest in the appointment that I should not perhaps otherwise have felt—and if I have not mistaken public feeling, has excited universal disgust—I feel great delicacy in addressing you on this subject, it is the first letter of the kind I ever wrote. the first time I ever solicited office either for myself or friends—& it is more to gratify Mr. Gaither than from any belief, that any thing I could say would influence the appointment, as I said above, I have confidence that you will do what you think right—& with that we should be satisfied. With great respect your

Friend and obt. Servt.

Isaac T. Avery

[Addressed:]

The Honble Willie P. Mangum
  Concord
    Cabarrus
      S. C.

politeness of   )
)
B. M. Gaither Esq.)

WPM-LC

B. A. Mangum to Willie P. Mangum

NOVEMBER 21st A. D. 1830

Sir,

Relative to the cart Wheels we were talking of; I wish You not to write to Berry, to make them; because, myself & Ephraim have been talking about making a trade.

He says he is willing to have work done in order, for me to save my money.

I have not commenced teaching school yct, in consequence of the people being so busy about sewing wheat, that they could not assist in building the house; though, the house is pretty well done, and I expect to commence sometime the following week. I shall have a very respectable school.

I am yours &c.

B. A. MANGUM[63]

[Addressed:]

Mr. W. P. Mangum
Orange
No. Ca.

WPM-D

Giles Mebane[64] to W. P. Mangum

HILLSBOROUGH
November 25th
1830

Hon"ble W. P Mangum
Dear Sir
I am directed to make known to you that according to the annual appointment of one of the two literary societies belonging to the University you have been chosen by your friends of the Dialectic Society to deliver an oration at Chapel Hill on

---

[63]One of Mangum's cousins in Orange County.
[64]Giles Mebane, 1809-1899, was the son of James Mebane of Mason Hall. A graduate of the state university, he practiced law in Orange and Alamance counties. He was in the legislature in 1844-1849, 1854-1855, 1860-1861, and 1877-1878. From 1862 to 1864 he was speaker of the senate and lieutenant governor. Grant, *Alumni Hist. of U. N. C.*, 423; *N. C. Manual*, 473-474, 483.

the day preceeding our next commencement—Inteligence from
you is requested if you can conveniently give it before the close
of the present college session

With respect and esteem
Your's &C

GILES MEBANE

The Honble Willie P. Mangum

[Address:] The Honebl Willie P. Mangum
Present

WPM-LC

W. M. Sneed to Willie P. Mangum[65]

RALEIGH Nov. 25th 1830

Dear Sir,

By accident I learned Monday Evening that Genl. Ward[66] had
dispatched an Express to you—We had determined to put you in
nomination on Tuesday—I say we vizt. C. L. Hinton, Alexander,
Gary, Williams, Mathews Wyche[67] myself & others—but it was
concluded that we would wait the answer It was received on
Tuesday after night—My Letter by the messenger was not delivered until yesterday at Breakfast—Upon the meeting of the
House at 10, Genl. Ward desired that the nomination should be
defered until this day—Alexander remarked (upon my telling
him I wished them indulged, for they were coming *gently* into
the fold) that it was like driving a gang of Patridges into the
nett—*Immediately* after the Journal was read this morning
Genl. Ward rose & remarked that an Election was to be made of
a most important officer at this Session—That of Senator to Congress, and that he nominated for that app^t. Willie P. Mangum
The Message from the Commons was then lying on our table—
having laid there on motion of Newland[68] from Tuesday to bal-

---

[65]See above, pp. 379-382, for the political maneuvers leading to this election.
[66]Edward Ward of Onslow County was a member of the legislature in 1806, 1810, 1811, 1815, and from 1822 to 1830. He was also a brigadier general of the militia. *N. C. Manual*, 833-834, 892; McIver, *N. C. Register*, 89.
[67]James Wyche was a member of the legislature from Granville County in 1828-1831, 1833, and in 1834-1835. *N. C. Manual*, 623.
[68]David Newland represented Burke County in the legislature from 1826 to 1830. In 1832 he was defeated for Congress by James Graham. *N. C. Manual*, 521-522; John H. Wheeler, *Reminiscences and Memoirs of North Carolina and Eminent North Carolinians* (Columbus, Ohio: Columbus Printing Works, 1884), 93-94.

lott on Monday next—I stated that it was *unusual* to make a nomination before the Senate had agreed to have the ballotting —and advised that the message be called up agreed to & then the motion of the Gen. from Onslow would appropriately follow— But he persisted—the nomination was made and ordered to be sent to the other house The Message was then called up assented to, and Genl. Jones[69] of Wilkes added to the nomination the name of Montfort Stokes—Thus we go I saw Genl. Jones this Evening—He told me that he had not have five words conversation with Genl. Stokes upon the Election—That he requested him to put his name in nomination That he could not well refuse, but that Stokes did not expect (as he told the other member from Wilkes)[70] that he (Jones) would vote for him—He is for you & will vote for you—Stokes is an arrant fool and he has (I learn) been told so by several, for running—No body will support him —The friends of Gov. Owen (& himself particularly) are quite reconcilled to your nomination You see Donnell is off—so the Coast is clear, as I told you in my letter from Warrenton—If Stokes friends can have any influence with him he will be withdrawn—If not—He *may* get 15 votes—Alexander says he should like to see you in Raleigh before the Election & told me to say so to you—If you *can*, come down Saturday or Sunday—

Your presence I think will assuage the acrimony of party spirit—I fear a contest between Owen & Spaight for Governor— I do not fear the result of the Election—but dread the bitterness of party strife—Carson[71] is here and all for you—I delivered your message—Indeed we are *all*—yes *all* for you—Come and see us & before the Election on Monday next—I am afraid you will be spoiled by the flattery and adulation of the Dastards—Can you believe that Fisher has given in his adhesion too?—I am told Bynum nominated you in the Commons about The time Genl. Ward did in the Senate—He was decidedly for you—I shewed him your letter early Monday morning—and he & Ward no doubt formed the plan of taking us all in, by a Coup de main, in the nomination—"That action deserves not much merit which is adopted from Necessity"—They *all* knew Owens friends would have supported you with a *very few* exceptions and were desirous of claiming the honor of nominating—Poor fellows let them have it—

[69]Edmund Jones represented Wilkes County in the legislature from 1802 to 1805, 1807 to 1812, in 1822, 1825, 1827, 1830, 1833, and from 1836 to 1839. He was also in the Council of State from 1822 to 1823. *N. C. Manual*, 432-433, 852-853.

[70]This was William Horton who was in the legislature in 1822-1823, 1829-1830, and 1833-1839. *N. C. Manual*, 853-854.

[71]Samuel Price Carson. See above, p. 196n.

It is now past Eleven—If I had time or space I would make a most *"obsequious* conclusion to your highness that will be—may be—no Election yet—

Your

W. M. SNEED

P S Give my kind esteem to your lady—and tell her I do sorrow for her repugnance to your returning to Congress—But I hope and believe that however it may operate upon her & you, it will eventuate in good, *great good* to the " *B L A N K S* she has given her husband

P.P.S. I am *really* afraid—you will be too proud of your Blushing Honors—But be sure come & see us before the Election—I have a great mind to write another Sheet—But tomorrow—

[Addressed:]
> Hon¹. Willie P. Mangum
>> Red Mountain
>>> Orange Cty.
>>>> N. C.

WPM-LC

Wm. Horner⁷² to Willie P. Mangum

ORANGE 28th. November 1830

Dear Sir

I promised Priestly H Mangum that I wou'd see you today & deliver to you a letter from him. But I dont feel very Well this morning so I send it by Boy Major—I was in Hillsborough yesterday nothing strange there worth stating—I will come over some day next week and see you.

Yours Respectfully

WM HORNER

Willie P. Mangum

N. B. Our Waggon landed home yesterday from Petersburg got for cotton $10.50 & 10.62½ Which is the highest market at this time.

W: H.

[Addressed:]
> Willie P. Mangum Esqr.
>> Orange N. C.

---

⁷²Justice of the Peace of Orange County.

WPM-LC

Copy of Letter Willie P. Mangum[73] *to Gov. Owen*

ORANGE the 1st. Decr. 1830

Sir

It is a leading principle upon which I have always acted, & I trust that no extremity shall drive me to compromize it. to *shew my hand* unreservedly in all my political transactions—

I have written two letters to Raleigh, the one addressed to your political friend C. L. Hinton Esqr. the Senator for Wake County, the other to Gen [Edward] Ward of Onslow, a member of the Senate, in which I have implicated your political principles in the strongest & most unequivocal manner—[74]

Though on no occasion should I have shrunk from this right & duty, yet I should not probably have exercised it, but for the reasons explained in those letters—

Those letters shall be as free to your inspection if desired, as I shall be ready to answer in any sort of responsibility for the liberty I have taken with you

I am Sir Your obt Servt.

WILLIE P. MANGUM

To Gov Owen—

[Endorsed:]
No 1.

———

WPM-LC

Willie P. Mangum to Edward Ward

ORANGE the 1st. Decr. 1830

My Dear General.

I have written to Gov. Owen—I wish you to know the substance—The following is a Copy of it—Towit. . . . [the omitted part is the same as the preceding letter]

———

[73]In Mangum's handwriting.
[74]In the days before this letter was written, Owen had promised to support Mangum if he saw that he could not defeat Donnell for the Senate. Donnell had made the same promise if he saw that he could not defeat Owen. Mangum's friends, Hinton and Sneed, therefore, delayed nominating Mangum in order that they might get the support of Donnell and Owen. This delay led a Donnell man to nominate Mangum before Hinton was ready. As a result Owen was indignant that his rival, Donnell, was to get credit for Mangum's election. Owen, therefore, bitterly opposed Mangum and almost defeated him. Enough Owen supporters finally voted for Mangum to elect him. The quarrel led to these hot letters. Boyd, "Draft of Life of Mangum," Chapter V, 1.

The within I write to Gov. Owen, upon the principle that I have no reservations *in these times* in political matters, & that I would not suffer the injury of being thought capable of doing a man an injury in private, which I would not dare do in public.—I hate mystery, subterfuge, & concealment.

Your friend
W. P. MANGUM

[Addressed:]
    Gen: Edward Ward
        of the Senate
           Raleigh
              No. Carolina.

WPM-LC

C. L. Hinton to Willie P. Mangum

RALEIGH Dec 2nd 1830

My Dear Sir

Your letter of yesterdays date was received last night about 10 clock, I would rather see you for three hours than any man in existence—John Randolph said save me from my friends and I will guard against my enemies, so you may say—for in the election for Senator there has been a complete somerset, for many of those who in the commencement branded you with the most odious names are now most clamorous for you—. there was no general concert, there was a rebellion[75] on the part of the friends of Owen, Donnel, Fisher & Jesse Speight[76] with a hope of bringing each on the turf. In the first place your situation was such as to be taken by the one and dropped by the other—. uncertain which was to assail or which to protect you—Owens friends first determined to run you believing you to be the strong man with Owens entire approbation—Halifax Cty, Gary, & J Williams firm for you regardless of the source from which your nomination might be made—I was requested to nominate you, which I delayed with a hope of bringing about a complete union, and at the request of some of Donnels friends. On the morning which the

---

[75]See the preceding letters.

[76]Jesse Speight, 1795-1847, who had represented Greene County in the legislature in 1820 and from 1823 to 1827, was at this time in Congress where he served from 1829 to 1837. In 1837 he moved to Mississippi and in 1845-1847 represented that state in the United States Senate. He was an ardent Democrat. *Biog. Dir. of Cong.*, 1553.

nomination was made Genl Ward rose in the Senate & Bynum in
the House immediately after the reading the journals, and announced you a candidate—this circumstance together with your
throwing yourself on the Roanoke interest was the beginning of
the present state of excitement which is greater than I have ever
witnessed in the Legislature—I feel unwilling to mention names,
but I know you have little idea of facts as they exist—nor can
you be correctly informed untill you meet with some impartial
friend who will give you a verbal statement and enter into a
more minute detail than can be done by letter—Alexander, Ship,
and others remain firm to you. Had you been nominated by
Owens friends they would have gone generally for you, and the
same opposition would have shewn itself on the other side—Your
angry feelings toward Gov Owen I know can never be allayed I
regret the occurrence. If as you say he has ever been your enemy
he has deceived me—for during the summer he frequently expressed his preference for you and unwillingness to be in your
way, and continued to do so untill you were put in nomination—
I then discovered that he faltered but believed it was owing to
the source from which the nomination came—. I highly respect
Gov Owen and should have supported him against any other man
than yourself—I have not seen him since his nomination, indeed
I was at one time placed in a situation in which I could not have
gone against him for yourself, whom every person knows is my
choice of the State—It is impossible to know how to act for the
best—some of your friends I think are doing you an injury by
their over Zeal — all feel enough on the subject — we were all
desappointed and mortified on the result of to days ballot. Mangum 86. Owen 97—I am a bad adviser I fear the suggestion I
made in my first letter in which I expressed my doubt as to the
policy of your coming down may have had some influence on you
if so I regret it, for I am now satisfied you would have been
elected if present to have stopped individuals and reports—My
respects to Mrs. Mangum tell her I have a son for each of her
daughters

                                              C L HINTON

[Addressed:]
    Honb^{le} Willie P Mangum
        Red Mountain
            Orange County
            N C

WPM-LC

R. M. Saunders to Willie P. Mangum

RALEIGH Decr. 3. 1830

My dear Sir—

We are thus far beaten in the election and our only relyance is on your aid—Your letter directing the withdrawal of yr. name was not rec^d untill Owens nomination & two ballots—having you tied at 89—yesterday Owen had 97—you 86—14 blanks—Last night our friends determined on a postponement untill Monday and have just succeeded in the Senate by a vote of 34. to 24—We think therefore that we have a right to call upon [you] to come here tomorrow—not in the character of a candidate—but as a friend to the *cause*—the intention is if you wish to decline a further ballot & Donnel or some other person cannot succeed to postpone untill the next session—this with your aid can be done —again I consider it as due to your own character to be here— both your sayings & yr. letters have been grossly misrepresented —The letter you wrote to Gov. Owen has been used as a *menace or challenge* & he has not thought proper to call either for Gen. Wards letter or Col. Hintons—You have met with *traitors*— when [you] had a right to expect friends—Caldwell [torn] done every thing in their power to defeat you—Judge Donnell is here —and a number of strangers will be here on Monday to attend the meeting of the Bank Directors &c—Donnell & friends are prepared to cooperate in whatever shall be deemed advisable— Fisher is acting in good faith towards you and directs me to say to you—that every thing like personal feeling is thrown aside & begs your attendance to aid & sustain the *cause* we all feel so deeply interested in—He feels confident your presence & nothing else can save us from Owens election—I view his success under the existing circumstances as fatal to our future prospects— where is the objection to your coming? Owen has mingled actively in the contest both by night & by day—You cannot again have the same means of defending yourself against the foul asperations & misrepresentations cast upon you—Dr. Smith[77] is here & no doubt in his *way* operating against you—Montgomery was against you at first—but has since done his duty—I again say your presence is due to yourself—your friends & the *cause*—

[77] James Strudwick Smith of Orange County.

unless you come we are beaten—if you come we will succeed or
at least defeat our opponents—

truly
Yrs
R. M. SAUNDERS

[Addressed:]

    Hon. Willie P. Mangum
        Orange

)
pr Boy)
)

WPM-LC

W. M. Sneed to Willie P. Mangum

Balloting for Senators in Congress.

[3 December 1830]

	Novr. 29th	Novr. 30.	Decr. 1st	Decr. 2nd.
	1st	2nd	3	4	5th.
Mangum	80	81	88	89	86
Stokes	37	32	21	11	1
Owen (not Nomd)	22	39	71	89	97
Genl. Speight Do.	[torn]	[torn]	3	......	......
Donnell	[torn]	[torn]	......	......	......
Scatg & Blanks	[torn]	[torn]	3	5	Bks. 6
Total	19[torn]	[torn]	194	194	
Majority	96	[torn]	98	98	
Fisher	......	[torn]	1	......	
J. W. Clark	......	[torn]1	......	......	
Toomer	......	[torn]2	......	......	2
Swain	......	[torn]1	1	......	1
Marshall[78]	......	1	......	......	[torn]
Spaight	......	[torn]	1	......	
Amos Weaver	......	[torn]	1	......	4

----

[78]This was Clement Marshall who was in the senate from Anson County from 1828 to
1831. *N. C. Manual*, 488.

My Dear Sir [torn]   Thursday 11 P. M.

It [torn]ing to me to be obliged to give [torn] regoing statement of the vo[te] [torn] Senator—I had no right to [torn] all
any good from the nomination of you by Ward & Bynum. It is all
over. I think nothing can prevent the Election of Owen—I wish
to God you had come down The slanders, venom & malice that
has been vented at you is without parallel in this day—Owen's
friends were much displeased at your nomination by the Donnell
men Every means was devised, as you see, to create division &
distrust—The two Spaights never voted for you until the balloting this day. The friends of Owen (& I suspect Owen has been
instrumental) have given it out that you sent a message by Gov.
Iredell when he returned from the West to Owen, that you would
not be a Candidate & that you wished him (Owen) to come forward and beat Spaight & Donnell—This has soured his friends
[torn] the two Spaights and several of [torn] guard—many of
Owen [torn] off & voted Blanks—Pos[torn] aver, as in the present cas[e] [torn] himself to be made the fa[torn]al of any party. Some of both si[des] (Owen & Donnell) proffered to him
l[as]t night to make him Gov. if he would carry his friends over
to th[eir] side. Poor fools they must hav[e] [k]nown (or ought
to have known) [that] the could not control a Le[torn]
[torn]iven to him. He was with-[torn] noming Docr. Montgom-
[ery] [torn] enough to say (as Danl. [torn] told me) that you
were not in heart friendly to Genl. Jackson—He (B) contra-
dicted it & *said* the Conversation took place between you & himself (Docr. M. not present) at May Orange Court. W. W. Stedman has given you many thrusts for some sentence you passed
upon a culprit when you were last on the Edenton Circuit—
Docr. M. voted for you, I doubt not on the last ballot for both the
Spaights did for the 1st Time—I cannot give further details—it
will do no good Excuse my manner—I have been so agitated all
day I have not been able to compose myself so as to sit down &
write to you—I thought I would wait until I could hear everything—I have just returned from Alexanders room—I told him
I should call upon Genl. Ward in the mornin[g] [torn] what he
meant to do w[ith] [torn]. He told me he had done so[torn]
[torn] is to give him an answ[er] [torn] morning—

The Con[torn] [t]alk is that Donnell or Fishers [torn] be
nominated tomorrow—I think it probable that Both will—I intend if either is—that I *will* withdraw your name—I have heard

nothing [torn] the Express that was [torn] on the day before
yester[day] [torn] [M]r. Saunders and Hay[wood] [torn] sent
not condescended to let [torn] a word—Genl. Ward never [torn]
your letter nor did he ever tell me a word about it—but *slily* &
sneakingly in the manner I have before told you of—nominated
you—If I could have had C. Hinton Col. Jo. Williams or Boddy[79]
to nominate you all would have been well or if you could have
come down on Saturday or Sunday last—Alexander tells me
Ward is very much displeased at some of his friends, (R. D. S.
& C Spaight and others) for the manner in which you were
nominated & their Turning round & voting against you afterwards

I shall indulge no regrets—but *I do feel* more than I can or
will attempt to express—I did feel dishonored by such *an association* as I have acted with in this Election—I mean very many
of the Spaight faction—& nothing but you [& your] name could
ever [torn] ced me to cooperate [torn]—

Saunders [torn] Dinner today present R. D. Sp[aight]
Fi[sher] & others. I do not know w[torn] or 8 in all[80]—

I will fold th[is]up & commence on another s[hee]—yours

W. M. SNEED

[Addressed:]

Honl. Willie P. Mangum
Red Mountain
Orange
(N. C.)

WPM-LC

Jno. Owen to Willie P. Mangum

RALEIGH Dec[r]. 4[th]. 1830

Sir,

I have received a letter from you dated the 1[st]. inst: the particular object or purport of which, I am at a loss fully to com-
prehend—unless it be—to inform me that you have traduced

N. C. Manual, 717-718.
[79]William .W. Boddie was in the senate from Nash County in 1820-1826 and 1828-1832.
[80]The postponement of the ballotting and renewal of friendly relations with Owen's supporters resulted in Mangum's election by the following vote: Mangum 103, Owen 84, scattering 8. McDuffie, "Willie P. Mangum," 41.

my political character in certain letters addressed to Charles L
Hinton esq, and Genl. Ward—to which you refer me for information. Any reference to those letters to ascertain the nature
and extent of the injury which you may have done my reputation, is unnecessary, since from your letter it is evident that you
seem to consider the charges contained in them as reproachful
to my character—

You conclude your letter communicating the fact that you had
assailed my character, by avowing "your readiness to answer in
any sort of responsibility for the liberty you have taken with
me"—This I am constrained to "consider an invitation to the
field of honor—["]

If I am right in this interpritation, and of its correctness you
must be the better Judge, Your letter leaves me no alternative
but to accept the call[81]—

My friend Louis D Henry esq,[82] will receive any communication you may be disposed to make, and is fully authorised to
conclude any arrangements which the matter may require.

I am Sir, your obd[t] Serv[t].
JNO. OWEN

To the Honb[le].
Willie P. Mangum

[Addressed:]
To the Honb[ble].
Willie P Mangum
Present—

WPM-LC

W. P. Mangum to Gov. John Owen[83]

RALEIGH December 8th. 1830.
Sir.

Your letter of the 4th. Inst. was handed to me on the morning
of the 5th by Mr. Henry & I have to express my regret that unavoidable engagements have delayed my acknowledgment of it
until this time—I cannot refrain from a strong expression of

---

[81]Mangum was willing to bring about a reconciliation. Louis D. Henry, David F. Caldwell,
and William M. Sneed were, therefore, able to mediate a peaceful settlement and prevent a
duel. McDuffie, "Willie P. Mangum," 41.
[82]Louis D. Henry, 1788-1846, was in the state legislature in 1821, 1822 and from 1830 to
1832. He was a presidential elector on the Democratic ticket in 1844. Ashe, *Biog. Hist. of
N. C.*, II, 163-167.
[83]In the handwriting of Mangum. Apparently this is a copy for William M. Sneed.

surprize at the interpretation, which you say you are "constrained" to place upon mine of the 1st. Instant, to-wit. to consider it "an invitation to the field of honor."—

It is alike due to myself; to the Judicial station[84] which I occupy, and to the moral sense of the whole community in which I live, to protest against an "intepretation" which would indicate on my part a total disregard of all the duties & obligations which I owe to either—Such an idea never entered my head, & it is to me wholly incomprehensible, by what rule of construction, such a meaning could have been imputed to my letter.

Having despatched peremptory direction to Raleigh to have my name withdrawn from the contest for Senator, before I wrote mine of the 1st. Inst to you; and without any knowledge of the fact; expecting that your name would be placed before the Legislature for that Station; I felt that it was my "right & duty" to comment upon what I understood to be your "political principles."—Comments of this sort, I viewed as being within the range of legitimate criticism of public men & their public principles, and according to this view, I stated to you in my letter that I claimed the exercise as matter of "right & duty."— Being unwilling however to make the *boundary* definitely & peremptorily, to which I might rightfully go; I preferred remitting that matter to your own judgment & sense of propriety—

I hold it as a maxim, never to touch the character of a Gentleman in any respect; without a due sense & recognition of every sort of just responsibility—Upon that ground I placed this matter—I think it was placed upon proper ground & there I must beg leave to let it stand.—

I deem it due to myself & waiving all etiquette, I deem it due to you to say, that the *motive* of my letter to you of the 1st. Inst., was to avoid the appearance & imputation of being capable of striking a blow in the dark, and of endeavouring to injure a gentleman by comments upon his political principles in a private, & insidious manner.

I have the honor to be
Your Mo. Obt. Sert.
W. P. MANGUM

The foregoing is a True copy of the Original
W. M. Sneed[85]

---

[84]The North Carolina law made duelling a crime.
[85]In Sneed's handwriting.

Tho, the last paragraph is in strict conformity with the fact, yet I have doubts whether it ought not to be suppressed. Will you give me your opinions on this; & suggest freely what you think fits the occasion, always having reference to what you think right & proper according to the sentiments of mankind in matters of this sort.

W. P. M.[86]

This note being delivered, Mr. Sneed was authorized upon the withdrawal of Gov Owens first letter which contained an acceptance of a supposed call, to reiterate what Mr Mangum had s^d. in his first interview with Mr Henry. That he (Mr M) had not to his recollection impeached or designed to impeach the integrity or personal honor of Gov Owen[87]—

[Endorsed:]
> No 3

[Enclosure 1]

We are authorised by the friends of both gentlemen to state that the rumor of a Challenge having passed between Gov. Owen & Judge Mangum is untrue—That some difficulty was supposed to exist between them which has been amicably adjusted and in a manner satisfactory and honorable to both Gentlemen

> LOUIS D HENRY
> W M SNEED
>
> Decr. 13th. 1830—

Honbl Mr. Mangum

WPM-LC

John Owen to W. P. Mangum

RALEIGH Dec 11th 1830

Sir,
    I have declined to receive your letter addressed to Mr Hinton, or to inquire into its contents—because to do either, after the

---

[86]In Mangum's handwriting.
[87]In autograph of Mangum.

receipt of yours of today, would seem to imply an injurious distrust of you, and to shew myself insensible to the obvious spirit of frankness and conciliation in which your last letter is written. In that letter you asure me that "you have never to the best of your recollection impeached or designed to impeach my integrity or personal honor." This is all the explanation that I could with propriety ask, or that you could with propriety give—To demand any thing further would indeed be to shew myself disposed to seek "occasion for further controversy." Permit me to assure you that had this frank disavowal of any reflections on my integrity or honor been earlier made, all correspondence of an unfriendly character between us, would have ceased with your second letter

I am your most obedient servant
JNO. OWEN

Honble
    Willie P. Mangum

[Address:] To
    The Honble
        Willie P. Mangum
        Present

WPM-LC

Thos. Jeff. Faddis[88] *to Willie P. Mangum*

SORM[a]. [?] 13th Dec. 1830

Dear Sir

Permit me to say to you that I have got able to explore the savage country without injury from which I have just returned; where I think the greatest corruption is going on I have ever witnessed; the whole of the chickasaw Lands[89] have become a merciless prey to a fiew of what the call inteligent Indians & Lords of speculators, who are purchaseing the Lands without money viz. with promises, & the Indian will have to depend

----

[88]Thomas Jefferson Faddis was a physician who represented Hillsboro in the House of Commons in 1831-1832. Grant, *Alumni Hist. of U. N. C.*, 191.
[89]In September 1830 Eaton and Coffee, as President Jackson's representatives, made a treaty with the Chickasaw leaders by which the Chickasaws agreed to live with the Choctaws. The treaty was never ratified by the Indians, but it was used as an excuse of the whites of Alabama and Mississippi to take up the lands which formerly belonged to the Chickasaws. Grant Foreman, *Indian Removal: The Emigration of the Five Civilized Tribes of Indians* (Norman, Okla.: University of Oklahoma Press, 1932), 195-197.

upon the result of a second sale for his money—The treaty as it now stands opens the greatest door to fraud & corruption ever before witness—do I beseach you make some enquiry into the matter. These Indians have a claim upon the protection of the government, I have strong contention with the Jackson men here & in the nation, but as yet they have stood off. I have written a letter to Mr. Henry Clay will you say to him of me what you conceive me worth

Yours

THO. JEFF. FADDIS

Honblr. W. P. Mangum.

[Addressed:] Honble.
Willie P. Mangum
Senator
Washington City.

———

WPM-LC

D. F. Caldwell to Willie P. Mangum

[1830]

Dr. Sir.

I regret to learn that an unfortunate difficulty exists between yourself & Govr. Owen. I feel too deep an interest in this matter, any longer to remain silent. I hope I shall be excused for offering my friendly mediation. I can not assume the responsibility of deciding so grave a matter, even if my umpirage were submitted to. I hope however you will acquiesce in this proposition; namely that the whole matter shall be left to the decission of mutual friends selected by yourself, or to mutual friends selected by a mutual friend. I have addressed a similar note to Gov. Owen.

Respectfully

D. F. CALDWELL.

Addressed:
Honble.
Mr. Mangum.

WPM-LC

Wm. M. Sneed to Willie P. Mangum

10 before 12

Dec. 22nd[90] [1830]

Dear Sir

I thought I would continue my letters—but I don't know what to write. Docr. Jas. S. Smith came down yesterday in time to give you a nuge under the short ribs—The Chatham Members[91] were opposed to you—Bynum was steady and Hearty—So was Col. very many others—Matthews, Nicholson,[92] Gary Jo. Williams all Franklin[93] & Warren.[94] The Cape Fear was as you supposed Jo. A. Hill voted for you until Owen was nominated— Though he did not like it—Genl Jones although he nominated Stokes voted for you—Wheeler (of H.) was up to the Hubb for Owen—so were several from that part of the Country because the Gov. was for opening Naggs Head—Obrian was for you— but I suspect it was only because the Donnell faction were so generally.

I thought when I made the Explanation to Jo. Hill & others about the nomination that it would have been satisfactory—it was so to him & a few others—but the *Wildfire* was kindled & no stop could be put to it—

I recall all I said in my last letter about the fauning & flattery that would be heaped upon you by your former enemies—as you said their did come a frost and considerable one it was this morning—But it came yesterday to your prospects—I little expected that your surmise might turn out History [William] Murchison of Cumberland said you were spoiled—That you thought you could get every thing you wanted—That you could go in and out when & when you pleased—but the 5th Ballott would shew—He said this morning the vote would be Owen 104 Mangum 93—Hill[95] of Stokes was warmly your friend throughout Martin[96] was opposed to you—Dodson[97] was steadily for you

---

[90]The date of this letter should be December 2. It was postmarked December 3.
[91]Joseph Ramsay was the state senator and Nathaniel G. Smith and Joseph J. Brooks were the members of the lower house from Chatham County.
[92]Colonel Thomas Nicholson represented Halifax County in the House of Commons from 1829 to 1831. *N. C. Manual*, 640.
[93]The representatives from Franklin County in the two houses of the legislature were William P. Williams, William Branch, and Gideon Glenn.
[94]Warren County's representatives were: John H. Hawkins, John Bragg, and Ransom Walker.
[95]John Hill, 1797-1861, was a member of the senate in 1823-1825, 1830, and 1831. He served in Congress as a Democrat from 1839 to 1841. *Biog. Dir. of Cong.*, 1097-1098.
[96]Robert Martin was in the state senate from Rockingham from 1829 to 1834.
[97]Stephen Dodson.

—The faction fixed Kerr[98] & Gwin[99] of Caswell for you and afterwards they were as noisy as anybody—Welch[100] was for Owen—Selby[101] of Hyde was for you until the last ballot—Harris[102] the same — It was *said* that you County men were all opposed I do not know it to be so—

I don't know when to quit—but I cannot write more than this side—Marshall[103] was for Stokes—I presume he voted for Owen the last ballot—An election was never conducted in such a miserable manner or poor wight of a candidate supported by such hetrogenious materials since old Adams time—

Well—if you have to abuse me for acts of Commission & omission Mrs. Mangum will have Commisation & forgive me as her great object is accomplished—you stay at home—A Tree is to be judged by its fruits—Although I brought forth the blossom—The fruit never came to perfection—and she may satisfy herself that the frost has nipped your bud so close. I do not think you will blossom again in at least six years—

Again excuse this Letter—*Nota Bene* I have endeavored to act with all the caution & prudence I could [m]uster & believe I did so—but fate, cruel fate determined the result—

Yours friend

W M SNEED

I don't know whether I
ought to ask you to answer this—but you
           have many, hearty & steady friends.

[Addressed:]

Willie P. Mangum,
     Red Mountain
          Orange,
               N. C.

---

[98]James Kerr of Caswell County.
[99]Littleton Gwinn of Caswell County.
[100]William Welch of Haywood County.
[101]William Selby, Sr., of Hyde County.
[102]Ransom Harris of Davidson County.
[103]Clement Marshall of Anson County.

1831

WPM-LC

W. M. Sneed to Willie P. Mangum

RALEIGH January 4th 1831

Honl. Willie P. Mangum
    Dear Sir
        The Convention resolutions[1] introduced this day week by
Dick[2] were taken up in Committee of the whole,—several small
amendments were made and the blanks filled up—The Speaker
then moved a substitute which proposed to submit the subject
of "Convention" or "no Convention" to the people at the next
election—This was lost by a large majority—I *believe* 37 to 26—
Upon Reporting the resolution to the house, and a motion made
for its indefinite postponement—the vote by yeas & nays stood
42 for & 21 against the motion—
    A similar string of resolutions was simultaneously introduced
the Commons and were also taken up this day while we were
discusing them in the Senate—Ransom[3] I understood made a
good speech in favor of them—In it he "pinched the toes, of Mr.
Speaker Fisher—Long[4] followed Pearson[5] and the Speaker has
the floor for tomorrow I am glad to see the Western gentlemen
disagree among themselves, and all most all of the Cape Fear
folks fall out with the West—when rougues fall out—you know
the rest—
    In the Senate speaker Caldwell, Martin and others expressed
their sorrow that Dick had introduced these resolutions—and
several of the Western gentlemen voted against them—so did
most of the Cape Fear people After it was all over—I told Dick
"Now do the honorable thing,—call up the appropriation Bill
and let us pass it"—He intimated that he would not move it himself but would vote for it—I have a *hope* a *very* faint one, that
this may yet be done—

---

[1]These convention resolutions called for a state convention to revise the constitution. This
was a part of the western pressure.
    [2]John M. Dick, 1791-1861, a lawyer of Greensboro, was in the state senate in 1819 and
from 1829 to 1831. In 1835 he was selected as a judge of the superior court and he served
until his death in 1861. Robert Dick Douglas, "Judge John McClintock Dick," *Founders and
Builders of Greensboro, 1808-1908*, compiled by Bettie D. Caldwell (Greensboro, N. C.: Jos.
J. Stone and Co., 1925), 29-41.
    [3]Ransom Harris of Davidson County.
    [4]William L. Long of Halifax County.
    [5]Richard M. Pearson represented Rowan County until Davis County was formed in 1836.
From 1836 to 1848 he was a judge of the superior court. After that he was on the bench of
the state Supreme Court. His opposition to Jefferson Davis during the Civil War is well
known. *D. A. B.*, XIV, 360; Ashe, *Biog. Hist. of N. C.*, V, 295-310.

I am *ashamed* to say that there is no hope entertained of passing the resolution for the repair of the Statue[6]—

All the Bank Bills have submitted to the Guilotine of the Commons Kerr of Caswell introduced a new one this day in the Senate—I heard it whispered, that it was intended to substitute Martin's Bill for it—pass it & they hoped the Commons would eventually pass it into a Law—I wish we were all at home—For we do, and have done, and will do, nothing but mischief so long as we stay here—

If I can find Time in the morning I will write y[ou a con] *fidential,* letter—If not then I[torn] in a day or two—No State Plot [torn] [o]nly relate to *me myself—*

> With Sentiments of Kindness
> I am your Obt. Servt.
>
> W. M. SNEED

[Addressed:]

> Honl. Willie P. Mangum
> of the Senat[e]
> Washington City.

WPM-LC

W. Montgomery to Willie P. Mangum

RALEIGH 7 [Jan.,] 1831—

My Dear Sir

Raleigh again In Ruins About 4. of the Clock this Morning, With in a few yards of the spot where the Fire in 1816 originated, the Fire was discovered. all Efforts to Extinguish it was Ineftual until It reached Mr. Stewarts dwelling house, on Fayetteville Street, the Spot where the First of 1816 was Errested, the Flames were Stopped Before the[y] reached the Corner House, on Fayetteville Street occupied by Marshall & Co. all the Buildings on the square nearly consumed, perhaps the number of buildings Consumed is 50— or 60—Most of the goods Were removed, the Lost is variously stated from $30—to $80,000 Dollars

---

[6]Possibly Canova's famous statue of Washington which had been placed in the State House in 1821.

Many Houses were Blown up. No serious accident that I have Heard of Occurred, Many Narrow Escapes, We shall probibly adjourn about this Day week, or sooner
In Haste   Yours

W. MONTGOMERY

N.b   the Loss Estimated at)
      $200,000 I Just Learn)
            W M   )

[Addressed:]

Hon^rl. Wiley P. Mangum Esq
Washington City
D. C.

WPM-LC

John H. Hinton[7] to Willie P. Mangum

CLARKSVILLE, TENNESSEE.
January 31st 1831.

My dear Sir,

I think you will not fail to recognize in the signature to this hasty script the name of an old and an intimate associate of early life and an unaltered friend at every subsequent period to the present.

Many a year has now elapsed, my friend, since I had the pleasure of reading a scrape from your pen or of hearing from you otherwise than through the medium of the publick prints; and although *you* have not had the same means of knowing *my* fortunes and condition in life yet I flatter myself that the name "Hinton," with the associations it will necessarily occasion, has not entirely vanished from *your* mind.

How widely different have been the pursuits to which, in the wisdom of an all-wise and superintending Providence, our attention has been directed, notwithstanding the intimate connexion that subsisted between us in the time of our school-boy-gambols! Yet as widely diversified as they have been I am sure we have not ceased to cherish, with some degree of pleasure, a recollection of many of the scenes that always render such seasons interesting to every subsequent period of life.

---

[7] See above, p. 2n.

The only object of this brief and hasty scrawl is to elicit from you some account of yourself and yours unconnected with publick life, and to beg the favour of such communications from time to time as you may find it in perfect accordance with your convenience and feelings to make.

The Hon. Cave Johnson[8]—the representative from this district —my friend and neighbour, could give you any account you might be disposed to receive respecting us.

Hoping soon to hear from you, I have the honour to subscribe myself, with the highest regard and the best wishes for your happiness and prosperity.

Yours friend and
Most ob. Ser.

JNO. H. HINTON.

Hon. Willie P. Mangum,
    Washington City.

[Addressed:]

> Hon. Willie P. Mangum,
>   Senator in Congress
>   Washington City.

WPM-LC

Henry J. Cannon[9] to Willie P. Mangum

CHAPEL HILL January 31st 1831

Dear Sir

A communication was addressed to you some time since in behalf of the Members of the Dialectic Society, through their President, requesting you to serve as their Orator at the approaching Commencement of this University. We have not as yet received an answer from you. And as we will be reduced to the necessity of making another choice, should you not accept of our appointment, I am instructed by that body over which I have the honour at present to preside, respectfully to request you to favour us

------

[8]Cave Johnson, 1793-1866, a lawyer in Clarksville, Tennessee, was a Democratic congressman from 1829 to 1837 and from 1839 to 1845. He was Postmaster General in Polk's Cabinet from 1845 to 1849. *Biog. Dir. of Cong.*, 1151.

[9]Henry J. Cannon, 1811-1862, a native of Raleigh, became a planter and lawyer of west Tennessee. Grant, *Alumni Hist. of U. N. C.*, 97.

with an answer as soon as possible.[10] We feel asured Sir, that, should you accept our appointment, its duties will be ably discharged; and that you may accept it is the sincere wish not of myself along, but of the Dialectic Society at large.

Yours respectfully

HENRY. J. CANNON

[Addressed:]

>   Hon. Willie. P. Mangum
>   Red Mountain
>   Orange N. Ca

———

W.PM-LC

Bill of Sale of Wagon to Willie P. Mangum

[March 22, 1831]

State of North Carolina)
)
    Orange County   )

   I John J. Carrington by these presents for & in consideration of the sum of one hundred dollars have bargained, sold & transferred, & by these presents do bargain, sell & transfer to Willie P. Mangum his Executors, admrs. & asigns one new road waggon, and the Geer & cover.   To Have & to hold to said Willie P. Mangum his heirs, Executors & assigns forever.

The said Mangum agreeing to permit said Carrington to use said Waggon & Geer to remove his family to Tennessee— Witness my hand & seal this 22nd. March 1831.

JNO. J. CARRINGTON

Test.
[torn] Parker—

———

[10]During his political career, Mangum received numerous invitations to deliver the commencement oration at his alma mater. He declined all such invitations. The Rev. William M. Green, a future bishop of the Episcopal Church, delivered the oration for the 1831 commencement. Battle, *Hist. of U. N. C.,* I, 339.

WPM-LC

J. G. A. Williamson[11] to Willie P. Mangum

LAGUAYRA [VENEZUELA] 30th. April 1831.

Willie P Mangum Esqr.
                    Sir
    I perceive from my papers rec[d]. a few days since from the
U States that the Consulship at Tangiers and Tripoli have been
vacated by the death of Mullowny[12] and Mr Coxe, the latter has
been filled but I believe the other still vacant—May I therefore
ask the favour of you to write to the Secre[ry]. of State at Washington in behalf of my application for the same—
    I must frankly confess to you my great object of change is to
leave an office dependent upon fees, and in the execution of the
duties of which, from the limited Laws on the subject of Consuls,
that so frequently brings me in contact unpleasantly with my
countrymen; as a merchant I have every resident american
against me and as a Consul in exacting the mizerable fees of office, I gain the illwill of Cap[ts]—& owners of vessels, I must
therefore sacrifice one or the other, or loose both—You can form
no idea of the settled jealousy of american merchants against
Consuls, and the no small degradation we suffer in the eyes of
these people by attempting business—Not having to any extent
engaged in business, I find my expences greatly exceeding my
fees, so much so that I am compelled to return home, being unable to support myself with Standing without more means than
I have at my Command, my fees of office for the last 2½ years
not exceeding 200 to 300 $ pr year—
    There is no subject that requires more the attention of Con-
gress than the Consular system of the U States, either to abolish
it entirely or place Consuls upon a different footing—If they are
necessary then pay them, if not do not send them; All the large
commercial nations of Europe pay their Consuls—
    It is more particularly necessary in South America than per-
haps any where else, where so much effect is made by appearances—Any services you may be enabled to render me or any of
your friends among the Cabinet at Washington will be ading my

---

[11]See above, p. 208n.
[12]John Mullowny had been consul to Tangier since the early 1820's. McIver, *N. C. Register*, 141.

dear Sir further obligations to those I am already under to you
and will greatly oblige   Sir

Your Friend &
Obt Servt

J. G. A. WILLIAMSON

P. S. I have written Gen. Saunders[13] on this subject to Raleigh
N. B. The Register, Tho⁵ L Smith Esqr.[14] is an old acquaintance
& friend of mine at Washington I have written to him likewise—
Perhaps a letter addressed to him first, might answer some purpose, however I have more confidence in your application direct
than any other, except some old particular revolutionary friend
of the President—Col. Polk[15] in Raleigh could be of great service
to me—I have written to R. Potter of Oxford to give you his aid
—But Sir I am sattisfied the very document which you presented
to Mr Clay though Mr. Williams[16] at Washington to obtain for
me this situation & for which I am under so many obligations
would if on file at Washington, be sufficient upon calling it to
view, by note from you to the Secre⁺ʸ. of State, to obtain any
vacant Consulship on the Barberry Coast or any where else—

Asking your attension
I am Sir your friend
& obt svt

J. G. A. WILLIAMSON

I am personally acquainted with Mr Branch[17] & Mr Eaton[18] at
Washington—but slightly with either----*your earliest attention
to this will much oblige me*   W.

[Addressed:]

To the Honbl.
Willie P. Mangum
Stagville
Benehans Store
Orange County
North Carolina

---

[13]Romulus M. Saunders.
[14]Thomas L. Smith, a native of Virginia, had lived many years in Hillsboro and Raleigh
before he moved to Washington. See below Williamson's letter to Mangum, May 11, 1831.
[15]Colonel William Polk.
[16]Lewis Williams.
[17]John Branch was Jackson's Secretary of the Navy at this time.
[18]John H. Eaton.

WPM-LC

J. G. A. Williamson to Willie P. Mangum

Consulate of the United States
LA GUAYRA 11th. May 1831.

To Wilie P. Mangum Esq.
   Orange County
      N. C. Sir

Under date of the 30th. april last I addressed
you to Stagsville, on the subject of the vacancy of the Consulate
of the U States at Tangier—I have always prefered an appointment under the system of our Barbary Consulates, than one under fees alone in any other Country—My last papers informed
me Tangier & Tripoli both have become vacant by the death of
the Consuls of the U States at those places, the latter I observed
filled, but the first I do not think has been—under this impression I wrote you on the subject requesting your friendship & aid
to procure the same for me, and permit me now to repeat my
former solicitations—

I am well aware I may be pressing you into service too soon,
but Sir I know of no person to whom I could so well apply for
friendship in such a matter together with a general knowledge
of me as yourself or who could be able to render me more effectual service—

Under date of the 30th—I wrote to Thos. L. Smith, the Register at Washington to give me information, whether the situation
was filled or not, and likewise for his aid in the affair, he is an
old acquaintance, but he cannot do me the effectual service that
you can, at the same time I am well aware there is great intimacy between him and the Secre^{ty}. of State—Smith comes from
New York into office but is a Virginian, and whom you in all
probability well knew when he resided in Hillsboro & Raleigh—

A change in my situation here will at the same time give the
President an opportunity to gratify some merchantile application for a Consulate situation—

I find the day is gone by for consular offices to bring business
to the holder of it; There must be other causes of a more powerful inducement, which are not at my command—and if at my
command I would kneed no aid of office to succede—

To depend upon fees for support here, would *beggar* me, and
to attempt business would sink all my influence as Consul among
these people—besides the unceasing enmity that always arises in

such cases from my countrymen, *A merchantile Consul* is no enviable person, and to get along much has he indeed to suffer from all quarters—

I have written & shall write again by this opportunity, to Genl Saunders at Raleigh on the subject, to Genl Barringer & R. Potter likewise—What [course for me to] pursue to aid me in this affair can be best suggested by—yourself—An *immediate* notice of it the Secre^ty. State perhaps would be best—

Begging your pardon for this intrusion & acknowledging myself with my obligations I am already under to you—

I am Sir Your Obt. Svt—

J. G. A. WILLIAMSON

P.S. My Compliments to Mrs Mangum & family

[Addressed:]

To the Hon^bl.
    Willie P. Mangum
        Staggsville
           Orange County
               North Carolina.

WPM-LC

William Watts Jones[19] to Willie P. Mangum

OXFORD August 30, 1831

Dear Sir.

It is a fact, that Robert Potter, on sunday last, castrated Lewis Taylor the Methodist-preaching negro trader and a young man by the name of Wiley, for having illicit intercourse with his wife.[20]

I know, Potter is unwilling that an unfavorable impression should be made on the minds of his friends, of which he considers you one; and therefore I mention to you, that he has unreservedly, and it is believed penitently, co[n]fessed it.

[19]An attorney from Wilmington who served in the legislature from 1807 to 1815 and from 1825 to 1827. *N. C. Manual*, 719-720, 722-723.

[20]In the trial which followed, Lewis Taylor testified that Potter had accused seven other men of showing undue attention to his wife in order to obtain a divorce and as a result marry a rich widow in Washington. The court sentenced Potter to two years' imprisonment and a $2000.00 fine. In 1834 he was expelled from the House of Commons for cheating at cards. He left for Louisiana and later for Texas where he was killed. W. C. Allen, *History of Halifax County* (Boston, Mass.: Cornhill, n.d.), 187; *N. C. Free Press*, March 27, 1832.

The examining Court believing Wiley in some danger, refused to take bail; and I am (as there is no lawyer here at present) making out a case for Habeas Corpus.

Yours

WM. WATTS JONES.

[Addressed:]

The Honble Willie P. Mangum
Hillsboro' No. Ca.

W. P. Mangum to John H. Bryan[21]

HILLSBORO 31st August 1831

My Dear Sir,

Your favor of the 12th Inst. has just this moment been received, and it will give me much pleasure to be able to be of any service to your friend Mr. Shepard. I have not of late, had any correspondent at Washington, & therefore you know, that my accommodation will be esteemed as of but little value. It shall nevertheless be freely and cordially given—I shall avail myself of the earliest opportunity to write to Washington on the subject.—I had a slight acquaintance with Mr Shepard a few years ago, and as well on his account as to gratify your wishes, it would afford me much satisfaction to be of any service in this matter.—

I promise myself the pleasure of writing to you occasionally from Washington, & I trust I shall not in vain, endeavour to lay you under a like requisition—No assurance I trust, is necessary to satisfay you that I remember with much pleaure our former intercourse, characterized as it always was on your part, with liberality, magnanimity, & a sentiment of the most friendly conciliation.

Yours truly & sincerely

WILLIE P. MANGUM

[Address:] John H. Bryan Esquire[22]
Newbern
No. Carolina

---

[21]The original letter is in the John H. Bryan Papers, Duke University Library, Durham, N. C.
[22]John Heritage Bryan, 1798-1870, was in the state senate from 1823 to 1825 and a member of the U. S. House of Representatives from 1825 to 1829. *Biog. Dir. of Cong.*, 752.

WPM-LC

Stephen K. Sneed to Willie P. Mangum

OXFORD 31st Augt 1831

Dr Sir—

Robert Potter has committed a most outrageous and disgrace-
ful act upon Lewis Willie & Lewis Taylor of this county the particulars of which David Laws will give you; and Mr Thos H Willie father of Lewis W[illie] has requested me to write you, for
the purpose of employing you to assist the Solicitor in prosecuting Potter, which you will please to do,   In haste

Your friend Sincerely

STEP K SNEED

[Addressed:]

Honl.
Willie P. Mangum
Flat River
Orange
No. C.

)
David Laws)
)

_____

WPM-LC

John Chavis to Willie P. Mangum

RALEIGH Sepr. 3^d. 1831—

My dear Sir/

Is it my colour, or my insignificance or the gross ignorance,
which my many letters contain, is the reason why you have never
condescended to answer one of them? Or is it your distrust of my
professed firm, unshaken, unabating friendship for you & your
family? Or do you consider my friendship to be not worth your
notice? Be it as it may, I must plainly & honestly tell you that I
have ever been grieved, that you were the profissed political
friend of G. Jackson, because I ever believed him to be expressly

what he has proved himself to be—The letter of Gov. Branch,[23] has put the capstone upon the whole business of the Cabinet. It is a fair unvarnished statement of facts, clinching beyond the shaddow of a doubt, the statement of Mr. Ingham & Judge Bereon [Berrien] & you as an honest statsman (as I believe you to be) cannot keep sides with him any longer, therefore put on again, your full coat of Federalism, & not only support the election of Clay, but go forth to Congress with a full determination to support the renewal of the United States bank, to trample under foot the doctrine of Nullification, to support the Tariff in its main bulwarks, & to support Internal improvements, in a word to prove that you are an American in the full sense of the word—

I have told you to put on your coat Federalism again. You know that you have been for some time past, hoping & shifting about, showing your coat, to be sometimes Federalism, sometimes Democracy, sometimes Republicanism Now you know this wont do, because you know that no political stratagem whatever can shake the foundation of Federalism Then why will you be afraid & cast & shift about? If you will now repent of your sins & promise to do better I shall hope that those of the Washington school, will forgive you—But Oh this Potter[24] business was ever the like done before—guilty or not guilty? Please to drop us a line by Mr. Devereaux[25] & let us know the beginning & the effect, for the reports are as various here, as that abominable insurrection in Southampton;[26] was in its out set. For my part I cannot believe that either of the parties are guilty—

Please to give my best respects to Mrs Mangum & tell her that I am the same old two & sixpence towards her & her children, & that she need not think it strange, that I should say, that her children will never be taught the Theory of the English Language unless I teach them, I say so still, I learnt my Theory from Lindley Murreys[27] spelling book which no other Teacher in this part of Country Teaches but myself & I think it preferable to the English Grammar—

[23]On August 22, 1831, Secretary Branch wrote Edward B. Freeman of Halifax the reasons for his resignation from Jackson's Cabinet. His letter was printed in the *Halifax Advocate* and reprinted in other papers. In this letter he reviewed the controversy over Peggy Eaton. His chief complaint was against the President's dictation on social matters. *N. C. Free Press*, September 13, 1831.
[24]Robert Potter's attack on Lewis Taylor and Lewis Willie.
[25]Thomas P. Devereux, an attorney and large planter of Raleigh, served for many years as reporter of the state Supreme Court and as the Federal district attorney. Hamilton, *Papers of Ruffin*, I, 447n; II, 6n.
[26]The Nat Turner Insurrection.
[27]Lindley Murray, 1745-1826, after studying law amassed a comfortable fortune as a merchant. Retiring in 1783 and settling in England, he began writing spelling books and English grammars which were so widely used that it is estimated that about 2,000,000 copies were sold. *D. A. B.*, XIII, 365-366.

I see, my son Priestly as I expected is not elected. Yes & you may tell him from me, that unless he lay aside that stuborn unyielding disposition of his & become condescending & familiar he will never set the River on fire, neither for himself or his children.

I am your Obt Lble se^t—

JOHN CHAVIS

[Addressed:]

> Hon. Willie P. Mangum Esqr
> Orange

Mr. J. Holloway,

———

WPM-LC

Nathaniel J. Palmer[28] *to Willie P. Mangum*

MILTON N. C. Oct. 21st 1831.

Dear Sir,

You have doubtless ere this, received the two first numbers of my paper. I have commenced business here under circumstances peculiarly flattering. I have nearly 400 subscribers and my subscription list is rapidly increasing, I have much cause for gratitude towards you for your kind suggestions and advice. Rest assured they shall be remembered, and your kindness duly reciprocated, should opportunity ever occur. Enclosed in this you will receive a subscription list. Your good offices in advancing my interests in your section of country is respectfully solicited. Please write to me and inform me how you like my editorial remarks and selections. I am much in need of the advice of friends of experience and observation your opinions, whatever they may be, shall be received in the spirit of candour and friendship. No one is better acquainted with the feelings and interests of the people of this section of the State than yourself your suggestions, or your kind aid, either in the shape of Editorial articles, or communications is earnestly solicited. I should like to get the Printing of the laws of Congress, it is very desirable that some press in this section of the State should publish them. The Raleigh Star

---

[28]Nathaniel J. Palmer, a native of Orange County and a brother to John C. Palmer of Salisbury, established the *Milton Spectator* in 1831. Later he moved to Raleigh. W. W. Holden *Address on the History of Journalism in North Carolina* (Raleigh, 1881), 16; Hamilton, *Papers of Ruffin*, II, 190.

and Wetern Carolinian printed at Salisbury are the nearest presses that publish them. I fear my brothers of the Star are getting out of the right track I dought whether they are at heart with the Administration, perhaps, though it is wrong for me to Judge them. The Western Carolinian is a real Calhoun press, though to keep in with the people he still holds out Jackson colours. The people, however, are suspicious of him and are making efforts to start a Press in that place that will do justice to their interests and feelings. I have received a letter from my brother there, who informs me that a Mr. Jones[29] has the rise of 300 subscribers for starting a new paper in Salisbury. When you go to Washington please write me frequently and communicate interesting information to the people through the medium of my press. Please inform me whether you think there will be any chance for me to get the printing spoken of above

With Sincere regard your friend,

NATHANIEL J. PALMER.

Hon. W. P. Mangum
    Orange. N. C.

[Addressed:]

Hon. Willie P. Mangum,
    Red Mountain
        Orange County
            N. C.

P. S. A petition has been signed by nearly all the citizens of this place and vicinity for me to receive the appointment of Post Master here there is little doubt I expect, but that I shall shortly receive it

N. J. P.

---

[29]In 1832 Hamilton C. Jones, an able lawyer and future Whig leader of Salisbury, established the *Carolina Watchman* to combat the nullification views of the *Western Carolinian.* Johnson, *Ante-Bellum N. C.*, 771-772.

WPM-LC

Otway Burns[30] to Willie P. Mangum

BEAUFORT CARTERET CO. N. C. Octo 31. 1831

Dear Sir.

Mr. Henry M. Cooke, the Collector of this Port having declared his intention of leaving this place the next spring for the Western Country & consequently will resign his appointment, which will leave a vacancy in the Collectorship of this District. To supply this vacancy the friends of the administration in & near this place are about proposing Mr. James E. Gibble, the present Inspector & Dy Collector

May I be permitted to solicit of you, as a particular favor to myself & our friends, your support in behalf of Mr. Gibble

Mr. Gibble is a gentleman of the very first respectability & one whom the people are anxious to serve; he has filled for several years the office of Inspector & Dy Collr. which he now holds, in a manner that has met the entire approbation of the community.

No service which you could render this community particularly the merchantile & Jackson's part of it, would be more highly appreciated than forwarding the appointment of Mr. Gibble.

Mr. Gibble in addition to his eminent qualifications is an old & firm supporter of the present administration—But the person who is applying in opposition to Mr. Gibble can boast of neither friendship to the administration nor super eminent qualifications.

Your particular attention will confer a particular favor on My dr, Sir,

Your Obt Servant

OTWAY BURNS

[Addressed:]

The Honble
Willie P. Mangum
U. S. Senator
City of Washington.

---

[30]Ottway Burns, 1775-1848, was a successful privateer in the War of 1812. He was in the legislature as a representative of Onslow County in 1821-1822, from 1824 to 1829, in 1831, and from 1833 to 1834. His vote in 1835 for the west in the constitutional convention made him unpopular in the east. As a result he was never elected to another political office. *D. A. B.*, III, 308.

Thomas Alston to James Webb[31]

WAKE CTY 17ʰ Novemʳ 1831

Dear Sir

Baldy Nicholls who has overseered for Genˡ Cameron has my Bond for one hundred and thirty Dolls due the Twenty fifth day of december next and if Judge Mangum will take it up when due —I will take his Bond with such security as you may think good for the balance of my claim against him, payable the first day of October next—provided the Judge will allow the annuel renewels of the interest—or I will take Mʳ. Canes[32] note payable at that time on the same terms—I will thank you to write me directed to Wake Forest Post office

Yours respectfully

T ALSTON

Doctor James Webb,
Hillsborough

[Endorsements]   )
            Jaˢ Alston)
)
        Ths. Alston

————

WPM-D

William Gaston to Willie P. Mangum

NEWBERN Novr. 30th 1831.

Dear Sir

I learn from my friend Mr. Louis Leroy[33] of Washington in this State that he has sent or is about to send on to Congress a Petition for the refunding of certain duties which have been paid under peculiar circumstances of hardship. Permit me on the part of Mr. Leroy to request that you will take the trouble to examine into the nature of his case and to yield it your aid shoud you find it a fair claim.—I write in haste—being very unexpectedly chosen by a majority (tho' a bare majority) of my townsmen to

---

[31]The original is in the James Webb Papers, University of North Carolina.
[32]William Cain, Sr.
[33]See below, Mangum's letter to Gaston, January 19, 1832.

represent them in the General Assembly.—It is impossible for me to decline such a call however much I could have wished it had not been made.—

You will necessarily be much occupied during the winter and will have little leisure for correspondence, but if you can now and then give me an intimation of what is going on in the political world you will gratify my curiosity to peep thro' the loopholes of retreat upon the mighty Babel and behold its stir.—

Respectfully your's

WILL: GASTON.

Honble. W. Mangum.

[Addressed:]

Hon:

W. Mangum   Free
    Senator in Congress.

WPM-LC

Hud. Van Noorden³⁴ to Willie Mangum

[Nov. 30, 1831]

Dear Sir

When I had the pleasure at this place of being introduced to you by Genl. Speight, I did not expect, that I should so soon have occasion to solicit your assistance; this however is the case at present;

I am one of the unfortunate sufferers by the French Spoliations³⁵ before 1800; to a Considerable amount & have like the rest long time since petition'd Congress for remuneration of my losses, & as long since as April 1826 send to Mr. Macon then one of our Senators the vouchers of those Claims, which were by him delivered to the select Committee appointed to report on those

---

³⁴See below, Van Noorden's letter to Mangum, November 30, 1832.

³⁵In the years before 1800 the French government, acting under the alliance and commercial treaties of 1778, seized American ships and cargo. The United States maintained that the treaties of 1778 were abrogated. By a convention of 1800 the United States and France agreed that the treaties of 1778 were abrogated and the claims of the citizens of the two nations were repudiated. American claimants after 1800, therefore, maintained that the Federal Government by the convention of 1800 and by the Louisiana Purchase assumed the responsibility of paying the claims. In 1825 the Court of Claims held the Federal Government liable. Several proposals were presented to Congress for the repayments, but each effort failed until 1885. Not until 1915 were all the claims finally settled. John Bassett Moore, *A Digest of International Law*, 8 vols. (Washington, D. C.: Government Printing Office, 1906), VI, 1022-1025.

Claims, & have remained there since as he last informed me in dec. 1829; I since Wrote to his successor M[r]. Iredell[36] who communicated to me the report of the committee last Session, & that before, which were in three or four instances all favorable to us; but there it appears to remain, as the Senate has not further acted on it; While the nations in Europe, British, Spanish, Danes, & in two instances, the French (one very lately) have settled & paid for Spoliations on our Citizens; the United States in this case in the oldest of all those Claims & having taken our private property for public use, have hitherto withheld to make us just Compensation, our Claims are now upward of thirty years Standing, & many of us, *my Self for one,* are grown *old* & poor by this unwarrantable delay;

[Be] so good to inform me as soon as Convenient the prospect we have this session; & if any more or further application on my part is needful; & may I request further your assistance in the passing favorable of these Claims, when they shall be taken up, which by some movements appears will be during this long session,

and as there have lately been established in the City by Some Speculative Gentlemen, offices, for attending to this business, & Collect those Claims, for a very high Commission; Some even requiring one half of the proceeds recovered; may I here beg your friendly advice as to the necessity of employing Such assistance; I have hitherto been in the habit of transacting my own business, and expect in case of danger of losing my Claims, which are just, and well authenticated; it would grieve me to lose a great part of that, for which I have been suffering So long;

Be so good to excuse the trouble I take the liberty to give you, as early as this on entering in your place; & again requesting the favor of your answer as soon as Convenient;

I am with great respect
Your obed[t]. Serv[t]
HUD. VAN NOORDEN
Greeneville Nov[r].*. 1831

The Hon Willie Mangum

[Addressed:]

Hon Willie Mangum
Senate of the U States
Washington City

---

[36]James Iredell.

16

WPM-LC

W. M. Sneed to Willie P. Mangum

RALEIGH Dec^r/ 2nd. 1831—

Dear Sir,

Yours of the 26th. Ult^o. came to hand the next Evening—you dont know what serious offence you have offered to my dignity and Talents—To bestow compliments upon the little & puerile talent of scribbling little familiar recital of "little" passing occurrences, and to exalt such an effort into the high sounding character of my "Forte" and *thereby* to overlook and underate the *other numerous* and & [*sic*] *wellfounded* claims to Honor, distinction, not to forget "exaltation" which I know *"justly"* belong to me, is an offence which, If I dared *lay aside* my undoubted claims to *Christian charity & forbearance,* I would resent and revenge as a man of Honor should—

Perhaps on the eve of your departure to "Gotham" well knowing that you would be obliged [to] lay aside the plain, blunt spoken, Honest North Carolina Gentleman Farmer, You would commence the "wiley" artful & fulsome Politician which you know you have to assume when located in that great & Majestic *emporium*—of all that is fair Honest & upright among its residents or visitors—

If the punishment be not adequate to crime I will forgive the ballance—

I have just returned from the House you will have seen that Miller was reelected yesterday—We have had 3 Ballots for Sol^r Genl to day vizt.

	Scott,[37]	Pearson,[38]	Waddell,[39]	Obrien[40]	Blanks
1st.	52	77	26	32	2
2nd	49	77	29	38	
3rd	43	73	32	42	1

The Blank in the last Ballot had the name of Obrien on one side & Pearson on the other—

You will no doubt have heard that Mr. Gaston is elected in place of C. G. [Spe]ight Dec^d[41] Gaston 146—C. Sheppard[42] 145—

[37]John Scott was elected December 7. *Journal of the Senate, 1831,* p. 34.
[38]Richard M. Pearson.
[39]Hugh Waddell, 1799-1879, was a member of the legislature in 1828, 1830, 1836, and from 1844 to 1846. In 1836 he was elected lieutenant governor. Grant, *Alumni Hist. of U. N. C.,* 639.
[40]Spencer O'Brien.
[41]Charles B. Speight, the senator from New Bern, died before he took his seat. *N. C. Manual,* 568.
[42]Charles Biddle Shepard.

There was one more vote than the number of voters—Mr. G. has not yet arrived—He was expected this forenoon—It is now night —& he has not come

Mr. Calhoun came into town yesterday and left here today at 2—He was visited by a great many & all that I heard speak of him were very much pleased with him—Gov. Iredell carried him down to see the two Houses in Session—I understand a Public Dinner was Tendered but refused—Gov. Iredell told me he wished him to stay to a party at his House this Evening, but he declined it—He is a great man—Superb Talents &. &. "yet all this availeth me not so long" as I recollect N- I- N- I- A- N".[43]— I wish I could forget it—He says he thinks the point on which the Tariff men will unite is to establish the Constitutionality of that law—He spoke of the Clay & Johnson[44] men uniting and attending the parties given by each of these gentlemen on the afternoon and night that Mr. Clay was elected Senator—He thinks it augurs un[i]on upon Tariff and Internal improvement questions—Gov. Owen has gone I suppose home—He has gained neither character, nor standing for himself nor his friends—He was severely "rasped" for interfering as he did in all the Elections at the beginning of the Session—His friendship & active exertions for Muse[45] as engrossing clerk lost him the place—

Leak[46] is nominated for Sol[r]. in opposition to Troy[47]—It wont do—

Van hook[48] took his seat this morning for [the] first time— Col. Mathews[49] is confined to his room by Rheumatism—

From my hearing nothing of it for several days [torn] no opposition will be made to Stoke[s].

I received [a] letter Dick & Steph [torn] the night before last — They each the [torn] will do but little in Granville — You p[torn] through Oxford since the failure to [torn] thing at the proposed meeting [torn] heard little or nothing about [torn] that was likely to be taken and [torn] expect from your letter & some oth-[torn] matters that I should have been ca[torn] but I pres[ume] such a course is [torn] I think if Wy[che] were withdrawn [I could] be elected—and if I was nomina[ted at] a gen-

[43]He refers to Ninian Edward's support of Calhoun and his attack on Crawford in 1824. See above, p. 141n.
[44]Richard M. Johnson of Kentucky was an ardent supporter of Jackson.
[45]John B. Muse was Governor Owen's private secretary.
[46]Walter F. Leake. See below, p. 446n.
[47]Alexander Troy of Columbus County was elected December 3. *Journal of the House of Commons, 1831*, p. 166.
[48]R. Van Hook.
[49]Isham Matthews.

eral meeting he would [torn] to leave the Contest—but without [torn] under every circumstance I think [torn] say no do any thing in the mat[ter]

I have [scri]bbled until I have [torn] late and h[av]e nothing more to [torn]

Your Friend

W. M. SNEED

[Addressed:]

> Honl. Willie P. Mangum
> of the Senate
> Washington City

WPM-LC

R. M. Saunders to W. P. Mangum

RALEIGH Decr. 3^d. 1831.

Dear Sir—

I have a son about 15 years of age, & who is tolerably well advanced in his studies, whom I am anxious to get into the Academy at West Point—I enclose you a certificate from his teacher of his [sch]olarship &c—I should take it as a s[in]gular favour if you could unite w[it]h Mr. Brown⁵⁰ in recommending him—His name is Franklin⁵¹—I have also written to my friend McLane as I am unknown to the Sec^y. at War—The Legislature is getting on as usual—It is said tha[t t]he House appropriation will fail in the [S]enate—through the Cape Fear & Western interest—tho—they will not be able to carry the convention—I doubt if Stokes⁵² is opposed—Miller⁵³ & Troy reelected solicitors —The ballot today Pearson 68, Scott 52—O'Bryant 38, Waddell 35—result doubtful—tho' I believe Pearson will be defeated—Scotts chance bad—I shall be glad to hear from you

Very respt.

Yr. Obt Servt.

R. M. SAUNDERS.

---

⁵⁰Bedford Brown.
⁵¹Franklin Saunders was at West Point as a cadet from 1833 to 1837. He served in the Seminole wars of 1837-1838, and in the Mexican War. From 1838 until 1846 he was a civil engineer. From 1850 to 1855 he served as assistant engineer of the North Carolina Railroad. Cullum, *Biog. Reg. of Officer of U. S. Military Academy.*
⁵²Montfort Stokes was opposed for governor by Richard D. Spaight. Stokes won. *Journal of the House of Commons, 1831,* p. 183.
⁵³Stephen Miller.

Honl. W. P. Mangum,
Senate.

[Addressed:]

Hon. W. P. Mangum,
Senate
Washington City

[Enclosure]

James Grant Junr.[54] *to Romulus M. Saunders*

RALEIGH Decr. 3, 1831.

My dear Sir

It affords me much pleasure to answer your letter concerning the scholarship of your son Franklin. During last session of this year, he studied, the whole of Ovid, Gould's Grammar & Hoopers Prosody in Latin, Greaca Minora, Greek Grammar & Prosody in Greek. In the prosecution of these studies he was diligent attentive, regular & highly distinguished in a class of six of all whom were good scholars. His moral character has been unexceptionable [*sic*] since he has been under my tuition & I must congratulate you on having so industrious & intelligent a son. He will study next session (unless you wish otherwise) Greek Testament & Greaca Majora. Virgil Adam's Roman Antiquities, Potter's Greacian Antiquities Arithmetic & Algebra.

I am your
obt. Srvt,

JAMES GRANT JUNR.

Precp. of R. Academy

[Addressed:]

Genl. Romulus M. Saunders,
Present.

---

[54]James Grant, Jr., 1812-1891, received the A.B. Degree in 1831, the A.M. in 1836, and the LL.D. in 1878 from the University of North Carolina. He left Raleigh in 1831 for Salisbury where he became the principal of the Salisbury Academy. Later he moved to Iowa and became a political leader of prominence. Grant, *Alumni Hist. of U. N. C.*, 230.

WPM-LC

Willie P. Mangum to Charity A. Mangum

WASHINGTON CITY:
Saturday morning 3rd. decr. 1831.

My dear Love.

I have arrived at this place safely, though detained on the road & disappointed in several of the Mail arrangements. The day I arrived at Oxford, I sent home my horses immediately—But learning afterwards that I should have to travel in the Stage all the night of Monday to get to Roanoke, I hired a sulkey & two horses, & on Monday travelled 47 miles to Monroe on Roanoke, where I slept Monday night, & tuesday morning got into the stage & travelled without stopping until Wednesday night to Potomac Creek, where I was detained more than a day—The old boat had burst its boiler—The new boat had not got on that line—And the only one to be used was a very large & old steam boat, which could not get up Potomac Creek, the tides being very low—At length however through snow & ice I got here yesterday—I am not at a hotel & have not got a boarding house. My object is to get into some good private boarding house—I shall write to you next week more at large—You must write My Dear, every week—I have been so much fatigued & with the loss of sleep I am unwell a little, only a little feverish—

My dear, I think much of you & our dear little children—Tell my dear Sally, that if she wants her Father to love her, she must try to learn as fast as she can—You must get Flannel to go next to her skin—

Fathers dear little Patty, must be a good girl & mind Mother—Father will try to bring her something, if she will be good—Mother must write Father a letter to let him know whether his little daughters are good children—

Give them some good kisses for Father—

My dear Love, remember me often as I do you—Be cheerful—And feel and know, that you are dearer to your husband than all the world besides.

I am My Love Yours most affectionately

W. P. MANGUM

Poor Patty, does she mind well? Does Sally mind well? I hope you will tell me yes—

Let me know how Orange goes on—

W. P. M.

[Addressed:]

Mrs. C. A. Mangum
Red Mountain
No Carolina

———

WPM-LC

Willie P. Mangum to Charity A. Mangum

WASHINGTON CITY December 8th, 1831.

My dear Love

Last Saturday morning I wrote you a line to inform you of my safe arrival, knowing that you would feel solicitude for my safety in the Stage Coaches and the Steam boat—

The weather since I arrived has been extremely cold, more severe than has been known for many years, so early in the season. It has been within two degrees of being as cold as it was in the coldest time of the severest part of last winter.

Things have changed a good deal since I left here—The new canal which is making through the City, with other causes, have carried the most of the business, fashion &c from Capitol Hill, to Pennsylvania Avenue & other portions of the City.

The members of Congress have generally followed the stream of business and fashion—and the most of them, indeed, almost all, have boarding in the dense parts of the City.—I am growing too old to care for those things, and have set myself down snugly in a small mess on Capitol Hill — with old General Samuel Smith[55] of Baltimore & four other gentlemen.—I know nothing of what is going on yet—I have made no visits—The weather has been too bad, & though this morning looks as if we shall have a fair day, there is 2 inches of snow on the ground—Mr. Clay is here, & looks well & like an old friend. The influenza is almost

———

[55]Samuel Smith, 1752-1839, a lieutenant colonel in the Revolution and major general in the War of 1812, was a member of the House of Representatives from Maryland from 1793 to 1803 and of the Senate from 1803 to 1813 and from 1822 to 1833. *Biog. Dir. of Cong.*, 1541.

universal—I have some cold—but slightly, not giving me head
ache, but disturbing the bowels—I mean to avoid all exposure &
be entirely regular & abstemious in my habits

I am now looking for a letter from you My Love. I constantly
almost think of home, of you & and our dear children, when not
engaged in business—I live three stories high in perfect retirement, where I hope to read & study more than I have ever done
at this place—You must write to me My Love, once every week,
once every week, [sic] and if you shall fail to do so, it will much
disappoint me.

Tell my dear child Sally, that Father wants to hear from her—
that he will be so pleased, if mother can write to Father that she
tries to learn her book well & tries to write well, and is a good
child, & minds her Mother & is kind & good to her little Sister
Patty—Remember the flannel for Sally. I trust you have got it
before this.—Tell my dear Child Patty, that Father loves his
little child—that Father wants her to be a good child, and that
Father will be so sorry, if she is not good, & mind her Mother—

Give my dear Sally & Patty three kisses each for Father & if
they have been good, give them more—

I want measures taken to hire a negro—You can get Mr.
Brinkly to attend to it—You can learn from Harrison Parker[56]
when the boy at Mrs. Mizes will be hired—If he can be got, I
prefer him—If not some other—Encourage Orange & let me
know how he goes on—Let him give you an account what he
has done & write to me

I shall write to you often my Dear—Take care of yourself, be
cheerful. Remember me often My Love, and always be assured
of my Love & affection, as I have no doubt of yours—

May God bless you & our dear Children.

Your affectionate husband

WILLIE P. MANGUM.

[Addressed:]

Mrs. Charity A. Mangum
Red Mountain
No. Carolina.

---

[56]Mangum's Aunt Clara Mangum married David Parker. Their son was Harrison Parker,
a well-to-do planter in Orange County.

WPM-D

William H. Haywood, Jr., to Willie P. Mangum

At night
Thursday 14 Dec. 1831.

Dear Sir/

I would trouble you with a long letter about our doings here if you had not forfeited a right to it at least for the present by your total neglect of me. So it is however the world over—to grow rich—or *great,* makes a man forget his friends whose lot is cast in a humbler sphere.—'Thinks I to myself this is quite a censorious—perhaps presumptions—train for a mere member of Poor Carolina's Assembly to address a Senator in Congress & more especially when my main object is to beg what I never begged for myself. I have a young friend & connexion here reading law with me and his character is just of that description that I can recommend him without exception—His history is shortly this—He is the son of a widow in Newbern who is the sister of Mrs. H's mother—Edward Graham Benners—His mother has strived hard to educate him and fit him for helping himself— he is a smart—pious—industrious & competent young man and of his own head & imagination is fired with an anxiety to do something for himself—His views are humble and I should be greatly favored if you can aid him in procuring some under Clerk's office in Washington—Without a certainty he is not able to go on—indeed I should have to advance him the means. Excuse me then if I intreat you to aid my views & his in this respect.—He is just the man that ought to be helped on in this world I assure you—is manageable teachable and smart,—19 years old—A place that would support him decently & leave a chance to study his profession is all he wants & you may have cause hereafter to be highly gratified at having advanced the views of such a youth—I improve this opportunity of returning thro. you to Genl. B.[57] & to Mr. Brown[58] my thanks for the notice they have taken of me.—They with Rencher[59] & our other friends in Congress who know me will aid you in this affair of honourable charity I hope, & excuse the liberty I take in pressing it upon them—Such applications I expect are frequent at W. City

---

[57]Daniel L. Barringer was in the House of Representatives from 1826 to 1835.
[58]Bedford Brown was in the Senate from 1829 to 1840.
[59]Abraham Rencher.

but probably the chance may offer to meet this as it comes from *Carolina*—

Jackson grows on me every day—Let us know *at once* if any thing is to come of a proposed Convention to nominate Vice Prest—that we may look to having *N Caro* properly represented.

Your friend

WILL. H. HAYWOOD JR.

[Addressed:]

> The Hon.
>> Willie P, Mangum
>>> Senate of U. S.

[Endorsed:]

> Answered 19th Dec.

Willie P. Mangum to Joseph Gales Jr.[60]

WASHINGTON 17th. dec. 1831.

Dear Sir

Your note of this morning has just been handed to me & I beg leave to assure you that I shall feel much pleasure, in having it in my power to be useful to your friend, both on your account & the peculiarity of his fortunes & condition. —

I have constantly kept myself free to act in this matter—save in an intimation that I should aid Dawson[61] of Capitol Hill in the first instance—

This of course I shall feel bound to do. But as he will very probably be *thrown out,* early in the Contest. I shall then be at liberty, & in that case I shall take much pleasure in aiding with my Vote, Mr. Walker.[62]

Gen Smith[63] & Col. King[64] of this mess, who have better means of forming a correct judgment than I have, of the prospects of Mr. Dawson. both I believe, think he has but little prospect of

---

[60]The original is in the Ford Collection, New York Public Library, New York, N. Y.

[61]A. R. Dawson was being considered for assistant doorkeeper of the Senate. He was defeated. *Register of Debates,* 22 Cong., 1 sess., p. 10.

[62]S. P. Walker was being considered for assistant doorkeeper of the Senate. He lost to Shackford of Missouri. *Register of Debates,* 22 Cong., 1 sess., p 10.

[63]Samuel Smith served as a Senator from Maryland from 1803 to 1815 and from 1822 to 1833.

[64]William R. King was the Senator from Alabama from 1819 to 1844.

success. When in the progress of the contest that shall become apparent—my vote will then be given for your friend—And should I have it in my power (of which however there is but little probability) I would carry to him any additional aid.

Yours respectfully & truly

W. P. MANGUM

[Addressed:] Mr. Joseph Gales Jr.
Washington

End.: W. P. Mangum
Dec. 19, 1821

WPM-LC

John H. Bryan to Willie P. Mangum

NEW BERN
Dec. 17, 1831.

My dear Sir,

Mr. Amos Wade a reputable merchant of this town has a memorial before the Congress praying a remision of duties on the cargo (Molasses) of the Brig Remittance of this port.—The memorial is in charge of Mr. Speight of the H. or R. and states the facts & reasons of his petition.—He & Mr. Gaston (to whom he applied for assistance) have requested me to invite your attention to it.—Your aid as a Senator of his State is solicited.—Mr. Wade is a worthy citizen and hopes if his case can be fairly brot. before Congress that he will obtain relief.—

I should be glad to hear from you.—

Yrs truly

JN. H. BRYAN.

[Addressed:]
To
The Hon:
Willie P. Mangum
U. S. Senate
Washington.

WPM-LC

John Scott to Willie P. Mangum

HILLSBOROUGH Decr. 18th. A. D. 1831.

My Dear Sir.

Yours of the 11^{sh} Inst. came to hand by last night's mail. The warm interest taken by you in my late struggle, increases the obligation I was already under to you, for the many proofs of sincere friendship so often heretofore manifested. In compliance with your wish, I will now give you "an account of the details the currents and counter Currents, the whys & the wherefores & all that"—

On my arrival at Raleigh, on Sunday evening before the meeting of the Legislature, I soon discovered that all the accounts of the hostile movements of my quondam friend R. M. S.[65] were but too true. He was at Guion's[66]—going from group to group & taking this member & that member, to one side, for consultation. By 10 oclock that night I was told, upon authority, to be relied upon, that he would not be a Candidate. On Monday I discovered that among the members East, West & South, out of the Circuit, the common belief was, that I was not the choice of the Circuit,[67] & that a large majority of it, was desirous of a change—this seemed to be in every body's mouth. Pearson & his active friends besieged every room in Town. The whole Cape Fear & the extreme West united with Gov. Owen & D. F. Caldwell busy night & day rallying & discipling them. On Tuesday night Waddell[68] arrived & *discovering* that I stood *no possible chance of success*, kindly took the fight off my hands, & undertook himself to beat Pearson. So at it we all went, every man for himself. Messrs: Dick,[69] Hill[70] (of Stokes) & Kerr[71] of Caswell undertook to ascertain my strength in the Circuit, & reported that of 33 votes they were authorised to say that 21 were for me. This formed the basis of our future operations & was urged with zeal by my friends. Waddell took but a small portion of the Cape Fear votes, but a much larger portion of the North East interest, than I had anticipated. It seemed (how it was brought about, I say not) that he was supported by many

[65]Romulus M. Saunders.
[66]Guion's Hotel in Raleigh. Johnson, *Ante-Bellum N. C.*, 152.
[67]See above, W. M. Sneed's letter to Mangum, December 2, 1831.
[68]Hugh Waddell.
[69]John M. Dick.
[70]John Hill. See above, p. 400n.
[71]James Kerr served in the senate from 1830 to 1840. *N. C. Manual*, 544.

under the belief that he is a thorough bred Democrat of the old
Jefferson School,—opposed to a Convention & withal, an Eastern
man in feelings as well as by birth, & education, Miller,[72] Wilson,[73] Spaight,[74] Sawyer,[75] Boddie,[76] Singleton,[77] Gen[l]. Montgomery[78] &c: started with me. Seawell,[79] Haywood,[80] Askew,[81]
Fisher,[82] Obrien[83] & the Roanoke generally, excluding Naggs-
head, all fell in about the close, except the federal interests,
which clung to Pearson, to the last. On the 8th Ballotting when
Pearson[84] rec[d]. his highest vote, he & his intimate friends, were
convinced that he could not succeed, & held a consultation as to
the course they should take, in the event that Waddell, or any
other candidate, should take the lead, next day. They determined
that if Pearson could not be elected, no one else, should beat
me, & that if necessary, they would withdraw him, & all support me. When the vote stood on the 8th ballotting 86   76   31
(Obrien withdrawn) Waddell & his friends were going the
rounds, all night, urging my 76 friends to have the goodness to
drop me & take him!—saying that of his 31 friends, at least 22
were for Pearson rather than Scott. To which it was replied
that it was unreasonable to insist that 76 should yield to 31, &
further that if Scott were withdrawn, Pearson's election was
inevitable, because nearly the whole of the Circuit members
would go over to Pearson,—he being their next choice, after
Scott &c: Waddell still persisted in asserting the impossibility
of Scott's success & predicting that on the next ballotting, the
East would rally upon him &c:—but 94 votes to Scott and but
21 to himself, showed the fallacy of his calculations. As soon
as it was ascertained that Pearson was to be beaten, my good
old friend R.M.S. again took the field (*at night*) to rally
Obrien's friends, & to start him again. Pearson & his friends
upon Consultation thereupon, resolved, that the moment when
Obrien should be nominated, Pearson should rise himself, &
withdraw his name, & all hands go for Scott. *Why* Obrien was
not nominated again, I have, as yet, rec[d]. no information. "All's

---

[72]William L. Miller.
[73]Louis D. Wilson.
[74]R. D. Spaight.
[75]Samuel T. Sawyer.
[76]George Boddie, Jr.
[77]Thomas S. Singleton.
[78]William Montgomery.
[79]Henry Seawell.
[80]Will H. Haywood, Jr.
[81]George O. Askew of Bertie County.
[82]Charles Fisher.
[83]Spencer O'Brien.
[84]Richard M. Pearson.

well that ends well"—After the election, all parties shook hands
cracked their jokes; & so ended the struggle.

As to the temper of the public mind, at Raleigh, on the subject of the Tariff, I can say but little. *I think*, that the members generally, are ready to cooperate in any measure, which
may be found necessary to adjust that question, and would make
any concessions to preserve the Union. In North Carolina, I
know of but one feeling, a feeling of the deepest horror, at the
very thought of a dissolution of the Union. Nothing however
has occurred, this Session, to elicit any feeling or expression
of opinion that might serve you, as a guide, on the subject. But
I surely hazard nothing in saying, that this State, will sustain
you under any responsibility you may encounter with a view
to adjust the Tariff Question, and remove the fearful perils that
await the continuation of that discussion.

Yours sincerely

JOHN SCOTT.

[Addressed:]

The Honble.
Willie P. Mangum
U. S. Senate
Washington City.

———

WPM-LC

Fr. Jones[85] to Willie P. Mangum

But wants mail sent to Monroe.[86]
[Postmarked White Plains,[87] Va.]
[21 Dec., 1831]

My Dear Sir;

I have to acknowledge the receipt of your favour, inclosing
the Presidents Message, & its accompaniment. I am truly thankful for the pamphlets, as my papers containing the contents,
were not received, owing to the derangement of the mails, consequent to the freezing of the Roanoke. That river is now closed

[85]Francis Jones, a graduate of Hampden-Sydney, was justice of the peace for Warren County. McIver, *N. C. Register*, 40.
[86]Monroe was near Jones' home in Warren County.
[87]Near Monroe.

with ice, at the Stage Ferry, & the mails & passengers pass through my plantation & cross the river where the ice is not stationary.

I was much gratified to see, in the message, that the President had abated his hostility to the U. S. Bank. I was certain that he would not veto any Bill, which might be passed, for a renewal of its Charter. I see that the Baltimore convention has unanimously recommended H. Clay & Jno Sergent, for the highest offices known in our government. I know not your opinion of these men. It will not do to divide & distract the Nation on that Question. Believing as I do that Jno. C. Calhoun is the most distinguished man, in the Nation, I should greatly prefer that he should be run against old hickory, if there were to be any opposition. Had I have known when Mr. Calhoun had passed my house, I should certainly have gone out to the road, to shake him by the hand.

A part of the "Roanoke State,"[88] has been lately choosing a Representative, to fill the vacancy, occasioned by the resignation of Robert Potter.[89] You know the Candidates. A friend, from Warrenton, has just now informed me that the contest was between Hawkins[90] & Mann.[91] Hawkins got 927 votes & Mann 860.. Pope & Wyche were far behind. Our venerable friend, N. Macon, was at the polls, as cold as the day was. There was but a thin election. I give you a state of the Polls.

	H	Mann	Wyche[92]	Pope[93]
Granville	354	42	446	37
Franklin	215	267	89	13
Nash	3	547	10	7
Warren	355	4		

I did not learn the Vote of Pope & Wyche in Warren.

We are invited to a vension feast at Wm. Eatons'[94] this Christmas. I wish you could be with us.

Extreme cold weather has prevented much communication in our neighborhood. The Mercury has been as low as 25°*. I shall

---

[88]This term was applied to the congressional district composed of Franklin, Granville, Nash, and Warren counties.

[89]Potter resigned because of his crime against Wiley and Lewis. See above, p. 410.

[90]Micajah T. Hawkins, 1790-1858, served in Congress from 1831 to 1841. He was a Democrat. *Biog. Dir. of Cong.*, 1077.

[91]Thomas N. Mann, a member of the House of Commons in 1822 and 1823, was an able attorney in Nash County. Grant, *Alumni Hist. of U. N. C.*, 411.

[92]James Wyche.

[93]Probably L. H. Pope of Halifax County.

[94]Father of William Eaton, Jr., of Warren County. William Eaton, Jr., served in the legislature and the state convention several times from 1838 to 1865. From 1851 to 1852 he was attorney general of the state. Hamilton, *Papers of Ruffin*, II, 269n.

be thankful for as many documents as you can conveniently send me, to Monroe.

Sincerely yours
FR. JONES
Decr. 21. 1831.

*10.12

P. S. I was in Raleigh yesterday Week. The Governor was elected; Stokes had 98 votes, 96 necessary to a choice; R. D. Spaight 83, 11 blanks & 1 or 2 scattering. The Bill to appropriate money to rebuild the Capitol, was defeated, or postponed in the Senate.

F. J.

[Addressed:]

	Honorable Willie P. Mangum	White Plains Va.
	U. S. Senate	Dec. 21.
Mail.	Washington City	

WPM-LC

W. Montgomery to Willie P. Mangum

RALEIGH N. C. Dec. 23, 1831.

My dear Sir

On yesterday the appropriation Bill was Lost in the Commons 68- against & 65 for it that question is Settled for the present Session, the State Bank Bill passed the Senate on yesterday on its second reading 33- for & 27- against—3 absent members, 2 against it and one for it,[95] it is Believed it will pass the Commons, there is Bills Before the Commons for three other Banks a Individual Capital one at Salisbury, one at Newbern, and one at Edenton, what will be there Fait I do not [k]now I am strongly inclined to think that they will Be Lost[96] there seems to be a strong disposition to place the State Banking Concern In the Hands of the people that it May be under the Contral of Publick

---

[95]The bill passed the second reading in the senate on December 23 and the third reading on December 24. On December 27 the bill was indefinitely postponed in the House of Commons by a vote of 64 to 58. *Journal of Senate, 1831,* p. 69, 71; *Journal of House of Commons, 1831,* p. 212.

[96]Bills to establish the Farmers' Bank of North Carolina, the Merchants' Bank of North Carolina, and the Bank of Albemarle were postponed indefinitely, January 2, 1832. *Journal of House of Commons, 1831,* p. 222.

opinion, and the profit, Be a Joint Concern, and the Loss (if there Be any) the same—

We will probably not adjourn Before the 15th of January. We will pass the railroad Charters,[97] I think certainly, I would Like to get a Copy of the Balitmore and Ohio Railroad Charters, & also any Information on the U. S. Bank that you May deem Important. My resolution is on the table yet & will take it up some time next week or week after, it will not pass I Fear I Have an Idea of Modefying it, By restricting the Bank if renewed to Issues not under $100, and prevent [?] the Issues of [illegible] checks Signed By officers of the Branches, & as far as possible to Exclude Foreign Stock Holders, and With these restriction with a few others I will Consent to renewal, For I am for a U. S. Bank But would prefer it Based on the Funds of the U. S. Intirely, and to be Confined to the opperation of the treasury Department, and Commercial purposes, Sutch a Bank as that I am for. Will you Consult Mr Brown on the Subject and advise Me, We Elected a throughrough republican Council throughout the First Ballot,[98] yours with great regard and Esteem

W, MONTGOMEY

[Addressed:]

The Honbl- Wiley P. Mangum
    Washington City
        D. C.

[Endorsed:]

Ans^ed 28th Dec^r.

WPM-LC

Robert J. Yancey to Willie P. Mangum

OXFORD, (N. C.) Dec. 24th 1831.

Hon. Sir—

I take the liberty of requesting that, if it should not interfere with your convenience, you would be kind enough to furnish

[97]The North Carolina Railroad, the Cape Fear and Yadkin Railroad, and the Tarborough and Hamilton Railroad companies were incorporated. *Laws of N. C., 1831*, pp. 32, 39, 46, 115.
[98]Nathan B. Whitfield of Lenoir County, Meshack Franklin of Surry, Owen Holmes of New Hanover, Alfred Jones of Wake, George Washington Jeffreys of Person, William Williams of Warren, and Robert C. Watson were elected to the Council of State, December 21, 1831. *N. C. Manual*, 431-432.

me with such public documents as you may suppose will prove useful to me as Editor of the Oxford Examiner. I feel reluctant to trouble you, Sir, but I know of no other of the delegation from the State to whom I could apply with as much confidence, relying upon your accommodating disposition and affable manners. Should you not deem it objectionable, I would be much honored if you could furnish for the Examiner such information upon the affairs at Washington, as you might deem useful to your Constituents, and beneficial to the public, and which cannot be conveniently procured thro the public prints.

You will be good enough to excuse me in these applications; and charge it to my desire to render the paper over which I preside as useful as possible. Believing you would be pleased at my success, I have ventured to make these request of you, calculating more confidently upon your kindness than I could on that of any other individual. My prospects are tolerable for a village paper—and but for that unfortunate affair of publishing that libellous address of Potter,[99] I might safely calculate upon tolerable success. Many of my friends were much disappointed and mortified at that instance of bad Judgment, or rather injudicious yielding to urgent circumstances. I am rather astonished myself that I ever suffered it to appear; but I was borne away by the deep and intense excitement which prevailed —at the time. I viewed it as a case in which I must risk my personal interest and safety to gratify the consuming desire of the public to hear every thing connected with the affair. What may be the result I don't know—however, I hold myself in readiness to abide whatever the law and the Court may say is *necessary* under the circumstances. But I humbly conceive that as it is so well known that I was not disposed to inflict injury upon any one, and only yielded to what I then thought was required by the circumstances of the case, (which sentiment was expressed in the paper in which the adress appered) I do not think a rigid enforcement of the law upon *me* would answer any of the ends of justice. I believe every individual concerned does me the justice to say that my motives were good. I beg pardon, Sir, for troubling you with my affairs, and hope to find excuse in your indulgence.

You will doubtless hear by the papers all that I could tell you about our State Affairs, and therefore I shall not trouble you

[99]See above, p. 410.

further than to present my most profound respect, and subscribe myself,

Sir, your obt. serv^t.

ROBT. J. YANCEY JR.

Ed. *Examiner,* Oxford.

To the Hon. W. P. Mangum
      Senator in Congress.

[Addressed:]

To the Honorable Willie P. Mangum

U. S. Senator

Washington City

D. C.

Oxford
Decr. 26.

WPM-LC

Samuel S. Hinton[100] to Willie P. Mangum

ASHVILLE ALA. December 25, 1831

Hon.
    Willie P. Mangum
        Dear Sir.
        From the great [torn] interesting subjects which will be presente[d] to the consideration of the present Congress, and the formiable array of talent (particularly in your Department) it is generally presumed that many able and eloquent speeches will be delivered. Perhaps it may be the Congress which will settle the complicated policy of our Country, and produce the salutary consequences of allaying the obduracy of party and sectional feelings, and settle into quietude and repose the political fury which for a year or two has threatened the disolution of our Union. Such at least are the fond hopes of every individual who cherishes a veneration for our institutions. The ability and influence which are discoverable in the Senatorial Hall are highly calculated to discharge this respon-

---

[100]Samuel Smith Hinton of Wake County, after receiving his A.B. degree at the University of North Carolina, moved to Alabama. Grant, *Alumni Hist. of U. N. C.,* 285.

sible task and I fear it never will comm[an]d again such a [varie]ty of wisdom—or whose [torn]
it with so hearty an [torn]   himself the reputed Father of the [Am]erican System is a member of your Honorable Body, and the indications of a Tempest which have arisen from this System have become too visible to have escaped his vigilant eye. He will not remain inactive upon this important occasion, but bring into requisition towards an adjustment the weight of his influence and the subduing power of his eloquence. He is a man I hold in the highest esteem and [torn] in a land of the *rankest* Jacksonism, since [torn] *opportunity* to exhibit toward him my unboun[de]d admiration. But this is digressing. I have every reason to believe he is disposed to comprom it in part his Tariff principles for the continuance of harmony though he firmly believes it to be the correct policy of our country I can discover no means calculated to produce this desired result than for the leaders of this policy to relax a little their sturdy grasp. The Anti-Tariff Convention in Philadelphia[101] has been a complete abortion, or to use more respectful terms towards that Honorable assemblage, has been ineffectual. No other consequence could have been anticipated, when it was to be borne in remembrance, that a majority of the States were not represented, and those that were, the number was very disproportionate, and *even then* entertained contrary and discordant opinions. I entertain no doubt, however but a modification will be made the present session of Con[gress.] [torn] -line will have by no m[torn]

The U. States Bank w[torn]   [torn]   and will I can say elicit [torn] splendid displays from your Body, particularly from Messrs. Clay and Webster. It is too favourite a Bantling of Mr. Bentons to permit it to remain undisturbed in its swaddring clothes throughout this session.[102] I discover he has made it a theme of conversation in public and private from St. Louis to Washington, and has very satisfactorily (no doubt to himself) proved among the many impositions it has practised upon the

[101]From September 30 to October 6 about 200 delegates from fifteen states met at Philadelphia. Warren R. Davis of South Carolina was the promoter. Clashes between nullifiers and anti-nullifiers developed. All delegates, however, were against the tariff. Memorials of Thomas R. Dew and William Harper against the tariff were drawn up to present to Congress. C. S. Boucher, *The Nullification Controversy in South Carolina* (Chicago, Ill.: The University of Chicago Press, 1916), 112-113, 164-165.
[102]In the 1820's Thomas Hart Benton became a champion of hard money. After Jackson came to office he waited for some time for his chief to speak up. Finally in February, 1831, he boldly challenged the wisdom of the recharter of the Bank and supported hard money. His speech was printed and circulated among farmers and laborers. Thereafter he became the spearhead of the attacks on Biddle and the Bank. Arthur M. Schlesinger, Jr., *The Age of Jackson* (Boston, Mass.: Little, Brown, and Co., 1946), 77, 80-82.

community that the small no[torn] which [torn] issued by its Branch are sp-[torn] that an individual indicated for their forgery c[ould] not be convicted as they were *illegal*. And pledges his reputation for the correctness of a decision upon a case of this kind which recently occurred in Ohio. Had he suspended his opinion until he saw this matter adjudicated by Judge Baldwin[103] in Philadelphia, it would have at least learnt him discernment enought not to be so hazardous of his character. I read his speech during the last session with uncommon attention, for I am apprised of my youth and solicitous to establish correct principles, yet I must confess his arguments afforded no conviction of its inutility. I am willing to abridge the charter of the Bank in a small degree not from an apprehension of an illegal exercise of any of its privileges, but to dispell the fastidious fears of a great number. As yet I am certainly of the opinion that it is an establishment essentiall ye[t in th]e language of Mr. Hamilton at [torn]   to [torn] of our country, and could [torn]   in [torn] abolition unless another *less* objectionable could be substituted. A Bank of the character which Genl. Jackson recommended in his former message to be regulated and controulled by individual who receive their appointment from the Executive, would be committing into their hands the custody of our suffrages. Perhaps the President has been so severely lacerated for his recommendation that he has abandoned his original idea, for I see no mention made of *his* Bank, though he says as regards the present [torn]   [w]ill retai[n] the same opinion. There a[re a] variety of other subjects which I am anxious to gain information upon but the limits of a letter preclude their mentioning—but indulge the hope you will contribute the light of your experience and your exertions in remitting to me all the ablest speeches in Congress upon the most important subjects, also the principal Reports of the Committees. You may consider it strange that a request of this kind should be made of you from an individual who is no longer an inhabitant of your State yet my apology will be found in not being acquainted with the members from this State, excepting Mr. Mardis[104] who is gentlemanly in his deportment respectable as a Lawyer, praeteria nihil (I mean no reflection) and cannot therefore give me that insight into the political movements which will be carried on in Congress.

[103]Henry Baldwin, 1780-1844, was a member of Congress from 1817 to 1822. From 1830 to 1844 he was a justice of the Supreme Court.
[104]Samuel Wright Mardis, 1800-1836, was a member of the Alabama legislature from 1823 to 1825 and 1828 to 1830. From 1831 to 1835 he was in Congress. *Biog. Dir. of Cong.*, 1287.

I therefore indulge the hope you will inform me in relation to the forms which the parties are resolve [torn] into and the general impressi[on] [torn] next Presidential election—A le-[torn] you often during the session would be *more* than [*ac*]*ceptable* to

Your obt. Servt

SAM. S. HINTON

WPM-LC

James Martin, Jr.,[105] *to Willie P. Mangum*

SALISBURY Dec. 27th 1831.

Dear Sir

I received by the mail the Public Documents transmitted to the 22d Congress by the President, which you done me the kindness to send to me.

The prospect presented to the mind by the message and those Documents is highly gratifying. The near approach of the extinguishment of the national debt—the flattering account given of our commercial relations with other powers, and the likelyhood of a long continued peace are subjects of the most pleasing reflections: The Picture given of our internal concerns is also consolatory. But I apprehend as to that, some more favoured part of the United States was sketched, than our own native State. I have not perceived the evidences of a growing prosperity in the State generally. If a judgement is to be formed from the price of property and we take land and negroes for the criterion the reverse will be found to be the case. There has been for several years and still is a declination in the price of Land,[106] and since the prohibition of the slave trade to Luisiana by their last Legislature, it will cause a still greater decline in the value of slaves and consequently a still greater depression in the value of Land. For altho our crops have been abundant, cotton our staple is distressingly low—yielding us at home only about seven cents to the pound. I must except out of this view the same of the min-

[105]James Martin, Jr., was a judge of the superior court from 1827 to 1835.
[106]North Carolina's plight in this period was constantly referred to by the press and leaders. In 1789 North Carolina ranked third in population in the Union. By 1830 the state ranked fifth. The total valuation of land was less in 1833 than in 1815 although much more land was under cultivation in the latter year. W. K. Boyd, *History of North Carolina: the Federal Period*, 83.

ing districts.[107] They participate in a larger share of prosperity than they have done for years Indeed as to them it is some thing like the manufacturing Districts to the North—Much labour turned into a different channel from that of Agriculture and the wants of the hands are to be supplied from the farms—It furnishes them with a home market of cash at better prices than heretofore obtained I have no doubt also that the iron business yields a fair profit in places where ore is good and abundant.[108] But as to our other concerns a downward course of depression marks their progress.

Much and great interest is felt as to the proceedings of the present Congress—I regard it as among the most important of its sessions—The Tariff is the great subject upon which the eyes of the public are turned. That it will be modified I have but little doubt. I[t] would seem that all parties express themselves favourable to a modification and reduction. Messrs. Clay and Adams—The President and Secretary of the Treasury seem to unite as to the principle of reduction or modification. I suppose the difficulty will be in the detail—and Sir as to that I am pleased to see that so many of our distinguished men agree likewise that the details of the measure should be met by a disposition to conciliate and to compromise. Do not our affairs call in as especial man[ner] for this temper of mind in the members of Congress? How often has this most useful of all social qualities preserved the great society of the States. You know how eminently it was displayed by the framers of the Constitution, Dr. Franklin was one of the master Spirits who stilled the Storm. Mr. [torn] in his secret debates mentions an anecdote of the Dr upon that occasion— "That when a Carpenter wished to form a joint between two planks he shaved a [little] from each one"—So when there are conflicting interest each should yield a part. In this spirit I most sincerely hope that this vexed question will be settled. As to my own part I do not anticipate any material change in our great staple Cotton from any modification—perhaps a small rise may be affected if we are permitted to import goods at a cheaper rate —upon the ground that the cheaper, the more are consumed and if we import more the[y] can afford us something more for our cotton in exchange. As to the duty of one cent on bar iron I believe that this part of the is benefitted by it—It secures the

[107]For an account of the gold industry, see F. M. Green, "Gold Mining: a Forgotten Industry of Ante-Bellum North Carolina," *The N. C. Hist. Rev.*, XIV (1937), 1-19, 135-155.
[108]Iron was produced in Chatham, Lincoln, Gaston, and Montgomery counties. Boyd, *Hist. of N. C.: Federal Period*, 343.

makers in their trade and from the number and rivalship among them, it has almost excluded the Swede iron and given us our own in retail at five cents the pound—and by the Load they will delivered at 4½ cents which is cheaper that it has ever been before—I mean in this town. But perhaps I am running too much into detail and my paper admonished me, of the same thing
Permit me to add that I am with much esteem
respectfully Your obt. Servt—

JAMES MARTIN, JUR.

[Addressed:]

The Honbl.
Wilie P. Mangum
Washington City.

WPM-LC

William Gaston to W. P. Mangum

RALEIGH Dec. 31st. 1831

My dear Sir

I am exceedingly reluctant to be troublesome to any friend, and feel a repugnance which I can hardly overcome to address you on the subject of this communication. Yet I know not any individual in Congress who I think will more readily excuse the freedom.—My townsman and neighbour, Mr. Robert G. Moore, made application some time since to get his son admitted into the West Point academy, and I readily gave a testimonial in favour of the youth. By the last mail I received a letter from him stating that this application was now renewed, and begging that I would write to some acquaintance in Congress to aid him in it.—I know Mr. Moore better than his Son. He is a very well informed and upright man, engaged in the instruction of youth and highly respected in his station. I am sure that all he says may be relied on.—Why I can not tell—but he apprehends that Genl. Speight does not take an interest in the application.—If you can serve him without impropriety or inconvenience I beg of you to do so.—

I have never seen an assembly more respectable for talents, or one which could do more good for the Country than the present

—were it not distracted—torn asunder by miserable sectional jealousies.—The unfortunate position taken by the West that they will use the question respecting the continuance or removal of the seat of government as a measure of coercion on the East must I fear prevent any arrangement in respect to constitutional amendments.[109]—It necessarily leads to a refusal on the part of the East to enter into any accommodation.—My poor State!—but I am interrupted.—

Believe me respectfully and truly
Your's—

WILL: GASTON

Hon:
    W. P. Mangum

[Addressed:]

        Honble
            W. P. Mangum
                Senate of the U. States

Endorsed:
    Enrolled as of January 1831 [1832]

1832

Postmaster General to Willie P. Mangum

WPM-LC

[WASHINGTON, 2 Jan., 1832]
The Honorable Mr. Mangum of the Senate is informed by the Postmaster General that he has this day appointed
    William Cain Junr Postmaster at Hillsboro: Orange Co. N. C. vice Richard L. Cook, resigned.
Post Office Department,
    2 day of Jany 1832
[Addressed:]
    Hon:
        Mr. Mangum N. C.
            of the Senate

------

[109] He refers to the threat to move the capital from Raleigh after the burning of the Capitol in the summer of 1831. Johnson, *Ante-Bellum N. C.*, 32.

WPM-LC

B. Bullock¹ to Willie P. Mangum

KNAPP REEDS² Jan 13th 1832

Dr Sir

I was at your house two days ago your lady was labouring under a slight cold the Balance of the family were all well except Frank who had Broke his leg about four Inches above the Ankle —he is doeing verry well he will soon walk again

I Received a letter from Peter³ the 11th of this Instant dated the 15th Decr in which he says he is sure he Cant pass his January Examination. Since he has recovered his health he says he has got on verry well.

I understand when Boys are found deficient at their first examination if they want to Remain they are put back Six months to give them another trial Should this be Peters situation will you be so good as to use your influence with the Secretary of War to Continue him another year or till it is fairly ascertained whether he Can get on or not.

We have had Extrem cold weather. Wheat not up yet. Roads impassable no money amog us; the Legislator got the Devil in it and we are all going down together.

was I the west I would Rise in Mass and force a Convention.⁴ I have never Seen the wrong so plain before. I will write you again in a few days State my law Case and give you an account of a Fight between Doctor Montague and Erasmus in which Erasmus was shot through the arm and Montague Stabed with a sword Cain[cane] in several places and beaten with a stick.

With Respect and Esteem your most
obedient Servant

B. BULLOCK

[Addressed:]

Hon. Willie P. Mangum
Washington City

---

¹Dr. Benjamin Bullock, the father-in-law of Walter A. Mangum.
²This was a post office in western Granville County not far from Mangum's home.
³Peter Bullock, the son of Benjamin Bullock, was a cadet at West Point but was dismissed in 1832. Later he went with Walter A. Mangum to Mississippi where he was accidentally killed by Walter. "Report of Select Committee on Military Academy at West Point, Mar. 1, 1837" in *House Documents*, Report No. 303, 24 Cong., 2 sess., 934.
⁴He refers to the demand for a constitutional convention to change representation in the state legislature.

WPM-LC

H. G. Burton to Willie P. Mangum

HALIFAX Jny 15th A D 1832

My Dear Sir

I have not yet had the honor of receiving the first line from any of you great men, during the present session—and what is still more extraordinary I have not yet seen The Presidents Message or any of the reports of the Setry!—about the time they were published I was on broad river where we have no Post office, and before I reached the East they had become old and destroyed—so that I have become thoroughly convinced that the whole machinary of Government can move on without the direction or aid of so important—ant [*sic*] a personage as the one now addressing you—but to be serious, Capt Henry Garrot with whom I presume you are acquainted is desirious of obtaining the appointment to take care of the Live oak⁵ in Florida, (it is understood there will shortly be a vacancy) he is a worthy good fellow, who served during the war and discharged his duties faithfully—he is in very reduced circumstances and has a most aimable family who stand in need of assistance his lady is one of the most Industrious individuals with whom I am acquainted —as you know he was unfortunate as a merchant—If it meets your approbation I hope you will interest the Delegation in his behalf—for I do not see how Mrs. Garrot will be able to support so large a family from her own exertions—of course I have but little news worthy the attention of a Politician as a desertation upon gravel and Slate could be used to little advantage in directing the affairs of the nation If Mr Clay becomes a free trade man and The Secty' as I understand recommend[s] Internal Improvements &c, I shall begin to think with Mr Balche that the Post of hono[r] is on the fence—

With much
Esteem Yours
H. G. BURTON

---

⁵In 1827 the House Committee on Naval Affairs recommended that a plantation for producing live oaks be established. Congress made the necessary appropriation for a plantation near Pensacola. This was never more than an experiment in this period of anxiety over the supply of live oaks for the navy. Great tracts of public lands were set aside for preserving live oaks. The navy kept these for the future and bought most of its live oaks from private lands. In 1832 Congress ordered a full report from the Secretary of Navy on the available live oaks. John C. Rives (ed.), *An Abridgement of the Debates of Congress from 1789 to 1856* (New York, N. Y.: D. Appleton and Co., 1859), XI, 275-277; House Doc. no. 23, 22 Cong., 2 sess., 59 pp.

[Addressed:]

The Honble
Willie P. Mangum
Washington
D. C.

WPM-LC

Will H. Haywood, Jr., to Willie P. Mangum

RALEIGH 16 Jany 1832.

Dear Sir,

I had the honor to receive a short letter from you some days ago and I have delayed replying till now because I have been unceesingly engaged in legislative business at home—In the midst of greater business nothing I am sure could draw your attention better but the circumstances of its being 'home'! Our Legislature adjourned on Saturday morn'g after a long and profitless session —Indeed I should be satisfied if I could persuade myself that the proceedings of our General Assembly were in effect no more than neutral—I very much fear that feelings which have heretofore existed are very greatly strengthened—East & West are parties —which have long distracted all our counsels. They are now as I fear perpetuated—Our Western friends have declared for years that they deprecated this State of things and opportunity was offered to prove their sincerity this winter—Had they availed themselves of it & offered the proper sacrifice to the State's weel much strength would have been added to their cause, & bright honours would have attached themselves to that section—There is however no disguising the fact that they have taken a new I think a false position—United with other interests they have cast off their 'first love'[6]—If you allow yourself time for such trifles you will perceive in my speech—recurrence to former days & times—and the Hon. Mr. *Leak* in reply has made the precious confession that *your Convention of 1823,* met here to prepare tempting *baits*[7] not to advance the principles you all professed—

---

[6] To gain the support of the Cape Fear representatives, the West proposed the removal of the capital to Fayetteville in exchange for the support of a constitutional convention by the Cape Fear section. Boyd, "Antecedents of the Constitutional Convention," 174.

[7] Walter F. Leake said that, as a member of the committee which framed the changes of 1823, he and others from the West were primarily concerned with the increase of representation from the West. He said that he and the others of the West agreed to have the convention at Raleigh as a means of gaining support of that city. *Debates in the Legislature of North Carolina on a Proposed Appropriation for Re-Building the Capitol, and on the Convention Question in the Month of December and January, 1831-1832* (Raleigh, 1832), 48.

I want to know if *you* back him!—He appealed with great confidence to his associates and you had the *honour* of being *one*—

The *West* being somewhat destitute of a leader suited to the occasion found one[8] among the *Cape Fear* delegation. I suspect you & our friend Mr Brown will be obliged to come back to the General Assembly to keep us straight.—If your leisure should tempt you to read my Speech on the appropriation bill it may perhaps strike you that I said nothing on the subject of *Convention*—It was a subject w[h] did not properly attach itself to the question—the course of our Wake Senator[9] to the contrary notwithstanding—When the *lash* is removed I have no hesitation in disclosing my sentiments on that subject tho: I confess that recent events are forcing me into new notions about it.—

You'll see that our Pres[t]. is not without friends here! In the small minority which voted against the Resolutions some were influenced by the belief that as a Legislature we must not touch the subject.—We have had a meeting here since then (Gov Stokes Ch[m]. very bad taste by the bye!) at which we endeavored to secure a full delegation at Baltimore to choose a candidate for Vice President!—Some who were named will not go most probably but a failure to do it they are to name one in their stead who is to be commissioned by *Central Com:*—

It will not escape your notice that we are wonderfully filled with the notice of making *Rail Roads in N. Caro.*—Unless we can do something of the kind we are gone!—I was prepared to give up myself as a victim to publick prejudice or anything else to attempt something grand *by the State*, but such a feeling was rare in our body & so the attempt was not made. Orange Co. I hear is much engaged in this subject—We had some difficulty in procuring the app[n]. to repair the *Statue*[10]—If W. Gaston had not been in the house I doubt very much if success would have followed the effort. He worked on the house—got us in a *glow* & we actually applauded him by loud cheers.—Hence the large majority in H. of C.—The Senate this year was a cold-blooded body.—

Our poor little City—1/4 burnt up—is very gloomy and all our people are absolutely forced into a cold sullen opposition to everything like *changes*.—Freemen are hard to *drive!*—

[8]Louis D. Henry of Fayetteville.
[9]Henry Seawell.
[10]The Canova statue of Washington was broken in the fire of the state house on June 21, 1831. R. D. W. Connor, "Canova's Statue of Washington." Publication of the North Carolina Historical Commission, *Bulletin* No. 8, (1910), 96 pp.

I will not venture to give you any expression of my experience in the *new* life of a politician—It would take up much of your time to hear me and I should probably be set down as a *querulous man*.—It is not the *thing* I thought it was tho: I had not given it a very lustrous aspect before my minds eye.—S. C^t. [Supreme Court] sits & All must here be forgotten.—Our *Counsellors*[11] are quite Democratick eno. don't you think so?

We never got any national politics before us—unless it was some foolish resolution about publick lands—They passed *sub silentio* when I was out of the house—I hardly know now what they were and I doubt much if many there did notice them more than I—Can you guess what will be the *ratio* of representation! Allow me here to entreat that you will make it your particular business to have the Census of N. Caro. re-examined—readded—& compared with itself. Don't make a noise about it but I think 'tis probable there is an unintended mistake in it to *our prejudice* —A few members may make a great difference to us too.—Have this done without naming me as I only gathered the thought from an accidental conversation with a Grand Juror at *Last Fed: Court* and thinking it important I have not forgotten it.— It is a very easy matter for a Clerk to cut his eye over pages & say 'Aye' all is right without having troubled himself to do as he ought. See to it!—I have gained many law suits by looking into the *papers* and I do not know that *cases* of *State* require less attention to produce similar results & if you can make for North Caro: an increase in her population that will save a Representative 'twill be Worth all the Nag's head prospects!—McKay[12] 'tis said here *will not resign* though he is unable to go on to W. City —I do not think Judge Johnson will be able to go on this Winter —He is still here an invalid.—

Please let Mr. Brown know that I am indebted to him for a Document sent me—& Genl Barringer of H of R. too please remind that I thank him for his favors—he has been attentive to me in this regard & when a thing of interest occurs here likely to compensate him I will not forget to make the acknowledgment directly.—

I am not so near and therefore I cannot judge as well as you can still I am not without hope of many happy riddances from the Tariff exactions—I think a great deal will be gained if

---

[11]Council of State.
[12]James J. McKay, U. S. district attorney, was elected to Congress in 1831. He served in Congress from 1831 to 1849. He was a Democrat. *Biog. Dir. of Cong.*, 1265.

these taxes are removed even from the articles consumed by the *wealthier*—The *minority* however just their cause ought not to be too stout.—

What do you think of Polk of Ten: an old college friend of mine—Write me frankly.—Is McDuffie thought to be aspiring after anything? Will Van B. nomination be successfully resisted! If it is I do not doubt that N. Caro: will take him up at once for Vice Prest. Have you ever looked in the State Dept. to find out what good friend it was who represented me as so odious to the publick here that it would be ruinous to the administration to honor me in any way? I should like to know who it was— Rencher told me it was done by *some one* but he did not certainly know by whom?—

I have seen no one directly from your house lately and therefore I am unable to say how your 'folks' are but your friends here are well and I

am still your friend & obt.
Serv.
WILL H. H. JR.

[Addressed:]

Willie P. Mangum.
In Senate of U. S.
Washington City.

WPM-LC

Priestley H. Mangum to Willie P. Mangum

HILLSBORO' Jan: 16th. 1832.

Dear Sir:

Yours of the 6th. Inst. came to hand by the last mail; and in answer, I have to say, that Rebecca has been in bad health some three months.—For the last three or four weeks, she has been almost constantly confined to her bed. The attending physician seems to be at a loss as to the real nature of her disease; and we all would have continued in ignorance on the subject, if nature, the best physician of all, had not ultimately made a full demonstration of the cure.—The crisis has passed by . . .[13]

----
[13]About two pages from the original letter are omitted. The part omitted is a detailed description of Rebecca's symptoms. This portion of the letter has no historical value and the details are too intimate to include.

You speak of cold weather at Washington—Here we have had a December, unparallelled by any other within the recollection of our oldest citizens, in its intense, uniform cole, & its snow and ice. The ice remained one month to a day, & it fell at first on the 6 & 7th of December. Now the weather is mild & open.

I have been so engrossed with painful reflection on the uncertain and critical condition of Rebecca's health, that I hardly know anything of the passing political events of the Winter. They have made some noise, & done but little in our Assembly. The burning of Raleigh & the undertaking to repair the statue of Washington are, I believe, the most striking & important events that have occurred there. The re-election of our Friend Scott, & the *put down* of Gov: Owen in consequence of his revengeful, pragmatical interference, this winter at Raleigh, with matters that a lofty mind & a good heart would not have touched—are to me not the least pleasing incidents of the day.—

In regard to *general politicks,* I hope you will not go ahead of public opinion in No. Ca. Whatever may become the settled policy of the Government on the subject of *protection, Now* is not the time for the public servants of this State to speak of *unconstitutional resistance.* For our people are ripe for no such thing—and nothing short of *tangible* oppression would wean them from the Union.

I should like to hear from you in regard to the Sec: of the Treasury; whether he has improved to your fancy since you saw him some years ago; whether he too is to be considered too selfish to be a patriot,—Other matters touching distinguished *actors* at Washington, & the political currents, I should like to hear of, as your convenience will permit.

Yours respectfully

P. H. MANGUM

[Addressed:]

  The Hon.
   Willie P. Mangum
    (of the Senate)
     Washington City
      D. C.

WPM-LC

W. Watts[14] et als. to Willie P. Mangum

WILLIAMSTON 17 Jany 1832-

Hon: Wilie P. Mangum
    Dear Sir,
            At a meeting of the citizens of our village lately held,
we the undersigned were appointed a committee respectfully to
address you and our representative Mr. Branch on the subject of
our Mails, and request your friendly co-operation in endeavouring to relieve us of the inconveniences under which we labour—
    We addressed a letter to Gov. Branch by our last mail inclos-
ing a plan of change to which we most respectfully refer you—
    We trust in your forgiveness, for transcending the limits of
strict propriety, in thus asking for a favor of other than our immediate representative—From the circumstances which have
transpired between him and president Jackson we are apprehensive that he does not maintain the weight and standing with
the Post Master General, to which his merits and talents entitle
him, and that his solicitations in our behalf would be treated
with indifference or neglect—We hope then you will not look
upon our petition as intrusive, or that Gov. Branch will consider
it in the slightest degree a reflection upon himself or conceive,
that our confidence in him is in the least diminished—We are
driven to extra measures to obtain our rights—Petition after petition has been forwarded to the Post Master General, and never
the word have we yet received—Petitions too, signed by almost
every individual on the road from Scotland Neck to Plymouth,
yet we are unworthy of that gentlemans notice—We were never
before the present administration, heard to utter a single complaint—Mails were as liberally supplied as the size of our village
could reasonably insure—Nor for slight causes are we disposed
to murmur—But why our mails have been lessened in number
while those of our neighbouring towns have been multiplied, we
are at loss to assign a plausible reason— In an excited state of
feeling we are ready to conjecture, that the system of proscription extends to communities as well as in individuals—However
this may be, it is a signal oversight—; much to our detriment,
premeditated or fortuitous—Nevertheless, we are still unwilling
to believe in any intentional neglect—

---

[14]William Watts was a member of the House of Commons from Martin County in 1829-
1830. *N. C. Manual*, 693-694.

17

Our little village has been progressively improving, though we admit in a very humble degree, for three years past—Not in population & houses only, but in commercial affairs—While our more favored neighbors, have not only been stationary, but some one of them at least, is in a retrograding condition—

Our reading community too, truly not large, yet is more numerous than usual for the same population—And many there are among us, who abstain from subscribing to some of the numerous journals of our country, solely on account of the teasing delay in our mails—And even, those that are now taken will probably be soon discontinued altogether, as bearing only the news trite & stale, that has already been antisipated by some communicative passenger—

But it is in mercantile concerns that we vitally suffer—Our merchants a very respectable portion of the community, labour under serious disadvantages—Advices from their correspondents reach them, almost always one whole week later than those only 20 miles off—How goading to their feelings! how oppressive to their interests and indirectly to the community needs no comment—A check is thus put to generous exertion and industrious enterprise—Speculation and liberal adventure belongs not to them but to our more fortunate neighbours—

Many of our citizens, planters, are in the habit from usage immemorial, of making shipments, the products of their own farms, to distant markets on account of the facilities of navigation—Speedly advices from the vacillating state of the markets is essentially important to their success & prosperity—And having suffered, so repeatedly, by pursuing a course, which was once lucrative, they have partly abandoned it, and submit with murmers to reduced prices and the accumulated incidental charges from shipment & storage—We could go farther, and state the evils that the labouring people themselves, suffer who get naval stores and sell them daily or weekly for an subsistence; but we abstain, and will not longer wear your patience, and generous disposition, in relating the injurious consequences that flow from this infrequent inter-communication; nor would we have gone thus far were they not so strictly applicable to us—They are truly speaking, evils and oppressions; and to them, so far, we have the additional mortification of inattention on the part of the Post Office Department—We much regret that the position of affairs places us under the necessity of calling your attention from graver deliberations, to a mater of such

seeming unimportance;—and in conclusion, again respectfully ask your friendly assistance in aiding our much respected and honorable representative, in relieving us, as far as practicable, of the serious oppression and inconveniences, under which, from the present existing state of the Mails, we are necessarily burdened—
We remain, dear Sir, very respectfully, your most obedient
& Humble servts—

WM WATTS
J B Wade
Jas. D. Briggs   James Shaw
D. W. Bagley
C B Hassell
Edwin S. Smithwick
Asa Biggs[15]
Thomas W. Watts.

Wm Store N. C.
17 Jany

[Addressed:]

Hon. Willie P. Mangum
Washington City
D. C.

WPM-LC

James W. Jeffreys[16] to Willie P. Mangum

RED HOUSE N C. Jany 19th 1832
My Dr Sir
It falls to my lot to write you again concerning a matter of some importance to me, and your county town Hillsboro—I hope you will not deem me troublesome, because it is thro you or persons acting in the same capacity that we have to call upon; upon matters of great importance to us—
There is a prospect of the mail from Milton to Hillsboro. is to be carried in two horse stages. There was a petition sent to

[15]Asa Biggs was later a member of the national House of Representatives from 1845 to 1847, in the Senate from 1858 to 1861, and a federal judge from 1858 to 1861. *D. A. B.,* II, 262.
[16]James W. Jeffreys was a planter and manufacturer in Caswell County. *Hillsborough Recorder,* Sept. 9, 1825.

the Post office department to have this mail carried in 2 horse stages—My object in writing to you is to beg of you to interceed for me at the Post office department, and endeavour to procure the contract for me as the present contractor will not be able to conduct in such style as the nature of it requires—My object in wishing to get it is to have a direct line of stages from this section of the state to Raleigh and our Seaboard towns. Fayetteville, Newbern, and Wilmington—I hope you will make this application for me as I hope it will be the last that I shall have cause to trouble you—I wish to know whether you have abandoned the idea of procuring a mail route from Oxford to Hillsboro—It is an object much desired by the people of Hillsboro and the vicinity—I have heard that it was rumored in Hillsboro that the route had been established and that you had procured the contract for me— I am afraid the news is too good to be true—

If you have not made the application I hope you will do it soon as I wish to convince the people of Hillsboro that they have not been shown that justice which the importance of their town requires of the Post office Department—

If you can get your petition granted which you can easily do,—I wish to put the line in complete operation. or sooner if requested by the 1st of April—

I shall be happy to hear from you as soon as convenience—

Very Respectfully
JAS. W JEFFREYS—

Red House N. C.
    Jany 19th 1832   Free

[Addressed:]
Hon Willey P. Mangum
Washington City
    D. C.

Willie P. Mangum to William Gaston[17]

WASHINGTON CITY 19th. January 1832

My dear Sir,

I received your favour early in December inviting my atten-

[17]The original is in the William Gaston Papers, Southern Collection, University of North Carolina.

tion to Mr. Leroy's case.[18] I have examined his memorial with care and presented it to the Senate. The principle has been hitherto recognized by Congress which reaches his case—It is now under reference to the Committee of Finance—I have no hope of a favorable report, nor of a more favorable disposition of it by Congress.

Believeing however, that it would be more satisfactory to Mr Leroy, I gave him his claim that direction with the view, that the final action of Congress might be had on the subject.—

Yours of the 31st. ult. came to hand in due course of mail.— I took the earliest opportunity of calling at the Department to ascertain whether the name of young Mr. Moore[19] was on file.— I found it on file with a note that he was recomended by you.—

So far from regarding your request as in any wise "troublesome," permit me to assure you that it would give me much satisfaction to serve you in any way in my power and I trust you will command my services freely & without reserve, in any matter in which you may suppose I can be useful to you or any of your friends.—As matter of Courtesy the nomination of one Cadet by a Senator is generally respected. Should therefore Mr. Anderson[20] of Hillsborough, fail to present an application of which he spoke to me last Autumn, I shall with much pleasure present Mr. Moore as my nominee.—

Having heard nothing from Mr Anderson since my arrival here, I think it very probable, that he has declined offering the name referred to.—

It is not believed that the present session of Congress will be useful—almost every thing seems to be considered with reference to its probable influence upon party interests.—I have but little hope of any essential & satisfactory modification of the laws of import.—Indications are now more unpromising than they were two or three weeks ago. The Ex-president Mr Adams, it is believed will take strong ground upon principles of free trade—His course and deportment have strongly tended to disabuse him of many prejudices.—I know no Gentleman in Congress who is more generally acceptable to all parties.—And he seems to have placed himself in that position without seeking it & without effort.—

I think it is to be very much regretted that the U. S. Bank

[18]See above, p. 417.
[19]See above, p. 442.
[20]William Anderson. See below, p. 519.

has come before Congress at this session.—I regard the continuance of that institution as of almost indispensible necessity—

By deferring its application to next Session I have no doubt,
with but slight modification (to save appearances) it would have
met with Executive favor.— It is *now* more than doubtful
whether it will.—And the whole may ultimately take the appearance of a trial of strength between Gen. Jackson & the Bank—
In that case. the Bank will go down—For Gen J's popularity is
of *a sort* not to slaken at present.—I hope for the best results
from the wise & patriotic counsels of Mr McLane[21]—

Accept with assurance of my
entire respect & esteem
WILLIE P. MANGUM

[Endorsed:] W. P. Mangum
          Jany. 19th 1832

[Address:] William Gaston Esquire
         Raleigh
            North Carolina

Free
W. P. Mangum

WPM-LC

Thos. H. Willie[22] to Willie P. Mangum

                   January 20th 1832 OXFORD GRANVILLE
Dear Sir, In view of the pressing & important throng of public
business with which your attention must be occupied at Washington, I feel some hesitation at the Idea of interrupting you
with any of my domestic affairs But under a grateful recollection of your past favours, promptly confered, & your kind sympa-
thies to me expressed I am induced again to trouble you

A kind of uncertain report prevails in this section that Robert
Potter, while a member at Washington, passed for a single man,
and in that character paid his addresses to a lady of wealth &
family & was to have been married to her this winter.[23] It is
said the ladys name is Lovet. The object of my letter is to re-

---

[21]Louis McLane was Secretary of Treasury from 1831 to 1833.
[22]See above, pp. 410, 412.
[23]See above, p. 410n.

quest you as soon as convenient to inform if you have learned
or heard of any such Report at Washington and the particulars
of it It is also said here that an acquaintance of his from N Carolina had informed the lady, that Potter had a family here &
that the information had frustrated his plan Be so good as to
give me information about this (if you can) as soon as convenient

    With sentiments of sincere Esteem I Remain your
                Most obdt Servt &C
                        THOS H WILLIE

[Addressed:]

            The Hon. Willie P. Mangum
            Washington City

_____

                                        WPM-LC

        C. H. Jordan to W. P. Mangum

                        22nd Jany 1832
Dear Sir
    It is the request of a number of persons in this county that
you cooperate with Gen Barringer and Mr Brown (both of
whom I expect have been written to on the subject) in trying
to establish a weekly mail from Blackwalnut Halifax Va to Roxborough in this county There are a number of persons in the
neighborhood of Hugh Woods, who would gladly subscribe for
news papers if they had the facilities which other neighbor-
hoods posses of geting them, in fact eighteen or twenty have already said they would, they have not only said so but they
manifest no little anxiety about the matter. The nearest post
office to Woods, is six miles which is Williamsville—Roxborough
is seven—Black walnut ten and Bennett's Store twelve or fourteen; in the circuference of these places are a number of persons destitute of public information and that solely for the
want of the means by which it could be obtained. There is already a horse route from Halifax C. House Va to Bennett's Store
which intersects the northern and Richmond mails at the former
and the Petersburg at the latter place. The proposed route
would give us the northern and eastern papers by those routes

and the southern news by intersecting a southern mail at Roxborough. We propose calling the office at Woods,—Woodsville, myself postmaster and Mr Woods will convey the mail once a week for the sum of Fifty dollars—The distance from Blackwalnut to Roxborough is about nineteen miles. Get it established if you can

Yrs respectfully

C. H. JORDAN

Hon. W. P. Mangum

[Addressed:]

Hon W. P. Mangum
Washington City

[Postmarked:]

Williamsville, N. C.

WPM-LC

William Potter[24] *to Willie P. Mangum*

[Jan. 22, 1832].

My Dear Sir:—

When I left home I expected to procure a situation in the Patent Office; but I have been disappointed—I find that there is no vacancy at present—and that if Congress consent to furnish more engrossing Clerks, in that Office, thirs' will not be permanent situations.

I had frequently been invited to Asheville, by the Postmaster of that place, and advised by a Mr Allen,[25] member of Assembly, to establish myself there, and I have partly yielded to their solicitations. I have issued a Prospectus, imperfect as it is, for the publication of a paper in Ashville, and I have but one favor to ask of the "Jacksonian Republicans"—and that is, the loan of $100 for 6 months, (from *Sundry* individuals, who will contenance my proposed undertaking.)

---

[24]William Potter published the *Raleigh Constitutionalist* before he began the *Jacksonian Republican* at Asheville. In 1847 he published the *Pittsborough Communicator* which later became a temperance newspaper under the name of the *Fayetteville Communicator*. N. C. *Free Press*, Mar. 13, 1832; Johnson, *Ante-Bellum N. C.*, 804.

[25]James Allen served in the legislature as a representative of Buncombe County in 1827, 1829, and 1831-1832. F. A. Sondley, *A History of Buncombe County, North Carolina* (Asheville, N. C.: The Advocate Press, 1930), II, 802.

I am now at sea—and probably a boistrous sea—without any pilot—distant, far distant from the good counsels of relations or connections—the safety of my barque, therefore, depends upon *chance*. Under these circumstances sheer necessity compels me, which I do with the utmost reluctance, to ask your aid in procuring the assistance of Mr. Kendall, Mr. Barry, Isaac Hill, and others of the Jackson ranks.—If each of 5 persons would subscribe for 10 copies, at $2, or, would advance me 20$, which would make one hundred dollars, I should, with the assistance of Mr. Coleman,[26] P. M. of Asheville & others of that place, be enabled to commence operations almost immediately—for I am now in treaty for a Press and materials, already in No. Carolina, which are offered me for one-third their value—they are the property of Col. Allison[27] of your county, and they are now lying idle at Milton.

I want to publish just such a paper as is *required* in No. Caro. a consistent Jackson republican and State's Rights paper—an *Independent* paper—one that will give to the unfaithful politician his due punishment—and reward the meritorious—and in place of crowding in *light reading* and anecdotes, to furnish important extracts from all our most valuable periodicals and journals—and to advocate the *Convention question* of our State —just such a paper is needed at Asheville. It must be published in the Western Section—and there is no other place in the West that will answer for a Press. I was assured by a gentleman living in Fayetteville, that if the Constitutionalist, or any other paper of that stamp, would come out *boldly* for a Convention, and the removal of the Seat of Government to that place, 500 Subscribers could be procured to it, in addition to its then No. Subscribers. If you will aid me, I assure you, you will not be disappointed in my publication—for it shall be what it professes to be—and your kindness shall long be cherished in a grateful bosom.

With an anxious solicitude for your happiness, &c. I am, Dr. Sir,

Yrs. Sincerely,
WM. POTTER.
22d. Jany. '32.

---

[26]John H. Coleman was the postmaster at Asheville.
[27]Colonel Joseph Allison of Orange County was in the legislature in 1830-1834, 1835, 1838, and 1842. *N. C. Manual*, 740-741.

Honl. W. P. Mangum.

I would be glad if you would endeavor to procure for me, the publishing of the Laws of the U. S.—and request Mr. Barry to give me a part of the advertising custom from his Department.

W. P.

[Addressed:]

The Hon. Willie P. Mangum,
Senator U. States, N. C.
Washington City.

———

WPM-LC

William Gaston to W. P. Mangum

Raleigh Jany. 23rd. 1832

My dear Sir

I am so strongly impressed by the prompt and kind manner in which you have attended to my communication in behalf of the son of my townsman M^r. Moore, that I can not deny myself the pleasure of informing you of the gratification it has given me . . [O]ur apprehension that the present session of Congress w[ould b]e productive of little good to the country has grieved but not [m]uch surprised me. Party combinations and factious interests ever have been and always will be most pernicious in free governments, and at the present day seem to have a predominance seldom before witnessed. Let us hope however that they are not all powerful. Public virtue is not extinct, and whatever difficulty it may find in causing its voice to be heard amidst these contentions, it should not forbear its efforts to command attention. I am much gratified at the intelligence contained in your letter respecting the course and deportment of the Ex-President. In common with a large portion of those with whom I was accustomed to act I had taken up strong prejudices against him. Of the injustice of some of these prejudices I became convinced several years since, and the conviction that I had done him wrong in the estimate I had formed of his motives renders me the more solicitous now to appreciate his worth.

With you I believe the continuance of the Bank of the U. S. of almost indispensable necessity. I *know* that no[th]ing but this institution could have cured the pre[sent?] money disease in N°. Cᵃ. and have a full conviction that if it be not upheld a state of things must ere long arise more extensively dangerous than what we have heretofore witnessed. I am mortified and pained too at the want of stability and permanency which a failure to renew the charter would stamp upon all the institutions of our country. How far it was expedient for the friends of the Bank to press the subject upon the consideration of the National Legislature at this session you have far better means of judging than myself. But indeed it is melancholy to think that the individual who fills the high office of President of the U. States (well-meaning as no doubt he is) must be coaxed into the performance of a sacred duty by assurances direct or direct that the supremacy of his popularity is unquestioned.—

We have had a very active session in the State Legislature, which has terminated in few practical results.—The understanding direct or indirect between the West and the Cape Fear was strong enough to defeat measures against which they were arrayed but not powerful enough to carry any of their own. The Legislature has sins of omission to answer for, but it committed little or no positive mischief.—

I take a very deep interest in the survey ordered to be made for a Central Rail Road. It is of vast importance that it should be prosecuted under the superintendence of some one whose skill in the art and practical good sense will command confidence in his recommendations. Whether after the railroad reaches Neuse between Smithfield and Raleigh it shall take up the valley of the Neuse pass by Hillsborough to Haw River and up the Allemance to Guildford &c, or leave Neuse below Raleigh and strike across towards Pittsborough or Haywood are very interesting questions. The most economical plan of constructing a rail road through the Pine Forests below is a matter on a right decision of which the success or failure of the whole scheme may greatly depend. The board of Internal Improvements is anxious to get a fit Engineer. You will greatly oblige me and the Board by using the opportunities you possess of discovering one who may be recommended and can be obtained. I have heard Genˡ. Swift[28] formerly at the head of the Engineer Department spoken of. Can [yo]u

---

[28]Joseph Gardner Swift, 1783-1865, one of the early graduates of West Point, was in charge of the fortifications of New York after the capture of Washington in the War of 1812. He resigned from the army in 1818 and became the surveyor for the port of New York and chief engineer of several railroads including the Baltimore and Susquehanna and the New York and Harlem. From 1829 to 1845 he was civil engineer in the government service in charge of harbor improvements on the Great Lakes. *D. A. B.*, XVIV, 247.

learn his qualifications for the undertaking and [whe]re he is
to be found?—

I pr[a]y you to believe me very respectfully

Your friend & obed^t. Servt.

WILL: GASTON

Hon: W. P. Mangum

WPM-LC

R. M. Saunders to W. P. Mangum

RALEIGH Jany 23rd- 1832

My dear Sir,

I read with much interest yr. favour of the 18th. instant—We
were all here on tiptoe in consequence of the rumour stated by
the Intell^r. of the rejection of Mr. Van Buren's appointment[29]—
& tho' the injunction of secrecy may have forbid your disclosing
particulars, your assurance that the appointment will in all probability be confirmed removes in some degree the anxiety felt
upon the subject—I am well satisfied his rejection by Mr. Calh.
or his party would for the present at least damn Mr. C's prospects in N. C.—Indeed I heard men come out for V- B- on the
receit of the news that I had not expected—I think with you,
that *he* should not be brought forward at this time for V- President, unless indeed he should be rejected & in that event the development of public sentiment will controul matters—I am decidedly opposed to Dick Johnston,[30] he wants character & talent
—& his constitutional notions are too wild for us—I wish you
may not be deceived in Judge McLean[31]—I always believed him
more over-rated than any man in the nation & his opinions as
reported show him totally incompetent for his present station—
But I fear he is not a *sinsere* man—a letter of his sometime last
summer to some persons in Phil^a. shewed that he was looking to
the presidency & what was worse proved him to be a *common
welfare* man in his constitutional opinions—besides I doubt, his
being *bona fide* for Jackson—and I have no idea of electing a
man who would go into the V-pre^y——to further his own views or

---

[29]Mangum voted for Van Buren's confirmation as minister to Great Britain.
[30]Richard M. Johnson of Kentucky.
[31]John McLean.

those of another at the expence of the president—I have no confidence in *him*—yet if the party have or if I be mistaken I am prepared to give way—I had thought myself, if Wilkins[32] or Dallas[33] acted with becoming forbearance upon the subject of the tariff & manifested an honest disposition for a proper modification—one of them should be taken up—sound policy dictated the gratification of Pennsy[a]—but if they link themselves to that selfish—H. Clay I am done with them—I have long believed Clay prepared for any thing to advance his own views & to effect it he would bargain with the devil—a large majority of those who have been selected as Delegates from this State, will go into the Convention uncommitted & perfectly disposed to select a man who will give Gen[l]. Jackson a bona fide cooperation in his administration & no one else in my view ought to be selected—

I suppose Dr. Carson[34] will select his Brother Sam, should he not attend—I shall write to Franklin[35] & Forny[36] & get one of them (in the event of their not going) to select you)—and Gallaway or Humphreys will select Brown—whether I go or not must depend on the necessity of the case—I cannot afford to do so unless I see that I can be of some good—which I likely might be with many of the delegation—

You have no idea of the unprecedented depression of the [prof]ession—fees in this circuit have fallen off 50 per Cent—I shall therefore feel the more solicitous for getting in my son at West point—my respects to Brown—to whom you may show this—

truly yrs

R. M. SAUNDERS

Hon: W. P. Mangum

---

[32]William Wilkins of Pennsylvania was United States Senator from 1831 to 1834.
[33]George M. Dallas who later ran on the ticket with Polk.
[34]John W. Carson of Rutherford County. Ashe, *Biog. Hist. of N. C.*, II, 60.
[35]Probably Abner Franklin who was state senator from Iredell County in 1827-1828. *N. C. Manual*, 662.
[36]Peter Forney, 1756-1834, was a presidential elector in 1804, 1808, 1816, 1824 and 1828. He was in Congress from 1813 to 1815. Ashe, *Biog. Hist. of N. C.*, V, 98-102.

WPM-LC

H. Van Noorden[37] to Willie P. Mangum

[GREENVILLE, N. C., 24 Jan., 1832]

Dear Sir

on the 30ᵗ. Novʳ. last I took the liberty to write you this inclosed, as I have not yet had the pleasure to receive an answer,
& the letter was Sent from my house by a negro to the Post office
in Greeneville I am fearful it has not reached you;—

I have Since Seen by the newspapers, that the matter therein
mention'd was committed to a Special Committee of the Senate
Supposed to be friendly to the cause, but have not yet Seen that
any report has been made by them; I was however yesterday
informed by Some of my fellow Sufferers of Washington in this
State, that a Speedy and favorable report was expected, & that
in case of acceptance by the Senate & house of representatifes
the memorials would be placed on a dockett in the order as
presented, & as my petition with the vouchers were as long Since
as April 1826 delivered by Mʳ. N. Macon to the then appointed
Select Committee, I should reasonable expect in that case, to
find an early place on Said dockett, except that in that long in-
terval of time my memorial & vouchers have been mislaid, may
I beg your friendly attention to examine, whether that—memorial & Vouchers are on the list of the early Claimants; as in case
they Should have been mislaid, another memorial and Copy of
the vouchers should be immediately sent in; my Claims Consist
in the Capture, & Condemnation of the Schooner Betsey & Cargo
of Specie & Bills in 1796, and in the Capture and Condemnation of the Cargo of Schooner Bell in 1797, the Vouchers Send
on, & delivered to the Committee, are Copies of the Condemnations, & protest's against Said Captures & Condemnations of
Said Vessels & Cargos;—no further Vouchers were then considered necessary, but will in due time be Send on, My *present
anxiety* is, that the matter may appear properly memorialized
before the Senate; to this give me leave to beg your attention
& further to Solicit your assistance to the passage of the bill as
before requested

And requesting to be favored with an answer, as early as may
be Convenient;—

---

³⁷See above, p. 418.

I remain with due respect
Your obedt Servt.

HAD VAN NOORDEN

Pitt County near Greeneville
24ᵗ. Janʸ. 1832
Honˡ. Willie P. Mangum[38]

———

Willie P. Mangum to Jesse Person, Esquire[39]

SENATE CHAMBER 25ᵗʰ Jan: 1832

My dear Sir

I have time only to say that I have received your letters, with the receipt enclosed.

I learn from Gov. Miller[40] of the Senate that Mr Presly[41] has just arrived in this City. I shall attend to your business and let you know the result at the earliest period.

I have not time to give any news. Nor indeed is there much except what you see in the public prints—The Senate will take an obstinate stand, I fear, against any substantial modification of the Tariff—The worst spirit is indicated.—

Accept the assurance of my most
friendly, & respectful consideration

WILLIE P. MANGUM

Address: Jesse Person Esquire
Louisburg
North Caroline

Free
W. P. Mangum

Postmark:
City of Washington
Jan. 26

---

[38]A copy of the letter of November 30, 1831, was enclosed. It is omitted here because the original was published above.

[39]The original is in the A. Burt collection, Duke University, Durham, N. C. Jesse Person was an attorney in Louisburg. McIver, *N. C. Register*, 46.

[40]Stephen Decatur Miller, 1787-1838, a member of the House of Representatives from 1817 to 1819, was governor of South Carolina from 1828 to 1830 and United States Senator from 1831 to 1833. *Biog. Dir. of Cong.*, 1315.

[41]I. B. Presly. See below, Mangum to Person, Feb. 22, 1832.

WPM-LC

Willie P. Mangum to Mrs. Charity A. Mangum

Monday Morning 30th. January 1832

My Dear Love.

The last letter I received from you came to hand the day before yesterday but bore date the 14th Jan. so that it had been 14 days on the road whereas it ought only to be from Sunday until the next friday or Saturday—

The letter is permitted to lay by a Week I suspect in the office,—You had better write a line to Mr. Vanhook[42] to know at what time you had better send letters.

I regret to hear that Hinton has thought proper to leave our school—And I do not think he has treated me well—Sally must go to some school. It will not do for her to remain at home this year. It is impossible for her to be instructed by you with any effect—I must fix upon something—in the meantime let me know if any other teacher is to be had in that neighbourhood.

Last Tuesday the weather changed suddenly and became the coldest that perhaps I ever felt—Mr. Adams the late President I understand, says that last Thursday was a[s] cold weather as he ever experienced in Russia—The thermometer was twelve or 13 degrees *below* zero—It hardly ever gets down to zero in North Carolina The freezing point is (I believe) 31 degrees *above* zero —so that you may judge how cold it was—It has been but little warmer since—Saturday night It began to snow continued to snow yesterday—& last night It rained a little and now the snow is about 4 Inches deep with a crust strong enough to bear a man—I have not been out of the House since yesterday morning—I continue well—Several persons have frozen to death in this weather in & about this City—and the poor people are almost literally freezing for fuel—The poor wretches hang about these Cities, fall into every evil habit & drag a most wretched existence when with little labour in the Country the[y] might live well.

The boy stands by me with a basket to carry letters to the Post Office—

Give my love & a kiss to Sally & Patty—& believe me my Love your devoted & affectionate husband

WILLIE P MANGUM

---

[42]Robert Vanhook of Person County.

[Addressed:]
>Mrs. Charity A. Mangum
>Red Mountain
>North Carolina

WPM-LC

William Polk to Willie P. Mangum

RALEIGH Feby. 1, 1832.

Dear Sir,

I have read with some attention the proceedings of C[ongre]ss in regard to the petition of the President and Directors of the Bank of the U. States for a recharter of s^d. Bank; and from what I can gather from the debates the Newspapers observations, find myself intirely at a loss to form an opinion what will be the result. I am anxious to have some reasonable grounds to enable me upon investing some money in a Stock, yielding a profitable dividend, and had determined to buy Stock of the U. States Bank—But should the petition be rejected, there is good reason to believe the Stock will fall perhaps below par. Those residing at the seat of Gov^t. and especially those on whom depend the passage of the Bill for a recharter, are much better enabled to give a correct opinion as to the result, than we who are at a distance; I have therefore taken the liberty to ask your opinion whether the Congress will pass a Bill for a recharter, in its present form, or with modifications, and what these most probably [will] be and should the Bill pass is it believed the President will give it his sanction. You will oblige me by giving your opinion as soon as a probable conjecture can be formed what is to be the result.

>Accept the assurance of my
>respect a[nd] esteem
>Yo [torn] Obt.
>WILL. POLK.

[Addressed:]
>The Honble
>Willie P. Mangum
>Washington City

[Endorsed:]
Answered 11th Feby 1832.

WPM-LC

Nathaniel G. Smith[43] to Willie P. Mangum

BUNKER HILL HARDEMAN COUNTY
TENNESSEE Feby. 1st 1832

Hon. W. P. Mangum
Dear Sir

You will probably be surprised at the caption of my letter, pecuniary considerations, with a desire to live comfortably, induced me to quit the sterile soil of N. Carolina my native State, (for which bye the bye I expect ever to cherish feelings of the highest regard) and seek a home in the more fertile region of the West. I have selected this county at least for a temporary residence, and probably a permanent one. From the intimacy formerly existing between us, to say nothing of our affianced connexion, may I not indulge the hope, that you will *officially* interest yourself for a particular friend and relation of mine, as far as is compatable with your publick duty.

My friend, Mr. Green Pryor of this County has enclosed a memorial to President Jackson directed to congress, asking for indeminfication of the United States for certain moneys paid by him to the government for a certain Fractional section of land in the State of Mississisippi Claiborn County, purchased in the year 1818 of a Mr. Isham Arthur, who had entered the land at two dollars an acre (government price) having been surveyed by a government officer and by him computed to contain, (said fractional Section) 440 Acres bounded by big black River &C the Said Mr. Pryor and his Brother Peter Pryor conceiving the big black to be the correct boundary, and also knowing from its locality it would on a re-survey overgo the originial estimate—gave Arthur a considerable advance on his purchase—thinking government *bound in justice.* to issue patents to the purchasers, under the survey of their officer and by order of the Department, at least after the money should have been paid to the proper receiving officer, all of which has been strictly complied with by Mr. Pryor the petitioner (Please to bear in mind Mr. Arthur, the original person who entered said land, had only paid one fourth part of the price, & Mr. Pryor paid the remaining three fourths out of his own pocket to Government) Several years after the purchase, the Department ordered a re-survey,

---

[43]See above, p. 245.

whereby it was ascertained that the original plat of Survey was incorrect and that the traverse of the big black River is much farther North than the original plat represented it to be—from a report made to Congress by the committee to whom it Pryor's memorial was referred Decr. 29th-1830—they seem to act under the impression that perhaps the former survey was fraudulently made—if it were neither of the Mr. Pryor's were in any ways accessory to it for they lived in Tennessee—[And] here permit me to say to you that I [know] Green Pryor well, and have known him for several years, and can conscientiously say I believe him as honest, virtuous and gentelmanly man as lives—and a man above collusion—for his character more particularly I refer you President Jackson & the Hon—James K. Polk—& Mr. [John] Bell who all know him personally—when the matter shall be communicated to Congress you will please attend to it—and also be good enough to attend the meeting of the committee—every word Pryor sets forth in the memorial may be relied as fact—for he is a man of undoubted veracity—he wishes to get a patent for the whole of the survey—or his money reimbursed—in fact he has not yet even a right to the 440 Acres—he appeals to the Justice of his country—to the magnanimity of Congress—excuse the length of my epistle—Should be glad to hear from you any time—Direct to Bolivar Tennessee—

Respectfully &C,

NAT. G. SMITH

Please endeavor to explain this matter to your friends and aid in any other way you may deem most advisable if consistent with your views of policy and oblige

Yours truly

N. G. S.

[Addressed:]

Hon. Willie P. Mangum
Senator in Congress
Washington

Mail)

WPM-LC

Lewis Cass to Willie Mangum

DEPARTMENT OF WAR
Feby. 3. 1832

Sir,

In answer to your letter of yesterday, I have the honour to state, that North Carolina will be entitled to nine additional Cadets, at the Military Academy, at the commencement of the next Academic in June. In their selection every attention shall be paid to your recommendation in favour of Mr. William Cameron.[44]

with great respect,
I am, Sir,
Your ob Servt.

LEW CASS

Hon. Willie Mangum
U. S. Senate.

—————

WPM-LC

James Iredell to Willie P. Mangum

RALEIGH Feb.ʸ 4ᵗʰ. 1832

My dear Sir,

I am anxious to hear from you what is going on in the political world—I *ought* to be done with politics & am trying to wean myself from them—but according to the vulgar saying "an old coach horse loves a smack of the whip"—I read the newspapers, but I have been long enough at Washington to know that one gathers but a superficial view of matters by consulting them— I feel a curiosity to know what is passing behind the scenes, where I have sometimes been admitted myself—I have no claim upon you, for I am a miserable correspondent but you would much gratify me by letting me as much as you can into the mysteries of the inner temple—If I know myself, I have no object but the good of my country in any of my political aspirations—I know you have no other—We exchanged our political

—————

[44]William Cameron, the nephew of Duncan Cameron, withdrew the same year of his appointment. He lived in Hillsboro. *House Document*, Rep. No. 303, 24 Cong., 2 sess., 95.

ideas too freely about twelve months ago to leave me any doubt
upon that subject, even if it were possible I could have entertained it before—First, then, (for I deem it first in importance)
what is to be done with the Tariff?[45] If the principle of the
Protective System is to be preserved, in my opinion the Constitution & liberties of our country are gone—If Congress assumes
to itself the power of taking the profits of one man's industry
& putting it in the pocket of another, then I say we had better
be under the government of the "Autocrat of all the Russias"—
The despotism of the latter would at least be equally diffused
among all his Subjects, as he would have no interest to oppress
one portion & favor another—That of the former would be
regulated solely by the interest of the majority—therefore the
burthen would be exclusively on the minority—Upon this subject I am for no compromise of principle—But I forbear, for
we have already discussed this topic, yet it is one on which my
tongue or my pen is always apt to "grow wanton"—In my opinion at this time all presidential or political questions are sub-
ordinate to this—Why does not General Jackson *come out* upon
it! Why is this studied equivocation in all his messages—Who
can understand on which side he is?

I have seen only one side of the debate on the nomination of
Mr Van Buren—I cannot say I should have voted against him,
but I do say as far as I have yet seen the discussion his opponents have made out what we lawyers would say was a "strong
case." of this opinion I know are some of the most intelligent
men I know here, who have no *party* feeling of any sort to bias
them—Towards Mr V. B. *personally* since I have been acquinted
with him, I have never had any but the kindest feelings—But
I have never admired his political *management*—I have always
detested "New York politics" in which he has borne so conspicuous a share—& what have we seen lately! an open avowal
by one of his partisans that the *republican majority* in New
York have for years been *governed* by *three* individuals—and
by whom are these *three* influenced?—If influenced by *one* individual then the government of New York is essentially a *monarchy*—if the *three* act on their own responsibility & from their
own motion, then it is an *oligarchy*—Is this *republicanism* to be

---

[45]North Carolina leaders were consistent in their opposition to the tariff. In 1827 the legislature resolved that it was inexpedient for Congress to increase the duties on imports. With
Jackson's election they expected a reduction. When that did not come, they were disappointed, although most of them refused to desert Jackson. Iredell, however, became a leader
for nullification.

engrafted into our United States' administration—I cannot trust the man who has always been andeavoring to flatter & fawn upon the *People*, professing his *democracy* while in fact he has continued to fasten upon them a machinery (pardon *me* if I allude to the *caucus* system) by which two or three men (it may be *one* man) govern them, not under the name of *Kings*, but of *republicans*—By the bye, let me tell you of the Caucus that was held here for the nomination of delegates to the convention at Baltimore to *choose* a Vice President—It was held in pursuance of a notice for the citizens of Wake to attend a political meeting & members of the Assembly & other citizens were invited—I took no part in the meeting but was present a part of the time—about forty or fifty members were present & about as many citizens of Wake—These undertook to nominate delegates to the Balitmore Convention—What was this, a caucus or not? & What authority had they to nominate delegates? I know it gave offence to *many* Jackson men, who were members of the Legislature—*whole hog Jackson men*—Can you tell me who is spoken of as Vice-President? I have believed myself from the first that this convention was proposed originally & exclusively for the purpose of nominating Van Buren—I see his hand in it —I see in it the New York political machinery—Is it not of the utmost importance to the South that we should have a Vice-President of our principles?—I have never yet seen an election of President in which I thought the choice of a Vice-President so important.—Can Gen¹. Jackson in all probability live thro' another term &, if he can, is not his mind becoming daily more & more debilitated?—Who are spoken of except Van Buren?—

If you paid much attention to the proceedings of our Legislature, you must have observed that your Senator Dr Montgomery introduced early in the Session resolutions in opposition to the U. S. Bank—They were never called up—The Doctor was afraid to do so—I have no doubt they would in either house have been rejected by a majority of three to one—whether right or wrong, that Bank is at this time very popular in our State—I believe, indeed I know, it has done us vast good and as yet we have felt no evils from it—where is the check upon the State Banks, if not to be found here! I mean not theoretically but practically?

There is no doubt of the vote of this State for General Jackson's re-election—If Mr Van Buren is run with him by the Baltimore convention, there will assuredly be two tickets for the Vice Presidency in this State at least—Let us have an Anti-

Tariff man, an open, plain-spoken, candid man of talents, I care not where he comes from (I should perhaps myself prefer him from the North) & he will I think obtain a majority in this State, even of the Jackson Party—Van Buren in my opinion *cannot* get the vote of No Carolina for Vice-President—Mark my prediction—

Tell our mutual friend L. McLane that I often think of my intercourse with him with great pleasure—& regret that I am so bad a correspondent as to have lost deservedly the instruction & delight I should have derived from his letters—If he could be nominated as Vice President, I am satisfied he would receive an almost unanimous support in No Cᵃ.—I had learnt to esteem him long before I knew him & a personal acquaintance only added warmth & strength to my former feelings towards him— His being in the administration is almost the only thing which has saved me from anti-Jacksonism, tho' I have not the slightest disposition to turn to *Clay*—

Having a leisure evening, just at the termination of our Supreme Court, I have written to you rather garrulously—I know you will excuse me & when we differ we shall differ in good temper—

My best respects to Brown—I hoped he would have let me hear from him this session, but not the scrip of a pen have I had from you or him—

Will you be so good also as to remember me to Messʳˢ. Tazewell, White, Hayne, Tyler & King,⁴⁸ Benton, Dickerson⁴⁷ &c— I could spend my time very pleasantly with you, but the *"augusta res domi"*—

Do let me hear from you & believe me

very Sincerely
Yours

JA. IREDELL

[Addressed:]

The Honorable
Willie P. Mangum
Washington City

---

⁴⁶William R. King.
⁴⁷Mahlon Dickerson was the Senator from New Jersey from 1817 to 1833. *Biog. Dir. of Cong.*, 904.

WPM-LC

John H. Bryan to W. P. Mangum

New Bern
Feby, 7, 1832

My dear Sir,

A very worthy lady of this town Mrs. (George) Ellis[48] is interested in the claim upon France for spoliation prior to 1800, and has requeseted me to invoke your aid in behalf of the claims. —I should be glad to learn their state and the prospect of compensation &C—

I should be pleased to hear from you occasionally and to receive documents of interest—

respy & truly
yr friend

Jn. H. Bryan

[Addressed:]

To—
The Hon—
W. P. Mangum
Senate
Washington City

WPM-LC

Wm. S. Ransom[49] to Willie P. Mangum

Raleigh N. C. Feb. 8th 1832

My dear Sir

From our paper of yesterday you will see the stand we have taken relative to the late important question which has so agitated and divided, and I may also be allowed on this occasion to say, although apparently incongruous, coalesced, many of the grave Seigniors of our Confederacy—I am well aware, as you very justly remarked in your kind letter to us, that ours is a trying and critical situation—You, with discrimination which is creditable, foresaw, and pointed out many of the dangers and perplexities we would have to encounter—But alas! Sir, you

---

were wholly ignorant of our real situation—that knowledge
from experience in the ways of men, which most men of your
course of life gain, enabled you, to judge pretty accurately of
what would be the trials of man *generally,* in attempting at an
early age, unassisted, to take a bold and independent stand, to
impress correct principles on the minds of an ignorant and per-
verse community and to acquire a laudable distinction in the
attempt—Your memory did not descend even to your own
knowledge of the people who surround us—You dwelt but little
on the life of a poor & involved but independent man — surrounded by people who differ with him in politics, envy him
for what they think his talents, hate him for his fearlessness
and fear him for his temerity. By such people am I surrounded
and still partly dependent on them—The federal party, here,
(for it still exists) and those who bask under their smiles and
grin for their bows—The *Iredell-Calhoun junto*—The timid ad-
herents of the *Star,* that would fain illume the dexterous Southern Nullifier—The many and strong friends of the Register,
that Organ of Clay and echo of the Intelligencer, obtained by a
long residence and deceitful conduct both in public and private,
are all, with a few who personlly, but without cause, dislike
us, virulently opposed to us and the prosperity of our Press—
Scarcely an individual here has dared speak in our support All
appear as if fearful some boon would be sought, some favor
asked—Disdainful glances, yea, even chilling looks of contempt
and illiberal remarks have been the record thus far of our
honest and strenuous exertions to promote the interests and
raise the standing of our State.

With a perfect knowledge of our poverty attempts have been
made to break up our establishment by impressing those with
whom we have *been compelled* to deal on a credit with the belief, that it could not stand long, and that even its friends viewed
ours as but an ephemeral plant which would bud & bloom but
for a day then fade and wither and die—This has caused a pressure of our debts and a total destruction of our credit and it is
even difficult to get workmen to issue the paper—we have between 6 & 700 subscribers and not over 60 of them have paid
and we cannot yet demand it. if we could only get $500 for one
year would have no earthly difficulty afterwards. It would add
to our independence—relieve us from the humiliation we now
feel, impart to our energies renovated vigor and stimulate us to
nobler exertions—Without it we cannot stand; with no money

to buy paper or pay workmen what chance have we to meet other demands, even to live ourselves. We do not expect in several years to make money, we just wish to live and give to our State a voice and reputation not before heard. In making our choice among the politicians of the day we never thought to be paid for it. but if there be any who are of our way of thinking and are able and willing to lend us $500 for one year only we would be greatly obliged, unless we can get it & that too in the course of ten days I fear we will have to sell out for our life is past all endurance at this time I know it is not in your power to advance the means we need yourself but you no doubt can be the means of procuring it for us. We hope soon to hear from you. Suppose you see Blair[50] who did aid us a little at first or some one who knows of these things. Tell Genl. Speight[51] his favor came to hand this morning

My Respects &c to Genl Hawkins[52] & Mr Hall.[53]

> With great esteem, Sir, Yr
> Obt Svt Respectfully
>
> W^m. S. RANSOM

Hon: W. P. Mangum

P. S. Mr Charles R Ramsey[54] is my Partner. M^r. R is a grand son of Dr Ramsay the historian of S. C.—He has been in the Navy several years My friends who know are much pleased with him. I estimate him verry highly myself—

> W [S] R

Let us hear from you Soon

[Addressed:]

> Hon: Willie P. Mangum
> Washington City

WPM-LC

J. G. A. Williamson[55] to Willie P. Mangum

ROXBORO Person County No. C. 11 Fe[by]. 1832

Honl.
    Willie P. Mangum
        Washington.
Sir

I have sugested to Genl. Barringer that a short correspondence on his part with several merchants of New York, Philadelphia & Baltimore, would I think shew more clearly to the President the necessity of such an appointment as I seek than any thing I could say upon the subject, and would strip the question entirely of the interest that would seem to hang around it from my statement;

I am well aware your influence is great at Washington and fell satisfied your friendship in this affair can do much for me and it will be adding to the many obligations I am already under to you

I am Sir with great respect

Your obt. Sert.

J. G. A. WILLIAMSON

[Addressed:]

Honl.
    W. P. Mangum
        M. of the Senate
            Washington

———

WPM-LC

Willie P. Mangum to Mrs. Charity A. Mangum

WASHINGTON CITY 11th February 1832

My dear Love.

Yesterday evening I received your letter of the 3rd. Instant, & was very glad to hear that you & our dear children were well. I am tolerably well with [the] exception of sore lips broken out

———

[55]See above, pp. 407-410.

with fevers [torn] some feeling of inward fevers. I have [been] very much engaged for some time, have [torn] sleep, & by that means became feverish—

We have a debate [torn] on upon the [ta]riff that completely [torn] attention here.

I spoke two [torn] subject—towit: tuesday & We[nesday I] had been so engaged in studyin[g the subje]ct & collecting materials, and made [torn] effort 2½ hours each of [tho]se days— being in all nearly 5 hours,[56] that I became excited feverish & slightly indisposed.—

I was not exactly pleased with my own effort—Yet I have reason to believe, that the almost universal opinion of the Senate is that it was eloquent & powerful.—

I understand that Gen. Smith got up a subscription of members to have several thousand copies of the speech printed in Pamphlets.[57]—I shall never be able to prepare it for the press in half so good a form as it was delivered.—

When it will appear I know not.

Brinkley can be warranted without me.—He will have to stay the execution.—He can procure security when it is known that he has conveyed his property to secure the debt.

However he had better let a judgment go against him & not stay it.—They cannot sell his property before I get home—It is conveyed to me in trust to secure that debt.

When I come home I will have it fixed in the best way for him.

I have no objection to B[torn] some ground in the mountain fiel[d] [torn] it don't [torn] with my crop [torn]

I [torn]whether to plant [torn] or all [torn] If there were ground [torn] I don't [torn] apart of the crop [torn] better [torn] cotton—My father [torn] be consa [torn] in the matter. He will be [torn] able to judge, seeing in what way the land is prepared—

I have much business now on hand & can write you but little.—I constantly think of you My Love, & had rather see you & spend a week with you, than to see all the world besides—

The time though it goes slowly, I hope will bring us together

---

[56]Mangum's speech on the tariff on February 7, 1832, was well received by his constituents. It was restrained in language but strongly against the tariff. The *Carolina Watchman* (Fayetteville) declared that the speech would raise Mangum in public esteem. It was widely distributed. McDuffie, "Willie P. Mangum," 44.

[57]*Speech of the Honorable Willie P. Mangum (of North Carolina) on the Tariff. Delivered in the Senate of the United States on the 7th and 8th of Feb. 1832, on Mr. Clay's Resolution in relation to the Tariff* (Washington, D. C.: Printed at office of Jonathan Eliot, 1832), 26 pp.

in health & with hearts of the best & warmest affections.—I
cannot tell My Dear, how completely you are identified with all
my affections—When I look out upon the moral waste created
by human selfishness, I can withdraw my eye with the consolation, that there is one spot of green on which it may rest—
that there is one heart warm true & devoted—& may God, long
—long preserve it in cheerfulness & peace—Tell my daughter
Sally that I shall [expect her] to read well in her books—Poor
[Patty, must] learn her A. b. C's.—Give them [each a] kiss—
And tell them they must be [good] children—
   I don't know where [torn] to me & let me know [torn]
                         Your affectionate [torn]
                              W. P. [torn]

                                              WPM-LC
         R. J. Yancey, Jr.,[58] *to Willie P. Mangum*

                                   OXFORD Feb 11th 1832
Hon. Sir.—Having been requested to write to Yourself and the
Hon. M. T. Hawkins in relation to the establishment of a Mail
between Oxford Chapel Hill and Hillsboro I have forwarded a
memorial to Mr. Hawkins, numerously signed, upon the subjects, to be presented to the P O Department—offering also
such suggestions as have occurred to meyself as well as others.
On the part of the Petitioners I have respectfully to solicit that
you will use your influence in aid of our wishes. Your own
knowledge of the localities &c. will render useless any thing
offered upon that head. I will therefore only ask that you will
consult the good of the people by enforcing with your influence
their application—A note, or personal recommendation from a
gentleman holding your elevated station, will weigh much with
the Department. With good wishes for your health and prosperity, I remain your humble serv't.
                         R. J. YANCEY, JR.
                              Examin. Office,
                                   Oxford
Hon. W. P. Mangum

N. B. What is the *political* world coming to? Van Buren *re-*

---
[58]Yancey was the editor of the *Oxford Examiner.*

jected![59] I am disappointed, and *fear* he will be made V. President. For one I would greatly prefer a Southern man—Judge Smith,[60] P. P. Barbour, Drayton,[61] or some man from our own North Carolina—Van Buren "went the whole" for the Tariff of '28—must we support a President who will pull down the U. S. Bank, who will *collect* our money, to *divide* it with others and ourselves, who is a friend of a "Judicious Tariff" alias a *Protecting* Tariff, and a Vice President who favors all these *oppressive* schemes also? I go for Jackson because we cannot better ourselves—but we have every hope, and reasonable hope too, that we can secure the second officer to our interest—Then let us not abandon our interests to sooth the feelings of the rejected minister.

R. J. Y. Jr—

[Addressed:]

Hon. W. P. Mangum
Washington City
D. C.

———

Willie P. Mangum to William Polk[62]

WASHINGTON CITY 11th. February 1832

Dear Sir,

I have received your favour of the first Instant, and now offer you the best opinion I am able to form in relation to the recharter of the United States Bank.

You will have seen a copy of the Bill reported by the Committee of Ways and means in the House of Representatives.

I can entertain no doubt that the bank has been gradually losing something of its popularity here, during the Winter. yet it is as little to be doubted that a Bill in some form will pass both branches of Congress.—In regard to the modification, it is impossible to form more than a vague conjecture.—The diver-

[59]He refers to the Senate's rejection of Van Buren as minister to Great Britain.
[60]William Smith, 1762-1840, a native of North Carolina, served as judge of the South Carolina Circuit Court from 1808 to 1813, and in the Senate from 1816 to 1823 and from 1826 to 1831. In 1829 and again in 1836 he was offered an appointment as associate justice of the Supreme Court by Jackson, but he declined. He opposed the tariff but never supported nullification. As a result Calhoun had him defeated in 1830 for reelection to the Senate by Stephen D. Miller. In 1833 he moved to Louisiana and then to Huntsville, Alabama. In 1829 the Georgia electors voted for him for vice president. *D. A. B.,* XVII, 359-361.
[61]William Drayton of South Carolina.
[62]The original is in the Correspondence of the Polk Family of North Carolina, Library of Congress. See above Polk to Mangum, Feb. 1, 1832.

sity of opinion upon the proper limitations & restrictions, is very great & in many respects, crude, & it would seem not well considered.—

Almost the whole of the South will in the Senate, be opposed to an extension of the Charter with the exception of Louisiana, & one from North Carolina.—Alabama would go for the recharter, with some essential & some *Whimiscal* restrictions, & so also would one Senator from Georgia.—

I think however it may be safely stated that the Charter in some form will be extended by the vote of both branches of Congress—Yet from the best information that can be obtained on the subject I think the President will veto the Bill, if it shall be passed this session.—My information on this subject, I know is not of a description to command entire reliance.—I believe the President abstains from conversation on the subject—Yet my opinion is strong, that he will not approve any Law on the subject that may be passed this Winter.—If the Bill shall pass, and the President shall place his veto on it, I think it will greatly endanger the ultimate fate of that institution.—

If final action of either branch of the Legislature, could be delayed until the next session, I have no doubt that he would approve a Bill with no very essential modification.—

Under every aspect of the case I should suppose that it would be hazardous to make investment at the present prices of stock.

I think it is to be deeply regretted that an application was made at this session of Congress—and altho I feel assured that the application was wholly unconnected with political consideration, yet it is equally obvious that the question will be pressed with party views.[63]

You know the President—The officer cannot be wholly divested of characteristics peculiar to the *Man*.—If it shall enter his mind that advantage is sought to be taken at this exigency, it is impossible to estimate its effect upon him.—He may regard it as a trial of strength between his popularity & that of the institution—he will not shrink from the Contest, & in that Contest the fate of the Bank will certainly be sealed for the *present*, & possibly *forever*.

Nothing can prevent his reelecton in my opinion — I have assurance upon which I fully rely, that his course upon this subject, will make no difference as to the result of Penn^a.—

---

[63]Mangum was not entirely consistent in his position on the bank. At first he was for a recharter but eventually he spoke and voted against its recharter. McDuffie, "Willie P. Mangum," 45, 47.

The spirit evinced by the opposition, instead of shaking; it is believed, adds strength to the President.—Permit me to offer you my congratulations upon your safe return home & be pleased to accept the assurance of my entire respect.

WILLIE P. MANGUM

[Addressed to] Col. William Polk
               Raleigh,
                  North Carolina

———

WPM-LC

Robt. B. Gilliam[64] to W. P. Mangum

OXFORD, 13th February 1832.

Dear Sir:

You will excuse me for reminding you of the importance of having the exceptions to the answers of Hawkins[65] & others, filed by the next term of our Superior Court.—I have spoken with Mr. Dexereux,[66] & he consents to the course you desired, but expressed a hope that it would not be delayed longer than the necessity of the case required. It is on this account, that I am induced to remind you of the near approach of our Superior Court.

I remain Very Respectfully
Your Friend

ROBT. B. GILLIAM

Hon W. P. Mangum
          Washington

[Addressed:]

To the Hon: Willie P. Mangum
    City of Washington

———

[64]An Oxford attorney who later carried on an extensive correspondence with Mangum.
[65]Probably Micajah T. Hawkins.
[66]Thomas Devereux.

WPM-LC

Henry Seawell to Willie P. Mangum

RALEIGH 14th Feby 1832.

Dear Sir

I wrote you some time during the session of our State Legislature upon the subject of Mr David Thompsons wishes to be
appointed one of the [torn] of the public land. In my letter I
[torn] make several speculations upon the pol[itica]l results of
the general government & was induced to venture more freely
in the hope of getting your views—I have as yet received no
answer, & after imputing your silence to the pressure of the
importance business of congress, have thought it was possible
my letter may not have reached you—the many hard things I
have heard of the corruption of the post office department, without having any reason to believe them is my best foundation for
these being said, necessarily excites a curiosity to know, whether
my letter did reach you—there were many idle things said in
it, in the spirit in which we have been accustomed to talk, that
I should be very sorry should be subject to the inspection of
strangers—In my letter to you I said something in relation to
the French treaty & the commission growing out of it—
I have recently seen that the commission is about to be
filled—The time I spent at Washington in that kind of business;[67] the relation which the duties have to the former persuits
of my life, to say nothing of my willings to shake hands with
the bar, would render an appointment every way desirable, and
you would confer on me by your aid, a kindness, singularly
acceptable There are of the Senate several gentlemen who on
former times I counted, as my personal friends, and to serve
whom I should feel much pleasure [havi]ng flattered myself
with the belief that they [torn] [a]ltogether indifferent towards
me, I cannot omit re[pea]ting their names, under the impression that I was not mistaken, & that they would feel a willingness to render me a helping hand. I allude to Gov. Forsyth, Mr
Tazwell, Col Benton, & Gov. Dickerson.[68] With Mr. McClain[69]
the Secretary of the Treasury I had an acquaintance, which tho
limitted as to our intercourse, was nevertheless of such a character as induced me to regard him as not altogether indifferent

---

[67]See above, p. 269.
[68]Mahlon Dickerson was in the Senate from New Jersey from 1817 to 1833.
[69]Louis McLane.

towards me—These gentlemen were originally of the Crawford party when I first had the honor of their acquaintance; & perhaps that sort of vanity we all of us have, that flatters us with the belief of our good standing with those we know, who are of high standing in the Country, may have had its effect on me in relation to them.—I have thought it not amiss to mention them, that you may act as you think most advisable in communicating my wishes to them—I shall write this day to Mr Browne upon the same subject—The subject of the rejection of Mr Van Buren tho occupying much of the political conversation of the day, has as yet reached no crisis—nor can any one say what public opinion is. I have only seen two or three speeches. Neither yours or Mr. Browns have come to hand. I do not believe the Country can [illegible] the matter—The U. S. Bank is a subject of deep interest, and with the most intelligent part of the community, I think three fourths are for it. The effect it has evidently had in this State upon the currency, by operating upon the local banks & forcing them to become able to redeem their notes, has placed this medium upon a footing of respectability so different, that [visi]ble to every eye; & none seem to oppose it [torn] who feel the loss of profits by the deminution of the [torn] of the local banks, or who are striving to bring through the legislature, the people's Bank, as they call it in this State—The people of this State, now get, generally, U S money for their produce at market—this they can send to any state without loss, & the constant emigration to the west, to say nothing of the travelling backwards & forwards, to & from the frontier States, upon matters of business, are opportunities of reminding every body of the difference now, & a few years back, when a traveller out of the State, coud not buy his breakfast with the money which circulated in his own neighborhood. I should be very glad to hear from you, & shall always feel great pleasure to hear you feel happy.

  fare well

   God bless you

      HENRY SEAWELL.

Honl. Mr. Mangum.

[Addressed:]

   Washington City.

WPM-LC

George O. Askew[70] to W. P. Mangum

BERTIE COUNTY N. Carolina
February 17th 1832

Dear Sir,

I have lately seen to my great mortification the rejection of
Mr. Martin Van Buren, as minister to England, but I take great
pleasure in seeing that you, and Mr. Bedford Brown, were not
among the opposition. None of my acquaintance, or your friends,
were disappointed when we saw in the public prints, that you
were ably contending for the confirmation of that appointment,
which would have done honour to our country and saved the
feelings of our venerable President, in whom, the people in
North Carolina, yet confide notwithstanding all that the representative from this district in congress can say to the contrary—
Yes sir, your people glory in the vote you gave on that nomination, and the side you took in the debate. It seems clearly to
me that the reasons given by Messrs Webster, Clay, Chambers,
Ewing, and others, for voting against the nominee were intirely
erroneous, an attempt, to make [torn] people abroad believe,
that the instructions given to Mr. McLane was about to prostrate
the honor of this nation at the foot of a King, sir, I can assure
you the event of that treaty viz, that of opening the West India
trade is now sensibly felt to the advantage too of North Carolina espicially this part of the state from which part a large
quantity of lumber is shipped—I have written you these few
lines for the purpose of asking you to be so good as to send me
a copy of the debate on Mr. Van Buren's nomination as minister to the court of St James—I was opposed to Mr. Calhoun be
fore I now am very much strengthened in my opinion. Your
people will sustain you in the course you took on that subject—

I am your friend
GEORGE O. ASKEW

Turners Road N C
23 February 1832

Hon. W. P. Mangum

[Addressed:]   Hon. Willie P. Mangum
Senator in the congress
of the United States.

---

[70]Member of the legislature from Bertie County.

WPM-LC

Willie P. Mangum to Charity A. Mangum

WASHINGTON CITY
Saturday morning 18th Feby
1832

My dear Love

I received your letter yesterday and at the same time received one from Mr. Chaves.[71] I regret very much that Sally is not at school.—I still think that Hinton[72] did not act well towards me. As to the complaint in the neighbourhood, it is rediculous; & he had nothing to do but to act in such a way as to put it down. I have been thinking a good deal upon the subject.—Mr. Chaves made a proposition to me; but being from home, I cannot do anything in it.—It would cost too much, unless 9 or 10 scholars could be got, and even then [it] would cost $40 or $50.—I prefer doing nothing in the matter until I return home, when I hope I shall be able to make arrangements more satisfactory— In the meantime if the school in the neighbourhood is near enough you had better send Sally as a day scholar when the weather is good—so as to keep her learning something—You can keep her reasonably employed when at home, & when it will suit you can occasionally send her to school—You will do in this as you think the best. I do not wish her too much confined, but still I do not want her to fall into idle habits—

In regard to the letter to me from Hardeman Duke, you can tell Aunt Agga, that the matter is before Congress and is not yet acted upon—That I will attend to it as soon as I can *do* anything—Whether the law will pass I cannot tell, but believe it will.—

You can get E. G. Mangum to set some copies for Sally, and let her write occasionally.—Her writing to me was very well done and give her a kiss for me for it.—And don't forget to give a kiss also to My dear daughter Patty.—

I am not now entirely well—I have a little fever, from being vaccinated. The matter was put into my arm this day week, and it is formed into a pustule and begins to give me some fever— The small Pox is in this City, and is now in a house not more than 200 yards from me.—It has been here for some time— After I heard of it, I could not get any vaccine matter for more

---

[71]John Chavis.
[72]A. M. Hinton had a school at Hillsboro which he gave up in 1832.

than 2 weeks. I was a good deal alarmed—kept close, until I could get the matter, and apply it so as to take—There is now no danger—I did not mention it to you, lest you might feel uneasy.

The weather begins to get a little softer—The winter has been the worst, take it all together that I ever saw—

Congress is very busy & still engaged in the discussion of the Tariff.

I am becoming very anxious to see you My Love, and really for more than a week, I have had a very strong inclination to come home. I could do it by loosing 7 or 8 days—But I should be so fatigued & worn down that it might make me sick—Upon full consideration I have given up the idea—I think of you My Dear Love & of our dear children often, & with a heart full of affection—Take good care of yourself, be cheerful, & let us hope to meet well, When I may close in my arms my dear wife with warm & deep affections felt by both & cherished by both.—Are you growing fat? let me know—

To day & tomorrow Congress does not meet—I shall be in my room almost all the time—How happy should I feel if that time could spent with you—May God bless you My dear—dear Love— & make you as happy as you deserve. I have been more afflicted in my feelings this week, than I ever was in public life at any time, by the determination of Congress to remove the *remains* of Gen Washington to the Capitol on his hundredth birth day next Wednesday the 22nd Feby I felt the deepest abhorrence at the idea of removing his remains, of violating [torn] & silent mansions of the dead—& to bring those remains & place them in the Capitol where the vilest & worst passions of human nature are constantly finding vent—

The proprietor of Mount Vernon has declined giving his assent. I rejoice at it—I cannot well describe my feelings on the occasion—

I, with many other Gentlemen, wrote immediately to the Gov. of Virginia wishing him to prevent it, if he had to march his militia & do it by force.—

Tell me my Love whether you grow & whether you enjoy as much health as usual.—Think of your husband & cherish for him your love and affections—often in the silent watches of the night, my mind strays far away & rests upon the bosom I love, & the heart which is dearer to my affections than all the world beside.

Your affectionate husband

WILLIE P. MANGUM

[Addressed:]

Mrs. Charity A. Mangum
Red Mountain
North Carolina

WPM-D

Jesse Person to W. P. Mangum

LOUISBURG N. C. Febr 20th 1832—

Dear Sir;

I fear that you have met with some difficulty in the settlement of my business with Mr Presley[73] not having heard from you since the 25th of Jany If he is there yet please settle with him if possible no doubt but he got my letter which I wrote to him to settle with you as soon as he reached there or so soon thereafter as he applied at the office.—If he is yet there and has not come to see you Please drop him a note informing him of your othority to settle my business with him.—yours Respectfully,

JESSE PERSON

The Hon. Willie P. Mangum

Address: The Hon Willie P. Mangum
Washington
City.

Free

[From]
Louisburg N. C.
Feb. 20th 1832

---

[73]See above, p. 465 and below, p. 496.

WPM-LC

J. Grant[74] to B. Brown & W. P. Mangum

RALEIGH No Ca 25th February 1832

Honbl Bedford Brown & Willie P. Mangum
        Gentlemen,

Your letter addressed to Governor Stokes with the accompanying documents, were handed over by him to me, with a request that I should correspond with you, & furnish if practicable the Vouchers necessary to ensure the success of our claim at the War Department.

I avail myself of the first opportunity of sending on Seven Bundles, containing 39 Packets the result of my labours, which I hope you will receive in good condition & in due time: They are of a very miscellaneous character & possibly some of them may be duplicates of others already sent, not having kept a list of those sent on by Mr Sneed;[75] I preferred having a double sett to the risk of not having sent on all within my reach.

On the Original Pay & Receipt Rolls previously sent on, I observed many names whose claims were not receipted for by any one; From the circumstance of those now sent on being detached, I infer these are the persons not receipted for on the Original Pay Rolls, they being absent I presume at the time the Paymasters attended in their respective Counties for the purpose of paying them, had to send on Powers of Atto. by some Friend to Raleigh to receive their pay: if this should turn out to be the fact, those Vouchers now sent on are additional ones, not heretofore presented at the Department: Would it not be well before you surrender the Papers, to call at the 3rd Auditor's Office & obtain one of the Pay & Receipt Rolls mentioned in the *list* which I have prepared & sent on the Papers now forwarded to ascertain if that is not the fact.

On the second Page of the Statement & Remarks as passed on by Govr Cass the present Secretary at War, accompanying the one furnished by Mr Hagner,[76] both of which I now send you; it is remarked that Governor Hawkins[77] had called the attention of the War Department to an account paid by the State to

---

[74]James Grant, Sr., the father of James Grant, Jr., who taught Franklin Saunders, was state comptroller from 1827 to 1834. *N. C. Manual*, 442.
[75]Robert Snead was clerk of the Committee of Public Claims. Walter Clark (ed.,) *N. C. State Records*, XXII, 863.
[76]Peter Hagner.
[77]William Hawkins was the governor of North Carolina from 1811 to 1814.

the United States Contractor for rations furnished to a Company of Militia ordered by the Governor to garrison Fort Hampton: It is further remarked "from Col Long no testimony is adduced respecting this company, & the rolls afford no evidence of its having been received by him into the United States service: I have now sent on many Papers on file in this Office by Col Long[78] & Maj^r King both U States Officers, which I hope will afford the evidence desired; I see no reason why a United States Officer should file his Papers in this Office, unless they were intended as Vouchers for the State.

It will be borne in mind that every three years & frequently Oftener there is a change of Governor; Mr Goodwin[79] Comptroller during the whole of the time of passing upon & entering the Vouchers & accounts in relation to this claim died in 1821; In his latter days he had become quite intemperate & his Books afford no correct guide to direct us in ascertaining the true State of this account: Col Hawkins[80] his successor was a man of but little skill in accounts, & it is a fact notorious that he gave himself no trouble about these maters; Many of the parties themselves whose vouchers are imperfect are since dead; hence the great trouble, confusion & delay in arranging the account for settlement; when I came into Office every thing was involved in mystery, it was all new to me & there was no one left, (the Treasurer[81] having just died) to inform me on the subject: With these dim & imperfect guides to direct me I turned my attention to the claim in 1828, from long familiarity with the Vouchers & intense reflection on the subject I have acquired some knowledge of it; I regret that I did not propose to the last Legislature, (they bearing my actual expenses Only) to come on & assist you at the Auditors Department, for you may rest assured, with your other duties to attend to, it will give you no little trouble, I think however by reading attentively the Statement & remarks furnished by Mr Hagner, with the letters of Gov. Hawkins herewith sent, or perhaps by reference to the whole corespondence copied in the letter Book of the Secretary at War, you will be able to inform yourselves of the nature of the claim so as to enable you to present it fairly before Congress.

[78]Probably Nicholas Long.
[79]Samuel Goodwin was the comptroller of North Carolina from 1808 to 1821. *N. C. Manual*, 442.
[80]Joseph Hawkins was comptroller of North Carolina from 1821 to 1827. *N. C. Manual*, 442.
[81]John Haywood.

I wrote Col Robards[82] (for the bills & explanations) he being one of the purchasers of Powder & Lead which is mentioned in the late Statement furnished: "Leonard Henderson & others for Powder stated to have been supplied & forwarded from Granville to Governor Hawkins" &C) I have enclosed to you his letter in reply: The difficulty which he mentions exists with many Other accounts; hence the necessity at this late day of Legislation on the subject, to supply any legal defect of evidence.

It will be perceived by Gov Hawkins letters that early application was made & pressed for the settlement of these claims; The Treasury (which is not the case now) was then Bankrupt and the payment waived, because they were not then able to meet the claims of the States; it is time that ours should be closed, & perhaps there could be no time more propitious than the present, no less on account of the ability of the General Government, than the misfortunes & the consequent additional demands for money by North Carolina.

I perceive from the Governors letter Book, he has written you, that he has lately understood, that the United States has a larger demand against No Ca for moneys advanced during the Revolutionary War, than the balance *now* claimed by us: I am at a loss to conjecture why his Excellency should have introduced this subject, particularly at this Juncture; certainly if *they* dont remind *us* of old scores, *we* should not invite them to do it; I do not know for I have never thought to ask him, how he derived that information; I presume however it must have been derived from myself; When I first undertook the investigation of the account in 1828 & brought the subject before the Legislature, some one then observed that Governor Franklin[83] when Governor of the State, had forborne to press the claims, saying it would only remind the General Government of a larger amount due by us for moneys advanced during the Revolution: That might have happened as it now does, owing to the difficulties thrown in the way the U S accounting Officers in the settlement of that claim: We have never obtained our Just rights; for I observe in overhauling the musty papers in my Office for Vouchers in relation to our present claims, others of Revolutionary date have been found, transmitted to & filed in this Office, with their seals unbroken to this day never having been

---

[82]William Robards was the state treasurer from 1827 to 1830. *N. C. Manual*, 442.
[83]Jesse Franklin was governor of the state from Dec. 18, 1820, to Dec. 18, 1821. *Biog. Dir. of Cong.*, 978.

acted upon at all: no wonder we are in arrears; then as now I presume there were changes of Public Officers; This sad truth awakens in me some melancholy reflections: In me the early flowers of youth are fast fading away & the frost of a long dark winter is falling on my tongue & freezing my very vitals; age begins to stiffen my limbs & dark mists are vailing the fields of vision, & soon the Stern Mandate of Death will call me to my long Home; I beg pardon for this digression, it is a train of thought which never fails to accompany the investigation of old musty documents.

Be so good as to acknowledge the receipt of the Papers sent; & as soon as convenient I should like to know whether they are considered material evidence for us

> I remain Gentlemen, with senti-
> ments of respect your very Obt
> hum[b] Serv[t]
>
> J. Grant
>
> P. S. Retain the two   )
> Statements with the Re-)
> marks, they will be mate-)
> rial for us until the   )
> acct is closed —   )
>
> J. G.

[Addressed:]

> Honb[s] Willie P Mangum & Bedford Brown
> Senators &C
> Washington City

Samuel Carson and Willie P. Mangum to John Branch[84]

[25 Feb., 1832]

Sir

We have according to the request of Gen[l] Speight[85] & your-

---

[84]The original is in the Division of Library and Archives, Department of Education, Nashville, Tennessee.

[85]On February 4, 1832, Jesse Speight's letter on the reasons for the rejection of Van Buren was published in the *Raleigh Constitutionalist*. Speight said that the reason given for the rejection of Van Buren was his instructions to McLane about the West Indies trade. These instructions, he continued, were approved by the Cabinet. Branch had denied this. Speight said he had learned from Jackson that he had given the instructions himself. Speight, therefore, concluded that some who were former friends of the President (meaning Branch) had "played a bold fist in the dark." This angered Branch. *N. C. Free Press*, Mar. 13, 1832.

self had a conference as your mutual friends, upon the subject of Gen¹ Speights letter published in the Raleigh Constitutionalist.

We are of opinion that in as much as Gen¹. Speight has disavowed to us in the most unqualified terms, any—the slighest disrespectful reference to you or your conduct—that it would be giving to the thing an importance to which it is not intrinsically intitled to make any publication on the subject at this time.

Should subsequent occurances make it necessary to the vindication of your character or conduct to make any publication. the memorandum in your possession of Gen¹. Speights prompt & Frank disavowal of any disrespectful refference to you, will be entirely sufficient to disabuse you of any unwarantable inferences.

very respectfully
your Friends & Obᵗ. Serᵗ.s

WILLIE P. MANGUM
SAML. P. CARSON

Feby
28ᵗʰ. 1832

WPM-LC

Spencer O'Brien to Willie P. Mangum

OXFORD 26th Febrʸ 1832

Dr Sir,

I had designed writing to you ere this, but have been prevented by one engagement or other.

We begin to feel a good deal of solicitude on the result of the question of rechartering the U. S. Bank. We shall in all probability, have a meeting in this place on the subject; and if you think it will have any, the least, good effect, it shall not be neglected. *My* principal motive in encouraging this meeting, is induced from the fact, that our representative, (Mr. Hawkins) who is "all the hog" for the *Jinral*, has committed himself, against what I know to be the sentiments of the District, & the State.

The fate of Dr Montgomery's resolutions[86] is conclusive as to the latter. It is true the vote was not taken on the question, but for the strongest of reasons. The Dr. clearly ascertained, from every indication in-doors & out, that they would have been strangled by an overwhelming vote; and so he let them rest. In the H. of Commons, their fate would have been no better, if as good.

The rejection of Mr. V. B's nomination by your body, has produced a good deal discussion among us, but perhaps, will settle down, without producing any material results. You will have the most of the fuss among yourselves, & when you get home may be surprized to find that a great many have either not heard of it, or attach no importance to it one way or the other.

Your remarks have not yet been published, that I^{ve}. seen, tho' I was pleased to learn the ground you took (viz') admitting, that the instructions were objectionable but denying them to be good ground for rejection &c. Your friends here-abouts; have been looking out with some anxiety for your remarks.

I perceive by the administration papers, that it is highly probable, this 'affair' will have the effect, to cause Mr. V. B to be nominated by the Convention as Vice President. Would not this be carrying the vindication too far for for the dictates of policy? I will offer you my testimony by way of exhibiting the ominous of this querey so far as our State is concerned.—The subject of the Vice Presidency was a good deal canvassed in private circles this winter in Raleigh. I frequently introduced the subject myself among the members, by way of ascertaining the strength of those spoken of. I can assure you then Mr. V B. will be so much dead weight to Genl. J. His conduct on the tariff question of "28 has been treasured up in judgement against him.[87] Judges Smith & Barbour, are the favorites in this State— three to one in favor of the former.

For the Lord's sake, can't Genl. J. get some other Editor than Blair in this time of trial? Can't you manage, by hook or crook, to buy up Gales & Seaton? If you can do no better send to Europe & import some decent & talented man. There are a great

---

[86]On December 3, 1831, William Montgomery proposed in the state senate that a special committee be appointed to report on the amount of notes in circulation, the specie in banks, and the dividends received by the states. This was not called up for a vote. *Journal of Senate, 1831*, p. 25. See above, James Iredell to Mangum, Feb. 4, 1832.

[87]North Carolina, like most of the South, was hostile to Van Buren. Before the convention the leaders of this state supported Philip Barbour for vice president. A. C. Cole, *Whig Party in the South*, 14.

many friends of the administration, who wish to take a Government paper—but can't stand Blair. Some time ago, I offered a red-hot Jackson man, my Globe for his Intelligencer, & even *he* asked me $3 to boot!!!

We have had various & contradictory accounts of this scene in the Senate between Messrs—Clay & Smith. To arrive at truth through the medium of the press is one of the morally impossibles, and will take it as a singular favor, if you will describe it to me. The account in the Globe makes Mr Clay to figure very much to his prejudice. Now, altho', on most political questions I differ from Mr C. 'toto coelo', yet I have ever admired his splendid talents, his bold, chivalrous & manly bearing—and perhaps, I may add, that when I most differed from him, I most admired his fearless & uncompromising spirit in what he deemed to be right. I am therefore, unwilling to believe u[ntil] convinced by stronger testimony than Blair's, that h[e did] any thing on the occasion alluded to, beneath the dignity of a Senator, and unworthy of himself.

Is it understood in Washington, that the Genl. will veto the Bank bill? We have heard here that he swore in his wrath, that he would immediately after the rejection of Mr. V. B. I trust it is not so.

What do you think will be the fate of Mr. Clay's resolutions[88] in the Senate? I perceive you made your appearance in that debate & hope you were satisfied with your effort on that occasion.

I should be pleased to hear from you as early as convenient, on these subjects & any others you may think would interest me.

Very Respectfully

SPENCER O'BRIEN

W. P. Mangum, Esqr—
Washington City

[Addressed:]

The Honble, Willie P. Mangum
of the U. S. Senate
Washington City
D. C.

---

[88]Clay proposed that import duties on non-competitive goods be reduced and that those on free competition articles be increased. G. G. Van Deusen, *The Life of Henry Clay* (Boston, Mass.: Little, Brown and Co., 1937), 251-252.

WPM-D

Willie P. Mangum to Jesse Persons

Senate Chamber 28th Feby 1832.

Dear Sir.

I have just received the enclosed letter from Mr. Pressley—
I shall this instant send to him an answer of which the following is a copy

"Senate Chamber 28th. Feby 1832.

"Sir

Mr. Person has authorized me to allow you any compensation, which is reasonable—

In case of disagreement, I should be ready to submit to the decision of either Gov. Miller of the Senate, or Mr. McDuffie of the Ho of Rep.

I trust this course will be satisfactory to you—

Yr. Obt Servt

WILLIE P. MANGUM

I. B. Pressley Esq.
at Brown's Hotel"

If this course is not agreeable to you, write to me immediately—
I doubt very much whether the money will be forthcoming.

I am Dear Sir Yrs truly

W. P. Mangum

Jesse Person Esqr.

Address: Jesse Person Esquire
Louisburg
North Carolina

Postmark:

City of Washington
Feb. 29

WPM-LC

Jno. S. Lewis[89] to Willie P. Mangum

COLUMBUS GA March 1 1832

My dear Judge—

Your very kind attentions to me in Washington & Carolina encourage me to address you with the security of older & more confirmed acquaintance—Keeping as you do an eye upon passing events, You are no doubt aware that the Creek Indians as well as their Cherokee brethren are upon the eve of emigration westward—I have just returned from a convention of Chiefs at which in sublime council it was determined to sell their lands— They have concluded we understand to send a delegation, & dispose of their country en masse as a nation, with the privilege of taking reserves individually—& enjoying, if they wish it, the rights of ordinary citizenship—If the treaty is concluded on the proposed terms i. e. of taking reserves, as there is no doubt it will be—there will be a commission appointed, consisting (it is understood) of one white man & four Indians to appraise their reserves when they dispose of them—My object in writing you, is, to commend to your attention & patronage the claims of Mr Hardaway for the appointment of commissioner. He is a gentleman of undoubted competency, of unblemished integrity, one upon whose character suspicion has never breathed the slightest taint. That he would fill the post with ability & satisfaction to the community I have not the slightest doubt—You will pardon my importunity My dear Sir, when I insinuate that I have a personal interest (along with the rest of the community) in this matter: for there is a much better chance of purchasing land under the commission of an upright man than of one guided by unfair & corrupt favoritism to a few—You are too well acquainted with this wicked world not to know, that this latter latter [sic] is an event by no means improbable—You will smile, my dear Sir when I assure you, I have penned this under the united annoyance of fever & headache, contracted at this aforesaid Indian Council—We flatter ourselves that by the exertion of your Influence with the President & his friends & an union of counsels with the Virginian or Georgia delegation you can render us essential service—Remember me to my relatives in Carolina,

---

[89]John S. Lewis was solicitor general of Challahoochee Circuit in 1842. Miller, *Bench and Bar of Ga.*, II, 575.

& tell them I will not despair of occasionaly seeing them—You are all well I hope—

Very truly & respectfully yr friend

JNO. S. LEWIS

[Addressed:]

Hon. Wiley P. Mangum
Washington City
D. C.

―――――

WPM-LC

Ann Johnson[90] to W. P. Mangum

Warren Co: March 2ᵈ. 1832

Dear Sir

You will pardon me I hope for troubling you upon a subject of individual claim upon the government especially when I state that my object is to acquire information from you—

I am informed that in a treaty made by Genl: Jackson as comm: of the *United States* with the Creek Indians some time about the years 1815 or 17[91] the Indians reserved a tract of land included in the purchase as a donation to Col. Benj: Hawkins[92] late *Indian agent* in *Georgia* & that the Senate of the U. S. *ratified the treaty as made*— My children & myself are in right of the late Gov. Hawkins of this state legatees of Col. B. Hawkins & of course entitled to a distributive proportion of the land given to the above said Col. B. Hawkins by the treaty above alluded to—Now sir you will confer a considerable favour upon my family as well as myself by obtaining a copy of the treaty & giving your opinion (so soon as it may suit your convenience) as to the plausibility of our claim—

Yours &c.

ANN. JOHNSON—

―――――

[90]Anna Hays Johnson was the daughter of William Johnson who owned Shocco Springs in Warren County. *Hillsboro Recorder,* June 18, 1823; *N. C. Press,* June 19, 1832.

[91]Jackson made the treaty at Fort Jackson after the Battle of Horseshoe Bend in 1814. John S. Bassett, *The Life of Andrew Jackson,* 2 vols. in 1 (New York, N. C.: The Macmillan Co., 1829), 332.

[92]Benjamin Hawkins, 1754-1816, a native of Warren County, North Carolina, was on Washington's staff in the Revolution. He served in the continental congress in 1781-1784, 1786, and in the Philadelphia constitutional convention of 1787. In 1785 and from 1796 to 1816 while he was in Georgia he negotiated with the Indians for the Federal Government. *Biog. Dir. of Cong.,* 1076.

[Addressed:]

Willie P. Mangum Esq.
Congressman at Washington
Dist. of Columbia
U. States.—

Willie P. Mangum to William Gaston[93]

WASHINGTON CITY 2nd March 1832

Dear Sir.

I trust you will pardon my delay in communicating to you the result of my inquiries in reference to the practicability of procuring the services of an efficient & scientific engineer to survey the route of the contemplated railroad in North Carolina. The contemplated work is worthy of the united effort of every part of the State, and I suppose it to be every way important to procure the services of some able & practical man to superintend the surveys.

The best information I have been able to obtain, indicates Gen. Swift,[94] formerly at the head of the United States Corps of Engineers, as the best qualified individual for the service, whose services can probably be procured.—

Gen. Swift is now superintending the improvement at Oswego on Lake Erie, and is daily expected to be in this City.—

Col. Abert[95] of the Engineer Corps, has had much experience, & is believed to be well qualified to estimate justly the merits of all who are distinguished in that line in the U. States.

He speaks of Gen. Swift as being eminently qualified & perhaps the best qualified man in the country.—All the other information I have been able to obtain is to the same effect. It is believed that Gen. Swift could be employed.—

I am wholly unacquainted with the powers, or the means of the Commissioners[96]—in truth I have not yet read the act of

[93]The original is in the William Gaston Papers, University of North Carolina.
[94]See above, p. 461n.
[95]Probably he refers to John J. Obert who was appointed to the U. S. Military Academy from Virginia. He was at West Point from 1808 to 1811. In 1814 he was appointed major as topographical engineer. He served as assistant to the geodetic survey of the Atlantic Coast in 1816-1818. From 1829 to 1861 he was in charge of the Topographical Bureau at Washington. Cullum *Biog. Reg. of Officers of the U. S. Military Acad.*, I, 101.
[96]The governor was authorized by an act of the legislature to have surveys made to determine the routes of the North Carolina Central Railroad and the Cape Fear and Yadkin Railroad provided each survey did not cost more than $4,000. *N. C. Laws, 1831*, p. 32. In the *Comptroller's Report for 1832-1833*, p. 11, Francis W. Rawll was paid $1,446.34 for one survey and $1,100.00 for the other.

Assembly nor do I know anything of its details—who is to contract with an engineer &c, &c.

I shall have an interview with Gen. Swift on his arival—and if I can in any way be useful, be good enough to indicate to me the manner.

I write in haste, supposing that you may feel it necessary to communicate to me more detailed information. I shall be glad to hear from you again on this subject, as soon as it shall be convenient.

Nothing of moment has occurred, save what appears in the public prints.

Accept Dear Sir the assurance of my entire respect & regard

WILLIE P. MANGUM

Mr. Mangum

WPM-LC

Martin Read [?] *to Willie P. Mangum*

HALIFAX TOWN N. C. 2nd of March 1832.

Judge Mangum
        D[ear] Sir
                    Having no personal acquaintance with Mr. Brown, the ot[her] Senator from our State, and always entertaining the great[est] respect for your tallents and publick services, I hope the free[dom] here used, by way of opening an occasional intercourse with the Senate of the united States through you, will not be considered an intrusion on my part. I do not claim it as a right deriveable from the representative relation in which you stand, to correspond with you. But I simply wish you to know that there is one, among many in the eastern part of your state, particularly, who has ever hailed your appointment to office as fortunate event, one, in which we might confidentially rely and trust all of our rights; and who would be happy to receive any communication that your leisure time may permit you to make, or that you might deem useful to be made known here.

The subject of the Vice Presidency is an all absorbing one here, as you will perceive from the communications to the roanoke advocate herein inclosed. Governor Branch has been proposed as a suitable person to fill that office, by two correspondents of the Roanoke Advocate, and I am under the impresion that the delegates to be chosen shortly at P. P. Herveys'[97] in this county, to meet others from this Electorial district, to form a Jackson ticket for President and Vice President, will be instructed to place Governor Branch on the latter. I am in favour of the nomination of the Governor for reasons that I shall not now trouble you with. I am highly gratified at the hopeful prospect of being relieved of the tariff, I have ever been an antitariffite, believing it unconstitutional, preventing what its name imports it is to do, and oppressing the poor of every section of the Union; and particularly the South. For simplicity and truth upon the subject, I do not recollect to have seen a prettyer essay than is contained in the Advocates hereby sent, over the signature of a Nullifer. With the ballance of the communication I have nothing to do in this epistle, but upon the unconstitutionality of the tariff, I think it conclusive.

The rejection of the no[mina]tion of Mr. Van Buren you will also see has caused [torn] emotion, but I believe it is only with those w[ho] hope to see him in the presidential chair, mo[st] of us are indignant at the maner the rejection w[as] effected, and thoug we are opposed to him as presiden[t], we, for the sake of the feelings of the President, whom we are bound to re-elect, would willingly have had his appointment confirmed. The resignation of the exSecretary, striped of ulterior Views, is to us totally incomprehensible, and was the first thing to awaken suspicion here, that all was not right.

Very respectfully your obt humble Sevt.

MARTIN READ. [?]

[Addressed:]

Judge Mangum
Senator in congress
Washington cty
D. C.

---

[97]Peyton Harvey was postmaster at Hill's Bridge in Halifax County in 1823. McIver, *N. C. Register*, 68.

WPM-LC

R. M. Saunders to W. P. Mangum

TARBORO'—March 3. 1832

Dear Sir,

I did not, as I flattered myself I should hear from you at Martin[98]—while there I received from Gen[l]. Iredell the enclosed copy of a letter from Gov. Branch—The original of which I shall receive at Pitt[99]—not wishing to delay my answer I take the liberty of inclosing it to you—which you will do me the favour of handing to Gov. Branch—I have written it without the benefit of consultation—tho' I trust you will not consider me as having gone too far—

Public sentiment here & at Martin decidedly against the Senate's rejection of Van Buren—

very sincerely

R. M. SAUNDERS

I had to open this   )
after sealing it—   )
having omitted something—)

[Addressed:]

Hon. W. P. Mangum
U. S. Senate
Washington City

———

WPM-LC

[ENCLOSURE]

TARBORO. March 3rd. 1832

Sir.

Your letter of the 20th. ultimo has been forwarded to me by your friend from Raleigh[100]—In reply to which I have the honor to State —at the time of writing the communication of which

---

[98]Martin County.
[99]Pitt County.
[100]Before February 20, 1832, Saunders wrote an article for the *Star* criticising Branch for disclosing a confidential conversation with Jackson. Saunders based his evidence of this being a confidential conversation on a statement made by Poindexter in his speech. February 20, 1832, Branch wrote Saunders for an explanation. When Saunders learned from Forsythe's speech that he had been unfair to Branch he wrote this letter. Later each accepted the other's explanation. *N. C. Free Press*, Apr. 7, 10, 17, 1832.

you complain, I had not seen "the remarks of Gov. [John] Forsythe in the Senate of the United States, on the nomination of
Martin Van Buren," but my impressions were produced by the
printed speech of Gov Poindexter.[101]

From the conversation as detailed by him, & the relation in
which you then stood to the President (supposing you to be the
person alluded to) I did consider the condemnation of a character, if not strictly confidential, as not authorizing a disclosure on your part. Under this impression, which I still entertain, I penned the article in the Star.—Yet I do not hesitate to
say, I consider you above disclosing a conversation which *you*
might deem confidential, or of giving information in any matter,
which you would not be willing to avow to the world.

I have the honor to be &c

R.M. SANDERS.

Hon. John Branch
      Washington City.

P. S. As I did not see Gen Iredell, as I suppose he will inform
you. I return my answer through the hands of my friend Mr
Mangum—
'The foregoing is a copy of a letter delivered by me this the
23rd. March 1832. to Gov Branch in Wash: City.

W. P. Mangum.

[Addresed:]   copy

      Hon John Branch
          Washington City

WPM-LC

Willie P. Mangum to Charity A. Mangum

Saturday morning
3rd. March 1832.

My dear Love.

I have been greatly disappointed in not receiving a letter from
you yesterday at the regular time—I hope to get one this morn-

---

[101]George Poindexter of Mississippi.

ing—The mail not yet come—I have been fearing that some
thing is the matter. I trust not. I have been more or less unwell
for more than a week. I am getting almost entirely well—&
should have been so, had I not been out necessarily the night before last—God Bless you My Dear Love & our dear children—
May the smiles of Heaven cheer & sustain you, & that we may
come together in health—As the weather begins to look like
Spring, my thoughts turn on home constantly I wish the time
were here to go home—I want to see you as much or more than I
ever did in my life—& press to my bosom all that is dearest to
me & that I most love in this world— Farewell   W. P. M.

WPM-LC

John Bragg[102] to Willie P. Mangum

WARRENTON March 4th 1832.

Dear Sir:
Yr. very friendly letter in reply to my first was duly recd. I
avail myself of the earliest intermission of professional engagements since its receipt to acknowledge my obligations for the
kind terms in which you express yourself towards me and to
return my thanks for the generous solicitude you evince in the
accomplishment of the object which was the subject of my first
letter & which I still have very much at heart—
A few days since I transmitted to Genl Hawkins, with a request that he would exhibit them to you, an *application* accompanied by such documents as I thought might facilitate the
object in view. I am apprehensive that possibly I may have been
too late—but my own absence and that of Judge Hall whose
certificate I desired to procure necessarily caused the delay—I
hope however for the best—You will pardon me for saying that
I rely mostly on yourself for assistance in this business—tho'
the papers were not enclosed directly to you—being the *immediate* constituent of Genl. H— *courtesy* seemed to require that he
shd be consulted.
You conclude yr. last by enquiring what I think of V. B.'s rejection—I think it was the result of a factious combination—

[102]John Bragg, 1806-1878, a lawyer in Warrenton, served in the House of Commons from
1830 to 1834. In 1836 he moved to Alabama and represented that state in Congress from
1851 to 1853. *Biog. Dir. of Cong.*, 729.

the fruit of Clay's ambition & Calhoun's malice—We had a Jackson meeting here last week the proceedings of which will be published in the Papers—from them you will observe my own individual opinions & I think I may safely say the sentiments of the whole "Roanoke Country" as you have been wont to call it. We remember not to forget those who, it gives me pleasure to say, so truly reflected our wishes by their votes on the Nomination—

Permit me to congratulate you on your late stand against the Tariff—This single effort more than compensates for all the anxiety & trouble experienced in effecting yr. election—let me recomend to you to have yr. speech printed & extensively distributed at least throughout Nᵒ. C— The great misfortune of this Tariff system is that its *modus operandi* is insidious and deceptive—you and I perhaps may understand it, but the great mass of the people are profoundly ignorant of its true and real character—They feel its debilitating & paralyzing effects but they cannot *see* any external eruption.—They want light to enable them to judge correctly & to convince them of the deadly nature of the disease under the imperceptible influence of which they are fast wasting away—

I think with you that on this subject there shᵈ be concert of action in the So.—If the Tariff is not modified this session—(of which I think present indications justify no hope) I do not hesitate to express the opinion that the Anti-tariff states shᵈ call a Convention, with the purpose of making out at once *an issue* on this agitating question—It is in vain to reason longer— ambition & avarice never yet listened to argument—

What a miserable spectacle does Congress at this time exhibit to the world—instead of deliberating upon the necessities of the nation—instead of endeavoring by a new & enlightened & dignified course of legislation to render the country peacable & prosperous at home & respectable abroad, we are daily disgusted by the pitiful antics of a parcel of puny political gladiators— reckless of all consequences animated by the blind fury of party rage—and striving with all their might for the mere paltry & ephemeral advantages of temporary party supremacy—

The more I see of the progress of our Govᵗ. the more am I convinced that our experiment will fail—I fear *signally* fail—I shᵈ not be surprised if *we* even shᵈ live to see the day when all that can be said of us will be *'illiumfuit'*—'Tis true I hope for better things—but 'tis *but hope*—

It is rumored here that Branch & White[103] are to fight—from their quarrels in the House I do not see how they can avoid something of the kind—Do write me & give me the *on dits* of the day—Dont the President mean to nominate another Minister to G. B^r—or will he [illegible]—& not trust again to the Senate?

I have just heard of the death of our friend Genl. Williams[104] he died to day (Monday) about 2 O'Clock—no more—

Yr. friend & obt Srvt.

JNO BRAGG

Warrenton N C
6 March 1832

[Addressed:]

> Hon: Willie P. Mangum
> U States Senate
> Washington

WPM-LC

John Chavis to Willie P. Mangum

March 10th. 1832

My dear Sir/

It is four weeks to day since I left your house, at which time, Mrs. Mangum & myself wrote to you respecting my Teaching School for you. It was agreed also, that as soon as Mrs Mangum rec^d your answer, she was to write to me. I promised her also, that I would not engage to Teach for any person or persons until I rec^d. a letter from her. Yesterday week was our mail day, when I expected her letter & no letter came, Yesterday I sent to the post Office & no letter came. Supposing that she had written, and her not receiving my Answer. I wrote to her to day that I had rec^d. no letter from her, fearing that she might think that I neglected her Interest & that of her children. I expected an answer from you also: but it has not come to hand—I have

---

[103]In the preceding sessions of Congress, Joseph M. White of Florida, accused Branch while Secretary of the Navy of suppressing important documents on the quantity of live oaks growing on public lands in Florida and of unduly increasing the salaries of agents. This brought on much controversy but an investigation in July exonerated Branch. *N. C. Free Press*, Aug. 14, 1832.

[104]General William Williams died Mar. 4, 1832. He was a member of the Council of State from Warren County. *N. C. Free Press*, Mar. 13, 1832.

thought it probable that you might disapprove of the Terms I mentioned. If you did, they were founded upon what you told me, that a school could be got in your neighbourhood of Twenty five scholars at ten dollars each, And I supposed that Thirty six dollars is [illegible] be quite a reduced price. At any rate, I expected that if you disapproved of my Terms, that you write to Mrs. Mangum to make me a proposition and it may be done, as no letters have come to hand—

So anxious am I, to Teach your children the Theory of the English language, that I am truly sorry that I had not told Mrs. Mangum to write to you, (or written so myself) that if nothing else could be done, that I w^d. come & Teach Sally alone, for the same you w.^d have to give for her board in Hillsborough, provided you w^d. board me & let me have a horse occasionally [to go] & see my family. This I w^d. do with the expectation of getting a school in the neighbourhood the next year & I w^d. do it yet, if I could be assured in a few days that it w^d. meet your approbation. I made this statement to her in to days letter—

I fear that my promise to Mrs. Mangum will prevent me from geting a school at all, for I put off attempts to this day; but I must set out on Monday to see what I can do. & if I sh^d. be disappointed, I have stated what I will do for you so that I shall expect an answer to this letter to be left at the post office of Rogers's store—

Mr. Holmes[105] in the senate, appears to use a knife, almost too sharp for sore shins, But Oh my son, what will you do with the overwhelming eloquence and masterly disquisitions of Mr. Clay? The Tariff is a tough question. but I still say, that you may modify it, but let it be extensive. I am already of the opinion that the senate did right in the case of Mr. Van Buren Pray put neck & shoulders to the renewal of the Charter of the United States bank, for if you fail to do that, you will at once sever the bones & sinews of the nation—What do you think now of the imprisonment of the Missionarys in the state prison of Georgia?

Please to give my respects to my son—Abraham Rencher & to Gen. Barringer—& tell them I w^d. be glad to receive a letter from them. Tell them if I am Black I am free born American & a revolutionary soldier & therefore ought not to be thrown intirely out of the scale of notice

---

[105]John Holmes was the Senator from Maine from 1820 to 1827 and from 1829 to 1833. *Biog. Dir. of Cong.*, 1110.

I am your Ob^t. Hb. Sv^t.

JOHN CHAVIS

[Addressed:]

Hon. Willie P. Mangum Esqr
In Congress
Washington City.

———

WPM-LC

S. F. Patterson[106] to Willie P. Mangum

WILKESBORO' N. C. March 11th 1832

Dear Sir—

The speech of Colo Benton on the state of the currency which you were so good as to send me, I have received, and read with much pleasure, and I hope some profit—The view which Colo B has taken of the subject, certainly evidences great labour and extensive research, and shows that his investigations have been carried to the extent required, in order to enable him to arrive at fair and just conclusions—I had myself in the course of my little dealing with the world, often wondered why it was that from the time the United States Bank went into operation, up to within the last three or four years, we had so little United States paper in circulation in the Southern Country; and when paper of that description began gradually to become more plenty, it should almost all consist of the Branch Bank orders of which Colo B speaks—Never had I been able to solve the mystery until I read his speech—

Although I would be opposed to an extension of the present charter of the Bank of the United States, yet my limited observations have led me to believe that an institution founded on similar principles was almost absolutely necessary for carrying on the financial operations of the Government with ease, convenience and safety—and that a renewal of the charter with such modifications and restrictions as would avoid many of the difficulties and objections which have been urged against it,

---

[106]Samuel Finley Patterson, 1799-1874, later was an anti-Jackson leader who was active in railroad developments and in banking. He was state treasurer from 1835 to 1837, president of the State Bank, president of the Raleigh and Gaston Railroad, and frequently a member of the legislature. Ashe, *Biog. Hist. of N. C.*, II, 328-334.

might under the existing circumstances of the country be deemed adviseable—So far however as North Carolina is concerned, I conceive that we would be but little affected by it, either one way or the other—The withdrawal of the Branch at Fayetteville, unless the business transacted there should be very speedily closed, I do not believe would seriously injure it debtors —certainly not to such an extent as materially to affect the price of property—

I am convinced, that generally heretofore, we have had too much Bank Capital in this State—more than could be *profitably* employed, and more than the commercial transactions of the country actually required—, As a proof of this, we need only refer to the fact that, the local Banks for the last two or three years have only been able to declare a dividend of from three to four per cent—In fact I believe the Bank of Cape Fear has not declared any dividend for the last twelve or eighteen months, and the State Bank I understood when at Raleigh last winter had about $400,000—of its bills lying idle, which it was anxious to loan, but could not obtain borrowers—the charter of these Banks will not expire until 1839, before which time I have no doubt others will be incorporated on some plan, or their charters extended—

You are apprized I presume before this time of the proceedings of a meeting held in this place about the 1st. Feby. (a copy of which was directed to be sent to you, Mr Brown & Mr Williams) for the purpose of appointing delegates to meet in convention the delegates from the other counties in this District, to select a suitable person to be placed on the Jackson electoral ticket and at which a resolution was adopted relative to the rechartering of the U. S. Bank—The meeting, though small, was highly respectable, and most of the persons present expressed their opinions upon the subject—All were in favour of an institution having the same objects in view which are professed by the friends of the U S Bank, but none were completely satisfied that, that institution had attained those objects—and all were opposed to a renewal of the charter, without important modifications and additional restrictions—

I have considered it due to you to say thus much in regard to the character and opinions of that meeting (the substance of which you may communicate to Mr Brown) as I presume you are both unacquainted with most of the persons who were there—

Our Superior Court commences tomorrow morning, Judge

Donnell and most of the gentlemen of the bar have arrived—I
have not seen any of them, but understand they are well—

Be pleased to accept my best wishes for your health and
prosperity, while I remain,

very respectfully your
most obt Sert.

S. F. PATTERSON

Hon W. P. Mangum

[Addressed:]

Hon: Willie P. Mangum
Senate of the United States
Washington

Mail)   D. C.

WPM-LC

Dillon Jordan, Jr.,[107] to Willie P. Mangum

FAYETTEVILLE March 14th 1832

Dear Sir

Pursuant to a resolution of the Administration Meeting held in this town on the 8th Inst I have the honour,
herewith to enclose you the annexed Extract from its
proceedings—

Your ob[t]. Serv[t]—

DILLON JORDAN JUNR.

"Whereas it is the undoubted right of the freemen of our land,
freely to express their opinions of the conduct of those to whom
the administration of the affairs of its Government are Committed: And Whereas we as a portion of the free citizens of
the United States, have witnessed with pleasure an anxious
desire on the part of Andrew Jackson, our venerable and worthy
Chief Magistrate, to promote the harmony and prosperity, and
also to preserve unsullied, the honor and integrity of the Union.
We therefore, cheerfully add ours, to the many other testimo-

---

[107]Dillon Jordan, Jr., was a member of the House of Commons from Cumberland County
from 1833 to 1837. *N. C. Manual,* 577.

nials of popular approbation, of the Measures of his administration; and of popular confidence in his public and private vertues.

Be it therefore Resolved,

That the confidence of this Meeting, in the firmness and patriotism of Andrew Jackson, is unimpaired, and that we cordially approve of his able and efficient administration of the affairs of the General Government

Resolved,

That we cheerfully unite with our fellow citizens in different Sections of the Union, in recommending Andrew Jackson for re-election, and that we will use all honorable endeavour to accomplish so desirable an object.

Resolved,

That the proposed Baltimore Convention for the purpose of nominating some tried Republican citizen, to be placed on the Jackson ticket, for vice President, has our entire approbation, as providing the surest means to secure harmony and union among the great republican party in this Country; and that we as a portion of the people of North Carolina, approve of the appointment of Delegates to that Convention, made by the State Meeting in Raleigh,

Resolved,

That we will support such person as that Convention may nominate for the Vice President at the approaching election—

Resolved,

That we have full confidence in the talents and patriotism of Martin Van Buren, of New York, and that we believe he is eminently qualified for the appointment to which he was recently nominated by the President; and view his rejection by the Senate of the United States, as an attempt not only to prostrate a talented and eminently useful citizen, but also to embarrass the administration of Andrew Jackson, and to obstruct our negotiations with the Government of Great Britain—

Resolved,

That we approve the course which our Senators the Hon. Bedford Brown, and the Hon. Willie P. Mangum pursued in relation to that nomination; and that as a portion of their Constituents, we tender them our acknowledgments, for vindicating by their *vote,* as we believe the will of a large majority of the people of

North Carolina; and that a copy of this and the foregoing resolutions, be forwarded to them b[y the] Secretary of this Meeting."

"From the Minutes"

DILLON JORDAN JUNR
Secretary

[Addressed:]
            To the Honorable,   [Endorsed:]
                Willie P. Mangum   Answered
                    Washington City   20 March '32

WPM-LC

John Martin[108] to Willie P. Mangum

Wilkes County 16th March 1832
Dear Sir   Your favour Came to hand by the last mail and I
hasten to acknowledge the favour and it would give me pleasure to be honoured as one of your Correspondants. When I sit
down to write to a Member of Congress, I am always at a loss
what to say for they being at the fountain head of information
I feel that I have nothing to Communicate. I find that the Tariff
is the all absorbing question with you and I am sorry to see that
a sperrit fare differant from that which I had hoped would prevail, is exhibited by the advocate of the protective Cistem, I had
expected that a Spirit of Compromise and mutual Concession
would have been produced and that unjust and Ruinous polity
modifyed or abandoned, and once more that harmony would
have been Restored amonge the states of our union, but I fear
that the Sistem will preserved in all its odious features, if that
should be the Case I fear the Consequences, for do not believe
that the South can or will bear up under its oppressions and
injustice
    The Jackson party are geting into Confusion in this part on
the subject of the Vice Presidency, a meeting of Delegates took
place at Wilkesborough on tuesday last from all the Countys
Composing this Electoral District for the purpose of nominat-

---

[108]John Martin was a member of the legislature from Wilkes County in 1806, 1813, and
1831. *N. C. Manual*, 852-854.

ing an Elector of President and Vice President and we Desolved
without making any nomination. The subject will be taken up
after the meeting of the Baltimore Convention and if Van Buren
should be nominated by that meeting it is my opinion that it
will Create an irreconcilable split in our Ranks. Certain persons
had Commenced working the wires in favour of Van Buren
which was the principal cause of our late meeting disolving of
itself without doing the business that they had been delegated
to do.

I see from the public papers that Congress has ordered the
printing of a Report made to the British Parlement on the Subject of Rail Roads and other Accompinying papers, I should feel
myself under obligations to you if you would send me a Coppy
for I am desirous of obtaining all the information on that subject that I possible Can, for I hope that a Rail Road at no verry
distant will Releave North Carolina from her embarress state

I am Dear Sir your with Esteem

JOHN MARTIN

The Honourable Wiley P. Mangum.

Jonesville N. C.
March 17 1832

Jonesville N. C.
March 17 1832

[Addressed:]

The Honourable Wiley P. Mangum
Washington City

WPM-LC

R. M. Saunders to Willie P. Mangum

RALEIGH March 18th. 1832

Dear Sir—

I came home last night from Tarboro' tho' I hear no [ne]ws
here—I did not receive your letter directed to [Gran]ville untill
I was preparing to leave for Tarboro'—I should have written
you in reply from Tarboro'—but expected daily to hear from
you [ref]erence to the letter I had before written [to] that place
inclosing the one to Govr. Branch [I] certainly should not have
embarrassed you with it—had yours been received before inclosing it—I could not anticipate any difficulty in the mere

delivery of my letter & if things took a belligerent result I intended relieving you from any responsibility by selecting some other friend—I still flatter myself that you found nothing in my reply to prevent its delivery—as you know it is unpleasant to be placed under obligations to those not of our [thinking] in matters of this kind—I should like however to hear if it was received & by whom received—I have received from Mr. Brown the warrant for my son[109]—for which I beg to tender to you both my best acknowledgements—It is still uncertain whether I shall go on to Baltimore—tho it seems to be the wish of many of our friends that I should do so—

I begin to think the sentiment in the State stronger for Van Buren than I expected—still there is a strong opposition—

All regret the decision of the Georgia question[110] & none that I hear are disposed to aid in its support with the exception of Western Gales—

Respectfully yrs—

R M SANDERS

[Addressed:]

Hon¹. Willie P. Mangum
Washington City.

WPM-LC

T. C. Mathews[111] & J. P. Freeman to Willie P. Mangum

ELIZABETH CITY March 20, 1832.

Dear Sir!

The undersigned have the pleasure to inform you that they have been selected a comitee to announce to you the passage of a resolution of which the inclosed is a copy by a large & respectable assemblage of the friends of the present administration, citizens of the county of Pasquotank recently held in this place, approbatory of your vote in the Senate on the nomination of M. VanBuren Esqr. as the diplomatic representative of our government near the court of St. James

---

[109]He refers to Franklin Saunders' appointment to West Point.
[110]He refers to the controversy over the removal of the Creeks and Cherokees. See below, p. 515n.
[111]Thomas C. Mathews of Pasquotank was a member of the House of Commons in 1834. *N. C. Manual*, 748.

The undersigned beg leave to add an expression of their individual respect and esteem and to subscribe themselves

Very Respectfully
Yours—

T. C. MATHEWS
J. P. FREEMAN.

[Addressed:]

Hon. W. P. Mangum
Washington
D. C.

[ENCLOSED]

Resolved unanimously, That this meeting do highly approve of the conduct of our Senators, the Hon. Bedford Brown and Hon. W. P. Mangum, on the nomination of Martin Van Buren Esqr as Minister near the Court of St. James, and that Drs. Isaac P. Freeman and Thos. Colville Mathews be appointed a committee to express to those gentlemen the news & feelings of this meeting upon that subject.

WPM-LC

W. Montgomery to Willie P. Mangum

ALBRIGHTS, N. C. March 24th 1832

Dear Sir

Will you permit a Friend to Console you In your Trouble, at Washington, We are somewhat Excited Here. But I presume nothing In Comparison with the Excitement at Head Quarters. Some are predicting a Speedy Dissilution of the union, under the great Excitement which seems to pervade the whole government, and calculate that the Decision of the Supreme Court, against georgia, will Be all sufficient to Complete the Matter.[112]

---

[112]After gold was discovered in the Cherokee country, Georgians were more anxious than ever for the Indian lands. The state laws were in force. Jackson had removed the troops which Adams had placed there to protect the Indians. As a result the Indians brought their cases to the Supreme Court. Marshall in the first case, Cherokee Nation vs. Georgia, declared the Indians could not sue. In this case Georgia had arrested an Indian criminal. In the other case, Worcester vs. Georgia, Marshall declared Georgia's laws in the Cherokee region void. Georgia was rebellious. Jackson refused to enforce this decision. For a good account, see U. B. Phillips, *Georgia and State Rights: A Study of the Political History of Georgia From the Revolution to the Civil War, With Particular Regard to Federal Relation* in the *Annual Report* of the American Historical Association for the year 1901 (Washington, D. C.: Government Printing Office, 1902), 76-82.

19

I Hope For Better things. I do not fear a Dissolution. But I do Feel greatly For the Situation in which our venerable Chief Magistrate is placed By it. But I Hope georgia, will Relieve Him, By setting at Liberty those scoundrils, they Have suffered, considerable, and it was Justly due them.

I see you Have Been Bandying the Subject of the united States Bank, and the House Had appointed a Committee to go and Investigate the affairs of the Institution,[113] Do promise me one of these reports, or rather two For there will no Doubt Be two, and I Want Both Sides. I now Hope and Believe that should the Charter Be Renewed, it will at Least remove some of my objections to that Institution, I am for a National Bank, to be under the Controul of the Nation, Not of a Few Northern Men whose Interest and feelings are at points with ours of the South. Could the power of Managing the Institution, Be reciprocal, among the States, I would not so much Care as to the distribution of the Capital, or Stock, But Banks are Like Mechinery a Main Wheele Drives all, and the Stock In Banks seems to constitute this Main Wheel. 25 Min does Move the Main Wheel, 13 or Even 7 May, all of whom May reside in philadelphia, and from ther rule. We Might Infer that they were Imported Eastern despots. But they are now In Hands, that will Cry aloud and spare that What are you going to do with the tariff. Will you Be able to give the South any Relief or will Clay succeed In His Wishes to make the Southern Burden Heavier. I see you are determined to give Him nothing, We look up to you with great anxiety on that subject, your Experience Has given you Mutch Light in that Matter.

Last Week at our Court was a week of Mutch Consultation, and speculation as regards our County Candidates. It is said that Doctor Smith and Myself will Have a race, for the Senate. I dislike the Controversy, But do nor fear the result. Allison,[114] Mabane,[115] Stockart,[116] Roan,[117] Mangrum,[118] Wm McCauley &

---

[113]In February 1832 Nicholas Biddle decided to induce Jackson to approve a recharter. He, therefore, let Jackson's supporters know that he would agree to the changes they recommended in this charter. This would hurt Clay's political ambition, but Biddle would save his bank. Benton then induced Jackson to have an investigation first. This would give ammunition for an attack on the bank or reason for supporting a recharter. Consequently on February 23, A. S. Clayton of Georgia introduced a resolution in the House for an investigation. Speaker Stephenson appointed a committee which was unfavorable to the bank. The members did not know much about banking and as a result they soon failed to prove any weaknesses. Nevertheless they succeeded in making political capital. R. C. H. Catterall, *Second Bank of the United States* (Chicago, Ill.; The University of Chicago Press, 1903), 227-231.
[114]Joseph Allison was in the state senate from 1830 to 1834.
[115]James Mebane.
[116]John Stockard. See above, p. 312n.
[117]Possibly Nathaniel Roan of Caswell County.
[118]Priestley H. Mangum was elected in 1832.

Doctor Craig,[119] are all spoken of for the Commons. For Sheriff
Allison Mangrum, Jams Forrest,[120] Wm. Wilson, Go. Laws, John
Freeland,[121] James Turrentine,[122] and Joel C. Yancey.[123] Robert
Potter Has Been sent up to be a Citizen In orange for two years.
I visited Him in prison the Evening after He arrive. He was Just
robert potter Without alteration. We Made a Move relative to
an Election, We Called a Meeting of the Friends of the A. J. s.[124]
on tuesday of May Court, to Make arrangements for an Elector
for our District. I do not now whether granville and person
will Do the same or not, I Hope they will, But Little talk as
yet who we will put on the ticket. My name Has Been Mentioned Some say I am two mutch of Van Buren Man. I think
we may have some Dificulty as regards the Elector. I wish you
would Help us out.

What have you Done with Joseph Thompsons papers. If you
Have gotten the Money send it to Me, for Him.

Yours with the Highest Esteem &c.

W. MONTGOMERY

Write me Soon.

Albrights N. C.
March 24th 1832.

[Addressed:]

The Honbl. Wiley P Mangum
Washington City
D. C.

WPM-LC

Thomas Burgess[125] to Willie P. Mangum

HALIFAX N. C. 26th. March 1832

My Dear Sir—

I have to reproach myself with great remissness in delaying

---

[119]John Craig was in the legislature from Orange County in 1811 and from 1813 to 1815.
In 1815 he was speaker of the lower house. *N. C. Manual*, 464.
[120]James Forrest was in the legisalture from Orange County in 1835. *N. C. Manual*, 741.
[121]One of Murphey's creditors formerly from Petersburg. Hoyt, *Papers of Murphey*, I, 65.
[122]James Turrentine was sheriff of Orange County from 1831 to 1837. *N. C. Laws*, 1831-
1837.
[123]One of Murphey's creditors in 1823. Hoyt, *Papers of Murphey*, I, 243.
[124]Possibly an Andrew Jackson society.
[125]Thomas Burgess was an attorney from Halifax who held many town and county offices
before he was elected to the House of Commons in 1819. He served in the legislature in 1819,
1821, 1822, and 1823. Grant, *Alumni Hist. of U. N. C.*, 86.

so long to acknowledge the receipt of the Pamphlet, containing Gen¹. Hayne's speech on the Tariff, which you did me the honor to send me.—

May I further trespass on your kindness by asking an additional favor— There resides in this village a Free man of color, of exemplary conduct & irreproachable character, who is a good Barber & musician, & has a Wife & five small children,— all of whom, by his industry, & economy, he has purchased from their former master—as he cannot liberate them by the laws of this State,¹²⁶ he is very desirous to remove with his family, to some Town in the North Western States, where he can set his Wife & children free, raise & support them by his calling, & be exempt from the oppression & restraint necessarily incident to a slave holding State.—He has asked my advice as to the place of his removal, & being ignorant of the local laws of the Free States in relation to colored people, & not knowing where would be the most eligible spot to locate himself & pursue with most advantage his occupations, I have, of course, declined advising him on the subject.—But feeling considerable interest in his Welfare, I have taken the liberty to request of you to procure the necessary information from your acquaintances in congress, & write me the result—I propose myself taking an excursion, the ensuing summer, thro' some of the Western States, & if your report be favorable, this free fellow will accompany me—

A great excitement has prevailed in this part of the State in consequence of the rejection, by the Senate, of Mr. Van Buren's nomination—But having retired from the bar, & from public life, I did not participate in it to any great extent—

Accept assurances of my esteem & respect—

                                        T BURGES

Judge Mangum)

[Addressed:]

            The Honᵇˡᵉ
                Willie P. Mangum
                    In the U. S.' Senate
                        Washington City

---

¹²⁶As a result of the change of sentiment on slavery in the early 1830's, the North Carolina legislature tightened the laws on manumission. David Walker, a North Carolina Negro living in Boston, wrote his *Appeal in Four Articles* to incite the slaves to insurrection. This raised the feeling to what Bassett calls "summer heat." To manumit a slave, the owner was required to give a bond of $1000.00 that the freed slave would conduct himself well as long as he remained in the state and that he must leave within ninety days. John S. Bassett, *Slavery in the State of North Carolina* (Baltimore, Md.: The Johns Hopkins University Press, 1899), 30.

WPM-LC

Walker Anderson[127] to Willie P. Mangum

HILLSBORO' March 28th 1832

My dear Sir!

I acknowledge with sentiments of sincere gratitude the receipt of your letter containing intelligence of the successful issue of young Mr. Cameron's[128] application for a commission in the U. S. military academy—You have laid our whole family under obligation by your friendly offices in this matter & in particular have done an act of great kindness to my Aunt[129] whose children are numerous & whose means of providing for them are very slender—I hope that William will not do discredit to your kind interference in his behalf & to avert so unpleasant a result, I have urged upon him & will continue to urge upon him the valuable suggestions in your letter.

I should have replied to your letter sooner, but waited a mail or two that I might at the same time advise you of the receipt of the commission from Gen: Barringer—it has not however yet come to hand, & as I presume the possession of it will be essential to Mr. C's admission at West Point, I beg you will remind the General of sending it on—

With sentiments of sincere regard
I am my dear Sir
Your friend & Servt

WALKER ANDERSON

[Addressed:]

To the Hon: W. P. Mangum
Washington
D. C.

WPM-LC

Wm. Cain, Jr., to Willie P. Mangum

HILLSBORO— 29th Mar 1832

My Dear Sir

---

[127]Walker Anderson, 1801-1857, was head of a girls' school in Hillsboro before he became professor of logic and rhetoric at the University in 1853. From 1851 to 1853 he was chief justice of the Supreme Court of Florida. Grant, *Alumni Hist. of U. N. C.*, 13.
[128]William Cameron.
[129]For many years Ann Owen Cameron taught music in Hillsboro. *Hillsborough Recorder*, Aug. 9, 1825.

Not hearing from you I presume you did not understand me in saying I did not know what you intended in sending two signatures—What I meant was this,—Whether you wished to make two notes or seperate notes due at different times and for different amounts because if you only intended it for one, one signature would have been sufficient—

I send you herewith Ten Dollars, with which I wish you to purchase me on the 2ⁿᵈ April (I wish you to purchase particularly on that day, it being my birth day) a lottery ticket in a Lottery, where the largest prize will be at least twenty thousand Dollars and send it to me with instructions to the Lottery vender to send me an account of the drawing—

All of our friends are as well as usual, Mr. Davis[130] with his family will leave here about this day two weeks for the Gold region[131]

Your friend in haste

WM. CAIN JR.

P. C. after buying the lottery ticket
if there should be enough money remain-
ing send me or subscribe for the best paper for me. I leave it
to your Judgment.

W. C.

[Addressed:]

The Honbl. Willie P. Mangum
Washington City

Free Wm. Cain Jr. P. M.

WPM-LC

Jos. B. Hinton[132] to Willie P. Mangum

WASHINGTON, N. C.
31. March 1832.

Honl. Sir,

Our acquaintance it is true is very limited—for I have no recollection, of being in your company, except for a few minutes,

---

[130]Cain's brother-in-law, Edward Davis.
[131]Near Charlotte.
[132]Joseph B. Hinton was clerk of Beaufort County Court in 1823, and state senator in 1829-1830 and 1832. *N. C. Laws*, 1824, appendix; *N. C. Manual*, 497.

several years since in the Town of Greenvill. When I was in
the Legislature, altho I heard of your being in the City, I had
not the good fortune to enjoy the pleasure of any of your company. But altho' our acquaintance is thus limited, you are one
of the Representatives of myself & of the whole State—and as
such, I will respectfully ask of you the favour of assisting Genl.
Speight and my other friends in Congress, to procure for me,
the Superintendency of the Beacon Island Hospital in this State,
should one be erected there. I trust I am as well qualified as
many of the profession who may or may not ask for it; and I
refer you to my friend Gen¹. Speight for the testimonials concerning my qualifications—and the public wish, here—in the
neighbourhood of that Hospital.

Here, however, an objection may meet me—I did not vote for
you—as Senator—no—but I did—as Judge. And your public
character, and from what I have seen of your personal worth,
I should cheerfully have voted for you as Senator—had I been
differently circumstanced. Gov. Owen & myself had been often
together throughout the year—preceding—he had been civil &
indeed kind—& his National & State politicks, in the main,
appeared to me to be unexceptionable—altho' not a splendid man
himself.—my support was *sought & promised*.—After your name
was given to the Legislature, my brother—Dʳ Potts of Tarboro'
wrote me—by all means to support you—inasmuch as all in our
quarter & particularly Edgecomb—"were Mangum men"—but I
was compelled to act differently & so informed him—because
of the pledge or promise I had previously made—& made without a suspicion that your name would be held up for the honor.
R. D. Speight & Gov. Owen & Gen¹. Stokes. I took it for granted
would be the persevering competitors.

But, my dear Sir, no Carolinian can not but be proud of the
Senators who now represent her in the Fed¹. Government—and
as my services in the Legislature are not done—if I live—
another day, may find me recording this sentiment.

If you can feel free to do this favour for me, I shall shew that
I know how to be grateful. Believe me to be yours with much
respect & esteem. & Your servant

JOS. B HINTON.

Honl. Judge Mangum.

[Addressed:]

Honl. Judge
W. P. Mangum
Senator in Congress
Washington City.

———————

WPM-LC

R. M. Saunders to Willie P. Mangum

RALEIGH March 31st, 1832

My dear Sir/

I returned last evening from J[o]hnston Court & found yours of the 24th & 25th. I h[a]ve to express to you my thanks for the interest you have taken in this business & my approbation of your course—As to Gov. B's[133] threatened publication, I have no fears—If he assails my honor he will of course expect to answer for it—I acknowledge my opposition to Gen. J— in the Crawford contest and it is likely in the ardour of my speeches I may have used strong & reproachful language—But I deny most unequivocally of ever saying any thing against Mrs. J—I had a sister living in a mile of Gen. J's—the families were friendly[134] & a brother of mine married a family connection of Mrs. J's—I am certain therefore that I neither felt or uttered an unkind sentiment respecting her—

I learnt with surprise & indignation Gov. B's allusion to our correspondence—Is the man deranged? Or has he lost every feeling of honor? I may have been deceived in confiding in the honor of such a man—but if he has character enough left to publish my letters (I have no copies) they will not injure me, but disgrace him. There can be no doubt as to the character of that correspondence—I wrote him from Salisbury—labouring at the time under much depression of spirits—I stated that as he knew I had lost my estate & had a growing family—and that had the right to expect better things than it was in my power to bestow—that I was anxious to get into some situation, for which I might be qualified & which promised a permanent support—But that I had not supported Gen. J. for the sake of office & I disliked to be consid-

———————

[133] John Branch.
[134] Saunders and his brother, Franklin Saunders, at one time lived in Sumner County, Tennessee. He returned to North Carolina and left three half-brothers in Tennessee.

ered even an applicant—*but threw myself upon his friendly feel-ing*—It was some time before he answered this letter—when he did, he gave me assurances of friendship &c—about the time of Mr. Grahams death, & after my election of atto. Genl.[135] I again wrote to Gov. B.—expressing my [torn] the health of my circuit, —the difficulties [I] had to meet with & desired his interest for the appointment of Comr. of the Land office—but charged him not to embarrass Gen. J. with my name—He after some time answered this letter—saying the office was filled before the receipt of my letter & then renewing in a more particular manner his offer to serve me—very fortunately for me—I thanked him in reply but declined all farther application—expressing myself satisfied with my situation—as I had then removed to Raleigh—Such Sir, is the correspondence which he now has the meanness to talk of publishing—to prove me an office seeker—My danger is that I have no copies of my letters—May I add to my obligations by requesting you to call on Gov. B. & say to him as he has named the [sub]ject of our correspondence to you that I demand it as an act of justice that he suffers you to read my letters & to take copies of them for my use—Thank God, I believe I can say with truth, tho' struggling against the tide of fortune for the decent support of an interesting family—that they submit quietly to my reason & that my support of Gen. J has been & will continue to be as disinterested as most of my neighbours—most willingly would I abandon political strife but the active part I have heretofore taken & the course which others persue seems to render it impossible—Bet Gov. B. is the last man to denounce others as an office seeker—who but for place, would now be a humble justice of Halifax.—

A word as to the tariff—when it was seen that the New York Senators[136] had gone with Mr. Clay—it produced here a strong senti[ment] amongst those friendly to Mr. V. B.—I did not hesitate to say openly, if that was the game they intended to play, I was off & I believe now if that course is persevered in N. C. is [torn] to him—that Barbour[137] or Wilkins[138] will be [ta]ken up —I have all along urged that I was certain Mr. V. B.'s feelings were with the South & that he would go as far as practicable in relieving our just grounds of complaint. But if I am to be met by

[135]He was attorney general from 1828 to 1835. *N. C. Manual*, 444.
[136]In three votes in March on Clay's tariff resolution, the New York Senators, Charles E. Dudley and William L. Marcy, voted with Clay. *Register of Debates*, 22 Cong., 1 sess., 591, 626, 629.
[137]Philip P. Barbour.
[138]William Wilkins of Pennsylvania.

the votes of his personal friends, & they bind themselves to Mr.
Clays chariot, then I say let them go & we will take care of ourselves—Such I know is the general sentiment in this State.

I can do nothing with the Star—I have thrown a hasty article
or two in the Constitutionalist & as that [is] considered more
the organ of the Van [B.] party the effect may be better—you
will know how to bring it to bear—

I think it likely I shall be at Baltimore[139]—Mr. Franklin[140] or
some one else will select you to act for them—Willis Alston is
endeavouring to get a nomination—but I will put a damper on
him—Nash[141] has moved & I will draw a preamble & resolutions
for Franklin—

> Very sincerely
> Yrs
>
> R. M. SAUNDER—

Your speech is read with approbation.

[Addressed:]

> Honl. W. P. Mangum
> U. S. Senate
> Washington City.

———

WPM-LC

A. Lockhart[142] to Willie P. Mangum

ANSON COUNTY April 3rd. 1832

Dear Sir,

I yesterday Rec'd. your speech on the Tariff, in Pamphlet form,
with gladness. Though with some surprise, as I did not know
that you knew there was Ever such a man living on earth as A.
Lockhart tho, permit me Sir to tell you that I have had my Eye,
as it were, on you ever since your Honourable. manly, & independent speech in Congress on behalf of Genl. Lafayette,[143] and
was very much in hopes I should have seen you in Anson while
you were on the bench. I was very much pleased at your being

---

[139]Baltimore Democratic convention.
[140]Abner Franklin.
[141]Frederick Nash.
[142]Adam Lockhart was a member of the legislature from Anson County in 1804 when he
was 36 years old. Hamilton, *Papers of Ruffin*, I, 460-461.
[143]See above, p. xx.

elected in the Senate, Govr. Owen ought not to have canvassd for the Senate, the office of Gov. of N. C. is Honourable to Gentlemen, I have just read your speech on the Tariff, your remarks accord precisely with my views & wishes on that & the other subjects, may god grant you success—your voat in the Senate on Mr. Van burens nomination &c. has echoed in N. C. much to your praise, as also to Mr. Brown, the stroke that has fallen on Mr. Van Buren, was I have no doubt, aimed at one of the best men —man that only pretends to stand will fall as long, &c.

Judge I am no Politician, tho have professed to be what I call a republican & have not deviated one hairs breadth since the beginning, which is upwards of 40 years, I was a full Jeffersonian & am equally so a Jacksonian. Jeffersons Administration, and Jacksons, so fare, has been my glory, I never expect to see him Genl. Jackson, tho, he as a man, that I wish never to fall, hath my whole heart in his support, please give my best respects to Mr. Brown & Mr. Bethune[144]

Judge I wish you good health, may you be Inspired with Political understanding doing all things that pertain to Public good & like the Dove to his ark, safe return home to your family & Constituents—

I am D. Sir yours most Respectfully

A. LOCKHART

Wodesboro N C
April 5th

[Addressed:]

The Honorable Willie P. Mangum Esquire
City of Washington

WPM-LC

Rob H. Burton[145] to W. P. Mangum

BEATY'S FORD April 4th 1832.

Dear Sir

I have noticed in the proceedings in Congress, many resolutions to place persons upon the pension list. I presume this has

[144]Lauchlin Bethune, an agriculturist from Cumberland County, served in Congress from 1831 to 1833. *Biog. Dir. of Cong.*, 697.
[145]Robert H. Burton, 1781-1842, an attorney, became superior court judge in 1818. He served one year. In 1830 he was elected state treasurer but he declined to serve. Ashe, *Biog. Hist. of N. C.*, III, 41-42.

been occaioned by the circumstances of these cases being such as to exclude them by the laws relating to pensions. With this belief I beg leave to trouble you with the case of an old man a neighbour of mine. Some two or three years ago he petitioned for a pension and forwarded the necessary papers. He was answered that he had not served a sufficient length of time to entitle him to a pension. The case with him was that at the time of peace he was prisoner, and although detained longer after peace than made up his time, he was not enroled. The case I allude to is in the name of John Kidds.[146] You will find his papers filed in the office of the Secretary of War. The date of his enlistment is truly stated as furnished by our secretary, where his name appears as informed by Mr. Hill. Upon inspection of the papers and a consideration of the case, I would take it as a favor if you would have him a pension allowed, if you think he deserves it. You would confer a favor on the old man who I know stands in much need of assistance to live—Perhaps you may think it strange that this application is made to you instead of our representative A year ago I wrote to him on the subject, to which no attention was paid & fearing it might not again I have taken the liberty of troubling you—

Our Country affords no news worth your notice. We are all anxiously waiting to see what will be the situation of our Country when a determination of the tarif, Georgia case &c is made.

I should like to hear from you at any time.

Very respectfully
Yours &c

ROB H. BURTON

Beatties Ford N C
   April 5th
    Mail.)

[Addressed:]

The Honble. W. P. Mangum
Washington   Free
Cy

---

[146]John Kidd was a private in Carter's Company of the 10th Regiment of North Carolina Continentals. He enlisted on August 1, 1780, and served for eighteen months. Walter Clark (ed.), *N. C. State Records*, XVI, 1098.

WPM-LC

C. P. Mallett[147] to W. P. Mangum

FAYETTEVILLE. 4th April 1832

To/

The Honble

W. P. Mangum

Dear Sir

I received the copy of your speech which you were kind enough to send me and I send you herewith a copy of the Observer—in which it has been noticed, and I can assure you if the Editor of this paper did not feel his remarks to be true—they would never appear there—In renewing our acquaintance—since you have "The Honble" due to your calling—it brings to my mind an anecdote, I read not long since—One of the Judges on the English bench—recognised—in the person of a man. arraigned at the bar for some misdemeanor—an old acquaintance —and one with whom he had participated in early life in many a frolic—and may be other—bad tricks—after some remarks—he asked him. what had become—of such and such individuals who had associated with them—they are all hung may it please your Honor except you and me—

When I think of our associates in school boy wantonness—I find very. very few—who are maintaining even a decent stand in the world. and it often has the effect (and I hope it may produce it more and more) to humble me before God—Who.s restraining grace has made me to differ—when I had and have all within me which has ever sent a soul to Hell. I hope to have the pleasure of seeing you before this Session adjourns—

I am Respectfully.

C. P. MALLETT.

[Addressed:]

W. P. Mangum

147Charles P. Mallett was a police commissioner of Fayetteville in 1823. McIver, *N. C. Register*, 84.

WPM-LC

John Hall[148] to Willie P. Mangum

WARRENTON April 4th— 1832

D^r. Sir

I received your speech delivered in the Senate which you were good enough to enclose me, it is approved of much by all that I have heard speak of it—

I have Just read a piece in the Globe of the 31.st—of March, it is a discussion of the Cherokee question by an unknown person—curiosity leads me to know the name of that man, tis a question —that I do not pretend to understand but I am confident that writer is no stranger to it—it is in my estimation the ablest examination of it I have seen—the language is sober intelligent & Judicial—a certain other man in examining the subject must have got some of his words and imagery from the hot beds of Shakespear, excuse the liberty I take in asking you if you know the name of the author of the piece in the Globe of the 31st— of March—

I am with regard   Y^r. Obt. ser^t

JN HALL

Warrenton N° Car
4 April 1832
Mail - -

[Addressed:]

The Hon   Free
   Willie P. Mangum
      In Senate of the U States
         City Washington

WPM-LC

Robert B. Gilliam[149] to Willie P. Mangum

OXFORD, 5th April 1832

Dear Sir:

I address you on behalf of Mr. S. Forsythe & Mr. Henry W. Jones. I have agreed that your Statement of what passed be-

[148]See above, p. 10n.
[149]See above, p. 482.

tween you and the late Nicholas Jones, relative to Saml. Forsythe's becoming Bennett's security in his suit against Maben,
shall be received as evidence, without the trouble of taking your
deposition.—You will therefore confer a favor on those gentlemen, by making out as circumstantial a statement as your memory will permit & forward it to me, in time to reach Oxford, before our May Court.

I may take this occasion to thank you for your kindness in
sending the pamphlet containing your speech on the Tariff—And
may I not be permitted without indelicacy to say, that I read it,
not with satisfaction merely, but with pride, & ever with exulta-
tion. I have heard a number of persons speak of the effort, as
well those who are your acquaintances, as those who are not, &
with *but one solitary exception,* they speak of it in terms of un-
measured praise.—The exception I allude to, is a *tariffied* cox-
comb, whose habitation if he has any, is some distance North of
Mason's & Dixon's line. We begin to hope that old North Carolina, *modest* [&] *unpretending* as she is, will not always remain
in the back ground.—

I feel well satisfied, that if a bill, based upon the principle of
Mr. Clay's resolutions, or upon any thing akin to it, becomes the
law of the land, that *nullification,* or something more decisive &
efficient will become the order of the day in this part of the Country. I know not from what cause it proceeds, unless it be from a
spirit of desperation, but the fact is, that the people here would
prefer the tariff of '28, with all its abominations, to the *compromise* which Mr. Clay in his gracious condescension, has con-
cocted to allay the *discontents* (that is the word I believe) of the
South.—I trust that you will continue to raise your voice, to
warn our oppressors of the inevitable tendency of perseverance
in keeping up their ruinous policy—Every day the clamor of dissatisfaction grows louder, & the determination not to endure, becomes more settled & decisive.

At this time the most frequent subject of conversation & discussion, is the Georgia qu [torn] am at a loss to know how it
will end.—[Torn] appearances, it seems that the authorities of
[torn] resist the Mandate of the Supreme Cou[rt] [torn] the
shedding of blood. How is the quest[ion] [torn] adjusted? All
my feelings are on the [torn] [Geor]gia, but I cannot see how
she is to [torn] thority of the Court, without the exercise of
practical nullification—& then you know [torn] crumbles to
pieces, like a lump of loose [torn]

Hoping better things for the country, that [torn] to expect,
I remain with high reg[ard]
Your friend

Robt. B. Gi[lliam].

Hon. W. P. Mangum
    Washington.

[Addressed:]

    To
        The Hon: Willie P. Mangum   Oxford N. C.
        Washington City   Apl. 5.

WPM-LC

John Long to Willie P. Mangum

LONGS MILLS April 5th 1832

D Sir
    I have read the speech you sent me on Mr. Clay's resolutions.
I believe you have reasons sufficient to induce you to believe
that I have always been your friend in your political undertak-
ings I can therefore take the liberty of communicating my opinion of your remarks. As to the constitutionality of the Tariff. I
never doubted a moment and if I had it is too well settled by the
deliberate acts of Congress sanctioned by the people to raise it
as an objection now it is the expediency the people will look at
and nothing else they care not for the constitution if they like
the effects of the measure now what effects has it produced? has
it destroyed the rev[torn] (as we supposed it would) have articles of Necessity become cheaper or dearer? and if they were
no cheaper how much more does a common farmer pay under the
Tariff of 1828 than he did under the Tariff of 1816 (with which
all *appeared satisfied)* not a cent more on Salt, Sugar, Coffee,
Nails, Hats, Shoes, On Iron about the ¼ of a Cent [torn] that
in proportion; molasses double (now *reduced)* I admit the increased duty on molasses was the greatest tax No. Ca. ever paid
on any one article but who laid it, was it not her own representatives and those too who were most clamorous against the Tariff, if our Senators had voted against it it woud not have been
laid. But some of the delegation publicly said they would make

it as bad as they coud with a View to making the people mad.
Now I say that an ordinary farmer who perhaps raises a load of
flour to sell a little pork and some corn, is not necessarily Taxed
2/6 more under the law of 28 than he was in 16. and as to the
duty on laths and orther goods you may tell the people they pay
[torn] or 100 per. Cent duty they only want to know how much
their Coat costs them, they will then compare the price with
what they gave for a coat of the same quality in 24. It cant. be
denied but it will be found now at least 50 per. Cent cheaper,
wheather it be domestic or foreign they cant. tell, they dont.
know, they dont. care, its enough to know the fact that its
cheaper and as good.

I can assure you as far as my knowledge extends you are quite
mistaken in supposing the people of No. Ca. are so hostile to the
Tariff I have not conversed with a single individual on the subject who is opposed to it.[150] and you may rely on it in my humble
Opinion its the only System which can save the poorer class of
people from starvation and the remainder from insupportable
parish taxes. (Now you¹, say this is strange & extravigant) But
Sir perhaps you are not so well acquainted with poor folks as I
am I ask you how a poor Widow with ½ doz. small child[ren]
entirely dependant on her exertions is to even exist (education
out of the question) can she support them by her wheel and loom
I say she cannot if she works 16 hours in 24. and never sick : who
woud employ her Spun thread is now furnished from abroad for
a less sum than woud buy her provisions while she woud spin the
same amt. I say then her children must become chargeable to
the County for no person will or can afford to raise them for
their labor. Those in easy circumstances are apt to spurn at the
poor and indigent, but the common labourer who knows nothing
more than to labour and cant, get employment at that even at $5
pr. mo. I assure you is in a bad state this is the situation of
thousands as this time, and why is it so? because we are all engaged in aggracultural pursuits, consequently have reduced the
price of grain & cotton so low that no person can afford to hire
hands to cultivate either I woud this day rather give a man as
much Land as he coud cultivate rent free, then to hire him at 5$
a mo. find him, find him a horse plough &C— The farmer who
does his work with his own individual hand may barely live, but
if he hires or has it done by slave labor (which is infinitely

---

¹⁵⁰Long was from Randolph County where there was considerable home manufacturing.

worse) he must get in debt. You seem to depreciate the Idea of little girls being confined to labor in the factories this its true woud be horid to parent[s] in fluent circumstances, and at the first blush wor[se] then death to such children as have been accustomed to Idleness & Luxury, But it is not expected that many such woud be employed its those (and plenty of those there are) who woud prefer it to a worse situation, I do believe if there is not some employment offered to many of our citizens whereby they can be supported our parish Taxes will in time be insupportable. Then I say let us divide our labour be "customers to our customers" so that all can be more profitably employed. Its said the Tariff has reduced the price of cotton, the British by; way of retaliation won^t give us as much for it who can believe such stuff the British do as they always have done buy of us what they can^t. do without as cheap as they can. Raising cotton was once a profitable business (and never more so then it ought to have been for I contend no man can afford to raise cotton for less than $25 p^r Cwt.) But large Capitalists engaged in the business without stopping to inquire into the Value of their stock were content in raising it for much less in enormous quantities still they have gluted the Market this every body must know is the true cause; and that every bail of cotton manufactured in the U. S. must have some effect on the price abroad, I have frequently heard even members of Congress urge [a]s an objection to the Tariff that it woud prohibit [torn] goods and we shoud thereby be deprived of the revenue, Now if we coud get the revenue without paying for the goods there woud be something in it but before we receive this revenue we must pay 3 or 4 times the am^t. of it for the goods—This reminds me of a circumstance I once Witnessed; a man in the Town of Fayetteville put up his house & lot at auction it sold for $10-000 (which was much more than he expected) When he went to settle with the Auctioneer, whoes regular commissions was 5 p^r- Cent finding it amo[unted] to $500—he declared it woud ruin him to pay it and appeared quite dissatisfied that his property sold so high. Now Sir, in my humble Opinion the whole of Our Southern Opposition to the Tariff may be traced to the principle of Slavery I Verily believe if we had nor never had any slaves we shoud all been Tariff men before this time, and when we become convinced that slaves are not worth owning (and not untill then) we will dispose of them in some way "If the slave will not run a way from the master the master will from the slave["].] Our Southern planters have been accustomed to receive great sums of money by the Culture of Cotton their expenditures have been proportionate by gluting the market their income is greatly reduced the Value of their Lands & Negroes proportionably reduced they find their circumstances much changed, they hold their Lands & Negroes and are determined to do nothing but rais cotton indeed they can^t. do any thing better unless they woud adopt the Home System this they think they can^t. do because their Negroes know nothing but the raising of cotton. constantly complaining their Northern Neighbours are making all the money (and they are too) and yet refusing to enter into this profitable business with every advantage in their own hands; Yes I veryly believe there are many of the Northern manufacturers now quaking with fear that the System will be entered into throughout the U- S- [torn] ts just as popular as they woud wish it to be they are sufficiently incouraged to make money— let us growl as much as we may they know we will buy their goods. What did Webster tell us in 24 when discussing the Bill "those regularly engaged with sound capital needs no further protection pass the Bill and you will induce others to embark 'till we who now, oppose the measure will be instructed to ask still further protection" Sure enough it was so, (for this Webster has been called inconsistent). My individual opinion on the Tariff was always what it N[torn] is this my first circular will prove, but for it I was denounced and opposed by every politician [torn] the state 'till I was in some degree made to yield ([torn] I only regret) tho my faith was not changed, I woud now carry the principle further than perhaps any body else, I woud entirely preclude every foreign article of consumption that can be made or produced in this country; and as those which cannot are mostly articles of luxury I woud Tax them well—rather than admit any foreign goods which we have the means of making I woud support the govern^t. by direct Taxation.— do this send off the Negroes & the Union is safe, all who woud work coud be profitably employed and I am confident every article woud be better and therefore those engaged in farming woud be paid for their labour and all coud live comfortably there woud be no clashing of interests in different states to quarrel about. You say M^r. Clay does the President great injustice in supposing there were different impressions in the [torn] as regard his Tariff principles. You undoubtedly think as you say, but I know to the contrary I know it was the constant business of many of Jackson's friends previous to & since his

Election to impress it on the minds of the people that he was opposed to [t]he tariff and I further know that in many instances they succeeded yes you can find many who will now tell you they voted for him on that ground alone, this is not all I heard one [of] the Electors in a public speech say he knew Jackson to be opposed to the Tariff. in fact it must be admited he himself did lack candor on that Subject, I believe that was the true reason o[f] his leaving the Senate to prevent his views from being known on that subject.[151] One of his friends from Tenesee Electionered with me on that ground, told me he was Authorised to say Jackson had gone his *Neplus Ultra* on that subject (afterwards *denied* it) At the time Jackson was elected I cared but little about it, took part in the Election more th[an] to vote, I apprehended no evil from his adm[inis]tration, believed him to be Honest &C. coud see n[o] inducement for him to act incorrectly. But I must acknowledge I am disappointed and I do humbly conceive his administration has not on[ly] been a continual scene of confusion & mystery and entirely occasioned by such of his Own friends and himself as he choose to aid him,[152] But I say him and his active partizans have cherished and undeviatingly practiced on the most despotic unchariti [t o r n   ] ever avowed in any civilised Country I say he has struck a blow at the first principles for which our forefathers fought & Bled   The right of *free suffrage*   Yes he has punished hundreds for daring to vote their true sentim[ents] where woud such a principal lead to and the m[an] who woud practice upon it in the capacity of the great representative of the Nation acts unworthy of [torn] station. I will not undertake to trace his administra[tion] to me it appears to be replete with wrongs, he has [s]carcely left any thing undone calculated to render hi[s] administration contemptable. But he must be re-elected [torn] the party is gone if it were not for that he coud be dispensed with. Now is there a man in the world who really thinks Jackson a well qualifyed man to serve [torn] — dent another 4 years. You know Sir he never [torn] —able. and I was told a few weeks ago by Gov. Stokes that he was informed by an inmate of the Presidents own house that he was Very infirm and serious doubt were entertained of his lasting long &C. that the

---

[151]In the Senate in 1824 Jackson voted twenty-two times for amendments which supported the protectionists' position and only four times for lowering rates. Bassett, *Life of Jackson*, 344-345.

[152]Long became a strong Whig. He had served in Congress from 1821 to 1829 when Jackson came to power.

Election of Vice President was of much importance that it woud behove the party to stick to Van Buren &C. well if they expect V- B. to act as President why [n]ot elect him at Once—Oh *Party Party* what a [r]uinous monster. Altho I coud have intire confidence in H. Clay & J Sergent, I woud much rather see some persons Elected who had no party If the people coud only come to the determination of demolishing parties and act in concert so as to Elect Judge *Marshall* President and some clever fellow V- P. what a glorious movement. I do not condemn the Senate for rejecting V. B. tho I shoud have voted as you did [t o r n] on different principles. After the [torn] made by the Presd^t. thro. M^r. [t o r n] —ons were his Own. I woud have g[torn] him the whole responsibility, I do not see how the Senate drew the distinction between V. B. & L-McLean, after the Presidents avowal, but I suppose they did not believe the President. Now Sir I have sketched off this hetero[g]eneous Mass as Ideas occurred to me after reading [y]our speech not at all in an inteligable form or [sc]arcely so it can be understood. With an intention of [cor]recting and writing it over. But on a little reflection [torn] know its quite unnessary and perhaps worse then [torn], and that I am writing to an old friend & acqua[int-a]nce who knows how to make every allowance you must [k]now I consider you a friend or I woud not have written [so] frank. I have therefore determined on just sending this[?] [p]roof sheet, with a solemn injunction that you will not show it or speak of it to any person but burn it [as] soon as you have read or looked over it

Yrs [torn]
Jo[torn]

WPM-LC

J. G. A. Williamson to W. P. Mangum

WASHINGTON Sunday morning 15^t April 1832

Hon^l W. P. Mangum
  M. of the Senate
    Sir
      I called on you yesterday and subsequently found your senate door closed, therefore failed in seeing you, I leave here

to day for Ba[tm]- & Phile[a]——I called on Mr Livingston[153] and I am satisfied he *knows & feels* the importance of the suggestions made him on the subject of Venezuela, but from his immense vocations they may soon loose their effect—the only difficulty that seemed to present itself in sending an agent as proposed or rather superading it to the Consulate at LaGuayra, is how or in what way the same, is he to be paid—I am *clearly satisfied an agent will be sent,* and in a conversation yesterday morning with Mr Archer C. of the C. of F. R.[154] house of R—, I am now confirmed in the opinion above that the Gov[t]. will send such an agent — With this impression then it would seem to me my claims[155] might be very justly pushed upon the President & Secre[y]., and I feel well satisfied with your influence *they cannot deny* them—Your colleague Mr Brown very kindly & frankly offers me his weight in this matter and all of the *house* to whom I have named the subject—give me the same assurance—Can I therefore ask you to push my claims with my other friends in this affair, let whatever new turn the Gov[t]. may take in this matter—I am clearly satisfied a great effort will be made in your house from its general temper to break down the appropriation to Mr. Moore[156] as minister to Colombia & insert in its place two Charges, one to New Grenada & the other to Venezuela—Should such a thing take place of which I can scarcely believe, let me ask you not to forget me—

I am solicitous to reside in that Country (Venezuela) one year more, and then return to my *native country,* and cannot succede In getting the Gov[t]. to sallar[y] [?] my office and remove it to Caracas & superadd more duties than consular, I have but little inclination to return again—*But I am perfectly satisfied some kind of political agent will be sent to Venezuela*—and in that event should it not be me, I will most certainly hand the Gov[t]. my commission—

I am your Friend

J. G. A. WILLIAMSON

P. S. I should be glad to hear from you to Phil[a]- of the movements on the appropriation Bill—

W—

[153]Edward Livingston was Secretary of State from 1831 to 1833.
[154]William Segar Archer was in the House of Representatives from 1820 to 1835. At this time he was chairman of the Committee on Foreign Relations.
[155]Williamson was again seeking an appointment as consul.
[156]Thomas P. Moore was minister to Colombia from 1829 to 1833. *Biog. Dir. of Cong.,* 1330.

WPM-LC

Charles Callaghan[157] to Willie P. Mangum

PHILA^a. 16th—April 1832

Sir

I have read your speech published in the Globe of 14th.. Ins^t. and consider it a most able exposure of the oppressive operation of the existing Tariff of protection—but I am of opinion there does exist a nunfavorable balance of Trade,—occasioned by the excessive circulation of Bank paper in what has been termed the North East of the Confederacy—this paper is the measure of value for all we receive from foreign nations which creates the prices on which the importer founds his calculation—it has been proved that its increase of circulation enhanced prices and that its contraction reduced the value of all merchandise—hence as there has been a gradual augmentation of our paper circulation for the last two years, prices have been in that condition as to warrant an import of more foreign labor than we can find of our own to pay with estimating all the freights & profits which may be supposed to have been made—the difference is a debt or what is termed by merchants a balance of Trade against us—

It is estimated that our debt to England at the present moment is to wit

Amount to be remitted for Sales of Merchandise

	$20.000.000
Bank U States Stock held there	9.000.000
U States Loan held there	10.000.000
State Stocks held there	5.000.000

44. million dollars

It is the shipment of our Stocks of which no return is made to the treasury department which prevents a knowledge of the sum we run in debt to England, owing to the large amount of paper money sustained by the annual collection of $30. million of impot Taxes by the aid of the Banking system—The scarcity of money now existing arises from this balance of Trade because those who have to pay that portion of it now due have ascertained they can pay it at the cheapest rate with Specie, or Bills of Exchange when the premium does not exceed 9 pCent—but

---

[157] A Philadelphia Whig leader who corresponded with Mangum and W. A. Graham.

as bills of Exchange arise from the shipment of merchandise they have been exhausted and are now scarce at 10 pCent prem⁰. —nor can they be created because our Cotton 1ᶜ. & Stocks estimated here in our paper currency, when realized in the currency of Europe will loose 15 a 20 pCent—therefore our debts will be paid in Specie as far as our Ten or 15 million of Dollars will go, unless in the operation of exporting it the Banks contract their issues to such a limit as will cause merchandise to fall to such a price as will cause its shipment in preference—this measure on the part of the Banks will so reduce the value of the assets of their debtors, as not only to loose their money, but to cause the foreign creditor to receive a dividend on the principle—

I am of opinion that under a low rate of Tariff and a sound Currency, composed of half paper & half coin we should sell more to foreigners than we should buy, and that Europe would become in debt to us and the balance of Trade in our favor—but this may never be the case so long as the national currency is in the hands of 350 Corporations who are paid by Law for excessive issues.

I am with great respect
Your most obᵗ Ser.
CHARLES CALLAGHAN

This thing of a balance of Trade may be confined to nations who make use of paper money for currency—
I refer to Bueynos Ayres where their paper Dollar estimated or reduced to Silver coin is worth only 15 cents.

Brazil   50 cts

Veneuzela   75 cts

Our own Country where we have 100 million, paper money and but 15 millions of Coin
The currency of Mexico is Gold & Silver—
Spain has no balance of Trade against her because her currency is Gold & Silver—
France has no balance of Trade against her because her currency is 90 parts coin & 10 parts paper.

[Addressed:]

Honˡ. Wilie P. Mangum
U S Senate
Washington City

Willie P. Mangum to Charity A. Mangum

WASHINGTON CITY
Thursday morning 19th April 1832.

My dear Love.

I am tolerably well. I am not yet quite well of cold, but much better—The weather has been wet, cloudy & rather cold for several days—I hope it will be warm soon—The Spring I learn is very backward with you. When I shall get home it is impossible to say, some talk of July. I·still think it will be early in June— My Colleague has gone home to Caswell. I mean Mr. Brown— Mr. Alexander[158] went to Warren to see his Wife—& so you see, I am almost the only one who stands at his post—I want to go home very much. But the business is not of a character to allow of my absence.

I hope my Love you remain well & also our children—Kiss them for me. Poor patty must not forget Father. — My Dear Love remember me often, and always believe me

Your affectionate husband

W. P. MANGUM

Mrs. Charity A. Mangum—
[Addressed:]

Mrs. Charity A. Mangum

———

Willie P. Mangum to Charity A. Mangum

WASHINGTON CITY
Sunday morning 22nd. April 1832.

My dear Love,

Your last letter mentioned that you had been disappointed in receiving my letter at the regular time—I don't know how it happened, I suppose by some fault of some Post Master on the route, for I have never missed writing every week.—When your letters have been delayed, it has caused me so much anxiety that I have been unwilling to give you a similar cause.

---

[158]Mark Alexander of Virginia.

I am tolerably well, but it does seem that I cannot get entirely well of cold—The immense Stone building—the Capitol, has so much chilliness about it, & the rooms for business are kept so warm that between them, I have almost constantly had more or less cold. The weather now is warmer, thought not as warm as I could wish. We have had a week of cloudy weather, a good deal of rain—& not a fair day until yesterday. This morning is again cloudy, & looks as if it would rain.—

When I shall get away from here is entirely uncertain—Congress seem determined to do no business scarcely—Both houses have been engaged about the most insignificant things for several weeks—I still think we shall break off without having done much, though more than half those you meet say we shall be here to take the 4th July dinner—I don't think so. The weather will be so hot—& the Congress halls so disagreeable, that I think they will break off—I hope My Love, that you spend your time agreeably as you can—You must not have a *great ball* before I can get home.—It would not look well to be so enjoying yourself without giving me an invitation.—When is the time you *calculate* to send out tickets.—

Last night I had the sweetest love dream that I have had in a dozen years.—I would tell you, if I were not ashamed—But here it is—I thought you & I were together in a beautiful garden, with a great many beautiful flowers & green leaves, & walks, with pretty borders of green grass. that you were sitting on a seat fixed for visitors. that I was walking before you.—It seemed to me, that you & I had been seperated some how, I could not tell how. yet I had such an impression—my heart was full of love & seemed as if it claimed you, but still I felt it necessary to court you again, though I had all along some confused idea that I had a claim to you.—I took a seat near you & in due form opened a courtship—after I had talked some time—I thought you turned to me with the sweetest look, took one of my hands in both yours, and said, "do you not know that you are dearer to me than all the world."—I was never more in love in my life. I threw my arms about you, & kissed you, over & over again— after a little I thought you said that was not quite right. I said, are you not mine?—you said with a smile, I will be—The next I remember we were walking side by side, one of my arms around your waist & one of yours around my waist.—I never in real life felt a more thrilling freshness of love—or felt more happy in the idea that it was returned—I even now remember with a thrill of pleasure, my feelings as I thought you turned to me, took my hand, & asked me if I did not know you loved me better than all the world—

This is a dream—But my Love, it is also reality, for though in real life, the scenes of our loves are never so enchanting— yet the heart can feel it in our poor home as well as in the courts of Princes—& better too—My dream did but little justice to poor little Patty & Sally I never once thought of them. You must give them a kiss for father & tell them to be good children, & not forget their father. If he did not dream of them he often thinks of them.

My dear Love I never wanted to see you more than I now do. May God bless & preserve you in tranquility & happiness—& that when we meet as I trust we shall in health, that our loves may be as warm, as fresh & delightful as was mine in that beautiful garden.

God Bless you My dear & beloved wife

WILLIE P. MANGUM

[Addressed:]

Mrs. Charity A. Mangum
Red Mountain
North Carolina

———

WPM-NC

Petition of Will. H. Haywood et als

[April 23, 1832.]

To the Post Master General of the United States.

Your petitioners who are Citizens of Raleigh in North Carolina & of Wake County in said State respectfully represent that they believe the publick good calls for some changes in the running of the mail stages from the City of Raleigh to Salisbury by the way of Pittsboro & Ashborough—the route is numbered in the published contracts 2143.—

The mail stage on this route arrives here upon the present plan *twice* a week and leaves here twice a week only. Leaving here only twice a week & the means of information to the people in *west* from the Country *North* of this City is detained for several days—further the main line of Stages coming through the Eastern part of our State from Newbern arrives here upon the arrangement lately made *thrice* a week and this western line failing to connect itself with that makes the improvement valueless to the whole Western part of our State—Also it not infrequently happens that passengers & mails coming by the Stages from North South or East are necessarily detained from 2 to 4 days at this place

If the arrangements of your department to advance other publick interests will not forbid the expenditure of increasing the times for arrival & departure of the mail Stages before referred to—Your memorialists respectfully recommend that the Contractor on route No 2143. be directed to run a mail Stage *thrice* a week from Raleigh to Salisbury via Pittsboro & Ashborough and that the times of its arrival & departure at & from this place be made to correspond with the departure & arrival of the Stage which comes from Newbern to this place—an additional convenience will be secured upon this change to all our Merchants who reside in the Western part of North Carolina—They will not be detained here at all on their journey to the North, for by the plan we here suggest the Western Stage can be made to arrive at this place every second day in time to take a Stage to the North.—

Your Memoralists confidantly refer you to the Representatives from the Western part of our State for information in the premises and particularly for the strong claims which the increasing wealth & population of that part of North Carolina furnish in aid of these suggestions.

Raleigh N. Caro. 23ʳᵈ.. April 1832.

Will H. Haywood Jr[159]	Richard Smith
Jo. Gales & Son	W. W. Miller
W. J. Whoon	Bu Daniel
Wᵐ. Hill	Jno. B. Muse
Lawrence & Lemdy	C. S. Selman
Robert Cannon	Geo. W. Haywood
B. S. King	Robᵗ. H. B. Brazill
Th. S. West	D. Lindeman
Willie Jones	R. Tucker

---

[159]Most of those who signed this petition were prominent citizens of Raleigh. Will H. Haywood, Jr., for instance, was a future United States Senator.

Chas. Manley
Tho Fobles
C. Dewey
Mm Mcpheeters—
James Litchford
J. C. Stedman
J. Peace
Robert Harrison
James Newbon
Patridge & Handford
Will: Peck

Theo. Hunter
Wm P. Hinton
M. Cooke
John O Parke
Bernard Dupuy
Alfred Williams
H H Cooke
J Coman
Thos G. Scott

WPM-LC

E. B. Smith[160] to Willie P. Mangum

HALIFAX, May 4 1832

Dear Sir

I enclose to you the petitions and affidavits of Robt L Whitaker[161] and Jethro [Harper] who pray to be placed upon the list of pensioners of the United States. Mr Whitaker is a half brother of Judge Norwood and a highly respectable man— Harper is an obscure individual and very poor. I have known both the gentlemen for many years and have no doubt of the truth of their statements and those who have deposed in their favour. As these gentlemen are constituents of Gov. Branch I would have forwarded the papers to him but for his absence from Washington at this time. Be pleased to lay them before the proper authority and let me know the result. The petitions are rather badly drawn, but in copying them I did not feel myself at liberty to make alterations or additions.—

You will see from the papers that Will P. Williams has been chosen to represent this electoral district in the Baltimore Convention—He is said to be a good Van Buren man but goes to the convention untrammeled

Respectfully yr. obt. Servt.

E. B. SMITH

Hon'ble W. P. Mangum

---

[160]E. B. Smith was clerk of the superior court in Halifax County.
[161]A private in the Revolution, he was placed on the pension list of 1835. Walter Clark, (ed.), *N. C. State Records*, XXII, 90.

[Addressed:]

To
The Honourable Willie P. Mangum
City of Washington

[Endorsed:]

Senate Chamber—7th. May 1832.

Mr. Edwards.[162]

Inclosed are two cases for pension. You will oblige me by having them as early examined as may be convenient. & let me know the result.

Yr obt Sert

W. P. MANGUM

———

WPM-LC

J. G. A. Williamson to John S. Menkin

PHIL 6th May 1832.

Mr John S Menkin [or Minckin][163]

Sir

I have been waiting with considerable impatience to hear from you and your movements.

The note I gave you for Sec^ty McLane I felt great anxiety to get an answer it is of much importance to me, because it is so ultimately conneted with my purse as well as character as counsel at LaGuayra—How do you come on and what are you about, can you move the waters—I trust you will be able to do so—What says the old man of [the] white house, so much behind [torn] best man in Washington, to aff—[torn] you can do more than [torn] the rest—

[torn]   Your friend

J. G. A. WILLIAMSON

[Addressed:]

Mr. John S. Minckin
(Washington City

---

[162]James L. Edwards was commissioner of pensions.
[163]Unable to identify.

WPM-LC

Willie P. Mangum to Charity A. Mangum

WASHINGTON CITY,
Saturday Night 15 Minutes before
Midnight, the 12th. May 1832.

My dear Love.

I have just returned from the great falls of the Potomac between sixteen & eighteen miles from the city, and being very much fatigued, I have determined to write you a line to night, fearing that I may not rise early enough in the morning to write by the mail now so early—I am in perfectly good health, & have increased in flesh to a weight greater than for the last 18 months.—I have got clear of my cold & cough, & the warm weather has been most favorable to me.—A party was made up yesterday, (the senate having adjourned over until Monday) to go up the Cheasepeake & Ohio Canal to the great Falls of the Potomac.

Two boats went up carrying about 200 persons, male & female—The day has been fine & clear & warm.—We dined at a Tavern at the end of our Trip, and a little after 4 O-clock set out on our return; arrived at Georgetown at ten OClock & then took a stage for Capitol Hill, a distance of three miles.—We were delayed on our return, by accident happening at one of the locks of the canal.—I have been a good deal amused during the day, & was especially gratified in viewing the rugged scenery at the Falls—I notwithstanding felt melancholy, & almost constantly thought of home, & the dear objects of my affection.—I begin to feel the strongest anxiety to set out for home, but the prospect is yet distant.—It is impossible to form any correct opinion as to the time of the adjournment of Congress—Not one of the several of the most important subjects has been taken up.—Both parties seem to be afraid to approach the Tariff.—The question is of immense moment. all feel that it is so, and as the very worst spirit prevails, each party seems apprehensive of the fatal consequences of a false movement on the subject.—

I fear that the 20th June is the earliest period that any prospect exists of getting off.—It may be earlier—but I think it is more probable that it will be later.—

I hope My Dear Love, that you feel easy under it, and endeavour to keep your mind quiet & tranquil.—I trust My Dear.

that if your Confinement shall happen before I get home, that you will go safely through it—Indeed I have the fullest confidence that it will be so.—Give Father's kiss to his children—& always feel My Dear Love, that my heart & my affections constantly turn from the Glossy appearences of this gay & heartless world, to our humble home, & that I feel that there exists all that is most dear to me, as well as most loyal & true to me.— May God bless My Love—often think of me—& believe me your most affectionate husband.

WILLIE P. MANGUM

[Addressed:]

Mrs. Charity A. Mangum
Red Mountain
North Carolina

WPM-LC

Willie P. Mangum to Charity A. Mangum

WASHINGTON CITY
Thursday morning 24th. May 1832

My dear Love.

It is now only three days short of six months since I left you and home.—This day eight years ago I turned my back upon Washington for home after what was then deemed, an extremely long session—I am yet wholly unable to state the time when Congress will adjourn—It will be I think, at least a month from this time—The most general opinion is, that it will be about the 3rd or 4th of July—I have no hope that I can get home before your Confinement[164]—an event that I naturally look to with anxiety, but with hope and confidence.—I do not indeed feel any apprehension.—I don't think that you are ever likely to have a dangerous birth— A great deal depends upon a peculiar constitution & habit of body, which always shews itself more or less at every birth— and in your cases nothing has ever appeared calculated to beget apprehension — take good care of yourself, My dear Love—be of good heart and cheerful spirits—and always cherish in your heart the belief of your husband's constant &

---

[164]Mary Sutherland Mangum was born July 8, 1832.

tender affection & solicitude for you; that you are dearer to his heart and affections than all the world besides, and feeling a firm reliance on the Ruler of Heaven & earth, you will pass through with firmness & safety— The most of people do not regard such an event with any sort of apprehension— and if I loved you less tenderly, I should feel less anxiety— But My Love, you are not only necessary to my happiness, but also to the virtue & well being of our dear little children,— You owe it to us all to preserve equanimity & cheerfulness, & may God protect & sustain you in body & mind, and enable us to meet again with hearts full of affection.—

You will of course make the necessary preparations and you must have the best attendance you can get.— And somebody ought to be in readiness to send for help if it should be necessary—

I should think Mrs. Leathers would be the best you can get, if she can be procured— You had best have some one to stay with you, if you can.—

I write in haste—thinking you may send in the middle of the week to the Post office—and if so you will get this.—

I am in very good health—I have not been in better for six or eight years— I have been careful of myself & of habits almost intirely regular— Since I got rid of my cough, which was caused by the extreme severity of the winter & too much care of myself, I have been very well— Tell Fathers children they must be good—give them my kiss—

God bless you my Love, Think often of your husband, affectionately & kindly, as yours most affectionately

WILLIE P. MANGUM

[Addressed:]
   Mrs. Charity A. Mangum
    Red Mountain
    North Carolina

Willie P. Mangum to Duncan Cameron[165]

SENATE CHAMBER 24th. May 1832

My dear Sir.

I suppose it will be agreeable to you to be informed that your

---

[165]The original is in the Cameron Papers, University of North Carolina.

brother John A. Cameron Esqr.[166] has this moment been unanimously confirmed by the Senate as Judge of the Western district of Florida, that is to say Pensacola. The salary is now $2300 p^r. annum. I have been in correspondence with him this winter, and have recently seen a Gentleman from Vera Cruz, being a member of a mercantile house in which Maj^r. Cameron resides.—This gentleman brought me a letter of introduction from whom I learnt much of the revolutionary state of the Country and the disastrous influence of that unsettled condition upon the profits of the consulship.—Your brother's condition in every way undesirable, whether in regard to the emolument, or the insalubrity of the position: & but for the pay he receives as a political agent, his compensation would be wholly incompetent to enable him to live decently and comfortably.

Major Cameron's letters to me have borne strong evidence of his dissatisfaction with his situation; and his friends here have been anxious to avail themselves of the earliest occasion to place him in a more eligible situation.—It was believed that the vacancy on the Bench at Pensacola, presented a favorable one, and the President was induced to make the nomination.—

The United States Bank question, for renewal is now before Congress. I mean the Senate, & will pass both branches—I think it will be vetoed—It will ultimately be approved in the event of Jackson's election (of which but few entertain any doubt) and the passage of it again after the next election—I think it to be regretted that it is now pressed—Political considerations however will urge it — & the danger lies, in the effect the veto may have, backed by the popularity of Gen. J. upon the passage of the Bill hereafter.

The Tariff will be modified it is believed; and it is hoped the modification will be of a character to tranquillize, to a great extent, the excitement existing in the South. Congress will not adjourn probably before the 3rd or 4th July — I write in great haste & simply to state the fact of your brothers appointment to the bench —

Be pleased to present me respectfully to M^{rs}. Cameron, & accept Dear Sir, for yourself the assurance of my entire respect & regard

WILLIE P. MANGUM

[166]See above, p. 260n.

WPM-LC

Duncan Cameron to Willie P. Mangum

ORANGE N. C. June 3rd 1832

My dear Sir,

The last mail brought me your esteemed Letter of the 24th ulto.

I am much gratified by the information it gave me of my Brother's appointment to the office of a Judge in the territory of Florida — and am greatly obliged by your friendly agency in the attainment of an object so important to, and desirable by himself his family and friends.

I regret to learn from your Letter that the President will probably put his *veto* on the Bill for renewing the Charter of the Bank U. States, in the event of its passing both houses of Congress—as far as I understand them—the *best* Interests of the U. States demand a *prompt* renewal of the Charter—delay (after it has passed in Congress) will produce pecuniary embarrassments exceeding in extent and degree all that can *now* be anticipated.—If the President will at some time hereafter approve the Bill—he ought to do it at *this* time, disregarding all political considerations, or the necessity of political parties—it is a subject so *deeply* affecting the general welfare—that it should be regarded by itself *only*.

I have seen and read all the Reports made by the Committee of investigation[167]—but have not seen the *documents*—if you have a copy of them to spare, I should like to get it.

All here remember you kindly and respectfully—and I am with great regard,

My dear Sir

Yrs. mo: truly

DUN: CAMERON

Stagville N C
    4 June

[Addressed:]

The Honble.
    Willie P. Mangum Esq.
        U. States Senate.
            Washington City

---

[167]See above, p. 516n.

WPM-LC

W. Montgomery to Willie P. Mangum

ALBRIGHTS N. C. June 6th 1832.

My Dear Sir

Our Court produced 6 candidates your Brother,[168] Mr. Mebane,[169] J. Allison, & J. Stockart Doctor Smith[170] and Myself In the Senate, & I Learn that Doctor Craig[171] Will. Be a Candidate in the Commons there is warm work pending Between doctor Smith and Me, He Has Made the attempt, as I Expected to Rally the Clay Men against Me, In private, but with the Exception of Joshua Johnson, He Has Failed Henry and George Hurdle was Hard pressed to go But they are My warmest Friends, at this time it seems to be generally Admitted that Allison is Certain, there Seems to be no general Expression about the others, only that Mebane will Be Hard pushed if Elected. We Had a Meeting, and Done No more than appoint 5 delegates, to attend a State Convention the 19th Inst. at Raleigh, Priestly, Waddle, Mabane Allison, and Walker Anderson, were appointed and are to Report to an adjourned Meeting at Hillsborough, on the 4th of July, where something deffinite relative to the vice P. Will be Done, What shall We Do, I Cannot go for V. B. Without a Certainty that He Will go for a Modification of the Tariff. and that is the general Expression. Here Barber[172] seems to be the promanent candidate at this time, I Fear We Will be Cheated out of the Election By the people. I understand Thomas Little was at Baltimore and He is pledged to go for Van B. you may Have seen Him, We are all Confusion. and the Clay Men stiring it, all the[y] Can and are In High Spirits at Least as regards there prospects for the vice P. I am Willing to Make some sacrifice, for Jacksons safety did I now How to do so. I am anctious to Hear from you, and shall Hold Myself and all under My Controul, uncommi[tt]ed, until the Last Moment, to wait your Advice, as to the proper Course for us to pursue, I think from what I Can Hear that, the Eastern part of N. C. Will Nearly all go against V. B., I now But Little about the West, But I think it is quite probable that, the Convention at Raleigh the 19th Int. Will nomi-

---

[168]Priestley H. Mangum.
[169]James Mebane.
[170]James S. Smith.
[171]John Craig.
[172]Philip P. Barbour.

nate Barber or some other Man than V. B.[173] you Will get the result of that Meeting, In time to write Me Before the Meeting at Hillsborough which I wish you to Do.

I understand Mr. Shab [torn] is gone on to West Point, it is all well, it would Have Been greatly against Me to Have went on, you May Continue the application For Me. if you think proper, your with great regard and esteem

W. MONTGOMERY

Albright N. C.
   June 6, 1832

   [Addressed:]

Honr. Willie P. Mangum Esq
Senator from N. C. In the
Congress of the United
Washington City

WPM-LC

Francis Jones[174] to Willie P. Mangum

[7 June 1832]

Dear Sir;

After defering my fixed determination from time to time, I have now undertaken to write to you. I thank you for the Documents &C. sent me, & particularly for your Speech on the Tariff. It is a bold & manly defence of Southern interests. I hear of the late speech of Mr. [George] McDuffie, on that subject that it has given great offence to the Ultra Tariffites. I see through the Papers, that the North & East are greatly dissatisfied with Mr. McLanes' Bill.[175] I further see that most of the South is equally so. Can this vexed question be so settled, as to reconcile the two parties & sustain the Union? I fear it cannot. I fear the friends of the Union have great Cause to believe that the Cupidity of the Northern Manufacturers will risque the worst. The Union must

---

[173]The Anti-Van Buren leaders held a state convention in Raleigh in June 1832. Orange was the only western county represented. The convention praised Jackson and condemned Van Buren. Philip P. Barbour was nominated for vice president. Herbert D. Pegg, "The Whig Party in Ante-Bellum North Carolina," (Ph.D. Thesis at the University of North Carolina, 1933. A typescript copy is in the library at the University of North Carolina), 5.

[174]Francis Jones, a justice of the peace from Warren County. McIver, *N. C. Register*, 40.

[175]In March 1832, McLane as Secretary of the Treasury presented to the Chairman of the Committee on Manufactures in the House of Representatives a tariff bill which would repeal the bill of 1828 and after March 3, 1833, would limit the revenue bill to government expenditures. The act was designed to reduce the tariff revenue to $12,000,000 a year and to distribute the rates so as to afford adequate protection to all great national interests involved. This became after some changes the Adams Bill or the Tariff of 1832. McMaster, *Hist. of the People of the U. S.*, VI, 137-138.

(if possible, on honourable terms) be preserved: Esto perpetua. I have been reading, this morning the Debate, in the Senate, on the Bill for rechartering the U. S. Bank—I am pleased to think that it will pass with many modifications. I should be gratified to have your Opinion on these two questions, as to the ultimate course that will be adopted. I am a constant reader of the proceedings of Congress & can, with truth, say that I am proud of the Course taken by you. I have written to our Friend, Genl. M. T. Hawkins, to try & get my Son, John M. Jones, a birth in the Military Academy, at West.-Point. I also informed him, that I should write you on the subject. As it is a public Institution & free for N. C. as well as other States, I hope you will see no impropriety in aiding me. I doubt not your willingness unless the request be improper.

A Member of your body, The honorouble G. M. Bibb,[176] is an old School mate, room rate, & sometimes bedfellow of mine. Will you present him my best respects, & tell him I read his Speeches & notice, his votes with great pleasure. I yet have the *kindest feelings* for him, & should be pleased to hear from him, & much more so to see him.

You will see through the News-papers that *our people* are many of them dissatisfied with the nomination of M. V. Buren, as V. President. I believe that the pack was stocked. I do not believe that the people of N. C. are transferable. Cujum pecus? I fear you will be disappointed in geting a puppy from my slut, in time. She has been in heat, but will have no whelps. As a planter you must have heard of the cold & wet weather of last month, so unfavourable to the cotton crop. Indeed the present Month, so far, is no better; It has been almost cold enough for frost, for a week, & the cotton looks very badly. I shall be much pleased to hear from you, & believe your sincere Friend

FRS. JONES
June 7, 1832

Monroe N. C.
7 June
mail

[Addressed:]   Honorable Willie P. Mangum
U. S. Senate
Washington- City

---

[176]George Motin Bibb went to Hampden-Sydney and William and Mary colleges in the 1790's. He was United States Senator from 1811 to 1814 and from 1829 to 1835. From 1844 to 1845 he was Secretary of Treasury. *Biog. Dir. of Cong.*, 698.

WPM-LC

Richard Hines[177] to Willie P. Mangum

HERMITAGE near
SPARTA N⁰. Cᵃ. 20th June 1832

Hon: Willie P. Mangum
     Dear Sir

My friend W. R. Swift[178] esq. the bearer of this expecting to spend some time in the District I take pleasure in introducing him to your acquaintance in him you will find a gentleman of extensive information amiable feelings and high character and although his is not a native a real N⁰ Carolinian in heart
—his acquaintance in this part of the State is both extensive and
respectable and his information various and correct on the subject of the Vice Presidency he is with a very large majority of
this section of the State for Mr. Barber—

Although a private I have been an anxious looker on of men
and things at Washington and I must confess I do not see in the
present excited state of the Country and parties how the great
question of the Tariff is to be settled so that all will submit none
can doubt that a large portion will dissatisfied—In your speech
on that subject you certainly expressed the feelings and opinions
of a very large majority of the people of this State and whether
they will be satisfied with a reduction short of the actual necessities of the Government is more than I can say—The contest in
this State for the Vice Presidency will be warm and bitter and
judging from present appearances likely to produce great political changes both in the State and individuals as all other parties
will probably soon be merged in the Tariff or anti-tariff and Van
Burin or Barber what will be the result God only knows but hope
it will all end in our Countrys good—

With Great Respect
I am most truly
Your Obt. Servt

RICHD HINES

[Addressed:]

Hon. Willie P. Mangum
Col: Swift)   Washington D C

---

[177]See above, p. 222n.
[178]He was actively working for Calhoun's election as president in 1824. He lived in Beaufort, N. C.

WPM-LC

W. H. Haywood, Jr., to Willie P. Mangum

RALEIGH 22ⁿᵈ. June 1832.

Dear Sir/.

I have rec'd yours dated 31 May. and I thank you for it & the trouble you have taken on yourself to procure for me the documents I need—they are not yet rec'd but I hope they will be in due time

I am totelly unfit for the business of politics I believe—that my views of correct legislative duty will not consist with remaining a member of Assembly you will perceive by a perusal of a circular which I have distributed here. a copy I enclose to you for the mere gratification of your curiosity.[179]—

If my letter to you. which I always write without much reflexion—conveyed the idea that Mr M L's plan[180] for an adjustment of the Tariff ought to be *entirely satisfactory for all time to come.* then I was unfortunate in the selection of my words.— To my mind no doubt presents itself that the real question we have to decide is whether there shall be mutual concession or disunion—for the latter alternative North Carolina is not prepared & I trust in God she never will be. We have not in these parts the slightest relish for it and in South Carolina we are furnished with strong evidence that a dozen men may wield the weapons of popular discontent at the outset of a political strife —which will soon become too potent for the feeble grasp of the agents by whom it was called into existence—God grant it may not hurl them with all against whom it was first employed in the profoundest abyss of destruction. In *no event*—for *no cause* must we consent to shiver the beautiful Vase! We have now laid hold on it & threatened to toss it against the hard rock of *nullification* until the pride of some ambitious men may prompt them to hurl it regardless of consequences. Depend on it my Dear Sir the patriot might stand forth and fight with his *friends.* We must talk to *discourage* this dangerous faction in So Carolina—not to insult & make desperate — not to cheer & countenance them either.—Our dangers are not unlike those of a family of brothers —one or two has become dissatisfied—jealous of nearly all the rest. the language of defiance is begun to be used on both sides— a brother or two who are out of the scrape & have taken sides

---

[179]The copy is not available.
[180]See above note 175 of this chapter.

with neither *must intercede for the sake of the whole* . . 'Tis much better to 'endure the ills we have than fly to others we know not of'—Under the influence of these feelings (and they are those of nearly *all* our people) I have thought it best—a source of satisfaction even (in that sense *'satisfactory')* to adopt the plan which Mr M L. report suggests—I have not the material or the love of politics which will enable me to wade thro: the details. but 'tis a peace offering & I am decidedly of opinion that we should heartily embrace it.—The same faults which afflict Mr. Clay's party—to a degree have visited the Calhoun party—they are 'Ultra'—and this is very far from my notions of correct American politics—The "American System" truly is this —*"Be moderate in your measures & politics"* . . Good God! Can it be possible that the American States men will so far forget the true principles of this really american feeling as to exasperate our people & force them to a fight for *paper* blessings— when all the solid advantages of real liberty are enjoyed by every individual in the Union!—There is not to my mind a finer picture of real moral sublimity any where recorded on the pages of mere uninspired history than the forbearance which the Bostonians practiced to the British troops immediately preceding the Battle of Lexington—they waited for the shedding of blood — though the whole country had declared for the cause of Mass[ts]..! they stood with arms in hands—quietly rec'd the sneering mandate of a pround commander—"Rebels disperse"—yet they fired not—nor fled—yet when the British troops had sacrificed a few martyrs to the great cause—they rallied and fought a fight of resistance that will live forever—but I hope no longer than the *Union & Govern[t]..* which were cemented by the blood of this same sacrifice.—Shall the chivalrous—patriotic South Show less greatness—and less forbearance to their *OWN LAWS* & those who are charged with the execution of them?—The Yankees did not begin to fight because they were *vexed*—but they fought - - - I forbear — these are comments that would better commend themselves to the minds of a friend who was disaffected—I do not believe you to be such a one & therefore I desist —

It is not possible for any govern't to be established [that] will be free of injustice real or supposed—for governments are the creatures of restless—imperfect men. And there never was that Govern[t]- which did not manifest the ambition—or cupidity of a ruling power.—I cannot agree with you. I am not willing to be persuaded that "ours has degenerated into a joint stock Company for many purposes & the distribution of patronage"— Yours is a warm temperament—you have been mixing in the agitation of party strife & political discussions—you have not given play to the natural goodness of your own disposition even —much more your station is not one that allows the cultivation of that greatest personal & political virtue—Charity—(I do not say so in reproof—for I have neither the right or disposition to venture it to you.) But it is a natural infirmity—Have you not oftentimes looked back upon the opinions you had formed of the motives of men as witnesses or suiters & been surprized at the errors into which your judgment had been betrayed by your excited feelings?—My good friend a man at W. City—whose whole soul is wrapped up in the consideration of the great publick measures agitating in that body is not qualified (—pardon the liberty of a friend—) to judge accurately of the motives & conduct of his associates—The govern^t. that is conducted on the principles of his party he thinks safe & sound—if it be on those of his opposing party he very honestly persuades himself 'tis corrupt.—Allow me to enquire Is there a *Senator* in our Congress who on any great question has been yet convinced by argument in that Hall to change his opinions? Has not each one gone to his place with the dogged purpose to sit out argument—resist conviction & do as he has all along thought before? Is not change of opinion now denounced as the crime of *deliberate inconsistency?!!* Take an example. Have not we of the South held up to publick *execration* as a base & dishonest trafficker—a contemptible chuckler to party power several distinguished citizens of the country who have first *opposed* & then *supported* the Tariff? Is that man alive who does not dread such denunciations— if he be he does not merit confidence for he is insensible! Thus do we not denounce the man who changes his views—*Why then? how is it* that we will argue to persuade men to come over to *our* sides! *We have shut their ears by our own acts—Were they to change, we have taught the majority to damn them!*— 'Ex uno disce omnes'.—According to my poor judgment we find in these things the root of all our bitterness — Our Senate Chamber is fast letting in these bitter waters—consultation—thought—& argumentative conversations are being superseded by factions, party feuds; and infuriate assaults upon a govern^t of which the same Senate forms a conspicuous part are the not uncommon exhibitions that invite there the Men & Women of the city—And there are "few lookers on in Venice" but when they are to be delighted with an abuse of the *Prest.*^{t} - - a review of "Southern treason"—or of Georgia *resistence to the Union'* or a well directed blow or two at the *"damned yankees"*—Am I not supported by your own observation of the facts—that nobody comes to look until he has been apprized that there's a chance to see a fight.—

As respects the Vice Presidency—I am resolved to go for the nomination—but I confess I will not in any way approve the manner of his support in one respect However much the Senator who voted against him as Minister may merit reproof it is better that Van B were hung three times over than the people taught not to respect that great body.—I will sustain them tho: I think they did wrong—not because I go for the party there—but for the whole Senate as a part of the country's govern'^{t}-. If ever the Senate furnish a means to party spirit to inspire the great body of the people with jealousy to them or rather disrespect for that branch of the Government we are hopelessly Gone.—I regret that we are obliged to differ about the propriety of refusing support to Van B. on account of any course the N. York delegates in Congress pursue about the Tariff—If the *Tariff notions* of Mr. Van B. are just cause to reject & disregard his nomination I do not for my life perceive why consistent men do not carry it out & *oppose Jackson*—If they would do so the question then would be fairly before the people—Van B. is I understand quite as much anti-Tariff as Mr. President;—besides it is a question of fair dealing. We sent our Delegates to the Convention—all agreed that Van B is most likely to succeed on the Jackson ticket —and how are *we* to draw back after taking the chance—this seems to me a crooked policy and after full & honest reflexion I will not myself pursue it, tho: I blame nobody else for doing as they think right—

I declare to you that I think it one of the dangers to our gov^t.. to let it enter into our consideration at all *where* a man lives. We learn to speak of different parts of our beloved country as though it contained our enemies & not our brothers Men of reflexion ought to guard against it & I deprecate the appeals which are made to these prejudices on the subject of this election & all others—It habituates our people to bad feelings & sentiments that are neither noble or just—for this cause above all others I regret the nomination of Mr. Barbour.—I am not less opposed to an abuse of the Senate to excite favour for Van B.—I will candidly confess that I do not like the signs of seeing *Calhoun's* friends—& Clay's in this State to a man united *against* Van B—. The close of this sheet admonishes me that I am trespassing on you—and verily on reading over my sheets I find I have almost written you a speech—I do not know whether we shall agree or not one thing I know is that we have differed before now & have '*agreed to differ*' & hope if we should differ we may not 'disagree'.—We are like to have a warm contest in this State for V. Pres^t—and poor North Caro: distracted about every thing else will not be able to unite even on this—A very respectable number of very respectable gent^n.. met here this week & nominated the *V^a Judge*[181] but I am quite as much against his *ultraism* as Van B's tariffism.—Head men of a *party* are very different men when they become the head of the nation—Where is the Pres^t.. who has not found it necessary to conciliate? Who doubts that Jackson is more for us now about tariff than he was when elected—Why?. So will any tariff man become who is supported by the South—But as respects the V. Pres^t.. in the name of common prudence what can *he* do—Mr Calhoun is against the tariff *now* quite enough as one would suppose. has his being V. Prest helped us one farthing on that subject for 8 years? The answer is ready.—Did not Mr Madison change his course on U. S. Bank? Did not Federalists & Democrats of distinguished talents change sides on that question at different periods? Has there been room left for doubt that a large part of the South & all of New England have change sides about the Tariff—I have been amusing myself today with a half doz pages of extracts from the complaints about the Tariff when Southern members carried it!!.— By the bye they talked then quite strong about *Disunion!*

I wish Congress would do something with the Tariff & adjourn —I am selfish enough to wish so if only for the sake of a chance to hear you talk over the matters of the last winter & this Spring & Summer.—I have been on the eve of getting into the Stage & riding to W. City just to see & hear but I have been weak eno: to be deterred by the fear of being suspected to rank among the humble suppliants of Executive bounty—Iredell[182] at the State Convention this week presided—he is a warm Barbour man—& he "goes the whole hog" for Nullification—

We have no State news—except that P. H. M.[183] is a candidate

[181]See above note 173 of this chapter.
[182]James Iredell.
[183]Priestley H. Mangum was elected to the state senate.

for the Assembly—but as he deserves so well to be elected I fear it will not occur—no other reason—he knows best & no doubt writes you—Seawell is opposed in Senate by Busbie[184]—I suspend the intention I had at first to give any opinion of the result —You don't care much about it.

There is evidently some machination going on in Orange against Barringer[185]—but by whom or how I know not—Though I have written you this long letter I have not done the like before in a long time—I have written you with an honest freedom that I hope you will excuse—without knowing how far or wherein we differ—One thing is sure you know I never desert *my friends* for trifling differences in politics—

Respects to Rencher[186] if you [blot] thanks to Dr Hall for his speech which I have rec'd & had—republished in paper here— *It is good — very good —*

Yours truly

W H H jr

5 July.

I wrote you this letter some days ago & laid it aside & neglected to send it—It will serve to remind you that I do not slight or undervalue your correspondence — We hope to see you soon

W H H jr

WPM-LC

J. G. A. Williamson to Willie P. Mangum

PHILA^a- 27 June 1832

Mr W. P. Mangum
    Senate of the U States
        Washington.
            My Dear Sir
                After parting with you on Monday evening, that night I left for Phila. and arri^d- tuesday night—and have been put in possession of sundry letters from Venezuela, and New York, sev-

[184]Johnson Busbee was a member of the House of Commons from Wake County in 1824 and 1827. From 1838 to 1839 he was a member of the Council of State. *N. C. Manual*, 436, 830.
[185]Daniel L. Barringer was reelected to Congress.
[186]Abraham Rencher.

eral on the subject of my visit to Washington, a particular friend
of mine from LaGuayra the place of my location in So America
has arrived in N York & from his intimacy with the *particular
friends* of Genl Santander[187] there, who has embarked for Car-
thegena the principal sea port for New Grenada, he informs me
the Genl. *has requested* Genl. Jackson to send to the three de-
partments of Columbia to wit Venezuela, New Grenada and the
Equator *Consul Generals,* you will perceive the Genl. thinks that
the President Can do these things without the aid of Congress,
he is therefore much mistaken as to the powers of the Executive
who unlike the Presidents of the South American Gov[ts]. have no
extraordinary powers—but that such a recommendation may &
will perhaps have some influences *may be* great weight with the
Secre[ty]. of State, at least to induce him in accordance with my
wishes & the memorials I have presented from the merchants of
New York & Phila[a]. of which you are aware, to persue the direct
measure I ask—

It is all essential, it is a point among commercial men there
can be no difference of opinion—I advise you of this in aid of
my application, and that you may use it in your interviews with
Mr Livingston on the subject—Nothing I can assure you would
give me so much satisfaction as the reception of the commission
I ask with a positive support out of the contingent fund until
the orders of Congress on the subject and it would add further
to the obligacions I am already under to you which I should be
pleased to acknowledge—

If not why as you proposed previous to me leaving Washington—

To stop short now in what I am a little informed upon both in
language and the usages & customs of the Colombians or might
perhaps say of all South America, would seem to cloud my hori-
son of expectation and like almost all my other attempts to be
useful, become mere castles in the air—

I have another reason which perhaps could be urged upon the
executive & the Secre[ty]. of State, it is to collect all & every material I can in the histories of Venezuela (Colombia) from which
something by a proper head might be digested either privately

---

[187]General Francisco de Paula Santander had been vice president under Bolivar when Colombia and Venezuela were united as New Granada. He soon broke with Bolivar but shortly
after the latter's death he returned from Europe and in October 1832 became president. He
refused to use an American vessel which Jackson offered to reenter his country. T. P. Moore,
the American minister, felt this was due to the influence of Jackson's enemies. E. Taylor
Parks, *Colombia and the United States 1765-1934* (Durham, N. C.: The Duke University
Press, 1935), 109, 119-121, 160-163.

for the Gov^t. of the U States or publicly in publishing a sketch
of that interesting country, to the writer, and one so little known
—This being private I did not think proper to broach it to Genl
Jackson or Mr Livingston, and at the moment of my last interview with you it escaped among many other reasons in conversation—To do this I must have means, and so far as my limit re-
sources allowed & time I have & did collect some matters & facts
when residing there—

I have no idea the Gov^t. will send Consul Generals to Colombia
or its dissolvg parts, as they must be first created by the Congress; under the new proposed change or revisal of the Consular
System of the U States the Laws upon that subject must be al-
tered to admit this or any other departure from things as now
stand—The reduction of facts & C on this subject I know is now
before one of the Clerks in the Secr^{ty}. of States department—
However my dear Sir whatever course the executive may think
proper to adopt on this subject, let me beg you to urge my claims
—Nothing can have a more salutary effect on this affair than a
personal interview, you then have two powers over the President. & Secr^{ty}. *personal* and political, they cannot resist both—

An appointment perfectly independent as I ask would give me
an opportunity of endeavoring to obtain not only private but
public confidence, it would gratify my pride and stimulate my
ambition, and open entirely a new career of usefulness to my
Country and pleasure to myself—

The letter referred to from N York can be relied on as I know
the Gentleman is not strictly speaking (entre nous) a *Santan-
daristan* [?], I place more confidence in it—That it may have
some effect there is no doubt, as I am well assured the President
& Secr^{ty}. repose great confidence in the Genl. views he has respecting Colombia—I am ab [illegible] my dear Sir that you will
not forget my claims and as I repose more confidence in success
upon this subject than all of the N. C. de——ion, Backed by my
friend Brown——.

Let me hear from you & oblige Sir Your Friend—

[Addressed:]

J. G. A. WILLIAMSON

To the Hon^l
W. P. Mangum
(Senate of the U. States
(
(Washington City

WPM-LC

Matthew St. Clair Clarke[188] to Willie P. Mangum

[9 July, 1832.]

Honb. W. P. Mangum Esq.
    U. S. Senate.

Dear Sir

I have written a note to Mr. Frelinghuysen, who is on the Com[ee] on the Library, to which Forces Memorial and my own was referred—

I have requested that Com[ee] to report a Resolution to be passed by the Senate alone directing the Secretary of State to contract with us for fifteen Hundred Copies of our Work—without saying at what price—I am satisfied the Department will do what is right. Mr. Livingston is exceedingly interested in work—so are Cass and Taney[189] My acquaintance with Mr. Woodbury[190] did not authorize a conversation. I spoke to the President last summer. He, like every one else, could hardly credit me, when I told him that the Congressional Revolutionary Documents had never been printed—and said it certainly ought to be done—

I have this work much at heart—knowing full well, that the true history of those times never can be written without it.

I am humbled when I hear it said that an Italian (Botta)[191] has written our best History—

Let these Documents be properly brought out and I undertake to prove error in every History—We have them all and in each one I can shew mistake—

There is not one of them which takes hold of the Fundamental truth of our Revolution—I am desirous to prove to the world that Revolution *in favour of* Freedom, is not to be elaborated in St. Stephens Chapel not the Chamber of Deputies, but in the hearts of the People—knowing—feeling—and determining their own rights—I want to bring out the facts, and then let some abler hand build up our History, as the Greeks & Romans did their Temples "for Posterity and the Immortal Gods—"

---

[188]Peter Force and Matthew St. Clair Clarke collected and edited the *American Archives*, which was planned to include 20 volumes. Congress failed to appropriate sufficient money and so only 9 volumes were completed. The publications were continued later. *D. A. B.*, VI, 512-513.

[189]Roger Taney.

[190]Levi Woodbury.

[191]Cairo Guiseppe Botta, *History of the War of the Independence of the United States of America*, 3 vols. (Translated from the Italian by Geo. A. Otis. Philadelphia, Pa.: Lydia P. Bailey, 1820-1821).

Your Obt. Servt.

M. St. Clair Clarke.

Monday Morning
    9. July 1832

[Addressed:]

Honb. W. P. Mangum,
        U. S. Senate.

July 21st. 1832—

Jany. That if she will condesind to board out Sally & send her to a men of my stamp, I can have her boarded at an excellent

---

WPM-LC

John Chavis to Willie P. Mangum

My dear Sir/

As no man is his own keeper, nor does he know what he is to come, therefore I will not make a positive promise, but my present impression is, that this shall be the last letter I ever will write to you, untill I get one from you I will not write this, if it was not owing to genuine friendship founded upon Mrs. Mangum and her children—I wish you to tell her, that the die is cast, I cannot come to Teacher for her. I have built a school house and at three or three & a half dollars a month at most the tuition eight dollars. That I have an anxious & particular desire to Teach her the Theory of the English Language, which she never have made arrangements to be stationary at home. That I shall house, within about three quarters of a mile of my school house the way to it is a dry ridge way, not a drop of water intervening, will be Taught unless I Teach her; because, no other person in this part of the Country Teaches it but myself, and my manner I deem far preferable to the English Grammar. I wish you to commence Teaching for the next year, on the first monday in make this statement to Col. Horner[192] & tell him that I want his daughter Juliana for the same purpose & tell him that I do confess, that I did not know the English Alphabet, radically [?] even when he came to school to me. I only want your daughters about twelve or eighteen months & then you may send them to any other school you please—

---

[192]William Horner.

I disapprove of three of your votes. Van Buren, the Bank & the fast day. but my greatest grief is that you should be in favour of the election of General Jackson for the Presidency. If it was not for the opinion I have of your honest Integrity, I should believe that you were certainly seeking for a diplomacy, which God you may never get for the good of your family. Let G. J. be elected & our Government is gone, and even in its present situation, it would require a Hamilton, a Jay and an old Adams, bottomed upon G. Washington to repair its ruins. This Clay knows, & nothing but conscious integrity & a united love of Country, could possibly induce him to undertake the management of such a rotten & decayed Government. I hope he will be elected, & even if he should, I shall pity his situation I had a promising crop, but having but little or no rain for about ten weeks, it is almost ruined. & what makes the case still worse, I have my last grist in my meal tub, & not a cent a money & what I am to do, God only knows—

I have the satisfaction to tell you, that Benjn. Rogers has, of his own accord become as friendly with me as ever he was. What wrought the change in him I cant tell. There has been no sale, & I expect will not be My respects to Mrs. Mangum & tell her never expect to see her at her house any more or again. If you will write direct your letter to be left at the post office at Rogers store—

I am your Obt. Hbl. Svt.

JOHN CHAVIS

[Addressed:]

Hon. Willie P. Mangum Esq
Orange

To be left at
Roundhill N C

WPM-LC

John Chavis to Willie P. Mangum

August 8th. 1832—

My dear Sir/
Your very friendly and satisfactory letter came to hand yesterday, and I embrace the earliest moment to answer it—

You appear to think, that I have become unsound in politics. If to be a genuine Federalist, is to be unsound in politics I am guilty. But pray how has it been with yourself? how often have changed your Federal coat for a Democratic or Republic one? & have not your friends, since you were last elected to Congress, been charged in the publick funds with the duplicity for electing you to Congress knowing you to be a Federalist? and have I not often browbeaten you for your shifting conduct? And how could you have the daring impudence, to tell me, in broad open day light, that I had become unsound in my politics? Are you not a pretty handsome fellow? No Sir, I w^d. have to know, that I am the same genuine, undeviating, unshaken lump of Federalism, that I ever was, that I have never deviated a single hair's breadth, from Dan to Beersheba. and which? because I believe that Federal policy, to be the best, that ever was adopted, in this or in other Country, of a free and elective Government. That there is no other policy that can stand the shock & vicissitudes of human nature. I do not believe that mankind are capable of living under, either a Democratic, or a Republican Government. The bonds of such Governments are not sufficient to restrain the corruptions of human nature. The volcano will burst. & the lava spread far and wide its destructive ruins. But after what I have said, I do candidly confess, that such is the state of things, that I am not capable of forming a correct Judgment what is the true policy of the day. therefore the course that I do pursue is, to form the best judgment, of the characters of those who are to administer the affairs of the Government, and they are those whom I believe to possess the greatest share of intelligence, experience, honesty & integrity, bottomed upon the love of the best Interest of the Government. And upon this principle it is, that I have ever been opposed to the election of G. J. from the beginning to this day. I believe him to be an honest man, but there is no other trait in his character, in my estimation that qualifies him for the seat of a Chief Magistrate. Therefore I cannot in consciens & honesty be in favour of his reelection now I appeal to you as a Gent^n. of candour & penetrating understanding, to begin at his cradle, & point out to me, the regular traits in his character up to the seat he now fills & shew me what it is, that constitutes him a dignified character, and one who is fitly qualified to fill the seat of a chief Magistrate I have made the appeal, but you wont make the attempt, & why? please you know too well that you cannot scrape up, those traits, in his character that will constitute him a dignified high minded honorable gent^n. You know also, that if you were to make the attempt that the annals of the nation w^d. contradict you. And above all, your own Ideas of propriety & dignity of conduct w^d. also forbid you to make the attempt for it w^d. only be an attempt. I could multiply, but I forbear & why? because you know the man & moreover it w^d. be treating you, like an upstart novice Teaching Hanibal the art of war. In a word, from what I have stated you may easily conceive, why it is, that I am so mortified, & killed that yourself & my two sons Priestley & Renchr, should be so attached to G. J. & to his re-election—For honesty integrity & dignity is my motto for character—But you say, his reelection is sure, & should he be elected, that liberty & the constitution will be safe, God grant it; but what you found your judgment upon, I cannot conceive, unless it be, that you have found him to be of such a subservient & Teachable disposition, that yourself & others of his friends, will or can have so much influence over him as to keep him in *the Track,* upon [no o]the[r] ground, I think, you can possibly believe it. It is time to come to Mr. Clay, but before I proceed I you must know, that I have never seen the moment when I was, as much opposed to G. J. as I was to Mr Clay untill I saw his address to his constituents. That address convinced me judgmentally, that he was an honest intelligent, & tried patriot & of inflexible integrity. Also that the Annals of the Nation have uniformly declared him to be a mighty & dignified character. Fulfilling all his deplomacies with judgment & inflexible integrity & I believe, that his worst enemies do not deny his capability of managing the destinies of the Nation because they may wield him in other respects. You are the first, that I ever hinted that this situation was impaired, it may be so, but I shall risque it upon the principles, I have above stated. You may blame me if you will, but I must be honest to myself & my Country—

I will now give my reasons, for saying, that the reasons which G. J. gave for puting his Veto on the bank bill was not worth a gourd button; I shall speak according to my understanding, & if I am wrong I would thank you to rectify my mistakes. In the first place he appears to hold out the Idea, that the people were taken on surprize, that it was not expected that an attempt w^d. be made at that session, to renew the charter of the bank, that the members of Congress had met, without the knowledge of the sentiments of their constituents upon that subject—

If I am right in my cenception, this could not be the case; For when I w^d. ask, was there a press in the union, but was teeming with Notices on the subject, Memorial after memorial, for and against its renewal, & how would the people be taken upon surprize, as the Members of Congress came unprepared to act?

In the second place, like Mr McDuffee,[193] in his arguments against the Tariff systim, placing the southern Farmers precisely upon equal & upon the same footing in all respects, with the exporting & importing Merchant, which Mr Appleton[194] show clearly, is not the case, that the parties are as distinct and as different, as light is from darkness &C. In like manner has G. J. placed the people at large precisely upon the same and equal footing in all respects with the stockholders of the U. S. bank, which is not, nor cannot be the case. Suppose for argument sake, that the Directors of the [bank] should, by bad management destroy the credit of the bank, & their paper become null and void (if you please) would the stockholders, presume to apply to the people at large, to aid them in restoring the credit of the bank? By no means, & why, because they w^d. know assuredly that they w^d. meet with an objection at the door of the application—that all the Interest the people had or could expected to have was the use of their paper as a circulating medium. That if they had destroyed their own Interest it was their own fault & not theirs. But it appears from G. J. reasoning he will not have it so, but endeavours to persuade the people that their sacred rights & privileges are about to be jeopardized, that he as their fostering father is endeavouring to protect & rescue them from such ruinous consequences—In the third place. I do not conceive the impropriety, which G. J. seems to have with respect to Foreigners holding stock in the U. S. bank. We are upon friendly & amicable terms with the British nation. We *live*, & deal reciprocally and act as brethren, as it were, in all respects, and is there any more impropriety in their holding stock in the bank than in their holding other property in this Country—or in the Americans holding property in their Country? If any should object to this statement, let him read Jays Treaty. Besides it appears plain, that at the time the bank was instituted, that such was the hostility against it, that it was difficult to obtain American stock-holders sufficient to carry it

[193]George McDuffie.
[194]Nathan Appleton, 1779-1861, was a member of Congress from Massachusetts from 1831 to 1833. *Biog. Dir. of Cong.*, 646.

into effect. Foreigners knowing this, & foreseeing the great advantages such a bank w^d. be to the Americans & themselves were willing to become stockholders, having full confidence in the American stockholders & Directors And here I w^d. ask under what shaddow of pretence could the American Stockholders set up to refuse such Marked friendship and confidence? It was also foreseen, that such joint sock w^d. not only accellerate & ficillitate Merchantal opporations, but w^d. accellerate & facillitate the fiscal concerns of the American Government, & that ultimately their paper, as a circulating medium, w^d. become equal to Gold & silver in both Countries, which has actually come pass. [torn] has objections respecting warlike operations I will [torn] as all lent which can never fall to the bottom of any place. so that upon a review of the Whole case, I concluded that his reasons were nothing more nor less, than a electioneering scheme well calculated to blind the people & shroud them in their ignorance, and therefore not worth a gourd button; but at the same time, I [do n]ot acknowledge that Van Buren is a [torn and illegible]

As to your votes I never doubted for a moment the purity of your motives but as I believe you to be like other men fallible I believe you were wrong, & in Van Burens case, I did not believe that you could possibly believe him to be a high minded honourable & dignified character possessed of inflexible integrity, & therefore ought not to be trusted in so important a mission & what you now say of him proves the correctness of my Idea—

As to your bank vote, my opinion was that you had voted against it in toto, which I know to be wrong, because it is evident that it is the back bone rib bones & sinew of the fiscal concerns of the Government, but now you say that all will go for the bank next Congress but I hope not a national bank to be within the controll & authority of the executive—

And as to your fast vote,[195] I never thought of the constitution, or of its having any connection with Church & state, for that is a case that I am as much opposed to any person whatever what I felt was, that you should be opposed to the worship of God, in any form—

I am glad to find that Mrs Mangum has increased her family and is well. I am [torn] you will write again shortly, tell Mrs Mangum she must send me word what for crop she has got—

---

[195]On June 28, 1832, the Senate voted on a resolution to ask the President to call a day of humiliation and prayer because of the cholera epidemic in Asia. Mangum was one of the thirteen who opposed the resolution. *Register of Debates*, 22 Cong., 1 sess., 1132.

You can get boarding at Mr Soloman Thompson near at hand & a respectable house, I know of no Lady that I w^d. recommend a friend to trust a daughter sooner than Mrs Thompson. Mrs Tignal Jones[196] alias Amelia [torn] has requested me to give her respects to Mrs Mangum & to tell her that she has three sons [torn] to match with her daughters. Col. J[torn] knows of your votes I am your [torn]-ly

JOHN CHAVIS

[Addressed:]
   Hon. Willie P. Mangum Esqr—
     Orange
To be left at
Roundhill P. O.

Willie P. Mangum to unidentified person[197]

    Orange Co. N. C. 10th. August 1832
Dear Sir.

Please to send your country paper published twice a week. to *"Harrison Parker Esqr. Red Mountain"*[198]—He is a man of substance & will enclose you the subscription on the receipt of the paper or send it by me at the meeting of Congress.—

Every thing is quiet & firm here—The Veto has to encounter here only a few thousands—mostly those whom the people have uniformly regarded either with distrust or as their enemies—The President is protected here from his enemies by a wall of brass aye, a gulf of flame—There is but little feeling as to the Vice Presidency—If two Jackson tickets shall be run, I think the regular nomination will succeed—If a resort shall be had to the mode adopted in Virginia, (of which I have just seen some indication) Barbour may prevail.—

If two tickets shall be run, the people will not I think, suffer anything to take even the appearance of endangering the Genl.—

But in truth, no opposition here to him can be supported by even a respectable portion of strength.—

   Accept the assurance
    of my respect & esteem

    WILLIE P. MANGUM

[196]See above, p. 321n.
[197]The original is in the Historical Society of Pennsylvania, Philadelphia, Pa.
[198]See above, p. 426n.

WPM-LC

W. A. Tharpe[199] to Willie P. Mangum

PARIS, [Tenn.] August 19th. 1832

Dear Sir.

I have seen during the late session of Congress that you were ag[t]. the renewal of the U S Bank charter, I suppose you was governed by constitutional objections, if so you and old Hickory both acted correctly, though as I conceive not for the best interests of the community. The U S Bank is and has been the most valuable moneyed institution I have ever known of. Such a Bank as the President recommended in his first Message to congress I cannot approve of, That Bank or institution that belongs to every body, belongs to no body and consequently must and will be neglected and abused. I shall be pleased and highly gratified to have your opinion on this important matter, if you spoke on the subject I have been so unfortunate as not to see your speech published.

I had the pleasure last winter of seeing your speech against the American sistem or Tariff. I was much pleased with it. it contained more real and convincing argument than any that has been published, however there was one and but one error or rong position taken, that I cannot now call your attention to, (I cannot find your speech) and perhaps that was an error of the printer or reporter.

Gen[l]. Carrington[200] informed me that you have some little matter of business in this country or about Nashville that you wish me to attent to, you have only to inform me and I shall with pleasure use my best exertions to serve your best Interest.

Gen[l]. Carrington & Family were all well about two weeks since, he is highly pleased with his removal and local situation. I have settled him on an excelent tract of Land and have made provision for his & his Wife's life time' on it, which is known to him, he has seen and read the instrument, which appeared quite satisfactory.

When I was about to set out for this country I was rather afraid that myself and Family would be unhealthy here, that fear has measureably subsided we are and have been very healthy since we left Neuse River and I sincerely hope we shall continue so.

---

[199]See above, p. 88n.
[200]John J. Carrington.

I am Dear Sir, Your
        Sincere and devoted Friend

                                    W. A. THORPE
Hon. W. P. Mangum.

P. S. I have no doubt but it is known to you that myself and
your Brother was engaged in the gold Hunting business, I have
never seen your Brother Walter since he returned from the
Mountains. I therefore know nothing about the business it may
have been a loosing business, if so, and you will ascertain the
amount of my part of the loss I will immediately pay it, I expected to have seen your Brother Walter before I left N. C. My
Boys told me When they came home that he said he would be to
see me in a few days. I suppose his other engagements prevented
his comeing, and that he would of written to me if he had of
known my address

                                    W. A. T.

[Addressed:]

            Hon. Willie P. Mangum
                Rid Mountain
                    N°. Cª.

                                    WPM-LC

            Chs. Fisher to W. P. Mangum

                        SALISBURY 24th August 1832
Dr. Sir.
    ˙You will see by the w. Carolinian, the result and the whole
history of a very large anti-Tariff meeting held here on Thursday last.[201] We obtained a glorious victory, but we have now
rallyed against us. all the *Clay-men, Tariff-men,* and *consolida-
tionists,* and the few *Van Buren* men have joined them. Our first
battle was in the Borough election, where they made use of the
most extraordinary means to elect their man. Mr Craig succeeded by one vote,[202] tho, they talk, nay say, that they will con-

---

[201]The anti-tariff meeting was held August 23, 1832. Hamilton C. Jones, an anti-nullifica-
tionist, had recently established the *Carolina Watchman* to combat the states' rights views of
the *Western Carolinian* edited by Burton Craige. At the meeting, Jones presented nationalis-
tic resolutions which Craige and Fisher opposed. A heated debate followed with D. F. Caldwell and Jones on one side and Craig and Fisher on the other. Fisher's resolutions favoring
a strong states' rights view prevailed. *Western Carolinian,* Aug. 27, 1832.
[202]Craige was elected to the House of Commons.

test his seat—and I believe they will, from the fact that they are sending out letters to every part of the State—They are trying to rally the Cape-Fear interest for Alexander—If other influences are kept off, we fear nothing for the result, but we have a most bitter, & indefaticable set of men to contend with. Craige by his boldness & spirit has given mortal offence to Caldwell & the set. & they will spare no pains to defeat him in the Legislature. He feels uneasy and looks to his friends. & to those who approves his political course to give him a helping hand. I was glad to see your Brother elected;[203] he is with us in this awful crisis in the fate of the South, and I know will sympathize with his political friends struggling here in this nest of———

How do you come on, and what are the political prospects around you? An attempt was made here last week (Court Week) to get up a clay-meeting to nominate a Clay-elector, but failed— I think, Caldwell, and the other Clay-men here, will join the Van Buren ticket—H. C. Jones Editor of the "Carolina Watchman" a paper recently got up here by *Martin*[204] & *Caldwell*, has half-way come out for V. Buren,—Judge Martin is said to be the author of a piece in that paper, that advocate the broad doctrine of *consolidation,* and the whole clan go the same way—

One of the constant arguments used here in favour of the Tariff is,—the *majority* has adopted it, and the *minority* must submit quietly, and to complain is little short of treason.

If you approve of the recommedation of our meeting, will you take some pains to get the plan carried into effect in Orange?— Let me hear from you—

Yours respectfully &C.

CHS. FISHER

I cannot be here at our Supr. Court intending to start to Geo. in a few days, say 10th Septr—but if *you & Rencher* could be here, and make public addresses, it would be most desirable. Can you come?— Rencher will be here.

[Addressed:]
The Honbl.
W. P. Mangum
Hillsboro
No. Ca.

---

[203]Priestley was elected to the state senate.
[204]James Martin, Jr., was superior court judge from 1827 to 1835.

WPM-LC

W. Montgomery to Willie P. Mangum

HILLSBOROUGH N. C. August 29, 1832.

My Dear Sir

I have Been greatly disappointed in not Seeing you Here this Court. You Have doubtless Heard of the affair of Col Childs[205] and Myself, He Has Made some False Charges against Me, and Finds Himself, under the Necessity of Changing His Charges He now Says He Can Make Me out a Nullifyer By you or By Letters that I should Have wrote to you, during the Last Session, Barringer[206] I understand is the Man that Says He Saw a Letter of Mine to you, Last Session. I write you this Letter to apprise you that the attempt is Making to Injure Me through My private Correspondance to you; this is in Characterestic of the General, I will Be down on Monday of Superior Court, when I Have Mutch to Communicate to you,

the people about this plce and County will not agree to give you and, Mr Brown a Dinner We are determined a Few of us to do.

With great regard and

Esteem
Your
Most
obedient
servt

W, MONTGOMERY—

[Addressed:]
Judge Mangum,
Red Mountain
N. C.

———

WPM-LC

Walker Anderson et als. to W. P. Mangum

HILLSBORO' Sept: 12th 1832

Sir!

At a late public meeting of a number of your friends & fellow citizens of the county of Orange, resolutions were passed ex-

---

[205]Colonel Sam Childs was a justice of the peace of Orange County.
[206]Daniel L. Barringer.

pressive of the confidence & esteem with which your political
course during the late session of Congress has inspired your
constituents—and the undersigned were appointed a committee
to be the organ of the expression of these sentiments and to request you to favour your friends of this vicinity with the honour
of your company at a public dinner to be given on any day that
may suit your convenience— We take pleasure in acknowledging
particularly the zeal and ability with which you have resisted
the encroaching usurpations of that party in the national
councils which seems to have devoted us to ruin—and tho' the
illegal exercise of power rendered your patriotic labours inef-
ficient to the end to which they were directed, we are proud
of the lustre they have reflected on our State & respectfully
tender to you the tribute of our highest admiration & esteem—
We have the honour to be your friends & fellow-citizens

Walker Anderson   )
Sam Child   )
W. Montgomery   )
Allen C. Jones
V. M. Murphey
John Scott

[Addressed:]

The Hon: W. P. Mangum

WPM-LC

John Chavis to Willie P. Mangum

Sept. 24th. 1832—

My dear Sir/
    My heart is grieved to the bottom, at hearing of your name
so bandied as it is respecting the Tariff. The Bank vote and
the presidency—
    I see from the last Register that you intend to take up the
Tariff on the 11th. of next month at Hillsborough—I write therefore to request you for the satisfaction of the people, to explain
what I am about to state & what Col Drayton's address[207] has
brought fresh to my recollection, which I believe to be a noto-

---

[207]See above, p. 480.

rious fact that the southern people through their deligation was the true cause of the establishing of manufacturers & the protecting system. Now if this be the case, it is clear to me that it is with a very ill grace indeed, that they should complain so heavily as they do against the northern people & their deligation for wishing to continue the protecting system when they themselves palmed it on them contrary to their wish and intention, in the first instance; that when they were pursuing a definite course for a livelihood they call their attention irresistibly to make their investments in Manufactories Tho I one of the northern delegation, as much as feel for the southern people, I would to the last day of my life reject the repeal of those duties, which w^d. be the overwhelming destruction of my constituents to gratify the southern people for their own acts. Now if the southern people through their delegation, however mortifying it might have been, had honestly & candidly confess their error & plead mercy & if the northern people through delegation, this w^d. have been honourable and plausible, & might have had, a commiserating tendency. but the head revolts at being blamed unjustifiably & will repell indignantly any application for a relief of grievances brought against them in such an insulting manner—

The Bank bill, There is one Item in the Presidents Veto which has ever been mysterious to me in all such cases, & that is, the boon the stockholders make on their papers. That my meaning may be understood, I will place you as the stockholders, & myself the people We come to you to borrow each of us a $100 you direct your Directors to lend it to us. We receive those sums which answers all our purposes equal to Gold & silver. Then to put the matter in the strongest light; suppose you make, as a boon a million of dollars for 100 what possible injury do you do us? is the first question I wish answered. Ought we not to be thankful for the deliverance you afforded us, & so rejoice at your gain? is the second question to be answered? & not to complain—

The Presidency. Can it be possible my son that you are yet the friend of the reelection of G. Jackson I should suppose that taking into view all his other Tread me down acts, the nominating of Gwinn [?] after his expected rejection, ought I think to send in your view of his domineering & despotic disposition. Oh my friend you cannot conceive what I suffer on yours Renchers & Priestley and tho. I have good reason to believe the latter has intirely turned his back upon me yet I love him & his character & that of his [illegible]. How you can conceive that G. J. is a high minded honourable wise & dignified character one who fitly qualified to fill the chair of the chief Magistrate I cannot conceive, & therefore I lament daily—My respects Mrs Mangum

JOHN CHAVIS

[Addressed:]

Hon. Willie P. Mangum Esq—
Orange
To be left at
P. O.
Red Mountain

————

WPM-LC

John Chavis to Willie P. Mangum

Oct 1st 1832.

My dear Sir/
    I hasten to inform you, that Mr. John Hunt of Greenville,[208] came to see me this morning to let me know, that the Orange Presbytary to which I belong had entered into a resolution to support me & my wife during life and had appointed a Committee to make arrangments for that purpose.[209] I told Mr. Hunt that I was thankful & would accept of the offer; but that I was in debt, and could not go untill next fall or winter—That I thought I had a prospect of making a school for the next year which wᵈ. be sufficient to cover all my debts provided my neighbours would patronize me as they ought to do, But should they not, I wish you to know that I will Teach for you the next year provided you can make such a school as will justify me to leave my family to take care of themselves. If you wish me to Teach for you, it wᵈ. be well for you to try your Strength forwith & write to Roger's store. In the meantime I shall try my strength here & should you prove the strongest party I shall certainly serve you—
    You are to recollect that school must not exceed a quarter of a mile from your door & let it be less if possible & your pay-

---

²⁰⁸A John Hunt of Granville County was clerk of the House of Commons from 1778 to 1806. *N. C. Manual,* 453-462.
²⁰⁹See above, pp. 155, 315-317.

ments must be at least half yearly The school to commence on the first Monday in Janʸ.

I view this Presbyterial arrangment as a merciful providence for which I am thankful—

My respects to Mrs. Mangum & believe me to be yours very Sincerely

JOHN CHAVIS

P. S.

Should I teach for you I will endeavor to see you before you go to Congress.

[Postmarked:]
Rogers Store Oct. the 5th

[Addressed:]
    Hon. Willie P. Mangum
        Orange
To be left at
Red Mountain P. O.

WPM-LC

J. W. Wright[210] to John Scott

LAURENS Bladen County October 12th 1832

John Scott Esqr.

Dr. Sir.

I expect to start in all next month a number of Slaves, either to Mississippi or Louisiana, to make an establishment for my son James M Wright,[211] who sets out on wednesday week to select a spot for permanent residence. He has been engaged here for a short time in the practice of the Law & as far as I can judge with favourable prospects. He will pursue his profession in one or other of those states. With Judge Mangum our Senator I have not the pleasure of a personal acquaintance, he is however known to me as a gentleman & a public man. Deducing therefrom his entire capability of serving me, I ask the favour of you to apply to him for letters in behalf of my son James M Wright to some of his friends of Mississippi & Louisiana. With you Sir I feel at liberty to be as frank as I am

[210]J. W. Wright was connected with the Cape Fear Bank.
[211]James Wright graduated at the University in 1826.

friendly—He finished his legal course with judge Tucker of Virginia & from testimonials there & elsewhere I have reason to believe he has uniformly been well received in the best circles—Such incidents are mentioned for no other purpose than to relieve judge Mangum from any difficulty, accompanied with an unreserved assurance on my part, that such a favour will neither be abused by him or lightly esteemed. If those letters cant be conveniently procured & forwarded in time for his departure Still forward them direct to me near Elizabeth town, & I can send them to him so as to answer every purpose. I should like my friend to meet with you again at Raleigh, if devotion to my private affairs would admit.

Very respectfully & sincerely your friend

J. W. WRIGHT

[Addressed:]

John Scott Esquire   Elizabeth Town N. C.
Hillsborough Orange Co   16th Octr.
Mail   North Carolina

Chs. R. Ramsay[212] to Willie P. Mangum[213]

RALEIGH Oct. 19th 1832.

Dear Sir.

An unusual press of business requiring my exclusive attention, has prevented me from responding sooner to your [torn] kind favor of the 17th of August. Its contents gave me much pleasure, while the sentiments were duly reciprocated by one who has long cherished a veneration for your talents and [mer]eted worth— one who feels grateful for the kind interest which you manifest towards him, and whose greatest ambition will be to merit a continuance of your good-will.

Assurance of esteem and approbation from a source entitled to so much respect, is peculiarly flattering [to] the feelings of a young man, who has just embarked on the theatre of public life, dependent upon his own merits and exertions, unaided by the advantages of wealth or family in[fluen]ce and is an ample remuneration for the wounds inflicted by the heartless and un-

---

[212]See above, letter of W. S. Ransom to Mangum, Feb. 8, 1832.
[213]The original is not available. A typed copy is available in the Mangum Papers, State Department of Archives and History, Raleigh, N. C.

charitable, who adopting their own narrow and bigoted minds, as a standard to judge of the motives of others, condemn every thing that is not in conformity to [their] taste and every body who may have the boldness to [think] difficulty from them.

You will perceive Sir th[torn] come in for a share of that abuse and oblog-[torn] almost invariably the inheritance of every person who is so regardless of his happiness as to sub-[torn] reputation to the caprice of the pupulace [torn] one who has outlived the susceptibility of early [torn] or whose sensibilities have become deadened by a lon-[torn] with the cares of public life, such attacks would [torn] an uneasy emotion; but I must acknowledge, that they [torn] me a great source of annoyance, and productive of much [disa]greeable reflection, which makes me frequently desirous [of] withdrawing from the editorial corps.

In assuring the entire con[trol of the consti]tutionalist[214] I was actuated more by necessity [torn]-action. Gladly would I have resigned my int-[torn] establishment and relinquished a situation at [torn] with my inclination and interest. I have st-[torn] to sustain the press—and more than once I ha[torn] of shipwreck—ready to yield everything [torn]-hout funds—without credit—an [ex]pensive establishment, already tottering under incumbrances to keep up, You can form some idea what my inducement were to continue the paper, and what the nature of my feelings were when left along to contend against a strong and active party, many of whom reckless of their own destiny, were intent on gratifying their vindictive dispositions by consigning me to ruin. Among the many foul and unwarrantable aspersions, which have emanated from the oppostion is that I control a pensioned press; whereas I had been actuated by pecuniary considerations, all the inducements were on the other side and the indignation manifested by the friends of Mr. Barbour at the course pursued by me with regard to the Vice Presidency, arose more from my refusal to be governed by their advice and permit my press to be subsidised to their use, than any actual belief in the [c]harge which they have conjured up.

I am glad to see Sir that you let your [torn]-ay against Nullification, I was fearful from the [torn] which were rife, that you had caught the [South] Carolina epidemic; tho' I have

---

[214]*The Raleigh Constitutionalist* began Nov. 15, 1831. Winifred Gregory (ed.), *American Newspapers 1821-1936 A Union List of Files Available in the United States and Canada* (New York, N. Y.: The H. W. Wilson Co., 1937), 505.

never seen any [torn] your public acts to warrant such a belief. I [torn] the pertinacity with which you cling to your anti tariff p-[torn] and hope that they will prevail, & that they wi[ll materialize] I feel almost certain, if due moderation [torn] exercised; but I am fearful the rashness of our [ne]ighbours will only have a tendency to widen the [b]reach between the North and South. The partisans of Mr Calhoun among the annonymous scribe [in] the Star, who has taken exceptions at your refusing to considering one of their party, doubtless ranks, deem Nulli[fica]tion & State Rights inseperable, To be a State rights [torn] they say, it is essential to espouse the doctrine of [Nullifi]cation; but this is merely an ad captandum flourish [torn] [sh]ows the true nature of the principles by which the[y] [torn] [actu]ated. Excuse thie hasty scrawl,

I am Respectfully
Your Obt Servt

CHS. R. RAMSAY

Wilie P. Mangum.

[Addressed:]

Honl. Wilie P. Mangum
Red Mountain
N. C.

WPM-LC

Mullard L. Felt to Willie P. Mangum

MERCANTILE LIBRARY
NEW YORK Oct 25—1832

Dear Sir

The Directors of the Mercantile Library of this city have instructed me to invite you to deliver a lecture before their Association at some time during the Months of Jany or Feby of next year, and to offer you as compensation One hundred Dollars.

Many of the most eminent men of this country, as well as Mr. Thackeray, now on his way over from England will lecture in this city during the winter before our own & the Historical Society of the State and your name, Sir, would add very materially to the e'clat of the occasion. Your appearance too, would highly gratify a large number of your warm friends & admirers, among whom we are proud to number ourselves.

I hope that you will be able, notwithstanding your numerous & pressing public engagements, to give our application an early & favourable consideration,

Respectfully
Your obt. Servt—

MULLARD L. FELT,
Corresponding Sec'y

Hon. Willie P. Mangum

WPM-LC

John Chavis to Willie P. Mangum

Nov. 3ᵈ 1832—

My dear Sir/

It is with heart felt satisfaction that I have to inform you that I had the oppy & the pleasure of reading your friends answer to Albermarle. At first, for a few hours, I felt mortified, at his attack, but shortly, I felt glad, that he had done it, because it wᵈ. afford you an oppʸ to answer for yourself, & answer much of the calumniations branded against you. Your being called a Nullifier was not unexpected to me. I knew that wᵈ. be the case from your strong expressions in your speech of the Tariff Bill. And when you mentioned in your address at Hillsᵇᵒ.[215] I was not at all surprised and when you denied the charge & said that there was but one Nullifier in the state, I believed that you meant G. Iredell, & I believe that Albermarle to be the man—

I thought much upon the subject, whether it be best for you to answer, or to get some friend to do it for you who was adequate to the Task. I however concluded that the latter wᵈ. be the proper course therefore I am pleased—

To hear you traduced is killing. I can blame and scold you myself but I dont like other people to do it. If I think you to be wrong in any case I dont want other people to think so, & there-

---

[215]On September 19, 1832, at a public meeting in Hillsboro, Mangum made a strong speech against nullification. He had been accused of being a nullifier. *N. C. Press,* Sept. 25, 1832.

fore I am so tormented at the thoughts of your being in favour of the reelection of G. Jackson, & what almost takes my life is, that I cannot believe that you view him as an honourable digni- fied and affectionate character & why you sh^d. wish him to con- tinue in the seat of the chief Magistrate I cannot conceive—I sincerely pity Mrs. Mangum, because I believed that she loves you as wife ought to love a husband, & therefore it must mortify her to the centre of her heart to think of your favouring the pretentions of such a character as she conceives G. J. to be. Please to give my respects to her, & tell her that the United states w^d. be too poor to induce me to vote for the reelection of G. J. And if she has not got a Lockchain, to send borrow one and chain you to her door, & prevent you from going to the Polls on Thursday to give a vote so degrading & debasing to her & her children. Good heaven! Why is it that W. P. Mangum has become so infatuated? What has become of his discriminat- ing powers of appreciating the respectability of characters? Let him take G. J. from his cradle up to his reappointing Guin to the Secretary office of the sale of the Indians Lands & see if he cannot discover a host of blots of the deepest dye in his character—undeserving a chief Magistrate? Has he lost sight of the honour & dignity of his Country? but I must lower my sails, for my feelings w^d. willingly carry me from my own, to the European Countries, where I should meet with shame & confusion of face, were I in favour of the reelection of G. J.—

But to return. Your reasoning & Mr Calhouns appears to me, to be pretty much a par. and I cannot clearly understand you. You appear to make a distinction between the states & the people of the states, That the states took the liberty to unite to support by the U. States constitution the Union & Laws of the General Government but not the people of the states. That the states are sovereign states and accordingly have a right to act independently of any Laws of the Government, in which their domestic affairs are concerned. Then I suppose you mean that in that case the states & the people bound to obey any Law unitedly only in the case of War—

I recollect that at the time the Constitution was forming the great question was between the sovereignty of the states, & a consolidation of the states, that the ultimatum was the states should be sovereign so far as to make their own Laws & to govern themselves; but at the same time they were by the Con- stitution under the Guardianship of the G. Government—That if their rights & privileges were infringed by any domestic or Foreign power the G. Government was bound to protect them, Also that the G. Government was to enact Laws for the general good & the people of the States were bound to obey these Laws, precisely in the same manner, as the people of each state are bound to obey the Laws of their respective states. Also in precisely, in same manner if the states are dissatisfied with any Laws of the state, they have a just right to complain, & to have the Law repealed & if the Legislature will repeal it, well & if not they must peaceably submit, & be Governed by the Law because it is a Law of their own chosing as it was done by representatives of their chosing. Just so by the Laws of the G. Government. The people of the several states are are [*sic*] bound to obey the Laws of the G. Government because they are enacted by representatives of their own chosing but if upon complaint of any Law, they cannot get it repealed why in that case they bound to submit & make the best of a bad bargain. This has ever been my understanding of the state and G. Governments But according to you and Mr Calhoun? I have ever been mistaken & I cannot see how or in what manner I am mistaken—

I shall expect a Long letter from you before you go to Congress—

One thing I must say to you in conclusion. That I am truly sorry that I am so ignorant & yet take so deep an Interest in the welfare of my Country, but nothing short of a Loss of my senses or death can possibly prevent me. so that if I am troublesome to you you must ascribe it a love of country. Please to present some of the cream of my love to Mrs. Mangum & her children, & believe me to be your undeviating & unshaken friend

JOHN CHAVIS

P. S. I am sorry that your writer did not give Albermarle a slap of the jaws for his low lived, pitiful despotic objection to your keeping the company of Federalist Adams & Clay men. He deserved not only a slap of the jaws, but a peak of the Butt

[Addressed:]
        Hon. Willie P. Mangum Esqr
            Orange
To left at
Red Mountain P. O.
    Mail

WPM-LC

W. M. Sneed to Willie P. Mangum

OXFORD 4th Novr. 1832.

Hon. Willie P. Mangum
    Dear Sir,
    Enclosed I send a paper containing sundry affidavits in Support of the claim of Majr. Pleasant Henderson[216] for a pension under the act of 7th June 1832—
    I shall thank you and Mr. Brown to make a certificate on the paper & transmit it to the Secretary at War—I know you will both feel a pleasure to render the old man a favor—
    Be pleased to present my respects to Mr. Brown—

Accept an assurance of my
Respectful Regard

Yours

W. M. SNEED

WPM-LC

John Mushat[217] to Willie P. Mangum

CHARLOTTE 13th Nov. 1832

My Dear Sir
    You will by this time have perceived that there is a vacancy in the *Judgeship* in Arkansas territory by the death of Mr Bible— M[y s]tate of health, the condition and situation of my fam[ily] and many other circumstances unite in rendering such a situation desireable—you have been for a considerable time acquainted with my character and situation and well know the political course I have steadily pursued—Any influence you can find yourself at liberty in exercising in my favor will be gratefully acknowledged—Our Elections have gone in favor of the administraton beyond our most sanguine expectations—Even the County of Iredell in which I reside long noted for its *Anti-republicanism* has given a majority in favor of the Jackson and Van buren Ticket, of nineteen votes which with one hundred and

---

[216]Major Pleasant Henderson, 1756-1842. See Walter Clark (ed.), *N. C. State Records,* XXII, 129-131, for an account of his military service.
    [217]John Mushat was a teacher at the Statesville Academy before he studied law. Coon, *Doc. Hist. of Educ. in N. C.,* 187-188.

fourteen given for the Barbour ticket show'd a majority in favor
of the present chief magistreate of one hundred and thirty
three—Nothing new—Judge Swain is now at this place discharging his duties as Judge—he has recovered in a great degree
from the injury sustained by the overturn of his sulkey—In
haste I am Your's Very Respectfully

JOHN MUSHAT

[Addressed:]
> Hon. Willie P. Mangum
> Washington City

WPM-LC

Jos. S. Watson[218] to Willie P. Mangum

GRANVILLE Novem: 19th 1832

Dear Sir:

I saw Saml. Richardson the plaisterer; he promised to start
to Orange on *Sunday,* but does not leave here till today. Sam is
a good workman, but is not altogether I apprehend quite as
"stirring" as you would like. A little firmness on your part will
if *necessary* set all things right.

Perhaps you have seen a piece in the Oxford Exam. Signed
"South East" and the reply of "South" in the last No.—That
you may understand some allusions in my reply it will be necessary to inform you that the Author of S East is Sandy Harris[219]
a man of less standing and character than other man in Oxford.
He wrote his piece with the belief that I had participated in the
previous communication, & so expressed himself to a friend of
mine, & then coming out & calling me yr. "Catspaw" made it a
personal matter as to me, & I Retaliated. The *"Contingent"*
authority &c alluded to in my communication is designed to
point him to a recent "faux pas" of his in relation to the Baltimore Convention—Sandy *was* first a nullifier after reading Mr.
Calhouns expose—And then a warm *Clay*—and *Tariff* Man—

218Editor of *Oxford Examiner.*
219Sandy Harris was a member of the House of Commons from Granville County in 1834
and led the fight to expel Robert Potter from the legislature. He moved to Texas. Jack
Poinsett got him in Indian service. He moved to Philadelphia where he developed a law
practice. He became an adviser to Lincoln. He was an uncle of Addison Mangum. In 1834
he challenged Mangum to a duel. Mangum brought libel suit against Harris. Hamilton, *Papers of Ruffin,* II, 202-203. See below, Watson to Mangum, July 9, 1834.

But having been asked by Genl Bryan[220] to go on to Baltimore in his place, he became a *Barbour* man—went on to Baltimore, but before the Convention went into session the Genl. unfortunately came on & took his seat & excluded Sandy.—

Hated by almost every individual in this community and hating all himself in return, he deals largely when he *can* in vituperation, defamation & petty slander, & would if it were worth while wage war with all mankind—

In haste Yrs truly

Jos. S. WATSON.

[Addressed:

Hon. Willie P. Mangum
Red Mountain
Orange.

WPM-LC

W. Montgomery to Willie P. Mangum

RALEIGH N. C. Novr. 20th 1832

My Dear Sir

We Met on yesterday and Elected W. D. Moseley,[221] of Lenoar Speaker of the Senate and L D Henry[222] Speaker of the Commons. We addopted the new Mode of Electing Speaker in the Senate, Without nomination, on the First Ballot Mosely got 29 out of 58. Wilboun[223] 5 & Sewell[224] 8. two or thre others were voted upon the Second Ballot Mosely got nearly all the other officers of the House, were all Elected without opposition. In the Commons Henry and Sawyer[225] were Nominated, Henry got 69 and Sawyer 52—

---

[220]Joseph H. Bryan.

[221]William Dunn Moseley, 1795-1863, was a student at the University with Mangum. He served in the state senate from 1829 to 1837 and was speaker from 1833 to 1836. In 1837 he was defeated for Congress by Charles Shepard. Shortly thereafter he moved to Florida and became that state's first governor, 1845 to 1849. *National Cyclopedia of American Biography*, XI, 377-378.

[222]See above, p. 395n.

[223]James Welborn was state senator from Wilkes County in 1795-1811, 1818-1821, 1823-1824, 1828-1829, 1832, and 1834. In 1835 he was a member of the state constitutional convention. Wheeler, *Reminiscences*, 397; Battle, *Hist. of U. N. C.*, I, 822.

[224]Henry Seawell.

[225]Frederick A. Sawyer was a member of the House of Commons from Pasquotank County in 1832. *N. C. Manual*, 748.

Many names are spoken of for governor Spaight and Burton
I think are the More prominant Branch is not Mutch talked of.
I think that the pull will Be Between Spaight and Burton. We
will Have the appropriation, Bank and Convention question Before us soon.

Glorious news from all quarters for Jackson—He will get two
Hundred and upwards. Do write me when you will Be Here,
there is Mutch Inquiry about you, and a great Wish Expressed
By your old Friends, that you would visit us.
In Haste I am yours truly,

W. MONTGOMERY—

[Addressed:]

Honbl. Willey P. Mangum
orange County N. C.

WPM-LC

George Blair[226] *to Willie P. Mangum*

FRANKLIN LOUISIANA
8th of December 1832

My Dear Judge

I believe you are in my debt, on the correspondence account,
but as I am seeking a favour, not confering one, it will not do
for me to be over punctilious & withal I suppose, you have so
many demands upon you, in that way, from your constitutents
at home that you have very little time to devote to those abroad,
but I beg you to bear in mind, that I still hail from the good old
Town of Edenton, in the good old State of North Carlina & that
in comeing to Louisiana, I neither relinquished my allegiance to
my native State or my claims upon you as my representative I
want the situation of Purser in the Navy for which I was an
applicant last winter & which I think the recommendations I
then offered ought to have secured me, but as I was not appointed, I have determined to renew my claims & to that end
have written to my brother in law Major Sawyer[227] & other
friends at Raleigh requesting them again to forward from that
place a strong recomendation of me, which I will back with some
of the best names from this State & these added to the influence

---

[226]George Blair was a member of the House of Commons in 1829-1830 before he left North
Carolina. *N. C. Manual,* 559.
[227]Frederick A. Sawyer.

of my friends in Congress from North Carolina & the services
which I have rendered the Government out here, in the course
of which I have braved Cholera, Yellow fever & every other
disease of this pestilential climate, will I trust, be sufficient to
induce the President to grant me this small favour, the last
which in all probability I shall ever ask of him & should he
nominate me to the Senate I rely upon Mr. Brown & yourself,
to see me safely & speedily through that body & as from my
having the same name, as the Editor of the Globe, some of the
opposition may suppose me a relation of his & vote against me
on that ground, you will please be careful to have it understood
that I am not related to, connected with or even known to that
Gentleman—

I congratulate you on the result of the Presidential election,
a result glorious alike to the electors and the elected. Who but
Gen Jackson would have had the courage, to veto the bill rechartering the Bank of the U. S. and who but Gen Jackson could
have withstood the overwhelming influence of that corrupt
Aristocracy? We are anxiously looking for the Presidents message on the opening of Congress, which is expected to develope
his sentiments on the South Carolina excitement and the real
friends of the old Chief, have no fears, but he will pursue the
course pointed out by wisdom and moderation: I think South
Carolina premature, but if the tariff policy is not abandoned,
the Southern States will be driven to separation and in this
sentiment Louisiana concurs, with the exception of her seven or
eight hundred Sugar planters, who are as avaricious as the
Lowells & Appletons of Massachusetts—Do write me soon &
fully & let me know *candidly,* what chances I stand for the
Pursership & believe me, my dear Judge

Most Truly
Your friend

GEO. BLAIR

Address me, Care of Messrs. Rhodes & Peters
New Orleans.

[Addressed:]
>To the Honble
>>Willie P. Mangum
>>>of the Senate of the United States
>>>>Washington City
>>>>>D. C.

WPM-LC

Willie P. Mangum to Charity A. Mangum

WASHINGTON CITY
Saturday night 15th Decr. 1832

My dear Love.

I was a good deal disappointed in not receiving a letter from you this morning. I hope I shall receive one tomorrow morning & hear that you & our dear children are all well.—You, I trust, my dear, will not fail to write to me at least every week. For, though in the midst of a city full of all sorts of people, yet I feel melancholy & lonely when I do not hear from you.—It is vain to disguise it, that all we see & hear in public life is empty and unsatisfying—& that home & our own fireside, and our family as they are most dear to the heart, are also best calculated for its real enjoyment, if it be not most grossly perverted & corrupted—

I have been most deeply mortified at public events here, since I last wrote—The weak & foolish Cabinet of the President has undone all the good that we hoped from his message—The whole concern is deficient in talent and good practical sense. His proclamation is violent & dangers in its principles.

Sunday morning 16th-

I stopt last night, because I began with but little candle.—I hope to hear from you this morning my Love.—It gives me more satisfaction to read the prattle of one of our children from your pen than to hear the best Congress Speech.—Mr. Russell[228] who was at our house has resigned his midshipmans warrant, and I got him appointed to another & a better office—I had expected he would go home in a few days to Granville, & I wished to send you a few things—whether he will go home now is uncertain— The little bell is ringing for breakfast & as it is only 15 minutes & I have to shave, I must close hastily. I am still in the City at Mrs. Requelle's—But I have a strong inclination to return to Dawson's to morrow—nobody is there in my old mess but Gen. Smith. If I go back, I hope to carry Mark Alexander of Va—It is much more convenient especially in bad or wet weather—

---

[228]William F. Russell, who was a student from Granville at the University of North Carolina in 1824, became a midshipman in 1826 and resigned in December 1832. He became a member of the legislature in 1842. Callahan, *List of Officers of U. S. Navy*, 478; *N. C. Manual*, 623-624.

Has the painter come? How does Stagg go on? I heard from Walter—he goes on well, as far as I heard. Kiss Fathers daughters for him. Tell them to be good & obey Mother, or I will not love them so well—Remember me, My Love, with affectionate kindness & always as your

Affectionate husband

God bless you

W. P. MANGUM

[Addressed:]

Mrs. Charity A. Mangum

Red Mountain

North Carolina.

WPM-LC

J. L. Bailey[229] *to Willie P. Mangum*

RALEIGH December 25. 1832

My dear Sir

My friend Fred: A. Sawyer, whom you know & who is a member of the legislature is desirous of procuring some diplomatic appointment in South America—Some vacancies have occurred in that country recently and by your friendly aid, together with his other friends at Washington perhaps he could get an appointmen[t]. He would be glad to obtain the situat[ion o]f a **charge** or secretary of legation—M[r Saw]yer is a man of talents, a good french sch[olar] & tolerably well versed in the Spanish *l*anguage—If you can assist my friend in this way I shall consider it a favour conferred upon myself—

And now my dear friend what do you intend doing at Washington this session—The times are awful and if the principles contained in Genl Jacksons proclamation,[230] are the correct principles of this Gov. the days of our Republic are numbered [torn] will force certainly be resorted to & will S[outh Caro]lina be put down at the point of the bayonet—I trust not—I know that you will never give your assent to such violent, and as I con-

---

[229]John L. Bailey, 1795-1877, was a member of the legislature as a representative of Pasquotank County in 1827-1828, and 1832. Later he moved to Hillsboro and Asheville. He taught law at both places. His law students became some of the most influential lawyers of the state. *Ashe, Biog. Hist. of N. C.*, IV, 53-54.

[230]He refers to Jackson's proclamation against nullification.

ceive unconstitutional measures—Your brother read me your letter & you intimated that you would sooner resign than sanction the mad projects of the administration—Do not resign, your countrymen will sustain you[231]—Your feelings & sentiments are correct and will meet with a hearty response in the bosom of many true Carolinians—We are playing the devil here —we are throwing ourselves in the arms of the enemy, we are doing that which which [sic] will meet with *their* entire approbation—we are denouncing So Carolina—[Reso]lutions will pass, we cannot help it [torn]-ning So Carolina—Genl Jackson hates [illegible] Car[olina] so do his parasites here—and So Carolina must be put down because one distinguished individual[232] is obnoxious to the President.—

Excuse this scrawl — I [hardly] know what I write — Mr. Settle[233] has been elected circuit Judge in the place of Swain[234]— There were no persons in nomination but Settle, Hogg[235] & Saunders[236]—There are many candidates for [the] Supreme Co bench—It is impossible to say who [will] succeed—Gaston declines running—Toomer[237] [is] the most prominent—Please answer that part of my letter relative to Mr Sawyer before I leave here — Let me know whether there is any vacancy & whether Mr. Sawyer would stand any chance if he were to [torn] Washington—and if you have tim[e] [torn] what you think the administration will [torn] against So Carolina—You will get Gov. Hayne [pr]oclamation by this mail—

I remain truly & sinc[erely]

J. L. B[AILY]

Honbl W. P. Mangum
Washington

[Addressed:]

Honbl. W. P. Mangum
Washington City

---

[231]North Carolina leaders were opposed to the tariff, but when South Carolina passed its ordinance of nullification the North Carolina legislature declared South Carolina's position revolutionary and subversive. In the senate the vote was 49 to 8 and in the House of Commons it was 98 to 22. Pegg, "Whig Party in North Carolina."

[232]John C. Calhoun.

[233]Thomas Settle, 1789-1857, was a member of Congress from 1817 to 1821, judge of the superior court in 1832, and several times a member of the legislature. *Biog. Dir. of Cong.*, 1508.

[234]David L. Swain.

[235]Probably Gavin Hogg, an attorney of Bertie County. McIver, *N. C. Register*, 46.

[236]Romulus M. Saunders.

[237]John D. Toomer.

WPM-LC

James Seawell[238] *to Willie P. Mangum*

FAYETTEVILLE 26th. December 1832.

Dear Sir,

While I address you upon the subject of this letter will you allow me to tender you my apology for the trouble it imposes upon you and to add that I am aware in the absence of a previous acquaintance I am excluded from a just claim to your particular friendship.

I am desirous of obtaining a Consuls appointment provided I could be favored with a situation where its commercial advantages should present to a man of business reasonable prospects of success &c

I am not at present apprised of a vacancy that would inable me to make a direct application, But would be content with a situation at any one of the Commercial Cities within the jurisdiction of the South American Republics or at *Vera Cruz* and would prefer if I could get it the *Avanah.*

In soliciting from you sir, this favor could I obtain your friendship and influence you will place me under obligations to you which with grateful recollections whenever in my power I should gladly reciprocate.

The public mind here appear to be almost entirely ingrossed with the affairs of South Carolina and whilest we deplore with regret the truly unfortunate attitude which that State has prematurely assumed We rely with confidence on the wisdom of Congress and the sound discretion of our chief Magistrate to avert the horid evils incident to a civil war,—my private opinion, however is, that by a degree of forebearance on the part of the Nation the affair will yet turmenate harmlessly,

I am dear Sir, with my best wishes
Yours truly & obt Srvt—
JAMES SEAWELL

[Addressed:]
The Honable
Wilie P. Mangum
of Congress,
Washington
D. C.

---

[238]James Seawell was a member of the House of Commons from Fayetteville in 1833-1834. Later he was connected with the Cape Fear and Yadkin Railroad. *N. C. Manual,* 574.

A

Academies, course of study, 423. *See also* education in North Carolina.

Adams, John Quincy, adminstration criticised, 231, 240, 272; election prospects in 1824, 83, 116, 161, 173; invites Mangum to reception, 95; levees of, 234; on tariff, 455, 460; unpopularity of, 268.

Adams, M. and Co., attachment against Mangum's property, 334.

Adams, W. H., on Barringer-Mangum pledge, 64.

"Albemarle," attacks Mangum's stand on tariff, 581.

Albemarle, Bank of, mentioned, 434.

Albert, James, military land claims, 95.

Albert, Lois, military land claims, 95.

Albert, Mary, seeks military bounty land of husband, 95.

Albright, Alexander, appointed agent for Counselman inheritance, 80, 86; letter from, 86.

Alexander, Adam R., sketch of, 76.

Alexander, Mark, mentioned, 539, 589.

Alexander, Wiliam J., helps elect Mangum as Senator in 1830, 379, 380, 385, 386, 390, 393; letter to, 374; mentioned, 379.

Allen, James, sketch of, 458; tries to have newspaper established in Asheville, 458.

Allison, Joseph, candidate for House of Commons in 1832, 516; owns newspaper press, 459; sketch of, 459.

Alston, Absalom, family matters, 256; letter from, 256.

Alston, James J., mentioned, 362, 369, 417; receipt from Mangum Trust Fund, 370, 371.

Alston, Thomas, aid in settling Mangum's debts, 362, 369, 370-371, 417; court cases of, 36; letters from, 36, 362, 369, 417; receipts from Mangum Trust Fund, 362, 371.

Alston, Willis, favors the registration of banks, 93-94; letters from, 319, 323, 329; mentioned, 524; opinion on presidential election of 1828, 319, 323-324; opinion on the sectional feelings dis-

played in Congress, 319; opinion on tariff, 319, 324, 330; sketch of, 93.

American Archives, mentioned, 562.

American Farmer, mentioned, 130.

American Party of Pennsylvania, nominates Mangum for President in 1848, xxxviii.

Anderson, Walker, endorses Mangum's course in 1832, 573; letters from, 519, 573; seeks nephew's appointment, 519; sketch of, 519.

Anderson, William, considered for West Point appointment, 455.

Anti-tariff meeting at Salisbury in 1832, 571-572.

Appler, Jacob, family matters, 249, 320; letter from, 249.

Appleton, Nathan, views on tariff, 567.

Archer, Wiliam S., asked to change Venezuela consulate, 536.

Arkansas judgeship sought, 584.

Armstrong, James W., describes life at West Point, 309; letters from, 212, 305, 309; seeks West Point appointment, 212, 305.

Arthur, Isham, land purchases of, 468.

Ashe, Paoli, P. and Co., interest in Deep River Bridge Co., 20, 151; land purchases in Haywood, 17.

Askew, George O., letter from, 485; reaction to the Senate's rejection of Van Buren's nomination, 485.

Atkins, Nicholas, supports pension claims of Titus Turner, 158.

Atkinson, Henry, mentioned, 87.

Avery, Isaac T., letter from, 382; sketch of, 382; supports appointment of Burgess Gaither, 382-383.

B

Badger, George E., befriends John Chavis, 315; candidate for attorney general in 1826, 219; candidate for Congress in 1826, 300; fee in Cherokee land case, 381; letter from, 301; opinion on legal matters, 90, 301; opposes Jackson's South Carolina proclamation, 590; reports on Mangum's popularity, 301; sketch of, 15, 90.

Bailey, J. L., approves Mangum's opposition to Jackson, 590-591; letter from, 590.

Baldwin, Henry, mentioned, 439.

of, 209; supports spoliation claim, 474.

Bryan, Joseph H., member of Spaight Faction, 379.

Bullock, Benjamin, attends Mangum's mother, 359; difficulties with Mangum, 368; invites Mangum to his home, 291; letters from, 291, 444; sketch of, 291; writes about his son's failures at West Point, 444.

Bullock, Peter, sketch of, 444.

Bullock, Thomas, sketch of, 200.

Bunyan, H. B., letter from, 100; seeks military pension, 100.

Burgess, Thomas, letter from, 517; seeks aid for a free Negro, 517-518.

Burke County Court Clerk, vacancy of, 376-378, 382-383.

Burns, Ottway, letter from 416; supports James E. Gibble for appointment, 416.

Burton, Alfred, sketch of, 375.

Burton, H. G., asks Mangum's support in senatorial race, 374; befriends John Chavis, 316; candidate for governor in 1832, 587; debts to Mangum, 308; family news, 154; letters from, 154, 190, 202, 220, 298, 308, 374, 445; offers financial aid to Mangum, 190; recommends Henry Garrot for appointment, 445; seeks legal advice, 130-131, 154; sends to Mangum a resolution on Indian lands, 220; sketch of, 154; views on presidential election of 1824, 190.

Burton, Robert H., letters from, 378, 525; recommends a candidate for appointment, 378; seeks pension for John Kidd, 526; sketch of, 525.

Busbee, Johnson, candidate for state senate in 1832, 559.

Bynum, Jesse A., part played in Mangum's election in 1830, 379, 382, 386, 390, 393, 400; sketch of, 94.

C

Cain, Ann Lillington, mentioned, 23.

Cain, Charity A., see Mangum, Charity A.

Cain, Martha Ann, describes the life at Virginia springs, 35-36; letter from, 35; mentioned, 19,

35, 227, 229, 299; receives slaves from her father, 288.

Cain, Mary, sketch of, 19.

Cain, Sarah Alston, mentioned, 19, 142.

Cain, William, Jr., letters from, 337, 338, 519; made postmaster, 443; sketch of, 4; views on Mangum's debts, 337, 338, 519.

Cain, William, Sr., deeds slaves to Mrs. Mangum, 43; gives property to Martha Cain, 288; mentioned, 97, 358; signs Mangum's notes, xvii, 313, 337, 338, 370.

Caldwell, David F., letters from, 207, 399; mentioned, 375; offers to mediate the Mangum-Owen controversy, 399; part played in Mangum's election in 1830, 379, 391; reports on sectional conflict within state, 402, 430-431; sketch of, 207; supports Clay in 1832, 572.

Caldwell, Joseph, sketch of, 3; students' attitude toward, 6.

Calhoun, John C., courts favor of Mangum, 234; in election of 1824, 83, 89, 91, 97, 105, 108, 111, 116; mentioned, 415, 555; social graces of, 234; visits Raleigh in 1831, 421, 433.

Calhoun party in North Carolina, 555.

Callaghan, Charles, letter of, 537; opinion on currency, 537; opinion on tariff, 538; sketch of, 537.

Cambreling, Churchill C., sketch of, 262.

Cameron, Ann Owen, teaches in Hillsboro, 519.

Cameron, Duncan, declines being candidate in 1824, 138; letters to, 8, 82, 172, 313, 337, 338; mentioned, 105, 259; prominence in state, xvi; sketch of, 56; started Mangum in law, xvii; starts Mangum in politics, xviii; supports United States Bank, 549.

Cameron, John A., appointed judge, 548; letter from, 278; seeks support for newspaper, 278; sketch of, 260; visits Washington, 266, 275.

Cameron, Paul, becomes pupil of Mangum, xvii.

Cameron, William, sketch of, 470; West Point appointment, 470, 519.

Camp, John G., authorized to collect debt, 363.

Coleman, John H., mentioned, 459.
Collector of port at Beaufort, appointment to, 416.
Collins, William, suggested for appointment, 348, 350.
Columbian College, bill to relieve, 245.
Coman, Matthew J., letter from, 282; seeks appointment, 282; sketch of, 282.
Commission under Ghent Treaty, its activities, 269-270.
Congressional aid to Columbian College, 245-246.
Congressional campaign of 1823, 51-52, 53-59; of 1825, 171, 183 184, 193-197; of 1827, 291-295, 300.
Congressional Caucus of 1824, 91, 116, 121, 123, 138.
Congressional reservation line, see Tennessee lands.
Congressional Revolutionary documents, editing of, 562.
Connor, Henry M., property claims of, 165-166.
Connor, Henry W., letter from, 196; property claims of, 196; sketch of, 196.
Connor, James, involved in law suit, 165-166.
Constitutional amendments, on electoral system proposed, 91, 221, 231, 232, 238-239, 241, 262, 266, 287, See also sectional conflict.
Consular appointments, 205-206, 264, 281. See also John G. A. Williamson.
Consular service, recommended changes in, 407, 409-410, 477, 536.
Cooke, Henry M., plans to resign as collector of port, 416.
Cooke, Richard L., mentioned, 23.
Corey, Benjamin, sells printing press, 265; visit to Washington, 289.
Cotton, low prices of, in 1824, 114; in 1831, 441.
Council of State, applied to for appointment, 297; Democratic members of, 448.
Counselman, George, property of, 86.
Counselman, Jacob, inheritance claims, 80, 86.
Court circuit, see superior court circuit.
Cozart, Robert, tries to collect debt, 328.

Crafton, Bennett, war record of, 177.
Craig, James A., approves Mangum's congressional course, 132; candidate for legislature in 1832, 550; letter from, 132; sketch of, 132.
Craig, John, in legislature, 517.
Crawford, W. H. and the election of 1824, xxi, 83, 84, 85, 89, 91, 93, 97, 105, 108-109, 111, 113-116, 118, 129-130, 138, 141, 146, 160-161, 169-171, 173-174, 184, 314-315.
Crawford party to stand aloof on the Adams Administration, 231.
Creek land claims, 498.
Creek removals, 497.
Creek treaty causes excitement in Congress in 1825, 230; under Jackson, 498.
Crudup, Josiah and Congressional campaign of 1825, 171, 183, 184, 193-197; letter to, 346; mentioned, 300; printed circular of 1825, 193-195; sketch of, 53.
Currency, weaknesses, 537-538.
Cuthbert, Alfred, sketch of, 85.

D

Dallas, George M., considered for Vice President, 463.
Daniel, Beverly, letter from, 98; proposes economy in government, 99; proposes relief for West Point cadets, 99; sketch of, 98.
Daniel, Joseph J., changes in court circuit schedule, 352, 353, 364-366; sketch of, 10.
Davidson, William, letter from, 361; recommends Samuel Hutchinson for appointment, 361; sketch of, 361.
Davis, Catherine, xv. See also Mangum, Catherine Davis.
Davis, Edward, mentioned, 23, 30, 520.
Dawson, A. R., seeks Senate office, 428.
Dawson's boarding house, 231.
Decatur, Susan, claims of, 253-254, 257; letters from, 253, 257.
Deep River Bridge Company, contract for subscribers to build bridge, 150-151; mentioned, 17, 20.
De Lacy, John D., sketch of, 13.
Desha, Robert, has controversy with William Brent, 319.

Forsythe, Samuel, mentioned, 528.
Fort Boyer battle, mentioned, 257.
Foster, Thomas F., sketch of, 173.
Franklin, Abner, considered for delegate to Baltimore Convention in 1832, 463; supports Mangum, 524.
Franklin, Jesse, and pension payments, 491.
Franks, W. J., sketch of, 20; sues A. D. Murphey, 20.
Free Negro, restrictions placed on, 215, 517-518; suffrage of, 240-244.
Freeland, John, candidate for sheriff, 517.
Freeman, J. P., letter from, 514; sends resolutions of Pasquotank meeting, 514-515.
French spoliation claims, 418-419, 464, 474, 483.
"Friends of Andrew Jackson," 517.

G

Gaillard, John, health of, 235.
Gaines, Edward P., involved in controversy over military precedence, 321.
Gaither, Alfred M., sketch of, 6.
Gaither, Burgess S., considered for Burke County clerk of court, 376-378, 382-383; sketch of, 377.
Gales, Joseph, 211, asks for copy of Mangum's speech in 1826, 289; has Mangum to dinner, 211; seeks an appointment, 296-297; sells books to Mangum, 33; sends Mangum's account, 276; sketch of, 13.
Gales, Joseph, Jr., letter to, 428.
Gales, Thomas, indebted to Mangum's father, 2; letter from, 2; sketch of, 2.
Gales, Weston R., mentioned, 208.
Gales and Seaton, asks Mangum to furnish copies of his speech, 206-207; letter from, 206; **mentioned**, 182.
Gallatin, Albert, as vice presidential candidate, 120, 122, 262.
Garner, John, letter from, 224; requests *National Intelligencer* be sent, 224.
Garrot, Henry, recommended for an appointment, 445.
Gary, Roderick, supports Mangum for Senate, 375, 380, 382, 385, 389, 400.

Gaston, William, advises moderation, 460; favors the United States Bank, 460-461; letters from, 417, 442, 460; letters to, 454, 499; makes possible the repair of the Canova statue, 447; mentioned, 150, 429; recommends candidates for West Point, 442; reviews work of legislative session, 442-443, 461; thanks Mangum for appointment, 460.
Gatlin, Alfred M., sketch of, 168.
Georgia, Cherokee controversy with, 529; Creek controversy with, 514; protests the tariff, 338-340; slaves seized by the British, 113-114, 137, 269-270.
Gibble, James E., endorsed for collector of port at Beaufort, 416.
Giles, John B., sketch of, 196.
Gilliam, Robert B., favors Mangum's tariff speech, 529; letters from, 482, 528; opposes nullification, 529; seeks legal assistance, 528-529.
Gilmer, George R., sketch of, 173.
Glynn, A. G., letter from, 251; recommends an instructor for the University, 251.
Gold mining in North Carolina, 440-441.
Goodloe, Daniel R., sketch of, 219.
Goodrich, Chauncey, asks assistance in collecting a debt, 325, 363; letters from, 325, 363; mentioned, 329.
Goodwin, Samuel, seeks pension, 490.
Graham, William A., praises Mangum, xxxv.
Grant, James, discusses Franklin Saunders' education, 423; letters from, 423, 489; seeks military claims, 489-490.
Granville County election in 1826, 291; in 1831, 421.
Graves, Barzilla, sketch of, 62.
Graves, John W., marriage of, 5.
Green, Thomas J., letter from, 331; sketch of, 331; suggests Mangum run for the Senate, 331.
Green, William M., letter from, 357; reports death of Mangum's mother, 357-358; sketch of, 357.
Greene, John H., letter from, 340; mediates Mangum-Seawell quarrel, 71; urges Mangum to run for attorney general in 1828, 341.
Grimes, Pherraby, letter from, 25; seeks pension of husband, 26.

Grimes, William, military record reviewed, 126.
Guion's Hotel, mentioned, 430.
Gwinn, Little, supports Mangum for the Senate, 401.

H

Hagner, Peter, sends a petition to Mangum, 489.
Hailes, William, sketch of, 321.
Halifax Minerva, mentioned, 265.
Hall, John, approves Mangum's speech on the tariff, 528; letter of, 528; sketch of, 10; views on Cherokee controversy, 528.
Hall, Thomas H., letter from, 221; mentioned, 476; sketch of, 191; views on Monroe's claims, 221.
Hamilton, J. G. de R., publishes sketch of Mangum, vii.
Hamilton, Robert and Co., make Mangum their agent, 18.
Haralson, Archibald, business relations with Mangum, xvi, xxiv, 17, 18, 37; friendship for Mangum, xvi; sells property, 17; sketch of, 17.
Haralson, Herndon, appointed commissioner of Deep River Bridge Co., 151; sketch of, 20.
Hargis, Thomas N. L., attaches Mangum's property, 333; invites Charity A. Mangum to a party, 25; sketch of, 25.
Harper, Jethro, seeks a pension, 543.
Harris, Ransom, favored Mangum for the Senate, 401; favored a state constitutional convention, 402.
Harris, Sandy, engages in newspaper controversy, 585.
Harts and Wright, account with Mangum, 1.
Harvey, Peyton, mentioned, 501.
Hatteras inhabitants, seek relief, 222.
Hawkins, Benjamin, Indian claims of, 498; sketch of, 498.
Hawkins, Joseph, opposed for comptroller, 208; seeks pension, 490.
Hawkins, Micajah T., candidate for Congress in 1831, 433; mentioned, 476, 482, 552.
Hawkins, William, helps with pension requests, 489.
Hawks, Francis L., sketch of, 296.
Hayne, Robert Y., mentioned, 123, 234.

Haywood, John, helps settle John Chavis' financial difficulties, 155, 184; letters from, 155, 260, 283; letters to, 248, 266, 412; recommends friend for appointment, 260, 283-284; sketch of, 41.
Haywood, William H., Jr., criticises Van Buren's opponents, 556-557; discusses law cases, 121, 136; estimates strength of presidential candidates in 1824, 111; favors a change in mail route, 541-542; letters from, 92, 118, 135, 336, 427, 446, 541, 554; recommends Edward G. Benners for appointment, 427; reviews efforts to change state court system, 446; reviews the proceedings of the legislature in 1832, 446; sketch of, 92; views on efforts to change state constitution, 446; views on the presidential campaign of 1824, 93, 137; views on the tariff, 554; views on nullification, 554-555.
Haywood, town of, mentioned, 14, 17, 150.
Heartt, Dennis, asks Mangum to write for his paper, 112; depressed by unpopularity of Adams' administration, 164; letters from, 112, 216; seeks lottery ticket, 216.
Henderson, Archibald, sketch of, 23.
Henderson, Elizabeth, mentioned, 5.
Henderson, J. M., letter from, 346; recommends T. D. Watts for an appointment, 346.
Henderson, John L., sketch of, 342.
Henderson, Lemuel, applicant for clerk of county court, 360.
Henderson, Leonard, seeks pension, 491; sketch of, 262.
Henderson, Mark M., asks aid for postmaster, 81; letter from, 81; sketch of, 81.
Henderson, Pleasant, seeks pension, 584; sketch of, 155.
Henderson, Thomas, introduces A. R. Alexander, 76; letter from, 76; sketch of, 76.
Henry, Louis D., champions cause of the West, 447; mediates between Mangum and John Owen, 395-397.
Hentz, Nicholas M., appointed to faculty of University, 273.
Hepzibah meeting house, mentioned, 53.
Hermes, mentioned, 257.

McLane, Louis, letter from, 195; mentioned, 248, 483; recommended for Vice President, 207, 473; resolution on Panama Mission, 289; reviews results of congressional election in 1825, 195-196; sketch of, 195.

McLean, John, mentioned, 462; sketch of, 315.

McMurray, William, in charge of Person post office, 145; letter from, 145.

McPheeters, Rev. William, reputation as a teacher, xvi.

M

Macon, Nathaniel, alarmed at centralization, 109; health of, 229, 233, 235, 249, 267; letter from, 305; letter to, 174; mentioned, 109, 177, 183; opposes a gift to Lafayette, 183; opposes governmental extravagance, 306; regrets Mangum's defeat in 1828, 305.

Mail route changes, 424, 451-452, 453-454, 457, 479, 541. *See also* post routes.

Mallett, C. P., letter from, 527; refers to school days, 527; thanks Mangum for his speech, 527.

Mangham, James C., letters from, 84, 113; reports on family matters, 84; views on Crawford's chances, 84-85, 113.

Mangum, Arthur, relation to Mangum, 1; property of, 47.

Mangum, B. A., discusses farm, 384; letter from, 384.

Mangum, Catherine Davis, illness and death of reported, 357-360; *See also* Davis, Catherine.

Mangum, Charity A., discusses family news, 142-143, 225, 227-228, 247, 254-256; discusses social life, 227; letters from, 142, 225, 227, 247, 254; letters to, 4, 19, 21, 23, 28, 35, 124, 140, 186, 191, 208, 210, 228, 235, 248, 259, 268, 274, 277, 367, 424, 425, 466, 477, 486, 503, 539, 545, 546, 589; marriage of, xvii; mentioned, 359, 424; sketch of, 4; slaves granted to, 43.

Mangum, Ellison G., asked to teach Mangum's daughter, 486; purchases land, 47; sketch of, 332.

Mangum, Martha, mentioned, 367, 368, 424, 541.

Mangum, Mary Sutherland, birth of, 546.

Mangum, Priestley, H., advises Mangum of circuit court schedule change, 366; advises Mangum to remain loyal to Crawford, 97; advises resignation, 300; as student, xvi; candidate for legislature, 516, 550, 559; defeated for office, 414; informs Mangum of his mariage plans, 97, 118; informs Mangum of his mother's illness and death, 358-359; letters from, 44, 46, 96, 117, 133, 164, 261, 299, 300, 341, 358, 366, 449; letter to, 14; receives account, 27-28; replaces William Cain on note, 337; reports family news, 118, 134-135, 358, 449; seeks appointment, 341; sketch of, 14; urges Mangum to move to Hillsboro, 44, 318; urges him not to exceed sentiment, 450, views on legal matters, 46; views on constitutional amendment, 262-263; views on Mangum's speech, 262; views of Webster's judicial bill, 262.

Mangum, Rebecca Sutherland, health of, 449; mentioned, 277.

Mangum, Sally Alston, birth of, 103; education of, 486; mentioned, 186, 191, 225, 228, 424, 486, 541; praised, 247, 255.

Mangum, Walter Alvis, business affairs of, 371; debt to, 332; health of, 225; legal suit against, 335; letter to, 309; mentioned, 14, 359; moves to Tennessee, 571, 590; sells cotton in Petersburg, 255; sketch of, 14.

Mangum, William Person, as merchant, xv, 1, 2, 359.

Mangum, William Preston, birth of, xii, death of, xli.

Mangum, Willie Person, chronological data on: chronology of, xi-xiii; biographical sketch of, xv-xliii; birth and early life of, xv-xvi; education of, xvi-xvii; member of Dialectic Society, 7; A.B. diploma, 7-8; reads law, xvii; license to practice law, 9-10; marriage, 14-16; enters politics, xviii; in legislature, xviii, xxxiii; elected judge of superior court, xviii; business ventures, xxii; unhappy as judge, 21; congressional campaign of 1823, xix-xx, 51-69; circular letter in campaign of 1823, 57-62; quarrel with Henry Seawell, xx, 40-41, 70-76, 77-

Moore, Thomas P., appropriations for, 536; sketch of, 95; views on presidential election of 1828, 323.
Morse, Jedidiah, mentioned, 280; sketch of, 272.
Moseley, W. D., sketch of, 586.
Mount Tirza Post Office, established, 218.
Murphey, A. D., campaigns for the legislature in 1817, 9; letters from, 20, 215, 271, 280; letter to, 341; mentioned, 150; seeks assistance for his history, 215, 217, 272, 280; sketch of, 9.
Murfree, William H., discusses legal matters, 32-33; letter from, 32; sketch of, 33.
Murray, Lindley, sketch of, 413.
Muse, John B., candidate for clerk, 421; encloses Mangum's commission, 354, 355; letter from, 355; sketch of, 355.
Mushat, John, letter from, 584; seeks an appointment, 584-585.
Naggs Head Party, opposed Mangum in 1830, 400.

N

Nash, Frederick, as judge, 299; letter from, 351; mentioned, 312; moves his residence, 524; reviews legislature's proceedings, 351-352; sketch of, 297.
National politics 1831, discussed, 438.
Negroes, see free Negroes.
Neuse River and Navigation Company, brief history of, 11; list of subscribers, 11-13.
Newland, David, sketch of, 385.
Newlin, John, letter from, 162; mentioned, 107; seeks to change mail route, 163; sketch of, 162.
New Monthly Magazine, mentioned, 42.
Newspapers established, 265, 285, 414, 435, 458-459, 474, 475-476, 571-572, 578-579.
New York lottery ticket sought, 216.
New York Mercantile Library, 580.
New York politics, North Carolina reaction to, 471.
Nicholson, Thomas, sketch of, 375; supports Mangum for Senate, 400.
North Carolina, against Van Buren, 494, 512-513, 514; economic plight of, 369, 440; education, agitation for improvement, 192;

governor's race in 1831, 434; legislative action in, 82, 83, 91, 207-208, 215, 217, 219; legislation on railroads, 435; legislation on state banks, 207, 351, 403, 434-435; legislature's proceedings in 1823, 82, 83, 91; in 1825, 207-208, 215, 217, 219; in 1828, 351; in 1830-1831, 402-403, 420-421, 422, 430-432, 434-435, 442-443, 446-447; opposition to tariff, 471; population decline in, 440, 448; reaction to Georgia-Cherokee controversy, 515; reaction to Jackson's proclamation against South Carolina, 590; reaction to nullification, 591; railroad survey in, 499; reaction to Senate's rejection of Van Buren as minister to England, 462, 484; resolution of legislature on Cherokee lands, 220; support for United States Bank, 508; war accounts irregular in, 490-491.
North Carolina Central Railroad, 499.
North Carolina Geological Survey, 272.
Norton, Ebenezer F., sketch of, 363.
Norwood, William, letter from, 364; offered exchange courts, 365.
Nullification, endorsed, 501; press on, 415; sentiment on 372, 450, 529, 554, 573, 585.
Nullification party in North Carolina, 580.
Nullifiers in North Carolina, 475.

O

Obert, John J., recommends an engineer, 499.
O'Brien, Spencer, candidate for solicitor in 1831, 420; letter from, 493; sketch of, 379; supports Mangum for Senate in 1830, 379, 380, 400; views on national politics, 493.
Olmsted, Denison, reports on geology of North Carolina, 272.
Orange County, candidates for sheriff, 517; legislative candidates in 1817, 8-9; in 1832, 516, 550; map of, see list of illustrations; meeting to endorse Mangum's conduct in Senate, 574.
Orange Presbytery supports John Chavis, 576.

608 INDEX

Presidential election method, *see* constitutional amendments.
Presly, I. B., business with Jesse Person, 488; compensation of, 496; trip to Washington, 465.
Press in North Carolina on Jackson, 415.
Price, Chandler, circular supporting Jackson in 1826, 291-295.
Pryor, Green, seeks refund on land purchases, 468-469.
Public documents sought, 436, 437, 440.
Public land claims, 468-469.
Pullen, Samuel H., sketch of, 42.
Pullen, Turner, helps settle John Chavis' financial difficulties, 184.

R

Race horses of Sam Yarborough, 276.
Railroad charters, 435, 447.
Rainey, Lemuel, claims of, 153.
Raleigh Academy, attended by Mangum, xvi.
Raleigh Constitutionalist, in financial difficulties, 475; mentioned, 458-459, 579.
Raleigh Democratic convention, 551.
Raleigh fire of 1831, 403, 447.
Raleigh, political factions, 475.
Raleigh, *Register*, mentioned, 475.
Raleigh, Star, mentioned, 579-580.
Raleigh-Hillsboro mail route, changes in, 102, 126-127.
Raleigh-Oxford mail route, changes in, 198.
Raleigh-Person mail route, changes in, 104-105.
Raleigh-Roxborough mail route, changes in, 162-163.
Raleigh-Salisbury mail route, changes in, 541-542.
Ramsay, Charles R., helps edit Raleigh *Constitutionalist*, 476; letter from, 578; praises Mangum, 579; seeks aid for newspaper, 578-579.
Ramsay, John A., sketch of, 151.
Ramsay, Joseph, opposed Mangum in 1830, 400.
Rand, Nathaniel, supports Titus Turner's petition, 178.
Randolph, John, returns to the Senate, 235.
Randolph-Clay duel, mentioned, 274, 275.

Ransom, William S., asks aid for newspaper, 476; explains his newspaper's stand, 474; letter from, 474.
Reaction to Mangum's tariff speech, 524, 527, 528, 529, 530, 537.
Read, Lethe E., discusses social life, 4; letter from, 4.
Read, Martin, letter from, 500; views on vice presidential nomination, 500-501.
Register of Debates, mentioned, 206.
Reinhart, E. W., desires to establish a newspaper, 285; letter from, 285.
Removal of state capital considered, 443, 446, 459.
Rencher, Abraham, mentioned, 427, 507, 559; sketch of, 322.
Requelle, Mrs., boarding house, 589.
Revolutionary War claims, 489-492.
Roane, William, candidate for county clerk, 378, 382; sketch of, 376-377.
Roanoke Advocate, mentioned, 265, 501.
Roanoke country in politics, 381, 390, 433, 505.
Roanoke elections for Congress, 433.
Robards, William, helps mediate Mangum-Seawell quarrel, 75, 78-79; letter from, 78; letters to, 75, 77, 79; purchased powder and lead, 491; sketch of, 53.
Roberts, William, sketch of, 315.
Robertson, John, letter to, 169.
Rogers, Allen, mentioned, 316; sketch of, 270.
Rogers, Benjamin, donates land to John Chavis, 316.
Rogers, John, asks aid against creditors, 168; letter from, 168; sketch of, 167; success as school principal, 189; views on national politics, 168.
Ross, Joseph, inquiries about Mangum's note, 313; letter from, 313.
Roxborough-Halifax mail changes, 457-458.
Ruffin creditors *vs.* Ruffin trustees, 301.
Ruffin, James, marriage of, 228.
Ruffin, Thomas, appointed judge, 203; letters to, 108, 130, 159; sketch of, 10.
Ruffin, William, letter from, 185; sketch of, 185; views on the pres-

idential campaign of 1824, 185-186.

Ruffin, William K., attends St. Mary's School in Baltimore, 159; letters from, 139, 277, 348; plans to go to Switzerland, 139-140, 277-278; recommends friend for appointment, 348-349; sketch of, 139.

Russell, William F., sketch of, 589.

S

St. Mary's School, attended by William K. Ruffin, 159.

Salisbury anti-tariff meeting, 571.

Salt Sulphur Springs, visited by the Cains, 35.

Santander, Francisco deP., mentioned, 560; sketch of, 560.

Saunders, Franklin, appointment of, 514; scholarship of, 423; sketch of, 422.

Saunders, Romulus M., campaign methods of, 430-431; controversy with John Branch, 502-503, 513, 514, 522; helps elect Mangum as Senator in 1830, 391, 394; introduces Judge Farman, 363; letters from, 363, 391, 422, 462, 502, 513, 522; mentioned, 123, 285, 374, 408, 410; recommends his son for West Point, 422; reviews the maneuvers in the senatorial race of 1830, 391; sketch of, 35; views on vice presidential candidates in 1832, 462-463, 522-523; views on the tariff, 523.

Sawyer, Frederick A., nominated for speaker in 1832, 586; seeks a diplomatic appointment, 590.

Scott, John, candidate for solicitor general in 1825, 217, and in 1831, 420; letters from, 216, 430; letter to, 577; mentioned, 15, 97, 304; reports on legislative proceedings in 1825, 217, and in 1831, 430-431; reviews the political maneuvers in the legislature in 1831, 430-431; sketch of, 18.

Scott, Thomas, sketch of, 199.

Scott, Wingfield, and controversy over army command, 321.

Seaton, Augustine, sketch of, 296.

Seaton, Sarah W., sketch of, 185.

Seawell, Henry, letters from, 40, 269, 355, 483; letter to, 70; mentioned, 381, 447; seeks appointment, 269-270, 356, 483; sketch

of, 16; success as a lawyer, 16. *See also* Mangum, W. P., quarrel with Seawell.

Seawell, James, letter from, 592; seeks appointment, 592.

Sectional conflict in North Carolina, 54, 105-106, 240, 442-443, 444, 446, 459, 461.

Selby, Joseph J., accounts with Priestley and Willie P. Mangum, 14, 26, 27.

Selby, William, Sr., supports Mangum for Senate, 401.

Senatorial instruction, *see* instruction of North Carolina Senators.

Senatorial race of 1830, xxv-xxvi, 372-373, 374-376, 379-382, 385-387, 389-394.

Settle, Thomas, nominated for judge, 591.

Shaw, Willie, receives post office contract, 229.

Shepard, Charles B., mentioned, 420.

Shepperd, Augustine H., candidate for judge, 299, and for solicitor general, 217; opposes a free Negro bill, 215; sketch of, 16.

Shipp, Bartlett, supports Mangum for the Senate, 390.

"Sir Archy," mentioned, 276.

Skinner, J. S., mentioned, 130.

Slave patrol in Hillsboro, alerted, 373-374.

Slaves deeded to Charity A. Mangum, 43, and to her sister, 288.

Slaves of Mangum taken to Mississippi, 577-578.

Slave sale, 288.

Slave scare of 1830, 373.

Sloane, John, sketch of, 182.

Small states *vs.* large states struggle, reviewed, 239.

Smith, E. B., letter from, 543; seeks a pension for friend, 543; sketch of, 543.

Smith, Franklin L., sketch of, 349.

Smith, James S., campaigns for the legislature in 1817, 8-9, and in 1832, 550; candidate for Congress in 1826, 300; letters from, 182, 188; mentioned, 269; opposes Mangum in 1830, 391; practices medicine, 359; seeks academy teacher, 189; sketch of, 8; views on national politics, 182-183.

Smith, Nathaniel G., letters from, 245, 468; seeks refund for public land, 468-469; supports federal aid to Columbian College, 246.